Shadows of the Workhouse

JENNIFER WORTH

PHOENIX

This edition published for
Index Books Ltd

A PHOENIX PAPERBACK

First published in Great Britain in 2005
by Merton Books
This paperback edition published in 2009
by Phoenix,
an imprint of Orion Books Ltd,
Orion House, 5 Upper St Martin's Lane,
London WC2H 9EA

An Hachette UK company

A CIP catalogue record for this book
is available from the British Library.

Typeset by Input Data Services Ltd, Bridgwater, Somerset

Printed and bound in Great Britain by Clays Ltd, St Ives plc

The Orion Publishing Group's policy is to use papers that
are natural, renewable and recyclable products and
made from wood grown in sustainable forests. The logging
and manufacturing processes are expected to conform to
the environmental regulations of the country of origin.

www.orionbooks.co.uk

Praise for Jennifer Worth

'These are powerful stories delivered with sweet charm and controlled outrage' *Times Literary Supplement*

'Worth is a vivid writer with a talent for the sting in the tail . . . a highly readable book – and a must for social planners
Evening Standard

'Jennifer Worth has a gift for storytelling and a keen eye for the evocative' BBC: *Who Do You Think You Are?*

'Worth is indeed a natural storyteller – in the best sense of the term, with apparent artlessness in fact concealing high art – and her detailed account of being a midwife in London's East End is gripping, moving and convincing from beginning to end . . . *Call the Midwife* is also a powerful evocation of a long-gone world . . . and in Worth it has surely found one of its best chroniclers' David Kynaston, *Literary Review*

'A chilling insight into life for the average mother [in the 1950s]' *Sunday Express*

'This delightful memoir brings to vivid life London's East End . . . full of humour . . . Worth's talent shines from every page'
Sainsbury's Magazine

'Worth's book made me cry in a railway carriage'
Matthew Parris, *Spectator*

'A candid, poignant memoir . . . this gripping narrative includes breech babies, adulterous relationships, urban pig-breeding and a surreal strip show in a brothel' *Townswoman*

'In her marvellous new book . . . [t]here are desperately sad stories here, but tales of great hope too. Or ordinary people living, giving birth and building their families despite enormous hardship and poor sanitation. And of midwives delivering superb care in the toughest conditions' *East End Life*

'Nobody who reads *Call the Midwife* will ever forget it'
The Woman Writer

Jennifer Worth was a nurse, midwife, ward sister and night sister from 1952 until 1973, working mainly in London. Her first passion was – and still is – music, and she is a Fellow of the London College of Music. She taught piano and singing for about 25 years but retired from teaching in order to concentrate on writing. She still sings in choirs all over England and Europe. She plays her piano (a 1904 Bluthner) daily, and is a present studying all the piano works of J. S. Bach – a long-term project. She has been married for forty-five years and has two daughters and three grandchildren.

By Jennifer Worth

Eczema and Food Allergy
Shadows of the Workhouse
Call the Midwife
Farewell to the East End

Dedicated with respect and gratitude to
Patricia Holt Schooling of Merton Books
whose vision, enterprise and courage led
to the first publication of these books.

ACKNOWLEDGEMENTS

Maysel Brar, for legal advice; Douglas May, Peggy Sayer, Betty Hawney, Jennie Whitefield, Joan Hands and Helen Whitehorn for advice, proof-reading, typing and checking; Philip and Suzannah, for everything; all the kind people who have written to me about the workhouse system, particularly Kathleen Daley and Dennis Strange; Chris Lloyd, Bancroft Library, Mile End, London; Jonathan Evans, Royal London Hospital Archives, London; Eve Hostettler, Island History Trust, the Isle of Dogs, London E14; Jean Todd, Allan Young and Jeff Wright for help with archive pictures; London Metropolitan Archives, London EC1; Hackney Archives, London N1; Camden Local Studies and Archives Centre; The Local History Collection of Gravesend Library, Kent; Peter Higginbotham for his help in checking the material on the history of the workhouse.

CONTENTS

PART III: THE OLD SOLDIER

Part I

WORKHOUSE CHILDREN

NONNATUS HOUSE

Nonnatus House was both a convent and the working base for the nursing and midwifery services of the Sisters of St Raymund Nonnatus.* The house was situated in the heart of the London Docklands and the practice covered Poplar, the Isle of Dogs, Stepney, Limehouse, Millwall, Bow, Mile End and parts of Whitechapel. I worked with the Sisters in the 1950s. It was a time, shortly after the Second World War, when the scars of the devastated city could be seen everywhere – bomb sites, blown-out shops, closed streets and roofless houses (often inhabited). It was a time when the docks were fully operational, and millions of tons of cargo poured in and out every day. Huge merchant vessels sailed up the Thames, to be piloted into the wharves through a complex system of canals, locks and basins. It was not unusual to pass along a road within a few feet of the towering hulk of a merchant ship. Even in the 1950s about sixty per cent of all cargo was unloaded manually, and the ports teemed with labourers. Most of them lived with their families in the little houses and tenements around the docks.

Families were large, sometimes huge, and living conditions cramped. In fact, by today's standards, the living conditions would be considered Dickensian. Most dwellings had running cold water, but no hot water. About half had an indoor lavatory, but for the other half the lavatory was outside, usually shared with other families. Very few homes had a bathroom. A bath was taken

* The Midwives of St Raymund Nonnatus is a pseudonym. I have taken the name from St Raymund Nonnatus, the patron saint of midwives, obstetricians, pregnant women, childbirth and newborn babies. He was delivered by Caesarean section ('*non natus*' is the Latin for "not born") in Catalonia, Spain, in 1204. His mother, not surprisingly, died at his birth. He became a priest and died in 1240.

in a tin bath placed on the floor of the kitchen or living room, though public bath houses were also frequently used. Most houses had electric light, but gaslight was still common, and I have delivered many a baby by this flickering light, as well as by torchlight or hurricane lamp.

It was a time just before the social revolution of 'the Pill', and women tended to have many children. A colleague of mine delivered an eighteenth baby to one woman and I delivered a twenty-fourth! Admittedly these were extreme cases, but ten babies was quite common. Although the fashion for hospitalisation for a birth was fast gaining ground, this "fashion" had not affected the Poplar women, who were slow to change, and a home birth was still preferred. Earlier in the century, even as little as twenty or thirty years previously, women were still delivering each other's babies as they had done in earlier centuries, but by the 1950s, with the advent of the National Health Service, all pregnancies and births were attended by trained midwives.

I worked with the Sisters of St Raymund Nonnatus, a religious order of Anglican nuns with a history dating back to the 1840s. This was also a nursing order pioneered at a time when nurses were commonly regarded as the dregs of female society. The Sisters, bound for life by the monastic vows of poverty, chastity and obedience, had been in Poplar since the 1870s. They started their work at a time when there was virtually no medical help for the poorest of the poor, and a woman and her baby survived or died unattended. The Sisters lived a life of ceaseless dedication to their religion and to the people whom they felt were in their care. At the time when I worked at Nonnatus House, Sister Julienne was Sister-in-Charge.

Convents tend to attract within their portals ladies of middle years who are unable to cope with life in one way or another. These ladies are always single, widowed or divorced, and lonely. They are nearly always gentle, timid and shy, with an immense yearning for the goodness which they see in the convent but cannot find in the harsh world outside. Usually they are very devout in points of religious observance and have an unrealistic or romanticised idea of monastic life and long to be part of it. However, they often do not have a true vocation that would enable them to take the life vows of poverty, chastity and obedience. Nor, I suspect would they possess the strength of character necessary to live within these vows. So they hover on the fringe, neither fully within the world, nor withdrawn from it.

Such a lady was Jane. She was probably around forty-five when I met her, but she looked much older. She was, tall, thin, aristocratic in appearance, with delicate bone structure, beautifully sculpted features, and refined manners. In another context she would have been an outstanding beauty, but her excessive dowdiness made her look plain and nondescript. It was almost as if she did it on purpose. Her soft grey hair could have curled prettily around her face, but she cut it herself, so that it was jagged and shapeless. Her height, which should have rendered her distinguished, she reduced by bending her shoulders, so that her carriage and walk were stooped and cringing. Her large, expressive eyes were filled with nameless anxiety and surrounded by worry lines. Her speech was so soft that it sounded like a far-off twitter, and her laugh a nervous giggle.

In fact, nervousness was her chief characteristic. She seemed frightened of everything. I noticed that, even at meals, she did not dare to pick up her knife and fork until everyone else had done so, and when she did, her hands frequently shook so much that she would drop something. Then she had to apologise profusely to everyone, especially to Sister Julienne, who was always at the head of the table.

Jane had lived at Nonnatus House for many years and fulfilled a role that was neither nurse, nor domestic servant, but a mixture of the two. I had the impression she was a highly intelligent woman who could easily have trained as a nurse, and been very good at it, but something must have prevented her. No doubt it was her chronic nervousness, for she could never have taken the responsibility that is a daily part of any nurse's life. So Sister Julienne sent her out to do simple jobs, like blanket baths, or enemas, or delivering various things to patients. In doing these little jobs, Jane was all of a twitter with anxiety, going over and over her bag obsessively, muttering to herself such things as, "Soap, towels. Have I got everything? Is it all there?" Consequently it took her two or three hours to do a job that any competent nurse could have achieved in twenty minutes. When she had finished, she was pathetically eager for recognition, her eyes almost pleading for someone to say that she had done well. Sister Julienne always praised her small achievements, but I could see that it was a strain for her to be so constantly alert to Jane's craving for praise.

Jane also helped the nurses and midwives in the clinical room in small ways, such as cleaning instruments, packing bags and so on, and again she was irritatingly eager to please. Asked for a syringe, she would rush off and get three. Asked for some cotton-wool swabs for one baby, she would bring enough for twenty and then almost grovel as she handed over the item with a nervous giggle. This craven urge to please brought her no rest, no comfort.

It was all very disconcerting, especially as she was old enough to be my mother, and as it generally took her about three times as long as it took me to do a job, I refrained from asking. But she intrigued me, and I watched her.

Jane spent most of her time in the house, so one of her jobs was to take telephone messages, which she did with meticulous, and needless, over-attention to detail. She also helped Mrs B in the kitchen. This led to many a rumpus, because Mrs B was a quick and efficient cook, and Jane's dithering nearly drove her to distraction. She shouted at Jane to "put a move on", and then poor Jane would be paralysed with terror, faltering, "Oh dear, yes, of course, yes, quickly, of course." But her limbs wouldn't move, and she just stood stock-still, whimpering.

Once I heard Mrs B tell Jane to peel the potatoes and cut them in half for roasting. Later, when she wanted to put the potatoes in the oven, she found that Jane had cut every potato into about twenty pieces. She had been so desperately anxious to please by cutting them into exact halves that she couldn't stop and every half had been cut in half again, and so on until all that was left was a mound of tiny pieces. When Mrs B exploded, Jane fell back against the wall, pleading for forgiveness, shaking all over and white with terror. Fortunately, Sister Julienne came into the kitchen at that moment, saw the situation, and rescued Jane. "Never mind, Mrs B, we'll have mash today. They are just the right size for steaming. Jane, come with me, will you, please? The laundry has just come back and needs checking."

Poor Jane's eyes said it all – her fears, her grief, her gratitude and her love. I watched her go, and wondered what had happened to make her so fragile. Despite the kindness always shown to her by the Sisters, she seemed to live in a world of unfathomable loneliness.

She was very devout and attended Mass every day. She also attended most of the five monastic offices of the nuns. I had seen her in chapel, her fingers counting her rosary, her eyes earnestly fixed on the altar, half-intoning the words "Jesus loves me, Jesus loves me," over and over again, a hundred times or more. It is easy to scoff at such devotion. Women like Jane can be seen everywhere and they are always fair game for a cheap laugh.

I was with Jane on one occasion in Chrisp Street Market. It was just before Christmas and the stalls were laden with knick-knacks and curios – obvious Christmas presents. We approached one of these stalls. Lying in the centre was a small wooden object, about five or six inches long. It was nearly, but not quite, round and smooth, with a slight ridge running up the under side towards a pronounced rim. The tip was rounded, smooth and polished, with a small hole in the centre.

Jane picked up the object and held it between thumb and forefinger for everyone to see.

"Oh, what's this?" she said enquiringly.

Everyone fell silent and stared at Jane and the object. No one laughed.

The stall-holder was a fast-talking, street-wise coster of about fifty, who had been selling bric-a-brac most of his life. With a theatrical gesture he pushed his cap to the back of his head, took the fag out of his mouth and stubbed it out slowly on the edge of his stall. He glanced at his audience and opened his eyes wide with surprised innocence before answering: "Wha' is it, lady? Wha' is it? Why, lady, haven' chew seen one o' these fings afore?"

Jane shook her head.

"Why, it's a honey-stirrer. Vat's what it is, lady. An 'oney-stirrer, for stirrin' 'oney."

"Really? How interesting!" murmured Jane.

"Well, yes, very interestin', it is. They're old, you know, lady. Been around a long time, they 'ave. I'm surprised you ain't come across one 'afore now."

"No, never. You learn something new every day, don't you? How do you use it?"

"How do you use it? Ah, well now, allow me to show you, lady, if you don' mind."

He leaned forward and took the object from Jane's outstretched hand. The crowd, which had grown considerably, pressed forward, eager not to miss a word.

"Let me show you, lady. You sticks vis 'ere 'oney-stirrer in yer 'oney pot, and you stirs yer 'oney like vis" – he made a slight movement of the wrist – "an the 'oney, it catches on vis 'ere rim – you see vis 'rim 'ere, lady?" (He rubbed his fingers around it appreciatively.) "Well, ve honey, it catches on the rim, an' drips off, like."

"Really?" said Jane, "how fascinating. I would never have thought of it. I suppose it must be used a lot by country people who keep bees."

"Oh, yes, country people, vey use it all the time, wha' wiv all 'em birds an' bees an' all.'

"Well, I'm sure it must be very useful. Sister Julienne likes honey. I think I will buy this for her as a Christmas present. I am sure she would appreciate it."

"Oh yes. Sister Julienne will appreciate it all right, not 'arf she won't. If you asks my opinion, lady, you couldn't get Sister Julienne a Christmas present as wha' she'd appreciate more. Now, I was askin' four shillins for vis 'ere remarkable honey-stirrer, but seein' as how it's you, lady, wot's buyin' it for Sister Julienne for Christmas, I'll let you 'ave it for two shillin' and sixpence, an' you got a real bargain, I can tell you."

The coster beamed benignly.

"That's very good of you," exclaimed Jane as she handed over the money. "I must say I'm delighted, and I'm sure Sister will be delighted when she sees it."

"No doubt abaht it. No doubt at all. It's bin a pleasure doin' business wiv you, madam, an' I must say you've made my day, you 'ave."

"Have I really?" said Jane with a sweet, sad smile. "I can't think how, but I'm so glad. It's always nice to give pleasure to someone, isn't it?"

Christmas Day arrived. We returned from morning church and prepared the dining room for Christmas lunch. A tableau of angels adorned the table centre. Our presents were exchanged at lunch time and were placed on the dining table beside each person's plate. I found it hard to take my eyes off a small box, wrapped in silver paper, decorated with a red ribbon, resting beside Sister Julienne's plate. What was going to happen?

We were fourteen to lunch that Christmas Day, including two visiting nuns from North Africa, beautiful in their white habits. Grace was said, with a special remembrance for the gifts of the Magi, then we all sat down to open our presents. A chorus of "oohs" and "ahs" and little squeaks and giggles arose from the table, as kisses were exchanged between the ladies. Sister Julienne picked up the silver box, saying, "Now what can this be?" and my heart stood still. She removed the paper and opened the box. Just the flicker of an eyebrow, instantaneous and then gone, was all that betrayed her. She carefully put the lid back on the box and turned to Jane with a radiant smile, her eyes alight with pleasure.

"How very kind. A most charming thought, Jane. It is just what I have always wanted, and I am truly grateful. I will treasure it always."

Jane leaned forward eagerly. "It's a honey-stirrer. They are very old."

"Oh yes, I know. I saw that at once. A delightful gift and so like you, Jane, to be so thoughtful."

Sister Julienne kissed her gently and quietly tucked the box away beneath her scapular.

To all appearances Jane was a bit of a dimwit. It was her reading that gave me the clue that she was, in fact, exactly the opposite. She was a voracious, almost obsessive reader. Books were her only self-indulgence, and she handled them with loving care. I took to spying on her authors: Flaubert, Dostoevsky, Russell, Kierkegaard. I was astonished. Predictably, she had a daily discipline of Bible-reading, but beyond the Old and New Testaments her devotional reading was formidable: St Thomas Aquinas, Augustine, St John of the Cross. I looked at her with new eyes. Aquinas for recreation! This was no dimwit.

Yet if anyone came into the room whilst she was reading she would jump up, all of a dither, and throw down her book guiltily, saying something like: "Do you want anything? Can I get you anything?" or, on one occasion: "I was just about to lay the table for breakfast. I haven't been idle, really I haven't." This did not seem like the behaviour of an intelligent woman.

Later I discovered that Jane had spent twenty years in domestic service. She had been put into service at the age of fourteen, when life for a humble servant girl was very hard indeed. She had to be up at about 4 a.m. to fetch the wood and coal, clear the grates and light the fires. Then it would be a day of constant heavy work, at the beck and call of the mistress of the house, until ten or eleven at night, when she would finally be allowed to go to bed.

Jane had been hopeless at the job. However hard she tried she could never master the skills of simple housework. Consequently the mistress was always cross with her. She became increasingly nervous, breaking things, bungling things. She lived in a state of sheer terror that she would do something wrong, which she always did, so she was continually getting the sack and having to find another position – where the cycle started all over again.

Few domestic servants can have been less suited to the job than Jane. Her incompetence was monumental, although it is not uncommon for highly intellectual people to be baffled by the practicalities of everyday life.

Poor Jane! I once saw her trying to light a gas mantle. It took her forty minutes. First she spilled the matches all over the floor, and by the end she had broken the mantle, broken the glass shade, cut herself, set fire to a tea towel and scorched the wallpaper. No wonder she was always getting the sack.

I remember another occasion at Nonnatus House when Jane spilled a drop of milk on the floor. She trembled and whimpered, "I'll clean it up. I'll clean it up. I'll do it."

She then proceeded to wash the entire kitchen floor, including moving all the tables and chairs. No one could stop her. She insisted on doing the whole kitchen. I asked Sister Julienne why she behaved in this way.

"Jane was utterly crushed as a child," explained Sister; "she will never get over it."

Jane very seldom went out, and never left Nonnatus House for a night. The only person she was ever known to visit was Peggy, who lived on the Isle of Dogs with her brother Frank.

No one could describe Peggy as plump. Voluptuous would be a better description. Her softly rounded curves spoke eloquently of ease and comfort. Her large grey eyes, fringed with dark curling lashes, had a sensuous quality in their dreamy depths. Her smooth, clear skin glowed with radiance and every time she smiled, which was often, dimples enhanced her beauty, making you want to look upon her all the more. "Allure" might well have been her middle name.

Yet Peggy was not an idle lady of leisure, preserving her beauty with creams and lotions, or toying with men for her own amusement. Peggy was a charwoman. What with office cleaning in the early hours of the morning, her "ladies" in Bloomsbury and Knightsbridge, and restaurants and banks each afternoon, she was always busy.

Peggy cleaned at Nonnatus House three mornings a week and the house always smelled sweetly of wax polish and carbolic soap when she left. Everyone liked her. Her beauty was refreshing, and her smile raised the spirits. Furthermore, she sang quietly to herself as she polished and scrubbed. She had a pretty voice, and sang in tune. Her repertoire consisted of old-fashioned folk songs and hymns, the sort that children used to learn in schools and Sunday schools; it was a delight to listen to her. Her speaking voice was equally charming.

She was kind to everyone, and never seemed to get ruffled. I recall once when I had been out half the night (in my memory, babies always seem to have been born in the middle of the night, especially when it was raining!) and came in wet and muddy. I had been obliged to wait in Manchester Road for forty minutes, whilst the swing bridge was opened for cargo boats, and consequently was tired and ill-tempered. I crossed the hallway leading to the Clinical Room, not even conscious that I was leaving wet, muddy footmarks all over the fine Victorian tiles that Peggy had just buffed up to a glow. Something made me turn at the top of the stairs and I saw the mess I had made of her hard work.

"Oh, gosh – sorry!" I said, feebly.

Her eyes sparkled with laughter, and she was down on her knees in a trice. "Don't give it another thought," she said, affably.

Peggy was a good deal older than she looked. Her beautiful skin, in which the only wrinkles were laughter lines around her eyes, made her look about thirty, but in fact she too was approaching forty-five. Her supple body was as agile as that of a young girl and she was graceful in all her movements. Many women of forty-five would wish to look as youthful, so what was her secret, I wondered? Was it a sort of inner glow, a secret joy that irradiated her features?

Although they were around the same age, Peggy looked at least twenty years younger than Jane. Her softly rounded curves contrasted with Jane's stiff, angular bones; her clear, youthful skin with the other's dried-out wrinkles; her pretty blonde hair with Jane's ill-cut greyness. Her easy-going laughter was infectious, whilst Jane's nervous giggle was irritating. Yet Peggy treated the tall, angular woman with great tenderness, making allowances for her nervous twitter and general silliness, and often making her laugh in a way that no one else could. Jane seemed more relaxed when Peggy was in the house; she smiled more readily and seemed, if possible, less apprehensive.

Peggy's brother Frank was a fishmonger, known to all as "Frank the Fish". By common consent he kept the best wet-fish stall in Chrisp Street Market. Whether his ability to sell his fish was due to the excellence of the fish, the ebullience of his personality, or his commitment to hard work was not known. Probably his success was due to a combination of all three.

He slept little, and rose about three o'clock each morning to go to Billingsgate Fish Market. He had to push his barrow along the quiet streets, as very few working men had a van in those days. At Billingsgate he personally selected all his fish, having an encyclopedic knowledge of his customers' likes and dislikes, and he was back at Chrisp Street by 8 a.m. to set up his stall.

He was an effervescent bundle of energy and he loved his work. He brought fun and laughter to hundreds of people, and many dockers were served kippers for tea, simply because their good wives couldn't resist the bantering flirtation that fell from his lips as he slid the slippery fish into their outstretched hands, always with a wink and a squeeze.

He shut up the stall at 2 p.m. every day, and started on his delivery round. He kept no books, but carried in his head a detailed knowledge of his customers' daily requirements. He never made a mistake. He called at Nonnatus House twice every week and he and Mrs B, who was not a great admirer of men, were best of friends.

Frank was a bachelor and, because he was comparatively well off and always good-natured, half the ladies of Poplar were after him – but he just wasn't interested. "'E's wedded to 'is fish," they grumbled.

Frank seemed an unlikely friend for Jane, who was pathologically shy of men. If the plumber or the baker called at the house and Jane opened the door, she would go to pieces. She would chirrup and twitter around them, trying to be pleasant, but merely succeeding in being ridiculous. But with Frank she was different somehow. His ready banter and Cockney wit were tempered by gentleness and consideration, to which Jane responded with a shy, sweet smile and eyes filled with gratitude. Or was it love, my colleagues Cynthia and Trixie wondered. Did repressed, dried-up Jane also harbour a secret passion for the extrovert fishmonger?

"Could be," reflected Cynthia. "How romantic! And how tragic for poor Jane! He's wedded to his fish."

"Not a chance," said Trixie, the pragmatist. "If it were a case of unrequited love, she would go to pieces with him even more than she does with other men."

Once, after Jane had been to visit Peggy and Frank, she said wistfully, "If only I had a brother. I would be happy if I had a brother." Later, Trixie said, acerbically, "It's a lover she needs, not a brother." We all had a good laugh at Jane's expense.

It was only later that I learned the sad stories that brought these three people together. Jane, Peggy, and Frank had been brought up in the workhouse. The two girls were nearly the same age, Frank was four years older. Jane and Peggy had become best friends and shared everything. They had slept in adjacent beds in a dormitory of seventy girls. They had sat next to each other in the refectory, where meals for three hundred girls were taken. They had gone to the same school. They had shared the same household chores. Above all, they had shared each other's thoughts and feelings and sufferings, as well as their small joys. Today, workhouses may seem like a distant memory, but for children such as Jane, Peggy, and Frank the impact of having spent their formative years in such an institution was almost unimaginable.

THE RISE OF THE WORKHOUSE

My own generation grew up in the shadow of the workhouse. Our parents and grandparents lived in constant fear that something unpredictable would happen and that they would end up in one of those terrible buildings. An accident or illness or unemployment could mean loss of wages, then eviction and homelessness; an illegitimate pregnancy or the death of parents or old age could lead to destitution. For many the dreaded workhouse became a reality.

Workhouses have now disappeared, and in the twenty-first century the memory of them has all but faded. Indeed, many young people have not even heard of them, or of the people who lived in them. But social history is preserved in the accounts of those who lived at the time. Very few personal records written by workhouse inmates exist, so the little we do know makes the stories of people such as Jane, Frank and Peggy all the more compelling.

In medieval times, convents and monasteries gave succour to the poor and needy as part of their Christian duty. But in England Henry VIII's Dissolution of the Monasteries put a stop to that in the 1530s. Queen Elizabeth I passed the Act for the Relief of the Poor in 1601, the aim being to make provision for those who could not support themselves because of age or disability. Each parish in England was encouraged to set aside a small dwelling for the shelter of the destitute. These were known as poorhouses. It was a remarkable act of an enlightened queen, and crystallised the assumption that the state was responsible for the poorest of the poor.

The 1601 Act continued in force for over two hundred years

and was adequate for a rural population of around five to ten million souls. But the Industrial Revolution, which gathered pace in the latter part of the eighteenth century, changed society for ever.

One of the most remarkable features of the nineteenth century was the population explosion. In 1801, the population of England, Wales and Scotland was around 10.5 million. By 1851 it had doubled to 20 million and by 1901 it had doubled again to 45 million. Farms could neither feed such numbers nor provide them with employment. The government of the day could not cope with the problem, which was accentuated by land enclosure and the Corn Laws. Industrialisation and the lure of employment drew people from the villages into the cities in huge numbers. Overcrowding, poverty, hunger and destitution increased exponentially and the Poor Law Act of 1601 was inadequate to deal with the number of emerging poor. There can be no understanding of the poverty of the masses in the nineteenth century without taking into consideration the fact of a fourfold increase of population in one hundred years.

Victorian England was not the period of complacency and self-satisfaction that is so often portrayed in the media. It was also a time of growing awareness of the divide between the rich and the poor, and of a social conscience. Thousands of good and wealthy men and women, usually inspired by Christian ideals, were appalled by the social divide, saw that it was not acceptable, and devoted their lives to tackling the problems head on. They may not always have been successful, but they brought many evils to light and sought to remedy them.

Parliament and reformers constantly debated schemes to change and improve the old Poor Law Act. A Royal Commission was set up, and in 1834 the Poor Law Amendment Act was passed. Responsibility for relief of destitution was removed from individual parishes and handed over to unions of parishes. The small parish poorhouses were closed and the unions were required to provide large houses, each designed to accommodate several hundred people. The aim was that "the poor shall be set to work, and they shall dwell in working houses".

And so, the union workhouses were born. Each was to be run by a master and his wife, who were responsible for day-to-day administration, together with a number of paid officers, who assisted them. Overall responsibility for each workhouse was in the hands of a local Board of Guardians and they were financed partly by the local Poor Law rates and partly through government loans that had to be repaid. Running costs were to be met by local rates, but income could also be generated through the work of the inmates.

It can be argued that the workhouse system was the first attempt at social welfare in this country. Certainly it was intended as a safety net to house and feed the very poorest of society, and it laid the foundations of our modern welfare state. In this respect it was nearly one hundred years ahead of its time, yet the implementation of the high ideals of the reformers and legislators went tragically wrong, and the workhouses came to be dreaded as places of shame, suffering and despair. People would often rather have died than go there – and some did. My grandfather knew a man who hanged himself when the guardians informed him that he must go into the workhouse. Most of the labouring poor lived on a perpetual knife-edge between subsistence and destitution. For them, the workhouse represented not a safety net, but a dark and fearsome abyss from which, should they fall, there would be no escape.

The authors of the 1834 Act proposed separate workhouses for different categories of paupers, but within a year or two, economy and ease of management dictated that mixed workhouses became the norm. These were built to house *all* groups of paupers – the old, the sick, the chronically infirm, children, the mentally disabled – as well as able-bodied men and women who were unemployed and therefore destitute. However, such a great diversity of people under one roof and one administration was doomed to failure.

The original policy was that the workhouse should be a "place of last resort", therefore that conditions inside a workhouse should be less comfortable than a state of homeless destitution outside. Strict rules for admission were introduced and enforced nationwide, and these rules were intended to deter the idle and shiftless from seeking admission. But the result, in a mixed workhouse, was that all classes of paupers suffered. Nobody could come up with an answer to the question of how to deter the idle without penalising the defenceless.

In order that the workhouse really should be a "place of last resort" a rigid, inflexible system of discipline and punishment was introduced. Families were separated, not only men from women, but husbands from wives and brothers from sisters. Children over seven were taken away from their mothers. The official policy was that babies and children under seven could stay with their mothers in the women's quarters. But policy and practice often diverge and mothers and toddlers were frequently separated. The construction of the buildings was such that there was no access from one group of paupers to another. Heating was minimal, even in the depths of winter. People had to sleep in dormitories in which anything up to seventy paupers could be accommodated. For each, an iron bedstead, a straw palliasse and a blanket were provided; inadequate protection against the cold winters. Paupers were locked into the dormitory each night and the sanitary arrangements were disgusting. A coarse rough uniform, often made of hemp, which was very harsh on the skin and offered no real warmth in the winter, was provided. Paupers' heads were sometimes, though not always, shaved. Regulations permitted the hair of children to be forcibly shaved. This was intended for the control of lice or fleas, but was sometimes done as a punishment, especially on little girls, for whom it was a humiliation.

Food was minimal and meals frequently had to be eaten in

silence, the paupers sitting in serried rows. The quantity of food for a workhouse pauper in the middle of the nineteenth century was less than that provided for a prisoner in jail, although this improved towards the end of the century.

Paupers were only allowed to go outside the workhouse walls with the permission of the master, to look for work, or for special reasons such as attending a baptism, funeral or wedding. In theory a pauper could discharge him- or herself from the workhouse, but in practice this seldom happened because of their abject poverty and the limitations of available work.

All these rules, and many more, had to be obeyed on pain of harsh punishments, which included flogging, birching, with-holding food, and solitary confinement. Complaints about the daily living conditions were usually dealt with by punishment. Deference to the master, his wife and the officers was required at all times.

It is easy at this distance of time to be critical, and to sneer at what we call "Victorian hypocrisy". But we should remember that this *was* the first attempt at a form of social welfare, and mistakes will always be made in any pioneering venture. Numerous reports were commissioned and published during the century of workhouse existence and many attempts at reform and improvement were made.

These evils had been designed to deter the indolent from entering the workhouse. The tragedy was that in a mixed work-house with one administration, one central building and one staff, the rules, regulations, and punishments applied universally, with the result that old people, the sick, the crippled, the mentally disabled, and children, suffered dreadfully. The atmosphere inside a workhouse was not only stifling to the human soul, but destroyed the last shreds of human dignity.

Another great problem that led to the ill repute of workhouses was the staff. In the early years none of them had any training or qualifications. This could not be expected, because there was no precedent, but the unfortunate result was that it opened the floodgates to all sorts of petty dictators who enjoyed wielding power. The masters had unlimited authority, and their character determined the lives of the paupers, for good or ill. Rules had to be obeyed, and the Master could be a good and humane man, or he could be harsh and tyrannical. The "deterrent rules" ensured that the only qualification required of applicants for the posts of Workhouse Master and officers was the ability to enforce discipline. Many came from the armed forces, reflecting the controlling and disciplinary role that was expected of them.

The "work" aspect of the system rapidly became an acute and intractable problem. The sale of goods was not the primary purpose of the Poor Law Act, but to generate some income for the day-to-day running of the workhouse items and produce made by the paupers were sometimes sold in the open market. This led to protests from employers in the private sector, on two counts: firstly, that goods produced in the workhouses by cheap labour and sold in the marketplace would seriously undercut them; secondly, that the resulting loss of business would affect their employees, who would either have to accept reduced wages or even lose their jobs. This would be a dire outcome when, in most cases, and unlike their workhouse counterparts, they had families to support. On top of these difficulties there was, of course, the problem (still alive and well in the twenty-first century) that in a free-market system work cannot be created out of thin air. Although the British industrial economy was booming throughout the nineteenth century, it was subject to periodic recessions that threw unskilled labourers out of work in their thousands, thus swelling the workhouse population. So pointless, profitless work was introduced to keep the paupers busy. For example, stone-breaking was required of the men. Industrial England could break stones using machinery, but the paupers had to break granite with a mallet. Animal bones could be ground into powder for fertiliser by machine, but paupers had to grind bones by hand. In one workhouse there was a corn mill for men to push round and round for hours on end, but it had no function; it was grinding nothing.

The women did all the cooking and laundry for their fellow inmates. "Scrubbing" is a word I have encountered frequently in this context. Hours of scrubbing vast lengths of stone floors, corridors and stairs was a daily requirement. Sewing sails for sailing boats, by hand, and picking oakum for caulking ships were further tasks that fell to the women and children. Oakum was old rope, frequently impregnated with tar or sea salt, which had to be unpicked by hand and tore the skin and nails. The fibres were then used for filling in the cracks between the wooden planks of ships.

The 1834 Poor Law Act required elementary education (basic numeracy and literacy) for children three hours per day, and a schoolmaster was employed by each Board of Guardians. When the Education Act of 1870 was passed, children were removed from the mixed workhouses and placed in separate establishments and had to attend the local Board School.

Under the 1834 Act a qualified medical officer was required to attend the sick, but nursing was carried out by untrained female inmates. In large groups of enclosed people who were not allowed out, infectious diseases spread like wildfire. For example, in the 1880s in a workhouse in Kent, it was found that in a child population of one hundred and fifty-four, only three children did *not* have tuberculosis.

One hears about "the insane" crowded into workhouses. I think workhouse life bred and fostered its own insanity. I once heard, in the 1950s, what used to be called "the workhouse howl" emitted from the throat of a woman who had been a workhouse inmate for about twenty years in the early twentieth century. It was a noise to make your blood run cold.

Medical infirmaries were also available for the hospital treatment of the poor who could not afford to pay a doctor or to go to hospital. But the infirmaries came to be feared almost as much as the workhouses themselves, and were regarded as places of disease, insanity, neglect and death. Medical and nursing staff were of the lowest order, and were frequently brutal and ignorant – it was work which no doctor who valued his career would undertake. The attitudes of medical and nursing staff, who were careless of the lives of paupers, reflected the mores of the time.

The stigma of illegitimacy has destroyed the lives of millions of unfortunate young women and blighted those of their children. If a girl's lover deserted her, and her parents could not, or would not, support her and the child, the workhouse was often the only form of relief available. The baby would be born in the infirmary. After weaning, the girl would be encouraged to leave the workhouse with her baby to seek employment. But this was usually impossible to find because of the limited labour market for women, further restricted because of the presence of a baby. The girl would also be encouraged to give her baby up for adoption. Many girls were medically certified as "hysterical" or "of unsound mind" or even "morally degenerate", and the baby would be forcibly removed and brought up in the workhouse. The young mother would be expected to leave, find work outside and contribute to the poor rates to offset the cost of keeping and educating the child. If she could not find work, she would have to return to the women's section of the workhouse. The system was heartless and stupid, but those were the rules, and they reflected the social attitude that a "fallen woman" should be punished.

It was one such story that brought Jane to the workhouse when her mother was dismissed for an illicit liaison with her employer.

JANE

"We'll have to watch that one, saucy little madam. Did you hear the way she spoke out of turn at breakfast?"

"Don't you worry, my dear. I'll break her before she leaves here."

The Master and Mistress were talking about Jane, who had been in the workhouse since birth. It was rumoured that her father was a high-class gentleman, distinguished in Parliament and at the Bar. When his wife found him in bed with a servant girl, the girl was immediately dismissed and went to the workhouse, where Jane was born.

The baby stayed with her mother to be breast-fed, but was removed when weaning commenced and was then taken to the infants' nursery. The mother returned to the women's section of the workhouse and never saw her baby again. Thus Jane was entirely reared by the institution and knew no other life.

It was a harsh, repressive existence, but no amount of smacks or punishments could subdue Jane's bubbling laughter and *joie de vivre.* In the playground, she chased the other children, or hid and jumped out on them with a delighted "boo". In the dormitory she crept under the beds and poked the mattresses of sleeping children with a stick. Her behaviour caused uproar and an officer would run in with smacks and orders to be quiet. Jane always got smacked, being the cause of all the trouble. But she cried herself to sleep, then giggled and did it again.

As she grew, her high spirits got her into endless trouble. Docility and obedience were expected from the children at all times, and if there was any deviation from this, naughty little Jane could generally be found at the centre of it. Who was it that tied Officer Sharp's shoelaces together as she sat darning socks, so that she fell over when she stood up and took a step? No one knew for certain, but as Jane had been seen in the vicinity, the little girl got a good smacking for it. Who was it that climbed the drainpipe in the playground? Why, Jane, of course. And who mixed up all the boots in the dormitory so that everyone had the wrong sizes? If it wasn't Jane, it might as well have been, so she got the punishment.

Jane's great misfortune was that she stood out. In a group of children she could not be overlooked. She was a good deal taller than average, and also prettier, with her dark curls and clear blue eyes. Worse than this, which was bad enough, she was a great deal more intelligent than most of the other children, and the Master and Mistress feared an intelligent child. They told the officers to keep an eye on her.

"Keep in line, don't straggle. Heads up, now. Don't slouch."

Officer Hawkins would show them how to do it!

The girls were marching to church one Sunday morning. It was a very long crocodile, consisting of nearly one hundred girls. Jane, halfway along on the outside, watched fat old Officer Hawkins strutting along like a penguin and with an instinctive gift for mimicry she copied the walk, head thrown back, arms flapping, feet splayed. The girls behind started to giggle. A hand shot out and hit Jane on the head with such force that she fell through the column of girls on to the road on the other side. She was hauled up and hit again and then pushed back into line. Her ears were ringing and lights were darting before her eyes, but she had to keep marching. She was six years old.

"Where did it come from?" demanded the Master, his eyes bulging, his face turning red. "Who is guilty of this piece of insolence?"

He was looking at a sketch of himself, on a page torn from an exercise book. It was a remarkable drawing for a child, but the Master couldn't see it that way. All he could see was himself with an exaggerated moustache, a square head, small eyes, and an exceedingly large stomach. The picture had been circulating among the girls for three days, causing endless amusement, which only added to the Master's fury.

He assembled all the girls in the hall and addressed them from the pulpit. He reminded them that they were paupers who must respect and obey their betters. No act of disobedience, disrespect or insubordination would be tolerated. He held up the pencil drawing.

"Who did this?" he demanded, menacingly.

No one moved.

"Very well. Every single girl in this room will be beaten, starting now, with the first row."

Jane stood up. "I did it, sir," she whispered.

She was taken to the discipline room – a small, square room with no windows and no furniture except for one stool. Several canes were hanging on the wall. Jane was beaten severely on her bare bottom. She could not sit down for several days. She was only seven years old.

That should be enough to break her spirit, thought the Master to himself with satisfaction. But it wasn't. He couldn't understand it. Why the very next morning, he had seen her, with his own eyes, dancing across the playground, as though she hadn't a care in the world.

The reason why Jane's spirit was not broken was that she had a secret. It was her own special secret and she had told no one else except Peggy. She locked it in her heart and hugged it to herself. It was this glorious secret that filled her with such irrepressible joy and exhilaration. But it was also to be the cause of her greatest disaster, and her life-long grief.

The rumour that her father was a high-born gentleman in Parliament must have reached Jane's ears when she was a little girl. Perhaps she had heard the officers talking about it, or perhaps another child had heard the adults talking and told her. Perhaps Jane's mother had told another workhouse inmate, who had passed it on. One can never tell how rumours start.

To Jane, it was not a rumour. It was an absolute fact. Her daddy was a high-born gentleman, who one day would come and take her away. She fantasised endlessly about her daddy. She talked to him, and he talked to her. She brushed her hair, and cast a flirtatious eye at him, as he looked over her shoulder, admiring her curls. She ran down the playground as fast as she could, because he was standing at the other end, admiring her strength and speed. He was always with her. He was everywhere.

She had a very clear picture of him in her mind. He was not like any other man she had seen at the workhouse, not like the coal man, nor the baker, nor the boiler man. They were ugly and short, and wore rough working men's clothing and cloth caps. He was not like the Master or any of the officers. Jane's little nose wrinkled with disgust at the thought. Her daddy was quite different. He was tall and slim with fine features and pale skin. He had long fingers; she looked at her own slender hands and knew that she had inherited her daddy's fingers. He had lots of hair – she didn't like bald men – and it was a soft, grey colour, always clean and nicely brushed. His clothes were nothing like the awful stuff worn by the workmen she saw, and her daddy didn't smell of sweat the way they did. He always wore beautiful suits smelling of lavender, and he wore a top hat and carried a walking-cane with a gold crest on top.

She knew just what his voice sounded like also – after all, he was constantly talking to her – it was not rough and grating like other men's voices; it was musical and deep, full of laughter. She knew this because he was always laughing with her and making fun of the Master and the officers. His eyes had twinkled with amusement, and he had called her 'his clever girl' when she had drawn a funny picture of the Master.

So how could Jane be unhappy? The more they beat her, the closer she drew to her daddy. He comforted her when she cried at night. He dried her tears and told her to be a brave girl. She swallowed her tears quickly, because she knew that he liked to see her smiling and happy, and she made up a funny story to amuse him, because she knew that he liked her funny stories.

She had also invented his house. It was a beautiful house with a long drive and fine trees in the grounds. There were steps up to the front door and, inside, the rooms smelled of beeswax and lavender. There were pictures on the walls and fine rugs on the floors. Her daddy took her by the hand and led her through the rooms, one by one. He told her that one day he would come and take her away from the workhouse, and they would live together in the beautiful home with the long drive and fine trees.

Jane was seven years old when she began to attend the local council school. She was very proud – it was a big, proper school for big girls and Jane loved it. It brought her into contact with a life outside the workhouse which she had not known existed. It also introduced her to learning, which she loved, and her young mind began to expand. She realised that there were thousands of things that she could learn and she absorbed and retained her lessons quickly. Excellent reports of her progress were sent back to the workhouse. The Master was not impressed. A request from the school's headmistress for Jane to be allowed to take piano lessons, as she showed an unusually good ear for music, was refused, the Master saying that no workhouse pauper should be singled out for special treatment. A request that Jane should be allowed to take the role of Mary in the school's nativity play was refused for the same reason.

Jane was bitterly disappointed at this, chiefly because her daddy would have been so proud to see her playing Mary, and she cried herself to sleep for several nights, until he whispered to her that the silly old school nativity play was not worth crying over. She would have the chance to perform in many more, much nicer plays when she came to live with him in the beautiful house with the long drive.

The workhouse girls were kept apart, as much as possible, from the other girls at the school. This was because several local mothers had complained that they did not want their daughters mixing with 'them workhouse bastards'. This segregation was a source of great pain to many of her friends, but not to Jane. She laughed at the rule that workhouse girls should not play in the same playground as the other children, and tossed her dark curls scornfully. Just let them wait. She would show them. All those dreary girls whose fathers were dustmen and street-sweepers and costermongers. They would be sorry one day, when they saw her daddy, a high-born gentleman, drive up to the school in a carriage. She would run up to him, and all those dreary girls would see her. He would pick her up, kiss her, and take her to the waiting carriage, and all the girls would see and be jealous. The teachers would say to each other: "We always knew that Jane was different."

Jane was fortunate in her class teacher. Miss Sutton was young, well educated and eager. In fact, to say that she possessed a missionary zeal for teaching the poorest of the poor would not be overstating her dedication and enthusiasm. She saw in the vivacious Jane unusual qualities that she was determined to promote. The child learned to read and write in about a quarter the length of time that it took the other children, so whilst Miss Sutton was engaged with the rest of the class, who were learning the alphabet and painstakingly spelling out words, she asked Jane to write stories for her. Jane did so with great joy and fluency, picking up any subject Miss Sutton suggested and weaving a delightful child's story around it. Several of these stories were shown to the Headmistress, who commented: "There is an unusual mind at work here," and she obtained a copy of *A Child's Garden of Verse*, which she handed to Miss Sutton for Jane's use. The child was enraptured by the rhythm of the words and quickly learned many of the poems by heart, which she recited to her daddy when they were alone together.

Miss Sutton also introduced Jane to history and geography, using a children's encyclopedia as her textbook. These lessons had to be surreptitious, because Miss Sutton was employed to teach reading, writing, and arithmetic. Furthermore, she was canny enough to suspect that if she requested extra lessons for Jane, the request would be refused and that would be the end of history and geography for Jane.

Miss Sutton took the wise step of introducing one volume at a time, with the words, "I think you will enjoy reading this. When you have done so, write me a story about it, and we will talk about it at lunch time."

Jane adored Miss Sutton, and their lunch-time conversations about kings and queens and faraway places were the high point of her day.

The children's encyclopedia was her treasure. There were ten large volumes, each beautifully bound in dark blue with gold lettering, and she pored over each one with a hungry mind. She loved the books, their feel and touch and smell, and wanted to keep them, but she knew she couldn't; they were kept in the classroom cupboard, but she knew that Miss Sutton would let her see them any time she wanted. To Jane these books were sacred. Every word she read was – must be – gospel truth, because it was written in the "'cyclopedia".

One day she came across a long word she had not met before. She traced it with her finger and tried to say it to herself: "Par" – that was easy; "lia" – what did that mean? "ment" – that was easy, too; but what was it all put together? Suddenly, like a lightning stroke, it came to her: *Parliament*. People had said her daddy was in Parliament. She devoured the relevant pages as though her life depended on it. In the background the other children were reciting C-A-T, D-O-G. Jane heard nothing. She was busy poring over information on Parliament and the British Constitution. She didn't understand it all, but that didn't matter, it was about her daddy. Like one possessed she read on. She turned a few pages; and then she saw him. The picture leaped towards her. It was her daddy, as she had always known he would look: tall and slim, with slightly grey hair, a thoughtful face, but kindly. He was wearing a beautiful frock coat with tails, just as she had always known he would, with slender trousers and elegant shoes. He was carrying a top hat and a walking-cane with a gold crest. He had long, slender fingers just like she had. She kissed the page.

The lunch bell sounded. Miss Sutton roused her.

"Come on, Jane, time for lunch."

"What is Parliament?" demanded the child.

"The Houses of Parliament are where His Majesty's Government sits. Now come along to lunch."

"Where are these Houses? Can I go? Will you take me?"

Miss Sutton laughed. An eager pupil is the breath of life to a dedicated teacher.

"I will tell you as much as I know about Parliament. But you must have your lunch first. You want to grow to be a big strong girl, don't you? Come back to the classroom after lunch."

After lunch Miss Sutton did her best to explain to the understanding of a seven-year-old that the Members of Parliament made the rules that govern the country.

"Are they very important people, and very important rules?" the child enquired.

"Very; there are none higher in the land."

"More important than the workhouse Master?"

"Oh, much. Members of Parliament are the most important people in the land, after the King."

Jane's breath was coming fast. She seemed unable to contain her excitement. Miss Sutton was watching her closely with astonishment. Jane looked up at her teacher, her blue eyes flashing through dark lashes (extraordinary, the vivid combination of blue eyes and dark hair, thought Miss Sutton). Jane's white teeth showed as she bit her lower lip. One of her milk teeth had come out and she drew air in through the gap with a sucking sound, then poked her tongue through it and wiggled it around. A smile spread across her face, as she whispered, confidentially: "My daddy is in Parliament."

Miss Sutton was, to say the least, taken aback. She was too

fond of the child to reply, "Don't be silly," but she felt it necessary to say something to dispel this illusion.

"Oh, come now, Jane, that cannot possibly be."

"But he is, he is, he's here in the book. I've seen him."

She turned a few pages on and pointed the artist's impression of a Member of Parliament.

"That's my daddy. I know it is. I've seen him lots and lots of times."

"But Jane, that is not a real man. That's just a drawing to show the clothes that a Member of Parliament might wear. That's not your daddy, dear."

"It is, it is, I know it is!" Jane began to cry, and jumped up. "You don't know anything. You don't know my daddy. I do, and I know it's him." Jane ran from the classroom in tears.

Poor Miss Sutton was troubled by this scene, and discussed it with the Headmistress. They agreed that Jane's reaction was just the longing of a highly imaginative child for a father she had never known. The Headmistress advised channelling Jane's thoughts in other directions and said it would be best not to mention Parliament again. That way Jane would forget about it.

Alone, Jane had also decided upon a similar course. She would never again mention her father to anyone, except Peggy. No one, not even Miss Sutton, was worthy of being let into her secret. She pretended she had forgotten all about the lunch-time conversation and carried on as though it had never occurred. But now she knew the book and the page where her daddy was to be found, and whenever she could, she went to the cupboard and opened the page, to gaze upon him with rapture in her heart. If anyone came near, she turned the page quickly, pretending she was looking at something else.

SIR IAN ASTOR-SMALEIGH

Sir Ian Astor-Smaleigh was a true philanthropist. He was an Oxford man who had devoted most of his life, and a considerable part of his fortune, to improvement of living conditions and life expectancy among children in the poorest areas of London. He was a founder member of the Oxford Philanthropic Society for the Improvement of Poor Children, having formed a charity dedicated to the provision of holidays for workhouse children. This work was also close to the heart of his wife, Lady Lavinia. They had made a systematic study of the workhouse system, and though they acknowledged that conditions had improved a great deal since the 1850s, they had seen with their own eyes hundreds of grey, unsmiling children crowded into workhouses and orphanages and were determined to do something about it. The idea of an annual holiday was Lady Lavinia's. Surely, she argued, two weeks by the sea for unwanted children, with healthy air and sunshine, was not too much to ask of society?

The opposition was loud in its scorn. "Holidays! For pauper children! What next? Let them learn to be grateful that they are given food and shelter."

Sir Ian and his lady battled on. When it was proved that one of the causes of rickets was lack of sunlight, they knew that this information could be used to further their cause. Were not many workhouse children afflicted with rickets? And were they not advocating a holiday in the sunshine?

Eventually they won the debate and, to their overwhelming relief, the committee passed, by a narrow majority, the resolution that money should be set aside for holidays for the children of one London workhouse. Additional funds were approved for a further five, if the experiment proved successful.

Suitable premises were found in Kent. These consisted of a series of large barns and sheds that could be adapted as dormitories for the children, who would sleep on straw mattresses on the floor. One of the sheds could be converted into a kitchen. The sheds were situated in fields that ran down to the sea. Sir Ian and members of the committee travelled to Kent to inspect the site and the accommodation. It all seemed perfect.

Sir Ian's next visit was to the workhouse selected for the experiment, in order to address the children himself and tell them of their good fortune. He wasn't going to hand over that pleasant task to anyone else, he told his wife. Was it not he who had haggled with the committee, hour after hour? Now he was going to have the reward of seeing the children's faces when they were told.

Accordingly Sir Ian had taken the train from Oxford, and was in a cab bound for his destination in the East End. He told the cabman to halt about a mile from the workhouse, because he wanted to walk the rest of the way in order to absorb the atmosphere. He attracted much attention in the London streets. He was tall and slim and well dressed. He was also clean. "Vere's a toff, nah, do-goodin'," was one of many whispers as he passed. Sir Ian was unaware of the sideways glances. His mind was fixed on his mission and he was determined that, in years ahead, the holiday project would be expanded to all workhouse children, nationwide.

The crocodile of little girls was returning from school. Jane was about halfway along the line, humming to herself as she marched along. She was looking at the pigtails of the little girl in front of her, watching them bounce up and down and wondering why they bounced more times than each step. "There must be some reason," she was thinking. She looked up, and her heart stopped beating. Pigtails, marching, the street, the buildings, the very sky itself vanished from her universe. Her daddy was on the other side of the street, walking straight towards the workhouse. She stood stock-still. The girls behind piled into her, causing commotion in the line.

"Get along there," shouted Officer Hawkins and hit her on the head. She neither heard nor felt a thing. Her daddy had turned into the workhouse gate and was walking straight towards the main door. She knew that it was him. Not a shadow of doubt. He was exactly as she had always known he would look, and exactly like the picture in the book – tall, slim, grey trousers, a frock coat, a top hat and a walking-cane. He had come to take her away, as he had always said he would.

Joy, unspeakable joy, flooded through Jane, with a rush of love impossible for a mere adult to describe. The intensity of a child's feelings is quite beyond our understanding, though we have all been children. Jane was almost suffocating with the power of her emotions. She felt that something huge and unknown was inside her and she was going to burst wide open.

"Get on there, I told you."

Another clout round the head, and Jane ran a few steps to catch up with the others. The door had closed behind her daddy, and the girls marched round the back to their usual entrance and stood in line for inspection before being told that they were to go to the hall.

Jane didn't stand in line with the others. She rushed straight upstairs to the dormitory, colliding with an officer on the stairway. She was flushed and breathless, but she grabbed the officer's hand, almost shouting.

"Quick, quick! I must have a clean dress and a clean apron!"

The officer was not used to being spoken to by a child in that manner. She shook Jane off.

"Don't be stupid. You'll have a clean dress on Sunday. Not before."

The child stamped. "But I must, I must! My daddy's downstairs, and I want a clean dress and apron before I see him."

"Your what?"

"My daddy. He's downstairs. He's in the Master's office. I saw him go in."

There was something so intense, so urgent and compelling about the child, that the officer gave in, and Jane was supplied with a clean dress and apron, against all the rules. She rushed to the washroom and washed her face and hands, brushed her hair until her curls shone, then flew downstairs to join the other children.

The officer plodded downstairs and told her colleagues of the extraordinary scene. They agreed that the child was mad, but one, with a snigger, said, "She may be right. Everyone says Jane's father was a high-born gentleman. Well, there's a fancy-lookin' gent gone in Master's office. We don't know what for." And she rubbed the side of her nose suggestively.

The girls filed into the hall and sat in rows, the youngest at the front, and the oldest at the back. Jane sat in the fifth row, her eyes fixed on the door where she knew her daddy would enter. She was burning with expectation.

The door opened and Sir Ian walked in, followed by the Master. Her heart stopped beating again. Yes, it was him, the same grave yet kindly face, the same smooth grey hair, and the same deep-set eyes with a smile at the corners. She sat up straight and tall. She was taller than the other girls anyway, but she increased her height by her posture. Her eyes were aflame with love, her mouth was slightly open, her teeth gleamed white as she smiled.

Sir Ian spoke to the children from the pulpit. He could see right down the long hall, with the massed young faces staring up at him. Most of the faces looked glum and unresponsive, and it is always difficult to address an audience from whom the speaker feels no wave of sympathy. He had a joyful message to impart; he had hoped for a joyful response. But most of the girls looked straight ahead, no emotion registering on their features. However, there was one little girl, sitting in the middle near the front, who looked really animated. Sir Ian therefore did what many public speakers do; he fixed his attention on one face in the audience and spoke to that person alone. He spoke of the coming summer and how hot London became at that time of year. He said: "I am going to take you away in the summer."

The little girl stifled a gasp, her eyes alight.

He spoke of the countryside and the seaside, and said: "I am going to take you to a beautiful place by the sea." The little girl could scarcely contain her emotion as he continued: "You will be able to paddle and swim, and build sandcastles and collect shells."

The little girl in the fifth row was now breathing fast, alternately clenching and stretching her fingers.

Sir Ian said, "We will do all this when the summer comes."

The little girl gave a sigh of delight as he stepped down from the pulpit. He felt pleased with himself. Overall, it had been a good address, and a good response.

The Master had also seen Jane's reaction and made a silent note to reprimand her about exhibitionism. He had not yet heard from his subordinate officers about the clean dress and apron.

The girls stood up to leave the hall. One by one they filed past the Master and Sir Ian. It was at this point that Jane lost all control of herself. As she passed, she rushed out of line and flung her arms around Sir Ian's waist, crying, "Thank you, Daddy, thank you, thank you," then she burst into tears, sobbing into his waistcoat.

He was surprised by this, and not a little touched. He ruffled her pretty hair and murmured, "There, there, my child. Don't take on so. You'll go to the seaside, and have a lovely time."

The Master tried to apologise and pull Jane away, but Sir Ian restrained him, saying that it was to the child's credit that she showed so much gratitude. He patted her hair and shoulders and took out a fine lawn handkerchief to wipe her eyes.

"There, now, dry your eyes. You can't go spoiling your pretty little face with tears. Let's see you smile. That's better."

The girls continued to file past, but Jane still clung to him.

The Master was standing beside them, seething with fury. After all the girls had left the hall, Sir Ian finally disentangled Jane's arms from around him. "There now, little one," he said, "off you run. Join your playmates. And I promise you will go to the seaside in the summer time."

Jane reached up and touched his face, and breathed the words: "Oh Daddy, I love you, Daddy, I love you so much."

She whispered it very softly, for him alone, but the Master heard every word. He said, out of the side of his mouth, to an officer: "Take her to the punishment room." He then escorted his guest to the boys' section, where Sir Ian gave his second address.

Jane ran to join the rest of the girls. They were agog with excitement and she was the centre of attention. She entered, proud and confident, her eyes dancing.

"That's my daddy. He's going to take me away."

They crowded around, chattering. Most of the girls believed her, although some of the older ones didn't. "Don't be silly. We're all going on holiday, not just you."

Jane replied haughtily. "Oh well, perhaps he will take some of you as well. He's very rich. But he's my daddy and he's taking me specially. After that we will live together in his big house."

An officer was standing right behind her. Jane was not aware of it while she spoke, but when she saw the girls looking over her shoulder, she turned round. The officer grabbed her.

"You come along with me, my girl. The Master wants to see you."

Jane's heart leaped. Her bright eyes looked over to the other girls. "There, you see! My daddy's going to take me away now. That's why the Master wants to see me."

The officer looked grim and most of the girls looked nervous. Only Jane was happy as she walked confidently away with the officer.

She was taken to the punishment room. The door was opened, she was pushed in, then the door was locked from the outside.

Jane was surprised, even startled, to find herself in a small room, about eight feet square, with no windows except the slit of a fanlight high up on one wall. There was no furniture, except for a three-legged stool sitting alone on the stone floor. Around the wall hung several canes of different lengths and a leather-thonged whip which had three tails, with a small lead pellet attached to the end of each tail.

She couldn't understand it. Why should they want her to wait here? Still, what did it matter, she thought to herself. She could still feel her daddy's kind, warm hands as he caressed her hair, and the sound of his voice as he called her "my child". What did it matter? What did anything in the world matter but that she had told him she loved him and he had called her his child and promised to take her away?

Jane sat down on the stool to wait.

Sir Ian Astor-Smaleigh returned to Oxford that evening full of philanthropic satisfaction. It had been a wonderful day. All the arrangements had been agreed with the workhouse master, the dates settled, the travelling arranged, catering organised, even the clothing supplier had been contracted. No wonder he was pleased. Over three hundred desperately poor children would benefit. He would be able to give a full and satisfactory report to his committee.

Lady Lavinia read his face as he entered the house. She shared her husband's happiness. The maid brought in a late meal and they sat down to discuss the day's work. He told her how he had addressed the children twice, first the girls and then the boys. They were poor, grey little things, he said, with very little life or vitality about them, not like their own children, who tumbled all over the place, and couldn't be contained. She protested that their children were not all that bad – "but do go on, dear."

"However," he said, "there was one little girl who seemed different. She was full of life. She was hanging on to every word as I spoke. She didn't take her eyes off me and she was obviously overcome with joy at the news. In fact she ran up to me afterwards to thank me."

Sir Ian had been on the point of saying that the little girl had called him 'Daddy', but then he thought better of it. After all, women were funny creatures and you never knew what they might think once they got an idea into their heads.

Lady Lavinia asked what the child was like.

"Oh, I don't know. Those damnation workhouse uniforms make all children look alike. I know she had dark hair. That's all I can say. But one thing I do know for certain: she was the only one to come up and say 'thank you' personally."

Lady Lavinia smiled fondly at her husband. "It does her much credit," she said, "and you can be sure of another thing: there is one little girl for whom this will be a day to remember."

A DAY TO REMEMBER

Jane waited for nearly two hours in the punishment room. This was because the Master had to accompany Sir Ian to the boys' section, after which many practical arrangements had to be sorted out. Then the Master wanted his supper, and a chance to discuss Jane's wickedness with his wife.

Two hours is a long time for a small child to wait alone in a closed room (Jane was eight years old). She grew hungry and fidgety. She was not particularly worried or frightened, in fact her mind was still buoyant. Her daddy had cuddled her and called her "my child".

She heard a key in the lock, and jumped up expectantly, smoothing out her apron and running her fingers through her curls, her face eager. The Master and a male officer entered. Her face fell.

"Where's my daddy?" she asked in a little voice.

The Master was bent on vengeance, and her question only added fuel to his fury. He took two steps across the room and hit her full in the face. She fell against the wall.

"You wicked girl. I'll knock that nonsense out of you."

But Jane was a girl of spirit, and now that she had her protector, she wasn't afraid of anyone. Her eyes gleaming, she faced the Master.

"I'll tell my daddy on you," she shouted.

The Master hit her again, harder this time. "Sir Ian Astor-Smaleigh is *not* your father. Do you understand? Now say it after me: 'Sir Ian Astor-Smaleigh is *not* my father.' Say it."

Now at this point a very curious thing happened. Curious to an adult, that is, but logical to the mind of a child. Children frequently hear something quite different from what has actually been said, particularly if it is something new and unrelated to anything else in their experience. (For example, throughout her childhood, my daughter thought our telephone number was "fried potato". She had heard us say "53280".)

Jane thought the Master had said: "See a nasty smelly is not my father." It didn't make sense. She stared at him in sullen amazement.

"Say it, say it," shouted the Master.

She didn't say a word, but just looked at him.

The Master repeated the whole sentence, and demanded she say it, his hand raised threateningly.

The child continued to stare at him in amazement. "A nasty smelly?" she exclaimed, her tone raised enquiringly.

"You insolent little bastard," the man roared. "First you insult Sir Ian, and now you insult me."

To the officer: "Undress her."

The officer grabbed her and started to undo the buttons of her dress. At this Jane really became alarmed and tried to pull away.

"Stop it, let me go. I'll tell my daddy on you, I will."

"Oh, the wickedness! Has she no shame?" muttered the officer, and continued to undress Jane until she stood naked before them. She was crying and frightened now, but still she resisted as much as her puny strength would allow.

"Hold her hands tight and turn her around," ordered the Master, selecting the leather-thonged whip from the wall. Jane saw him take it down, and screamed.

"No! No! Don't! Let me go! Da—"

The first lash fell across her back, knocking all the breath out of her. Pain like fire shot through her body, and the second stroke fell before she had time to breathe. When the third fell, with excruciating pain, Jane realised what was happening. She gathered all her strength and pulled hard at the hands holding her screaming, "No, stop it. Daddy, Da—"

The fourth lash fell with added force. The three lead pellets at the end of the thongs cut into her back.

The pain was like nothing we can imagine. A flogging across the back and shoulders causes indescribable agony because the bones, which are a mass of sensitive nerve endings, are only just beneath the skin surface, and there is very little soft tissue to protect them. The leather thongs were hard and cut the skin, exposing the bones to further pain and injury. The lead pellets struck in random places, tearing the flesh.

By the fifth lash, Jane began to lose consciousness. All her weight fell on to the arms of the officer who held her, and she vomited down his trousers.

"Dirty little thing," he exclaimed, and jerked his knee upwards, catching her in the mouth. Her teeth clamped together over her tongue, which was lolling forward, and blood trickled out of her mouth.

Still the Master continued his self-appointed task. He had intended twenty lashes of the whip, but his wife had cautioned him, saying, "You don't want to kill her. Questions might be asked. Ten lashes will be enough to teach the girl the lesson she deserves."

Jane felt no more pain. She was only conscious of a terrible jolt to her body each time the lash fell. She could hear and see nothing beyond a red mist that swam all around her.

Eight . . . nine . . . ten. The Master brought down the last stroke with satisfaction. The officer let go of Jane's hands, and she fell to the floor. She had wet herself, and she slid into the urine that was mixed with vomit and blood.

"Get a couple of the women to take her to the dormitory. She is to come to my office at eight o'clock tomorrow morning, before she goes to school."

The Master issued the orders, hung the whip on the hook, and left the punishment room.

A nurse and a female officer came to collect Jane and take her up to the dormitory. The nurse was shocked with what she saw but the officer, who had seen it all before, was very blasé.

"She'll get over it. A good beating never did a child any harm. 'Spare the lash and spoil the child.' Come on. Get up on your feet, you lazy girl, and put your dress on."

The nurse was horrified. "You can't put a dress on with her back like that. She needs lint and gauze and ointments."

"Well she won't get them," said the female officer, with finality in her voice. "The Master would never stand for favouritism."

The nurse took off her apron and wrapped the child in it. Jane could barely stand, let alone walk, so the nurse carried her upstairs to the dormitory. She laid her on the bed, face down, and fetched a bowl of cold water. She sat beside the bed for hours, bathing the girl's back with cold water to reduce the blood flow and restrict the terminal capillaries, so reducing the inflammation.

In spite of the pain Jane fell asleep. The nurse continued to bathe her back and all the girls crept into the dormitory, subdued and silent. They slipped into bed, and only a few whispers were heard. One of their number, the brightest and liveliest, had been terribly flogged, and a wave of shock and horror united them in silence.

A little girl with blonde hair crept up to the nurse. She was crying piteously. She said her name was Peggy and she laid her fair hair against Jane's dark curls, whispering to her, kissing her, and sobbing. She asked the nurse if she could help, and so she took a cold sponge and bathed Jane's back just as the nurse showed her. Together, the stunned and silent nurse and the weeping little girl ministered to the stricken Jane, until Peggy was so tired that she too fell asleep.

It was probably this action on the part of the nurse and her child helper that saved Jane's life. All night she drifted in and out of consciousness, and the nurse sat up with her through the long hours whilst the other girls slept. Sometimes Jane moaned in pain, and moved her limbs. Sometimes she let out a weak cry of "Daddy". Sometimes she took the nurse's hand, and held it fast. The blood on her back was clotting, the nurse noted with satisfaction, and the child could obviously move her legs, so at least her spine had not been broken. The hours slipped past.

The Master had ordered that Jane should report to his office at 8 a.m. before school. But Jane could not be roused. The Mistress was called and she, although secretly shocked by the child's appearance, declared that she was shamming, and pulled the mattress so hard that Jane fell out of bed onto the floor, where she lay, immobile. The Mistress then looked coldly at her, turned her with her foot and declared that she could have the day in bed, but must be ready for school the following morning.

Thinking to be helpful, the nurse (who knew nothing of the background), said to the Mistress as she was leaving. "The child has been calling for her daddy all night long, madam. Do you think it would be helpful if we were to fetch him?"

To her surprise the Mistress exploded. "Her daddy! Oh, the iniquity, the sinfulness! Will there be no end to this child's wickedness?" and she stormed off to tell the Master this latest revelation. Something else must be done to purge Jane of her lies.

Jane was not able to go to school the next day, nor for many days after that. Gradually the pain eased, and her mind began to clear. She was able to stand, and to take a little food. She barely spoke, and scarcely raised her eyes from the ground.

The Mistress came to the dormitory to tell her that all this shamming would not be tolerated a moment longer and she must go to school, but first the Master wished to see her. Jane went deathly white and started to shake all over. She attempted to follow the Mistress out of the dormitory, but her legs gave way, and she sank to the floor. An officer hauled her to her feet and dragged her downstairs. As she approached the door of the Master's office Jane vomited the contents of her stomach all down her apron. The Mistress was furious.

"We'll soon have that off you," she shouted, and tore off the apron.

The Master sat at his desk and eyed Jane up and down. The officer kept hold of her, or she would probably have fallen.

"You wicked child. You monstrous liar. It seems there is no end to your depravity. In spite of just chastisement you persist in calling Sir Ian Astor-Smaleigh your father. If you ever do so again, I will flog you again. But, at my wife's request, I will not do so now. You see how good and kind the Mistress is to you, and how little you deserve it. For the time being, as a reminder to you of your wickedness and as an example to the others, you will be deprived of your dress and apron, and you will wear a sack. Now go. And remember, if you say that Sir Ian Astor-Smaleigh is your father one more time I will flog you. And the next time I will show no mercy."

Jane was taken away to the laundry room and her dress removed. A sack with three holes, for head and arms, was put on her with string tied around the waist. Her hair was shorn as close as possible, so that she looked nearly bald. She was sent to school like that.

If Miss Sutton was horrified at her appearance, she was even more horrified at the change in the child's behaviour. The little girl sat shivering and cringing. Each time Miss Sutton went up to her, she reacted with terror. In fact she seemed terrified of everyone, even the other children who spoke to her. She did not read, and she barely joined in any of the lessons. If she held a pencil, her hand shook so much that she was unable to write. The most alarming feature was her total silence. For two whole weeks she said absolutely nothing.

The Headmistress wrote to the Master of the workhouse, asking what had happened. He replied to the effect that he had absolute authority over the workhouse children and was answerable to no one. He reminded the Headmistress that he was a member of the Board of Governors of the school. If there was any interference, he was in a strong position to complain to the Chairman about the conduct and competence of the Headmistress. No further action was taken.

Humiliations were heaped upon Jane. She started bedwetting.

The workhouse punishment for this was that the offending child would be stood on the detention platform, which was at the front of the dining hall, visible to everyone, holding her wet sheet. The child had no breakfast that day. Morning after morning, throughout the winter and spring, Jane, shorn of her hair and wearing a sack tied with string, stood miserably, conspicuously on that platform, clutching a wet sheet. Day after day she went to school with no breakfast. This morning penance continued with monotonous regularity.

The scars on Jane's back healed more quickly than the scars on her mind. In fact, her mind and personality never did fully recover. She was never seen to smile, nor heard to laugh. Her buoyant, bouncing step changed to a cringing shuffle. Her flashing blue eyes were scarcely seen, because she would look up briefly, fearfully, and then look down again quickly. Her voice changed to a whisper. Her precocious level of schoolwork changed to average or below average in the class. Miss Sutton was heartbroken, but however much she tried to encourage Jane to write stories for her, as she had in the old days, she had no success. Jane would put her hands up to her mouth, cast fearful sideways glances at her teacher, and whisper: "Yes, Miss Sutton." But after half an hour the page would still be blank.

Jane's mind was largely blank as well. She had very little memory of the events that led up to her flogging, and she hadn't the faintest idea why it had occurred. She went through it all in her mind, over and again, round and round, an endless repetition of thought that got her nowhere. Everything was confused. Nothing made sense.

She was clear in her mind that it had something to do with the day her daddy had come to the workhouse and told her that he would take her away in the summer. But why had the Master been so cross with her? Her daddy wasn't cross, so why should the Master be cross? Why had he flogged her, and made her wear the sack? She tried and tried to think what she had done wrong, but could think of nothing. And why had the Master shouted several times: "See a nasty smelly is not your father?" This was the biggest puzzle of all. "A nasty smelly?" What did it mean? Her daddy wasn't a "smelly". Her daddy smelled of lavender, as she had always known he would. She had cuddled him and smelled the lavender. She had never called the Master or Mistress nasty smellies, so why had he flogged her? Like a swarm of wasps these thoughts buzzed in her mind all the time, day and night, until she felt she would go mad with the buzzing.

But not for one moment did Jane, in her thoughts, impute any blame to her daddy or cease to love him. In fact her love grew stronger and more real because she had seen him and touched him, and he had stroked her hair, called her "my child" and said he would take her away in the summer time. The spring came, and Jane knew that the summer would follow. It would not be long now. She only had to endure and be good, and not get into any more trouble. Her daddy would come, as sure as the summer sunshine, and take her away from the workhouse for ever. This fragile dream she clung to. It was her one solace in her misery and bewilderment.

May, June, July. The summer days were drawing out. There was a buzz of excitement amongst the workhouse girls – they were going on holiday. It had never happened before. Jane's crushed spirits rose a little, and occasionally she allowed herself to lift her eyes from the floor.

August arrived, and preparations were made. Summer dresses and sandals were provided. The girls could talk of nothing else. There was a fever pitch of excitement. The day for departure arrived.

The girls were standing in the dining hall after breakfast and everything was ready.

The Mistress entered. "Right, now. Form a line and march out quietly. We will proceed to the station."

The girls stepped forward.

"Not you. Stay where you are."

The Mistress pointed at Jane. The other girls marched out.

Sick disappointment took possession of Jane. She saw the last girl leave, as she stood in her place. She heard footsteps echo down the corridors and doors banging. Then silence.

Now it was that Jane's heart finally broke. Hitherto her suffering had been physical. Now the torture was mental, emotional, and spiritual. The utter desolation of rejection was hers to savour. Her daddy was not going to take her away. Her daddy did not love her, or want her. That was why she was there in the workhouse. He had put her there because he did not want her and she would never see him again. She knew it in her heart.

Throughout the long weeks, alone but for the porter's wife who brought her food twice a day, Jane lived with this bitter knowledge. She had nothing to do, day after day; no books, no toys, no pencils and paper. She cried herself to sleep alone in the dormitory; ate alone in the huge refectory; went out alone in the yard (euphemistically called a playground) and walked around the walls. She spoke to no one except the porter's wife, twice a day.

The other girls returned, sun-browned and happy. Jane heard stories of the seaside and paddling and catching crabs and building sandcastles. She didn't say a word.

The knowledge of rejection, of being unwanted, is more terrible to live with than anything else, and a rejected child will usually never get over it. A physical pain entered Jane's body, somewhere in the region of the solar plexus, which ached all the time and from which she would never be free.

Unknown to Jane, Sir Ian and Lady Lavinia had visited the children's holiday camp. They had played with the children by the sea, organised races for them across the sands, hired a man with a donkey to give them rides and read stories to them in the evening. They were very happy with their work.

At the end of the day, Sir Ian asked the Master: "I have not seen that pretty child who came up to thank me when I first met you. Where is she?"

The Master was nonplussed, but his resourceful wife stepped forward with a curtsey. "The child has an aunt, sir, who always takes her on holiday each year. I assure you, sir, that at this very moment the child is playing happily on a beach somewhere in Devon." She curtsied again.

"I am glad to hear it," said Lady Lavinia, "but for my part, I am sorry not to see the child. My husband spoke most highly of her."

After they had left, the Master said. "What a blessing we did not bring that wretched child. If she had gone running up to that man in front of his wife, and clung to him and called him Daddy, heaven knows what trouble it would have stirred up."

And on this occasion – who can tell? – the Master may have been right.

FRANK

Give me a boy for the first five years
of his life, and I will make the man.
Rousseau

Frank had but a dim recollection of his father. He remembered a tall, strong man, whom he held in awe. He remembered his big voice and huge, rough hands. He could remember once tracing the veins on the back of this vast hand with his little fingers, and looking at his own smooth white skin and wondering if he would ever have hands like that. To be like his father was his only ambition and he worshipped him. In the later, sadder years of his childhood he tried desperately to remember what his father had been like, but a phantom that comes and goes could not have been more elusive and only the dimmest memory remained.

He remembered his mother much more clearly; his sweet, gentle mother who was never strong because she was always coughing. He remembered the sound of her voice as she sang songs to him and played with him. Above all, he remembered her cuddles as she put him to bed and lay down beside him.

In the winter his mother hardly went out of doors because of her weak chest and his father would say, as he went off to work, "Now you look after your mother while I'm away, Frank lad. I'm relying on you to take care of her for me." And Frank would look up at his god with big solemn eyes and accept the task as a sacred duty.

When a tiny baby was born – so tiny that everyone said she would not live – Frank was four years old. He had been an only child all his life and could not conceive of any other child entering his world. Many boys of that age become very jealous of a new-born baby, but not Frank. He was mesmerised by this tiny creature, hardly bigger than a teacup, who could move and cry, and who needed so much care. Not for a moment did he resent the hours of attention given to the baby. In fact, he liked to help. The most fascinating thing of all was to watch his mother breast-feeding the baby, and he tried never to be far away when this mysterious and beautiful ritual was going on. He kept very quiet, crept close to his mother and watched, spellbound, as the baby sucked and the milk oozed from the nipple.

The baby was premature and sickly, and for a long time her life hung in the balance. His father said to him, many times: "You've got a special job to do, young man. You've got to look after your little sister. That's your job now, lad."

So Frank watched over her, and hardly went out to play with the other boys in the court, because he was so busy looking after his little sister.

The baby didn't die. She gained strength and became quite robust, although she always remained small. She was christened Margaret but was called Peggy, because Margaret seemed too long a name for such a small baby. After the christening Frank's father said, "You done a good job there, son; and I'm proud of yer."

Then catastrophe struck. In those years typhoid was raging through East London. His huge, strong father, who had never known a day of illness in his life, was hit by the disease and died within a few days. His mother, who had never been strong, was spared and so was the baby. His mother went out to work, cleaning offices. She left home in the early hours each morning, and again each evening, leaving Frank to look after Peggy, who was by now a toddler.

One day Frank ran home from school (he didn't think much of school, regarding it as a waste of time) to take over the domestic responsibilities from his mother, so that she could go out to her job. It was cold and she was coughing badly, but she went nonetheless. Money had to be earned, or they would be homeless. Frank did as he had so often done before: he put some wood that he had found on his way home from school onto the fire, made some tea for himself and Peggy, played with her and, as the fire was dying, he undressed her and put her to bed, creeping in beside her for warmth.

In the middle of the night he woke up, aware that something was wrong. It was pitch-black, and the quiet was terrifying. He could hear Peggy breathing, but that was all. Something was missing. Nausea seized him as he realised that his mother was not there. In a panic he felt all over the bed, but the side where his mother usually slept was empty. He called out in a small voice so as not to wake Peggy, but there was no reply. He crept out of bed and found the matches. He struck one and the flame leaped up, lighting the whole room momentarily. His mother was not there. Blinded by tears, he crept back into bed and held Peggy in his arms.

The cold had badly affected his mother as soon as she stepped outside. She was asthmatic and bronchitic, and had been fighting off a chest infection for several weeks. She had a mile to walk to the bus, and the freezing mist rising off the river had got into her lungs. She was thankful for the brief respite of sitting in the bus, but by the time she got to the building where she was employed, she felt more dead than alive. She went to the cleaning cupboard to get out her things, but the bucket felt so heavy that she could hardly move it. She asked permission to make herself a cup of tea, saying she would feel better with something warm inside her. The tea was indeed comforting, but the building was cold and she sat shivering in the basement, pulling her shawl around her shoulders and coughing. One by one the office workers left and she found herself alone.

Normally, this office took her about three hours, but after one hour, she had scarcely cleaned one tenth of it. She felt so weak she could scarcely drag herself around, and there was still the scrubbing to do. She returned to the basement to get the bucket – the one that had felt impossibly heavy when empty – and filled it with water. She pushed it along the floor with her feet and then lifted it up the stairs one by one, resting it on each stair as she did so. She reached the second storey this way, and then her failing strength must have given out. She fell down the stairs that she had climbed so laboriously, knocking the bucket over as she fell. She was drenched with water and lay on the stone floor all night. In the morning they found her dead at the bottom of the stairs.

Frank had never spent a night away from his mother. There was only one bed so they had all slept together even when his father was alive. He had never even contemplated a time without the comforting warmth of her body beside him. Now, in the dark and cold of the room, the bed felt like a hostile and alien territory, and he wanted to run away from it, run to the next-door neighbours, screaming. But there was Peggy to think of. She was quietly sleeping, unaware that anything was wrong. So he bit his lips, rubbed his fists into his eyes and cuddled up close to her.

He was six years old.

He must have slept, because it was daylight when he was awoken by Peggy crying. There was some milk and water left from the night before but it was cold and she pushed it away. He did not know what to do. He took a wet nappy off her, as he had seen his mother do, but then he didn't know what to do with it, so hid it under the bed. There was no more wood for the fire. He drank the cold milk himself and crept back into bed. They fell asleep again.

He awoke as a crowd of neighbouring women entered the room.

"Oh, it's a shame, oie tells ya."

"Poor li'l kids. Vey didn' ask 'a be born."

"Both dead in six months."

"It makes yer wanna cry, don' it?"

Frank looked around him in bewilderment and held Peggy defensively, pulling the blanket up higher.

A man entered the room. "Are these the children of the deceased?" he enquired.

A chorus of voices answered.

"Yeah, more's the pity."

"Poor li'l lambs."

"Vey don' know wha's 'appened."

"And is there no relative to look after them?"

"No' as 'ow I knows on, do you, Lil?"

"Nah, no one."

"They will have to come with me, and the effects sold to contribute to the Guardians' expenses."

He looked around the room at the meagre furniture – one bed, one table, and two chairs, a small cupboard, a washing bowl, a chamber pot, a candlestick, some tin plates and cups – all back-breakingly acquired by the father, to provide for his family.

"Will someone get them ready while I take an inventory?"

Two women stepped forward, and Frank grabbed the back of the bed, clutching Peggy. "Where's Mummy?" he asked plaintively.

"Yer mum's dead, luvvy, more's the pity."

"No, my dad's dead," he insisted.

"An so's yer mum, dearie. Found dead vis mornin' in ye office."

"Blue, she was," chorused the women to each other.

"Froze stiff, vey say, an' soakin' wet."

"Wet froo, an' all, and 'er wiv her weak chest."

"No' surprisin', is it?"

Frank looked from one to another, and horror struck his heart. Was his mother dead? He had promised his father that he would look after her! What had gone wrong? Peggy was beginning to whimper again. Kind hands were placed on him. He clung to the bars of the bedstead with all his strength and turned his back on the women, holding Peggy, who was beginning to scream now, between his body and the head of the bed.

"You will have to get him free," said the man. "They cannot stay here alone."

It took four women to loosen his fingers from the bars. A child's fingers can be incredibly strong if they are curled around something. Eventually two women were holding him and Peggy in their arms. He was biting and scratching and kicking in a hysteria of fear and rage. He shouted at the woman holding Peggy, "Give her to me. She's my sister. Don't take her away." Tears were streaming down his face.

"We will have to go. Does anyone know where the key is kept?" said the man.

The door of the room was locked, and they made their way downstairs. The woman holding Frank was badly bruised. They walked through the streets, collecting a crowd of onlookers as they went.

Frank and Peggy were admitted to the infants' section of the workhouse, where boys and girls under seven years of age were housed. They were undressed and bathed and treated not unkindly. In fact, Peggy's tiny stature and wispy blonde hair evoked a stream of sympathy from the women who received them. Frank had exhausted his fury, and sullenly allowed himself to be washed and his hair examined for fleas.

"We'll have to cut it off. You know the rules."

He submitted to having his head shaved, but when he saw a large woman doing the same to Peggy, he rushed at her and butted her in the stomach with his head. She collapsed onto a chair winded, then grabbed the boy and thrashed him soundly, whilst another officer shaved Peggy.

"It's a shame, cutting this pretty hair. But it will soon grow again."

Poor little Peggy looked like a tiny Martian when they had finished, and Frank sobbed with impotent rage.

The children were dressed in workhouse clothes and taken to the playroom to meet the other children. We would not call it a playroom today, because there was nothing to play with. It was just a large, bare room, about forty feet long by twenty feet wide, with high, uncurtained windows and rough floorboards.

"Now you play quietly with the others until tea time." The door was shut, and the officer left.

They stood shyly in the doorway, looking at about forty other children, all wearing the same clothes. Frank, acutely self-conscious that he and Peggy had no hair, tried to hide her under his jacket. A boy of about his age ran up to them, shouting: "You're new. You're new. Where've you come from? What's your name, baldy? An' who's this little squirt, then?" He pulled at Peggy's arm and tickled her scalp.

Frank flung himself at the boy, fighting with savage fury. All the rage that had been building up during the day was concentrated in his attack. The rest of the children stood back to watch the fun. The other boy was no slouch when it came to fighting and the two were evenly matched. There were no adults in the room to stop them.

Peggy was terrified and ran screaming to a corner, where she crouched down, hiding her head. A little girl with dark hair left the others, came over to her and put her small arms around the sobbing child. "Don't cry, please don't cry. They're only fighting. Boys are always fighting. Boys are awful. Here, sit on my knee."

The girl sat down on the floor and Peggy climbed onto her knees. She played with a long, dark ringlet hanging down near her face, and laughed when she pulled it and it bounced back up again.

The girl smiled happily. "You're like a little doll. I've never had a doll, but I've seen them. And you're better than a doll, because you're real, and dolls are only pretend. Will you be my friend? My name's Jane, and I'm four. What's yours?"

Peggy didn't say anything, but her tears stopped. Jane sat quietly, cuddling Peggy, and laughing to herself as she watched the fight.

The boys were roughly the same weight, but Frank had the advantage of cold, calculated fury and his need to defend his sister. He glanced at the other boys who were egging them on, and knew instinctively that if he lost this fight, Peggy would never be safe from their torments.

After a few minutes Frank's adversary was on the floor in a corner. "Truce. Give in. Hold 'im off," he called out.

Frank turned to face the others. He raised his fists defiantly. "Anyone else want a go?"

No one stepped forward.

Frank swaggered over to the corner where Peggy sat on Jane's knee. "Thanks," he said. "She's only two, and she's scared. Her name's Peggy and I'm Frank."

The girl had a merry laugh, open features and piercing blue eyes. Frank liked her, he liked the way she was nursing Peggy, and he saw the contentment with which the little girl responded to the older one. He knew that he could trust her. "Let's be friends," he said.

Over the next few weeks, the reality of his mother's death dawned upon Frank.

He would never see her again and pain inside reduced him to tears. Other boys laughed and jeered at him, but he only had to stick out his jaw and raise his fists aggressively, and they quickly backed off. Peggy did not seem as unhappy, because Frank was always there for her. Also, Jane had taken to her and petted and fussed over her, calling her "my little doll". Jane was indisputably the leader among the girls, so her protection meant a good deal.

Jane was good for Frank also. He liked her with the instinctive affection that recognises a kindred spirit. He approved of her gentle ways with Peggy, and he also liked her naughtiness. She was always playing tricks and pranks, making everyone laugh. She would jump out from behind a door when the officer opened it, shouting "boo", and then run away laughing. She was always caught and smacked, but nothing seemed to quench her high spirits. The day she climbed the water pipe in the playground and sat on the gutter and wouldn't come down was one of the funniest things Frank could ever remember. Fat old Officer

Hawkins had been on duty that day and got onto a ladder, then lumbered up it, with all the boys crowding around underneath, trying to see her knickers. When she finally got Jane down, she thrashed her soundly in the playground, and then again in the evening before bedtime, but Jane just rubbed her bottom, shook her curls defiantly, and did not seem to care.

The night times were the worst for Frank. Alone in a small, hard bed, with darkness all around, he sobbed silently for his sweet mother, whom he had adored with all the passion of boyhood. He missed the warmth of her body, he missed the smell of her skin, the touch of her hand, the sound of her breathing. He would creep over to Peggy's bed and get in beside her, where the smell of her hair would numb his pain, and they would sleep together till morning. This became their one comfort in the first months of their life in the workhouse.

A year passed. After breakfast one morning, Frank and two other boys were taken to the Matron's office. She said abruptly, "You are big boys now that you are seven, and we are taking you to the boys' section today. Wait in the hallway, and the van will come for you at nine o'clock."

The boys did not know what she meant, and the three of them sat on the bench, engaged in mock fights and ribaldry.

At nine o'clock, a man entered the front door and enquired, "Are these three to go?"

They were taken outside to a green van and told to climb in the back. It was all very exciting. They had never been in a van before, so they clambered in willingly, ready for adventure. The van started with a jerk, and they were thrown off the bench onto the floor. They shrieked with laughter. This was going to be a good day. A ride in a van! You wait till we get back and tell the others. The van stopped twice, and other boys of their own age climbed in. Soon there were eight boys, all shouting and skidding around the floor of the van as they turned corners, or pressing against each other to see out of the small back window in order to wave at people as they passed. Everyone turned to look, because motorised transport was comparatively unusual in those days. The boys felt very privileged, and infinitely superior to the people walking or travelling in horse-drawn carts and wagons.

Eventually the van stopped and the back door opened. Frank saw a very large, grey-stone building in front of him, and he did not much like the look of it.

"Where am I?" he asked.

"This is the boys' section. You come here when you are seven and stay until you are fourteen," said a tough-looking man, who was a workhouse officer.

"And where's Peggy?" he demanded.

"I don't know who Peggy is, but she's not here."

"Peggy is my sister and I look after her. My dad told me to."

The officer laughed. "Well, someone else will have to look after her. There's no girls allowed in here."

Still Frank did not understand. He was unsure, frightened, and he felt like crying, but he wasn't going to let the other boys see him, so he squared his shoulders, clenched his fists and put on a swagger as they were taken to the Master's office.

The interview was brief. They were told that they must obey the rules, obey the officers at all times, and that if they did not do so they would be punished. The Master then said, "You will be given your duties and lunch is at one o'clock. You will start school tomorrow."

Frank had wanted to ask about Peggy, but the Master so terrified him that he did not dare speak. He followed the officer to the dining hall with a feeling of panic in his heart that he had not known since the night when he had awoken to find his mother's side of the bed empty.

Lunch in a huge refectory with about a hundred and fifty other boys, some of them very big, was terrifying and he could hardly eat. He ate half a potato and drank some water, but it nearly choked him, and he could not stop his tears from falling. Some of the bigger boys pointed at him and sniggered. None of the male officers showed any sympathy. The three new boys who had come together were all considerably more sober now. The fun and high spirits of the van ride evaporated as the reality of the situation began to dawn upon them. They had left the small world and comparative kindness of the nursery, where there were women officers and nurses, for the harsh, often brutal world of the workhouse proper, where, for the next seven years, they would encounter only male officers.

Back in the nursery, after breakfast, Peggy looked around for Frank, but could not find him. She looked in the lavatory and the washroom, but he was not there. She looked in the classroom and under the stairs, but he was not in those places either. Bewildered and frightened, she stood on the bottom stair hugging the banister, and stamped her feet. An officer came up to her, but she screamed and stamped her little feet even faster.

"Poor little thing," remarked the officer to a colleague, "she's going to miss her brother, they were very close. She'll just have to get over it in her own time. There's nothing we can do."

Peggy was three years old and Frank had been with her all her life. She had not noticed the loss of her father, when she was eighteen months old, and had only the vaguest memory of her mother. But Frank was her world, her life, her security and she was utterly devastated. All day she stood on the bottom step, hugging the smooth, round balustrades, sometimes silent, sometimes sobbing. Sometimes she kicked the stairs and hurt her toe. Twice she wet herself, but still she wouldn't move. Jane tried to talk to her, but Peggy shook her shoulders and screamed, "Go away."

"Leave her alone," said an officer to Jane, "she'll get over it in a day or two."

Towards evening Peggy started to bang her head on the balustrade. It hurt, but she wanted it to. Perhaps Frank would come when he knew she had hurt herself. When he didn't come, she sobbed uncontrollably, then slipped down onto the stairs in a deep sleep. A nurse picked her up, carried her to the dormitory and put her to bed.

For the next three months, Peggy hunted for Frank every day. She always expected to find him, but never did. She asked everyone: "Where's Frank?" and was told that he had been transferred to the big boys' section, but she did not understand. She developed the habit of sitting alone in a corner and rocking herself. A nurse, who knew that this was a particularly frightening development in a lonely, insecure child, tried to comfort her. But Peggy would not be comforted. Each lonely night, she sucked her thumb and rocked herself and cried for Frank to come to her. But he didn't come.

As time passed, she stopped looking for Frank and asked for him less, until eventually she stopped asking. It was assumed that she had forgotten all about him.

It was to be nine years before brother and sister saw each other again, and by that time they did not recognise each other.

BILLINGSGATE

At the age of seven, Frank had entered an all-male world of petty rules, upheld by harsh, uncompromising discipline and gratuitous tyranny. Many of the workhouse officers were men who had been brought up in a workhouse themselves during the nineteenth century, when conditions for paupers were simply appalling. A child had to have a very strong constitution to survive the brutality, the work, the cold, and near-starvation. These men knew of no other way of life, and to them it was only natural to impose the same sort of regime on the boys in their charge.

Frank was immediately set to work on one of the numerous tasks assigned to paupers: cleaning potatoes, cutting cabbage, scrubbing out the huge cooking vats (only the smallest boys could get inside them), burnishing the stoves, cleaning the brass, and hosing down the vast stone floors of the kitchen – and woe betide any boy who got himself wet! The list was endless and the day long, starting as it did at 6 a.m. The boys also went to the local council school, so the work had to be done before or after school. Frank found that if his tasks were not finished before he went to school, he got a beating from the officer in charge, and if he stayed behind to finish the job, he got a beating from the schoolmaster for being late!

Small boys quickly learned to hide their tears. They knew that any sign of weakness would be seized upon by a bigger boy and mercilessly exploited. Bullying, constant intimidation and jeering were the only response a smaller boy would gain from tears.

Once, and once only, Frank asked an officer where Peggy was. The man must have told one of the older boys, perhaps maliciously, knowing what would happen. The same day, in the washroom, a chorus went up. "Peggy, Peggy, who's Peggy?"

"Peggy's his tart. What a fart!"

"Peg, Peg, peg your nose, what a pong!"

"Peggy's a stink."

"He has to put a clothes peg on his nose 'afore he can touch 'er."

Frank burst into tears, and a big boy came and pushed him over onto the slippery floor.

"Garn, you ain't got no tart, yer titch," said the boy, squeezing Frank's testicles so hard that he screamed with pain.

The officer came in and the big boy swiftly merged into the crowd, looking innocent.

The officer looked round and asked no questions. "Get up," he said curtly to Frank, "get washed and go to the dormitory."

Frank crept into bed and cried, as he did every night, for his mother and his sister. He had learned to make no sound when crying, so as not to attract attention, and to keep very still, so that he seemed to be asleep. But he often lay awake for hours, his heart bursting.

During these wakeful hours he often – nearly always, in fact – heard movements and soft footsteps, grunting and puffing and cursing sounds, as iron bedsteads rattled and straw mattresses squeaked. Each dormitory had an officer in charge who had himself once been a workhouse boy. The officer slept in a closed cubicle at the end of rows of beds, and each night a boy would slip quietly out of bed and go into the cubicle.

What can one expect if a crowd of boys are thrown together, with no escape and no female influence? All the boys were lonely. All of them were motherless. They had only each other in whom to find comfort and, let us hope, a little happiness because for them life would be short. From 1914 to 1918 the older boys in Frank's dormitory – those born in the 1890s – were destined to be sent straight from the workhouses of England to the trenches of France, to die as cannon-fodder in defence of King and Country.

*

It was September 1914. A costermonger by the name of Tip called at the workhouse and asked to speak to the Master. The Master was prim and pompous; the coster flashy and talkative. He explained, in a husky voice inclined to sudden squeaks, that his lad had gone off to the war, and he had been left without a boy, and a coster must 'ave a boy, how else was he goin' to do his trade, like, an' what he was lookin' for was a sharp little lad of about eleven or twelve, eleven being the preferential age, seeing as how they learns quickest, a boy who was a good worker, an' quick, an' it didn't matter about no book learning, because he never could see no use for that in the fish trade, and them as 'ad book learning never seemed to get on spectackiler in the trade, but he, Tip, would edicate the boy himself an' make a right sharp coster out of him, as how he could earn his living honest-like, an' keep his head up with the best, an' he would supply his lodgins an' his victuals, least as to say his doxy would, an' 'ad the Master got such a boy, who was hard-workin' an' willin'?

The coster delivered all this in a curious voice that growled and gurgled sometimes, and squeaked and whistled at others. The Master paused to think, and the coster, who never paused and could not conceive of anyone else doing so, started again, "An' he's gotta be strong, 'cause its no place for a wimpish lad, an the doxy'll feed him well an' keep his strength up, an'—"

The Master held up his hand to silence the man. "Just wait here, will you?" he said, as he left the office.

Workhouse masters were encouraged to off-load inmates in order to reduce expenses, but they were not allowed to turn them out onto the streets unless provision for their maintenance was assured. The apprentice system was the answer.

The Master thought carefully about the coster's request, and his mind fixed on Frank – he was eleven, he was strong, he was hard-working, he was obedient, and he was, according to his school reports, one of the "has ability but must try harder" type – the despair of every honest schoolmaster.

The boys were at tea, and Frank was called out.

"Now stand up straight, look lively and don't answer back," said the Master as he cuffed him round the ear. "There's a man here wants to see you."

They entered the office, where the coster was whistling. He had a beautiful, mellow whistle that seemed a most unlikely adjunct to his peculiar speaking voice.

"This boy seems to answer your requirements. I give you my assurance that he is hard-working. All our boys are trained to work."

The coster looked Frank up and down and sucked his teeth. He had only two, one in the upper and one in the lower jaw, both at the front, so he was able to vary his sucking with singularly comic effect.

He pinched Frank's ear. "You're a skinny li'l sprog. Can you lift a box of herrings?"

Frank didn't dare to answer back in front of the Master, so he just nodded.

"Ain' chew got a tongue, ven?" demanded the coster.

Again Frank nodded.

"Yes, he has and he can use it to good effect when he wants to," answered the Master.

"Vat's what I needs, a boy as can holler good and loud like, an' make 'em all sit up."

"This is the boy for you, then. He's got a voice like a foghorn," said the Master conclusively.

"I'll take 'im. An' if he don't come up to scratch, I'll bring him back next week."

Before Frank had time to say a word, he was whisked off to the clothes cupboards, his workhouse uniform removed, and ill-fitting street clothes put on him. The coster took him by the hand and they stepped out into the road together.

Tip was a flashy dresser. Not for him the drab greys and browns of working men. He wore green corduroy trousers and a shirt of vivid blue. His shoes were tied with enormous bows which bore no resemblance to the humble shoelace, and at his throat was tied a silk neckerchief of red and blue. His cap was not your ordinary cloth cap, as worn by the English, nor the beret favoured by the French, yet it bore a close similarity to the French style. Tip's cap could be described as a very large beret, made of the best velvet, and the colour, neither blue nor green, seemed to change with the light and movement. Tip considered himself a real swell, and his doxy admired him prodigiously.

He glanced down at Frank and his masculine vanity acknowledged that the boy was taking in his elegance. "You gotta look sharp in our trade, titch. No use lookin' like a bag 'o dirty washin'. The ladies don' like it. An' it's the ladies as wha' does the buyin', see? So you gotta please the ladies. That's rule number one. We'll 'ave to get you some new clobber. Can't 'ave you goin' round lookin' like vat, queering my pitch. The ladies would run away fritted, vey would. I knows of a Jew as what can fix you up cheap and natty like."

Tip had started the sentence in his baritone voice, but as he came to the end of it, the words came out in a series of high, unexpected squeaks. Aware that Frank was listening with puzzled attention, he explained.

"It's the toobs. The toobs what wears out with all that 'ollering. They gives out if you're a good coster, like what I am, 'cause they're too delicate to stand all that 'ollerin'. Vat's what I needs a boy for, to 'oller, along with other fings, lots of other fings, all of which I'll teach you, but 'ollerin' will be one of your first jobs. Now let's 'ear you 'oller. See vat li'l lad over there, playing in vat puddle? Well, you call out, loud as you can now, 'Hey, mucky, your mum's comin'.'"

Frank caught the spirit of things, and bellowed the words out with all his strength. The boy jumped up and ran round the corner like a greyhound.

Frank roared with laughter, and squeezed Tip's hand. "Vat's what I needs," said Tip. "Reckons as how you'll suit me, an' if you can pick up ve other tricks of the trade quick like, we'll get on famous. Now we're gettin' to my lodgings, an' my doxy's

Doll see, and Doll, she's a rare 'un, but she won' stand no lip from boys, see, so don' you give her no lip an' you won't feel the back of 'er 'and." Tip rubbed the side of his chin reflectively and muttered, "An' you don't wanna feel the back of 'er 'and, I can tell yer."

They climbed a dark and foul-smelling staircase to the fourth floor. A large and shapely woman ambled towards them. She wore a red skirt, frayed and dirty at the hem, and a purple blouse, high at the neck, with a row of jet buttons down the front against which a full bosom pressed, screaming for release. Black jet beads hung to her waist, and heavy black hair hung down around her shoulders. When she smiled, her teeth were also black, as though they had been painted to match her outfit. She looked at them both, then cried out, "Is vis the li'l workhouse kid, ven? Oh, look, he's thin, the pet," and she pressed Frank's head to her bosom, an experience which he found to be not unpleasant, though the smell could have been sweeter. "We'll 'ave to give 'im some pie dahn Dill's, eh Tip?"

"Let's ge' goin' ven," said Tip with a leer.

Doll twisted her hair up on top of her head in a fashionable coil (Frank watched, fascinated) and stuck several pins in. One of them had a bird on the end and this she settled on the top of her head.

"You bet, squire," she said with a wink. Then she leaned down to Frank. "He's a nice-lookin' li'l lad, bu' thin like. Oh, I don' like 'a see 'em so thin. What's yer name an' all, eh? We'll ge' choo some pie, ven. Howzat?"

It was nearly seven o'clock and the streets were filled with people. Apart from marching to school in a crocodile, Frank had not been outside the workhouse gates for years. He was filled with wonder and to linger was irresistible. Here, a family was fighting, the man and woman threatening each other with equal fury; there, some boys were playing skittles; yonder a woman was fetching water from the pump whilst a crowd stood around with their buckets, gossiping as they waited. Frank had not seen women for years, and couldn't take his eyes off them, until he realised with alarm that Tip and Doll were almost out of sight, and he had to run to catch up with them. They sauntered along, greeting people, chaffing children, Tip pinching the cheeks of young girls, Doll screaming across the street to another woman. They both dressed in a more gaudy fashion than any of their neighbours, and Frank felt proud to be with them, although neither looked round to see if he was still there.

They entered a beer shop, high-ceilinged, bare-walled, with a wooden floor. The serving counter was at one end next to a raised platform with a piano on it. The room was not particularly full, and Tip and Doll seemed to know everyone. Frank was all eyes and ears. This was the high life indeed!

"You standin' a top o' reeb [*pot of beer*], Al?"

"Sey [*yes*], I done a doogheno flash [*good deal*] today. But kool 'im [*look at him*]. Who's he?"

"My wen dal [*new lad*] Give 'im some reeb an' rater" [*beer and water*].

Frank took his beer and sipped it, puzzled. Conversation continued.

"Jack, 'e 'ad a regular tosseno tol [*bad luck*]. 'Ad a showful [*bad money*]. Bigger loof [*fool*] 'im."

"He musta bin flash karnurd [*half drunk*] at ve time."

"On [*no*], just a dabeno [*bad debt*].

Costers in those days spoke to each other almost entirely in back slang, incomprehensible to an outsider. This continued until well after the Second World War.

Frank's eyes rested on each of these big, confident men as he spoke, but none was as flamboyant or assured as Tip, and the seeds of hero-worship were sown in this young heart.

He drank his beer. No one seemed to notice him. He was hungry, and Doll, who was flirting with a man sporting a walrus moustache, appeared to have forgotten the pie she had promised him.

The beer shop filled up, cards were brought out and men sat

down to the serious business of gambling. A group of boys in a corner were engaged in the equally serious business of 'three ups'. A piano player started a tune, and everyone sang along, getting louder and louder at each chorus. A girl leaped onto the stage and started dancing with more energy and vigour than grace, accompanied by shouts and catcalls from the audience. The beer flowed and the laughter swelled. Exhausted, Frank fell asleep on the floor.

He was awakened by Doll, screaming, "Oh, the poor li'l nipper. 'Ere, Tip, you'll 'ave to carry 'im."

"Take me for a monkey?" said Tip, scornfully. He shook Frank hard and pulled him to his feet.

"Come on, there's a day's work ahead."

Doll was the worse for wear and hung onto Tip's arm as they walked through the streets. Frank, more asleep than awake, kept close behind them. They climbed the endless steps to the fourth floor, and a straw mattress and a blanket were pulled out from behind the big feather bed and put on the floor under the table for Frank, who was only too thankful to lie down anywhere. He went to sleep to the comforting and familiar sounds of grunting and puffing and rhythmic bed rocking.

Frank was awakened by a flannel soaked in cold water being thrown on his face. He leaped up and banged his head on the table. Stunned, he gasped: "What's up? Where am I?"

Tip spoke. But it was a very different Tip from the evening before. Gone the flashy clothes, gone the easy swagger and pleasant bonhomie. The morning revealed Tip the coster, Tip the businessman, Tip of the calculating, clever, ruthless eye for a bargain. "Out o' bed, sharp now. There's work 'a be done. Billingsgate opens at four, and it's three o'clock, an' we've gotta get the barrow an' the gear, an' be there. Get some clothes on, an' follow me."

Tip was already in his work trousers and was pulling on his heavy boots. Frank felt the urgency and leaped out of bed. He was still dressed from the night before and had only to find his boots. He pulled them on hastily and stood up straight.

"Good. Now take vat bag, an' we're off."

Out in the night air, Tip was electric with energy. He kept doing little runs and skips and punching the air with his fists. He gave several short, barking shouts, took in great lungfuls of air and blew it out noisily. He was working himself up to a fever pitch, and Frank caught the energy. He sensed that something significant was happening, and he ran along the dark, quiet street, alive to everything, tingling with anticipation.

They went to a tunnel under a bridge. Other men were there already and each man had a boy. They greeted each other in their own lingo. A door was opened, revealing a pitch-black cavern, and a naptha flare was lit with a match. The flame leaped up, revealing a stack of barrows, trucks, handcarts, donkey carts, bridles, hooks, chains, ropes, tarpaulins – a medley of wood and metal.

Tip growled to Frank, "Watch wot I takes, and be sure you remembers it. If you don't ge' the right gear, you can't do yer job, an' the tally bloke there, he'll cheat you if 'e can."

He selected what would be needed for the day, and paid the rental to the man with the flare. "Push this 'ere, an' let's get goin'."

A boy called out, "Hey, yennun – you."

Frank took no notice.

The boy kicked him hard. "Don't you answer ven, yennun?"

Tip explained. "He means 'new one'. That's you, see? Take no notice, we got work 'a do. You'll pick up ve lingo in no time."

In pain, and limping, Frank pushed the barrow. He had learned to hide all signs of weakness in the workhouse and it had stood him in good stead.

"Now, we mus' get a move on." Tip leaned his weight on the barrow and it sped over the cobbles, rattling on solid, iron-framed wheels.

Billingsgate was London's fish market, and lay on the north

bank of the Thames, east of the Monument. Fishing boats came in throughout the night and the market stalls, laden with fresh fish, were ready for business when the market opened at 4 a.m.

Tip's electric excitement is, if anything, intensified and every nerve in his body seems to be quivering. A fishy, seaweedy smell hits his nostrils, and he inhales deeply. "Beautiful, be-oootiful," he murmurs appreciatively.

The noise all around is intense. Above the babble of voices Frank can hear the shouts of salesmen, standing on boxes or tables, roaring out their merchandise and their prices. A Babel of competition.

"'Andsome cod, best in the market – all alive."

"Fine Yarmouth bloaters – oo's the buyer?"

"Eels O! Eels O! Alive O!"

"Wink, wink, winkles, best for tea."

"'Ere you are, guvner, fine brill, come an' look at 'em, guv. You won't find better."

"Over 'ere. Finney 'addock. 'Ad – 'ad – 'ad – 'addy 'addock.

"Now or never – whelks, whelks, whelks, I say."

On all sides everyone is asking "What's the price?" whilst shouts of laughter from salesmen and customers, bargaining and bantering, pepper the noise of the crowd.

Frank can see, in the semi-darkness of the sheds, the white bellies of turbot shining like mother-of-pearl; living lobsters, their claws flailing helplessly in the air; mounds of herrings with scales glittering like sequins; huge baskets piled with grey oysters, blue mussels, pink shrimps, sackfuls of whelks, their yellow shells piled up high; buckets of grey-and-white eels slithering and sliding all over each other.

Frank sees porters in strangely shaped leather helmets, rather like squashed pagodas, carrying fish baskets on their heads. Eight hundred tons of fish pour in and out of Billingsgate every day and all of it, down to the last herring, is unloaded and portered in this way. A man whose neck is 'set' can carry sixteen baskets, each weighing a stone, on his head. These powerful men are the backbone of the fish market, and their history is one of high romance. The quinquereme of Nineveh, laden with spices and precious oils, was unloaded in exactly the same way in medieval London. Caesar's galleys, rowed up the Thames by chained men, were berthed here, London's most ancient port, and unloaded by men such as Frank sees.

Frank flattens himself against a wall as one of these giants passes, shouting: "Move over – make way, please – gangway."

A thin man, trembling under the weight of his load, mutters, through clenched teeth: "Shove to one side, can' choo?"

Everywhere ragged, desperate-looking men and boys are clamouring for the job of porterage, hoping to earn a shilling or two before the day's end.

Through the arches of the open end of the huge covered building, silhouetted against the grey sky of dawn, Frank can see the masts and tangled rigging of the oyster boats and lobster trawlers. Sails, black against the skyline, shift and tremble. He sees the red caps of sailors as they draw in the sails. He hears the chug-chug of primitive engines as a throttle is opened. He hears the shouts of men as they unload their vessels.

"Keep close beside me," Tip growls, "an' listen to everyfink. Don't miss nuffink, see? You gotta learn how to buy."

He assumes a nonchalant air and saunters down the gangway, whistling as though he were on holiday. He passes through the arches onto the quayside, where the river glides black and secretive, and silver threads of light pierce the wakening sky. They clamber over ropes and rigging to the long row of oyster boats moored close along the wharf – known as "Oyster Street" in the trade – where the fishermen sell direct from their boats.

"No middlemen here. Best prices," hisses Tip out of the corner of his mouth.

Each boat has its blackboard and the master, in his white apron, walks up and down calling his prices. The holds are filled with oysters and sand, which a man turns over with a spade, rattling the masses of shells.

Tip discusses price with the master, shakes his head and walks away, saying loudly to Frank, "I knows of better oysters dahn ve sewers."

The oyster merchant shouts after him. Tip ignores the shouts, and clambers over shrimp nets and weights to reach a fisherwoman, with huge muscular arms, shouting the price of shrimps. The master of the vessel is behind her, filling a jug with shrimps and letting them fall back like a shower of confectionery. Tip breaks the head off one, and sniffs it.

"I wouldn't give that to my dog," he says and hands it to Frank, who doesn't know what to do with it.

Clambering over ropes, rigging, sails, cans of engine oil, netting, lobster pots, gangplanks, ladders, baskets, trays – all littered over the quayside in a seeming mass of confusion, Tip and Frank scramble the whole length of Oyster Street. Nothing is bought.

Six o'clock is approaching. Tip snaps into action, his nonchalance leaving him as fast as he had assumed it. He returns to the fisherwoman, and buys shrimps at half her asking price, oysters for a third. Brill and dab he buys, which he had earlier disdained as "poison", with a bucket of eels added, "to clear 'em".

Buying is over and the excitement has passed.

Tip hired a porter – a starved-looking man of sixty – and refused to pay the sixpence the man asked.

"Three pence, then," said the man, humbly.

"I'll gi' yer tuppence, take it or leave it. I can soon find another, stronger'n you, you miserable ol' skele'on."

The man took it, and staggered out of the gate to where Tip and Frank had left the barrow.

"An' now for breakfuss," said Tip.

A COSTER LAD

The woods are lovely and dark and deep,
But I have promises to keep,
And miles to go before I sleep.
Robert Frost

"Betty, my dear, I say, Betty, why you look charming' this mornin'. I'll draw up my chair here an' get close in by this nice, invitin' fire. An' you, Betty my love, can 'ave the infinite pleasure of supplyin' me with some good 'am an' heggs an', if you got some nice 'ot muffins an' butter, I'll 'ave 'em an' all, an' some of yer best Rosie Lee, good an' strong. Betty, my love – why you do look ravishin' this fine morning – you can look after vis young lad, like wot he was your own son. Bring him the same, cause 'e's new, an' there's a hard day's work ahead, an' likewise a man can't go to work on an empty stomick, no more can a boy."

Tip leaned back in his chair, put his feet on the table, and placed his order, with an expansive wave of the hand. Frank sat down to the best breakfast he had ever had in his life. After years of workhouse bread and margarine it tasted like nectar. The muffins oozed butter down his chin as he sank his teeth into them; the yellow yolk of the egg ran over the pink ham and he dipped his bread into it. He ate with concentrated enjoyment. Men and boys came in and sat down. Betty rushed around serving. The fire crackled and tobacco smoke filled the air. Voices merged into a quiet hum, and Frank fell asleep, his head on the table.

A heavy hand hit his shoulder. "Right now. It's eight o' clock, an' we gotter get a-goin' on the round."

Tip walked swiftly out into the yard and Frank staggered after him, rubbing the sleep from his eyes. They arranged the cart together, Tip instructing every move, securing the sides, the shafts, the step, placing the trays, the weights and measures, the knives, bags and torn newspapers. At each move, he would say: "Now don't forget this one."

They started the round. If Frank thought that life in the workhouse was hard, that was because he had not experienced life as a coster. From that day on he never stopped working and he never stopped loving every minute of it.

He hollered his way down the streets, bawling out the day's catch. Shrimps, mackerel, herrings, whelks – his high-pitched voice carried from one end of a street to the other. He learned quickly, and within a month he could gut a fish so fast you wouldn't see him do it. He charmed the ladies with his appealing eyes, so that they bought things they didn't want. He flicked a mussel from its shell with a twist of the knife, faster even than Tip. He could worm a whelk before it knew what had hit it.

The round was about ten miles' walking distance. Tip usually closed the barrow at about three o'clock in the afternoon. Anything left over was Frank's to sell. A tray was suspended round his neck and he went out alone. Tip would size up the value of the fish on the tray and say what he wanted Frank to get for it. Anything over that amount was commonly known as a "bunt", or "bunce", and the boy could keep the money. This was regarded as a coster boy's pay, because they received no wages for their work, food and lodgings being regarded as quite sufficient recompense for a day's labour.

Frank quickly discovered that this was to be the hardest part of his day's work. The tray was heavy and his legs soon felt heavy too. Buying was mostly over for the day, and customers were few, so they had to be first attracted, and then persuaded to buy. The fish was getting stale and nothing can disguise the smell or look of stale fish, especially in summer. Frank often had to trudge several miles before he had sold his stock and gained the money Tip demanded for it. Frequently there was nothing at all left over for his bunt. But on other occasions there was, and Frank was ecstatic at having earned himself sixpence or a shilling – a fortune for a boy who had never had anything of his own. To earn his bunt became his main aim, and often he did not return to the lodgings before nine or ten in the evening. He would then crawl under the table, dog-tired, and sleep until 3 a.m., when he was wakened to go to the market.

Frank picked up the lingo within a few weeks, and was soon talking fast and confidently in the incomprehensible jargon costers proudly shared. He assumed the devil-may-care swagger of the other coster lads. He copied Tip's easy-going banter with the ladies. He also copied Tip's flamboyant style of dress, achieved with a few cut-downs from the master-dresser and a few bits such as a neckerchief and shoelaces which he had bought himself with his bunts. His ambition in life was to buy himself a flashy cap.

He adopted the costers' attitude to money: "Spend it while you've got it, tomorrow you may die." He saw that costers worked very hard and that a good trader earned a lot of money. He saw this money being thrown around each evening in the pubs and taverns with extravagant ease. Any man who had had a good day wouldn't hesitate to spend his entire profit on drinks for his mates. If he'd had a bad day, another coster would buy for him. If any coster was in hard street, or was turned in by the police, there would be an immediate whip-round for him. No coster saved a penny, not even a halfpenny, for the future.

Costers didn't live in homes; they lived in lodgings, where they dossed down for a bit, and then moved on. The lodgings were always unspeakably squalid and cheerless, because costers and their women were hardly ever in them. Life was lived in the streets, the markets, the pubs, the penny hops, the penny gaffs, at the race tracks and in the bawdy houses. Life, with all its richness, was lived outside. Costers went back to their lodgings only for a few hours' kip, before the next day dawned and the markets opened.

Above all, Frank learned the trade. Unless he had been trained from boyhood, no man had the slightest chance of becoming a successful coster. The tricks and dodges, the graft and guile, were just as important to learn as the skills of buying and bartering. Frank learned all this lore from the other coster lads as they went around in the early evenings, selling off the day's 'left-overs' and trying to earn an honest bunt. He learned to cover his fish with parsley, to keep it smelling nice. He learned to squeeze a lemon over it, to improve the taste. He added a few nuts to his store, to increase his range. He learned to sell four pints of whelks as five, by taking a bit off the top of each. He learned where he could sell fish heads and tails, and the best times to find the buyer. He learned to mix dead eels with live ones to increase his stock by five to one, and "they don't notice one's dead until vey gets vem 'ome". He made the acquaintance of an unscrupulous pieman who would take eels that had been dead for two days for ready money. He learned that herring and mackerel look fresher by candlelight, so he carried a candle stuck in a turnip for dark evenings. He learned to wheedle and whine, saying his master would knock him about if he didn't sell his wares. He always sold.

By the age of twelve, Frank was as sharp as a terrier. He was up to every dodge in the business, and there were some who said he was as clever a man as Tip. He spent long hours in the markets, he knew the price of everything and forgot nothing. An expert in slang, he conducted all his business in the lingo. He could chaff a peeler so uncommon curious that the only way to stop him was to let him off. He was a master of his trade.

At the age of thirteen Frank decided it was time to go it alone. He wasn't going to give the best years of his life to a master, not he. He'd be his own master, do his own buyin' and sellin', and keep his own profits He'd show them how it was done.

He left Tip and Doll and moved into a common lodging house for men – the back room of a public bar that was open only to the water's edge. The floor was rough stone, the ceiling and walls unplastered. For twopence a night he could hire a straw mattress and a blanket on the floor. Any other lodgings would cost him tenpence a night. So Frank took it, reckoning that he would hardly be there anyway, and why waste good money on a place he only slept in?

The men were rough, obscene, vicious, and put the fear of God into the lad, but he was growing fast, was quick on his feet and good with his fists. He coped, but only just. His greatest terror was of being robbed. He had seen it happen more than once. A sobbing lad of about twelve stuck in his mind. The boy had been skinny and pale and had lost all his stock money overnight. If a lad can't buy, he can't sell. Frank gave him a shilling to buy some walnuts for the theatre trade, and learned to keep his stock money safe. He kept it in his socks and slept each night with his socks and boots on, and the boots tightly laced.

Most of the men in the lodging house were casual labourers, picking up a day's work if and when they could. All were unskilled. Frank considered himself an aristocrat, being skilled in the fish trade. He hired his own gear, bought his own stock, and sold in the streets, keeping all his profits which he spent on flashy clothes, fancy food, beer, girls, the penny hops, the penny gaffs and gambling . . . gambling.

By the age of fourteen, it would be safe to say Frank was a desperate gambler. All the coster men and boys gambled, but none more seriously than Frank. The love of the game was first in his thoughts and dreams, and not a spare moment would pass but he would toss a coin and invite a bet on it. He did not care what he played for, or who he played with, as long as he had a chance of winning. Every day he worked untiringly, spurred on by the thought of the money he would earn, which he could lay against the odds with the next gamester he met. Many a time he lost not only his money but his neckerchief and jacket as well, but nothing could dampen his ardour for the game, a run of continual bad luck making him more reckless than ever.

The coster boys would meet at various points to pitch against each other. They met under railway arches, in pub yards, on the quayside of the river, or even on the shingle when the tide was out. If ever a group of boys' backs and heads were seen crouching in a circle, it would be safe to say that it was a group of gamblers, and ten to one Frank would be in the middle, calling the loudest, the quickest, the fiercest.

"Sixpence on Tol."

"Sixpence he loses."

"Done."

"Give 'im a gen [*shilling*]."

"Flash it them [*show it*]."

Tol wins and the loser bears his losses with a rueful grin.

Now Frank goes into the ring and takes up a stance to toss his coins. His face is scornful.

"Sixpence on Frank."

"A gen he loses."

"I take that one."

"Owl [*two shillings*] on Frank."

"Kool Tol, he's fritted [*Look at Tol, he's afraid*]. Done."

Frank is cool and determined. He plays three up, and calls "Tails." The three coins fall, all tails up. Frank takes his winnings.

Betting starts again. Tol throws, calling "Heads." The coins fall, one head, and two tails. He throws again. The coins fall, showing three tails. Frank takes his winnings. Tol curses and spits, and throws again. "Heads." Again they come down tails. Frank wins. He stares hard at Tol.

"An half-couter [*half sovereign*] next throw."

A gasp goes up from the onlookers, and they bet among themselves for or against Frank.

"Done," says Tol defiantly.

Frank tosses. "Heads," he calls. The three coins fall, all heads up.

"You stinking fish," screams Tol, and pledges his jacket and his boots to honour the debt. He is getting aggressive, and the crowd presses closer. Tol jerks his elbow savagely. "I wish to Christ you'd stand back." Tol's lips are pressed together, his eyes anxious and watchful.

The tense atmosphere has attracted men to the scene, who start their own betting on the two gamesters.

Tol adopts new tactics to bring back his luck. He pushes aside the onlookers and shifts his position a quarter-circle to the right before throwing.

"I'll have it off you. A half-couter," he cries with bravado, knowing full well that he is pledging half his stock money.

"Done," says Frank, confidently.

Betting amongst the onlookers continues and Frank and Tol know that sovereigns are being placed on one or other of them.

Tol spits on the coins, then takes a halfpenny and tosses it on his hand to see what he should call. He then spits again on the three coins and shifts his feet defiantly on the cobbles. He tosses his three coins, calling out "Tails." The coins fall, all tails up. His features relax, and he looks round the circle with a triumphant grin. He puts on his jacket and boots with a triumphant air. Money changes hands among the spectators.

That throw marks the end of Frank's luck for the day. He tosses again and again and, four times out of five, loses. He can hear the bets of the men going against him, and grinds his teeth in fury. If it were an accepted part of gambling to murder your opponent, he would do so. Tol calls again and again. Every time Frank accepts and challenges in return. He loses all his winnings, all his earnings, his neckerchief, his jacket, he even pledges his magnificent velvet cap, vowing it will bring him luck. It doesn't, and he loses it.

With the cap in his hands, Tol stands up. He casts a contemptuous look at Frank, spits on the cap and throws it in the river.

"I'm off now to get a liner [*dinner*]."

He swaggers away to the admiring gasps of the boys and the amused shrugs of the men.

Seething with fury Frank vows revenge. "You wait, you scab, I'll 'ave you to rights. I'll muck you, you scurf, you," he screams.

The men laugh and saunter off. The boys lose interest. A new game starts.

Frank tried to strike a jaunty pose as he stood up, but with no jacket, no neckerchief and no cap, he didn't feel like the cold, calculating gamester any more. He turned quickly and walked in the opposite direction from Tol.

He walked for hours, not feeling the keen wind blowing off the Thames, his mind full of the next game, when he would get even. He'd show 'em. He'd 'ave the houses [*trousers*] off that lousy skunk. He'd get 'is money back, an' more. Hatred filled his heart when he remembered the insult to himself and his trade. Being called a stinking fish was more than a man could stand. He'd get even. His luck'd be back next week. Not for an instant did it occur to him that he had been a fool. The passion for gambling had him in its obsessive grip.

In anger and resentment Frank trudged on, unaware of his surroundings, hating everyone, scowling at those who passed. Ahead of him was a two-bit jerk of a little nipper in baggy trousers, and shoes down on the uppers, leading a little girl, not yet out of nappies, by the hand. He hated them both. The little girl was laughing as she toddled along on unsteady legs. Suddenly she fell and let out an exaggerated howl of pain. The boy bent down and helped her up. He wiped her eyes with his sleeve, and rubbed her knees, spitting on his fingers in order to clean them. He laughed and said: "All better now," but the little girl wouldn't be consoled. She rested her blonde head on his shoulder and put her arms around his neck. He picked her up and carried her into a court, and Frank saw them no more.

Life turns on little things. The momentous events in history can leave us untouched, while small events may shape our destinies.

Frank stood quite still in the street, suddenly feeling cold. The heat of revenge left him, and a cold uncertainty entered his heart. He shivered and leaned against the wall, feeling unexpectedly dizzy. What was it? Everything seemed so cloudy, so misty. What could it be? He didn't seem to be real any more. He touched his face and felt tiny soft arms around his neck. He breathed in and could smell the lovely scent of a baby's hair. Stunned, he wanted to run after the boy and the little girl, to find out who they were. But they had gone. Had he really seen them – a boy in baggy trousers and a tiny girl with blonde hair – or were they ghosts? He shivered and rubbed his eyes, trying desperately to recall something. But the mists of forgetfulness swirled around, and he could not remember what it was.

He made his way back to the lodging house, his mind in turmoil. He was Frank the coster; Frank the rising man; Frank the desperate gambler, feared by all. What did those kids in baggy trousers and nappies mean to him? Nothing! He tried to shake off the image. All right, he had a sister and she was in the workhouse. So what? That wasn't his fault, was it? Let her look after herself, like he'd done. Anyway, he hadn't thought of her for years, and, likely as not, she'd forgotten all about him. He hadn't asked his father and mother to die, that was their lookout, he'd got on all right without them. He shook off the thought of the boy and girl, and whistled his way back to his lodgings. He'd had nothing to eat all day, because he had lost his money, but he wrapped himself up in his blanket in defiance of hunger, and lay down on his palliasse. Sleep evaded him, however.

He heard the other men coming into the lodging room. He heard their cursing and swearing, their belching and farting, and he hated them. How could they be like that? A ghost of a man crept up to his bed, a big man who was strong and gentle. This man looked after his wife, who was frail and coughing. The ghost merged into the farmyard sounds and smells of the men around him, and Frank fell into a light sleep. For the first time in years he dreamed of his mother, whom he had loved so passionately. She was leaving him to go to work. With a cry of anguish he sat up in bed. He felt all over the bed for her, but she wasn't there, and then he remembered where he was and wept bitterly. He remembered now that terrible night when she had not returned, and he remembered holding little Peggy in his arms until the next day when they had been taken to the workhouse.

Memories came flooding back as he lay staring into the darkness: the court where they lived, the room they shared, his mother laughing and singing to him, or his mother coughing and his father anxious. The big ghost hovered over the place, but never quite materialised. He remembered the tiny baby, born not much bigger than a teacup. He thought of the times they had washed her, he and his mother, and put baby clothes on the little creature that were far too big for her. He remembered his mother feeding her, and he wept afresh at this strange and beautiful memory. He buried his face in the straw palliasse, as he had done so often in the workhouse, to muffle the sounds of his sobs. The ghost came nearer and seemed to want to speak to him but did not.

Frank woke at the sound of the other costers getting ready to go to market. What a crazy night! What had been going on? This was the real world. He threw a boot at his mate, and asked him for the loan of some stock money for the day. He knew that costers always helped each other out when one of them hit hard times.

At Billingsgate he was the cool, hard, professional buyer again. His eyes never missed a trick. His ears didn't miss a sound. He hollered his way through his round with double the usual energy and was sold out by 2 p.m. He found his mate to repay the loan. It was a point of honour for costers to repay a debt.

He counted his earnings. There was enough for stock money for tomorrow, and a tightener [*dinner*] today. He went to Betty's and ordered the best Kate and Sidney [*steak and kidney*], with spuds and two doorsteps [*thick lumps of bread*], followed by spotted dick [*currant pudding*] and custard, and a pint o' reeb [*beer*]. No. He thought again. Make that two pints o' reeb.

That's what a man needed inside im, some good grub. He hadn't eaten since breakfast yesterday, what with the game, and queer goings on. No wonder he'd felt funny. A man couldn't keep goin' without a good lining to his stomach. He sat down with his back to the door. Betty brought his food and pinched his ear, but somehow he didn't feel like responding and she retired, offended.

A big man came in. He had hired a boy to hold the bridle of his horse, and called out to the boy as he entered, "You look after her, lad, while I'm away."

Frank heard the words, and the ghost came back and sat down beside him. He remembered, at first dimly, and then as clearly as though it were yesterday, that he had promised his father that he, Frank, would look after his mother and his sister. The spotted dick nearly choked him, and he could eat no more. Did Betty hear him mutter, "I'm sorry, Dad, I'm sorry," as he glanced sideways, or was she imagining it? She certainly saw him brush a tear from his eye with his sleeve, and said to Marge, the cook, in her motherly way, "Vere's somefink up with vat young 'un. Can't eat 'is spotted dick, an' all. Sumfing's up, I tells yer."

Frank sat at the table for a long time, unable to move. The ghost left him, but the memories remained. His mother was dead but his sister, as far as he knew, was alive and in the workhouse. He thumped his fists on the table and dug his nails into his hands as he remembered the tyranny and cruelties he had endured. He prayed that it had not been as bad for his sister in the girls' section. Perhaps they were kinder to girls. He remembered the time they had spent together in the infants' section, and carrying her to his bed when she cried at night. He recalled fighting a bully who had called her "baldy", and he grinned with satisfaction. He remembered a little girl called Jane, who was a friend to them both, and he prayed that Jane had looked after Peggy when he had been transferred to the boys' section. He had never prayed before, but now he did so, and he vowed to heaven, his teeth and fists clenched, that if his sister was still alive he would find her and get her out of the workhouse. He would look after her as he had promised his father.

Betty came over, concerned, and cleared the table.

"How about a nice cup o' Rosie Lee, luv, good an' sweet? On the 'ouse, o' course."

PEGGY

Frank found himself in the workhouse once more. This time he was waiting in the Master's office. He had smartened himself up, as best he could in a communal lodging house, and was waiting with dread in his heart. Was she still alive? Children died in workhouses. He had seen it himself, and had heard stories from people he had met. If Peggy had died, he'd kill those responsible and swing for it. Footsteps came along the corridor, and he stood up.

Frank's first surprise at meeting the Master after nearly four years was how little he was! He had a childhood memory of a large, terrifying man, whose word was absolute law and who had the power to beat and flog for the slightest misdemeanour. Yet here was this flabby little man, about a head shorter than Frank himself, who looked as if he hadn't the strength to lift a bit of cod off a plate, never mind a box of them off a slippery quayside. Frank looked at his puny muscles and compared them in his mind with the lean and muscular men he had worked with for years, and nearly laughed out loud. Was this the terror of the workhouse, this pathetic-looking jellyfish?

But he had come for a purpose, and must be polite. He enquired about his sister: was she still alive? Yes, the Master replied, without giving anything away, she was. Frank gave a huge, shuddering sigh of relief. Where was she, then? The Master replied, guardedly, that she was in the girls' section, where she was well cared for. Frank's joy was unconfined. Here, in this very building? Could he see her, then? His eyes were eager. The Master was prim. No. Boys were not allowed in the girls' section.

Frank was nonplussed. "But I can't help bein' a boy," he blurted out. "If I was 'er big sister you'd let me see 'er, wouldn't you?"

The Master smiled, and agreed, but rules were rules, he said, with such finality that the interview ended.

Frank's joy at knowing she was alive was greater than his disappointment at not being allowed to see her. But he would see her – damn the Master – and he changed his round so that he would be near the workhouse gate at 4 p.m. when the girls returned from school. He hung around, shouting "whelks and eels" as the crocodile of girls marched past him. But he couldn't pick her out. There were a couple of dozen little girls with blonde hair, about the age that she would be, but even though he went every day for a fortnight and looked carefully at them, he couldn't recognise his sister. Several of the bigger girls giggled and nudged each other, winking at him as they marched past. Normally he would have flirted back, but he had no heart for flirting now. He changed his round again.

He sought another interview with the Master. On this occasion he had carefully prepared his questions. If he couldn't see his sister because of the rules, what were the rules about taking her away altogether? The Master was surprised at the boy's persistence and explained, condescendingly, that any relative could apply for the discharge of an inmate and, provided the applicant could prove that he could provide adequately for said inmate, the application would be considered favourably.

Frank's quick brain translated. "You means, if I can support my sister, I can get her out of 'ere?"

The Master nodded.

"An' what would you means by 'support'?"

The Master looked at the eager fourteen-year-old sitting before him, and smiled at the impossibility of his hopes. "I would say, firstly, that the applicant must be of good character and must have decent accommodation. He must prove himself able to support the inmate for whose discharge he is applying, and should have a reasonable sum of money saved against illness or loss of work."

"An' 'ow much would you call a 'reasonable sum'?"

The Master tapped his pencil, and smiled archly.

"Oh, I would say twenty-five pounds. That is a fair sum."

Frank swallowed. Twenty-five pounds! Ask a working boy today to save £25,000 and he might swallow and turn pale, just as Frank did.

The Master concluded the interview and assumed that he would see no more of the boy.

Frank dragged his feet miserably back to the lodging house. The obstacles seemed insurmountable. Why couldn't he just take her? When he entered the squalid doss-house, in which about twenty men slept and ate, he realised the Master was right. He couldn't possibly bring a girl here. He would have to be able to provide for her and find somewhere decent to live.

Frank then worked as he had never worked before, spurred on by necessity. He did his fish round, as ever, but instead of knocking off when he had sold it all, he looked into the fruit-and-nut trade, and hawked them around the pubs and theatres and music halls until ten or eleven at night. He doubled his income. He changed his habits and became something of an outcast from his old mates, because he never gambled, never flashed his money around by joining them in the tavern. They resented it and ridiculed him. He opened a Post Office National Savings Account. No coster ever saved. Conspicuous spending each evening in the pubs and taverns was their habit. But Frank wasn't interested in what the others did. He had opened the account because he knew that in a communal lodging house he would eventually be robbed. When he learned that he would earn four per cent on his investments he was thrilled and carefully worked out how many pennies that would be to every pound saved. By the age of fifteen he had saved eight pounds.

There is no doubt about it, Frank was a brilliant and imaginative coster. He went into the fried-fish market, arranging for the fish to be cooked at a baker's and employing a lad to hawk it around at a fixed rate, plus the bunting system. He looked into the roast-chestnut market and worked out that the hire of the gear would pay for itself around Christmas time. He was right.

By the age of sixteen he had twenty-five pounds in his Post Office account.

He then looked round for a room to rent for himself and Peggy. It had to be a decent room – on that point he was determined. His sister was not going to be dumped in any old hole. She would be twelve years old now, quite the young lady. He had not seen her since she was little more than a baby, but he visualised her as petite and pretty, and felt sure she looked like his mother. Mother and sister merged into each other in his imagination, a numinous female ideal, the guardians of his hopes and longings.

He found a room on the top floor of a house at eight shillings a week, plus two shillings for the rent of furniture. It was an upper-class house, he felt. There was a gas stove on the middle landing for everybody's use, and a tap in the basement, There was even a lavatory in the yard. He was well satisfied.

Frank stood again in the Master's office. He had on his best clothes and his Post Office book was in his pocket. The Master had not expected him, and was astonished when he saw the proof of twenty-five pounds saved in only two years. How had a boy of sixteen achieved it? He looked at him with new respect and said: "Your request will have to be considered by the Board of Guardians. They meet in three weeks' time."

He gave Frank the date and time of the Guardians' meeting and told him to come back on that evening.

Frank asked if he could see his sister, and was told curtly that he would see her in three weeks' time. Seething with frustration, he looked at his powerful fists and nearly knocked the man down. But he remembered he had to be "of good character", so thrust his hands behind his back. He would never get Peggy out if he hit the workhouse master!

The Guardians debated the application. It was unusual, but they agreed to release the girl, if she wished to go with her brother. Frank was called into the boardroom and interrogated.

They seemed satisfied and were especially impressed by the Post Office book. They told him to stand by the window, and Peggy was called away from her evening duties.

Peggy was in the washhouse, helping to prepare the younger girls for bed. It was a duty she loved – better than scrubbing the greasy old kitchen floors, or putting out smelly dustbins. She could play with the little girls, and there was always laughter when Peggy was putting them to bed. They had to laugh quietly, so as not to get into trouble, but, somehow, a bar of soap slithering across a stone floor seemed even funnier if you had to stuff a towel into your mouth to stop shrieks of laughter. Suppressed giggles double the fun for young girls.

Peggy was flushed with the steam and the laughter. Her blonde hair was damp and the wispy bits around her forehead curled upwards. Her apron was wet, and her arms soapy.

An officer came in. "The Guardians want to see you. Come with me."

She didn't know what the summons meant and had no time to feel alarm. She was shown into the big boardroom, where a group of gentlemen sat around an oval table.

Frank, standing inconspicuously by the window, watched her every step. She was taller than he had expected. He had imagined a tiny creature, because he remembered a tiny baby. But this was a grown girl in early puberty. He liked her dishevelled hair and laughing features, still damp from the washhouse. He saw, with a stab of pity, the fear and uncertainty as she stepped towards the oval table.

The Chairman said, not unkindly, "Your brother has made an application to remove you from the workhouse."

"My brother?" Peggy looked bewildered.

"Yes, you have a brother. Didn't you know?"

She shook her head. The anguish inside Frank made his legs turn to jelly. He leaned against the wall.

"Well, you have, and he asks permission to take you out of our care and to look after you himself. Do you wish to go with him, or do you prefer to stay here with your friends?"

Peggy didn't say anything, and a member of the Board said sharply, "Speak up, child, and answer the Chairman when he is good enough to speak to you."

Peggy's lip trembled and she began to cry, but still she said nothing. Frank's anguish had turned to dread. What if she did not want to come? It was a possibility he had not even considered.

The Chairman, who was kindly, with daughters of his own, said gently, pointing to Frank: "This is your brother Frank. It is to be regretted that you have not seen him since you were three years old, but now he has applied for your discharge and we, your guardians, are satisfied that he can provide for you. Do you wish to go with him?"

Peggy looked over towards the window, and saw a tall stranger. He did not mean a thing to her. Insecure children are terrified of change. She thought of the happy laughter in the washhouse, and her friends at school and in the dormitory. She stared at this unknown, unknowable young man, and her heart was set on her friends and the routine she had always known.

Frank saw rejection in her eyes and panic spurred his movements. Before she could speak, he stepped swiftly across the room.

"Stay where you are, you have no right—" shouted the Master.

Frank took no notice. He walked straight up to Peggy and stood looking down at her. Everyone in the room was hushed as brother and sister looked at each other for the first time in nine years. Then, slowly, he extended the little finger of his right hand and curled it round the little finger of her right hand. He held it close and grinned. "Hello, Peg."

The action stirred her memory as nothing else could have done. Holding little fingers was a special and intimate gesture from a childhood almost lost to her now. No one else had ever done that to her. She had forgotten all about it, but now she remembered. A dim, far-off memory of loss and longing stirred within her. She looked at this tall lad and the love that she had not known for years flooded her heart.

She squeezed his little finger in return, and smiled a smile of secret understanding. He saw the dimples in her cheeks, and knew that he had seen them before. Then with sudden, impetuous warmth, she threw her arms about his neck and leaned her head on his shoulder. The Guardians watched with breathless wonder. Even the Master was silent. The intoxicating smell of her hair sent a thrill through Frank's tense body and he relaxed, knowing that she was his sister, and that all would be well.

She did not hold him for long, but turned to the Chairman and curtsied. "I will go with my brother, if you please, sir."

Memories of early childhood dwell in a limbo that is neither forgetting, nor quite remembering. As Peggy danced along the pavement, looking up at Frank, she tried desperately to recall him, but could not. She looked up at his face, his hair, his smile, and tried to persuade herself that she knew him and could remember him when they were little, but she had to admit to herself that he was a stranger. Yet somehow he wasn't. His big, rough hand grasping her own felt familiar, his arm round her shoulders as he led her down a dark street was familiar too. Something in his touch struck a chord within her that she knew and responded to.

Frank was jubilant. He felt like a king. None of his mates could have done what he'd done. He had got her out of that place, his little sister, and he would never let her go back. She did not look as he had imagined, but that did not matter; she was better than he had imagined. He greeted several of his friends, who nudged each other and shouted, "Who's yer tart? Where'd 'ja find 'er? Any more like 'er fer us?"

Frank replied, good humouredly, "She's my sister, and there's no one in the whole world like her."

He took her back to the lodgings – in a respectable street, he pointed out. He was proud to show her the facilities of the house.

He led her up to the second floor and showed her the last word in luxury: the gas stove on the landing, where she could cook. They climbed two more flights of wooden stairs, and he proudly flung open the door.

It was a small attic room with a sloping roof and a garret window, in which a broken pane had been patched up with cardboard. The walls were unpainted and bits of plaster were falling off. The ceiling was yellow and stained with damp. The furniture, rented for two shillings a week, consisted of a rough wooden table and chair, a narrow iron bedstead with coarse grey army blankets, a wooden box, a candle stuck in a milk bottle, a jug and washbowl and a chamber pot. It looked fairly bleak, but children like small rooms, and to Peggy it seemed like heaven.

She threw her arms around Frank. "It's lovely, lovely. Are we really going to live here?" Her eyes filled with uncertainty. "Will I have to go back? Don't let me go back. I want to stay here with you." He folded her in his arms and said fiercely, "You'll never go back. Didja hear me? Never. Not as long as I can see to it. We'll be together, always. Vat's a promise, an' all. Now, let's see vat smile o' your'n, so I can see them dimples."

She smiled with trusting confidence, and he put his little fingers into the dimples.

"You'll 'ave to smile a lot more offen, yer know."

He brought in some wood and lit a fire in the narrow grate. Red and yellow flames leaped up, filling the little room with colour. He had bought some muffins and some real butter, and they sat on the floor by the fire, toasting the muffins on the end of a knife. They were so delicious she couldn't stop eating them and the butter ran down her chin. He chuckled and wiped it off with his finger. She took hold of his hand and licked the butter off his finger, looking up at him with melting eyes. A thrill ran through him, and he did not know what to say.

She murmured, "Muffins. Muffins and butter. Better than nasty smelly old bread and margarine. Can I eat muffins for evermore, Frank?"

"Course you can. Thousands of 'em. I'll see to that, you'll see. Muffins every day, if you wants 'em. An' candy, an chocolate, an' cakes an' all."

"And can I have jam and honey and cream?"

"Wha'ever you wants, my li'l sister, you can 'ave. You'll see."

"And pretty dresses?"

"Loads of 'em."

"And a carriage with four horses?"

"Of course. Six 'orses, and a coachman, an' all."

Peggy sighed with happiness. But something inside her stirred, and she clung to him. "But you won't go away? You won't let them take me away from you again, will you?" Her eyes were wide with terror. His eyes were serious and his voice firm. "No one can take you away from me, not no one, never. I've promised, haven't I? We'll be together always."

Satiated with muffins and warmth and the emotion of the day, her eyes began to close. Frank watched her closely, thinking he had never seen such a pretty face. She was so much prettier than the coster girls most of his mates had. They were rough-looking girls with loud voices and dirty hair. He leaned forward and touched her hair. It was like silk, and so fine he had to blow it, just to watch it move. She felt his breath on her face, and opened her eyes.

"Come on, little girl, it's time for you to go to bed."

Frank used the words he had used when he was six and she was two. A distant memory stirred and she giggled, and leaned back against the wall, kicking her heels against the floor.

"Can't make me."

He leaned towards her and took off her boots and socks, saying as he did so, "This little piggy goes to market. This little piggy stays at home."

She caught the rhyme and finished, "And this little piggy goes wee, wee, wee, all the way home. Home, Frank, not the workhouse but home, with you."

He undressed the sleepy young girl just as he had done nearly ten years before. He put her into the bed and she fell asleep straight away, snuggled into the warm blanket that he pulled around her.

He threw another log on the fire. He did not feel sleepy. He felt wide awake, teeming with emotions that tumbled into his conscious and subconscious mind. He had done it! He'd got her out. Out for good an' all. Hadn't that stinking workhouse master sat up when he'd showed him the Post Office book, and told him there were respectable lodgings to take her to? Frank looked proudly round the little room. This was real swell, this was.

He stroked the hair of the sleeping child, and a wave of tenderness swept over him. This was his sister. Was she really like their mother? He couldn't say. Already the shadow of his mother was fading as the reality of Peggy grew more distinct. How soft and pretty girls were. He stroked the smooth white skin of her arm and compared it with his own, all covered with black hairs. He took up her hand, then noticed with fury that it was all red and rough, her nails short and broken, with little cracks at the fingertips. The bastards. They'd got her scrubbing and doing heavy washing already! They'd better not come his way again, or he'd murder them! No – that was too good for them. He'd get the Master and the lousy officers scrubbing the floors themselves. They could scrub for years. That'd learn 'em! He swore angrily to himself, and vowed that Peggy would never have to work so hard again.

He got up and turned the log with his boot. Sparks shot up the chimney and the embers glowed red, making the meagre little attic look cosy. He looked around, and thought of the squalid men's doss-house on the waterfront where he had lodged for two years. Disgusting! Men were always coughin' an' spittin'. Men were always fartin' and belchin' an' swearin'. Always fightin' over nuffink, they were. It wasn't just Peggy who'd been rescued. Rescuing her had rescued him from that lousy, flea-ridden dump, and he was never going back. Never.

He sat down again beside her and listened to her quiet breathing. Men snored! Leastwise, all the men he'd ever known had snored like elephants. Enough to keep a person awake all night. Peggy let out a tiny puff as she moved in her sleep, and he held his breath. Was that how girls snored? The workhouse dormitory with seventy boys and an officer came to his mind, and he shut the thought out quickly. He didn't ever again want to think of it. It was too awful. They were both out now and they'd stay out. They belonged together. His jaw was set with determination as he looked into the future.

She would have to go to school. His sister was going to have a good education and grow up to be a lady. He'd see to it, he would. His sister wasn't going to be a common coster girl, like them poor little kids. Half-starved, half-frozen, unwanted kids, sent out for hours and hours to sell a few lousy apples or rotting pears that no one would buy and then they'd get beaten because they hadn't sold a thing. His sister would be a lady with book-learning and a posh accent.

The log shifted on the fire, and the sound broke his train of thought. Perhaps he'd better get some shut-eye. He'd have to be up at three to go to the market. It was more important than ever that his trading showed a profit. He could think about schools tomorrow. But he didn't want to disturb the magic of the moment. The firelight was fading, but he could see the dark curve of her lashes against her pale skin. He could see the slender white shoulder against the grey blanket. He leaned over and kissed it, very gently, so as not to disturb her. This was the best day of his life.

Quite suddenly he felt really tired. The excitement of the day had caught up with him at last. He pressed the log down into the ashes, undressed, and crept into bed, hoping not to wake her. But the bed was so small that he had to push her over to make room for himself. She sighed, and stretched out a sleep-warmed arm, which, feeling his body, curled around his neck and drew him towards her. She murmured: "Is that Frank? Is that really Frank, my lovely brother? Oh, I love you so much."

He kissed her eyes, her hair, her face, her mouth. He passed his hands down her slender body, and fire ran through him as he felt the circle of her tiny firm breasts and buttocks. She was neither asleep nor awake, but she loved him with all her heart and mind, with all her soul and her body. Their union was as inevitable as it was innocent.

TILL DEATH US DO PART

Peggy was singing her way through her scrubbing and polishing at Nonnatus House. It was always nice to hear her. Sister Julienne casually remarked, "You sound happy. How's Frank these days?"

"Frank? Well, he's had a bit of a stomach ache recently, but a dose of Epsom Salts will soon see that off."

A few weeks later she confided to Sister, "Frank's still got the stomach ache, Sister. Salts don't seem to do him any good. What else can I give him?"

Questioning revealed that Frank's stomach ache had lasted for six weeks. Sister advised seeing the doctor, but Frank would not go to the doctor. Men like Frank never do.

"I've never bin to a sawbones in me life, an' I'm not startin' now. I'll work it off, you'll see."

But he couldn't work it off, and a couple of weeks later he had to shut up his stall in Chrisp Street Market at 11 a.m. leaving half the fish unsold – something unheard of. He took a couple of codeine and slept when he got home, and felt sufficiently well to go to Billingsgate at 4 a.m. the next morning.

"There, I said I'd work it off, didn' I?" he said as he kissed Peggy goodbye.

But some of his mates brought him home at 7 a.m. The pain had got so bad that he couldn't continue. Peggy put him to bed and called the doctor, who examined him and advised hospital. Frank refused. The doctor assured him it would only be for a few days for tests. Peggy insisted and finally Frank acquiesced. Tests revealed the early stages of carcinoma of the pancreas. They were told it was inflammation of the pancreas and radium treatment was advised.

At Nonnatus House Peggy sought reassurance. "It's only

inflammation, and what's the pancreas, anyway? It's only a tiny organ in the body, they tell me; it's not like the liver or the stomach. The radium treatment will get rid of it in no time, I suppose. After all, the pancreas is not much bigger than your appendix, and thousands of people have their appendix out, don't they?"

We reassured her. What else can you do? We did not say that, in those days, no one had ever been known to recover from cancer of the pancreas. Frank was given the choice of hospitalisation for the radium therapy, or an out-patient visit twice a week. He stayed at home. He handed over the lease of his stall to a mate of his for three months, saying he would want it back when he had had a good rest and was better. He told Peggy not to give up any of her work, because he didn't want to be fussed. However, Peggy did give up most of her work, arguing that this would be the only time in their lives when he was not working six days a week, and they could treat it as a holiday. A bit of radium therapy would hardly get in the way and they could go out and about on the other days and have a good time.

However, Peggy continued her work at Nonnatus House. Perhaps she needed the proximity of the Sisters for reassurance and advice. She did not appear anxious, saying things like, "He's getting on nicely now, thank you, Sister," or, "We haven't been out anywhere, really. The radium seems to make him tired, so we stay in, and he likes to hear me reading to him. It's better than going out, we reckon."

One day she said, "He seems to get pain at night, but they've given him some tablets, and that'll do the trick, eh, Sister?" Another time she said, "He's lost a bit of weight. Good thing too, I tell him. 'You were beginning to get quite a paunch on you,' I said, and he laughed and said, 'You're right there, Peg.'"

Within a few weeks we were requested to take Frank for home nursing. Sister Julienne and I went to assess him.

Peggy and Frank lived in a prefab on the Isle of Dogs. These were small, ready-made buildings erected in huge numbers after the war, to house some of the thousands of people whose homes had been destroyed. The prefabs were put up as an emergency measure and intended to last only four to five years, but many of them lasted forty to fifty years. They were very pleasant, cosy and greatly preferred to the terraces that had been destroyed by the bombs. As we approached the prefab estate in the morning sunlight, it looked charming, with the low buildings, leafy trees full of sparrows and the river lapping in the background. It always surprised me that only a short distance from one of the biggest commercial ports in the world such quietness and peace could prevail.

Their tiny garden, about six to ten feet of space all around the house, was well tended, with flowers and cabbages and runner beans growing well. A vine was trained up the south wall and I wondered if they ever got any grapes worth eating. The front door opened straight into the sitting room, which was comfortable and pretty. It was also spotlessly clean. Peggy was obviously very house-proud.

She greeted us with her usual happy smile. "It's good of you to come," she said as she took Sister's cloak and hung it up. "He's in bed at the moment, but he's getting along nicely. He's had two weeks of the radium treatment now and he's getting stronger all the time. He says he'll be back at the market in no time."

We went into the bedroom and I was thankful that Sister Julienne was with me. Had I been alone, my reaction at seeing Frank for the first time in about three months would probably have betrayed my shock. He looked ghastly. He lay in the middle of the big double bed, his eyes sunken, his skin grey. He had lost so much weight that his flesh hung in wrinkles and he had lost most of his hair. I doubt if any of his mates at the market would have recognised him.

Sister went straight up to him, with her gentle warmth. "Hello Frank, how nice to see you again. We miss you at Nonnatus House, and look forward to your return. The other man's good, we've no complaints, but it's not the same as having you."

Frank smiled, and the skin pulled tight across his nose and cheek bones. His eyes, sunk deep into their bony sockets, gleamed with pleasure. "I'll be back right enough, Sister. It's only a few more weeks of this radium, an' I'll be on me feet again."

"Are you sure you won't go into hospital for the remainder of your treatment? It would be more restful, you know. The ambulance journey back and forward can be very tiring, especially after the treatment."

But Frank and Peggy were both adamant that he should remain at home.

Sister examined him. She carefully moved his emaciated body, the arms and legs that seemed to have insufficient muscle to lift their own weight. Was this the man who had lifted a hundredweight box of cod only a few short weeks ago? I went to the other side of the bed and caught in my nostrils the smell of death as I leaned over him.

Strangely enough, Peggy did not seem to notice how desperately ill he was. She seemed perfectly happy, and kept saying things like: "He's getting on fine," "He's getting stronger each day," or, "He ate all the milk pudding I made for him. That shows he's getting well, doesn't it?" I was struck by the fact that we all see what we want to see. Peggy appeared to have closed her mind to the reality of Frank's condition, to the extent that she literally couldn't see it. To her, Frank was exactly the same as he had always been, her brother and her lover. He was the beat of her heart, the blood in her veins, and the physical changes, obvious to anyone else, she just did not see.

It was arranged that I should call for home nursing twice a day, and that Sister would come any time that Peggy requested.

I do not know whether or not Sister Julienne noticed the sleeping arrangements in the little house. The prefabs were constructed in a rectangle with a single large room and two small rooms leading off it. These were intended as bedrooms, but one of the rooms in Frank's house was a dining room, which we could see through the open door. The only room used for sleeping had a double bed in it. If Sister Julienne noticed these things, and put two and two together, at no time did she say so. The Sisters had seen it all before, many, many times. In cramped living conditions, where a family of ten, twelve, fifteen or more lived in one or two rooms, incest was hardly surprising. Families kept their secrets and the Sisters did not comment or judge. I felt that there was nothing in human life that they had not witnessed in the seventy years they had worked in Poplar.

Later Sister said to me, "We will have to keep up this pretence that he is going to get better. The charade has to go on – treatments that will do no good, drugs that are useless – to give, the impression of medical competence and nursing care. 'Hope' lies in those treatments and, without hope for the future, most of our patients would find themselves in torment at the end."

One day when I called they were studying travel brochures received from Thomas Cook. Frank was very alert in his mind. His speech was slower and quieter, but his eyes were bright, and he seemed almost animated.

"Peg an' me, we thinks we'll go to Canada for a good 'oliday when the treatment's done an' I'm on me feet again. She's never bin abroad afore. I was in France and Germany in Hitler's war, an' I never wants 'a go near Europe agen. But Canada, now – big clean open spaces. Look a' this 'ere, nurse. Lovely pictures, aren't they? We reckons Canada's just the place for us, don't we, Peg? Who knows, we might stop there if we likes it enough, eh, Peg?"

She was sitting on the edge of the bed, her eyes glowing with happy anticipation. "We'll go on the Queen Mary," she agreed. "First Class, like a couple of swells."

They both laughed and squeezed hands.

Together Peggy and I helped him to the bathroom. It was difficult, but he still had the strength to get there. She washed him all over, because although he could get into the bath, he did not have the strength to get out. In clean pyjamas he sat in the sitting room looking at the plaster ducks flying across the wall, whilst Peggy and I changed the bed with the text over it, executed in big, childish embroidery stitches, 'God is Love'.

We had taught Peggy many essentials in the art of nursing, such as treating pressure points and dealing with pain or nausea. She was quick to acquire any small skill to make Frank more comfortable. I enquired about appetite, pain, bowels, vomiting, headaches and fluid intake, and left them happy with their plans for Canada. Should it be Vancouver or the Rockies? They couldn't decide.

The air was sweet as I left the little house, and the sounds of the huge cargo vessels, the cranes, the lorries, seemed far off. I thought of the thousands of powerful men working ceaselessly in that great port, and the fragility of life. Health is the greatest of God's gifts, but we take it for granted; yet it hangs on a thread as fine as a spider's web and the tiniest thing can make it snap, leaving the strongest of us helpless in an instant.

Frank received a six-week course of radium therapy and was taken twice a week by ambulance to the hospital. Both he and Peggy expressed wonder and a touching appreciation that all this was free on the new National Health Service. "It's lucky I got ill now, an' not a few years ago. I could never 'ave paid for all this expensive treatment." They seemed completely confident that it would be effective, probably because it was so elaborate. That he was getting weaker every day was put down to the temporary effects of the radium, which would pass when the treatment was completed. Everyone – that is, all the medical and paramedical staff, which must have totalled at least thirty people – kept the illusion going, though there was no corporate decision to do so.

Nausea is an unpleasant side effect of radium treatment and was something that Frank had been warned about in advance. He attributed his weakness and weight loss to the fact that he could not eat much. 'Cos a man's gonna get thin like, if he's not eatin' like what I'm not. Once I get some good grub inside me, an' keep it down, I'll pack the old weight on, you'll see."

Pain was another matter. The control of pain is the first

responsibility of anyone involved in the care of the dying. Pain is a mystery that we cannot fathom, because there is no measure. Everyone's tolerance of pain differs, therefore the correct dose of analgesic will differ. One must balance the strength of analgesic to the level of pain perceived and not allow the pain to develop beyond the patient's tolerance.

Frank was having half a grain of morphine three times a day. Later this was increased to four, then six times daily. It was sufficient to dull his pain to an acceptable level, but did not impair his faculties. He was interested in everything.

He once said: "Every mornin' I hear the fishin' boats come up the river. Can't get out of the 'abit of wakin' . In my mind I can see the sails, dark against the red sun, like wot' they used to be like, comin' quietly out of the morning mist. Boo'iful they was, just boo'iful. You've gotta have seen them sailin' boats to know wot' a lovely sight it was. Now I listen to the sounds of ve engines. I can tell you by ve sound if it's an oyster smack or a mackerel trawler. I can even tell you 'ow many deep-sea vessels from the Atlantic come in. It'll be good to be back at Billingsgate."

Peggy and I agreed that it wouldn't be long. He was getting on famously.

Peggy had given up all work now and never left his side, except for essential household duties. She spent hours reading to him. Frank had never learned to read fluently, and could barely write.

"Book-learnin's never been my strong point – but Peg, she's the scholar. I love to 'ear her read. She's got a lovely voice."

Peggy read about half a dozen of Dickens's novels in this way, sitting close to him, outwardly reading but inwardly attentive to every mood and movement. She was conscious of every shade in her loved one, ready to close the book if she sensed tiredness, or to change his position if she saw discomfort. Peggy knew almost before he knew himself what his needs were going to be.

Love permeated every nook and cranny, every corner and crevice of that little house. You could feel it as soon as you entered the front door, like a presence so tangible you could almost reach out and touch it. If there is one thing that a dying person needs more than relief from pain, it is love. I have seen, later in my career when I was a ward sister at the Marie Curie Hospital in Hampstead, unloved, unwanted people dying alone. Nothing can be more tragic or pitiful. And nothing is more hopeless or intractable for the nursing staff to deal with.

Love prompted Peggy to sing to Frank every evening, the old songs, the folk songs and hymns that they had both learned in childhood. Love prompted her to move the bed so that he could see the masts and funnels of the boats as they approached the docks. Love told her which visitors to admit and which to turn away from their front door. They grew even closer. They had always been one flesh; now they were one spirit, one soul. And all the time she kept up the pretence that he was going to recover. If she cried alone in the kitchen, he never saw it.

It was Frank who first startled me. We had just finished a blanket bath (he no longer had the strength to get to the bathroom) and he had asked Peggy for a hot drink and a hot-water bottle. As soon as he heard the kitchen door close, he said, "Nurse, you must promise me you won't let on to Peggy. It'll break her heart. Promise, now."

I was putting things away in my bag and my back was turned towards him. I didn't move or breathe. I had to respond in some way, but I couldn't find my voice.

"I want you to promise, now."

"What do you mean?" I said, eventually. I had to turn round, and he was looking straight at me, his sunken eyes bright in their dark sockets.

"I mean I'm not gonna get better an' I don't want Peg to know until she has to."

"But Frank, what makes you think you won't recover? The radium treatment ends next week and then you will begin to feel stronger."

I hated myself for this pathetic falsehood. I felt degraded by it. Why do we have to be like this? In India, apparently, a man often predicts his own death, says farewell to his family, goes to a holy place, and dies. Yet we cannot admit to someone that he is dying, so we have to play false, and I have been as big a deceiver as anyone.

He didn't say a word, but closed his heavy eyes. We heard the kitchen door open. He hissed fiercely, "Promise. Promise you won't tell her."

"I promise, Frank," I whispered.

He sighed with relief.

"Thank you." His voice was husky. "Thank you, now I can rest easy."

The radium treatment halted the malignant growth for a while, but could not be continued beyond six weeks, as it would destroy other organs. Frank's deterioration was rapid when treatment stopped. The pain became more intense, and the morphine was increased to one grain, then two grains every four hours. He could barely eat, and Peggy sat beside him feeding semi-solids into his unwilling mouth.

"There, Frank love, just another little spoonful, put some strength into you."

He would nod, and try to swallow. She washed and shaved him, turned him, cleaned his mouth and his eyes. She dealt with his urine and his bowels, and kept him clean and comfortable, all the while humming the songs he liked. He no longer looked at travel brochures, nor had the mental strength or interest to listen to Dickens, but he seemed to like to hear her singing. He rarely spoke and was drifting in and out of consciousness.

Frank was quietly slipping away into that mysterious border land between life and death where peace and rest and gentle sounds are the only needs. One day, in my presence, he gazed at Peggy for a long time as though he did not recognise her and then said, quite clearly: "Peggy, my first love, my only love, always there, always when I need you." He smiled and drifted away again.

More than anything else a dying person needs to have someone with them. This used to be recognised in hospitals, and when I trained, no one ever died alone. However busy the wards, or however short of staff, a nurse was always assigned to sit with a dying person to hold their hand, stroke their forehead, whisper a few words. Peace and quietness, even reverence for the dying, were expected and assured.

I disagree wholly with the notion that there is no point in staying with an unconscious patient because he or she does not know you are there. I am perfectly certain, through years of experience and observation, that unconsciousness, as we define it, is not a state of unknowing. Rather, it is a state of knowing and understanding on a different level that is beyond our immediate experience.

Peggy was aware of this and, in ways that neither she nor anyone could explain, she entered into Frank's mental state in the last few weeks and days of his life.

One day, as I was leaving, she said, "It won't be long now. I shall be glad for us both when it's all over." She did not look unhappy. In fact she looked as serene and as confident as ever. But all pretence was gone.

I asked her, "How long have you known that he was going to die?"

"How long? Well, I can't say exactly. A long time, anyway. From the time the doctor first said he should go into hospital for tests, I suppose."

"So you've known all the time, and never let on?"

She did not reply, but stood on the doorstep, smiling.

"How did you guess?" I asked, intrigued.

"It wasn't a question of guessing. I just knew, quite suddenly, as though someone had told me. I've had so much happiness in life with Frank, more happiness than anyone can expect. We're more than brother and sister, more than husband and wife. How could I fail to know that he was going to die?"

She smiled, and waved to a neighbour who was passing, and

replied to her enquiry, "Yes, he's getting on nicely, thank you; he'll be up and about soon, you'll see."

The last evening of his life came surprisingly quickly. Rash is the professional who will predict death. The young can die while your back is turned, yet the old and frail, who you think will die in the night, live on for weeks.

The late summer evening was beautiful as I approached the prefab estate. Long shafts of sunlight glimmered on the river and made the little buildings glow like pink marble.

Peggy greeted me at the door with the words, "He's changed, nurse. About an hour ago he just changed. Something's different."

She was right. A deep motionless stupor had come over Frank. He did not appear to be in any discomfort or distress. In fact I have never in all my experience known anyone to die in a state of distress. "Death agony" is a common idea, but I have never seen it.

Frank's breathing had changed. It was very slow and deep. I counted the breaths and there were only six per minute. He was slightly blue around the mouth, nose and ears. His eyes were open but unseeing. Peggy took his hand and grasped it firmly. She stroked his forehead with her other hand and leaned over him whispering, "I'm here, Frank. It's all right, my love, I'm here."

He seemed quite unconscious, but I saw his hand move as he gripped hers more firmly. What is this mystery we call the unconscious? I felt sure he knew she was there. Perhaps he could even hear her and understand her words. I felt his nose, his ears, his feet. They were quite cold. I felt his pulse; it was only twenty beats per minute. I whispered, "I'll stay here quietly. I'll sit over by the window."

She nodded. I sat down to contemplate them both. She was completely calm and relaxed. She did not look unhappy or even anxious. Every nerve of her concentration was focused on the dying man. She was with him in death as she had been in life.

His breathing rate dropped to four per minute and the hand

holding Peggy's fell limp. I felt his pulse again, but could not locate it, and when I did it was a feeble eight or ten beats per minute. I sat down again, and Peggy continued to stroke his face and his hands. The clock ticked steadily, and quarter of an hour elapsed. Frank gave a deep, deep breath, which made a rasping sound as it passed through the collapsed throat muscles. A little fluid oozed out of his mouth and trickled down the pillow. His eyes were still open, but a white film was collecting over them.

Peggy whispered, "I think he's gone."

"I think so. But wait quietly for a minute."

She sat unmoving by the inert body for about two minutes. Then, to our surprise, he took another huge, rasping breath. Would there be another? We waited for a full five minutes, but he did not breathe again. There was no pulse or heartbeat.

Spontaneously Peggy said, "Into Thy hands, Oh Lord, I commend his spirit." Then she recited the Lord's Prayer, in which I joined her.

Together we straightened and laid out the dead man's body. We closed his eyes. We could not keep his mouth shut so I tied the chin with a bandage to keep the lower jaw in place. We could take it off when rigor mortis had set in. We had to change the bed linen completely, because at the time of dying his bowels and bladder had emptied.

We washed him all over, and I said, "We will leave him in a shirt, put on back to front. The undertakers will bring a shroud."

She replied, "I've got one. I got it several weeks ago. I couldn't have left him indecent could I?"

She fetched a chair and climbed up to a small cupboard high above the gas meter. There was a box in it from which she extracted a shroud. We put it on him. I asked her if she would like me to contact the undertakers. She thanked me, and said she would be grateful. "But tell them not to come till tomorrow morning, will you, please?"

That was perfectly normal. In those days the deceased often lay in the house for a day or two as a mark of respect for the dead. Family and neighbours would come in to "pay their respects".

Throughout, Peggy was completely calm and tranquil. Her face and voice betrayed no sign of sorrow or loss. In fact I would have said she had an almost ethereal quality about her. I left her with a feeling of admiration.

At the door, she said, "If you see anyone, any neighbours, don't tell them Frank's died, will you? I'll tell them tomorrow. I want to tell them myself."

"Of course not," I reassured her, although I would have to report it at Nonnatus House.

Her anxiety passed.

"That's all right. It's just the neighbours, I don't want them to know yet. They can come tomorrow to pay their respects. But not tonight."

We smiled at each other, and I squeezed her hand. No one would come barging in tonight, not the undertakers, nor the neighbours, nor anyone. She could be alone with her thoughts and her memories. Would she like a couple of sleeping tablets?

She thought for a second. Yes, that would be a very good idea. I opened my bag and handed her a couple of Soneryl.

Peggy shut and locked the door when I left. She sat for many hours on the edge of the bed, unable to take her eyes off Frank, their life together tumbling through her mind. Her happiness had been perfect and complete, she had always known that, and now she was not going to be parted from him.

She pulled up a chair and climbed again to the cupboard above the gas meter and took out two more boxes, one very small, the other larger. She undressed and brushed her hair. She opened the larger of the two boxes and took out a white shroud, which she put on, tying the ribbons carefully at the back. She opened the small box and tipped out fifteen grains of morphine, to which she added the two Soneryl. She took a bottle of brandy and a glass from the bedside cabinet, and swallowed all the tablets in two or three gulps. She continued drinking brandy until she could no longer sit up.

When the undertakers arrived the next morning they could not get in. They broke the window and saw her dead, her arms around her brother.

AND THE MEEK SHALL INHERIT THE EARTH

The Reverend Thornton Applebee-Thornton had been a missionary in Sierra Leone for twenty-five years. He was enjoying a six-month furlough home in England, which he tried to spend mostly at the Applebee-Thorntons' country house in Herefordshire. This was not always easy, because his father, a widower of ninety who was looked after by two ladies from the village, was a retired Indian Army colonel who had never been able to understand his only son's priestly persuasion. In fact, he despised it, despised his wet and wimpish ways, and secretly felt aggrieved that he should be afflicted with such offspring. His only son, he grumbled to himself, might have had the decency to turn out to be more of a man than that poor thing with his dog collar and his sermons, a missionary pandering to the blasted natives.

"Bah!" he would shout, "kick hell out of the blasted wogs. That's the only way they will respect you. It's the only language they understand."

At which point his reverend son decided that perhaps it was time to visit his cousin Jack at his farm in Dorset; but cousin Jack had just retired to the South of France, leaving his son Courtney in charge of the farm and yes, of course, (the letter read) cousin Thornton would be more than welcome to stay if he could accommodate Fiona's busy programme at the riding school that they had just opened. A week at the farm convinced the Reverend Mr Applebee-Thornton that all this horsey stuff was not for him. Equally, the young couple decided between themselves that the poor old boy was really a frightful bore and they couldn't be expected to introduce him to their circle; perhaps Africa was the best place for him.

So he visited old school friends, and students from his days at theological college. They were delighted to see him, but sadly, after they had exhausted the shared experiences of thirty to forty years ago, found they had little to say to each other.

Perhaps a couple of weeks in Brightlingsea – or did they call it Brighton these days? – would be pleasant. The Metropole was comfortable and he enjoyed the sea breezes, but, as he sat on the front watching life pass by, he was forced to conclude that he had spent so long in Africa and given so much of his mind and energy to the mission that he had lost touch with the changes in England. Expecting the customs and manners, dress and behaviour of the 1920s, he was a little shocked, and more than a little pained by what he saw.

The Reverend Mr Applebee-Thornton was a bachelor – not, he was quick to assure his friends, by choice. He greatly admired, indeed revered, the fair and gentle sex, and would very much have wished the solace and companionship of a loving wife, joined in the felicity of holy matrimony as vouchsafed to his more fortunate friends and colleagues; but the fair ideal had not come his way. The truth is that the reverend gentleman was essentially a one-woman man, and the only woman he had ever fancied was, unfortunately, a nun. He had never spoken to her, beyond the sacramental words: "This is the body of Christ, take this ... " as he gave her the consecrated bread; but she was enshrined in his heart and when he was moved to another mission her memory went with him. But that was all a long time ago, he mused, as he watched the boys and girls flaunting themselves half-naked on Brighton beach, and times had changed. Perhaps one was out of touch?

He pulled a letter from his pocket. One of his old friends from theological college was the rector of All Saints', Poplar. The Rector would be delighted to see him, the letter read, and to show him around the parish. Would a couple of weeks be sufficient?

This was how the Reverend Thornton Applebee-Thornton came to be in Poplar at the time of which I write. As the mission in Sierra Leone was planning to introduce a midwifery service, the Rector suggested that his old friend might like to study the work of the Sisters of St Raymund Nonnatus. It seemed like an invitation not to be missed. Accordingly, the Rector contacted Sister Julienne, and arranged that conducted tours of our practice would start the following day, with visits, by arrangement, to some of our patients.

The Reverend Mr Applebee-Thornton came to lunch at Nonnatus House. We were about twelve at table that day. We were accustomed to luncheon visitors, mostly clergymen and sometimes retired missionaries, and it was always a pleasant change. The Reverend was a tall, distinguished man of around fifty. He was good-looking, with fine, slightly sharp features and a sensitive mouth. He had a full head of pure white hair and sun-weathered skin. He was very thin and I thought this was probably due to repeated bouts of dysentery and other intestinal infections. He ate heartily of the lamb stew provided by Mrs B, our cook, complimenting her with loquacious courtesy upon its excellence. He had a deep, kindly voice and kindly eyes that looked at each person around the table with intelligent understanding. If he spoke directly to anyone his attention was so focused, and so penetrating, that he seemed to be able to read the mind and character of the person he was speaking to.

Conversation was general. Sister Julienne asked him to tell us about the mission at Sierra Leone and he expounded on the size of the Christian community, the dire poverty of the natives and the work being done to found schools and hospitals. He spoke with fluency and charm, with not a trace of self-aggrandisement, to which he would have been entitled, having been a pioneer in a challenging and hostile environment.

He was fascinating. We all hung on his words, especially Chummy, our nursing colleague, whose burning ambition – in fact her only reason for training as a nurse – was to be a missionary. Eagerly she asked him about the plans to start a midwifery service, to which he smilingly replied that he hoped she would honour the mission by being their first trained midwife. Chummy's huge shoulders expanded with pride and joy. She closed her eyes and exclaimed, "Oh, I will, I will. You can rely on me."

He looked at her quietly and carefully, his pleasant eyes taking in her youthful enthusiasm. Many people reacted to Chummy's massive size and awkward gestures with ill-concealed humour, but not this gentleman. He leaned towards her and said softly, "I am quite, quite sure that we can rely on you."

Chummy's breath quivered out of her in a series of happy gasps and she could bring herself to say no more.

The Reverend Mr Applebee-Thornton turned to Sister Julienne. "Which brings me to the purpose of my visit today. What with the charm of the company and the excellence of the luncheon, I had almost forgotten that I was here to be shown around your district nursing and midwifery practice."

Was it an accident? Was it coincidence? Was it a mistake? Or was it devilish cunning? With a perfectly straight face, saucy Sister Julienne, whose eyes never missed a trick and whose mind was everywhere, looked coolly at him and lied through her teeth, without so much as a blush.

"I very much regret that none of the Sisters will be available to escort you on a tour of the district. I cannot express my regret too strongly, but we all have other duties this afternoon."

He looked disappointed and everyone else looked surprised. "It is a busy time for us," she continued, "and unfortunately none of my trained nurses can be spared for the purpose either."

The poor man looked uncomfortable, as though he were superfluous to requirements, and ought to be going.

"However, Jane is available this afternoon . . . "

At this poor Jane nearly fell off her chair, knocking over a salt pot and a dish of mint sauce, which slid greenly across the table. Sister Julienne appeared not to notice.

". . . And Jane, who knows the district well – perhaps better than any of us – would be delighted to accompany you."

She rose to her feet, and we all got up with her and stood

behind our chairs as she said grace. My eyes were lowered, but I glanced up and looked across the table at Jane. Her hands were not folded; they were clinging to the back of her chair and she was panting. Little beads of perspiration had broken out on her forehead and all in all she looked as if she were on the point of collapse. What on earth was Sister doing, I wondered. This was sheer cruelty.

In the hallway I heard Sister suggesting to Jane that she could take the Reverend to the Manchester Road and the Dockland areas first. Then they could look at Bow, Limehouse and the other parts of the district another day.

Jane went to fetch her coat and her legs were shaking. I saw the Reverend Mr Applebee-Thornton watch her closely as she walked in front of him. His face was thoughtful. Jane reached to take down her coat, but her hands twitched so convulsively that she could not take it off the peg.

"Allow me," he said courteously, and helped her to put it on. He put his hand on her arm and led her to the door. He turned and thanked Sister for allowing him such an excellent guide, who he was quite sure would be most helpful and informative. He opened the door for Jane with a slightly old-fashioned bow and murmured: "After you, madam."

They returned at tea time and he was full of praise, saying how informative Jane had been, and how greatly he valued the time she had so graciously spared him. Asked if he would like more conducted tours of the district, he said that there was no limit to his thirst for knowledge. Asked if he was quite happy with Jane as his escort – would he prefer a trained midwife on another occasion – he became profuse in stating his preference for Jane, who, he declared, was the perfect guide. Her erudition and encyclopedic knowledge of the topography and sociology of the area were more than he had dared hope for.

Jane appeared to accept her new role as guide for the Reverend Mr Applebee-Thornton, and carried out her duties with her customary attention to detail. Sister Julienne advised her to take a map, and to keep notes of what they had seen.

A week or two later, at lunch, Sister enquired how things were going. Jane replied eagerly, "Well, Pippin wants . . . "

She turned a deep red and her hands flew to her mouth. Stuttering, she tried to excuse herself. "I don't mean to be impertinent, Sister, but he asked me to call him Pippin. I said I couldn't presume to be so familiar, but he said that all his friends call him Pippin, and he would be hurt if I didn't."

To this. Sister replied, with exaggerated solemnity, that Jane had done the right thing, and must certainly call him Pippin, if that was his wish.

That same evening we were in the bicycle shed. Sister Julienne was mending a puncture, and I was tightening my brakes. To my great surprise, she said, "Where do you get your clothes from, Jennifer?" With the tyre lever grasped firmly in her small hand, Sister ripped off the outer tube.

"Well, I have a dressmaker. I don't usually go for off-the-peg stuff."

"But what store would you recommend for good clothes?"

I thought for a while. Sister plunged the inner tube into a bowl of water. "Liberty's, I suppose, in Regent Street."

"Ah yes, Liberty's. That sounds most suitable." She was turning the inner tube thoughtfully in the water, looking for bubbles.

"Jane needs some new clothes. I am going to tell her to get some. I wonder, Jenny, would it be too much to ask you to go with her? I'm sure she would value your advice. You need spare no expense, because Jane earns money but she never spends it."

No one could ever resist an appeal from Sister Julienne – certainly not me. More surprises were in store.

"And who is your hairdresser?"

"I always go to Chez Jacques in Regent Street, which just happens to be opposite Liberty's."

Her eyes lit up. She had found the puncture now; the water

was bubbling. But her real interest seemed to be in my hairdresser.

"Just opposite! Now, that's marvellous. It couldn't be more convenient. If you are in the area, could you take Jane to the hairdresser? She always cuts her hair herself, but I am sure she would look prettier if a good hairdresser attended to her."

Now, none of my nearest and dearest would suggest that I am quick off the mark when it comes to matchmaking. My poor mind doesn't work that way. Slow, they call me. But on that occasion the penny dropped. "It would be a pleasure, Sister. Just leave Jane in my hands."

Jane was dingy, drab and plain. Her clothes were about the worst I have ever seen. Her shoes were heavy, black lace-ups. Her stockings – tea-coloured lisle – were baggy. Her hair always looked a mess, and her skin was grey and deeply lined. To smarten her up would be quite a job.

After breakfast the next morning, Sister Julienne said: "Jane, you need some new clothes. Go with Jennifer this afternoon and she will choose some for you. You also need a haircut."

Jane meekly replied: "Yes, Sister."

It may seem extraordinary to speak to an adult in such a manner, but there was no other way of dealing with Jane. She was incapable of making even the smallest decision for herself and had to be directed in everything. I took my cue from Sister. I had thought carefully, and decided that a new look for Jane would have to be subtle. If I tried to dress her up like a fashion plate, the result might be disastrous. But first, the hairdresser.

Jane had never before been inside a West End hairdresser's and she hung back timidly at the door. But I only had to say, "I've made an appointment for you; you've got to come in," and she obeyed meekly.

I had a quiet word with Monsieur Jacques: "A gentle style, to frame the face, nothing exaggerated, no backcombing, something to suit a mature lady of quiet habits."

Monsieur Jacques nodded gravely, and took up his scissors.

As every woman knows, it's the cut that counts, and Jacques was a master-cutter. Had he ever achieved anything as spectacular as his reinvention of Jane? Perhaps the enormity of the challenge inspired him, for the result was little short of a miracle. Her natural curls moved in all the right places, her dingy greyness was now a confident iron-grey, with a softening of white at the temples. Jane looked at herself with astonishment in the huge mirrors, and as he flicked a wayward curl with his tail-comb, she actually smiled. Some of the worry left her face and she giggled. "Ooh, is that me?"

At Liberty's I looked out for a sales assistant who would not intimidate Jane. Some of them can be so smart and sharp they set the teeth on edge. A languid young woman with a drainpipe figure and a contemptuous eye shimmied across the carpet, but I steered Jane towards a homely-looking soul with a tape measure round her neck.

I explained the requirements, and she murmured reassuringly, "The unconscious elegance of a Hebe-Sports, with a little blouse or two. Leave everything to me." She deftly applied the tape measure to Jane's bony frame.

As promised, Jane emerged from the changing room transformed by a tailored suit in elegant grey. The tape measure breathed, "The iconic statement of the suit is in keeping with modom's splendid height. The subtle moulding of the skirt lends softness to the hips. Observe the detail of the pockets, rounding and moulding the line of the hips. Notice how the curve of the collar flatters modom's superb shoulders."

All of which was another way of saying that Jane's gaunt figure and prominent bones had somehow been concealed by the cut of the suit. She stood, meek and silent, passively allowing the collar to be adjusted a fraction of an inch.

One would have thought that the tape measure had by now exhausted her repertoire, but not at all. She was just winding herself up for a virtuoso performance.

"The slender figure and sublime height of modom are perfection for the timeless beauty of the true suit. Observe the effortless grace of modom's posture –" (Jane was drooping as usual.) "Good clothes reflect the creativity of their creator, striving for the zenith of creation. The true suit is visionary, in a restrained and dignified mode. Modom's intuitive understanding of the truly chic speaks volumes for her ineffable vision."

Jane looked utterly bewildered, and even I felt as though I were sinking out of my depth.

The tape measure cast a swift, professional eye over us both, absorbed the fact that we were floundering, and swiftly came in on the attack. "Observe how the silken threads pick out a million dancing lights, and enhance the flickering shades in modom's beautiful hair."

I had to agree that the colour certainly matched Jane's hair, although she stood silent, having no opinion on the subject.

The tape measure now turned to the drainpipe, who had joined us. "And now we must consider the passive and perfect necessity of the little blouse. Quintessentially, tara lawn is the first essential. Such a fine fabric – wouldn't you agree?"

"Oh, quintessentially essential," the drainpipe gushed as we crossed the floor to a room filled with blouses.

"The colour at the throat is all important. Modom requires understatement. The bold gesture is not for modom. Dusty pink, I think."

She pulled from the rail a pink blouse and held it against Jane's scrawny throat. The result was undeniably pleasing.

"Whilst the blue – muted, of course – draws attention to modom's fine eyes." A second blouse was held up. It was true. I had never before noticed how blue Jane's eyes were.

The tape measure drew forth yet another. "And what does modom say to mellow yellow?"

Jane had nothing to say, but the drainpipe ventured to suggest that perhaps mellow yellow was a little over-emphatic in its proclamation, and would not the merest whisper of lilac speak with quiet authority?

The tape-measure raised her manicured hands. "Lilac! Heavenly lilac! How could I forget?"

She signalled to the drainpipe, who trickled away and returned with a third blouse, of perfect fit and colour. Jane looked charming in all of them.

The tape-measure was rhapsodic. "Ah! the perfection of lilac. Queen Mary's favourite colour, and modom's truest friend. Lilac is a poem, a fragrance, a hint of nothingness. Modom cannot possibly miss heavenly lilac from her wardrobe."

These women certainly gave value for money and we took the lot.

Shoes, gloves, handbag and some decent stockings were all chosen in the same manner, and we were on our way east of Aldgate, back to Poplar.

Was Pippin likely to be aware of all the intense female activity that had been going on for his delight and diversion? Was he likely to see any difference? The sad answer to both these questions was probably "No". I have yet to meet a man who can give you even the vaguest description of what a woman was wearing ten minutes after she left his company. He would probably say, with an airy wave of the hand, "Oh, she was looking lovely in a green floaty thing," when she was wearing tight-fitting blue!

Jane changed for lunch and therefore it was to an all-female audience that she displayed the results of our outing. Cries of "Lovely", "transformed", "fab hair-do", went up all around, and Jane looked surprised, quietly gratified by all the compliments. Sister Julienne allowed herself a meaningful wink as she whispered to me, "Well done."

Pippin came at 2 p.m. prompt, and exhibited no surprise at Jane's appearance. Perhaps he saw no change! They left together for Mile End, the northerly border of our district.

Let us not enquire too closely into these guided walking tours, conceived and executed with a view to benefiting the native people of Sierra Leone. To do so would be a lapse of good taste.

Suffice it to say that the two-week stay at the Rectory was lengthened to six and that, day by day, bit by bit, Jane began to look more relaxed and happy, and less chronically nervous.

Pippin came to lunch one Sunday a few weeks later, and towards the end of the meal he said, "I will have to be leaving you all soon. My six-month furlough draws to its close, and I must return to the duties God has been pleased to entrust to me in Sierra Leone. Before I leave England I must spend a few weeks with my aged father in Herefordshire. These visits are not always easy for me, because we do not always see eye to eye, especially over the treatment of the native African. My father, now aged ninety, was an army officer in the African wars of the 1880s, and his principles I regard as harsh, whereas he regards mine as weak and mollycoddling. It can be very difficult."

He turned to Sister Julienne. "I was wondering, Sister, if you could possibly spare Jane for a couple of weeks to come with me? I feel that a feminine influence would ease the tension in an all-male household. With her charm and tact, and her gentle disposition, I feel that she could mollify my father in ways that I never could with my blunderings. Jane has already agreed to come if you can spare her. And I, for my part, would be eternally grateful." Jane's hand was resting on the table; he touched it lightly, and gave it a little squeeze.

She blushed and murmured: "Oh! Pip."

The visit started badly because the old colonel called Jane "a raw-boned horse" and Pippin was furious and would have walked out of the house without even unpacking. But Jane laughed and said she had been called worse than that in her time. Pippin raged on about "that impossible old man" until Jane went up to him, placed her fingers on his lips, and whispered: "Just be thankful that you have a father at all, dear."

In an agony of self-reproach he caught hold of her wrists and drew her to him. "May God forgive me. I am not worthy of you." He kissed her gently. "All my sins will be redeemed by your suffering, my wise and perfect love."

Later that evening the Colonel returned to horses when he referred to "that little filly of yours". Pippin stiffened, but his father carried on, "She's got good legs. Always a sign of pedigree in a horse or a woman. You can tell the breeding by the shape of the ankle."

The weeks passed well and the Colonel took to Jane. Her quietness appealed to him and he approved of her self-effacing habits. He barked at his son one evening: "Well, there's one thing to say. That little filly of yours is not going to drive you mad with a lot of silly chatter. Never could abide those magpie women, m'self; yackety-yackety-yak, all day long."

His son smiled and said, "I take it that we have your blessing, then, sir?"

"Whether you have my blessing or not, my boy, I can see you are set on the filly and nothing will make any difference. Go ahead, go ahead; your mother would have been pleased, God rest her soul."

The Reverend Mr and Mrs Applebee-Thornton returned to Poplar for a few days before they sailed for Sierra Leone. I have never in my life seen a woman so changed. She was tall and regal, her eyes were smiling, and calm confidence seemed to spring from deep within her. Pippin hardly took his eyes off her, and always referred to her as "my dear wife", or "my beloved Jane".

Of course, we had to have a party. Nuns love a party. They are very sedate affairs, ending at 9 p.m., in time for Compline and the Greater Silence, but they are fun while they last. Mrs B provided excellent cakes and sandwiches, to which we added a little sweet sherry, compliments of the Rector. The invitation was open to anyone who had known Jane and wanted to wish the happy couple well in their new life. About fifty people came, and some boys from SPY (the South Poplar Youth Club) provided music with their guitars and drums, which was considered to be very risqué. Pippin gave a delightful speech. The length of the phrases and the extravagance of the language – about pearls of great price, and the best wine being served last – was lost on many people; but the gist of the message was that he was the luckiest man alive, and everyone cheered.

Dancing had just begun when the telephone rang. I was first on call.

"Yes . . . yes . . . This is Nonnatus House. Mrs Smith . . . What address, please? How frequent are the contractions? Have the waters broken? Keep her in bed, please. I'll come straight away."

Part II

THE TRIAL OF SISTER MONICA JOAN

SISTER MONICA JOAN

Sister Monica Joan did not die. She developed severe pneumonia after wandering down the East India Dock Road wearing only her nightie one cold November morning, but she did not die. In fact, the incident seemed to rejuvenate her. Perhaps she enjoyed all the extra pampering and cosseting supplied by her Sisters and Mrs B, the cook. No doubt she enjoyed being the centre of attention. Perhaps penicillin, the new wonder drug, had pumped fire into her old heart. Whatever the reason, Sister Monica Joan, at the age of ninety, enjoyed a new lease of life, and was soon to be seen trotting all over Poplar, to the great rejoicing of everyone who knew her.

The Sisters of St Raymund Nonnatus was an Anglican order of fully professed nuns. The Sisters were all trained nurses and midwives, and their vocation was to work amongst the poorest of the poor. They had maintained a house in the London Docklands since the 1870s, when their work was revolutionary. Poor women in those days had no medical care during pregnancy and childbirth, and the death rate was high.

Midwifery as a profession did not exist. In each community local women, in a tradition passed on from mother to daughter, went around delivering babies. Such a woman was called 'the handy woman' and her practice usually consisted of 'lying-in and laying-out' (i.e. lying-in after childbirth and laying-out of the dead). Some of these women were good at their trade, and were caring and conscientious, but they were untrained and unregistered.

Against relentless parliamentary ridicule and opposition, many inspired women, including the Sisters of St Raymund Nonnatus, fought to have midwifery recognised as a profession, and for midwives to be trained and registered. Eventually, after a series of bills were defeated in the House, the women won, and the first Midwives Act became law in 1902. The Royal College of Midwives was born, and from that moment maternal and infant deaths began to fall.

The Sisters were true heroines. They had entered slum areas of the London Docks at a time when no one else would go near them, except perhaps the police. They had worked through epidemics of cholera, typhoid, tuberculosis, scarlet fever and smallpox, careless of being infected themselves. They had worked through two world wars and endured the intensive bombing of the Blitz. They were inspired and sustained by their dual vocation: service to God and service to mankind.

But do not imagine for one moment that the Sisters were trapped by their bells and their rosaries, and that life had passed them by. The nuns, collectively and individually, had experienced more of the world and its ways, more of heroism and degradation, of sin and salvation, than most people will experience in a lifetime. No indeed, the nuns were not remote goody-goodies. They were a bunch of feisty women who had seen it all, lived and loved and suffered throughout, and remained true to their vocation.

Nonnatus House was situated just off the East India Dock Road, near Poplar High Street and the Blackwall Tunnel. It was a large Victorian building and sat next to a bomb site. A third of all Dockland dwellings had been destroyed by the Blitz, and most of the derelict buildings and rubble had not been cleared away. Bomb sites became children's playgrounds during the day and dormitories for meths-drinkers overnight.

Overcrowding had always been chronic in Poplar, and it was said that Poplar housed 50,000 people per square mile. After the Second World War the situation was even worse, because houses and flats had been destroyed and rebuilding had not yet commenced, so people just moved in with each other. It was not unusual to find three or four generations of one family living in a small house, or fifteen people living in two or three small rooms in the tenements – the Canada Buildings or the Peabody Buildings or the notorious Blackwall Tenements. These were Victorian buildings constructed on four sides around a central courtyard, with inward-facing balconies which were the arteries of the tenement. There was no privacy. Everyone knew everyone else's business, and terrible fights would occur when the tensions of overcrowded family life erupted into violence. The tenements were bug-infested and insanitary. Some of the better ones had an indoor lavatory and running water, but most of the buildings had neither and infections spread like wildfire.

Most of the men worked in the docks. Thousands poured through the gates when they opened each day. Hours were long, the work was heavy, and life was hard, but the Cockney men knew nothing else, and they were tough. The Thames was the backdrop of Poplar, and the boats, the cranes, the sound of the sirens, the whisper of the water all formed part of the tapestry that had been woven into its cloth for generations. The river had been the people's constant companion, their friend and enemy, their employer, their playground and frequently, for the destitute, their grave.

Cockney life, for all its poverty and deprivation, was rich – rich in humanity and humour, rich in drama and melodrama, rich in pathos and, unhappily, rich in tragedy. The Sisters of St Raymund Nonnatus had served the people of Poplar for several generations. The Cockneys did not forget, and the nuns were loved, respected, even revered by the whole community.

During the time of which I write, an incident occurred that shook the very foundations of Nonnatus House. In fact, it shook the whole of Poplar, because everyone got to hear about it and for a time the local people could talk of little else.

Sister Monica Joan was accused of shoplifting.

My first intimation that something was wrong occurred when I returned from my evening visits, wet and hungry, and wondering why anyone was ever fool enough to be a district midwife.

What about a cushy little office job? I thought to myself as I pulled the bag from the carrier of my bike, knowing it would take me an hour to clean and sterilise all my instruments and repack the bag ready for use the following morning. Yes, that's it, I thought for the umpteenth time, a soft, cosy office job, with regular hours and central heating, sitting behind a nice smooth, desk, tapping at my Olivetti, and thinking about my date that evening; a job in which the maximum responsibility would be to find the minutes of the last meeting, and the biggest disaster a broken fingernail.

I entered the front door of Nonnatus House, and the first thing I saw was a great number of wet dirty footprints all over the fine Victorian tiles of the hallway. Large footprints in a convent? They were certainly very big, far too big to be those of a nun. Could it be that a group of men, had recently entered? It seemed unlikely at seven o'clock in the evening. And if the rector or any of the curates had called they were unlikely to leave dirty footmarks. If any tradesman had called in the morning and left such an unseemly visiting card, the mess would have been cleared up before lunch. But there they were – large dirty footprints all over the hall. It was inexplicable.

Then I heard Sister Julienne's voice coming from the direction of her office. Sister's voice was usually quiet and well modulated, but now it had a slight edge to it, either through anxiety or nervousness, it was hard to tell. This was followed by men's voices. It all seemed very strange, but I didn't want to linger, knowing that I had my bag to prepare before I could get anything to eat, so I made my way to the clinical room, where I found Cynthia and Trixie and Chummy deep in conversation.

Chummy had opened the door, apparently, to a sergeant and a constable who had asked to see the Sister-in-Charge. Chummy was all of a flutter, because she always went to pieces when any man entered the room, but chiefly because the constable was the policeman she had knocked over when she was had been learning to ride her bicycle. Intense embarrassment at the sight of him had rendered her speechless. The men had entered the hallway, and in her awkward confusion she had banged the front door so hard that it had sounded like a gun shot. Then she had tripped over the doormat and fallen into the arms of the policeman she had injured the year before.

Chummy was still in a state of such nervous distress that it was hard to get a word out of her, but Cynthia, apparently, hearing the bang of the front door and the noise of poor Chummy falling over, had come to see what it was all about. It was she, apparently, who had taken the policemen to the office and called Sister Julienne.

No one knew much more than that, but female speculation can make a great deal out of very little. Whilst we boiled our instruments, cut and folded our gauze swabs and filled our pots and bottles, our imaginations ranged over everything from arson to murder. Chummy was convinced the visit had something to do with her assault on the policeman, but Cynthia gently calmed her down, saying that there was no way a charge would be brought a year after the event, and his coming to Nonnatus House must be a coincidence.

We went to the kitchen for supper, deliberately leaving the door open, of course. We heard the office door open and heavy footsteps. We all pricked up our ears, but heard only a quiet: "Good night, Sister. Thank you for your time, and you will be hearing from us in morning." The front door closed, and four inquisitive girls were left in a state of unbridled curiosity.

It was only after lunch the following day that Sister Julienne asked us all to remain in our seats as she had something to say. Fred the boiler man and Mrs B the cook were also asked to the dining room, because the matter had to come out into the open, and Sister did not want rumours flying around that would undoubtedly be exaggerated.

Apparently, Sister Julienne told us, Sister Monica Joan had been in Chrisp Street Market and the owner of a jewellery stall had seen her fingering several items. He had heard from other stall-holders that one of the Sisters was "light-fingered" so he watched her, but pretended not to be doing so. He saw her pick up a child's bracelet, look around her and then deftly tuck it under her scapular. Then she had assumed her usual haughty aspect, head held high, and attempted to walk away. But the stall-holder stopped her. When he asked to see what she was holding beneath her scapular, she was extremely rude to him, telling him not to be so impertinent, and calling him a "boorish fellow". A crowd, of course, had gathered. The man grew cross, called her a "scraggy old God-botherer" and said she'd better hand it over, or he'd get a peeler. Whereupon Sister Monica Joan had flung the gold bracelet across the stall with a contemptuous gesture, crying: "You can keep your tawdry trinkets, you loutish lump. What do I want with them?" and stalked off with an expression of offended dignity on her fine features.

Mrs B exploded: "I don't believe a word of it. Not a word. He's a liar, vat bloke. I knows him, an' I knows as what he's a liar, I do. You won't get me believing a story like vat about Sister Monica Joan, you won't, love 'er."

Sister Julienne silenced her. "I'm afraid there is not a shadow of doubt about the truth of the matter. Several people are ready to testify that they saw Sister Monica Joan throw the bangle across the stall before she stalked off. But I'm afraid that is not all. There is worse to come." She looked around at us, sadly and we held our breath.

The costermonger, probably enraged at having been called a "boorish fellow" and a "loutish lump" went round other stall-holders who had talked about a "light-fingered Sister" and collected eight men and women who claimed that they had strong suspicions about her having stolen from them, or who had positively seen Sister Monica Joan take something small and hide it under her scapular. Collectively they had gone to the police.

Sister Julienne continued, "The police were here yesterday and this morning. I felt bound to confront Sister Monica Joan with their report, but she wouldn't say a word to me. Not a single word. She just looked out of the window as though she had not even heard me. I told her I was going to look in her chest of drawers, and she just shrugged her shoulders dismissively, and pursed her lips and said, 'Pooh to you.' I must say her attitude was extremely annoying, and if she behaved in that way to the coster, it is not surprising that he was so enraged."

Sister Julienne produced a suitcase from under the table, saying: "This is what I found in Sister Monica's chest of drawers," and she withdrew several pairs of silk stockings, three egg cups, a great quantity of coloured ribbons, a lady's silk blouse, four children's colouring books, an ornate hairpiece, a corkscrew, several small wooden animals, a tin whistle, a quantity of tea-spoons, three ornamental china birds, a bundle of knitting wool all tangled up, a necklace of gaudy beads, about a dozen fine lawn handkerchiefs, a needle case, a shoe horn and a dog collar. All of the items were unused, and some of them still had a label attached.

There was really no need for Sister Julienne to say, "I'm afraid this has been going on for some time." It was painfully obvious to all of us and Mrs B burst into tears. "Oh, the love, bless 'er, oh the poor lamb, she don't know what she's doin', she don't. Wha's going to 'appen to 'er, Sister? Vey wouldn't lock 'er up, not at 'er age?"

Sister Julienne said she didn't know. Prison seemed an unlikely outcome, but the costermonger was definitely bringing a charge, and Sister Monica Joan would be prosecuted.

Sister Monica Joan was a very old nun born into an aristocratic family in the 1860s. She had obviously been a strong-willed young woman who had rebelled against the restrictions and narrow self-interest of her social class, because she had broken away from her family (a shocking thing to do) around 1890 in order to train as a nurse. In 1902, when the first Midwives Act was passed, Monica Joan trained as a midwife and, shortly after, joined the Sisters of St Raymund Nonnatus. Her profession to a monastic order was the last straw for her family and they disowned her. But Novice Monica Joan didn't care a hoot and carried on doing her own thing. When I knew her, she had lived and worked in Poplar for fifty years and was known by virtually everyone.

To say that by the age of ninety she was eccentric would be an understatement. Sister Monica Joan was wildly eccentric to the point of being outrageous. There was no telling what she would say or do next, and she frequently gave offence. Sometimes she could be sweet and gentle but at other times she was gratuitously spiteful. Poor Sister Evangelina, large and heavy, and not gifted with verbal brilliance, suffered most dreadfully from the astringent sarcasm of her Sister-in-God. Sister Monica Joan had a powerful intellect and was poetic and artistic, yet she was quite insensitive to music, as I witnessed on the occasion of her shocking behaviour at a cello recital. She was very clever – cunning, some would say. She manipulated others unscrupulously in order to get her own way. She was haughty and aristocratic in her demeanour, yet she had spent fifty years working in the slums of the London Docklands. How can one account for such contradictions?

Whilst being a professed nun and a devout Christian, in her old age Sister Monica Joan had become fascinated by esoteric spirituality, ranging from astrology and fortune-telling to cosmology and centric forces. She loved to expound on these subjects, but I doubt if she knew what she was talking about.

At the time I knew her, she was verging on senility. The focus of her mind seemed to come and go, to shift and change. Sometimes she was perfectly rational, while at others it was as though she were seeing the world through a mist, trying to grasp, things half-seen. Yet I suspected she knew her mind was going, and occasionally used the fact to get what she wanted. Somehow she had a magnetic quality about her and she fascinated me. I loved her dearly and enjoyed spending time in her company.

When Sister Julienne solemnly told the group in the dining room that Sister Monica Joan would be prosecuted for theft, a wave of shock had rippled around the table. Novice Ruth cried quietly.

Mrs B protested vociferously that she wouldn't believe it. Trixie said she wasn't surprised. Sister Evangelina snapped, "Be quiet, we'll have none of that," and sat very still, staring down at her plate, but her temples were twitching, and her knuckles went white as she gripped her hands together. Sister Julienne said: "We must all commit Sister Monica Joan to our prayers. We must seek God's help. But I will also engage a good lawyer."

I asked if I might visit Sister Monica Joan in her room that afternoon, and permission was readily given.

As I mounted the stairs, my mind was in a turmoil. How would I be received by a lady who had been visited by the police, from whose chest of drawers numerous stolen items had been extracted, and who had been told that she would be facing prosecution?

Sister Monica Joan's room was not the customary cell of a nun, bare and plain. Hers was an elegant bed-sitting room with all the comforts due to a distinguished old lady. These were probably a great deal more than any other nun might expect, but Sister Monica Joan had a knack of always getting her own way. Since the pneumonia she had spent more time in her room, and I had been a frequent and happy visitor. But on this occasion, my heart was pounding with anxiety.

I knocked, and heard a sharp: "Enter. Come in, don't just stand there. Come in."

I entered, and found her at her desk, notebooks and pencils all around her. She was scribbling away furiously and chuckling to herself.

"Ah, it's you, my dear. Sit down, sit down. Did you know that the astral permanent atom is equivalent to the etheric permanent atom and that they both function within the parallel universe?" She seemed to have no recollection of what had been going on, for which I was profoundly relieved. If she had been in a state of remorse it would have been hard to know what to say.

I grinned and sat down. "No, Sister. I didn't know about the parallel universe, nor the permanent atoms. Do tell me."

She started to draw a diagram for my benefit. "See here, child, this is the point within the circle, and these bands are the seven parallels that are the unifying stability within the atoms that are the essence of the parallel universe wherein men and angels and beasts and others . . . I think."

Her voice trailed away as she scribbled furiously, her mind obviously racing ahead of her pencil. Suddenly she cried out, her voice squeaking with excitement: "I have it. Eureka! All has been revealed. There are eleven parallels. Not seven. Ah, the perfection of eleven. The beauty of eleven. All is revealed in eleven."

Her voice dropped to a whisper, and she raised her eyes to heaven, her features radiant. I felt again the magnetism of this woman, who could hold me in a spell just by moving her fingers or lifting an eyebrow. Her skin was so fine and white that it seemed barely sufficient to cover the fragile bones and blue veins that meandered up her hands and arms. She sat perfectly still, a pencil poised between two fingertips, the first joint of which she could bend independently of the rest of the finger. With eyes closed, she murmured, "Eleven parallels, eleven stars . . . eleven crowns," and I was bewitched all over again. I knew that many people could not stand her. They found her arrogant, haughty, supercilious and too clever by half – and, I had to admit, with some justification. Many thought she was an affected poseur, playing some sort of role, but I could not agree with that. I thought she was absolutely sincere in everything she said.

That she was utterly unpredictable was agreed by all, but now, it seemed, she was a shoplifter! I felt quite sure that she had no recollection of what she had been doing, and could not be held accountable for her actions. She was still murmuring, "Eleven stars . . . eleven spheres . . . eleven teaspoons."

Suddenly she opened her eyes and snapped, "Two policemen were here this morning. Two great big clomping fellows with their boots and their notebooks, going through my drawers, as though I were a common criminal. And Sister Julienne took it all away. All my pretty things. My colouring things, my ribbons, eleven teaspoons. I had been collecting them – eleven – just think, and I needed them, every one."

Grief seemed to overcome her. She didn't cry, but she seemed frozen with terror, and murmured: "What is going to happen to me? What will they do to me? Why do elderly, respectable women do this sort of thing? Are we tempted, or is it a sickness? I don't understand . . . I don't know myself . . . "

Her voice faltered, and the pencil dropped from her trembling fingers. She knew all right. Oh yes, she knew.

PHOSSY JAW

Nonnatus House was subdued and saddened as we awaited the prosecution of Sister Monica Joan for shoplifting. Even we young girls, always ready to giggle and joke about almost everything, were more restrained. We somehow felt it unseemly to laugh when the Sisters were suffering. Sister Monica Joan spent more of her time in her room. She did not go out of the house at all, seldom came down to the dining room, and really only left her room for Mass and the five monastic offices of the day. I sometimes saw her entering or leaving the chapel, but she hardly spoke to her Sisters. They treated her with gentleness, but she returned their smiles and kindly glances with a toss of her proud head as she went to her pew to kneel in prayer. We are all complex creatures, but prayer and downright rudeness seemed incompatible.

The only people she consistently spoke to were Mrs B and myself. Dear Mrs B, whose love of Sister Monica Joan was unconditional and unreserved, and who still didn't believe a word of it, was up and down the stairs all day, pandering to her every wish. Sister Monica Joan treated her more like a personal lady's maid than she had any right to, but Mrs B seemed perfectly happy with her new role, and nothing seemed to be too much trouble. She was heard muttering to herself in the kitchen one day: "China tea. I though' as 'ow tea was just tea. But no. She wants China tea. Now where am I goin' to get vat?" None of the grocers in Poplar seemed to stock China tea, so she went all the way up West to get it. When she proudly presented a cup to Sister Monica Joan, Sister sniffed it and sipped it, then declared that she didn't like it. Anyone else would have been furious, but Mrs B took no offence: "Not 'a worry, my luvvy. You just 'ave a slice o' vis honey-cake I made this mornin', while I run along and make you a nice pot o' tea, jus' as 'ow you likes it."

Sister Monica Joan could out-queen the Queen when she chose. Her attitude was serenely gracious as she inclined her head. "So kind, so kind." Mrs B glowed with pleasure. Sister broke a piece of honey-cake with her long fingers and delicately raised it to her lips. "Delicious, quite delicious. Another slice, if it's not too much trouble." Mrs B, fairly bursting with happiness, ran downstairs for the umpteenth time that day.

Sister Monica Joan fascinated me as she did most people. But she never treated me as a lady's maid. No doubt her instinct told her that it just would not work. We understood each other as equals and found endless pleasure in each other's company. During the uncertain weeks of waiting we had many conversations in her pretty room just after lunch, or before Compline. We talked for hours. Her short-term memory was faulty – often she did not know what day or month it was – but her long-term memory was excellent. She could clearly recall facts, incidents and impressions from her Victorian childhood and her working life in the Edwardian era and the First World War. She was highly intelligent and articulate and could express herself vividly, often in beautiful language that seemed to come naturally to her. As I wanted to learn more about old Poplar, I tried questioning her. But this did not work. She was not easy to pin down, and often took no notice of what I had said or asked. She had a habit of making statements unrelated to anything that had been said beforehand, like: "That rapacious old mongrel!" And then no more! The old mongrel had obviously come into her mind unbidden and then slunk away, his tail between his legs.

Sometimes she developed her thoughts and her words flowed easily. She would make a dramatic statement: "Women are the cohesive force in society." She picked up a pencil and balanced it delicately between her two fingertips, those astonishing fingers that she could bend at the first joint. Would she continue? To say a word might break her thoughts.

"And 'woman' in the slums is capable of taking on almost superhuman responsibility, from a very young age, that would crush most of us. Today they live in luxury – look at all the giddy young girls around us – they have no memory of how their mothers and grandmothers lived and died. They have no understanding of what it took to raise a family twenty or thirty years ago."

She glanced at the pencil and twisted it round with her thumbs. Privately I questioned the "luxury" in the tenements, but said nothing for fear of chasing away her memories. She continued.

"There was no work, no food, no shoes for the children. If the rent was not paid the family would be evicted. Thrown onto the streets by the law of the land."

She paused, and a memory flashed through my mind of something that I had seen only a few weeks earlier, when I was cycling back from a night delivery.

It had been about three o'clock in the morning, and I saw a group of people, a man and woman and several children, coming towards me, keeping close to the wall. The woman was carrying a baby and a suitcase. The man was carrying a mattress on his head, a rucksack and several bags. Each of the children, none of them over ten, was carrying a bag. They saw the headlights of my bike and turned their faces to the wall. The man said, his voice quite distinct in the darkness: "Don' chew worry. It's only a nurse," and I cycled past, not realising at the time that a dramatic and tragic event was taking place; an event that used to be referred to light-heartedly as a "moonlight flit". The family were anticipating eviction and fleeing unpaid debts. God only knows where they ended up.

Sister Monica Joan was staring at me, hard, and then she narrowed her eyes. "You remind me of Queenie – turn your head."

I did so.

"Yes, you look just like her. I was so fond of Queenie. I delivered her three children and I was with her when she died.

She was no more than your age, but she died trying to avoid eviction."

"What happened?" I whispered.

"She went into the Bryant and May factory that made matches. They were a lovely family, and I knew them well. No fights in that family. Her husband was no more than a boy when he was killed in a riverboat accident. What could Queenie do with three little children? The Parish would have taken them from her, but she wouldn't have it. She went into the match factory because they offered higher pay than anywhere else. Danger money, they called it, and wriggled out of any responsibility by saying the women accepted the danger when they accepted the pay. Wicked it was. Wicked. Death money it should have been called. Queenie worked there for three years and kept a roof over their heads and just enough to eat. We thought she would escape phossy jaw. But it got her, yes, it got her, and she died a terrible death. I was with her at the end. She died in my arms."

Sister Monica Joan said no more. Could I risk a question?

"What is phossy jaw?"

"There you go. What did I say? Young girls have no idea how women had to live and work. The matches were made from raw phosphorus. The women inhaled the vapour, and the fumes got into the mucous membrane of the mouth and nose. The phosphorus penetrated the bones of the upper and lower jaw. The bones literally sloughed away. In the dark you could see the woman's jaw glowing with a bluish light. There was nothing that could be done for these women and they died a slow and agonising death. Don't ask me again what phossy jaw is, you ignorant girl. It's what Queenie died of, trying to provide for her children, trying to avoid eviction."

She glanced at me, and clamped her teeth together.

"That's what we fought for. Girls like Queenie, hard-working, loving, young women full of life, who were driven to their deaths by the system. I was with her when she died. It was ghastly. The bones of her lower face crumbled away, and she suffered weeks of agony. There was nothing we could do. Her children went to the workhouse. There was nowhere else for them."

The rain fell quietly on the window, and she sat quite still. I could see the pulse beating sluggishly in her long neck, carrying the life-giving blood to her brain. "Draw the curtains, please, dear." I did so, hoping she would continue, but she only murmured, "It seems like yesterday, no time at all." And there was no more.

The memories of people like Sister Monica Joan should be cherished. I sat on the edge of her bed, my legs drawn up underneath me, and tried to interpret from her sensitive features what was in her mind. I did not want Queenie to fade from her memory, so I asked about the children going to the workhouse, but she became irritable and snappy.

"Questions. Always questions. You give me no peace, child. Can I not expect a little repose in my old age?"

She threw her head to one side with an affected sigh. At that moment the bell sounded for Compline. "There now. See what you have done. You've made me late for my religious duties."

She swept past me without a further glance and made her way to the chapel.

That evening I attended Compline. The lay staff at Nonnatus House were not bound to do so – we were not professed religious – but we could attend any offices if we wished to. I particularly loved the words of Compline, the last office of the day, and had been very affected by the story of Queenie, so I followed Sister Monica Joan into the chapel. Her behaviour was atrocious! She entered without so much as looking at anyone else, and did not take her usual pew but went straight to the visitors' seats, took a chair and sat with her back to her Sisters and the altar. Sister Julienne quietly came up to her and gently tried to draw her into the group around the altar, but Sister Monica Joan rudely pushed her aside and even drew her chair further away so that she was looking directly at the wall. Compline proceeded in this fashion.

Sister Julienne was obviously saddened, and the love and pity in her eyes showed that she knew something strange was going on in the mind of the old lady, which she was trying to understand. Perhaps it was advancing senility, or perhaps one of those mental illnesses that make people turn away from, and become aggressive towards, the people who have been closest and most dear to them. Quietly the Sisters left the chapel. The Greater Silence had begun. After that evening Sister Monica Joan always sat with her back to her Sisters, even at Mass.

The following afternoon I went to Sister Monica Joan's room after lunch, hoping that she would not turn against me as she had against her Sisters. She had enriched my life so much with her friendship, and I knew it would be greatly impoverished if that friendship were suddenly withdrawn.

She was sitting at her desk, alert and busy with her notebooks and pencil. She turned. "Come in, my dear, come in. This will interest you. The hexagon meets the parallel" – she was drawing a diagram again – "and the rays combine here . . . Oh bother!" Her pencil broke. "Fetch me my pencil-sharpener, will you, dear? The second drawer down in my bedside cabinet." She continued tracing the lines across the paper with her forefinger.

I went across the room to her bedside cabinet, happy that she was not excluding me from her affections. What made me pull open the third drawer down? It was not intentional, but it almost paralysed me, and for several seconds I thought I would choke. The open drawer revealed several gold bangles, two or three rings (one of the stones looked like a sapphire), a small diamond watch, a pearl necklace, a ruby pendant on a gold chain, a gold cigarette case, a couple of gold cigarette holders studded with stones, and several tiny gold or platinum charms. The drawer was only about two inches deep and no more than ten inches wide, but it must have contained a small fortune in jewellery.

Sudden silence can attract immediate attention. She turned round and saw me transfixed, looking into the drawer. At first she did not say anything, and the silence developed an ominous quality that was broken by her hissing: "You wicked girl, prying into my affairs. How dare you? Leave the room immediately. Do you hear? Withdraw, at once."

It was so shocking, I had to sit down on the edge of the bed. Our eyes met, mine full of grief and hers flashing with anger. Gradually the defiance crumbled away, and her old, old face assumed a tired, almost pathetic quality. She whimpered, "All my pretty things. Don't take them away. Don't tell anyone. They will take them all. Then they'll take me away, like they took Aunt Anne. All my pretty things. No one knows about them. Why shouldn't I have them? Don't tell anyone, will you, child?" Her beautiful hooded eyes filled with tears, her lips trembled, and the toll of ninety years descended on her as she crumpled into a sobbing wreck.

It took only a second to cross the room and hold her in my arms. "Of course I won't tell anyone. No one will ever know. It's a secret, and we won't tell anyone, I promise."

Gradually her tears dried, and she blew her nose and gave me one of her saucy winks. "Those great clod-hopping policemen. They'll never know, will they?" She raised one eyebrow and chuckled conspiratorially. "I think I will take my tea now. Go, child, and tell Mrs B that I will have some of that delicious China tea."

"But you didn't like the China tea."

"Of course I liked it. Don't be silly. You are getting muddled up, I fear!"

Laughing, I kissed her goodbye and made my way down to the kitchen to deliver the message to Mrs B.

It was not until later that evening that the awfulness of the dilemma hit me. What on earth was I going to do?

MONOPOLY

A promise is a promise, but theft is a criminal offence, and my pledge to Sister Monica Joan that I would not tell anyone about the stolen jewellery weighed upon me so heavily that I could hardly keep my mind on my work. Purloining a few pairs of silk stockings and handkerchiefs was naughty, but stealing jewels, some of them very valuable, is a serious offence. Normally nothing disturbs my sleep, but this did. If I told Sister Julienne, she would call the police again, and they would search Sister Monica Joan's room a second time, more thoroughly than before. Perhaps there would be other things hidden away, in a box maybe, or in the bottom drawer of the bedside cabinet. The gravity of the offence might be more than doubled. They might arrest her on the spot, old as she was. I blocked out such a thought. Sister Monica Joan must be protected at all costs. I would not tell anyone.

Antenatal clinic was particularly trying that week. There were too many women, it was too hot, and there were too many small children running around. I felt like screaming. We were clearing up afterwards. Cynthia was cleaning the urine-testing equipment, I was scrubbing the work surfaces.

She said: "What's up? You've not been yourself lately."

Relief swept over me. Her deep slow voice acted like a balm to my troubled spirits. "How do you know? Is it that obvious?"

"Of course it is. I can read you like a book. Now come on, out with it. What's up?"

Two of the Sisters were still in the clinic, packing up the antenatal notes and filing them away. I whispered, "I'll tell you later."

After Compline, when the Sisters had gone to bed, Cynthia

and I sat in her room with an extra helping of pudding left over from lunch. Briefly I told her about the jewellery.

She whistled. "Phew! No wonder you have been quiet recently. What are you going to do?"

"I'm not going to tell anyone in authority. I'm only telling you because you guessed something was up."

"But you can't keep it to yourself. You've got to tell Sister Julienne."

"If I do, she'll tell the police and they might arrest Sister Monica."

"You're not being rational. They won't arrest her. She's too old."

"How do you know? This is big stuff, I tell you. It's not just pinching a few crayoning books."

Cynthia was quiet for a while. "Well, I don't think they will arrest her."

"There you are, you don't know. You only think, and you might be wrong. If they arrested her it would kill her."

There was a bang on the door. "I say, you chaps, how about a game of Monopoly, what? No one in labour. All the babies tucked up in bed. What say you, eh?"

"Come in, Chummy."

Camilla Fortescue-Cholmeley-Browne. Descended from generations of High Commissioners of India, educated at Roedean and polished by a Swiss finishing school, Chummy represented the upper crust in our small circle. She had a voice that sounded like something straight out of a comedy and she was excessively tall, which caused her to suffer much ragging. But she took it all with sweet good nature.

Chummy tried the handle. "But the door's locked, old bean. What's going on? Something rummy's afoot, or I'm a brass monkey."

Cynthia laughed and opened the door. "We've got some pudding in here. If you want some go and get a dish, and while you're about it, tell Trixie."

When she had gone, Cynthia said to me, "I think we had better tell the girls. Neither of them is in authority so the police won't be called, and they might help. Chummy's father was a District Commissioner or something in India and Trixie's cousin is a solicitor, so they might know something about the law."

I agreed. It was a relief to be sharing the responsibility after all my silent anguish.

Both girls came in with a dish and a spoon, Chummy bearing the Monopoly board. We shared out the pudding. Cynthia sat on the only chair and three of us sat on the bed. The Monopoly board was laid out on the bed, supported by books to stop it sagging. I had been against playing Monopoly, but Cynthia said it would help relieve the tension, and she was right.

We sorted out our money and tucked it in piles under our knees while Cynthia told them the story.

Trixie burst out laughing. "What a scream! So the old girl's been pinching things left, right and centre. Tucking them under her scapular and no one would ever suspect. The cunning old vixen." She roared with laughter.

"You cat. Don't you call Sister Monica Joan names or I'll—"

Cynthia intervened. "I won't have you two squabbling in my room. If you want to start a row you can go elsewhere."

"Sorry," I muttered reluctantly.

"I'll be good," added Trixie; "I won't even call her a female fox. But you must admit it's a scream. I can just see the headlines: 'The Secret Life of a Naughty Nun'."

Trixie threw the dice. "Two sixes. I start."

"That's just the sort of thing I'm not going to allow to happen," I snarled. "The police are not going to be told." I moved my piece. "Liverpool Street. I'll buy that." I laid down my money with determination and took the card.

Chummy threw her dice. "This is a Council of War, and I'm with you, old horse. The important thing is to protect Sister Monica Joan from the machinations of the Constabulary, what? Mum's the word, I say. What ho! Not a syllable. Lips sealed."

Cynthia shook the cup slowly and thoughtfully, and rattled the dice. "Well, someone's going to find out, even if *we* don't say anything. The police will search her room again; they are not fools, you know."

"I've thought of that," I said. "Perhaps we could take the jewels out of her room and hide them."

"Don't be a fool." Trixie was always too sharp for my liking. "Then you'd be an accessory."

"What's that? I thought accessories were things like gloves and handbags."

"Accessories are the law. You can be an accessory before the fact, or an accessory after the fact. It doesn't matter if it's before or after; either way you'd be in for it." Trixie pushed the dice to her neighbour as she spoke.

Chummy shook the dice. "I'd say she's got to the root of the matter. If the jewels were in your possession, the Robert Peelers would say you'd egged the old lady on. Bally awkward situation, and you'd be as sore as a gumboil. No. We've got to prove that she didn't know what she was doing." Chummy moved her piece, but decided not to buy.

Trixie jumped on it in a flash. "I'll buy that. Come off it. That old girl's as sharp as a razor. She's got it all weighed up. No one suspects a nun, so she's in the clear – that's what she thinks."

"I'm not so sure." Cynthia moved her piece. "The Angel Islington. I'll buy that. I like the blue properties. I think her mind is definitely disturbed."

"Don't give me that one," Trixie snapped. "She's as crafty as they come. Look how she manipulates everyone to get her own way. She knows exactly what she's doing. Another visit from the police would do her good. I'll put a house on each of my properties please, Bank."

Chummy was Bank and sorted out the high finance. "Well, I can't agree, old sport. I think another visit from the police would give her a stroke."

"Of course it would." I threw the dice so hard they overshot the board and landed on the floor. "The police will never know. I'll see to that."

Cynthia, who, as the room-owner, had the right to sit on the only chair, retrieved the dice. "I have a feeling it's not as easy as that. You have to tell 'the whole truth and nothing but the truth'."

"That's only in court," I said, "and we're not in court . . . yet. Park Lane – I'll buy that."

"You're not thinking straight, idiot, I've already got Mayfair. It won't do you any good. Anyway, if you end up in court giving evidence, you'll have to tell the whole truth."

I decided not to buy Park Lane and Trixie gleefully snapped it up.

"If you don't, it's called 'obstructing the course of justice'. I've heard my cousin talk about that."

It was Chummy's throw. "I've heard of that one, too. It's the same sort of thing as 'withholding evidence', which is a serious offence. I say, this pudding's no end good. Is there any more, madam hostess?"

"No, but I've got some biscuits here in my wardrobe. Just let me move the chair and I'll get them. How about a coffee?"

Trixie shook her head. "I've got a much better idea. My brother bought me a couple of bottles of sherry for Christmas; he thought I needed cheering up, stuck in a dreary hole like a convent. We'll have them now. It will help the discussion. We've got to come to a sensible decision about this. Get your tooth mugs, girls."

Trixie slid off the bed and Chummy remembered some chocolates and crystallised ginger left over from a previous occasion. I ran down the passage to get my tooth mug and some figs and dates, to which I was partial.

We settled down again around the Monopoly board, which had wobbled with all the movement on and off the bed. After some argument about whose piece was where, and which houses were on whose properties, we poured the sherry, took handfuls of food, and continued the game.

Trixie was clearly winning. She had houses on Park Lane and Mayfair, and the dice fell in her favour. Everyone seemed to stop there and had to pay rent. Groans all round. The sherry slid down nicely, assisted by all the sweet food. Chummy made a general point that had been in all of our minds.

"Where do you think, the old lady got all those sparklers from? I say, this sherry's going down a treat. I always say sherry tastes so much better out of a tooth mug than one of those bally little glasses, what? Perhaps the dregs of toothpaste in the bottom of the mug give it that special flavour. I did a cordon bleu course, you know, but the teacher never mentioned that. If I ever go back there, I'll recommend it. Hell's bells! Go back five places – that puts me in jail!"

Trixie giggled. "We'll get Sister Monica Joan in jail before the night's out. Sorry! Sorry! Don't take on so. Just stirring it up. Have another sherry!"

Cynthia filled my mug. "Yes, where did she get it from? There's nowhere in Poplar that sells expensive jewellery."

Trixie had the answer – inevitably. "I reckon she's been going to Hatton Garden. It's not far from here, only a short bus ride. A pious-looking old nun going around the shops and warehouses. Easy. No one would think to suspect her, the wicked old thing."

"She's not wicked," I shouted. "Don't you dare. She's—"

"Now, now, you two. My turn and I collect £200 for passing Go. Come on, Bank. Wake up. I want my money."

Chummy jerked herself upright. "I'm beginning to think the police have to be told because of this business of withholding the course."

"The what?"

"The course of evidence, of course."

"You're not making sense."

"Yes I am. You're not listening."

Cynthia was carefully tucking her £200 down her bra. "I think you mean the course of justice."

"That's what I said."

"No you didn't. You said the course of evidence."

"Well, same thing, and it's an offence."

"What is?"

"Holding the evidence, old bean. And it's not allowed."

"You mean withholding the evidence."

"That's what I said."

"No you didn't. You said holding it."

"Look here, this is going round in circles. Anyway it's my turn." Trixie picked up a card from the pack. "So you reckon we've got to get the police in again?"

"Yes, because of obstructing, old thing."

"No you don't. You want to get the police in again because you fancy that policeman."

"I don't. Don't you dare." Chummy gulped down her sherry and went bright red.

"Yes you do. You're sweet on him. I've seen you go all coy and giggly when he comes to the house."

"You're a regular shower. You've no right to come out with whoppers like that, you gumboil, you."

Poor Chummy looked as if she were on the verge of tears, so Cynthia came to her rescue.

"You're just stirring it up again, Trixie. You haven't looked at your card yet. Turn it over."

Trixie did so, and gave a howl of anguish. "I'm ruined. I'm bankrupt. This isn't fair. Make repairs on all your houses. I shall have to sell. Give me another drink. I've got to think about this one." She took another mug of sherry and another chocolate.

"I'll take Mayfair and Park Lane off you at half-price," I said magnanimously.

"No you won't. I'm not selling at half-price."

"You've no option."

"That's what it is – obtion." Chummy was obviously thinking deeply, as she gazed into her mug. "Obtion – the course of justice. And it's an obtion, and you mustn't do it."

"There's no such thing as an obtion."

"Yes there is, and you mustn't obtion the justice of the course. I know it. My father told me. Someone he knew obtioned the justice course, and I can't remember what happened, but it happened."

"Well thanks for nothing. A lot of help, I'm sure. Look, I'm going to auction these. Does anyone want these priceless properties? I'll take eighty per cent. You won't get a better chance. All right then, seventy per cent, I'm not going to sink to half price, I'll have to do something else."

At that moment Chummy's legs got the cramp. They were too long to be kept in a confined space, and with a groan she stretched out, knocking the board for six.

"Well, that's that," said Trixie with satisfaction. "I'm the clear winner."

"No you're not. You haven't made repairs to your houses."

"I don't have to."

"Yes you do."

"Now don't you two start that again. Help me to clear up the board and the pieces. Chummy doesn't look as if she's going to be much help. There's a drop left in the bottom of this second bottle. Do you want to share it between you? I've had enough."

We did. Cynthia was shaking Chummy.

"Look, this is my bed. You go to your own bed."

Suddenly Trixie grabbed Cynthia's arm. "Oh my God! I've just had a dreadful thought."

"What?" we said in chorus.

"Chummy's on first call tonight."

"Never! Oh no! What's to be done?"

The three of us gazed at Chummy stretched full length, smiling sweetly and fast asleep on Cynthia's bed. We looked at each other, and looked again at the sleeping form.

Cynthia spoke. "I'll take first call tonight. There's nothing else for it. Trixie was out last night, so I'll take it if a call comes in. I've had less than you two anyway. We might as well leave Chummy here, and I'll sleep in her room. We must throw away these bottles and open the windows to let in some fresh air, in case one of the Sisters comes up here tomorrow. Go and open the windows on the landing, at both ends, and in the bathroom. We've got to get a good draught blowing through."

Thankful for Cynthia's common sense I went to open the windows. The cold air hit me like a pain, and my head began to reel. The window flew out of my grasp and struck the brickwork. Cynthia came up and secured it.

"I'm going to wash these mugs and wash out the bottles too, to get rid of the smell. You had better go to bed. You'll be on duty at 8 a.m. Don't listen for the telephone. I'll take any calls."

She went to Chummy's room and I to mine. For several nights I had lain awake, but that night I slept like a baby.

AUNT ANNE

As I entered Sister Monica Joan's room she glared at me. "I'll murder that fellow one of these days. You see if I don't. The dirty old goat!"

Strong language for a reverend Sister. It was intriguing, but I knew from experience that straight questions seldom got straight answers. However, if I entered Sister Monica Joan's world and, as far as possible, relived it with her, she would often recall whole scenes from long ago. So I said, "He's always up to something. What is it this time?"

"You've seen him at it?"

I nodded, and waited.

"He's always there. Lah-di-dahing around the factory gates in all his finery – silk shirt, bow tie and gold watch chain. I'll give him a silk shirt – I'll strangle him with his silk shirt, the old rascal."

This was going to be rich. She needed no prompting to continue. "Those poor girls in the shirt-making factories. They are the lowest paid of all the workers, and they work the longest hours, too. There's a grass bank outside the factory gate – you know the one I mean?" I nodded. "Well, he stands there in all his finery, twirling his moustache, and as the girls come out of the gate he throws coins, mostly copper, some silver, up the bank towards the wall, shouting. 'Scramble, girls, scramble for it.' And up the grass the girls go, shouting and pushing and laughing. There might even be a fight to get at a silver sixpence. The dirty old man."

I was beginning to wonder why such a philanthropic act should provoke such vitriol.

Sister Monica continued even more angrily. "It's degrading

them. Those girls wear no knickers, you know. How can they afford such a luxury? That's what he's after, the debauched old satyr. And when they are menstruating they have no protection. The blood just runs down their legs. The smell is supposed to be enticing. I don't know, perhaps it is. But it's degrading for those poor girls who scramble for a penny that will buy them a bun or a drop of milk. I can't bear to see women exploited in that way."

I finally understood what she was on about. "But women have always been exploited for their sexuality."

"Yes, I suppose so, and always will be, I fear. And no doubt some of them want to be. I dare say half the girls scrambling up the bank and sliding down with their skirts around their necks know what they are doing. But it pains me to see them degraded."

She did not continue with her thoughts, but asked me to go and see Mrs B about tea, which I did. When I returned to the room, Sister Monica Joan was not there. The jewels had been uppermost in my mind for days, so quietly I looked into the bedside cabinet. The drawer was empty.

As she had made no reference in the past few days to my earlier discovery, I had assumed that she had forgotten all about it. Perhaps I had fondly imagined that she had forgotten about the jewels. But now I knew she had not forgotten a thing and had taken the precaution of hiding them elsewhere. But where? Had she tucked them into her mattress? She was quite capable of cutting a small hole, stuffing them in and sewing it up neatly. No one would ever know.

Trixie's image of a crafty old vixen came to mind. Perhaps she was. Perhaps she was piling up wealth for some hidden purpose of her own. But at the age of ninety? It was hardly likely.

She swept back into the room in high spirits. No remorse, no shame that she had been caught stealing, no fear of future discoveries. Perhaps she had hidden them in the lavatory cistern or behind the bath.

Her opening comment was, as usual, quite baffling. "Twenty-seven dinner services, each with ninety-six pieces. I ask you, my dear, what sensible family could possibly need twenty-seven dinner services?"

Such a question requires a little thought before it can be answered.

Whilst I hesitated, she continued, "And fourteen sets of silver-plated cutlery. Would you believe it, every single piece, every fish fork or sugar tong, had to be counted and checked before it could be put away. Have you ever heard such nonsense? And they thought I would be content to spend my life counting fish forks."

I was beginning to understand. One had to get used to following sideways the many strands of Sister Monica Joan's thoughts. Perhaps the dinner services and the fish forks related to her family and her girlhood in the 1870s and 80s.

Her next statement confirmed this. "My poor mother was a slave to such possessions. For all her finery and 'Your Ladyship' she was more of a servant than her own servants. I doubt she knew a day of real freedom in her whole life. Poor woman. I loved her, and pitied her, but we never understood each other. My father ruled her life. Every move. Do you know, my dear, he had all her hair cut off and her teeth pulled out when she was less than thirty-five?"

I gasped: "How? Why?"

"She was never strong, always ailing. I don't know what was wrong with her, except perhaps that her corsets were too tight." Corsets. The accepted instrument of torture for women

"I remember it quite well. I was only a little girl but I remember my mother lying in bed with doctors present. One of them told my father that all her strength was going to her hair and her teeth and that they would have to go. She was never consulted in the matter, she told me many years later. Her head was shaved and all her teeth extracted. I was in the nursery and heard her screaming. It was barbaric, my dear, and ignorant. I was frightened when I saw her later: her face swollen; blood all over her pillow and sheets; a bald head. She was crying, poor woman. I was about twelve years old and something happened to me in that moment.

Something revolted inside me and I knew that women suffered through man's ignorance. As I stood by her bed, I changed from a carefree little girl into a thinking woman. I vowed I would not follow the pattern of my mother, my aunts and their friends. I would not become a wife whose husband could order that her teeth be pulled out, or who could be locked up like poor Aunt Anne. I would not spend my life counting fish forks. I would not be dominated by any man."

Sister Monica Joan's face assumed an expression of haughty defiance. The young can be very lovely, but the faces of the old can be truly beautiful. Every line and fold, every contour and wrinkle of Sister Monica Joan's fine white skin revealed her character, strength, courage, humanity and irrepressible humour.

I said, "Several times you have mentioned that your Aunt Anne was locked up. Why was this?"

"Oh my dear, it was iniquitous. Aunt Anne, my mother's sister, was put into a lunatic asylum because her husband was fed up with her!"

"What! You are joking," I retorted

"Don't you accuse me of joking, you saucy girl. If you are going to be rude to me you can leave the room." She turned her head and arched her eyebrows, slightly dilating her nostrils, the epitome of offended dignity, although I had a feeling she was putting it on for effect.

"Oh, come off it, Sister. You know that was just an expression. What happened to Aunt Anne? – that's what's important."

She turned to me and giggled like a child caught doing something naughty. But her expression quickly changed.

"Aunt Anne, dear Aunt Anne. She was my favourite aunt. Always pretty, always sweet and gentle with a soft laugh. When she visited the house she always came up to the nursery to spend time with us, to tell stories and play games with us. We all loved her. Then suddenly she came no more. No more."

Sister Monica Joan sat as still as a statue, gazing out of the window. The sun was shining and she moaned, "It's too bright, it hurts my eyes. Draw the curtain across, will you, child?"

I did so and when I returned she had her handkerchief to her eyes. "We never saw her again. When we asked our mother she just said, 'Hush, dears, we don't talk about Aunt Anne.' We kept thinking she would come back with her games and her stories; but she never did."

She sighed deeply and balanced her chin on her long fingers, lost in thought. "Poor woman, poor dear woman. She was defenceless."

"Did you ever find out what had happened?" I enquired.

"Yes, years later I found out. Her husband tired of her and wanted another woman. So he quite simply spread the story around that she was weak in the head and going mad. Perhaps he ill-treated her; perhaps his repeated insinuations really did unbalance her mind, so that she began to doubt her own sanity. We don't know, but it is not difficult to drive someone mad. Eventually her husband persuaded two doctors to certify that she was incurably insane. It would not have been difficult in those days. Perhaps the two doctors were cronies of his. Perhaps they were paid to certify. I do not suppose she was ever examined properly by an independent and impartial psychiatrist, as she would be today. It would have been very easy for him to choose his own doctors and the certificate was irreversible. Aunt Anne was taken away, taken from her children, who from then on were motherless. She was locked up in an asylum, where she remained for the rest of her life. She died in 1907."

"That is one of the most shocking stories I have ever heard," I said.

"It was not uncommon. It was a very clever way for a rich man to get rid of an unwanted wife. He had to pay for the asylum, of course, but that would not trouble a rich man. After a period of years, I don't know how many, he could get a divorce with no scandal. Easy!"

"And did the woman have no one to speak for her?"

"Oh yes, her father or a brother could, and probably would. It was not always plain sailing for an unscrupulous husband. But my grandfather, Anne's father, was dead, and there were no brothers, only four daughters in the family. So poor Anne had no one to protect her."

"Could her mother or sisters not speak for her?"

"Women had no voice in any matter. It had been the same for centuries. That is what we fought for." Her eyes flashed and she banged the desk. "Independence for women. Freedom from male dominance."

"Were you a suffragette?" I asked.

"Bah! Suffragettes. I've no time for suffragettes. They made the biggest mistake in history. They went for equality. They should have gone for power!" With a dramatic gesture she swept her arm across the desk, scattering pencils, papers and notebooks to the floor. "But I broke the mould in my family when I announced that I was going to be a nurse. Oh, you should have heard the rumpus. It would have been funny if it had not been so deadly serious. My father locked me in my room and threatened to keep me there indefinitely. Then he tried to insinuate that I was mad and should be confined to an asylum like poor Aunt Anne. But times were changing. Women were beginning to break the chains of their bondage. Florence Nightingale led the way and many others followed. I wrote to Miss Nightingale from my prison in my father's house. She was quite an old lady by then, but she was very powerful. She spoke to Queen Victoria on my behalf. I don't know what they said, but the result was that I was released from captivity. My poor docile mother never really recovered from the shock of having a rebel daughter. Nonetheless, I was thirty-two before I could break away from my father's domination and start nursing. That was when my life began."

The chapel bell rang for Vespers.

Sister Monica Joan took up her black veil and adjusted it over her white wimple. She turned to me with a naughty wink. "If my father had seen me as a nun, he would have had a stroke. But mercifully he was spared, because he died the same year that the old Queen died. Hand me my prayer book, child."

It was on the floor, along with the other items that had been pushed from her desk. I retrieved everything that was scattered around, placed them all on the desk and handed her the prayer book.

"Now for it," she said, her head held high, her eyebrows arched in a slightly supercilious curve. A mischievous grin crinkled the corners of her mouth and eyes. "Now for it," she said again as she swept out of the room.

There was nothing cringing or pathetic about Sister Monica Joan. She was going to battle it out to the end. If she couldn't face her Sisters in chapel, she would sit with her back to them, and if they didn't like it, they could lump it.

After the evening visits we took supper in the kitchen. This was a meal prepared by ourselves, because we all came in at different times. We were looking the worse for wear, particularly Chummy, who couldn't hold her drink but did not want to admit it, and had been protesting all day that she thought she had a touch of flu. Chummy was, in addition, torn by a feeling of guilt because she was supposed to have been on first call that night and it had been Cynthia who had gone out at the bleakest hour before dawn, 3 a.m. We sat down around the kitchen table, eating our peanut-butter sandwiches.

"They've gone," I whispered, in case any of the Sisters were in the hallway.

"What's gone?"

"The jewels, they've gone. They are not in the drawer."

Trixie eyed me dubiously. "Are you sure they were there in the first place? After all, we've only got your word for it. Perhaps you dreamed the whole thing. Sister Evangelina calls you Dolly Daydream, and not without reason."

"I did not dream it. I tell you, I saw them and now they've gone."

"Well she must have hidden them somewhere else, the cunning old—"

Cynthia stopped her. "Don't you two start on that again. I'm too tired to put up with you squabbling like a couple of children. Pack it in."

Chummy groaned and spoke in a weary voice: "I second that motion, Chairman. My poor bally head feels like a suet pudding that's gone cold and been warmed up again for the servants. Did I hear you say that the jewels have gone?"

"Yes."

"Well strike me pink."

Trixie was quick off the mark. "She's hidden them. It's as clear as daylight. She knows she's been rumbled, so she's hidden them again. You can't tell me she doesn't know what she's doing. Of course she does." Trixie cut another slice of bread and dug her knife into the jar.

Cynthia was less emphatic. "Well, this does throw rather a different light on things. I still don't think she knows what she's doing."

"Oh, go on with you. She pulls the wool over everyone's eyes. But she doesn't fool me for a moment," said cynical Trixie.

Chummy was licking the peanut butter off the knife.

"Premeditation. That's what the constabulary will be after. Were her actions premeditated or were they not? If we're going to protect Sister Monica Joan, Counsel for the Defence, that's what we've got to prove. But at the moment, my poor bally head aches so much I can't think straight. I'm going to bed. Who's on first call?"

"You are."

"Groan, groan and thrice groan. That settles it. I must get in a bit of the old sweet slumber before that accursed bell pitches me out onto the floor. Nighty-night all. Sweet dreams."

Cynthia stood up. “And I’m going to bed too. Don’t you two start quarrelling as soon as you’re alone.”

Trixie looked at me when they had gone. “I reckon there’s not much more to say. Chummy hit the nail on the head. Was it, or was it not, premeditated? Come on, let’s do the washing up.”

RECREATION HOUR

Recreation in a convent is a time when the nuns can let their hair down – metaphorically, of course. Usually the recreation hour lasts from 2 p.m. to 3 p.m. With the morning work completed, lunch taken and no religious duties to perform until Vespers at 4.30 p.m., the nuns are free. But "free" only within the discipline of the order. At Nonnatus House, during the recreation hour, the nuns withdrew collectively to their sitting room, where they would engage in needlework and polite conversation.

How these reverend ladies found time for it defeats me to this day. Each of the nuns seemed capable of packing forty-eight hours of work into every twenty-four and each of them did it with serenity and grace. Sister Julienne, for example, who was Sister-in-Charge, was not only the senior nurse and midwife with overall responsibility for the practice, but she was also in charge of the smooth running of the house. She was accountable for maintaining the monastic tradition of religious observance, instructing the novices, teaching the student midwives, acting as hostess to numerous house guests, handling convent finances and keeping the accounts. She took her fair share of district visits, including night calls, as well as finding time to engage in needlework and polite conversation during her brief hours of recreation when most people would want to lie horizontal with their feet up.

It was their practice, as I have said, for the nuns to retire to their sitting room after lunch. But occasionally Sister Julienne would say at lunch time, "I think we will take recreation in the nurses' sitting room today," whereupon the Sisters would look with a particular benevolence upon us girls, as though they were granting us some special favour. The nuns would then go to their cells (nuns sleep in cells, not bedrooms) to collect their work, and we would rush to our sitting room to clear away dirty plates, mugs, ashtrays, magazines, glasses, empty chocolate boxes, biscuit tins, hairbrushes, medical books (yes, occasionally, we put in a bit of study), and all the paraphernalia essential to the life of the average young girl.

The Sisters entered and we smiled sweetly, as though we hadn't been frantically clearing things away for the past five minutes. Sister Evangelina, not famous for her tact, glared around her, growling, "Well, Nurse Browne, I believe your mother is coming to visit you at the weekend. You had better tidy the place up before she comes."

"Oh, but we have just had a thumping good tidy up for you, Sister." Chummy was not offended, simply puzzled.

Trixie gave a shrill laugh and was about to speak, but Cynthia, the peacemaker, retorted, "We'll get out the Hoover, the polish and the dusters before the weekend, Sister."

Sister Evangelina snorted her disapproval and opened her workbox. Everyone did the same except Trixie and me. Neither of us owned a workbox; we did not sew or knit for recreation.

Sister Julienne was concerned. "Oh, my dears, perhaps you could each make a little tea cosy for the Christmas Fayre. Tea cosies always go down well. People buy them for Christmas presents."

Material, stuffing, scissors, needles and cotton were provided and conversation centred on the desirability of a large number of tea cosies to boost the convent's finances for the coming year. As well as everything else, the Sisters not only organised and ran a sale each year, but made a large number of the items to be sold. For many decades the finance for supporting the midwifery practice had, to some extent, depended on the monies collected at the Christmas Fayre.

The Sisters were making many small items considered to be useful or necessary in those days, such as handkerchief sachets, glove folders, pincushions, cushion covers, tray cloths, tablecloths, pillowcases and virtually anything else onto which a bird or a

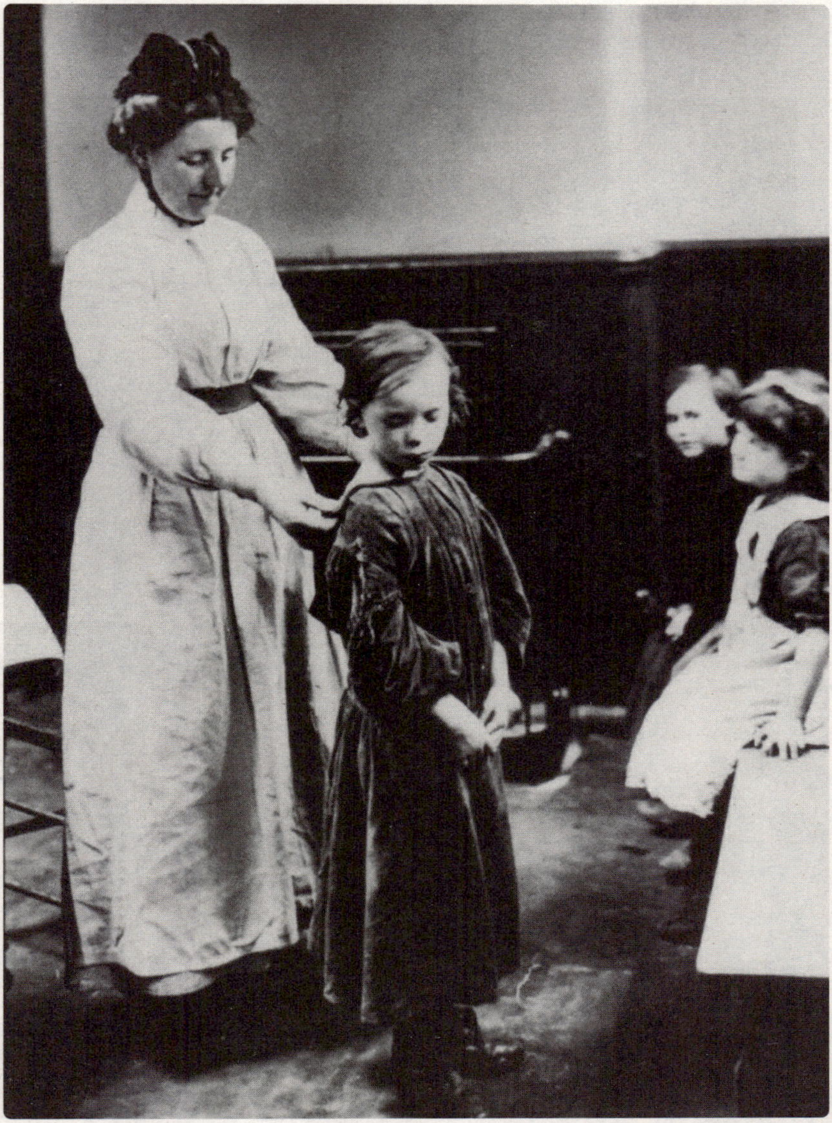

Hackney Workhouse c.1911. *Photo courtesy of the Corporation of London, London Metropolitan Archives.*

BELOW The Poplar Tenements, known as the Canada Buildings. They were bug-infested and closed in the 1960s. Joseph Collett lived here. *Photo taken in the 1950s by midwife Jean Todd.*

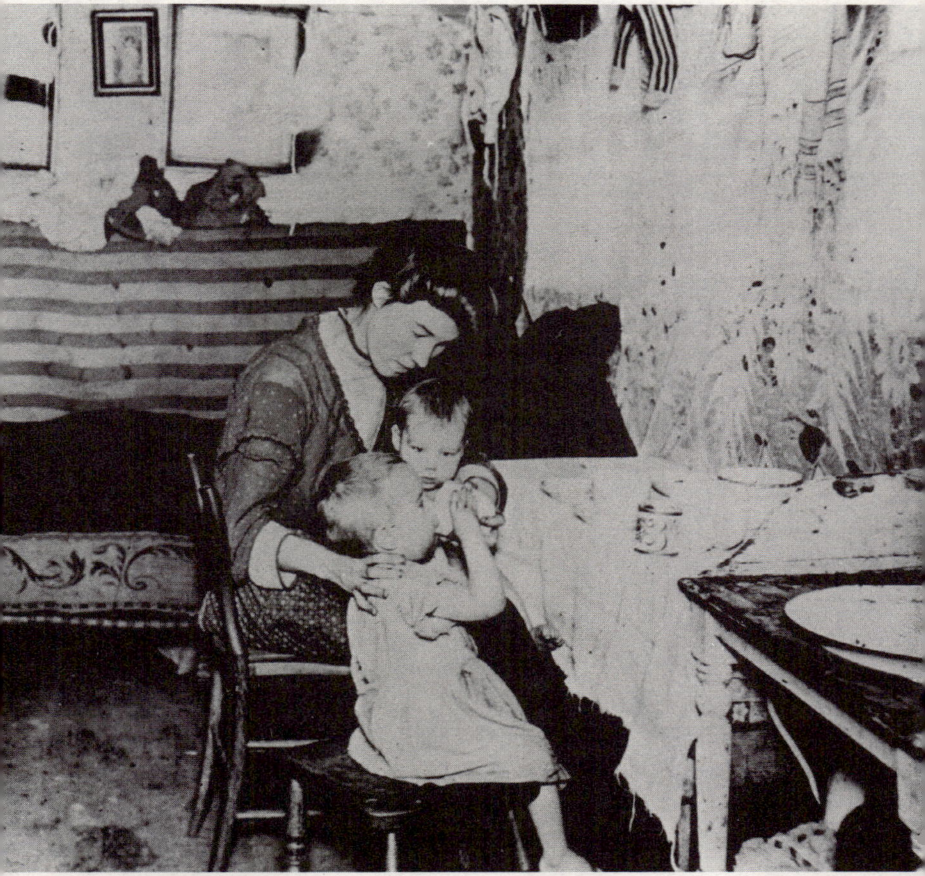

ABOVE Typical domestic scene, c.1900: they are poor, but not destitute. When I look at this I think of Frank and little Peggy when their mother was alive. *Photo courtesy of Bancroft Library, the Cohen Collection 1900–1910.*

LEFT Poplar Workhouse c.1905.
Photo courtesy of Bancroft Library.

Women picking oakum c.1890. Oakum was pieces of old rope untwisted and pulled apart; the fibres were used to fill holes and cracks in wooden boats and ships. Women and children were forced to do this work, which tore the hands and nails. *Photo courtesy of the National Trust Photographic Library.*

Workhouse boys with their schoolmaster c.1870. The Education Act 1870 required children to be taught the three Rs. This is a very rare picture of workhouse boys with their schoolmaster. *Photo courtesy of the Local History Collection of Gravesend Library.*

ABOVE Flat barges with their distinctive red sails were a common feature of the Thames and were in use for at least 200 years. Joe Collett's first job was as a bargee. *Photo courtesy of the Island History Trust Collection.*

LEFT The gambling school, Shadwell, c.1910–20. Frank was an addicted gambler and groups like this could be found everywhere. It was illegal and the boys have a furtive air about them, on the look-out for the police. *Photo by F C Wright, the Highway Clubs in East London, Bancroft Library. Courtesy of Jeff Wright.*

LEFT Hackney Workhouse babies, c.1900. At least these babies went out! A Royal Commission Report 1909 revealed that in many urban workhouses the babies never left the premises and that 40% died in their first year in the workhouse. Jane would have been taken out in a pram like this. *Photo courtesy of the Hackney Archives.*

BELOW St Pancras Workhouse, London c.1906. *Photo courtesy of Camden Local Studies and Archives Centre.*

Hackney Workhouse children c.1900. *Photo courtesy of the Hackney Archives.*

daisy-chain could be embroidered. Conversation centred on the saleability of each item for the Christmas Fayre. The need for a large number of chair-back covers puzzled me and, even more, the name by which they were called – 'antimacassars' – until I learned that they were intended to protect the back of a chair from the grease on men's hair. Many men plastered their hair with Brylcreem in those days and the oil used in Victorian times was Macassar.

I looked around me with pleasure. It was all very genteel and sweet; it could have been a scene from any period in history when ladies had almost nothing else to do. Sister Julienne was making rag dolls with great speed and efficiency, creating tiny waistcoats and shoes, fixing button eyes and snipping wool hair. Sister Bernadette was an expert in golliwogs. Children are not allowed to have such toys today, nor even to use the word, but in those days they were all the fashion. Sister Evangelina was hemming handkerchiefs, and Novice Ruth – what on earth was she doing? Novice Ruth had a wooden object rather like a large cotton reel. Four nails, without heads, had been hammered into the top. The Novice was plying heavy linen thread round and round the nails with a small blunt instrument and pulling the thread over the nails at each turn. Through the centre of the wooden reel a woven band emerged. It was already a yard or two long, but still Novice Ruth continued plying the thread and weaving.

What on earth was it? I watched, fascinated. She must have read my mind because she laughed and said, "You wonder what I am doing. This will be my girdle. I am approaching the time of my first profession, when I shall take my first vows. A Sister wears a woven girdle wound three times around her waist and, at the end, we tie three knots. This is a constant reminder of our three vows of poverty, chastity and obedience."

She had such a beautiful face and such a radiant smile. Her vocation clearly filled her with joy.

Conversation continued about the Christmas Fayre and who should attend the stalls. Mrs B as usual, was in charge of the cake stall, and Fred, the boiler man, always managed a very good stall selling second-hand tools, which attracted men to the Fayre. It was Fred's proud boast that he could sell anything. Give him a bag of bent, rusty nails and he would sell them for you.

The doorbell rang.

"Now who can that be?" said Sister. "We're not expecting anyone. Would you answer it, please, Nurse Browne."

Chummy laid down her expert embroidery and left the room. We continued talking about the Christmas Fayre, speculating if the band from the SPY Club could be asked to provide some entertainment. Should they be paid and, if so, how much? "How about tea and cakes?" someone ventured. "Wouldn't that be sufficient payment?"

"What on earth has happened to Nurse Browne?" Sister Evangelina grunted. "She's been gone at least five minutes. It doesn't take that long to answer the door."

At that moment Chummy re-entered the room. She was bright red. She took a step forward and kicked a waste-paper basket, which shot into the air, spilling its contents as it flew. It hit Sister Evangelina on the side of the head, knocking her veil and wimple sideways. The shock caused her to prick her finger and blood spurted over the handkerchief she was hemming.

"You clumsy fool," she shouted. "Look what you have made me do." She sucked her finger and waved the ruined handkerchief at Chummy.

Sister Julienne took charge. "Never mind, Sister, use the handkerchief to bind the finger or we shall have blood all over the other work. Better to spoil one item than half a dozen? Now, Nurse Browne, what on earth is the matter?"

Chummy opened her mouth and her lips moved but no sound came. She tried again with no success.

The Sisters were seriously concerned. "My poor child, do sit down."

Chummy sat down and again tried to speak. Her vocal chords finally responded and the words came out in a rush. "Please,

Sister, the policeman is at the door and he wants to see you."

Trixie gave a scream of laughter. "Didn't I tell you! There, look, Chummy's sweet on the policeman!"

Cynthia kicked her hard.

Sister Julienne looked troubled. "Oh dear, oh bother. I'll go at once."

We all looked at one another. Sister Julienne would only use such an extreme expression as "oh bother" in an extreme situation.

The knowledge that the policeman was at the door again gave me a nasty jolt. I had managed to lay aside the awful dilemma of the jewels found in Sister Monica Joan's room. I looked anxiously at Cynthia, who was embroidering a cushion cover and who refused to look up. All the Sisters were silently bent over their work. Chummy took up her sewing again but her hands were shaking so much that she could not control the needle.

Only Trixie spoke. "Well, now for it. They've come to take her away. There'll be a right old rumpus."

Sister Evangelina turned on her. "Hold your tongue, you thoughtless, loud-mouthed girl. Just keep quiet for once."

"Sorry, I'm sure." Trixie didn't look at all sorry.

I managed to catch Cynthia's eye and we exchanged a look of alarm. Novice Ruth stifled a tear and worked furiously at the girdle she was making. Sister Bernadette was stuffing a golliwog, poking the stuffing down hard into the legs. The clock ticked and no one spoke except for the occasional "Pass the scissors, please", or "Have you got the light-blue thread over there?"

The soft footsteps of Sister Julienne were heard and we all looked up expectantly, but she passed the door and went upstairs. Glances of real anguish were exchanged between the Sisters.

All the muscles around my chest and stomach seemed to tighten at once and I felt hot all over. "Could we open a window, do you think?" I enquired.

"I was about to suggest the same thing," said Sister Bernadette, and Cynthia, who was nearest to the window, stood up and opened it. The clock ticked on and we continued sewing. No one spoke.

Again footsteps were heard – descending the stairs this time. We all looked up, each with the same thought in mind. What were they going to do with her?

The door burst open and Sister Julienne stood there, her features filled with joy. "They are dropping all charges and taking no further action! Oh, the relief, I can't tell you the relief. I have just been up to see Sister Monica Joan to convey the news, although I am not sure that she understood what I was saying because she just looked at me in complete silence."

"Praise the Lord," said Sister Evangelina, sniffing hard. She blew her nose loudly into the blood-stained handkerchief and wiped the corner of her eye. "Let us praise the Lord for his mercy."

We were all overjoyed at the news, but Sister Evangelina displayed more emotion and relief than anyone else in the room. Her reaction brought home to me the genuine goodness and charity of the woman who had suffered so much from Sister Monica Joan's verbal cruelty. The apparent dislike between the two women was not of her making, and a less loving soul might have been indifferent, if not secretly glad, to see her Sister's downfall.

Sister Julienne sat down. "This calls for a celebration so I have asked Mrs B to bring up an early tea and we will have jam with our scones today."

Mrs B came bouncing in with a large tray. "There, din' I tell yer? As innocen' as a new-born babe, she is. An' them police, they wants their bleedin' 'eads (beggin' yer pardon, Sisters) bangin' together, vey do. An' I'd like to ge' me 'ands on vat lyin' coster, I would."

Sister Julienne burst out laughing. "You'll do no such thing. We don't want you had up for assault. Perhaps you would pour the tea, Novice Ruth, and pass the scones."

Mrs B withdrew. The tea and scones were passed round, not

forgetting the jam. Everyone was in festive mood.

Sister Julienne continued her story. "Apparently the legal adviser to the police has suggested that, due to the age of the suspect and the triviality of the items found in her room, the police might find themselves in a position of ridicule if they were to proceed with prosecution. The costers involved have been informed that a charge will not be brought by the Public Prosecutor but they would be within their rights to bring a civil action. Due to the fact that a civil case costs so much money and that they would be unlikely to get compensation, damages or costs, the costers have decided not to proceed." Sister Julienne gave a huge sigh of relief, caressing her cup as she raised it to her lips.

We four girls could not share the happiness of the Sisters. We knew something of which they were completely unaware. The knowledge of the jewels in Sister Monica Joan's possession weighed heavily upon us. I was terrified that Trixie would blurt out something ill-considered that would give the game away. Cynthia and I exchanged glances and clearly the same thought was going through her mind also. She was sitting near Trixie so she nudged her and I was grateful to see her mouth the words, "We'll talk later." A plan was forming in my mind to remove the jewels from Sister Monica Joan's room, take them to Hatton Garden and just leave them somewhere. My mind was racing – yes, that would be the answer, or perhaps I could leave them outside a police station a long way away, so no one would suspect. But where would I find them? The beastly things had gone from Sister's bedside cabinet. Perhaps I could talk to her about it. Would she see reason? It would be good to talk to Cynthia later; she was always so sensible.

Sister Julienne said, "I knew our prayers would be answered. I do so believe in the power of prayer. No need for a lawyer now, eh?" and she giggled, happily. I squirmed – if only she knew – and my resolve to find the wretched jewels and dispose of them grew firmer.

Tea was being cleared away, the sewing brought out again, and we all settled down to work.

The door opened. Sister Monica Joan stood at the threshold. She did not enter the room immediately but stood quite still, one hand resting on the door. She was wearing her full outdoor habit, with the long black veil, perfectly adjusted over the white wimple. She looked magnificent. Everyone stopped talking, laid down their sewing and looked up at her. Yet she did not move, her hand remained motionless on the door handle, her hooded eyes were half-closed, her eyebrows raised, and a slightly supercilious smile played around the corners of her mouth. She had a magnetic quality about her that forbade speech.

Then she moved for the first time; slowly and deliberately she turned her head, beautifully poised on its long neck, and scrutinised each person in the room with a level and unfaltering gaze. She looked each of us straight in the eye for a few seconds, then turned her head very slightly and looked at the next person. No one dared to speak or move. I have never seen a more riveting performance in my life.

It was Sister Monica Joan herself who broke the silence. She tilted her head slightly to one side and raised an eyebrow. A naughty little grin lit her features. "Greetings all. Did I ever tell you about the Thief of Baghdad? They boiled him in oil, don't you know; or perhaps they drowned him in a butt of Malmsey wine. One or the other, I'm not sure which; but they did him in, I'm sure of that."

Sister Julienne rose, both arms outstretched. "Oh my dear, say no more about that dreadful business. Not another word. It was all a misunderstanding and we have put it behind us. But come in and join our happy circle. I see you have your knitting bag with you."

Sister Monica Joan graciously consented to be led into the room. Sister Evangelina rose from her seat. "Have this chair, my dear; it is the most comfortable." Sister Monica Joan sat down.

The jewels! They flashed and glistened into my mind. They

had to be disposed of and now was the perfect time. Sister Monica Joan was knitting quietly and everyone else was sewing and chatting. There might never be such an opportunity again.

I excused myself and left the room. At the bottom of the stairs I removed my shoes, so that no one would hear footsteps. It was the work of a moment to reach Sister Monica Joan's room. Quietly I entered and wedged a chair under the handle, in case anyone tried to enter. The search started. I scrutinised every inch of that room, every drawer, every shelf, every cupboard; I felt all over the mattress, the pillows, the cushions; the tops and the hems of the curtains. I rummaged through her underwear and her habits – it wasn't seemly to pry into a nun's private things, but it had to be done. Nothing! Nowhere! My earlier thought about the lavatory cistern returned, and I raced along the corridor to the bathroom. Still nothing. I began to feel panic grip me; recreation hour must surely be drawing to a close. If one of the Sisters found me on their private landing or in their bathroom, there would be a lot of explaining to do. Running downstairs and replacing my shoes took only a few seconds, and I was back in the sitting room just as the ladies began to fold up their sewing and talk about the evening visits.

I muttered my excuses: "I'm sorry, Sister, I don't seem to have got on very well with the tea cosy. I don't think I'm much good at sewing."

Sister Julienne smiled. "That's perfectly all right, we can't all be good at the same things."

She turned to Sister Monica Joan. "Can I help you, dear? That is a lovely baby's shawl you are knitting. Can I help you put it away?"

She took the handle of the knitting bag. Sister Monica Joan grabbed the bag back. "Don't touch it, leave it to me." She pulled the side nearest to her, but the handle on the other side was caught over Sister Julienne's wrist. The seam burst and a shower of rings, watches, gold chains and bracelets was flung across the floor.

THE TRIAL

Total silence followed. The two halves of the torn knitting bag were held by Sister Julienne and Sister Monica Joan, who looked at each other for what seemed an eternity.

Sister Monica Joan was the first to speak. "Inanimate objects have a life of their own, independent of the creature, have you not noticed?" She glanced at each of us in turn. "And whenever an atom gets excited it creates magnetic fields."

"Are you suggesting, Sister, that these inanimate objects were somehow magnetised into your knitting bag, independent of human activity?" Sister Julienne's voice was sarcastic.

"Most certainly. 'There are stranger things in heaven and earth than are dreamed of in your philosophy, Horatio.'"

"Don't call me Horatio."

"Poof, hoity-toity." Sister Monica Joan was aloof. "The difficulty of comparative study is the incomprehension of lesser minds. But keep the trinkets. Use them well. In the latter days they will be interpreted in a mystery play, a drama, an allegory. Use them well, I say; they have their own life, their own force, their own destiny." And with that she floated out of the room.

Trixie's suppressed giggles exploded. She turned to me. "I believe you now. I thought your fevered imagination was working overtime. The cunning old . . . Sorry, Sister."

Sister Julienne looked at me. "How long have you known about this?"

"About two weeks." I was feeling very uncomfortable.

"And you said nothing to me?"

I could only mutter a feeble: "I'm sorry, Sister."

"Come to my office after supper and before Compline. We

must gather up these things." She bent down and started picking up the jewels. We all helped in silence.

It was difficult to concentrate on my evening round, and babies that would not feed seemed perverse and irritating. Part of me was glad that the secret, which had oppressed me for days, was at last out in the open. On the other hand I was furious with myself for not having managed to dispose of the jewels before Sister Julienne found them. The knowledge that she required me in her office later gave me an uneasy feeling, and my legs turned the pedals reluctantly as I cycled back to Nonnatus House.

As soon as I entered the clinical room I knew, from the atmosphere, that the police were in the house. Usually, after a day's work, a group of young girls would make quite a lot of noise, chattering and giggling as they packed their bags and cleared up; but not on this occasion.

Novice Ruth looked up. Her eyes were red and her voice seemed subdued. "You are to go to Sister Julienne's office at once," she said.

A sick feeling grabbed at my stomach. Cynthia said: "I'll do your bag. Leave it here, and don't worry."

I knocked on the office door and entered. The same sergeant and constable who had been assigned to the case earlier were present. The jewels were spread out on the desk.

Sister Julienne spoke. "Here is the nurse who has known of the existence of this –" She hesitated – "this . . . little haul, for more than fortnight."

My face was burning and I felt like a criminal.

The sergeant spoke to me, the constable taking notes all the while. They required my name, my age, home address, next of kin, father's occupation and many more details besides.

"When did you first see these jewels?"

"On a Monday afternoon, two weeks ago."

"Can you identify them?"

"Not really, I did not look closely enough."

"But are they substantially the same?"

"Yes."

"Where did you find them?"

"In the third drawer down of the bedside cabinet."

The constable looked back through his notebook. "We looked in the bedside cabinet, sir, and there was nothing there. They must have been placed there after our search."

"Just what I was thinking. And what did you do, nurse?"

"Nothing."

"Were you aware that these jewels are of considerable value?"

"I guessed they might be, but I didn't know."

Sister Julienne intervened. "Why did you not tell me?"

"I promised I wouldn't."

Sister Julienne was about to speak, but the sergeant silenced her.

"Who did you promise?"

"Sister Monica Joan."

"So she knew you had seen them?"

"Yes."

"And she made you promise not to tell?"

"Yes – no. She didn't make me promise. I just did."

"Why?"

"Because she was so upset."

"What was she upset about?"

"The jewels."

"Upset that you had found them?"

"I suppose so."

"Upset that she had been found out?"

"I don't know."

"Was she upset before you found them?"

"No. She was happy."

"And she was happy when you left her?"

"Yes."

"Why?"

I didn't want to answer. But he repeated: "Why?"

"I suppose she was happy because I had promised not to tell."

The sergeant looked at the constable. "Sister Monica Joan obviously knows what she has been doing. First she moves the jewels around to avoid detection and then when they are found, she is clearly relieved when a promise of secrecy is made."

He turned to me again. "At the time of finding the jewels, nurse, did you know that the police were investigating a charge of shoplifting brought by local costers?"

"Yes."

"And did it not occur to you that the jewels might be relevant to police investigations?"

"I don't know."

"Nurse, I won't insult you by suggesting you are stupid!"

"Well, yes, I did think they were relevant."

"Were you aware that withholding evidence during a police investigation is a criminal offence?"

My mouth went dry and my head began to spin. It is one thing to engage in underhand behaviour, but quite another to be told by a police sergeant that you have been guilty of a criminal offence. My voice was barely audible.

"I didn't know until a few days ago that it was a criminal offence."

"And what happened a few days ago?"

"I told the girls."

Sister Julienne exploded. "You told the girls and you didn't tell me. This is outrageous!"

"Why did you tell the girls and not the Sister-in-Charge?"

"Because I knew that Sister Julienne would have to tell the police, but the girls wouldn't."

"And what did the girls say?"

"I can't quite remember. We had a couple of bottles of sherry and I'm not sure what we said. It all got a bit confused."

The constable taking notes gave a chortle, that was quickly smothered when the sergeant stared at him.

Sister Julienne's blood pressure was rising fast. "This gets worse and worse. You girls had a couple of bottles of sherry when you were on duty! We will talk about this later."

I groaned in despair. Now I had got my friends into trouble too.

The sergeant interrupted. "Let's get back to the jewels. You decided to conceal the information from the police, but what did you intend to do?"

"I thought I could take the jewels from Sister Monica Joan's room and just leave them somewhere, in Hatton Garden, or outside a police station."

The sergeant and the constable exchanged glances.

"But I couldn't find them, so I couldn't do it."

"She had moved them from the bedside cabinet?"

"Yes."

"It's a very good thing for you, nurse, that you could not find the jewels. If you had done as you have suggested and been apprehended with the jewels on your person, you would have been in serious trouble."

I went cold. Theft, prison. The end of my nursing career. The end of everything.

The sergeant was watching me carefully. Then he spoke. "We are not going to take any further action, nurse. This is a caution, and will be recorded as such. You have been very foolish. I hesitate to call you a silly young girl, but that is what you are, and I hope this will be a lesson to you. You can go now."

I crept out of Sister's office numb with shock. To be called a "silly young girl" by a police sergeant when you think you are so mature and responsible is not a pleasant experience.

The girls pressed me for information. We sat round the kitchen table eating cheese-and-pickle sandwiches and home-made cake and I told them all about it. Narrowly missing prison was foremost in my mind.

"Not a chance, old scout. We'd have stood by you," said Chummy staunchly. Her loyalty reminded me of my own disloyalty – I had let the cat out of the bag about the sherry party. I was contrite in my apologies. Cynthia, as always, was soothing, pointing out that we were all in it together and no harm had come of it. She advised cocoa all round and an early night.

The jewels were taken by the police for identification and Hatton Garden jewellers who had reported losses over several years were asked to examine them. One man, Samuelson by name, positively identified a rope of antique pearls and a diamond ring as having been stolen from his stock a few years previously. He produced record books verifying his statement.

The testimony of costers who had seen Sister Monica Joan take small items from their stalls was also required. With their evidence, combined with that of Mr Samuelson, the police decided that, on a variety of counts, there was now a case against Sister Monica Joan. However, her mental fitness was in doubt, so a medical assessment was required.

The general practitioner who had known Sister Monica Joan for many years and who had attended her through her recent bout of pneumonia was consulted. He said that he was baffled and quite unable to decide whether or not she was senile, and advised obtaining the report of a psychiatrist.

The psychiatrist was a lady, a senior consultant in psychiatry at the London Hospital, who examined Sister Monica Joan twice at Nonnatus House. Her report stated that, in spite of her age, Sister's mind was remarkably clear. All her responses were swift and accurate; she was astute, observant and cryptic in her conversation; her understanding of past and present events was impressive; and she had a clear understanding of the difference between right and wrong. No evidence of mental deterioration could be found and the psychiatrist considered that Sister Monica Joan could be held responsible for her actions.

Having considered the two medical reports, the police decided to prosecute and they referred the evidence to Old Street Magistrates' Court for a preliminary hearing.

Three magistrates agreed unanimously that there was a prima

facie case of larceny, for which a younger person would undoubtedly have stood trial at the London Quarter Sessions. However, the presiding magistrate was exceedingly doubtful, considering the age of the accused. He had a grandmother of ninety-three who did not know the time of day nor even recognise her own daughter and he was very sympathetic towards extreme old age.

Whilst the charges were being read by the police superintendent, Sister Monica Joan sat between her solicitor and Sister Julienne, who was scarlet with embarrassment and kept her eyes lowered. In contrast, Sister Monica Joan sat upright and looked around her with haughty grandeur, every now and then exclaiming something-like "poof" or "tosh" or "fiddlesticks".

When the superintendent had finished, the presiding magistrate said, "You have heard the charges?"

"I most certainly have."

"And do you understand them?"

"Don't be impertinent, my man. Do you think I am stupid?"

"No, Sister, I don't. But I must be quite sure that you understand the charges brought against you by the police."

Sister Monica Joan did not answer. She looked towards the clock on the wall and raised her veined hand towards her chin like an actress posing for a photograph.

"I am not sure that she does, sir," said Sister Julienne quietly to the solicitor who stood up to speak.

But, before he could do so, Sister Monica Joan turned on them with quiet rage. "Do not presume to speak for me. Speak for yourselves. Bear witness to your own imperfections. We stand, each of us, alone and naked before the Judgement Throne, where none but the silent dead can testify."

The presiding magistrate was having second thoughts. This was very different from a grandmother whose conversation was confined to: "I'm ninety-three, you know, think of that, ninety-three." He addressed Sister Monica Joan very seriously. "Have you understood the charges brought against you?"

"I have."

"Do you plead 'guilty' or 'not guilty'?"

"Guilty! Guilty? Do you imagine, my good fellow, that I accept a charge of guilt from the hoi-polloi I see before me?" She sniffed scornfully and drew out a laced handkerchief from beneath her scapular, which she applied to her nose with an affected gesture, as though an unpleasant smell had assailed her. "Guilty indeed – huh? 'Let he who is without sin cast the first stone.' Does your small mind understand the hidden meaning of 'guilt'? Before you use the word again, it behoves you to find out, if perchance you are capable of such intellectual exercise, which I very much doubt."

Such rudeness to the presiding magistrate was Sister Monica Joan's undoing. Had she shown a little more humility, a little more uncertainty or even contrition, it is likely that, in their discretionary powers, the magistrates would have taken the matter no further. As it was, after a brief consultation, the decision was made to accept a plea of not guilty and to refer the case to the London Quarter Sessions for trial by judge and jury.

Sister Julienne was devastated by Sister Monica Joan's performance in the Magistrates' Court. She had hoped that the matter would end quietly there, but now the full publicity of the Quarter Sessions would have to be faced. But Sister Julienne was not a woman easily beaten. She prayed about the matter. The inspiration granted to her from a heavenly source was that the defence of mental deterioration should be strengthened. She consulted the solicitor and it was decided to obtain a third medical opinion.

Sir Lorimer Elliott-Bartram had an enviable reputation as a psychologist. He was well known in London, having given medical evidence in several legal cases. Sir Lorimer was getting on in years but not so far on that he could not maintain a thriving practice in Harley Street. In fact, the further on he got, the more patients came flocking to his doors and therefore the more money he made. It was all very satisfactory.

Sir Lorimer had qualified as a surgeon in 1912, and had had a distinguished record as an army doctor in the First World War – distinguished, according to the military commanders, as a first-rate officer and doctor; and distinguished, according to the men in the ranks, as a butcher.

Although Sir Lorimer had never qualified, nor attempted to qualify, as a psychiatrist, he had made a fortune in Harley Street by dabbling in psychotherapy, memory loss, personality change, mental block, hypomania, dypsomania, kleptomania and related subjects. He was a tall, handsome man with a deep, resonant voice that could easily adopt a silky tone. The majority of his patients were women.

There is an old saying in medical circles that if you want to make a study of invective, you should listen to two doctors talking about a third. In psychiatric circles Sir Lorimer, a mere psychologist, was regarded as a pompous old windbag and a chancer, who fuelled the tank of his Rolls-Royce with the blood of rich old ladies.

Oozing opulence, Sir Lorimer entered Nonnatus House and was taken to Sister Monica Joan's room. He kissed her hand and called her "dear reverend lady".

She murmured, "What a relief to meet a mature gentleman of experience and understanding."

He kissed her hand a second time, whispering: "I understand everything, dear lady, everything."

She sighed and smiled: "I am sure you do, Sir Lorimer, quite sure."

Later that day, just before Compline, I asked Sister Monica Joan if she liked Sir Lorimer.

She was sitting comfortably by the window knitting. Her face assumed a bright, plastic smile as she cooed, "He is charming, my dear, perfectly charming –" the smile vanished, and a hard edge entered her voice – "and determined to be so."

Sir Lorimer's report was very long and technically complex. For the benefit of the lay reader who is unfamiliar with medical terminology, I have attempted to summarise and simplify it. The report stated:

> Sister Monica Joan is a lady of the Leptosomatic type with a nervous affinity to the Cyclothymic make-up on the one hand and a tendency to Catatonic excitement on the other. Neologism and Disconnection, though slight, could not be discounted. Whereas elucidation of the former may throw light upon the latter, comprehension of the latter seldom throws light upon the former, from which it may be deduced that individual psychological symptomatology must be sought in personal biography. The Korsakaw Psychosis of Registration, Retention and Recall is important. A link between Retrograde Amnesia is consistent with the facility, richness and rapidity of association. Whilst Depersonalisation is not a factor, Dereal-isation is and Catatonic symptoms are not evidence of Cat-atonia, though significant to the trained mind. Kleptomania is consistent in Cyclothymic behaviour, but inconsistent with Leptosomatic tendencies.

Although they could not understand it, Counsel for the Defence and the Sisters were very impressed by this report.

The trial of Sister Monica Joan at the London Quarter Sessions attracted much attention. The public gallery was full. Many costers, and several jewellers from Hatton Garden, were present. Several older women, who remembered the accused as a young midwife and who owed their lives to her, had come out of sympathy. The press gallery was full. A shoplifting nun was good news to a hard-bitten reporter.

Sister Monica Joan sat in the dock. She was knitting quietly and seemed completely unconcerned with what was going on around her. Sister Julienne sat beside her, and attended throughout.

The usher entered.

"Silence in Court," he shouted. "Be upstanding for His Lordship."

Everyone rose to their feet – everyone, that is, except Sister Monica Joan, who remained seated. "Stand for His Lordship," shouted the usher.

There was no movement from Sister Monica Joan. The usher moved towards her, banged the floor with his staff and shouted louder.

Sister Monica Joan gave a surprised little squeak. "Are you addressing me, young man?"

"I am."

"Then let it be known that I will not be addressed in this rude fashion."

"Be upstanding for His Lordship," shouted the usher.

"Did your mother never teach you to say, 'please', young man?"

The usher swallowed hard and banged his staff down on the floor a second time. Sister Monica Joan sat immobile, her beautiful eyes half-closed, her lips pursed in disdain.

"Please stand up, madam." whispered the usher.

"That's better. That is much better. Courtesy is a virtue and costs nothing. I am sure your mother would be proud of you." Sister Monica Joan leaned forward, patted him kindly on the shoulder and rose to her feet.

Cheers from the public gallery.

"Be silent for His Lordship," screamed the usher, striving to restore his authority.

The judge entered, mumbled, "Please be seated," and everyone sat down, including Sister Monica Joan.

Counsel for the Prosecution addressed the jury. He outlined the facts as they were known and said that he would call as witnesses three jewellers from Hatton Garden who had lost jewellery, and eight costers who had lost sundry items from their stalls. He would also call a psychiatrist, who had examined the accused and considered her to be of sound mind and therefore responsible for her actions.

The three jewellers were all reliable witnesses. The first, a Mr Samuelson, stated that he had inherited the business with its stock from his father. A rope of antique pearls and a diamond ring had disappeared from the stock four years previously. The police had been informed. The stolen jewels had never been recovered until the police had contacted him recently saying that a cache of jewellery had been found, and asking him to examine the jewels. With the help of his record books, Mr Samuelson had been able to identify the pearls and the diamond ring.

The second jeweller stated that Sister Monica Joan had entered his shop three years previously and asked to see a tray of small items of little value, such as charms and trinkets. He had been called away to attend to another customer and left her alone with the tray, confident that, as the lady was a nun, it would be safe to do so. However, an assistant had seen the nun take a small item from the tray and slip it into her pocket. He had warned his employer, and together they had escorted Sister Monica Joan into a back room and challenged her. She had produced a small trinket, valued about two shillings, from the folds of her dress. The jeweller said that he had taken the item back and told Sister that he would not call the police on this occasion, but that she would not be admitted to his shop again.

The assistant was called to the witness box. He verified everything his employer had said and identified Sister Monica Joan as the nun referred to. He said that he had not seen her in the shop since that day but had noticed her wandering around other shops in Hatton Garden. He concluded that she must have remembered that she was barred from entering his employer's premises and therefore he rejected any suggestion that she was suffering from memory loss or senile dementia.

Sister Monica Joan continued to knit and displayed no interest in what was being said about her. Sister Julienne, on the other hand, seemed to be on the verge of tears.

The costers were called to give evidence. They were a colourful group of seven men and one woman. The first stepped confidently into the witness box to be sworn in, giving his name as Cakey Crumb.

"Could you give your first name please?"

"Well, I've allus bin known as Cakey. Wiv a name like Crumb, wha' would you expec'?"

"With what name were you christened?"

"Cuthbert."

Shrieks of laughter from the costers, which were silenced by the judge.

Counsel for the Prosecution continued: "Could you please describe your occupation?"

Cakey stuck his thumbs into the armholes of his colourful waistcoat and drummed his fingers on his chest. "I'm a business man. Managin' director of me own company. Bin a' i' since I was four'een, wiv a break for the war, when I was in the merchan' navy; 'orrible, va' was, real 'orrible. Never did like wa'er, I never. We was torpedoed an' 'undreds of men was frown in ve wa'er. 'Alf of 'em drowned. 'Orrible i' was to 'ear 'em cry for 'elp, poor sods. An' then another time we was . . . "

"Yes, Mr Crumb. I am sure the court would like to hear your reminiscences, but we must confine ourselves to the case against Sister Monica Joan. You are a business man, you say?"

"Yerst. Costermonger. I 'as me own cock sparrer, an' sells in ve park its."

The judge interrupted. "Did you say you sell cock sparrows in the park its?"

"No, no, m'lud. Cock sparrer is wha' we calls ve barrer an' park it is ve market."

"I see." The judge made a note. "Please go on."

"I sells ladies fings, and vis nun, she comes up to me stall an' afore you can blink an eye, she picks up a couple of bread an' cheeses, tucks 'em in 'er petticoats, an' is off round the Jack Horner, dahn ve frog an' toad, quick as shit off a stick. I couldn't

Adam an' Eve it, bu' vats wot she done. When I tells me carvin' knife wot I seen, she calls me an 'oly friar, an' says she'll land me one on me north and south if I calls Sister Monica Joan a tea-leaf. Very fond of Sister, she is. So I never says nuffink to no one, like."

The judge had laid down his pen long before Cakey had finished giving his evidence. "I think I am going to need an interpreter," he said.

The usher spoke. "I think I can help you, My Lord. My mother was a cockney and I was brought up with the rhyming slang. Mr Crumb has testified that he saw Sister Monica Joan take a couple of handkerchiefs – bread and cheese is the usual expression for handkerchiefs – off his sparrow, or barrow, and set off round the Jack Horner – corner, My Lord – down the frog and toad – meaning road – as quick as – I need not go on, my Lord, a harmless vulgarity implying no disrespect to Your Lordship – quick, stick – the rhyme is obvious my Lord."

"'I am beginning to understand. Ingenious, very. But what was all that about Adam and Eve? We are not talking about the Garden of Eden, you know."

"'To Adam and Eve it' is a very common expression my Lord. It means 'to believe it', or the negative. Mr Crumb could not Adam and Eve the evidence of his own eyes."

"You are very knowledgeable, usher, and I am indebted to you. But that was not all the evidence Mr Crumb gave the court, and it has to be written down for the record."

The usher was standing up stiff and straight and feeling very important. All eyes were upon him. "Mr Crumb said that he told his wife what had happened. There are several expressions for wife – carving knife, trouble and strife, Duchess of Fife spring readily to mind – and she called him a liar – holy friar, My Lord, and said she would hit him in the north and south – mouth – if he called Sister Monica Joan a thief – tea-leaf was the rhyming slang used by Mr Crumb."

"I understand now. Thank you, usher." The judge turned

towards Cakey. "Would you say that that interpretation is substantially correct, Mr Crumb?"

"Oh yerst, yers. That's Isle of White."

"I suppose I am correct in understanding that it is . . . right?"

The judge looked pleased with himself and smiled at Cakey. He motioned for the Counsel for the Prosecution to continue.

"When did this all occur?"

"Abaht a year ago, I reckons."

"And you never told no one – ahem, I mean, anyone?"

"Nah, nah. I'm no' daft. There'd 'ave bin a righ' 'ole bull and cow if I 'ad. I don't want me jackdaw broke, do I?"

The judge sighed and looked towards the usher.

"Mr Crumb did not tell anyone, My Lord, because he was anxious to avert a row with his wife, whom he felt was capable of breaking his jaw."

"Is this correct, Mr Crumb?"

"Gor, not 'alf, an' all. Got an Oliver Twist like a piston, she 'as. Knock yer 'ampstead 'eafs out soon as look at yer, she would."

"Mr Crumb, I was referring to the accuracy of the usher's translation, not to your wife's skill as a pugilist."

"Oh, I see. Well yers, 'e's got ve lingo taped an' all."

"Thank you, Mr Crumb. Usher, I should be grateful if you would attend closely to what the witness says and interpret for me, should it be necessary."

"Certainly, My Lord."

Counsel for the Prosecution continued. "Having said nothing for a year, why have you come forward now?"

"Because I earwigged some of me mates 'ad seen ve same sort of fing; vis ole blackbird goin' round ve markets, lookin' all 'oly like, bu' pinchin' fings off stalls and then scarperin'. So we goes to ve grasshoppers, an vey took it to ve garden gate."

"I understand your evidence as far as the grasshoppers, Mr Crumb," the judge interrupted. "Usher, perhaps you could enlighten me as to the meaning of the last sentence?"

"Grasshopper, My Lord, is rhyming slang for copper, which

Your Lordship may know is a colloquialism for the police. And the police referred the case to the magistrate – the garden gate."

"I understand." The Judge turned to Mr Crumb. "If the police are grasshoppers and magistrates are garden gates, what, may I enquire, is a judge?" he asked politely.

"Barnaby Rudge, m'lud."

"Hmm. Not too bad. Could have been worse, I suppose. We might have gone down in local terminology as a pile of sludge, or something equally unsavoury. All things considered, I think we have been let off quite lightly. Counsel, do you have any further questions?"

"No, My Lord."

Cakey Crumb stepped down from the witness box, and a costerwoman took his place. She stated that she had seen Sister Monica Joan take three skeins of embroidery silk from her stall and hide them under her scapular. She continued: "I didn't do nuffink abaht it because ve Sisters are well respected arahnd vese parts, an' in fact saved my life when I was younger. The silks only cost a shillin', an' it just didn't seem worthwhile to make a fuss. I jus' thought to meself – poor ole girl, she's goin' off 'er rocker – an left it; but when I heard from the other costers that she'd been pinchin' things left, right and centre, I decided to go in wiv them an' go to the police. After all, we got a livin' to earn, an' thievin' is thievin' whoever 's doin' it. We can't afford 'a be sentimental."

Five other costers told similar stories reporting the thefts of sundry items they had seen Sister Monica Joan take. Lastly, the coster who had instigated the proceedings in the first place was called. He told the court that he had seen Sister Monica Joan take a child's bangle from his stall and hide it under her scapular. When he had challenged her, she had flung the bangle across the stall and stalked off. Five people were called to the witness box, each one declaring under oath that he or she had witnessed this scene.

Things looked black for Sister Monica Joan, but she appeared completely unconcerned, as though the proceedings had nothing to do with her. She was knitting quietly, occasionally counting her stitches and noting them down on her knitting card. She would smile serenely at Sister Julienne who, in contrast, was in a state of real anguish.

The day's proceedings ended and the judge adjourned the court until ten o'clock the following morning.

On the second day, Counsel for the Prosecution called the psychiatrist to the witness box. She stated that she had examined Sister Monica Joan and could find nothing suggestive of senility or mental deterioration. On the contrary, she found Sister to be exceedingly quick and accurate in her responses. Her memory was good and she had a clear perception of right and wrong. In conclusion, the psychiatrist stated that, on the balance of medical evidence, Sister Monica Joan knew what she was doing and was responsible for her actions.

The general practitioner was less positive. He agreed with everything that his colleague had said but nevertheless had a feeling that something was amiss. He doubted if Sister Monica Joan could really be held responsible for her actions although he was unable to say exactly why. In conclusion, he said that the court should prefer the evidence of the specialists. He sat down next to the psychiatrist.

Sir Lorimer Elliott-Bartram was called to the witness box. Sister Monica Joan looked up from her knitting, caught his eye and gave him one of her ravishing smiles, then lowered her eyes demurely.

Counsel for the Defence asked the first question. "From your examination of Sister Monica Joan, would you say she is of sound mind?"

Sir Lorimer paused for a long time before speaking. His pause was calculated for maximum effect. The jury was impressed and leaned forward attentively.

"That is an interesting question and one to which I have given much thought over the years. On mature reflection, and after a lifetime of experience, with reference to Smellingworthy and Schmitzelburg on the subject and not forgetting the work of Crakenbaker, Corensky and Kokenbul as published in *The Lancet*, I have come to the conclusion that the sound mind is a figment of the imagination."

"What on earth is he on about?" whispered the general practitioner.

"He is making, it up as he goes along," the psychiatrist murmured.

"Silence in court!" warned the judge. "For the benefit of the jury, Sir Lorimer, please elucidate. A figment of the imagination, you say."

"Indeed I do. Which of us can contemplate his friend and say: 'He is of sound mind,' gentlemen of the jury? Which of us can gaze upon the wife of his bosom and say: 'Her mind is sound'?"

The jury took notes and shook their heads.

Counsel for the Defence continued. "Perhaps then you would say that the accused suffers from senile dementia?"

"Most certainly not," said Sir Lorimer indignantly. He was old himself and senility or senile dementia were words that he never used.

"I have heard the evidence of the psychiatrist and would point out that normal sensory perception is far from being an objective picture of reality, but is conditioned and modified by many personal factors both sensory and extrasensory. In my opinion, psychiatrists make the problems that are to be solved."

"Could you enlarge upon that, Sir Lorimer?"

"Certainly. Psychiatrists need to earn a living like everyone else. A similar syndrome can be observed in the fields of sociology and counselling. Left to themselves, most people will sort out their own problems. If it is suspected that someone else will sort them out, the problems multiply exponentially."

"The insufferable old hypocrite," whispered the psychiatrist.

Counsel for the Defence continued. "I have read your most erudite report, Sir Lorimer, and I am impressed by your reference to the Korsakaw Psychosis of Registration, Retention and Recall. Could you please enlighten the jury?"

"Certainly. A prominent feature of Korsakaw's Psychosis is that Registration may be interposed by Deregistration, preventing the proper interpretation of happenings. Retention for shorter or longer periods may differ markedly, and Recall may be either voluntary or involuntary."

"That rubbish goes back to 1910," hissed the lady psychiatrist. "He ought to be struck off. I wonder if the General Medical Council knows about him?"

"Silence in court," said the judge. "Please continue, Sir Lorimer."

"Not infrequently psychological experiences are important as regards the origin of psychological symptoms. It is possible to ascribe to the psychological experiences that determine the genesis of the psychological symptoms aetiological importance in the production of the whole."

"This is an example of the three Bs," mouthed the lady psychiatrist.

"The three whats?" replied her colleague.

"Three Bs – Bullshit Baffles Brains," she hissed.

Counsel for the Prosecution stood up. "May I enquire what all this has to do with the theft of valuable jewellery from shops in Hatton Garden?"

"Here, here!" chorused the jewellers in the gallery.

"Silence in court!" said the judge. "Sir Lorimer, with respect to your eminent position in the field of mental health, I was wondering the same thing."

Sir Lorimer continued. "Sister Monica Joan is a lady of great intelligence and fertile imagination. She was brought up in wealth and luxury. Association with her childhood is strong. If valuable jewellery was found in her possession, I have not the slightest doubt that, by the Korsakaw Psychosis, the lady thought that the jewels belonged to her mother."

"Her mother!"

"That is what I said."

"I don't believe a word of it," whispered the lady psychiatrist. "She put him up to it. I told you she is as sharp as they come."

"If it is true, it is a sign of senile dementia," her colleague muttered.

"Rubbish. The old girl's up to every trick."

Counsel for the Prosecution continued. "A remarkable theory, Sir Lorimer. 'Fanciful' would perhaps be a better description. But it does not get us any nearer to answering the question about how the jewels came to be in Sister Monica Joan's possession. Have you any theories, fanciful or otherwise, on that score?"

"No, I have not."

"No further questions, My Lord."

Sister Monica Joan had continued knitting placidly all afternoon, occasionally muttering to herself as she made notes on her knitting chart. Sir Lorimer stepped down from the witness box and she smiled at him again. The time had reached 4.30 p.m. and the judge adjourned the court for the day to reassemble at ten o'clock the following morning.

The court was crowded again on the third morning, when Sister Monica Joan was due to appear in the witness box. She was waiting in the dock, calmly knitting as before, and occasionally speaking to Sister Julienne, who was sitting beside her.

The usher entered and, before doing anything else, he went over to the nun and whispered, "When I call: 'Be upstanding for His Lordship,' would you be kind enough to stand up, madam, please?"

Sister Monica Joan smiled sweetly. "Of course I will," she said, and she stood with everyone else.

Counsel for the Prosecution opened the morning's proceedings. "I wish to call Sister Monica Joan of the Order of St Raymund Nonnatus to the witness box."

A buzz of excitement ran through the courtroom and the jury leaned forward expectantly.

Sister Monica Joan stood up. She wound up her ball of wool, stuck it on the end of the needles and placed it in her knitting bag, which she handed to Sister Julienne. "Would you make a note, dear. The next row will be row fifty-six. Slip one, knit two together, purl four, slip one, purl three, knit two together, pass slip stitch over, repeat to end."

"Yes, dear, of course I will." Sister Julienne marked the knitting card.

"Did I say purl four, slip one, purl three, knit two together, pass the slip stitch over?"

"Yes, you did, dear."

"That's wrong; it should be purl three *after* slipping the slip stitch over, not before."

"Oh yes, of course, that makes sense."

The judge leaned forward. "Have you ladies sorted out your knitting?"

"Yes, My Lord."

"Then perhaps we can start the morning's proceedings."

Sister Monica Joan made her way to the witness box. She looked completely composed; in fact she looked beautiful in her full black habit with the halo of white linen around her face. A small smile lightened her features and her eyes sparkled mischievously. Naughty Sister Monica Joan always enjoyed the limelight.

Counsel for the Prosecution opened. "The police report states that certain jewels were found in your knitting bag. Is this a true statement?"

Sister Monica Joan looked towards the jury, then to the visitors' gallery. She turned towards the judge and raised one eyebrow quizzically. Her composure held everyone captive as they waited for her reply.

Her voice, always clear, had a ringing quality. "Truth. The eternal mystery. 'What is truth?' asked Pilate. Mankind has been seeking the answer to that question for thousands of years. What would be your definition of truth, young man?"

"I am here to ask you the questions, Sister – not the other way round."

"But it is a perfectly fair question. Before we can establish the truth, we must have a definition of it."

Counsel decided to humour her: "Truth, I would say, is an accurate record of fact. Would you accept that, Sister."

"You have studied Aristotle?"

"A little," replied Counsel modestly.

"Truth. Truth is a movement of inexhaustible power, containing within itself divine truth. In the depths of space, matter is forever being formed into the heavenly bodies and transformed into the speed of light and disappears from our ken. Would you say that this is an accurate record of fact when it has disappeared from our ken?"

"I am not a scientist, Sister, but a lawyer, and I am enquiring about jewels found in your possession."

"Ah, yes, the jewels. The stars are the jewels of heaven. But are they fact? Are they truth or are they a chimera? Do we see the stars? We think we see them, but we do not; we see what they were light years ago. Would you say that the stars are an accurate record of fact, young man?"

"You see, she *is* confused," whispered the general practitioner.

"She's clever. She is deliberately trying to confuse the issue. That's what she's doing," the psychiatrist replied in hushed tones.

The judge interrupted. "Silence in court! Sister, this court is here to consider stolen jewellery. It is not here to discuss metaphysics. Please confine your answers to the matter in hand."

Sister Monica Joan turned her shapely head towards the judge. "Matter, and what is matter? Einstein says that matter is energy. Are these jewels matter? Are they energy, moving at the speed of light into cosmic forces beyond the limits of our consciousness? Are these jewels living matter, living energy, circling the earth in the full moon of April, or are they mere clods of clay, dull and lifeless, as postulated by the police?"

Although Sister Monica Joan was speaking to the judge, her

clear voice rang through the courtroom. An eloquent hand reached towards the jury, who sat spellbound although they did not understand a word she was talking about.

Counsel for the Prosecution continued. "But how did the jewels come to be in your possession, Sister?"

She turned on him angrily. "I do not know, young man. I am not a seer; I am but a humble seeker of eternal truths. These jewels, which seem to excite so much interest, have their own life, their own consciousness and their own energy force. When an atom gets excited it creates magnetic fields independent of human activity. Did they not teach you that at school, young man?"

Counsel, who was close on fifty, was beginning to look out of his depth. "No, madam, I was not taught that at school."

"Were you not taught that all matter is subject to the laws of gravity?"

Counsel refused to answer. "Sister, I am enquiring into stolen jewellery. Are you trying to say that jewels were magnetised or gravitated from jewellers in Hatton Garden into your knitting bag by their own volition?"

"I do not know. I am not a seer. Only God knows the whole truth. Questions, foolish questions all the time. You wear me out with your questions, young man. Can I not expect a little repose in my old age?"

Sister Monica Joan raised her hand to her face and tottered slightly in the dock. A gasp of anxiety was heard in the courtroom. She murmured: "May I sit down, My Lord?" and the usher ran forward with a chair. She smiled weakly. "So kind, so very kind; my poor heart." She raised her eyes appealingly to the judge and said softly, "Thank you, My Lord. Are there any more questions'?"

"No further questions," said Counsel for the Prosecution.

Sister Monica Joan had created a good impression in the witness box. Even though most of the jury did not know what she was talking about, her sincerity and conviction were compelling. Her age and frailty were appealing and their sympathy was with her. A verdict of not guilty seemed likely.

The Judge adjourned the court until 2 p.m.

Counsel for the Defence opened the afternoon's proceedings. "Are you sitting comfortably, Sister?"

"Most comfortably, thank you."

"I will try not to fatigue you with my questions."

"You are most kind."

"The jury has heard you say that you do not know how the jewels came into your possession."

"I do not."

"But were they really in your possession?"

"I possess nothing."

"Nothing?"

"No, nothing. I renounced all worldly possessions with my profession. Poverty is one of the vows of the monastic life."

"So you do not and cannot possess anything?"

"No."

"And you have never possessed the jewels in question?"

"Never."

Counsel for the Prosecution stood up. "Then what were they doing in your knitting bag?"

Counsel for the Defence was furious. "My Lord, I really must protest at this interruption, which is designed to intimidate the witness. I was coming to that point myself later, but without the bullying tactics adopted by my learned friend."

The judge allowed the protest, but nonetheless he leaned forward and said kindly, "Sister, if as a professed nun you cannot own or possess anything, can you account for the fact that a quantity of jewels were found in your knitting bag?"

"No, I cannot."

"Did you put them there?"

"I don't know."

"Well, if you did not put them there, who did?"

Sister Monica Joan looked vague and tired. "I don't know, My Lord. I suppose I must have."

"And where did they come from?"

Sister Monica Joan was crumbling fast. The day had been too long. Her sparkle and confidence were fading leaving a tired old lady who did not really know what she was saying. "I suppose they came from Hatton Garden, like everyone says they did." She leaned her forehead on her hand and sighed deeply. "I don't know why respectable elderly women do this sort of thing, but they do. Oh, they do, they do. Is it a sickness? Is it a madness? I do not know. I do not know myself."

A ripple of shocked sympathy spread through the courtroom. To incriminate oneself is sad, but for Sister Monica Joan to have done so was tragic. If a pin had dropped it would have been heard in the silent courtroom. The judge leaned back in his chair and sighed.

"'I adjourn the court for today. I will make my summing-up tomorrow. The court will reassemble at ten o'clock.

The atmosphere in the courtroom was tense the following morning. A verdict of guilty was a foregone conclusion in the minds of the jury. Could it be prison for a lady of such advanced years? Perhaps the judge would order confinement to a mental asylum. A recommendation for clemency was everyone's hope.

Sister Julienne was seated in court, her face white with shock and sorrow. On the other hand, Sister Monica Joan once more looked completely relaxed and unconcerned, knitting contentedly and smiling at people she recognised. She stood when the usher gave the order.

The judge opened the morning's proceedings. "Last evening, at seven o'clock, I was informed of new evidence which throws a different light on this case. The witness arrived in London this morning and is at present waiting outside. Call the Reverend Mother Jesu Emanuel, please, usher."

A murmur of surprise spread through the court. Sister Julienne gave a gasp and stood up when her Superior entered. The latter was a good-looking lady of about fifty with calm grey eyes. She walked purposefully to the witness box to be sworn in.

Counsel for the Defence spoke: "You are the Reverend Mother Jesu Emanuel, the Mother Superior of the Order of the Sisters of St Raymund Nonnatus?"

"I am."

"And you have been in Africa recently."

"I have been with our mission in Africa for the past year. I returned yesterday."

"Would you please tell the court what you have told me."

"On my return to our mother house in Chichester I learned that Sister Monica Joan had been accused of the theft of jewellery. I knew at once that this was a mistake. The jewels have not been stolen. The jewels belong to Sister Monica Joan."

Everyone started talking at once.

The judge ordered silence. "Please continue," he said.

"When a Sister takes her final vows, all her property is given to the order. In some orders this is irrevocable, but not so in ours. We hold the property in trust during the Sister's lifetime. If the Sister leaves the order, or has need of the property for any reason, the property reverts to her. Sister Monica Joan made her final vows in 1904. She had inherited great wealth from her mother, including a quantity of jewellery, which has been kept in the security vaults of the convent's financiers ever since. Sister Monica Joan is now a very old lady. It is the policy of our order to give special privileges to our retired Sisters, who have given a lifetime of service to our work. Knowing that Sister Monica Joan likes pretty things and that she would enjoy having her mother's jewels to play with, I gave them to her the last time I visited Nonnatus House."

"Have you any confirmation of this?"

"I have the certificate of withdrawal from the bank with me for Your Lordship's inspection."

Counsel for the Defence spoke. "The jewels have been checked against the certificate, My Lord, and they can all be accounted for."

The judge was handed the certificate, which he examined; then he said: "Did you not tell anyone about this, Reverend Mother?"

"No, My Lord, I did not, and in this respect I am entirely culpable. Sister Julienne was away on retreat at the time of my visit to Nonnatus House, or I would probably have mentioned it to her. Immediately after that, preparations were made for my visit to Africa and it slipped my mind. I am devastated that my action should have caused so much trouble. But frankly, it was not something that I regarded as important. I looked upon the jewels not as objects of monetary value but as pretty things that would give innocent happiness to a very old lady, bringing back memories of her childhood and her mother."

The Judge adjourned the court until two o'clock that afternoon to allow time for full consultation. The jeweller, Mr Samuelson, who had earlier identified the pearls and the diamond, was called, and he acknowledged that he might have been mistaken. It was agreed by all parties that if Sister Monica Joan had forgotten how she came to be in possession of the jewels, she could not be held responsible for her actions, whatever the psychiatrist might have said, and the charges of petty theft made by the costers was dropped.

After lunch the judge informed the court that the Prosecution had withdrawn all charges. There was wild cheering and hat-throwing in the public gallery.

The judge motioned to the usher to call for silence. Then he addressed the court. "I think I speak for the popular voice of this courtroom when I say how pleasing is the outcome of this case. Much needless strain and anxiety has been caused to the Sisters of St Raymund Nonnatus. However, I say to the Sisters, as I say to the police, the Prosecution, the doctors and everyone involved in this case, including the press and the wider readership beyond these walls: it is folly to jump to conclusions."

Part III

THE OLD SOLDIER

MR JOSEPH COLLETT

Sister Julienne and I left Nonnatus House and cycled towards the tenements, known as the Canada Buildings. We made our way to Alberta House, to a patient I had not met before – a man with leg ulcers that required daily dressing. Sister had told me the ulcers were severe, and warned that dressing such wounds in the patient's home was very different from doing so in a surgically equipped and sterile hospital. The man was a Mr Joseph Collett, aged over eighty, and he lived alone in one of the ground-floor flats.

We knocked at the door. There was no immediate response, but we heard movement inside. The door was opened by a very old and rather dirty man. He peered at us through thick-lensed glasses, and it was obvious from the way he was looking and trying to adjust his focus that he could not see at all well. Nonetheless, he must have recognised us, for he opened the door wide, drew himself up very straight, and bowed slightly, saying: "Mornin', Sister. I've been expecting you. Good of you to come. Who have you got with you today? Someone new?"

"This is Nurse Lee, and when I have shown her the routine, she will be looking after you."

He turned towards me, and put out a hand to touch my coat sleeve, as the partially sighted do. He couldn't quite see me, but he was obviously assessing my height and general contours, by which he would recognise me. "It's nice to have you here, young lady, and I am sure we are going to get on famous. Allow me, Sister."

He said this with old world courtesy, took her bag, and slowly walked with it to place it on the table.

"I've got the boiling water ready for you, and the flavine, and lint. I think you'll find everything's there."

Sister Julienne started unpacking her bag, and I looked around the room. The smell was none too pleasant, but I had got used to that in the tenements. The walls were a dirty beige, with wallpaper peeling off. The paint was dark brown, blistered and cracking. A small gas stove sat in one corner, by the stone sink. Next to the sink was a lavatory, which was an obvious addition to the room and not part of the original structure. The windows were so dirty that very little light could penetrate, and there were no curtains. An open doorway revealed the bedroom, with a brass bedstead. The whole area – living room, bedroom, kitchen area and lavatory – could not have been more than about fifteen to eighteen feet square, and there was no separate bathroom. It was quite adequate for an old man living alone, but I knew that many such tenement flats housed whole families. How did they manage, and stay sane?

A fire was burning merrily in the hearth and a hod of coal stood beside it. I noticed a tin bath full of coal under the sink. A very beautiful grandfather clock stood proudly against the opposite wall, next to a large wooden crate full of sticks and old newspapers. A heavy wooden table – the sort antique dealers would fight over today – filled the centre of the room, and some grimy plates and mugs were spread out on a newspaper. The room was full of old military photographs, prints and maps, and what looked like medals and trophies, yellowed with age and dirt. I concluded that Mr Collett had been a soldier.

Our patient sat down in a high wooden chair next to the fire, took his slippers off and placed his right foot on a low stool. He pulled up his trouser leg, revealing horrible blood-and-pus-soaked bandages. Sister Julienne told me to do the dressing, whilst she watched me. I knew everything had to be disposed of in the patient's house, so I placed newspapers on the wooden floor. I kneeled down and started to undo the bandages with forceps. The stench was revolting, and I felt nausea rising as I struggled to peel off the layers of bandage, which were stuck to each other with slimy fluid. I let them fall onto the newspaper, to be burned on the fire. The ulcer was the worst I had ever seen, extending upwards from the ankle for about six to eight inches. It was deep and suppurating badly. I cleaned it with saline, packed the cavities with gauze soaked in flavine, and rebandaged. Then the other leg had to be treated.

Mr Collett didn't complain whilst I was attending to his legs, but sat back sucking an old pipe with no tobacco in it, talking now and then to Sister Julienne. The grandfather clock ticked loudly, and the fire crackled and blazed. The siren of a cargo boat echoed through the room as I completed the second dressing and bandaged up the leg, with the quiet satisfaction of knowing that I had made this dignified old soldier more comfortable.

I cleaned up, saw that everything was burned, packed my bag, and Sister and I prepared to leave.

"Won't you stay for a cup of tea, Sister?" he asked. "It won't take me a minute."

"No, but thank you; we have other work to do."

I thought he looked crestfallen, but he said quickly, "Then I won't keep you, marm."

This old-fashioned use of the royal "marm" surprised me, but strangely it didn't sound out of place.

"Nurse Lee will come to you each morning from now on."

He laid his pipe on the mantelpiece and stood up. He was very tall, more than six feet, and stood very straight. He walked slowly over to the door and opened it for us, then bowed again slightly as we left.

Out in the courtyard the air smelled sweet and fresh. A horse-drawn coal cart entered, and a huge man jumped out, lifting a tiny child of about two or three onto the cobbles. The man strode through the courtyard calling in a distinctive and penetrating yodel: "Co-al, co-al," the second syllables rising a perfect fifth from the first. The long strides of the man took him swiftly through the court and the little boy, running as fast as he could to keep up, tumbled and fell. As he picked himself up, he lifted his fluffy blond head, and in a tiny, piping voice called out: "Co-al, co-al." A perfect fifth!

Women came out of many doors and hailed the coal man, who carried a bag, or half a bag, up the stone steps to the balcony where it was required. No one had a real bunker or space to store coal, so small amounts of half a hundredweight had to be bought frequently. Coal fires were to become obsolete due to the 1960s Clean Air legislation, but in the middle fifties they were the only form of heating for most people.

Inevitably, if you see a person daily in his own home over several months, you will cease to regard him as a patient and come to know him as a person. Treating Mr Collett's leg ulcers took about half an hour, during which time we talked and, as old people can always remember the distant past more easily than they can remember yesterday, we talked about his early life.

Mr Collett was not a typical Cockney in appearance, speech or manner. He was much taller than average, and had a slow, thoughtful way about him. His quiet dignity and formal way of speaking commanded respect and I never presumed to call him 'Joe'. He was a Londoner, first generation, and spoke with a London accent, but it was not heavy Cockney, typified by an idiosyncratic use of grammar and idiom. He told me his parents were country people from Sussex who had been tenant farmers. The family had been displaced by the Enclosure Acts of the nineteenth century and, unable to sustain themselves even at a subsistence level, they had drifted towards the city in search of work. They had settled in Croydon, where Mr Collett had been born in the 1870s, the oldest of eight children. His father had been a painter and decorator, and an unskilled builder's labourer. He was often out of work, because in the nineteenth century painting was a trade at the mercy of the weather. Paints had no chemical quick-drying components in them and would take about four days to dry, so in wet weather no painting could be done externally, and the men were laid off. The building trade was in the same position, because cement would not dry in less than three days.

"But my father was a good man," said Mr Collett. "He would not see his wife and children go without. There was always stone-breaking to be done for road-building and railway construction, and he would go to the yards and break stones all day. He would come home at night wet through, aching all over, with a few pence in his pocket that he had earned, and my mother would rub his back and chest with liniment and apply flannel soaked in hot mustard water to keep out the cold. He was a good man. He wouldn't go to the pub and drink away his money, like many we came to see."

Mr Collett shook his head in disapproval, and cut off a chunk of tobacco, which he proceeded to shred finely in the palm of his gnarled hand and stuff into a leather pouch, in which he kept a piece of apple peel "to keep the tobacco moist", he told me. I was fascinated by this tobacco, called shag or twist, which was sold in lengths. Shag was the tobacco my grandfather smoked, and the smell of it filled me with happy childhood memories. Tobacconists kept long coils of it, perhaps two or three feet long, like a curled, black sausage, and a few inches would be sawn off and sold to a customer. I thought the smell was lovely as Mr Collett shredded it in his hand (or perhaps it was just an improvement on the usual fusty smell of the room), and I encouraged him to cut it up and smoke the stuff, which produced clouds of thick, grey smoke when a match was applied. Incidentally, shag was the same tobacco that men often chewed. You would see a lot of old men chewing away with toothless gums, sucking the last drachm of juice from the tobacco, after which they would spit it out.

Mr Collett always asked me to join him in a cup of tea, and I always refused, for two reasons: I had never been able to drink strong tea, the unvarying brew of East Londoners; but, more importantly, the thought of drinking anything from the filthy mugs that I saw on the table made me feel sick. Neither of these reasons could I tell him, so I always said that I was too busy. He accepted this, but he always looked sad, and once he just nodded his head quietly and swallowed hard, as though there was a lump in his throat. I could see him, of course, better than he could see me, and if he had known that I was studying his face, trying to read his thoughts, he would have stood up quickly and turned away; but I was packing up my bag and watching him at the same time. There was a patient weariness and sorrow written all over his strong features, which made me think he was lonely, and that my visit was the bright spot of his day. I didn't like to leave him, even though it was always a relief to quit the all-pervading smell of the place.

Then I had a brilliant idea. Boiling water poured into those filthy mugs would melt the grease and accumulated dirt, which would then float to the top. If I asked for a cold drink, the dirt would remain stuck to the sides of the mug. It was foolproof. So I said that I didn't like hot drinks, but would enjoy something cold. I was thinking of orange juice.

His face burst into smiles, like the sun coming out on a grey day. "That's what you shall have, my maiden."

He stood up, and went to a small cupboard near the sink. He fumbled about, feeling for the things that he could not see clearly, and came out with two hand-cut crystal glasses and a bottle of sherry.

"Oh no, no," I protested, "I can't drink alcohol, not when I'm on duty. I meant orange squash, or something."

His face fell. The sun went behind the clouds. I realised how much it meant to him, and how little it meant to me. The scales are unevenly balanced, I thought. I laughed and said: "All right, I'll just have half a glass. But don't you dare tell the Sisters, or I shall get the sack. No nurse is ever allowed to drink on duty."

I sat down on the wooden kitchen chair by the big mahogany table, and we drank a glass of sherry together, sharing the secret of my disobeying orders. The light was dim, because of the dirty windows, but the fire glowed red, transforming the squalor into cosiness. Mr Collett's eyes gleamed with pleasure, and I had the impression that he was so happy he could hardly speak. Two or three times he dabbed his eyes with a filthy old handkerchief, and muttered something about having a cold in the eye.

That moment was significant in my life, because I understood that he had wanted to give me something, but had not known how. A cup of tea was all he could think of. My refusal had been a rebuff. By joining him in a clandestine glass of sherry, we had shared more than just the drink: we had shared a conspiracy of silence. It obviously meant more to him than I could have imagined, and I felt all my youthful pride and arrogance crumbling to dust beside his humble, unaffected joy in my company.

That day was the beginning of a friendship that was to last until his death.

As I left and stepped out into the court, a woman with a shopping basket was entering the flat next to Mr Collett's. She was old, but brisk and spritely. She looked up at me, challenge written all over her features.

"You seein' vat dirty old man agen – phew!" She spat out the sound, with a hiss.

"Nasty old bugger, I says. I'm tellin' yer, you Sisters oughta have somefink better to do than run around after him all the time. Phew!"

She spat on the cobbles again.

"Him, who is he, any road up? He's not nobody, he's not. He's not one of us, he ain't. Where's he come from? – that's what I wants 'a know. And look at 'ow he keeps 'is place. Filthy. It's disgustin', I says. He ain't not got no right 'a be livin' there among God-fearing folks as likes to keep themselves respeckable."

She nodded her head emphatically. The curlers under her scarf stuck out at angles, making her look particularly vicious. She smacked her gums together, and repeated "disgustin'" as though she were stating the ultimate in moral depravity, and disappeared through her doorway before I could say a word.

I was seething with fury. What right had this woman to speak to me, or anyone else, in that way about her neighbour? I felt deeply protective of Mr Collett, as obviously she would not hesitate to spread such venom about him to anyone who cared to listen. It was insufferable. He was dirty, admittedly, but no worse than many. And anyway, he was partially sighted. The sherry had left me with a warm glow inside, and this gratuitous attack on a gentle old man whom I respected sent my blood racing. No wonder he was lonely, if he had this woman as a neighbour.

I mentioned the incident over lunch at Nonnatus House, with great indignation.

Sister Julienne tried to calm me down. "We meet a lot of that sort of thing among the older people of Poplar. They are deeply suspicious of anyone from the next area of the Docklands, even the next street, sometimes. If we believed everything they tell us, we would believe everyone to be a murderer and villain, or a wife-beater and granny-basher. I cannot be quite sure, but I believe Mr Collett had two sons who died in the First World War. If this is the case, our deepest sympathy is due to him." She smiled at me quietly, and said no more.

The next day, a bottle of orange juice was standing on Mr Collett's table. Bless him, I thought, he must have made a special shopping trip on my account. I wanted to ask him about his sons, but decided it would be better not to. He could tell me if he so wished. I asked him to tell me more about his early life in Croydon, and about his family.

"It was a good life for children. Back then Croydon was a small place in the countryside. There were fields and farmhouses, and streams where the children played. We were poor, but not as poor as many, and my mother was always a good manager. She could make a meal out of a bone, she could, and my father kept an allotment, so we always had fresh vegetables. But it all came to a tragic end." He paused, cut off another chunk of tobacco, and filled his pipe.

I bandaged up his first leg, and started the second. "What happened?" I asked.

"My father died. The scaffolding on the building where he was working collapsed. Five men were killed. It was due to slipshod workmanship on the part of the scaffold-builders. There was no compensation for the wives and children of the dead men. My mother could not pay the rent, and we had to get out of the house. It was a nice house," he added, reflectively, and sucked his pipe. Clouds of smoke filled the room.

"I don't rightly remember where we moved to, but it was smaller and cheaper. We kept on moving to smaller and smaller places. I was thirteen, and the eldest of the children. I left school at once, and tried to get work, but in 1890 there was no work." He told me how he had tramped for miles trying to find anything: on the land, on building sites, with horses, on the railways. But there was nothing. "The only job I could get was in the yard where my father used to break stones in the bad weather. But it was piecework, and I wasn't really old enough or strong enough to break the granite boulders. I hardly got a thing for a day's hard labour. I remember my mother cried when she saw me at the end of the day. She said, 'You are not going to do this, my son. I'm not going to have you die as well.' The men were rough, you know, really rough, and they were all swinging fifteen-pound sledgehammers. Most of them were drunk. You can imagine the accident if a lad of thirteen had been hit instead of a stone."

I undid the second bandage. "So what did the family do?" I asked.

"We came up to London. I don't know why; perhaps my mother was told there was more chance of work for her, or for me. We came here, to Alberta Buildings. I can still see the old flat from here – that one on the fifth floor, second from the end, by the stairway. It was just one room, like this one, but with no water or lavatory, of course. I think there was gaslight, when we could afford to use it. It was cheap, but even at three-and-sixpence a week my mother had to work day and night to keep a roof over our heads. From the day my father died, my mother never stopped working." With the childhood memories flooding back to him, Mr Collett described how his mother did cleaning by day, portering, and took in washing and ironing. There were good wash-houses at Alberta Buildings in those days, he said. On top of that she took in mending for the second-hand-clothes dealers, did umbrella stitching in the winter and parasol-making in summer.

He went on to tell me that she had applied to the Poor Board for relief, but was told she was not of the Parish, and to go back where she came from. As a special concession, the chairman had offered to take three of her children, saying that she would then be relieved of the burden of having to feed them, and would have only five children left. The three children would be put in the workhouse. When his mother refused, they had called her ungrateful and improvident, and told her that she need not trouble herself to come back to them, because the offer would not be repeated. They sent her away, saying she would have to manage as best she could.

"She did manage, but I don't know how. She kept a roof over our heads, and provided enough food to keep us from starving. But we seldom had a fire, even in the coldest weather. We never had shoes, and our clothes were thin, and mostly in rags. All the families around us were just as poor, and it was made far worse by drunkenness. Most of the men drank, and that meant a lot of violence in some of the homes. Many women were in such despair they drowned themselves. Every week the cry would go up: 'A body in the Cuts,' and it was always a woman. You can imagine how the children felt . . . always scared their mother might be next . . ."

He sat thinking for a while, puffing his pipe, then chuckled. "It's a funny thing, you know, but children can accept almost anything when they feel loved and secure. In spite of being cold and hungry, my brothers and sisters were always laughing, always playing out in the court, always inventing new games. I never heard any of them complain. But I was different. I was thirteen when my father died; I remembered the old life and hated our new one. I hated seeing my dear mother working eighteen or twenty hours a day for a pittance. She would sit late into the night, sewing shirts by candlelight, in a freezing room, with no food inside her, all for sixpence. I resented the injustice of it. Of course, I was out each day looking for work, but times were hard and the best I could find were odd jobs, like holding a horse, or running errands, or sweeping out a yard.

"I tried to get work in the docks. You would think there was plenty of work in London's Docklands, wouldn't you? Well, there was, but there were thousands and thousands of men after the same work. I reckon there were ten men for every job – no chance for a young boy like me."

In those days such jobs as there were went mostly to the boys whose fathers and grandfathers had been dockers, Mr Collett explained. There were frightening scenes at the dock gates: hundreds of half-starved labourers, clad in rags, crazed and desperate, fighting for the chance of a few hours' work. Perhaps fifty would be taken on for the day while five hundred would be turned away to idle their time away in the streets. No wonder men were violent.

"At low tide there was always scavenging to be done in the mud. Some lads found things of value, but I never did. The best thing I found was bits of coal, washed off the barges, and driftwood. At least that made a fire for the evening.

"The worst thing was the way the gentry was so suspicious all the time. I was looking for honest work, but I was called "ragamuffin", "varmin", "lout", "thieving dog". Just because I was thin and ill-clothed and looked hungry, they assumed I was a thief."

Mr Collett's mouth tightened. His proud face stiffened at the memory of the insults. I had finished his second leg and sat back on my heels looking up at him, thinking that the accumulated experience of old age was much more interesting than the chatter of the young.

I had a glass of orange juice, whilst he drank a cup of tea. It was a good compromise, because he gave me a glass, which was dusty, but not filthy.

I was enjoying his company and conversation and didn't want to leave him, as he seemed so happy. On impulse I said: "I must go now, but it's my evening off tonight. Can I come and have a glass of sherry with you, and you can continue your stories?"

The joy on his face answered my question. "Can you come, my maiden? Can you come? I'll say you can come, and a thousand times welcome."

YOUNG JOE

Cycling back to Nonnatus House, I had misgivings about my quixotic suggestion of returning that evening. Medical people are warned about the difficulties that can develop when friendships with patients are formed. It is not something that is forbidden, but it is discouraged, and for very good reasons. So, after lunch, I spoke to Sister Julienne in private. She didn't look disapproving, or even particularly concerned.

"Well, having said you will go this evening, you cannot possibly fail him. That would be needlessly cruel. I think he is a lonely old gentleman and your visit will give him pleasure. Enjoy yourself. He is a very interesting old man, I have found."

With Sister Julienne's blessing, my misgivings vanished, and I cycled round to Alberta Buildings at about 8 p.m. with a light heart.

Mr Collett was so obviously overjoyed to see me that he seemed nervous. He had gone to some trouble, and put on a clean shirt and waistcoat and a pair of highly polished boots. Like all old soldiers, he had never got out of the habit of buffing and rubbing his boots to perfection and the whole room smelled strongly of boot polish. The dirty plates and mugs and newspapers had been removed from the table, and two fine crystal glasses and half a bottle of sherry had been put out in readiness. The fire burned brightly, casting flickering shadows over the dingy walls.

He said, "I was so afraid you wouldn't come, but here you are."

He walked slowly and carefully over to his chair. "It's good to have you here. Sit down. It's so nice to see you."

I was overwhelmed and a bit embarrassed by all this, and sat down awkwardly, not knowing quite what to say.

"You've come. You are here," he repeated. "Ah, this is so lovely." Obviously I had to say something. "Yes, I've come. Of course I have. I'm not going to run away, so let's have a glass of sherry, and we can talk about old times."

He laughed with delight, went over to the table and lifted the bottle. He felt around for the glasses and I moved to help him, but he said, "No, no, I can do it. I have to all the time, you know."

He poured out two glasses. His hands shook a little and he spilled a considerable quantity on the table, of which he was unaware. I realised that spilled food and liquid would probably account for much of the smell in the room. The rest was likely to be an uncleaned lavatory, unwashed clothes and the bugs that infested Alberta Buildings. I wondered if he had a home help.

But I wasn't going to think about that sort of thing. If he was unaware of, and quite content with his dirt, why should I criticise? Sister Julienne had told me to enjoy myself, and that I was going to do.

I took a sip of the sherry, and said, "Lovely. This is a cosy room, and you know how to make a nice fire. You were telling me about your childhood. I'd love to hear more."

He settled down comfortably in his wooden chair, and put his feet on the stool (ulcerated legs have to be kept raised as much as possible). He pulled out his shag and his penknife, and started cutting it up. I inhaled a sniff of the strong tobacco. He took a sip of his sherry.

"This is luxury. When I was young I would never have dreamed of such luxury. A fire every day! A warm bed at night! Enough food to eat . . . A welfare state that pays my rent because I am too old to work, and pays me a pension of ten shillings and sixpence a week, to buy all that I need, including a bottle of sherry when I want it. This is luxury my poor, dear mother never knew in all her life."

He was cutting up his shag slowly and carefully, holding it in the palm of his left hand and drawing the knife downwards. It looked alarming, as though he was going to cut his hand, because the tobacco was clearly tough and needed a lot of pressure. But from long practice he knew just when to ease the pressure, and he never cut himself. He worked by feel, not by sight. He slowly unravelled strands of the villainous-looking stuff with which he filled the bowl of his pipe. Next, he took a wooden spill, about eight inches long, from a pot at his side and stuck it into the fire. It burned up brightly, the flame leaping high into the air. He brought it towards him, sucking hard on the pipe, and the flame dipped downwards into the tobacco. He sucked and puffed contentedly, and smoke filled the air. Then he blew the flame out, and returned the half-burned spill to the pot, in much the same way that my grandfather used to do.

"Sheer luxury," he said, smiling contentedly. "I was telling you about our first years in Poplar, after my father died; how my poor mother had to work day and night; and how I couldn't find work, except odd jobs, to help her. Well, there was one job I got that was good fun for a lad who's looking for adventure.

"I was down the Blackwall Steps, waiting for the tide to go out, so that I could go scavenging. A man came along and said to me: 'Here, boy, can you cook a stew?'

"'Yes, sir,' I said (I would have said 'yes' to anything).

"' Can you skin a rabbit?'

"'Yes, sir.'

"'Bone a fish?'

"'Yessir.'

"'Make tea and cocoa?'

"'Yessir.

"'Clean a wick and fill a lamp?'

"'Yessir.'

"'You're the boy I want. My cabin boy's done a bunk. Can you sail today?'

"'Anywhere, sir.'

"'Be here at high tide. The *British Lion*'s the barge you want. A florin a week all found.'

"It was all so quick I hadn't time to draw breath. I raced back to Alberta Buildings, round to the washhouse where my mother was toiling away, and told her I had been hired as cabin boy on a Thames barge. My mother didn't look as thrilled as I had expected. In fact, she was dead against it. We had words, and I shouted at her: 'Look, I'm off, whatever you say, and I'll come back a rich man. You'll see.'

"So I ran back to the Steps, no extra clothes, nothing like that. Sure enough, at high tide, the *British Lion* came along, and I jumped aboard. It was the most wonderful time I had in my life, and I reckon every boy's dream. I was on the river for six months. The barge carried flints, coal, wood, bricks, sand, slates – anything. We would take a load of coal down to Kent, and pick up a cargo of bricks to bring back to Limehouse. In those days hundreds of trading vessels plied the river, huge ocean-going cargo boats down to one-man skiffs. You could always tell a barge by the red sail, and often the sail and the cabin were all that could be seen. The barges were so low that, with a full load, the whole deck would be under water. It's true."

He heard my incredulous gasp and roared with laughter, and sucked his pipe.

"People would stare from the banks, because honestly, all they could see was a red sail, and men paddling about knee-deep in water, with apparently nothing beneath them.

"I was as happy as a boy could be," he continued with another laugh. "I made the stews, trimmed the lamps, learned boat-handling, and didn't mind I wasn't paid. The skipper always said he would pay me after the next trip. After a bit, the mate whispered to me, 'That bloody monkey's not goin' 'a pay you. He never does. All the cabin boys do a bunk in the end.'

"That was a shock to me, that was. I had been counting up the florins in my mind, and had reckoned on one pound after working ten weeks, and two pounds after twenty weeks. I thought I was rich – except that I hadn't got the money. So I asked the skipper and he said, 'After the next trip, lad. When I'm in funds.'

"Well, the next trip came and went, and no money. Three or four more trips – no money. I got cross and resentful and told him if he didn't pay me, I'd do a bunk. He just smiled pleasantly, and said, 'After the next trip, Joe, the next trip, trust me.'

"Well, of course, I knew he wouldn't pay me, and the next time we reached Limehouse, I left the barge and didn't go back."

He paused, and sucked on his pipe, but it had gone out, so he scratched around in the bowl with a sharp implement that he pulled from his penknife, and lit another spill from the fire. The flame leaped upwards again, narrowly missing his eyebrows. I thought with alarm that he might one day set himself, and the whole building, on fire. His eyesight was not good, and his hands shook. I wondered how many old men in a similar state of infirmity were playing with fire in Alberta Buildings.

"If I had known what I was doing, I don't think I would have left the barge, pay or no pay. You see, I was happy and busy, which is what a boy needs. The skipper and his mate were nice men. We got on all right. I had enough food to eat, and a bunk to sleep on. What more can you ask in life? What does money matter? The trouble was, the skipper had hired me for a florin a week, so I was expecting it. If he'd asked me in the first place to join him to learn boatmanship and navigation, with no pay while I was learning, I would have accepted, and my mother would have been pleased. But he lied to me, and that was his mistake, and my misfortune."

Joe had left, fully expecting to find a similar job on another barge. But there were no jobs. The other barges supported just a skipper and a mate, but no cabin boy because the skippers could not afford to pay a boy. The *British Lion* only had the luxury of a boy because he was never paid. Joe hung around the water's edge and haunted the wharfs and jetties every day, begging to be taken on, but in vain.

After six months on the river, he was tanned and strong from long hours of work in the fresh air. He had trapped rabbits and caught fish, or pinched carrots and turnips from fields at the water's edge. He had grown taller and filled out, with good food inside him. The dense population of Poplar, the stuffy buildings and crowded streets suffocated him, and the lack of fresh air and sunlight nearly drove him to despair. Food was scarce, and he grew pale and thin again. On the barge, he had held himself upright, and his eyes had sparkled with the pride of his position as cabin boy. Returning to the streets of Poplar, he slouched and dragged his feet, his eyes dull and downcast. Worst of all was his state of mind as it dawned upon him that he was one of the myriad flotsam drifting around the Docklands, unwashed, underfed, ill-clothed, barely educated, with no realistic hope of anything better. He was fifteen.

Of all the jobs that a boy could aspire to, casual dock labour was one of the least viable and most depressing. Joe could, and no doubt should, have looked further afield, but after a taste of life on the river and the thrill of handling cargo, he saw himself as a river man. Most days, he would linger round the dock gates with a crowd of seedy, hungry, ignorant men, waiting for the chance of a job. Violence could explode at any time.

His poor mother worried about him, naturally. It had been a joy to see him fit, taller, stronger, after six months on the barge. When she learned that he had been cheated of his pay, she was justifiably furious. But there was nothing anyone could do, so she wisely said little and was thankful to have her son back, looking so well. But as the months passed, and she saw the degrading effects of poverty and unemployment biting deep, her worries increased. Furthermore, she now had to feed him. She earned her money mainly from washing. The two eldest girls had left school and worked in a shirt-making factory. Joe knew that he was fed on sweated female labour, and his proud young heart rebelled at the knowledge. At thirteen he had seen himself taking his father's role and supporting the family. Now, two years later, he had to acknowledge not only that had he provided nothing but also that he was a burden on the female wage-earners.

"It was when I was at my lowest that I met the recruiting

sergeant," he said. "But what time is it? I've been sitting here, talking nineteen to the dozen, and you, bless your heart, listening, as though an old boy rambling on is interesting to you. You mustn't mind me. I don't often get the chance to talk. I hope I haven't bored you."

At that moment the grandfather clock, solemn and stately, sounded the quarter hour.

"What time is that? Quarter past ten?"

"No. Quarter past eleven."

"Eleven! It can't be. Oh, how time flies when you are enjoying yourself. I've talked far too much, and you must go, my maid. You've got a day's work to do tomorrow, and you need your beauty sleep."

I had to assure him that he hadn't talked too much, that he couldn't possibly be a bore, that I was fascinated by his story and that I hadn't enjoyed myself so much in ages. Nonetheless, I had to go, but would certainly have another sherry with him, for the pleasure of his company, and in anticipation of hearing about the recruiting sergeant.

As I stood up, I glanced above the fireplace. I was surprised to see that a large area of the chimney breast was black – about two feet in an irregular circular shape. In addition, it seemed to be moving slightly, or shimmering, like oil on a damp surface. I had not noticed this earlier, and curiosity compelled me to take a couple of steps nearer to see what it was.

I saw, and I recoiled with horror, my hand over my mouth to prevent a scream escaping. The moving mass was thousands of bugs. I had heard that Alberta Buildings were infested with house bugs, but had not seen them before. They were behind the plaster of the walls and ceilings, where they crept along, infesting every level and every flat. They came out at night, attracted by the heat, and it was impossible to get rid of them. Only with the demolition of the Canada Buildings, a few years later, were the bugs destroyed.

I stood there, rooted to the spot, my eyes darting around me to other areas of the room, feeling these vile creatures were everywhere. I imagined I was itching. My mind flitted to a horrible incident during my training when an old gypsy woman had been admitted to the ward on which I worked. She was gnarled and weather-beaten, and her long grey-black hair was matted and unwashed. On the third morning after her admission, the white pillow was entirely black, and we found it to be literally covered with fleas. Thousands of them had hatched from the eggs in her hair, due to the warmth of the hospital ward. I was one of the young nurses who was told to clean her up. She was aggressively resistant, and the fleas were hopping everywhere. It took days to get rid of them, and to rid ourselves of fleas. No wonder I began itching all over when I saw the bugs!

Mr Collett could see neither the bugs on the wall nor the expression on my face, which was just as well. He rose, smiling, and held out his hand to say goodbye. With great difficulty I controlled myself and said goodbye, with renewed thanks for a lovely evening.

Outside, I shuddered, as much from shock as from the cold air after the warm room. I got on my bike and rode back to Nonnatus House. A hot bath was the only thing on my mind.

THE RECRUITING SERGEANT

Bugs crept and crawled through my dreams during half the night and seriously disturbed my sleep. I dreamed of a huge scaly creature that got bigger and bigger. It was poised to jump on me. It opened its horrible jaws and let out a ferocious "Aaaarrrgh". I awoke with a scream. It was the alarm clock. Shaken and trembling, I looked fearfully around the walls. No bugs. I pulled back the curtains and examined the whole room. None. "I can't go back there," I thought, "it's too horrible."

At breakfast, pale and heavy-eyed, I picked at my cornflakes in the big kitchen where we ate our breakfast at the large pine table.

"What the hell's the matter with you?" said Trixie, sharply. "I thought you had been to see an old man of nearly eighty last night. Or did we get it wrong? Is he nearly eighteen?"

"Oh shut up, you cynical cat," I muttered crossly, and told the girls about the bugs. They gasped with horror and Trixie, being the most affected, threatened to strangle me if I said another word. Cynthia gazed at me in sympathy, and Chummy said: "Great Jehosaphat! How perfectly ghastly. What did you do, actually?"

A suppressed sound came from somewhere in the region of the boiler. It was a kind of gurgling, a spluttering, like a valve leaking. We had forgotten Fred, the boiler man and odd-job man for the convent, who was crouched on the floor among the ashes. The splutterings became louder and more frequent, ending in a long-drawn-out wheeze. I could see that Fred understood and sympathised with my experience. But did he? He took a deep breath, threw back his head, and bellowed with laughter. His eyes watered. He coughed, and the fag shot off his lower lip to a distance of three or four feet. His skinny body fell forward onto his knees, and he shook with laughter. He took a grimy handkerchief from his pocket, wiped his eyes and blew his nose.

"You girls'll be the death of me, you will. Cor bli'! I'll shi' me breeks if you goes on like vis. You wai' till I tells ve ol' girl. She'll pee 'er drawers, she will. Likes a good laugh, she do, bu' can never 'old 'er water, poor soul."

I was deeply offended. This was not a suitable reaction to my experience.

Fred saw my expression, and went off into another paroxysm of wheezing and coughing. "Who' a lo' o' fuss abou' a few bugs!" he exclaimed when he could speak.

"There weren't a few, there were thousands," I said indignantly.

"Great Jehosaphat! How perfectly *ghastly*. Tell me, what did you do, actually?" he said wickedly, mimicking Chummy's plummy accent. She coloured deeply, and looked uncomfortable. Most of the Cockneys made fun of Chummy's accent, but Fred had not done so before. She was hurt, and I was cross with Fred on her account.

"I didn't do anything," I said sharply. "It's none of your business anyway, and I assure you it was perfectly ghastly, so there."

He curled up again in another paroxysm of laughter. "All righ', all righ', Miss Perfic'ly Ghastly, keep yer wig on, but don' ask me 'a git worked up. I've seen them bugs too offen 'a gi' excited."

At that moment the Sisters entered the kitchen, and wanted to know what was going on. I gave a graphic account, dwelling on the vast numbers of bugs, and my sleepless night, perhaps just exaggerating a little.

If I had expected cries of sympathy and horror, I was to be disappointed.

Sister Evangelina humphed. "Well there are bugs in all the tenements and in many of the houses. I'm surprised you haven't seen them before. Don't make a fuss. They won't hurt you."

Sister Bernadette added, "I was delivering a baby one night, by gaslight. I looked up and the gas mantle, which was fixed to the wall, had a circle of black around it, just as you have described. This was on the wall over the woman's bed!

Sister Julienne, who had kept her hand firmly over her mouth, to prevent herself from laughing, I suspected, especially after Fred winked at her, said: "It's a bit of a shock to us all, when we first see them. You have to understand that they live in buildings, and do not infest human beings. The real danger is that they are suspected of carrying typhoid, but as there has not been an outbreak of typhoid since the nineteen-thirties, I think you are quite safe. As for your never going back there, I'm afraid that is out of the question. You are going back this morning, to treat Mr Collett's legs." With that she left the kitchen to start her morning's work.

I dug my nails into the palm of my hand and clenched my teeth. I had hoped to be relieved of treating Mr Collett. If he had been told that another nurse would be taking my place, he would have had to accept it, and not see me again. What could I do? Nothing. But Sister Julienne was as firm as she was saintly and I had no choice but to go back. I realised I would have to take a grip of myself.

Cynthia whispered to me, "Come on. Let's go to the clinical room, away from Fred."

Her soft voice was reassuring, but her first words unexpected. "Now come off it. It isn't like you to get so worked up. If bugs are in all the tenements, we must work with them all the time, only we don't see them. Out of sight, out of mind. Now forget about it. You will probably never see them again."

I knew she was right. Her slow, gentle grin put everything into perspective, and we laughed together as we got our bikes out and pumped up the tyres. District work tends to blow the cobwebs away.

Mr Collett was smiling and happy when he opened the door. "Welcome, my lassie, and I hope you had a good night's sleep. Yesterday evening was the happiest time I've had for ages."

I didn't tell him that I had been awake half the night, but

wondered what his thoughts would have been if I had never come back. He would have suspected something, and supposed that he was to blame. I didn't like to think of the hurt he would have suffered.

As I undid the bandage, I remarked: "These ulcers are improving – why did you not have regular treatment before?"

"Well, I didn't like to bother anyone. I've had them for years, and always bandaged them myself. I had to see the doctor about my eyes, and he saw I was limping a bit and asked to see my legs. Then he arranged for you Sisters to come. I didn't ask for treatment. I never thought they were bad enough."

They were the worst leg ulcers I had seen, and he didn't think they were bad enough to justify a nurse's treatment! I asked him how they had started.

"It was gun wounds during the war. They healed up all right, but there was always a weakness. As I got older, little patches started, and then spread. But I can't grumble. My legs have been good to me most of my life. You expect these little things as you get old."

Little things, I thought, I wouldn't call these ulcers "little"!

The mention of gun wounds made me think of the recruiting sergeant, who had been driven from my mind by the bugs. "Last night, before I left, you said you would tell me how you met the recruiting sergeant."

He settled back comfortably in his big wooden chair. That morning he began a story that he continued in subsequent visits, often over sherry in the evening.

"Well, I was fifteen, going on sixteen, and I reckon if I hadn't met him, it would have been a life of crime for me. There was no work, and I'd met a lad who was into everything. He always seemed to have money. He was younger than me, but quicker and smarter. We palled up together. I'm not going to tell you what we did, because I'm not proud of it, but one day he suggested going up the West End, where the pickings would be better. I'd never been up West before. I remember feeling dazzled by the great buildings, the fine open streets, all the carriages, and ladies and gentlemen in their fine clothes. We went to Trafalgar Square and hung around. My eyes were popping out, especially at the sight of the soldiers in their crimson jackets and black trousers. One of them came over to where we were standing by a fountain. I was so flattered; I couldn't believe he wanted to talk to us."

He chuckled and blew a cloud of smoke across the room.

"I thought it was a special honour. No one had told me they were at it every day, on the look out for lads like me.

"'Nah then, nah then, my fine young man' (he was talking to me, not to my mate), 'aint a fine young man like you got nothing to do on a day like this?'

"I must have shrugged and grinned sheepishly.

"'Well then, did you ever see a soldier with nothing to do?'

"I hadn't, but then I had never seen soldiers before, and I was struck dumb with the honour of having this splendid figure of a man single me out for conversation.

"Then he asked me what I'd had for breakfast.

"Nothing," I said.

"'Nothing!' he roared, 'nothing! I've never heard nothing like it. Did you say *nothing*?'

"I nodded.

"'No wonder you're looking a bit skinny, begging your pardon for the liberty, squire, but one can't help noticing these things. Look at me, now.'

"He patted a well-filled stomach with appreciation.

"'Bacon and liver, and brawn and kidneys, with fresh farm eggs and field mushrooms. As much bread-and-dripping as a man can eat, with beer if your taste runs to beer at breakfast, or tea and coffee, with fresh cream and sugar from Barbados. That's the sort of breakfast a man needs to line his stomach for the day. And did you tell me you had *nothing*? That is unbelievable. *Unbelievable.*'

"He shook his head as though he honestly had never heard anything like it before.

"'Well now, young man, you come along with me. A special friend of mine runs an alehouse over there. As a great favour to me, I'm sure he can find you something to fill your stomach with. He's got a kind heart, he has, and when I tells him that my friend – if I can make so bold as to call you my friend – has had no breakfast, it will fair melt his tender old heart, it will . . . No, not you,' he said to my mate, who had edged forward at the mention of breakfast. He put his hand on my shoulder and led me to the alehouse.

"It was dark and smoky inside and, after the sunlight, I couldn't see anything, but the soldier led me to a table and sat me down.

"'Bill,' he roared, 'Bill. Does a man have to wait all day for a pint of porter? Look lively, man.'

"The fat, well-fed figure of the landlord emerged from the gloom.

"'A pint of your best for me, and for my friend – er – why, bless my soul, can you believe it, I don't even know your name. I've felt so comfortable with you, like I've known you all my life, but I don't even know your name.'

"I'm Joe Collett.

"'Joe! What a coincidence. My young brother's called Joe. And a tall, handsome young man he is, just like you. Oh, what a lad he is, my brother Joe. Such larks! Remember the larks we've had in here with Joe, eh, Bill? Those were the days. My young brother Joe joined the Dragoons, and now he's a commanding officer, with a servant and a carriage, and as much money as he knows how to spend. But I was forgetting. Now, Bill, my old mate, my young friend Joe has had a bit of a night of it, and has unfortunately missed his breakfast.'

"The landlord sounded astonished.

"'Missed his breakfuss? A man can't get through the day without a good breakfuss 'a warm him. That's terrible, that is.' He patted his large belly, and looked at me with a sympathetic face.

"The sergeant winked suggestively. 'There! I knew as how

you'd see the gravity of the sitivation, Bill. I says to young Joe over by the fountain there, I'll take you over to my mate Bill, I said, and he'll see you right. Now what have you got out the back there you've got a bit of spare of, that would satisfy young Joe? Not nothing too flash, like, because he ain't got much money on him at present.'

"I was alarmed. I hadn't got *any* money. But before I could speak, the landlord said, 'Call it on the 'ouse, sarj, on the 'ouse. It's an honour to entertain a Guardsman any time. And any friend of yours is a friend of mine. Now, young sir, would tripe and faggots, and a good chunk of last night's pease pudding fried up crispy-like, suit you?'

"I couldn't believe my luck. It sounded like a meal fit for a king.

"'Oh, an' do you like bread-and-drippin', young sir?'

"I loved bread and dripping!

"The meal arrived, and it was enough for two kings. I just ate and ate. The sergeant didn't say anything. He just smoked his pipe and drank his porter, and looked out of the window at the pigeons squabbling on the window sill.

"When I had finished, he said, 'You were hungry, squire.'

"I nodded, and thanked him warmly.

"'Don't thank me, lad. You heard what the landlord said: it's an honour to entertain a Guardsman. We gets that all the time, we do. We gets used to it. Treated like royalty, we are, wherever we go. No one can do enough for us. Did you ever see a soldier go hungry? Course not.'

"He puffed his pipe, and called for another pint of porter, saying, confidentially, 'Between ourselves, the ale in this house is real special. Old Bill brews it himself. If you are a konosser of good ales, young squire – and I am sure you are – I don't think you will be disappointed. Unless, of course, you prefer coffee after breakfast.' What a suggestion to a fifteen-year-old, going on sixteen!

"Bill brought two pints of porter, and I began to confide in the sergeant. I told him my father was dead.

"'Oh, your poor mother,' the sergeant said huskily, pulling out a handkerchief. 'My father died when I was a young lad – much younger than you, of course. I was sixteen when my father died, and my poor mother had a life of hard, hard work in order to keep us.' He blew his nose and dabbed his eyes. 'What would a man do without his mother? She sacrifices everything to bring up her family, and does without herself. A man can't do enough to repay his mother, he can't. My mother's settled comfortably in a nice little cottage in the country, which me and my brother John got her with our army pay.'

"'I thought your brother was Joe.'

"'I mean Joe. John's the other brother I haven't told you about. Here, Bill, more ale, and look lively.'

"'Did you say a cottage in the country?'

"He nodded.

"'Yerse. It was the least we could do for our poor old mum. My brother Joe and me – he's a good lad, he is – we saves up our army pay, and now she lives like a princess, our old mother does. Wants for nothing.'

"I thought of my mother, sitting up half the night, mending for a rascally second-hand-clothes dealer, going out at five in the morning to clean offices, and then toiling all day over the wash tub. I said, 'How do you get into the army?'

"He looked surprised, and raised his eyebrows.

"'Oh, was you thinking of an army career, then?'

"I nodded. 'But how do you get in?'

"He drew his chair closer to mine, and lowered his voice. 'It's not easy. I can tell you that for a start. You needs hinfluence. It's not what you knows, but who you knows, as the saying goes. It's a lucky day for you, squire, that you met me, because I've taken a real fancy to you, seeing as you are like my young brother Joe. How old are you, Joe? Seventeen, eighteen, eh?'

"'Seventeen,' I said. It was a lie, I was fifteen.

"'I thought as much. A good judge of age, I am. It's lucky for you you are seventeen, because you couldn't get into the army if you was only sixteen.'

"He leaned closer, and muttered out of the side of his mouth: 'Is your health good? No nasties, nothing like that, I take it?'

"I said my health was good.

"'Are you a Christian? The army won't have none of them heathens and hatheists.'

"I said I was Church of England.

"'Now, you're an intelligent lad, I can see that. Can you write your name?'

"I said I had been at school full-time until I was thirteen.

"'A scholar, my word. With your edifaction, sir, you will rise to the rank of brigadier general, you will.'

"He stretched out his hand, took my porter from me, and drank it himself.

"'If you are going to put pen to paper, young sir, you will need a steady hand. All the edification in the world aint going to help if your hand is shaking, on account of too much strong porter before lunch. Where was you planning lunch, by the way? Perhaps I can join you?'

"I said I hadn't any plans, but I was thinking about joining the army, and how could I do it?

"He leaned closer, and tapped his nose. He looked all around, before whispering, 'It's your lucky day, lad. I reckons as how I can help. I knows where the recruiting office is sitivated, and if I recommends you to the company's commanding officer – I'm very well thought of in higher command, I am – I reckons you would be in with a chance. Without me you haven't a hope. They'd turn you away as soon as look at you, they would. Come on, let's go.'

"Out in the sunlight, I blinked, and lowered my head from the glare, but the sergeant turned to me.

"'Right now, Guardsman Joe – what did you say your name was? Collett I must remember that – Collett. Guardsman Collett, stand up straight. Throw your head and shoulders back. Breathe deep, chest out. The soldiers of the Queen don't slouch around the place. Now, pick your feet up. Left, right, left, right. Eyes straight ahead. Left, right.'

"We marched across the square at a cracking speed. People fell aside. Everyone looked at us. I felt so proud. We passed my mate, who just gawped. I didn't turn my head to look at him.

"We entered the recruiting office, and the sergeant snapped his heels together with a crack like a whip, and shot his right arm up in salute to the officer who stepped forward.

"'Sah. Mr Joseph Collett, sah. Aged seventeen. Good health. Good education. Father dead, sah. Wants to be a soldier, sah. Highly recommended, sah.'

"There was a lot of saluting and 'sah-ing', and heel snapping, and the sergeant said, 'Right, young Joe. I'll leave you with the commanding officer. I'll be off now. Good luck, lad.'

"And I never saw him again."

With bewildering speed Joe had been hustled into the medical room, and asked to stick his tongue out and drop his trousers. A doctor gave him a quick look over, and passed him as fit. He was taken to a desk and told to write his name and address at the top of a printed form, then to sign his name at the end of the page. Confused but confident, Joe did so.

"Guardsman Collett, you are now a soldier in Her Majesty's Scots Guards. You will receive full uniform, full rations, full billeting, and a shilling a day. Here is a travel warrant to take you from Waterloo to Aldershot, which will be your first camp. You may go home now to tell your mother and collect your personal belongings. The last train from Waterloo goes at 10 p.m. If you are not on it, remember: you are now a fully enlisted guardsman, and failure to report at barracks will be counted as desertion, which is punishable by a flogging and six months in prison on bread and water. Here is your first day's pay of one shilling. Now follow the uniform sergeant downstairs, where you will be fitted with boots and uniform. Stand to attention, Guardsman Collett, and salute when you are leaving a superior officer."

In the wardrobe room Joe had been fitted up with full uniform and boots. He looked exceedingly handsome in the scarlet jacket and black trousers, and he gazed at his reflection with barely suppressed joy. He put the shilling and his travel warrant in his pocket, and was given a brown-paper parcel containing his old clothes. He was given directions to Waterloo Station and, with dire warnings about prison and flogging if he failed to turn up, was sent on his way.

Joe marched all the way back to Poplar, his newly acquired military swagger getting stronger with every step. His buttons gleamed, his boots shone, his red tunic dazzled the eye. People stood aside. Older men touched their caps. Small boys marched beside him, imitating his step. Best of all, young girls giggled and whispered and tried to attract his attention. But "eyes straight ahead", as ordered by the recruiting sergeant, was Joe's rule, and never once did he glance back, however enticing the female attentions. Girls had never looked at him before. "A soldier's life is the life for me" – and his young heart sang in tune to his step.

He marched into the court of Alberta Buildings, round to the washhouse, and flung open the door. The chatter stopped and a gasp of admiration went up from the women at the wash tubs. But his mother had her back to him. Turning round, she gazed uncomprehendingly at the figure in the doorway for a few seconds, as though she didn't recognise him. Then a low moan escaped her lips, rising to a terrible scream, and she fainted.

Joe rushed forward in alarm. Women crowded round. Water was splashed over her face and neck, and she opened her eyes, which, seeing Joe in his scarlet tunic, flooded with tears. She sobbed uncontrollably, unable to speak. A woman said, "You best get her back to your place an' all, Joe. Poor soul. She's that took she can't hardly stand, poor lamb. Oh Joe, you didn't never oughta've done it, you never."

Alarmed and bewildered, Joe helped his mother across the cobbled court and up the stone stairway to their flat. Doors opened, and women came out onto the balconies to witness the drama.

A neighbour brought in a cup of tea, and handed it to her with the words, "I've laced it with a drop o' somethin' soothin', Mrs Collett, to keep yer strength up. Lor' knows, yer goin' 'a need it," and she gave Joe a reproachful stare.

His mother drank the tea, and the sobs diminished. When she could speak, Joe asked her why she was crying.

She clung to him, and rubbed her swollen face on his sleeve. "A soldier, Joe! My eldest son, my comfort, my hope, a soldier. They draw them in, young men, thousands of them, every year. Cannon-fodder, they calls them, 'the scum of the earth'. They draws them in to die." Tears again flooded her eyes, and she wiped them away with her shawl.

"Go and ask Mrs Willoughby three doors down if I could have another cup of that tea, will you, dear? She's a kind soul, and won't mind, I know that. She feels for me. She's lost sons in the army."

Joe was not merely deflated. He was shattered. He had expected a hero's welcome. He took his jacket off, not wanting to step onto the balcony in scarlet, and fetched another cup of tea, laced with a drop of rum, which many good Poplar housewives kept for moments of crisis.

While gratefully sipping the tea, his mother said: "I 'ad four older brothers, and they all died in the Crimean War. I was only a little girl, and 'ardly remember them, but I remember my mother crying, an' 'ow she never recovered. The grief seemed to cling to 'er for the rest of 'er life. My older sister was engaged to be married to a young man who died at Sebastapol. The suffering was terrible, by all accounts – just terrible."

"But the Crimean War was ages ago," Joe protested; "it's all over and done with. The Empire's strong. There are no wars now. No one would dare attack the British Empire. And I'm a soldier of the Queen Empress, and proud of it."

She forced a smile. "You're a good lad, my son, and your

mother's a silly old fusspot. She's not going to spoil your last afternoon with tears. When do you have to report to barracks?"

He remembered the travel warrant and the shilling in his tunic pocket. He pulled it out and laid it proudly on the table beside her. "I'm paid a shilling a day and it's all for you. I get my billet and my food and my uniform, so I don't need money. I'll bring it all to you, and you won't want no more."

Poor woman! She had cried all over again. What mother wouldn't?

"You must keep some for yourself, my son."

"Nope. Not a penny. I done it for you, and you shall get the pay."

"My boy! Oh, my lad!" She kissed his hands and wiped her tears on his sleeve. "My dear boy. But I fear for you. My heart is heavy. I fear for you."

She finished the tea, and pulled herself together. The rum helped. The children would soon be in from school, and later the girls from the factory. She couldn't present a tearful face to them.

"You start getting your things together in a bundle, while I go down to the yard to wash my face. Then we'll use your shilling to buy some whelks and a loaf, and some real butter and a saucer of jam for the little ones. We'll have a real feast your last evening at home."

And that is exactly what they did. The younger boys were over the moon about their big brother's uniform. Each of them tried on the jacket, and the six-year-old pranced around the room with the jacket trailing on the floor and the sleeves flapping wildly. The sisters were agog with admiration. Suddenly Joe had become a man in their eyes. Only their mother was silent, but she kept a brave smile on her face.

Time passed all too quickly. The laughter, the cheers, the songs, had to come to an end. Joe had a train to catch from Waterloo at ten o'clock that night. He dared not miss it.

ARMY LIFE

Guardsman Joe Collett arrived at Waterloo Station at 9.30 p.m., along with about sixty other young men recruited that day. Each of them thought that he had been singled out for special consideration by a recruiting sergeant. They were all very poor boys and were surprised to see each other. None of them knew that the army was obliged to recruit twelve thousand men each year to make up the numbers, mostly lost through death.

Also at Waterloo Station were around a hundred girls, dressed to kill. Oh, the skirts, the ribbons, the laces, the tucks, the frills and flounces! Oh, the boots with dainty buttons, and the wide-brimmed hats, heavy with fruit and flowers and feathers! And what was that Joe saw? Could it be paint? Joe had never seen rouged lips and cheeks before, and he was enchanted.

The girls clung to the soldiers, two or three to each. Some of them carried a phial of gin or rum in their garters, and these were brought out with much skirt-rustling and mock modesty. There was only half an hour before the train was due to leave, but the girls knew how to use the time to advantage. Much can happen in half an hour, and each girl knew that the recruits had been paid a shilling that day.

Most of the new recruits had gone alone to the station, but some were accompanied by mothers, aunts or sisters. These young men were put to great embarrassment by the girls, who openly sneered at them, and cast bold, contemptuous eyes on their womenfolk. These good women were scandalised by the wanton behaviour of the girls, and tried to protect and warn their sons, which only made matters worse.

Joe, being alone, taller than average, and undoubtedly good-looking, was mobbed. He was offered a phial of rum which, laughing, he swallowed in one gulp. It went straight to his head. He clung to a brunette, who cuddled him, and led him round the station, singing. Joe felt he had never been so happy in his life. Two more girls joined them and led him out of the station into the little lanes. It was a quarter to ten. In the lanes the girls cuddled and kissed him, and fondled him all over. In his intoxicated state Joe felt that more than his blood was rising. It was then that the girls discovered that Joe did not have his shilling on him. They screamed with rage. They kicked him and pushed him and he fell against a wall, hitting his head. They tore his jacket off him, frantically going through the pockets, threw it on the ground – Joe's beautiful red tunic – and trampled it in the mud. He cried out, but could not stop them. They pulled his hair and scratched his face until the blood ran. They spat on him and then rushed off, with a flick of skirts, around the corner.

Dazed, bewildered and bleeding, Joe leaned against the wall. He tried to gather his senses, but couldn't think what had happened. His head hurt from the blow. He was sliding comfortably down the wall when a sharp noise penetrated his fuddled hearing. What was it? It was repeated. Dear heaven, it was the train whistle. Aldershot ... the last train ... must catch it ... desertion ... flogging ... prison. He snatched up his jacket, nearly falling flat on his face as he did so, staggered towards the station, hurtled towards the moving train, was pushed onto it by a porter and fell into a seat.

"Blimey, mate, you look as if you've had a good time," said his companion, with a sardonic grin.

The train gathered speed, and Joe fell asleep. He was awakened by a rough hand shaking him. "Wakey, wakey, Sleeping Beauty. You're a soldier now, and we're at Aldershot. You can dream of her another time."

Aldershot? What was that? Joe woke to see half a dozen grinning faces above scarlet tunics staring at him, and it all came back. He was a soldier now ... the recruiting sergeant, that was it. Head up, shoulders back, chest out, breathe deeply, no slouching now. He jerked himself upright, and pain split his head from ear to ear. He groaned.

The men roared with laughter. "He's only a kid, leave 'im be. He'll learn. Here, mate, give us yer arm."

Joe staggered off the train on the arm of his unknown companion, and a staff sergeant stepped forward. "Right men. In line. Roll call. Look sharpish."

The motley group of raw recruits shuffled backwards and forwards, sideways and hitherways, trying to make a line. The staff sergeant bellowed and swore and brandished his regimental swagger cane, trying to get them into military line. He was not successful, but had to make do with second best.

"Right, you horrible men. You wait till I get you on the parade ground. You'll damned soon learn how to form a line. Roll call."

An old duty sergeant stepped forward with two sheets of paper in his hand containing lists of names, which he proceeded to read out. His reading was not very good. No doubt the process would have been quicker if a duty sergeant who could read properly had been sent, but the ability to read was not an accomplishment that was rated very highly in the army.

He got through several simple names without mishap – Brown, Smith, Cole, Bragg – but then was stuck.

"Warrarramb . . ." he shouted.

No one answered.

"Warrarrnad" Louder.

No response.

"What you say?" yelled the staff sergeant.

The duty sergeant tried to look confident, and shouted "Warrarrandy"

No response.

The staff sergeant strode over to him, his cane swishing, his boots clicking, and snatched the paper. In the flickering gaslight of the station he squinted at the page. "Warrenden," he shouted.

A man stepped forward. Roll call proceeded in this manner. The duty sergeant did his best, but got stuck on Ashcroft, shouting

"Askafoot". Bengerfield, Willowby, Waterton set him stuttering, until everyone thought roll call would never be finished.

One man was missing. The name was shouted backwards and forwards several times, but no one stepped forward. The staff sergeant struck the calf of his leg with his swagger cane and, with great deliberation, pulled out a stub of pencil and underlined the name.

"It will be the worse for him," he said menacingly. "Right men, form a column, four abreast, quick march."

Forming a column for untrained men is as difficult as forming a line. The staff sergeant swore and cursed and used his cane liberally, eventually getting some sort of ragged column together. With a "left, right, left, right" they marched off.

It was four miles to the camp, which did Joe good. By the time he got there, his head had cleared from the effects of the rum, and ached only a little from the crack on the wall. The night air refreshed him, and the men surrounding him gave him a feeling of security.

The sentries at Aldershot Barracks leaped swiftly to attention when they heard the column approaching. An incomprehensible word was barked out by the staff sergeant, sounding something like "Awt". No one in the column thought it meant anything and continued marching. The four at the front were confronted by a menacing row of guards, each with a bayonet raised at forty-five degrees, and pointed directly at their stomachs. Another step, and they would have been skewered. They halted. The men behind carried on marching, straight into the backs of the men in front. About half the column fell on each other in this way. Being fresh from a sane world where this sort of thing is considered funny, they fell about laughing, but the staff sergeant failed to see the joke. He swore and raged at their imbecility.

The column re-assembled inside the gates and marched another quarter-mile to the billet, a grey rectangular building, four storeys high.

A short way off from this building the staff sergeant shouted.

"In a minute, I am going to say 'halt', and that means 'stop', and when I say 'halt' I want you to stop. Got it?" They continued marching.

"Awt." Half the men stopped, the other half didn't. The result was exactly the same as at the gate. The staff sergeant nearly went berserk. Somehow he managed to re-assemble them, marched them another fifty yards and shouted, "Halt."

This time everyone stopped.

"Right. In line."

This was no easier than it had been at the station. In fact it was harder, because it was pitch-dark. Men stumbled and fell over each other, muttering and laughing.

"Silence!" roared the staff sergeant.

"Silence yerself, yer bloody windbag," shouted a voice.

"Who said that?" roared the sergeant.

"Father Christmas," said the voice.

"Corporal, open the door," roared the sergeant.

The corporal on duty opened the door of the billet.

"Forward. Quick march," roared the sergeant, leading the way up four flights of stone steps. At the top, the corporal in charge of the billet opened the door, and the disorderly line of men entered.

"New recruits, Corporal, and a bigger bunch of stupid bastards I've never met." The staff sergeant turned to go. He turned to the men. "You wait. You just bloody wait. You'll wish you'd never been bloody born, you will." And with those pleasant words, he departed.

I roared with laughter at this story. We both laughed, Mr Collett and I. Nothing binds people more strongly than the same sense of humour, and the ability to laugh together. I was thoroughly enjoying my evenings of sherry and an old soldier's reminiscences. The British Army of the 1890s was not something I would have expected to find interesting, but in the firelight, with a good storyteller like my companion, the years came alive.

I was also aware that Mr Collett had become deeply fond of me, which was touching. One of the pictures on his walls was of a pretty young girl in 1920s dress. I understood that this was his only daughter, who had been killed in the bombing in the Second World War. Perhaps I was becoming a substitute granddaughter to him. I didn't mind. I liked him. He was a dear old man, and reminded me of my own grandfather, whom I had loved and admired deeply, and who had been more of a father to me than my own father. He had died a couple of years previously at the age of eighty-four, and I still felt the loss. If Mr Collett and I were both substituting another person into our growing affection, it was all right by me.

He refilled my glass. "Do you like chocolates, my dear? I bought a box of Milk Tray this morning, with you in mind."

He reached up to the mantelshelf, and felt for them. I was still a bit chary about eating anything, because of all the filth around the place, and once, when he had produced a grubby plate of biscuits, which I had seen him drop on the dirty floor and pick up, I had said that I didn't like biscuits. But an unopened box of chocolates was a different matter. Anyway, I loved them. After that, it was always sherry and chocolates. Incidentally, I never saw the bugs again, and after a while I ceased to look for them.

"So you got to your billet, and your head wasn't too bad. What happened then?"

"We were told to make up our cots. A soldier sleeps in a cot, not a bed. They are constructed in two halves, the bottom half of which pushes into the upper half. This allows for more space during the day in the centre of the billet. The corporal showed us how to do it. The biscuit, which is a soldier's straw-filled mattress, and two rough blankets, were folded on the top part of the shortened bed. We had no pillows, no sheets. Nothing fancy like that. The corporal told us the sip-but was on the landing."

"What on earth is a sip-but?" I interrupted.

"Oh, that's back slang for a piss-tub. There's a lot of rhyming slang and back slang in the army. At least there was in my day. It may have been dropped by now.

"I remember my first night very well. It was so new, so exciting, that I couldn't sleep. Apart from which I still had a headache from the girls pushing me against the wall. My thoughts were racing – those girls, my mother, the recruiting sergeant, the staff sergeant, the station, the march through the night. I must have dozed off towards dawn and in my dreams I vaguely heard a bugle call. Seconds later the corporal burst into the billet, shouting: 'Show a leg now, get out of it. Open those blasted windows and let some fresh air in. It smells like a bloody farmyard in here. Get out of it now, do you hear me?'

"Perhaps I didn't move, but the next thing I knew was that my cot collapsed, and I landed on the floor. The corporal had pulled the bottom half away from the top half, which was a very effective way of rousing anyone who did not leap out of bed the instant reveille was blown. This sounded at 5 a.m., summer or winter.

"The corporal ordered us to dress and put away our cots and fold the biscuit and blankets. I was in a daze, but the roar of the corporal kept me on my toes. He kept bellowing on about the blankets not being folded straight, and how, he'd never seen such a useless, slovenly bunch of recruits, and how we would be licked into shape and no mistake. He ordered two men next to the door to carry the sip-but to empty it down the drains and clean it at the pump, where it would be left until the following evening.

"'Right now. Stand by your cots. This is only the reception centre, where you are treated gentle-like. Later you will learn what army life is, when you have been sorted into the regiments what you have enlisted for. Get me. You will have an hour's drill before breakfast. Then your breakfast, then an hour's parade, then present to the colour sergeants for sorting. Got it? Right. In line. Down to the parade ground.'

"We got into some sort of line and filed down the stone stairs. In the darkness outside we could hear voices rather like the staff sergeant's barking out orders. We were put to physical exercises –

press-ups, star-jumps, squatting with straight back, step-ups. Imagine all that with a headache and no sleep! But I kept thinking this was better than hanging around the dock gates looking for work, and it was. The last quarter of an hour consisted of the most exhausting exercise so far – running with your knees lifted high at each step. After this, we were starving for our breakfast. This consisted of dry bread and sweet tea. It tasted delicious. After that we were led to the parade ground for another hour of drill. At 9 a.m. a bugle sounded and the colour sergeants marched onto the square, each followed by a duty sergeant carrying a list of names, which they read out in turn. The recruits were sectioned into their colours, and marched off. This happened every day, because the recruiting sergeants were busy enlisting unsuspecting young lads like me every day of the week.

"There were only four Scots Guards recruits that day. It's a crack regiment." (Mr Collett said this with great pride, lifting his chin high.) "We were taken in marching order to the quartermaster's stores, where we were issued with top-coat, cape, leggings, one suit of scarlet, one of blue for drills, boots, shirts, socks, and numerous pieces of regimental dress. We were issued with a rifle, bayonet, and two white buff straps, with pouches that could hold fifty rounds apiece. We were also issued with a busby, the tall fur headdress reserved for Guards. Everyone in the regiment was very proud of these.

"We – the four of us, that is – were shown to a whitewashed barrack room overlooking the square. A corporal was in charge of each billet, and a couple of older duty-men also kept billet there. They showed us how to fix straps for drill purposes, how to roll the top-coat and fix it to the kitbag, how to fix leggings, what cleaning materials we would need, how to place our cape and scarlet top-coat, when not in use, on the racks above our cots – even how the straps of the kitbag should hang from pegs above the head of the cot."

The pettiness of it all, the meticulous attention to detail, reminded me of my nurse's training. I told Mr Collett about it.

We were issued with three fitted dresses, twelve aprons, five caps and a cape. We were given precise instructions on how they must be worn at all times. The hem of our dresses had to be fifteen inches from the floor, no more, no less. Caps, which were flat pieces of starched linen, had to be folded and pinned to an exact shape and size. Aprons had to be pinned at an exact point above the bosom, and adjusted to the precise length of the dress. Shoes had to be black lace-ups, of a specific style, with rubber soles for quietness. Stockings were black, with seams. Belts and epaulettes were of differing colours, distinguishing the different years of training a student nurse underwent. Full uniform had to be worn at all times when on duty. I recall, in my first year of training, being ordered out of the dining room by a third-year nurse, because I had forgotten to put on my cap. Later, when I became a ward sister, I forgot my cuffs on one occasion when I went to the matron's office, and was sent back to the ward to get them before I could address her!

We discussed whether this sort of discipline was necessary. Mr Collett said: "Well, it certainly is for men, because large numbers of men living together can easily become like wild animals. Men are brutes at heart, and without the civilising influence of women they quickly revert to savagery. The discipline of the armed forces is the only thing that keeps them under control. I wouldn't have thought it was necessary for women, though, would you? But I maintain that nurses always look lovely, and so I approve of the uniform."

I chuckled at this. There is no doubt in my mind that the nurses' uniform of the early and middle 1900s was just about the sexiest thing ever invented. Nothing has surpassed it for allure. I was not the only young nurse to be acutely conscious of a heightened sex appeal when in uniform. Ironically, the draconian old sisters and matrons who rigidly enforced the uniform seemed to be unaware of the effect it had on the male sex.

Those were the repressive days when student nurses had to live in barrack-like nurses' homes, and be in by 10 p.m. No men were allowed, and a nurse who smuggled one in would be dismissed if she was caught. Student nurses could not marry. All this was to repress our sexuality, yet we were dressed up like sex kittens. With exquisite irony, in today's permissive society, when anything goes and nurses can do whatever they like sexually, the uniform has changed beyond all recognition, and the average nurse now looks like a sack of potatoes tied in the middle, often wearing trousers rather than sexy black stockings.

I asked Mr Collett how he coped with all the regulation of army life. Was he as bad as I had been in my early nurses' training? I must have driven the ward sisters mad. He laughed, and said he didn't believe it.

"But I had a hard time at first. We all did. The Scots Guards prided themselves on being a crack regiment, so we had more hours of drill, rifle and bayonet training, longer marches, and heavier pack-weights than other regiments. Also we had less time off. We were so exhausted in the evening that we seldom went to the wet canteen. Often I just made up my cot at 8 p.m. and went fast asleep until reveille.

"I had more money than I'd ever had. On a shilling a day I was able to send four shillings a week home to my mother. I knew that would pay the rent, and I swore to myself that I would always pay the rent, so that she need never again fear the workhouse. And I kept that up for years and years, even when I was married."

I asked him about his marriage.

"Well, after three months at Aldershot, I was given forty-eight hours' leave to go to see my family, before being posted to Plymouth. Across the court of Alberta Buildings lived a girl I had known for years, but she seemed so much more grown up than I had remembered her, and I reckon she must have thought the same about me. She was the prettiest little thing I had ever seen." He chuckled fondly, and slowly refilled his pipe. He rubbed it in his hands, and stroked his cheek with the warm bowl.

"We were only sixteen apiece, and forty-eight hours isn't long, but I knew she was the only girl in the world for me. We reached an understanding that she would wait for me until I was in a position to marry her. Long engagements were common in those days, and couples thought nothing of waiting ten or fifteen years before they could get married. As it happened we had to wait only three years." He lit a spill from the fire, applied it to the tobacco, and sucked hard. He looked thoughtful.

"It's a damned good thing I did meet my Sally during that forty-eight hours, because the promises we had made kept me clean while I was at Plymouth. It was a lively town, and ten or twelve regiments were garrisoned there, as well as sailors and marines. There were pubs and bawdy houses in every street, and prostitutes in every bar. I learned fast. You do in the army, and it didn't take long to figure out that if I went with one of them girls I was likely to pick up VD. That would have been the end of my army career, the end of my hopes for winning Sally and the end of the rent for my mother. So I kept myself clean. All the other chaps said I was mad, and I should enjoy myself while I could. But I saw enough of them go into the venereal wards of the sick bay to know they were the ones who were mad." He looked severe.

"But hadn't you better go, young lady? Are you going to be locked out at ten o'clock? I don't want to be getting you into trouble."

"I will go, but I want to hear about your marriage first," I said eagerly. "It sounds so romantic. Anyway, there are no restrictions with the nuns. They are much too sensible for that. Now tell me about how you got married."

He patted my hand fondly. "After Plymouth, I was posted to Windsor Castle, as one of Queen Victoria's foot guards. It was the best posting I had, and I loved it. There wasn't really a lot to do. It was all marching and square drill. There were several hours of sentry duty, day and night, but we relieved each other every two hours, and then we had two hours off, until the next relief. At Windsor Castle I started reading. I knew I was not properly educated, and wanted to do something about it. There was a library in the barracks, and I just read anything I could get hold of. It became a passion with me. The more I read, the more I realised how ignorant I was. I devoured history like other chaps devoured booze. I spent all my spare time reading, and it was a habit that never left me, until my eyes began to go, and it became impossible."

He looked sad, but perked up. "But I can listen to the wireless. There's nothing wrong with my hearing.

"Anyway, what with one thing and another, I loved it at Windsor Castle. Now, it's a funny thing, but in the army, I've noticed, the less work you have to do the more you get paid. We were paid ninepence extra per day for Royal Duties. I was now earning good money, and was able to apply to my colonel for permission to marry. He said I was too young, but when I told him that I had known the girl since I was thirteen, he relented. Married quarters were sometimes available to soldiers and their wives, and that was what I was after. I wasn't going to get married and have my Sal living in a room in the town, and me in barracks. The colonel said we would have to wait until a cottage became available, which we did, and within two years Sally and I were married at All Saints' Church, Poplar, just over the way there. I took her down to Windsor soon after. Our twins were born at Windsor Castle, and I was the proudest young father in the regiment. But our happiness was too good to last. News from South Africa was bad. Infantrymen were being sent out every week. I had a feeling, though I didn't say it to Sal, that my turn would come, and it did. On the first of November 1899 I sailed for South Africa."

SOUTH AFRICA
1899–1902

Mr Collett's legs were greatly improved with daily treatment. The ulcers were reduced from about eight inches in diameter to two inches. They were more superficial and were also drying out. Consequently, the smell in the room was improving. It was still dirty, with a faint whiff of urine hanging in the air, but the sickly-sweet stench had definitely gone. I realised that the smell must have been due to the suppuration of the wounds. If only he had sought treatment earlier, and not tried "do-it-yourself" remedies, the ulcers would never have got into such a state in the first place. I reduced the visits to alternate days, and then every third day, and the improvement was maintained.

Our sherry evenings continued as a regular feature, and I knew how much he loved my visits. He made no pretence about his joy at seeing me. I began to think that I was the only person who visited him and wondered about his family and friends. It was unusual, if not unknown, to see a Poplar man without either. Family life was close, and old people were valued. Neighbours lived on top of each other and were always in and out of each others' doors, especially in the tenements. Yet I never saw nor heard of anyone popping in on Mr Collett to see if he was all right, to ask if he needed anything, or just to pass the time of day. I wondered why.

He said to me once, regarding his neighbours: "I'm not one of them, you know. I was not born and bred in Alberta Buildings, so they will never accept me."

I asked him about his family. He said, simply and sadly, "I have outlived them all. It is God's will that I should be left. One day we will be reunited." He wouldn't say any more, but I hoped that as time went on he might.

One evening, I asked him to tell me more about the Boer War.

"I was drafted in the autumn of 1899. My poor Sally was heartbroken. We were so happy at Windsor. We had a nice little army cottage. She did washing and mending for the officers and earned some money that way. She was happy, and as pretty as a picture. What's that jingle now, let me think:

> The Colonel's wife looks like a horse
> The captain's wife is not much worse
> The sergeant's wife looks a bit slicker
> But the private knows how to pick 'er.

"Or something like that. Anyway, my Sal was the prettiest girl in the regiment. Our twins were born, and they were on their feet and running around, when the postings came. We knew it would be for a long time. Sally and the boys couldn't stay at Windsor, so they went back home to live with her mother. The flat is just above where we are sitting now. That's why I like living here. I can sit of an evening, and think of Sally and the twins, when she was so young, living right above me.

"We sailed from Plymouth. There were crowds on the quayside, cheering, waving, singing. Some of the lads were happy and excited at going, but my heart was heavy, and a lot of others felt the same. I reckon that single men make the best soldiers, because they have few regrets about what they leave behind."

He went on to describe the troopship, crowded with men and horses, carts and wagons, guns and munitions, food and supplies. The journey took five weeks. Discipline had to be very strict, because of living in such a close, crowded space. The men did hours of drill on deck. But they were in good spirits, because it all seemed like an adventure. "We were going to knock hell out of those Boer farmers who dared to defy the British Empire," he said.

They landed at Durban and were ordered to form ranks and

march. They weren't told where they were going, just told to march. They marched for eight days in full winter uniform in the boiling heat, carrying 150 lb packs. The sun burned down relentlessly, and flies and mosquitoes followed them all the way. There were no roads, so they marched through open scrubland, and along rough tracks. The countryside was beautiful, and wild, nothing like home, but they were too tired and too hot to take it in.

"I was in a Highland Regiment, as you know – the Scots Guards – and I'll tell you something: there is nothing in the world like the sound of the bagpipes to raise a man's morale, to lift his spirits, and give him strength. However tired and thirsty we were, the bagpipes at the front of the column only had to strike up and within seconds you felt your feet lift off the ground, your step lighten, your spirits rise, and every man-Jack was marching strong, in rhythm to the pipes." Mr Collett chuckled, straightened his shoulders, threw back his head, and swung his arms as though he were marching.

"There's a photograph of my regiment hanging on the wall over there, if you'd like to have a look."

I peered at the grey-and-yellow photo of a column of soldiers, which didn't really mean a lot to me, but I said it looked impressive.

"Yes, it was impressive, you're right. But, at the same time, it was insane."

I was surprised to hear him say that.

"Well, you imagine: going to war, and marching through open country, soldiers in scarlet, playing bagpipes! Talk about secrecy or surprise tactics! The enemy could see and hear us for God knows how many miles around. And we never saw them. All over South Africa columns like ours were marching, and being attacked by an unseen enemy. Yet the British generals still didn't learn. We carried on in our old swaggering ways, and lost countless thousands of young men because of it."

He told me they were ordered to climb a hill one night. He

didn't know where, because none of them were told, but it was steep and treacherous, more like mountain terrain than a hill. They had no special climbing equipment. They wore their military uniforms with full pack, as well as rifle and bayonet, and were wearing boots made for marching, not for climbing. Nor were the men trained for mountaineering.

By dawn they had got to what they thought was the top, only to find that there were higher ridges all around that were invisible from below, and in which groups of armed men were hiding. When the whole brigade had gained the first ridge, fire opened up from all sides, from cannons, rifles and long-range muskets. They were completely unprepared. Hundreds of men were mown down before they could retaliate.

"I shall never forget the scene," said Mr Collett. "The cries and screams were terrible to hear. We formed ranks and fired back, but our position was hopeless. We were in full view of an enemy we could not see. It was a day of gunfire, under a baking sun. No shelter, no water. Just relentless gunfire."

By nightfall the barrage from the guns died away, and in the darkness all that could be heard were the cries and groans of the wounded. "We tried to help them, but we were stumbling over rocks and dead bodies. In any case, there were no doctors or medical orderlies, no bandages or morphine, no stretchers – nothing." The men were ordered to retreat, and to leave the dead. In the sun the injured would die of thirst the following day. "That was the moment when I realised the truth of my mother's words, that we were just 'cannon-fodder'. Young private soldiers were ordered, time and time again, to march directly into gunfire, and High Command didn't give a damn how many died, nor the cost in human suffering." Mr Collett was trembling and his voice was shaky.

He bit his lip to control himself.

"And would you believe it, it was all unnecessary. Of course, we didn't know it at the time – the ordinary soldier didn't – but there had been no reconnaissance. There were no maps of the terrain, and no scouts had been sent ahead to assess the area or the heights of the various hills. If we'd had a ground map, the whole incident would never have happened. The British lost two thousand men that day, the Boers two hundred – all because there was no reconnaissance.

"I've read a lot of history in my life, and bad leadership seems to crop up time after time in the British Army. Of course, we had some good colonels, and generals as well, but it was always a lottery."

Mr Collett spoke with some bitterness about the effect in those days of the class system when, as he put it, only the aristocracy and upper classes could hold a commission, and they bought their rank. Working-class men could not afford to buy a commission. This meant that a young man with money, however stupid he might be, however lazy, or indifferent to army life, could buy a rank and be put in charge of other men. The tradition of an easy life for the officers, with nothing but parties and races, was well entrenched, and any friendship between officers and other ranks was forbidden. "They did not think of us as human beings," said Mr Collett. "We meant nothing to them. We were just 'the scum of the earth', utterly disposable.

"I don't know how it was that I wasn't killed. In my regiment, more than three-quarters of the men who went out to South Africa died, either in battle or in the military hospitals. Yet somehow I was spared."

Another killer was disease. Mr Collett had suffered slight leg wounds in one skirmish, and had a short stay in hospital. While he was there he saw a constant stream of men being brought in with what was called dysentery. It was, in fact, typhoid fever, due to infected water, and it spread like wildfire. At one stage it seemed to be out of control. He commented: "I don't know if anyone who caught the disease recovered, but I know that I never saw a man walk out. I only saw the bodies carried out – ten or twenty a day from one ward – and they were quickly replaced by as many new patients with the same disease. The small hospital that I was in had been built for three hundred patients, and it was carrying two thousand. There were nowhere near enough doctors or nurses to treat all those men, so most of them died. Three times as many men died in the hospitals as died on the battlefields. I don't know how it was that I didn't catch typhoid. I was spared for something worse."

I wondered what could be worse, and imagined the heartache and frustration of trying to nurse sick and dying men under such impossible conditions.

"Somehow I survived and had to take part in what was called 'the bitter end'. After two and a half years of fighting we were no closer to victory than we had been at the beginning. We couldn't engage the enemy. They were always hiding and attacking our lines, our communications, our stores, always surprising us. So our generals decided to attack their food supplies. This meant attacking their farms. A 'scorched-earth' policy was approved and we private soldiers had to carry it out. We hated it. Most of us felt degraded and emasculated, attacking women and children. We turned them out of their homes and burned their farms and barns. We killed their animals and burned their fields. Nothing was left after we'd finished. They were turned out to wander the veldt with no water, no food, prey to wild animals. I remember one young Boer woman with two little children and a baby. She was sobbing, begging us to spare her. I wanted to, but refusal to obey military orders is unthinkable. It would have meant execution by firing squad if I had done so. Perhaps I would have risked it if I had been single. But my money was going to Sally and the boys, and to my mother for the rent. What could I do? And even if I had disobeyed orders, it would have done no good. Other men would have carried out the job." He looked very grim and bitter.

"It was humiliating to us, and to our commanding officers. We were sent out to fight men, not defenceless women and children. We should never have done it. Never." Mr Collett clenched his hands tightly.

"It was a black time for the British Empire. Thirty thousand women and children died, mostly young children, and we were disgraced in the eyes of the world. We outnumbered the Boer fighting men by twenty-five to one, yet even then we couldn't win without attacking their homes, their womenfolk and their children.

"In the spring of 1903 I sailed for home, and I was discharged from the army in 1906."

"Did you regret your army years, or do you look back on them with pleasure?" I asked.

"Mixed feelings. The army certainly educated me and broadened my mind. I mixed with men from other backgrounds and experienced other ideas and points of view. Without the army, I would have been a casual dock labourer, mostly unemployed, so I am grateful for the work. With my army record, I was able to get a good job as a postman. And a postman I remained for the rest of my life until I retired with a pension to keep me comfortably in my old age."

His ingenuous simplicity had always charmed me. He looked upon his squalid, bug-ridden flat as comfort, even luxury; he was grateful for a modest pension that enabled him to buy food and coal sufficient for his needs. He saw himself as a wealthy man, who could afford to buy a bottle of sherry and a box of chocolates with which to entertain a young nurse of whom he had grown fond. He was completely content.

I leaned forward and squeezed his hand with affection. "I think it's getting late and I must go, but next time you must tell me about re-adjusting to civvy life. I guess your twins didn't know you?"

He didn't reply, but looked dreamily into the fire. "You go, my maiden, you go," he said, softly. I left an old man to his memories, the consolation of loneliness.

My next visit to Mr Collett was a morning about three days later. His legs had improved beyond all recognition and the ulcers were now completely dry. It was very gratifying.

On the mantelpiece, amid all the dingy and faded old photographs, was a gleaming white card, with a gold border and an embossed crown on it, requesting the pleasure of the company of Mr Joseph Collett and lady at the Old Guards' reunion at Caterham Barracks on a Saturday in June. I remarked on the card. He told me that for several years he had enjoyed going to the Old Guards' Day, but had not been able to go in recent years, due to his deteriorating eyesight and bad legs.

Impulsively I said, "Look, your legs are so much better now. It won't be any trouble for you to get around. Let's go together. It looks like good fun. It's not every girl has an opportunity like this, and I don't want to miss it."

He positively lit up. He took my hands and kissed them. "You darling girl! What a wonderful idea. It hadn't even crossed my mind. We'll go, and we'll make a day of it. I can tell you, the Guards do us old soldiers proud. What a day we'll have! What a day!"

I requested the day off well in advance, telling Sister Julienne about the invitation, and the plans. The girls were most intrigued; what on earth would it be like? Trixie suggested that a Young Guards' reunion might be more exciting, but wished me pleasure with my old ones.

The day itself dawned bright and fair. I was round at Alberta Buildings shortly after eight o'clock. Mr Collett was excited and chatty. He was dressed for the occasion in a faded old suit. His shoes had been polished, and he carried a new trilby hat. Most important of all, and by far the most impressive, he was wearing a row of medals on his chest. It had not occurred to me that he had medals, and I looked at them closely. He was proud and happy, telling me what each of them was for.

We took the bus from Blackwall to Victoria Coach Station, and then a coach to Caterham, arriving at about ten o'clock. I was excited, having never been inside a barracks before. For a young, inexperienced girl it was a stupendous occasion, and my excitement communicated itself to Mr Collett. We stayed very close together, because of the crowds, and I held his arm all the time as he couldn't see clearly. I had expected a rather solemn occasion with a lot of old men talking about old times. But it was nothing like that. It was an Open Day, with full military honours and pageantry. The reunion itself was an evening event.

The day was exhilarating. The British Army really knows how to put on a show. The colour, the flags, the pipes and drums, the drills. The scarlet uniforms, black busbies, the marching, with the pipe major throwing his staff high into the air. I was thrilled. Mr Collett had seen it all before, and couldn't see it very well this time, but he heard my cheers and was delighted.

Towards evening, when the marching and the drilling had ceased, and the tired crowds were starting to leave, I thought we would be leaving also. But Mr Collett pulled me back. "Now it is time for the regimental dinner. Come on, my beauty. This way. They'll see 'the privates know how to pick 'em'."

We went to the great dining room by special invitation. We were a little late, because Mr Collett's walking was slow. We passed young soldiers, who clicked their heels and saluted. We entered, the doorman took our card, and called: "Mr Joseph Collett and Miss Jenny Lee." There were about two hundred men and women seated at the tables. Heads looked up, and then a voice called out: "Gentlemen, now here is a really old guardsman." And everyone in the room stood up and raised their glasses: "To an esteemed old soldier."

Tears of emotion sprang from Mr Collett's eyes. We were led to the Colonel's table, and placed at his side. The dinner was sumptuous, and the Colonel and his lady so gracious to the old man. They talked about the Boer War, and Africa, and army life sixty years earlier. He was treated with the respect and recognition that he deserved so well.

FRANCE

1914–1918

The joyous day at Caterham Barracks cemented our friendship and I knew then that, come what may, I was bound to Mr Collett for life. We chatted and laughed all the way home, and parted at the bus stop near Blackwall Tunnel. He insisted that he didn't need me to go back with him, as he was perfectly capable of finding his way in the dark. It gladdened my heart to remember the respect, even deference, with which he had been treated at the barracks by the Colonel. He would not forget that day in a hurry.

One day, whilst treating his legs, I asked him about his life after leaving the army. I knew that Sally and the twins were living in Alberta Buildings by that stage. Did they continue to live there when he came back?

"No. I got a job in the Post Office you see, and so we had to move near to the sorting office in Mile End." He went on to tell me about his new life. Postmen had to sort their own mail in those days, and had to be in the sorting house by four o'clock each morning to receive the night mail. Sorting took a couple of hours, then they would be out on the road delivering until about 1 p.m. After a couple of hours off, they went back to sort and deliver the evening mail, which finished about 7 p.m. Mr Collett thought it was a good life.

"The twins were getting bigger. Pete and Jack were about six or seven, and the spitting image of each other. No one except their mother could tell them apart and even she got it wrong sometimes. They were lovely boys."

He bit his lip and swallowed hard, choking down the emotion.

"You've heard, I suppose, that identical twins often seem to live for each other. Well, I can tell you how true that is. They were two people, but I often thought that neither of them could be quite sure where one ended and the other began. They were always together, you couldn't separate them. They didn't seem to need anyone else. They even spoke their own language. Yes, it's true! We would listen to them playing, Sally and me, and they used different words with each other than they used with everyone else. It was a mixture of ordinary English and their own language. They could understand it, but we couldn't. You can never be quite sure what's going on in a child's mind, and identical twins are more of a mystery than other children. Pete and Jack lived in a world created by their combined imaginations, filled with giants and dwarves, kings and queens, castles and caverns. They didn't really have any friends. They didn't need them. They had each other."

"Didn't their mother feel left out?"

"You're right there, she did. The boys weren't lacking in affection, or anything like that. They were just totally self-sufficient. In fact, Sally once said, 'I reckon you and me could die, Joe, and they wouldn't notice. But if one of the boys died, I reckon the other would just fade away.'"

Tears glistened in the corners of his eyes, and he murmured, "Perhaps it was best, all for the best. The Lord giveth, and the Lord taketh away." He fell completely silent, lost in thought.

I had heard of two sons being killed in France, and looked at the picture of two handsome little boys on the wall. I asked, "Did you have any more children?"

"Yes, we had a little girl, and Sally nearly died in childbirth. I don't know what went wrong, and the midwife didn't know either, but my Sal was near to death for weeks after the birth. Her sister took the baby and wet-nursed her for the first three months, and the boys went to my mother. It frightened the life out of me, so I never let her go through it again. That's one thing you learn about in the army, if nothing else: contraception. I never could understand these men who let their wives have ten or fifteen children, when they could prevent it.

"But Sally recovered, thank God, and the children came home. We called the little girl Shirley – don't you think that's a pretty name? She was the loveliest little thing in all the world and a blessing to us both."

I did not need to see Mr Collet professionally more than once a week, because his legs were nearly better, but our sherry evenings continued, and during one of them he told me the story of Pete and Jack.

Young girls are not usually interested in war and military tactics, but I was. Wartime had shaped my childhood, but really, I knew little about war itself. The First World War was a mystery to me, and we were taught nothing about it in our history lessons at school. I knew that vast numbers of soldiers had died in the trenches of France, but so great was my ignorance that I did not even know what "trenches" meant. Later I met people who had suffered in the Blitz, and heard their first-hand stories, so when Mr Collett mentioned his sons' experiences I encouraged him to talk.

Pete and Jack had been sixteen years old when the war started. They had left school at the age of fourteen, and for two years had been Post Office telegraph boys, racing around London on their bikes delivering telegrams. They were known as "the flying twins". They loved it, were proud of their work, proud of the uniform, and were both healthy from all the fresh air and exercise. But in 1914 war started, and a national recruitment campaign was launched. "It will all be over by Christmas" was the government's promise. Many of their friends joined up, lured by the thought of adventure, and the twins wanted to go too, but their father restrained the boys, saying that war was not all adventure and glory.

1915 saw the launch of the famous poster of Lord Kitchener, pointing darkly out of the frame and saying "Your country needs you". After that, young men who did *not* join up were made to feel that they were cowards. Hundreds of thousands of young men volunteered, Pete and Jack among them, and marched off to their graves.

The men were sent for three months' military training in how to handle a gun and a grenade. Also how to care for horses and sword fighting for hand-to-hand combat were part of their training. Mr Collett commented wryly: "That just shows you how little the military High Command knew about mechanised warfare with high explosives!"

Men, boys and horses were packed into a steamer that stank of human sweat and horse droppings, and were shipped across the Channel to France. They were sent straight to the front-line trenches.

I said, "I've heard about this, front lines and trenches and going over the top and the likes, but what does it all mean?"

He said, "Well I wasn't there – I was too old. I suppose I could have gone as a veteran, but the Post Office was vital work, because all communications were handled by the Post Office, so I don't think I would have been released. However, I have met several men who were there at the front and who survived, and they told me the realities we never heard about back home.'

"Tell me about them, will you?"

"If you really want me to I will. But are you sure you want to hear? It's not the sort of thing one should discuss with a young lady."

I assured him I really did want to hear.

"Then you had better get me another drink. No, not that sherry stuff. If you look in the bottom of that cupboard you will find half a bottle of brandy."

I filled his glass, and he took a gulp.

"That's better. It upsets me, talking about it. My two beautiful boys died in those trenches. I reckon I need a bit of brandy inside just to think about it."

He finished the glass, and handed it back to me for a refill, then continued his narrative.

The things he told me that evening were deeply disturbing.

The trenches, I learned, were a series of massive dugouts intended as *temporary* camouflage in flat countryside that offered no natural protection for an army. In the event, they were used for four years of continuous warfare, and provided living accommodation for soldiers.

For months on end men were camped underground in trenches that were always damp, and sometimes waterlogged. Conditions were so cramped, and the men so tightly packed side by side, that the only way to sleep was to stand with their heads and shoulders learning over the parapet. Trench-foot (rotting of the skin caused by a fungal infection), frost-bite and gangrene were rife. The men endured filthy clothes, unchanged for weeks, and lice, millions of lice, that spread from one man to another and were impossible to eliminate. There was no sanitation, and drinking water was contaminated by mud and sewage. Hot food was an infrequent luxury. The rats were everywhere, thriving on an unlimited supply of human flesh as men died in such numbers that the living were unable to bury them.

Both armies were entrenched in their dugouts, often in a line only a hundred yards apart, and both sides were ordered to blow the other to smithereens. Men were being blown to pieces all around; arms, legs, heads were blown off; men were disembowelled, faces torn open, eyes shot out. If the men were ordered to leave their trenches ("go over the top" as it was called) and advance on foot towards the enemy line they would be heading straight into the line of fire and as many as 100,000 men could die in a single day.

And all the time, the cold, the damp, the hunger, the lice, and the stench of decomposition as rats gnawed at the corpses of the dead, drove the men stark raving mad.

"It's worse than I had thought, far worse," I said. "I can't even imagine it. I think I would have gone out of my mind in such a situation."

"Many did. And there was precious little sympathy for them."

"It is surprising that men did not simply run away. What was to stop them?"

"Desertion was punishable by death by firing squad."

In that instant I remembered my Uncle Maurice. He was a strange, withdrawn man subject to violent passions and irrational behaviour. He was potentially dangerous, and I had always been very afraid of him. My aunt told me that he had spent four years, the entire war, in the trenches and somehow miraculously survived. "Don't provoke him dear," she would say, and I could see that her entire life was devoted to trying to ease his mind and bring tranquillity to his life. She was an angel, and I thought at the time that he did not deserve her – but without her he would have been a nervous wreck, and probably even certified as insane.

She said, "He hardly even talks about the war, he bottles it up. Occasionally I can get him to talk about it, and I think it helps. But he still even now, thirty years afterwards, has dreadful nightmares. He screams and thrashes around the bed, and shouts to people in his dreams."

Having heard Mr Collett's descriptions of trench warfare I began, for the first time, to understand my Uncle Maurice, and my aunt's saintly devotion.

One day she told me the most dreadful story of all. Her husband had been ordered to join a firing squad of ten men to shoot one of their companions who had deserted and been captured. The victim was a boy of nineteen who had been so terrified by the noise of guns and the death happening all around him that his mind had snapped and he had run away screaming. He was quickly arrested, for he had not managed to stumble more than half a mile, then was court-martialled, and sentenced to death for desertion. All the men knew the boy and each one hoped and prayed he would not be ordered to join the firing squad. Ten men were selected and ordered to shoot the boy in cold blood, and my uncle was one of them.

*

I told the story to Mr Collett. For several moments he said not a word, but was busy cleaning out his pipe with a murderous-looking weapon, scraping and gouging the nicotine and tar from the encrusted bowl of his old friend. Then he blew hard down the stem and bits of black stuff flew into the air.

"That's better," he muttered "no wonder it wouldn't draw." Then he said, "Fill my glass, will you dear?"

I sloshed more brandy in, not knowing how strong it was. He took a sip and rolled it on his tongue, then said: "That is a dreadful story. It will remain with your uncle for the rest of his life. War brutalises a man. It is not surprising he was moody and violent. But you must remember two things: running away from battle has always been punishable by death. Military discipline must be harsh, or every soldier would run away; and secondly in a firing squad of ten men only one held a rifle with live ammunition – nine held blanks. So every man had a nine out of ten chance of not being responsible for the death of his colleague.

"I don't know what to think. I suppose it's as you say – military discipline must be harsh – but it's dreadful all the same. I find it almost unfathomable."

"Of course you do, my dear, you are in a profession that is devoted to caring for life, not destroying it. 'War is hell' – General William Sherman said that about the American Civil War a hundred years ago. It always has been hell and it always will be."

"My grandfather told me that his uncles had been in the Crimean Wars and never came back. The family never knew what happened."

"No they wouldn't. The common soldier was completely expendable, not even named. Did you know that after the battle of Sebastopol the bones of the dead were collected up in sacks and shipped back to Britain to be ground down into fertilizers that was sold to farmers for a profit."

"That can't be true."

"It is true. Perfectly true."

"It's disgusting! I think I'll try a shot of your brandy."

"Be careful. It's strong stuff."

"I'm not worried, I can take it." I boasted.

I poured some, and took a gulp as I had seen him do. It didn't just take the roof off my mouth; it set fire to my throat and gullet and windpipe. I started coughing and choking violently. He laughed. "I warned you."

When I had recovered, I said, "But that was a hundred years ago. They can't have been so callous after the First World War."

"Beautiful cemeteries were built all over Northern France, the graveyards of millions of young men. They rest in peace."

"Have you been there to see the resting place of Pete and Jack? It would be a comfort to you."

"No, they are not buried there."

"Where then?"

He sighed, a sigh so deep that all the sorrow of the world seemed gathered into it.

"We don't know what happened to them. A telegram, "missing presumed dead", was the message from the War Office. This was at the end of war. They had lived through three and a half years at the front, only to go missing presumed dead during the last few months. My Sally's heart was broken. Little Shirley was the only thing that kept us going."

He sat silent and still for a couple of minutes, sipping his brandy and sucking on his pipe. I did not care to interrupt his thoughts. When he spoke his voice was dull and resigned.

"About a year later we were informed that their bodies had never been found. Thousands of families received the same letter. You see men were just blown to pieces and nothing identifiable could be found. Or a trench wall might have collapsed and buried them alive; or they could have fallen and sunk into the mud and been sucked down, and the mud closed over them. We don't know. Millions of boys, on both sides, died and were never found. And millions of families are grieving still."

LONDON
1939–1945

I saw more of Mr Collett after that, but we never again mentioned the twins. He told me that Shirley, the pride of his heart, had had a good education, and passed the School Certificate, an achievement attained by very few East End girls in those days. This enabled her to go into the Post Office to be trained in accountancy and bookkeeping, to work as one of the counter staff. She also studied telegraphy and Morse code.

"It was two years of study," Mr Collett said. "The system was based on long and short sounds, or flashes of light. We spent many hours, the three of us, tapping and flashing messages to each other. Sally and I picked up some of the code, enough to learn the alphabet, but Shirley became a real expert. She had to be a touch-typist as well and could sit blindfolded, listening to a message being tapped out and typing the words with never a mistake. Then we darkened the room, and I sat flashing the code to her with a torch while she typed the message. Still no mistakes. Her skills were greatly valued when the Second World War came. In 1939 she was put straight onto the reserve Special Occupation List."

I asked him about his memories of the war and his admiration for Winston Churchill shone through.

"From 1935 onwards you had to be blind not to see that something was going to happen. Hitler was re-arming and mobilizing his troops, casting fear and unrest all over Europe. Unfortunately, most of our leaders seemed to be both blind and deaf. Only Churchill could see clearly and he poured out warnings, but his words fell on deaf ears, and the government refused to re-arm. Consequently, when war came in 1939, we were completely unprepared. We had the minimum trained army and navy, and virtually no equipment.

"Now, Churchill is a man who has interested me all my life. He is a contemporary of mine, and was also in the South African war. The first I heard of him was his famous escape from Pretoria prison, which electrified the troops, and the whole of England, when the news got back to London. The funniest thing about it was the letter he left behind for the Boer Minister of Defence. Something like: 'Sir, I have the honour to inform you that I do not consider your government has any right to detain me as a prisoner. I have therefore decided to escape from your custody,' and ending up: 'I remain, sir, your humble and obedient servant, Winston Churchill.'

"In 1916 Churchill became a lieutenant colonel of the Royal Scots Fusiliers (I was a Scots Guardsman, you remember). He served in the front line alongside his men, which was more than most of the officers did. After the war he dabbled in politics, but was never very successful. He made a lot of mistakes – but whatever he did, he did it on a grand scale, and he was always fascinating, a magnetic personality.

"I tell you, I have never been more relieved in all my life than when he became Prime Minister and Minister of Defence in 1940. He had moral strength and a command of words that put fire in your belly. He united the people to stand up to Hitler and fascism, even though we had only broken bottles and carving knives to fight with. I honestly believe that without Churchill we would have lost the war, and Britain would be a Nazi state today."

It was a sobering thought. I had always taken freedom for granted. I had been a child during the war, and had seen things through a child's eyes. It was not until after the war, when I was about ten years old, that I saw on a cinema newsreel the ghastly pictures of Belsen, Auschwitz, Dachau, and the many other death camps dotted across Europe. This was when I began to understand the evil we had been fighting.

Also, being a country-born child, I had seen very little of the war itself. We lived only thirty miles from London, but life was peaceful and untroubled. My mother took in evacuees, which was good fun as far as I was concerned. Food was scarce and I didn't see a banana or an orange until I was ten, but apart from that there might not have been a war going on at all. Where, I wondered, had Mr Collett spent the war?

His response was firm. London was his home and it was where he had remained throughout the war years. Sally didn't want to leave London either – it was where she had been born and bred. They both felt there really was no other option. This attitude was fairly typical of Londoners. In 1939 large-scale evacuations of women and children occurred, but within six months most of them were back. They couldn't cope with the countryside and returned in droves, preferring the risks of London to the quiet of the countryside.

I had heard a similar story from the Sisters. About seventy Poplar women, all of them pregnant, had been evacuated with two of the midwifery Sisters to Cornwall. One by one these young women returned, always giving the same reason: the silence got on their nerves; they were frightened of the trees and the fields; they couldn't stand the wind moaning. At the end of six months there were only around a dozen left, so the Sisters themselves returned to the place where they were needed the most – the heart of Poplar.

In 1940 Mr Collett retired from the Post Office. Straight away he joined the ARP (Air Raid Precautions) and Sally joined with him. In the early months of 1940 the duties were to see that government directives were carried out. This mainly involved checking that people carried gas masks, that blackout regulations were being observed, that sandbags were filled and that air-raid shelters were suitably equipped. At first, ARP wardens were often called snoopers and laughed at, but in September 1940 the Blitz started and their work really began.

For three long months London was bombed every night,

and there were sometimes daylight raids as well. Bombing was concentrated mainly on the Docklands, but this was also the area with the highest civilian population and hundreds of thousands of Londoners died or lost their homes.

If one looks at a map of London, the horseshoe loop in the Thames going round the Isle of Dogs is fairly obvious. From the air it is a landmark, and the German bomber pilots could not fail to see it. Bombs only had to be dropped on that target, and they were sure to hit either the docks or the housing around them. Thousands of tons of high explosive fell in less than three months. Poplar, housing up to 50,000 people to the square mile, was indeed a sitting target.

There were never enough air-raid shelters for such large numbers of people. In other parts of London people went into the Underground stations, but Poplar had none. The nearest underground was Aldgate. The government provided corrugated iron for people to build Anderson shelters in their gardens, but most Poplar people did not have a garden. Fortunately, many houses did have cellars, where people slept. The crypts of churches provided shelter for hundreds of people, and whole communities lived day and night in the churches. More than one baby was born in All Saints' crypt, as I learned from the Sisters. The overcrowding was terrible. Each person had just enough room to lie down, and no more.

There was always the fear that plague or disease would sweep through the shelters. Water and sewage pipes were frequently hit, but somehow they were always repaired, at least enough to prevent the spread of disease. Gas and electricity supplies were often hit too, but they were always patched up as well.

Mr Collett said to me: "Looking back it seems impossible, but everyone worked day and night, with amazing good spirit.

"When you are living in such conditions, close to death, every day is a gift. You are happy every morning to see the dawn break, and to know that you are still alive. Also, death was no stranger to us. Poplar people were used to suffering. Poverty, hunger, cold, disease and death have been with us for generations, and we have just accepted them as normal, so a few bombs couldn't break us.

"We were used to overcrowding, so the shelters didn't seem too bad. The loss of a house or rooms was no worse than eviction, and most people didn't have much furniture to lose anyway. A family would just move in with neighbours who still had a roof over their heads.

"It was an extraordinary time. Suffering and anguish were all around us, but so too, in a strange way, was exhilaration. We were determined not to be beaten. Two fingers up to Hitler, that was the attitude. I remember one old woman we pulled out of the rubble. She wasn't hurt. She gripped my arm and said: 'That bugger Hitler. 'E's killed me old man, good riddance, 'e's killed me kids, more's the pity. 'E's bombed me 'ouse, so I got nowhere 'a live, bu' 'e ain't got me. An' I got sixpence in me pocket an' vat pub on ve corner, Master's Arms, ain't been bombed, so let's go an' 'ave a drink an' a sing-song.'"

There was even more devastation when the firebombs came, and it was these that were responsible for Sally's death. Both Mr Collett and his wife had had a premonition, sensing that one of them would be killed, but they didn't know who, or when. The firebombs were small, and burst into flames when they hit the ground. They were easy to put out – it could be done with a sandbag, or even a couple of blankets – but if the fire spread it could set whole buildings alight. The government appealed for volunteer fire-watchers who would go to the top of tall buildings to keep a watch on the area around them. They gave the alert when a firebomb fell, and the men with sandbags rushed to the spot at once to put out the fire. These fire-watchers had to know the area well, and were mostly old people who didn't have the physical strength to deal with all the digging and heavy lifting required in the streets. Sally volunteered. He said: "She and others went up the highest buildings with nothing but a tin hat to protect them from the explosives and firebombs. One night the building Sally was in got a direct hit. I never saw her again. Her body was never found."

After telling me this sad story he paused, and stared into the fire, for a few minutes, then said softly: "She knew the risk. We both did. I'm glad that she was taken first, and not left on her own. Death is kinder than life. There is no more suffering beyond the grave. We will meet again soon, I hope."

He said the words "soon, I hope" a second time, and I didn't know what to say, so I asked him about his daughter.

Shirley's skills in Morse code and telegraphy were classed as a "special occupation". She joined the WAAF (Women's Auxiliary Air Force) in 1940 and entered the Intelligence and Communications Corps of the RAF. Her father saw a little of her when she came home on leave, but mostly he didn't even know where she was stationed, because all her work was highly confidential, and secrecy was tight. She had never married, and had always been very close to her parents. After her mother's death she threw herself into her work.

Mr Collett, too, found that hard work was the only remedy for unhappiness. After Sally's death he worked day and night, not bothering much about food or sleep. As an ARP warden he did anything and everything that needed doing: helping ambulance men, digging away rubble, carrying water, filling sandbags, and mending burst pipes. He went out at night when bombs were dropping all around, not caring if he was killed. He helped people out of burning buildings, got them to shelters, carried babies, pushed prams. "It was a hard time, but satisfying," he told me, "and all the while I fancied Sal was looking down on me, and sharing the experience."

Many of his experiences from those days he could still vividly recall. He told me about one little boy, about six or seven years old, he said he would never forget. The wardens had dug him out of the rubble he had been buried under for several hours. He was underneath the body of his mother. She must have thrown herself over her son in order to protect him, when the bomb fell.

She was quite stiff and cold, but he was safe beneath her. One does not know the psychological damage that such an experience can inflict, however. He said the boy's name was Paul. Mr Collett mused: "He would be in his twenties now, and I often wonder how he has grown up, and if there has been any lasting mental damage."

He continued his tragic story. "During the next five years I saw Shirley occasionally. She was flourishing. War has that effect sometimes. The unusual circumstances bring out the best in some people. All her intelligence and leadership qualities placed her in positions of command, and she thrived on it. I was so proud of her.

"In 1944 it seemed that the war was ending and we dared to plan for her demob and picking up our life again. But it never does to plan ahead in wartime. The V1 and V2 rocket attacks started. At Christmas 1944 I was told by the RAF that a rocket had fallen on the staff headquarters where Shirley was stationed, and that she had been killed. I have been alone ever since."

THE SHADOW OF THE WORKHOUSE

Jenny kissed me when we met,
Jumping from the chair she sat in . . .
Say I'm weary, say I'm sad,
Say that health and wealth have missed me,
Say I'm growing old, but add,
Jenny kissed me.
Leigh Hunt

Poplar was destined for change. Town planners had a new broom with which to sweep clean, and they were so successful that they swept virtually everything away. Poplar had survived the war, the blitz, the doodlebugs and the V2 rockets. The people had picked themselves up, brushed off the debris, and formed themselves into a community again, almost indistinguishable from the communities of their parents and grandparents. What finally destroyed Poplar was the good intentions of bureaucracy and social planning.

The tenements were to be demolished. In 1958 and 1959 notice was served to thousands of tenants and alternative accommodation was offered. This could be as far away as Harlow, Bracknell, Basildon, Crawley or Hemel Hempstead, which might as well have been the North Pole, as far as most of the older people were concerned. Social workers and housing officers buzzed in and out of the tenements all day with sheaves of forms and good advice and forced good cheer. The residents were not taken in. Most were wary or apprehensive. Some were distraught.

This was the time, and the only time, when I felt sympathy for Mr Collett's neighbour. She came up to me one day as I entered the court of Alberta Buildings and said piteously, "Vey sez we go' 'a go. Go where? Somewhere we don' know, somewhere a long way off. Somewhere no one'll know me, an' I won' know no one. It ain't right, it ain't. I've always paid me ren', you can look a' me book. Never a day la'e. I keeps me flat clean, like me mum used 'a. You can see for yerself. Can' chew do somefink? Ve Sisters 'ave a lo' of say in fings round here."

All the Sisters experienced scenes like this. The idea amongst the older generation that the Sisters would somehow intervene and help them save their little homes was touchingly persistent, but quite erroneous, of course. We tried to comfort the people as best we could, but I doubt if it did much good. The community was doomed. The people who had seen off Hitler by sticking two fingers up and carrying on were themselves seen off the premises.

Then the demolition men took over. The land became valuable. Big business stepped in. The ordinary people didn't stand a chance. Tower blocks were built, which were supposed to be so much better than the tenements. In fact they were the same thing, only far worse, because interaction between neighbours had been stripped away. The courtyards had gone, the inward-facing balconies had gone, walkways and stairways had gone, and upstairs and downstairs neighbours were strangers, with no obvious points of contact. The communal life of the tenements, with all its fraternity and friendship, all its enmity and fighting, was replaced by locked doors and heads turned away. It was a disaster in social planning. A community that had knitted itself together over centuries to form the vital, vibrant people known as "the Cockneys" was virtually destroyed within a generation.

But this was all in the future. We did not know, in 1959, that the effects would be so catastrophic to the Poplar people. We only knew what was happening at the time – namely that the Canada Buildings were to go. We discussed it endlessly over the luncheon table, and one of the nuns said, "Well, if the tenements go, it won't be long before we have to go, because we won't be needed here."

We all looked at each other with sadness, but Sister Julienne said, without a trace of regret: "For more than eighty years we have served God in Poplar. If we are no longer needed here, He will give us other work to do. In the meantime, I suggest we stop speculating on the future and get on with the job in hand."

When I next visited Mr Collett, a social worker was just leaving. She looked harassed, poor soul, and was besieged by women as she stepped across the courtyard. I felt sorry for her. What a job! You are on a hiding to nothing, I thought as I watched her go.

Mr Collett's legs were almost better now, and as he was quite capable of dressing the superficial wounds himself, I called only once a fortnight to check that there was no deterioration. His walking was much better and he was able to get about easily, which was entirely due to simple, regular treatment. Nursing is one of the most satisfying jobs in the world.

He was silent and thoughtful as I undid the bandages. I think we were both wondering what the other was thinking.

He was the first to break the silence. "You've heard, I suppose, that the Buildings are being closed? Yes, Of course you know all about it. I don't understand why. These buildings are sound. They were still here after the Blitz, when thousands of terraces went down like packs of cards. The Canada Buildings will last for centuries, yet they want to pull them down. All my ghosts will be cleared away with the rubble. Will they be laid to rest, I wonder? Will I?" His words sounded like a premonition.

"What are they offering you?" I asked.

He started, as though I had interrupted a dream. "Offering me? Oh, I don't know. Several things: a flat in Harlow; another in somewhere called Hemel Hempstead. I've got to think about it. I must say, it's very good of them to offer me anything at all. When I was a boy, if a landlord gave notice to quit, he was not obliged to offer you anything else. So I'm grateful for that, and I told the lady social worker so."

I smiled at his generous disposition. There can't have been many social workers at that troubled time who heard an expression of gratitude. "How long have you got to decide?" I asked.

"A few weeks. Perhaps a month. No longer. It's all very sudden."

It was indeed sudden. The sound of children playing was the first thing to go. Flats were vacated, and removal men were in and out of the courtyards; windows were boarded up; the stairways were left dirty and increasingly derelict; dustbins rolled across the cobbles. The constant hum of human activity was replaced by empty echoes as the courts picked up the sound of a single voice and threw it backwards and forwards, till it fell silent in the still air.

I wondered how much more I would see of Mr Collett. If he was going miles away to the countryside of Hertfordshire or Essex, how often would I be able to visit him? Our cosy evenings of sherry and chocolates and chats seemed to be coming to an end.

I popped in on him about a week later to ask if he had come to a decision. He had.

"I'm going to St Mark's in Mile End," he said. "When I was young, it used to be a workhouse. But that was a long time ago. Now it is a residential home for old codgers like myself. I think it will be for the best. The lady social worker tells me I will be well looked after. I'm going next week."

I was shocked and alarmed by the news. The shadow of the workhouse had darkened the lives of countless people for more than a century. Although officially closed in 1930 by Acts of Parliament, workhouses had merely lingered on under another name. I feared for Mr Collett, but I did not like to express my doubts, or even to sound negative, so I simply said: "I'll come and see you, I promise."

Back at Nonnatus House, I poured out my misgivings to Sister Julienne. She was thoughtful and looked grave, but said: "You must understand that this is his decision. He is intelligent, and I think he probably realises that he will not be able to manage to look after himself, alone, in a new place."

I was young and passionate, and argued the case. "But he's so much better now. He can get around without any trouble. Although his eyesight is dim, he's not blind, and he can find everything he needs."

Sister Julienne smiled her sweet, beautiful smile. "Yes, my dear, I know, but that is only because he knows where everything is, and habit makes it possible for him to continue living alone. In other surroundings he would be lost. It is the same for most old people."

My unease persisted, but I knew there was nothing I could do.

A few days later, when I was in the area, I thought I would pop in to arrange a final evening with my old friend. To my astonishment, the flat was empty. I peered through the curtainless window. Everything was the same – but different. Inanimate objects have a life of their own, especially when they are the daily companions of a living soul. Without that life, they take on a bleak, desolate appearance, like furniture piled up in a warehouse. I knew he was gone, and didn't need anyone to confirm it, although the woman next door stepped out, or rather shuffled out. Gone was her self-righteous aggression; gone, her busybody ways and manners. Instead she exuded a dull, helpless apathy and despair. Her voice was subdued. 'E's gorn. Vey took 'im vis mornin' wiv 'is case. Vey'll take me an' all, vey will." She shuffled back into her flat, and bolted the door. Poplar people never bolted their doors in daytime, unless they were afraid of someone.

At Nonnatus House, I felt a heavy sense of loss as I climbed the stairs. It had all been so sudden. My first thought was to go and see him at once, but then I dithered around, thinking that he needed time to settle in and get to know other people. Perhaps it was all for the best. If a thing has to be, it's best to do it quickly. He was a wise old man; he would not have agreed to go so soon if he had thought there was anything to be gained by delay.

It was about a fortnight later, after lunch, when I cycled up to Mile End to find St Mark's. I entered by the huge iron gate, and looked at the bleak grey buildings. I was accustomed to the old workhouse buildings, because most of them had been converted into hospitals or isolation units. I knew that they all had a particularly grim appearance, but I had never seen anything as forbidding as St Mark's. My heart sank as I looked around.

I enquired after Mr Collett. Perhaps I had imagined that some helpful, pretty young nurse in a natty little uniform would take me straight to him. Not so. The only person I saw was a rather dirty-looking porter pushing a trolley of bins. He spoke no English, but pointed to a door. Inside was a sort of office area with no one around. It was cold and high-ceilinged, with plaster cracking and crumbling off the walls. I called, and my voice echoed up the stairwell. Still no one came.

I wandered out, and through another door. A wide, empty corridor stretched ahead, with doors going off it. I opened one, and entered a large, square room, where a lot of old men were sitting around Formica-topped tables. For a room so full of humanity it was eerily quiet. Faces looked up at me, all blank and expressionless. I looked round, but could not see Mr Collett. Nor could I see anyone to ask about him. Some plates rattled, which indicated a kitchen, and I went towards the sound. Two young men were inside, but neither of them spoke English. They repeated the name "Collett" several times, but shook their heads. One of them indicated another building. I followed the advice, and was fortunate to meet a porter, who said, "You need Reception, dear, over there," pointing to the first door I had entered.

Back in the hall with the echoing stairwell I hung around, and "hello-ed" for about twenty minutes. Eventually a middle-aged man entered, carrying a sheaf of papers. I gave him my request.

He looked at me in astonishment. "You want to see a Mr Collett? Is that what you are saying?"

"Yes."

"Why? Are you a social worker?"

"No. I just want to see him. Have I come at the wrong time, then? Am I out of visiting hours?"

"No. We don't have any visiting hours. We generally don't get any visitors. I'll have to open the office and find out where this Mr Collett is."

In the office, he thumbed through piles of papers. "I think I've found him. Mr Joseph Collett. Is that the name you want? Block E, Fifth Floor. Go up that staircase you see opposite."

He pointed to a stone staircase. I climbed five flights and pushed open the heavy door, entering a room similar to the one I had seen on the ground floor. It was large, with about twenty Formica-topped tables and four hard-backed chairs at each table. Old men were sitting on most of the chairs, their arms on the table, staring at the man opposite. Some had their heads down, resting on their arms. No one spoke. The room smelt acrid with urine and body odour. The high windows let in light, but they were too high for anyone to see out.

I looked around until I saw Mr Collett at the far end of the room. He was looking down at the table at which he was sitting, and did not see me approach. I went straight up to him and kissed him.

He gasped, looked up, and tears filled his eyes. His lips trembled, and the tears fell. He whispered, "My maiden, my Jenny, you've come, then." He was too overwhelmed to say anything more.

The chair opposite was empty, so I sat down and we held hands across the table.

"I would have come sooner, only I thought you should have a chance to settle in, and get to know your companions. I'm so sorry if you thought I wasn't coming."

He muttered, "Yes . . . no . . . I mean, that's all right, my pet, that's all right. You're here, and I love you for it. I'm so grateful." He squeezed my hand.

I bit my lip, close to tears myself, and looked round at the cheerless room, filled with lethargic old men saying nothing. I didn't know what to say myself. We had never had any difficulty with conversation before; in fact, time had always seemed too short for all that we had to say. But now I was tongue-tied. I asked empty questions like: "Are you all right, then?" "What's the food like?" "Are you comfortable here?" to all of which he replied, bleakly, "Yes, I'm doing very nicely, thank you. You don't want to worry your head about me."

Minutes ticked by, and there were long silences. I knew I would have to go, because I had my evening visits to start at 4 p.m. It had taken me at least forty-five minutes to find him, and time was short. It had been only the briefest of visits, and I hated leaving him, as I tried, haltingly, to explain.

He said, simply, "You go, my maid, and don't mind me."

I kissed him again, and fled from the room. At the door, I turned. He was stroking the cheek where my lips had touched him, and his tears were falling fast onto the table.

I don't know how it was I didn't have an accident as I cycled back to Nonnatus House. I was filled with sorrow.

After supper, I spoke to Sister Julienne. She listened in silence to what I had to say, and didn't speak for a long time. Thinking she hadn't taken it in, I said. "You do understand what I'm saying, don't you? It is simply dreadful. He shouldn't be there."

"Oh yes, my dear, I understand all right. I was thinking of Our Lord's words to Peter, as recorded in St John's Gospel: 'When you are young, you go where you wish, but when you are old, others will take you where you do not wish to go.' This was taken to indicate the manner in which St Peter would die, but I have always thought that it is a general reflection about us all. For we all grow old, and very few of us retain our health and strength to the last. Most of us become helpless and completely dependent on others, whether we like it or not. Old age is a time when we learn the virtue of humility."

I didn't know what to say. I had often found myself in a similar position with Sister Julienne. She had a purity of thought and a simplicity of expression that were quite unanswerable.

She continued: "Mr Collett's tragedy is that all his family were killed in the wars. The tragedy is loneliness, not the surroundings, which I doubt he notices. What you see as intolerable living conditions may be all par for the course to him. If he were living in luxury in a palace, he would be just as lonely. You are his only friend, Jenny, and he loves you. You must stay with him."

I said that I had pledged myself to do that, and then I started to rail against the folly and inhumanity of turning him out of the flat where he had been comfortable and independent.

She stopped me in mid-sentence. "Yes, I know all that. But you must understand that the Canada Buildings have long been due for demolition. People are not going to put up with a bug-infested environment and insanitary conditions today. The Buildings must go, so the people must go. I am well aware of the fact that most of the old people who are being moved will not be able to adjust to new surroundings, and that many of them will die as a consequence. Which brings me back to the words of Jesus: 'When you are old, men will take you where you do not want to go.'"

She smiled at me, because I must have looked so sad, and said: "Now I must go and take Compline. Why not join us this evening?"

The beauty and timelessness of the monastic office of Compline eased my troubled soul.

"The Lord grant us a quiet night and a perfect end."

I thought of Mr Collett and all the other old men, isolated – even from each other – by loneliness.

"In thee, O Lord, have I put my trust. Let me never be put to confusion."

The candles lighting the altar were reflected on the windows, shutting the dark without, and enclosing the nuns within.

"Be thou my strong rock and house of defence."

Jews and Christians have drawn strength and wisdom from these psalms for two to three thousand years.

"Thou shalt not be afraid of any terror by night."

All those sad old men – were they afraid? Afraid of living, yet more afraid of dying?

"For He shall give his angels charge over thee."

Did they know any joy, in their joyless surroundings?

"Lighten our darkness, we beseech thee, O Lord."

Just hold them in your prayers, as Sister Julienne will in hers.

"Protect us through the silent hours of the night, so that we who are wearied by the changes and chances of this fleeting world may repose upon Thy eternal changelessness."

The Sisters left the chapel quietly. The Greater Silence had begun.

I saw Mr Collett as much as I could after that. I never stayed very long – half an hour perhaps, not more, and this was mainly because we both found it difficult to know what to say. The circumstances were just not right for cosy chats, and we were no good at small talk. Also the inertia, I think, was dulling the mind that had once been so alert. Knowing how much he used to enjoy radio documentary programmes and plays, I asked him if he listened to his wireless. He looked at me blankly, so I repeated the question.

"No, I haven't got my wireless. I don't know what they did with it. I don't think I could have it here, anyway, so it doesn't matter."

I asked what had happened to his things.

"I don't know. The lady social worker said she would look after all that. I suppose they were sold, and the money put into my account. I've got a bank account, you know. I gave her the number."

"Have you seen her since?"

"Oh yes, she came here. She is very pleasant. She gave me this."

He fumbled in the inside pocket of his waistcoat, and produced a bit of paper. It was a receipt for £96 14s. 6d. for the sale of furniture. I thought of the grandfather clock, the fine old table, and his high wooden armchair. Now all that was left was a piece of paper.

The big room with its high windows was oppressive, and the all-pervading smell of urine nauseating, but I doubt if the old men noticed this (after all, the sense of smell fades along with the other senses as age advances). The worst thing for them, I could see, was the boredom of having absolutely nothing to do, hour after hour, day after day. One or two got up and shuffled off to the lavatory, or to another room, which I was later to discover was the dormitory. But apart from that, they did nothing. A few played cards or dominoes, but the games never seemed to excite much interest. The *Daily Mirror* and the *Express* were passed around, and some of the men glanced at them but, from what I observed, most of them just sat at the tables, looking at each other. I never saw any other visitor, and I wondered how it was possible that so many old men could have no one at all who wanted to visit them. I saw only Block E, Fifth Floor, and I did not know how many other blocks and floors there were, filled with old men, seemingly abandoned, each day killing the time, until time killed them.

One day I asked Mr Collett where his pipe was and if he smoked it. He said, "We are only allowed to smoke on the balcony."

"Well, do you do so, then?"

"No, I don't know where the balcony is."

I felt very cross at such thoughtlessness on the part of the staff. They were not unkind, as far as I could see, but they were mostly Filipino or Indonesian young men, who spoke little or no English, and it obviously had not occurred to any of them to take a nearly blind man to the balcony and make sure that he knew how to find his way there and back.

"Well, let's go out to the balcony, then, and you can have a smoke, and we can get some fresh air at the same time. Have you got your pipe, your twist, and some matches?"

"Not on me. They are in my locker. I'll go and get them. You can come with me. I don't suppose anyone would mind."

He stood up, and felt his way along the tables to a short

corridor at the end of which was a wide double door leading into the dormitory. My experienced eye saw at once that it was the size of the average hospital ward, designed for twenty-eight or thirty beds. It held, at a rough guess, sixty or seventy. They lined each wall, and the far end wall also. They were small two-foot-six-inch iron bedsteads, with thin mattresses over sagging springs. Beside each was a tiny locker about twelve inches wide, and the beds touched the lockers on either side. I looked down towards the far end of the dormitory. There were no lockers, and the beds were so close to each other that, presumably, the only way the occupant could get in and out was by climbing over the end. Some were occupied by old men, who just lay there, sleeping or staring at the ceiling. My critical nurse's eye looked at the bed linen and blankets. All were filthy, and the stench of urine and faeces was evidence that fresh linen was a rarity. A ward sister would have had a team of cleaners in there in seconds. But I saw no staff at all that day.

Mr Collett felt his way along fourteen beds, and then went to the locker beside the fifteenth. I watched him, and noticed that he was walking with difficulty again. I thought, with alarm, about his leg ulcers – so much better, but only because of regular treatment. Was he still getting it? I looked around at the general neglect, and had misgivings. Perhaps he was treating the ulcers himself. I resolved to ask him before leaving that day.

He found his pipe and chuckled as he cradled his old friend in the palm of his hand. We made our way, first to the table where he had been sitting, and then to the balcony, counting the number of tables, and the direction he would have to take. I wanted to be sure he knew how to get there by himself. The door was big and heavy, with a metal safety bar, but he could manage to open it.

The fresh air was lovely, though cold, and the balcony was pleasant, but there was nowhere to sit down. I had to hold Mr Collett's pipe and matches whilst he cut up the tobacco. He filled the pipe and lit it, and, with a satisfied sigh, exhaled clouds of thick smoke. "Luxury," he murmured, "sheer luxury."

I noticed the way he was standing. It was not good. He was shuffling from one leg to the other, and taking a few steps backwards and forwards. I didn't like the signs. People with leg ulcers can usually walk, but standing still in one place is nearly impossible for them. I asked him how his legs were, and who was treating them.

"Well, I can do it myself."

"Yes, but do you?"

"Now and again, lass, now and again."

"How often? Every day?"

"Well, not quite every day; but enough, quite enough."

"Do the staff renew the dressings?"

"They looked at them when I first came here, but I don't recall since."

I was silent. Two months, no trained person dressing the ulcers or supervising his treatment. It was not good enough. I said, "I would like to have a look at them."

"Another time. Another time. I'm enjoying the fresh air, and the pipe, and, above all, your company. I know you'll have to go soon and I don't want to spoil it. You can look at my legs another day."

He was right. The time was drawing near to 4 p.m., and my evening visits. I could not linger, so I kissed him tenderly, and left him with his pipe, and a rare smile on his face.

THE LAST POST

Something told me that Mr Collett did not have long to live. I was anxious about his legs, but apart from that I could see that he would never adapt to the communal life of St Mark's. Sister Julienne had been quite right, I discovered. The unpleasant surroundings meant nothing to him at all. The tiny bed in a dormitory with about seventy other men was quite acceptable. In fact, he described himself as "Very comfortable. Doing nicely. They are very good to us here." So if he had no complaints about the conditions, I realised that I should not. His trouble was chronic loneliness, and the inability to adjust to change.

On two occasions when I visited I asked to see his legs, but he prevaricated, making different excuses each time, and I didn't think I could force the issue. The next occasion when I called he was not at his usual table. The man who generally sat opposite him pointed to the dormitory and said, "He ain't got up today."

I went to the dormitory, and in the fifteenth bed on the right Mr Collett lay motionless. I looked at him for a long time from the doorway, hating myself for hating the smell, and for not wanting to approach the bed. A sort of dread had entered my heart, and I wanted to turn and run.

He moved and coughed slightly, and this set me in action. I went up to his bed, kissed him, and whispered, "It's me. Are you all right? It's not like you to stop in bed."

He took my hands and kissed them, and murmured that he would be all right by and by.

I sat beside him, not talking, squeezing his hand from time to time, thinking, If he stays here, not moving, for several days he will get pneumonia, and that will be it. Pneumonia is the old man's friend, they say. A quiet and peaceful end. I hope he goes that way in his sleep. What greater blessing can we ask at the end of life?

Then it occurred to me that, whilst he was lying in bed, it would be easy to look at his legs, so I asked him if I could. He neither agreed nor disagreed, but seemed indifferent.

I pulled the blankets away from the foot of the bed, and the stench of decaying flesh rose to greet me. A rough, fluid-sodden bandage covered each leg, and I unwound them with difficulty. I had no surgical forceps, or scissors, and had to do it with my fingers. The bandages looked as though they had not been changed for a fortnight, and were stuck to the flesh underneath. As I tried to ease them away I thought I might be hurting him, but he did not move, nor show any sign of pain or distress.

At last the wounds were fully exposed. I had to grip the iron bedstead, and call upon all my nurse's training of discipline and self-control to avoid crying out. From the knee to the ankle there was no skin at all, just livid, suppurating flesh, oozing pus and blood. Daylight was fading fast, and the dim electric-light bulb hanging from the ceiling was no great help, but I thought I could see traces of black around the edge of the wound. I looked down at his feet. The toes looked greyish and swollen, one or two of them a darker colour than the others.

"Oh, my God, it can't be. Oh, please, no. Not him. It's not fair."

There was only one way to tell. I unfastened the brooch I was wearing and dug the pin deep into the centre of the wound on each leg. He didn't move. Then I dug it really hard into his toes. He didn't feel a thing. There could not be the slightest doubt: gangrene.

He said, "They are feeling better today. They've been giving me gyp the last few weeks, but they don't hurt now, and I guess they're getting better."

I had to control myself. Fortunately he could not see my face, but he was sensitive to my voice. "As long as you are comfortable, you just stay there. I'll go and get someone to put another dressing on, because I've taken the bandages off. I won't be long."

I raised the alarm, and later the superintendent and a doctor came to the dormitory, but in the meantime I had to leave for my evening work. After I had finished my visits, I cycled back to St Mark's and, for the last time, climbed the staircase to the Fifth Floor of Block E. Mr Collett had been transferred to Mile End Hospital.

I was relieved to hear it, and I cycled the half-mile down the road to the hospital in order to find out which ward he had been admitted to. It was too late to see him, but I was told that he was comfortable and sleeping.

Immediately after lunch the next day, I cycled up to the hospital and went straight to the ward. The ward sister told me that Mr Collett had been operated on that morning, and had not yet come round from the anaesthetic. The operation had been a mid-thigh amputation of both legs.

I was taken to the side room where he lay. The calm cleanliness and efficiency of the hospital was reassuring after the shambolic dirt of St Mark's. Mr Collett lay on spotless white sheets, his face calm and relaxed. A nasal tube was *in situ*, and a nurse was sucking the mucus from his throat with an aspirator. She then counted his pulse and checked the flow rate of the blood drip that was running into his arm. She smiled at me as she turned to go. Hospital protocol and discipline had the upper hand, and Mr Collett was now a part of it.

I sat with him for a little while, but he was fast asleep, and looked quite peaceful, so I left, resolving to come back after my evening visits, by which time he might have come round from the anaesthetic and would recognise me.

It was about 7.30 p.m. when I approached the ward, and the screams assailed me long before I pushed open the door. A harassed-looking staff nurse was on duty, and as I ran towards the side ward a frightened nurse whispered: "I think he's gone mad."

Mr Collett was sitting bolt upright in bed, his blind eyes staring, wide with terror. He was waving his arms and screaming: "Watch out, to your left, a grenade exploding." He screamed and ducked to escape an invisible missile flying over his head.

I ran to him, and took him in my arms. "It's me, Jenny. Me, I'm here."

He grabbed me with superhuman strength and pushed me down to the floor. "Get down, keep your head down. They'll blow you to bits. A bloke over there had his head blown off a minute ago. That one over there has lost both his legs. It's a terrible place to be. Gunfire all around. Down. GET DOWN!" He screamed with all his strength and hurled himself forward. The stumps of his legs twitched violently and he fell out of bed. He seemed impervious to the fall, and grabbed me, pulling me under the bed with him.

"Stay here. You'll be safe here, in the shelter. I'll keep a lookout for any other poor soul. Look out!" He screamed and looked up. "That plane, see, it's just dropped its load of bombs, they're coming for us. It'll be a direct hit." He screamed louder than ever, "KEEP DOWN!"

A doctor and two male orderlies rushed into the ward. The staff nurse had a syringe filled and ready. The orderlies crawled under the bed and held Mr Collett, who was fighting and screaming. The doctor injected a powerful anaesthetic and a few minutes later, Mr Collett rolled over onto his side, asleep, but the stumps of his legs twitched violently with involuntary nervous spasms.

We were all shaken and trembling. The two orderlies picked the old man up and put him back into bed. He looked peaceful again. The hospital staff left, but I sat by his bedside for a long time, crying quietly.

At nine thirty the night sister asked me to leave, saying he would be kept sedated all night, and telling me to ring in the morning.

Before breakfast, I rang the hospital, and was told that Mr Collett had died peacefully at 3.30 a.m.

*

There was no last post for the old soldier; no solemn drum roll; no final salute; no lowering of the colours. There was just a contract funeral, arranged by the hospital, leaving from a hidden area next to the morgue. A priest and one mourner followed the coffin, and we travelled in the hearse, next to the driver. I had not thought of flowers until nearly at the hospital gate, so I had bought a bunch of Michaelmas daisies from a street flower-seller. We were driven to a cemetery somewhere in North London. I don't remember where it was. I only remember a cold, bleak November day, as we stood on either side of the open grave, the priest and I, reciting the office for the burial of the dead: "Dust to dust, ashes to ashes." The men shovelled the soil over the coffin, and I laid the purple daisies on the rich brown earth.

CODA

It was many years later – perhaps fifteen or twenty years – when Mr Collett visited me. I was happily married, my daughters growing up, my life in full flow. I had not thought of Mr Collett for years.

I woke in the middle of the night, and he was standing at the side of my bed. He was as real as my husband sleeping beside me. He was tall, and upright, but looked younger than when I had known him, like a handsome man of about sixty or sixty-five. He was smiling, and then he said, "You know the secret of life, my dear, because you know how to love."

And then he disappeared.

Epilogue

In 1930 the workhouses were closed by Act of Parliament – officially, that is. But in practice it was impossible to close them. They housed thousands of people who had nowhere else to live. Such people could not be turned out into the streets. Apart from that, many of them had been in the workhouses for so long, subject to the discipline and routine, that they were completely institutionalised, and could not have adjusted to the outside world. Also, the 1930s were the decade of economic depression, with massive unemployment nationwide. Thousands of workhouse inmates suddenly thrown onto the labour market would only have made matters worse.

So the workhouses were officially designated "Public Assistance Institutions" and, in order to make them more acceptable, would be locally referred to by such names as "Glebe House", "Rose House", and so on. But in practice they carried on much the same as before. The label "pauper" was replaced by "inmate", and the uniform was scrapped. Comforts, such as heating, a sitting room, easy chairs and better food were introduced. Inmates were allowed out. The inhumane practice of splitting families was stopped. But still it was institutional life. The staff were the same, and the attitudes and mindset of the master and officers were stuck firmly in the nineteenth century. Discipline remained strict, sometimes inflexible, depending on the character of the master, but punishments for transgression of the rules were relaxed, and life was certainly easier for the inmates of the Institution than it had been for the paupers of the workhouse.

The buildings continued in use for many decades for a variety of purposes. Some were used as mental hospitals right up until the 1980s, when they were finally closed by the Prime Minister, Margaret Thatcher. Many were used as old people's homes, and my description of Mr Collett's last weeks in such a place in the late 1950s is by no means unique. I was giving a talk to the East London History Society about this book when it was first published, and a lady in the audience stood up and said, "Your description is not exaggerated. In the 1980s I was with a group of people taken round an old people's home which had formerly been a workhouse and the conditions you describe were exactly the same. This was, as far as I remember, in 1985 or 1986."

The infirmaries continued as general hospitals for many decades. But the stigma of the old association with the workhouses was never eradicated. During my nursing career I saw many times the fear in a patient's eyes who thought they'd been put in a workhouse, even though they were in a modern hospital. In 2005 I was giving a radio talk and I mentioned this. The interviewer said, "I know exactly what you mean. Only a few years ago, in 1998, my granny was taken to the infirmary. She begged and pleaded not to go because she thought she was being put in the workhouse. She was terrified, and I swear it was that which killed her." The stigma lingered and most of the old infirmaries in the country have now been demolished, or converted into commercial or residential buildings

We who live comfortable, affluent lives in the twenty-first century cannot begin to imagine what it must have been like to be a pauper in a workhouse. We cannot picture relentless cold with little heating, no adequate clothing or warm bedding, and insufficient food. We cannot imagine our children being taken away from us because we are too poor to feed them, nor our liberty being curtailed for the simple crime of being poor. There are very few records left to tell us what the lives of workhouse paupers were like. Every workhouse kept meticulous records – but these were official records written by administrators; the paupers themselves kept no records. Similarly there are very few photographs of the paupers. Thousands of archive photographs of the buildings, the guardians, the masters, their wives and officers can be found in council records; but there are virtually none of the paupers themselves. The few that we do have are tragic to behold. There is a blank, hopeless look on all the faces, the same dull eyes, the same death-like despair.

But before we condemn the workhouses as an example of nineteenth-century exploitation and hypocrisy we must remember that the mores of the time were completely different from the standards of today. For the working class, life was nasty, brutish and short. Hunger and hardship were expected. Men were old at forty, women worn out at thirty-five. The death of children was taken for granted. Poverty was frankly regarded as a moral defect. Social Darwinism (the strong adapt and survive, the weak are crushed) was borrowed and distorted from the *Origin of Species* (1858) and applied to human organisation. These were the standards of society, accepted by rich and poor alike, and the workhouses merely reflected this.

Is there anything good that can be said about the old workhouse system? I think there is. Thousands of children who would have died of starvation on the streets were housed and reared – brutally, perhaps, by modern standards, but they survived, and after the 1870 Education Act, they were also educated. Mass illiteracy became history, and within a couple of generations the population of Great Britain could read and write.

I recall one woman who was over eighty when I met her in the year 2000. She was an illegitimate child of a servant girl and her master. His wife discovered the girl's pregnancy and dismissed her. The girl went to the workhouse – that was in 1915. The old lady said to me, "I am grateful to the workhouse. I learned the value of discipline and good behaviour. I learned to read and write. No, I never knew my mother, but none of us did. When I was fourteen I went into service. But I bettered myself, and learned secretarial work in night classes, and became a secretary. I am very proud of what I have achieved. I don't like to think what might have happened to me had it not been for the workhouse."

Further Reading

Mayhew's London, by Henry Mayhew, edited by Peter Quennell. (Hamlyn Publishing Group, 1969)

The Scandal of the Andover Workhouse, by Ian Anstruther (Alan Sutton, 1984)

The Workhouse System 1834–1929, by M. A. Crowther (Batsford, 1981)

The People of the Abyss, by Jack London (London, 1903)

The Poor Law, by S. Styles (Macmillan, 1985)

Outcast London, by G. Jones, edited by G. Steadman (Oxford, 1971)

In Darkest London, by William Booth (London, 1890)

The Life and Labour of the Poor (nine vols.), by Charles Booth (London, 1880–1892)

Pauper Palaces, by Ann Digby (Routledge, 1978)

The Workhouse, by Norman Longmate (Maurice Temple-Smith, 1974)

Down and Out in Paris and London, by George Orwell

The Victorian Workhouse, by Trevor May (Shire Publication, 1997)

The English Poor Law 1780–1930, by Michael Rose (David and Charles, 1971)

Into Unknown England 1866–1913, edited by Peter Keating (Fontana/Collins, 1976)

'The Homeless' from *In Darkest England and the Way Out* (William Booth, 1890)

'On the Verge of the Abyss' from *In Darkest England and the Way Out* (William Booth, 1890)

'The Submerged Tenth' from *In Darkest England and the Way Out* (William Booth, 1890)

'The Bitter Cry of Outcast London', by Andrew Mearns (first published in *The Pall Mall Gazette*, 1883)

'A Night in a Workhouse', by James Greenwood (first published in *The Pall Mall Gazette*, 1866)

Workhouses of the North, by Peter Higginbotham (Tempus Publications, 1999)

Call the Midwife

A True Story of the East End in the 1950s

JENNIFER WORTH

Clinical Editor
Terri Coates MSc, RN, RM, ADM, Dip Ed

PHOENIX

A PHOENIX PAPERBACK

First published in Great Britain in 2002
by Merton Books
This paperback edition published in 2008
by Phoenix,
an imprint of Orion Books Ltd,
Orion House, 5 Upper St Martin's Lane,
London WC2H 9EA

An Hachette UK company

This is a work of non-fiction, and the events it recounts are true. However, certain names and identifying characteristics of some of the people who appear in its pages have been changed. The views expressed in this book are the author's.

A CIP catalogue record for this book is available from the British Library.

Typeset by Input Data Services Ltd, Bridgwater, Somerset

Printed and bound in Great Britain by Clays Ltd, St Ives plc

'Worth is indeed a natural storyteller – in the best sense of the term, with apparent artlessness in fact concealing high art – and her detailed account of being a midwife in London's East End is gripping, moving and convincing from beginning to end . . . *Call the Midwife* is also a powerful evocation of a long-gone world . . . and in Worth it has surely found one of its best chroniclers'
David Kynaston, *Literary Review*

'A chilling insight into life for the average mother [in the 1950s]'
Sunday Express

'Worth is a stylish and dramatic writer' Matthew Parris, *Spectator*

'This delightful memoir brings to vivid life London's East End . . . full of humour . . . Worth's talent shines from every page'
Sainsbury's Magazine

'Funny, disturbing and incredibly moving, *Call the Midwife* opens a window onto the fascinating and colourful world of the East End in the 1950s' *Mature Times*

'Jennifer Worth's entertaining and moving account of her experiences among the Docklands people balances sentiment with gritty realism' *Docklands News*

'A candid, poignant memoir . . . this gripping narrative includes breech babies, adulterous relationships, urban pig-breeding and a surreal strip show in a brothel' *Townswoman*

'[Worth's] moving account . . . is beautifully written . . . A book of memories which aims to elevate the profession of midwifery in the public consciousness' *Church of England Newspaper*

'In her marvellous new book . . . [t]here are desperately sad stories here, but tales of great hope too. Of ordinary people living, giving birth and building their families despite enormous hardship and poor sanitation. And of midwives delivering superb care in the toughest conditions *East End Life*

'Nobody who reads *Call the Midwife* will ever forget it'
The Woman Writer

'Descriptions of life which are not for the easily offended reader. No detail of either midwifery or prostitution is left undepicted in graphic detail' *Methodist Recorder*

'The Docklands in London's East End in the 1950s seems more like the nineteenth century than 50 years ago' *Good Book Guide*

'Sheer magic' *The Lady*

Jennifer Worth trained as a nurse at the Royal Berkshire Hospital in Reading. She then moved to London to train as a midwife. She later became a staff nurse at the Royal London Hospital, Whitechapel, then ward sister and later night sister at the Elizabeth Garrett Anderson Hospital in Euston. Music has always been her passion, and in 1973 Jennifer left nursing in order to study music intensively. She gained the Licentiate of the London College of Music in 1974 and was awarded a Fellowship ten years later. Jennifer married Philip Worth in 1963 and they live together in Herftordshire. They have two daughters and three grandchildren.

By Jennifer Worth

Shadows of the Workhouse
Call the Midwife
Eczema and Food Allergy: The Hidden Cause – My Story
Farewell to the East End

This book is dedicated to Philip, my dear husband

The history of 'Mary' is also dedicated to the memory of Father Joseph Williamson and Daphne Jones

ACKNOWLEDGEMENTS

All nurses and midwives, many long since dead, with whom I worked half a century ago

Terri Coates, who fired my memories

Canon Tony Williamson, President of The Wellclose Trust

Elizabeth Fairbairn for her encouragement

Pat Schooling, who had courage to go for original publication

Naomi Stevens, for all her help with the Cockney dialect

Suzannah Hart, Jenny Whitefield, Dolores Cook, Peggy Sayer, Betty Howney, Rita Perry

All who typed, read and advised

Tower Hamlets Local History Library and Archives

The Curator, Island History Trust, E14

The Archivist, The Museum in Dockland, E14

The Librarian, Simmons Aerofilms

CONTENTS

PREFACE

In January 1998, the *Midwives Journal* published an article by Terri Coates entitled "Impressions of a Midwife in Literature". After careful research right across European and English-language writing, Terri was forced to conclude that midwives are virtually non-existent in literature.

Why, in heaven's name? Fictional doctors grace the pages of books in droves, scattering pearls of wisdom as they pass. Nurses, good and bad, are by no means absent. But midwives? Whoever heard of a midwife as a literary heroine? Yet midwifery is the very stuff of drama. Every child is conceived either in love or lust, is born in pain, followed by joy or sometimes remorse. A midwife is in the thick of it, she sees it all. Why then does she remain a shadowy figure, hidden behind the delivery room door?

Terri Coates finished her article with a lament for the neglect of such an important profession. I read her words, accepted the challenge, and took up my pen.

INTRODUCTION

Nonnatus House was situated in the heart of the London Docklands. The practice covered Stepney, Limehouse, Millwall, the Isle of Dogs, Cubitt Town, Poplar, Bow, Mile End and Whitechapel. The area was densely populated and most families had lived there for generations, often not moving more than a street or two away from their birthplace. Family life was lived at close quarters and children were brought up by a widely extended family of aunts, grandparents, cousins and older siblings, all living within a few houses, or at the most, streets of each other. Children would run in and out of each other's homes all the time and when I lived and worked there, I cannot remember a door ever being locked, except at night.

Children were everywhere, and the streets were their playgrounds. In the 1950s there were no cars in the back streets, because no one had a car, so it was perfectly safe to play there. There was heavy industrial traffic on the main roads, particularly those leading to and from the docks, but the little streets were traffic-free.

The bomb sites were the adventure playgrounds. They were numerous, a terrible reminder of the war and the intense bombing of the Docklands only ten years before. Great chunks had been cut out of the terraces, each encompassing perhaps two or three streets. The area would be roughly boarded off, partly hiding a wasteland of rubble with bits of building half standing, half fallen. Perhaps a notice stating DANGER – KEEP OUT would be nailed up somewhere, but this was like a red rag to a bull to any lively lad over the age of about six or seven, and every bomb site had secret entries where the boarding was carefully removed, allowing a small body to squeeze through. Officially no one was allowed in, but everyone, including the police, seemed to turn a blind eye.

It was undoubtedly a rough area. Knifings were common. Street fights were common. Pub fights and brawls were an everyday event. In the small, overcrowded houses, domestic violence was expected. But I never heard of gratuitous violence children or towards the elderly; there was a certain respect for the weak. This was the time of the Kray brothers, gang warfare, vendettas, organised crime and intense rivalry. The police were everywhere, and never walked the beat alone. Yet I never heard of an old lady being knocked down and having her pension stolen, or of a child being abducted and murdered.

The vast majority of the men living in the area worked in the docks.

Employment was high, but wages were low and the hours were long. The men holding the skilled jobs had relatively high pay and regular hours, and their jobs were fiercely guarded. Their skills were usually kept in the family, passed from father to sons or nephews. But for the casual labourers, life must have been hell. There would be no work when there were no boats to unload, and the men would hang around the gates all day, smoking and quarrelling. But when there was a boat to unload, it would mean fourteen, perhaps eighteen hours of relentless manual labour. They would start at five in the morning and end around ten at night. No wonder they fell into the pubs and drank themselves silly at the end of it. Boys started in the docks at the age of fifteen, and they were expected to work as hard as any man. All the men had to be union members and the unions strove to ensure fair rates of pay and fair hours, but they were bedevilled by the closed shop system, which seemed to cause as much trouble and ill feeling between workers as the benefits it accrued. However, without the unions, there is no doubt that the exploitation of workers would have been as bad in 1950 as it had been in 1850.

Early marriage was the norm. There was a high sense of sexual morality, even prudery, amongst the respectable people of the East End. Unmarried partners were virtually unknown, and no girl would ever live with her boyfriend. If she attempted to, there would be hell to pay from her family. What went on in the bomb sites, or behind the dustbin sheds, was not spoken of. If a young girl did become pregnant, the pressure on the young man to marry her was so great that few resisted. Families were large, often very large, and divorce was rare. Intense and violent family rows were common, but husband and wife usually stuck together.

Few women went out to work. The young girls did, of course, but as soon as a young woman settled down it would have been frowned upon. Once the babies started coming, it was impossible: an endless life of child-rearing, cleaning, washing, shopping and cooking would be her lot. I often wondered how these women managed, with a family of up to thirteen or fourteen children in a small house, containing only two or three bedrooms. Some families of that size lived in the tenements, which often consisted of only two rooms and a tiny kitchen.

Contraception, if practised at all, was unreliable. It was left to the women, who had endless discussions about safe periods, slippery elm, gin and ginger, hot water douches and so on, but few attended any birth control clinic and, from what I heard, most men, absolutely refused to wear a sheath.

Washing, drying and ironing took up the biggest part of a woman's working day. Washing machines were virtually unknown and tumble driers had not been invented. The drying yards were always festooned with clothes, and we midwives often had to pick our way through a forest of flapping linen to get to our patients. Once in the house or flat, there would be more washing to duck and weave through, in the hall, the stairways, the kitchen, the living room and the bedroom. Launderettes were not introduced until the 1960s, so all washing had to be done by hand at home.

By the 1950s, most houses had running cold water and a flushing lavatory in the yard outside. Some even had a bathroom. The tenements, however, did not, and the public wash-houses were still very much in use. Grumbling boys were taken there once a week to have a bath by determined mothers. The men, probably under female orders, carried out the same weekly ablution. You would see them going to the bath-house on a Saturday afternoon with a small towel, a piece of soap, and a dour expression, which spoke of a weekly tussle once again waged and lost.

Most houses had a wireless, but I did not see a single TV set during my time in the East End, which may well have contributed to the size of the families. The pubs, the men's clubs, dances, cinemas, the music halls and dog racing were the main forms of relaxation. For the young people, surprisingly, the church was often the centre of social life, and every church had a series of youth clubs and activities going on every night of the week. All Saints Church in the East India Dock Road, a huge Victorian church, had many hundreds of youngsters in its youth club run by the Rector and no less than seven energetic young curates. They needed all their youth and energy to cope, night after night, with activities for five or six hundred young people.

The thousands of seamen of all nationalities that came into the docks did not seem to impinge much upon the lives of the people who lived there. "We keeps ourselves to ourselves," the locals said, which meant no contact. Daughters were carefully protected: there were plenty of brothels to cater for the needs of the seamen. In my work I had to visit two or three of them, and I found them very creepy places to be in.

I saw prostitutes soliciting in the main roads, but none at all in the little streets, even on the Isle of Dogs, which was the first landing place for the seamen. The experienced professional would never waste her time in such an unpromising area, and if any enthusiastic amateur had been rash enough to attempt it, she would soon have been driven out, probably with violence, by the outraged local residents, men as well as women. The brothels were well known, and always busy. I daresay they were illegal, and raided from time to time by the police, but that did not seem to affect business. Their existence certainly kept the streets clean.

Life has changed irrevocably in the last fifty years. My memories of the Docklands bear no resemblance to what is known today. Family and social life has completely broken down, and three things occurring together, within a decade, ended centuries of tradition – the closure of the docks, slum clearance, and the Pill.

Slum clearance started in the late 1950s, while I was still working in the area. No doubt the houses were a bit grotty, but they were people's homes and much loved. I remember many, many people, old and young, men and women, holding a piece of paper from the Council, informing them that their houses or flats were to be demolished, and that they were to be rehoused. Most were sobbing. They knew no other world, and a move of four miles seemed like going to the ends of the earth. The moves shattered the extended family, and children suffered as a result. The transition also literally killed many old people who could not adapt. What is the point of a spanking new flat with central heating and a bathroom, if you never see your grandchildren, have no one to talk to, and your local, which sold the best beer in London, is now four miles away?

The Pill was introduced in the early 1960s and modern woman was born. Women were no longer going to be tied to the cycle of endless babies; they were going to be themselves. With the Pill came what we now call the sexual revolution. Women could, for the first time in history, be like men, and enjoy sex for its own sake. In the late 1950s we had eighty to a hundred deliveries a month on our books. In 1963 the number had dropped to four or five a month. Now that is some social change!

The closure of the docks occurred gradually over about fifteen years, but by about 1980 the merchant ships came and went no more. The men clung to their jobs, the unions tried to defend them, and there were numerous dockers' strikes during the 1970s, but the writing was on the wall. In fact the strikes, far from protecting jobs, merely accelerated the closures. For the men of the area, the docks were more than a job, even more than a way of life – they were, in fact, life itself – and for these men, the world fell apart. The ports, which for centuries had been the main arteries of England, were no longer needed. And therefore the men were no longer needed. This was the end of the Docklands as I knew them.

In the Victorian era, social reform had swept through the country. For the first time authors wrote about iniquities that had never before been exposed, and the public conscience was stirred. Among these reforms, the need for good nursing care in hospitals gained the attention of many farsighted and educated women. Nursing and midwifery were in a deplorable state. It was not considered a respectable occupation for any educated woman, and so the illiterate filled the gap. The caricature figures of Sairey Gamp and Betsy Prig – ignorant, filthy, gin-swilling women – created by Charles Dickens, may seem hilarious as we read about them, but would not have been funny if you had been obliged, through poverty, to place your life in their hands.

Florence Nightingale is our most famous nurse, and her dynamic organisational skills changed the face of nursing for ever. But she was not alone, and the history of nursing records many groups of dedicated women who devoted their lives to raising the standards of nursing. One such group was the Midwives of St Raymund Nonnatus,* They were a religious order of Anglican nuns, devoted to bringing safer childbirth to the poor. They opened houses in the East End of London, and in many of the slum areas of the great industrial cities of Great Britain.

In the nineteenth century (and earlier, of course) no poor woman could afford to pay the fee required by a doctor for the delivery of her baby. So she was forced to rely on the services of an untrained, self-taught midwife, or "handywoman" as they were often called. Some may have been quite effective practitioners, but others boasted a frightening mortality rate. In the mid-nineteenth century, maternal mortality amongst the poorest classes stood at around 35–40 per cent, and infant mortality was around 60 per cent. Anything like eclampsia, haemorrhage, or malpresentation, would mean the inevitable death of the mother. Sometimes these handywomen would abandon a patient to agony and death if any abnormality developed during labour. There is no doubt that their working practices were insanitary, to say the least,

* The Midwives of St Raymund Nonnatus is a pseudonym. I have taken the name from St Raymund Nonnatus, the patron saint of midwives, obstetricians, pregnant women, childbirth and newborn babies. He was delivered by Caesarean section ("*non natus*" is the Latin for "not born") in Catalonia, Spain, in 1204. His mother, not surprisingly, died at his birth. He became a priest and died in 1240.

and thereby spread infection, disease and often death.

Not only was there no training, but there was also no control over the numbers and practice of these handywomen. The Midwives of St Raymund saw that the answer to this social evil lay in the proper training of midwives and control of their work by legislation.

It was in the struggle for legislation that these feisty nuns and their supporters encountered the fiercest opposition. From about 1870 the battle raged; they were called "an absurdity", "time wasters", "a curiosity", and "an objectionable body of busy-bodies". They were accused of everything from perversion to greed for unlimited financial gain. But the Nonnatus Nuns would not be put down.

For thirty years the battle continued, but in 1902 the first Midwives Act was passed and the Royal College of Midwives was born.

The work of the Midwives of St Raymund Nonnatus was based upon a foundation of religious discipline. I have no doubt that this was necessary at the time, because the working conditions were so disgusting, and the work so relentless, that only those with a calling from God would wish to undertake it. Florence Nightingale records that when she was in her early twenties she saw a vision of Christ, telling her that her life was required for this work.

The St Raymund midwives worked in the slums of the London Docklands amongst the poorest of the poor and for about half of the nineteenth century they were the only reliable midwives working there. They laboured tirelessly through epidemics of cholera, typhoid, polio, and tuberculosis. In the early twentieth century, they worked through two world wars. In the 1940s, they remained in London and endured the Blitz with its intensive bombing of the docks. They delivered babies in air-raid shelters, dugouts, church crypts and underground stations. This was the tireless, selfless work to which they had pledged their lives, and they were known, respected and admired throughout the Docklands by the people who lived there. Everyone spoke of them with sincere love.

Such were the Midwives of St Raymund Nonnatus when I first knew them: an order of nuns, fully professed and bound by the vows of poverty, chastity, and obedience, but also qualified nurses and midwives, which is how I came to be among them. I did not expect it, but it turned out to be the most important experience of my life.

CALL THE MIDWIFE

Why did I ever start this? I must have been mad! There were dozens of other things I could have been – a model, air hostess, or a ship's stewardess. The ideas run through my head, all glamorous, highly paid jobs. Only an idiot would choose to be a nurse. And now a midwife . . .

Two-thirty in the morning! I struggle, half asleep, into my uniform. Only three hours sleep after a seventeen-hour working day. Who would do such a job? It is bitterly cold and raining outside. Nonnatus House itself is cold enough, and the bicycle shed even colder. In the dark I wrench at a bicycle and crack my shin. Through blind force of habit, I fit my delivery bag on to the bicycle, and push it out into the deserted street.

Round the corner, Leyland Street, across the East India Dock Road and then on to the Isle of Dogs. The rain has woken me up and the steady pedalling calms my temper. Why did I ever go into nursing? My thoughts flit back five or six years. Certainly there had been no feeling of vocation, none of the burning desire to heal the sick that nurses are supposed to feel. What was it then? A broken heart certainly, the need to get away, a challenge, the sexy uniform with the cuffs and ruffs, the pinched-in waists and pert little caps. Were they reasons though? I can't tell. As for the sexy uniform, that's a laugh, I think as I pedal through the rain in my navy gabardine, with the cap pulled down well over my head. Sexy, indeed.

Over the first swing bridge that closes off the dry docks. All day they teem with noise and life, as the great vessels are loaded and unloaded. Thousands of men: dockers, stevedores, drivers, pilots, sailors, fitters, crane drivers, all toiling ceaselessly. Now the docks are silent, the only sound is the movement of water. The darkness is intense.

Past the tenements where countless thousands sleep, probably four or five to a bed, in their little two-room flats. Two rooms for a family of ten or twelve children. How do they manage it?

I cycle on, intent on getting to my patient. A couple of policemen wave and call out their greetings; the human contact raises my spirits no end. Nurses and policemen always have a rapport, especially in the East End. It's interesting, I reflect, that they always go around in pairs for mutual protection. You never see a policeman alone. Yet we nurses and midwives are always alone, on foot or bicycle. We would never be touched. So deep is the respect, even reverence, of the roughest, toughest docker for the district midwives that we can go anywhere alone, day or night, without fear.

The dark unlit road lies before me. The road around the Isle is continuous, but narrow streets lead off it, criss-crossing each other, each containing thousands of terraced houses. The road has a romantic appeal because the sound of the moving river is always present.

Soon I turn off the West Ferry Road into the side streets. I can see my patient's house at once – the only house with a light on.

It seems there is a deputation of women waiting inside to greet me. The patient's mother, her grandmother (or were they two grandmothers?), two or three aunts, sisters, best friends, a neighbour. Well thank God Mrs Jenkins isn't here this time, I think.

Lurking somewhere in the background of this powerful sisterhood is a solitary male, the origin of all the commotion. I always feel sorry for the men in this situation. They seemed so marginalised.

The noise and the chatter of the women engulfs me like a blanket.

"Hello luvvy, how's yerself? You got 'ere nice an' quick, ven."

"Let's 'ave yer coat and yer 'at."

"Nasty night. Come on in an' get warm, ven."

"How about a nice cup o' tea? That'll warm the cockles, eh, luvvy?"

"She's upstairs, where you left 'er. Pains about every five

minutes. She's been asleep since you left, just afore midnight. Then she woke up, about two-ish, pains gettin' worse, an' faster, so we reckons as 'ow we ought 'a call the midwife, eh, Mum?"

Mum agrees, and bustles forth authoritatively.

"We got the water hot, an' a load o' nice clean towels, an' got the fire goin', so it's all nice an' warm for the new baby."

I have never been able to talk much, and in this situation I don't need to. I give them my coat and hat, but decline their tea, as experience has taught me that, in general, Poplar tea is revolting: strong enough to creosote a fence, stewed for hours, and laced with sticky sweet condensed milk.

I am glad that I shaved Muriel earlier in the day when the light was good enough to do it without risk of cutting her. I also gave the required enema at the same time. It's a job I hate, so thankfully it is over; besides which, who would want to give a two-pint soap-and-water enema (especially if there was no lavatory in the house), with all the resultant mess and smell, at two-thirty in the morning?

I go upstairs to Muriel, a buxom girl of twenty-five who is having her fourth baby. The gaslight sheds a soft warm glow over the room. The fire blazes fiercely, and the heat is almost suffocating. A quick glance tells me that Muriel is nearing the second stage of labour – the sweating, the slight panting, the curious in-turned look that a woman has at this time as she concentrates every ounce of her mental and physical strength on her body, and on the miracle she is about to bring forth. She doesn't say anything, just squeezes my hand and gives a preoccupied smile. I left her three hours earlier, in the first stage of labour. She had been niggling in false labour all day and was very tired, so I gave chloral hydrate at about 10 p.m., in the hope that she would sleep all night and wake in the morning refreshed. It hasn't worked. Does labour ever go the way you want it to?

I have to be sure how far on she is, so prepare to do a vaginal examination. As I scrub up, another pain comes on – you can see it building in strength until it seems her poor body will break apart. It has been estimated that, at the height of labour, each uterine contraction exerts the same pressure as the closing of the doors of an underground tube train. I can well believe it as I watch Muriel's labour. Her mother and sister are sitting with her. She clings to them in speechless, gasping agony, a breathless moan escaping her throat until it passes, then sinks back exhausted, to gather her strength for the next contraction.

I put on my gloves and lubricate my hand. I ask Muriel to draw her knees up, as I wanted to examine her. She knows exactly what I am going to do, and why. I put a sterile sheet under her buttocks and slip two fingers into her vagina. The head well down, anterior presentation, only a thin rim of cervix remaining, but waters apparently not yet broken. I listen to the foetal heart, a steady 130. Good. That is all I need to know. I tell her everything is normal, and that she hasn't far to go now. Then another pain starts, and all words and actions have to be suspended in the enormous intensity of labour.

My tray has to be set out. The chest of drawers has been cleared in advance to provide a working surface. I lay out my scissors, cord clamps, cord tape, foetal stethoscope, kidney dishes, gauze and cotton swabs, artery forceps. Not a great deal is necessary, in any case it has to be easily portable, both on a bicycle, and up and down the miles of tenement stairs and balconies.

The bed has been prepared in advance. We supplied a maternity pack, which was collected by the husband a week or two before delivery. It contains maternity pads – "bunnies" we call them – large absorbent sheets, which are disposable, and non-absorbent brown paper. This brown paper looks absurdly old fashioned, but it is entirely effective. It covers the whole bed, all the absorbent pads and sheets can be laid on it and, after delivery, everything can be bundled up into it and burned.

The cot is ready. A good size washing bowl is available, and gallons of hot water are being boiled downstairs. There is no running hot water in the house and I wonder how they used to manage when there was no water at all. It must have been an all night job, going out to collect it and boiling it up. On what? A range in the kitchen that had to be fuelled all the time, with coal if they could afford it, or driftwood if they couldn't.

But I haven't much time to sit and reflect. Often in a labour you can wait all night, but something tells me this one will not go that way. The increasing power and frequency of the pains, coupled with the fact that it is a fourth baby, indicate the second stage is not far away. The pains are coming every three minutes now. How much more can she bear, how much can any woman bear? Suddenly the sac bursts, and water floods the bed. I like to see it that way; I get a bit apprehensive if the waters break early. After the contraction, the mother and I change the soaking sheets as quickly as we can. Muriel can't get up at this stage, so we have to roll her. With the next contraction I see the head. Intense concentration is now necessary.

With animal instinct she begins pushing. If all is well, a multigravida can often push the head out in seconds, but you don't want it that way. Every good midwife tries to ensure a slow steady delivery of the head.

"I want you on your left side, Muriel, after this contraction. Try not to push now while you are on your back. That's it, turn over dear, and face the wall. Draw your right leg up towards your chin. Breathe deeply, carry on breathing like that. Just concentrate on breathing deeply. Your sister will help you." I lean over the low sagging bed. All beds seem to sag in the middle in these parts, I think to myself. Sometimes I have had to deliver a baby on my knees. No time for that now though, another contraction is coming.

"Breathe deeply, push a little; not too hard." The contraction passes and I listen to the foetal heart again: 140 this time. Still quite normal, but the raised heartbeat shows how much a baby goes through in the ordeal of being born. Another contraction.

"Push just a little Muriel, not too hard, we'll soon have your baby born."

She is beside herself with pain, but a sort of frantic elation comes over a woman during the last few moments of labour, and the pain doesn't seem to matter. Another contraction. The head is coming fast, too fast.

"Don't push Muriel, just pant – in, out – quickly, keep panting like that."

I am holding the head back, to prevent it bursting out and splitting the perineum.

It is very important to ease the head out between contractions, and as I hold the head back, I realise I am sweating from the effort required, the concentration, the heat and the intensity of the moment.

The contraction passes, and I relax a little, listening to the foetal heart again – still normal. Delivery is imminent. I place the heel of my right hand behind the dilated anus, and push forward firmly and steadily until the crown is clear of the vulva.

"With the next contraction, Muriel the head will be born. Now I don't want you to push at all. Just let the muscles of your stomach do the job. All you have to do is to try to relax, and just pant like mad."

I steel myself for the next contraction which comes with surprising speed. Muriel is panting continuously. I ease the perineum around the emerging crown, and the head is born.

We all breathe a sigh of relief. Muriel is weak with the effort.

"Well done, Muriel, you are doing wonderfully, it won't be long now. The next pain, and we will know if it's a boy or a girl."

The baby's face is blue and puckered, covered in mucus and blood. I check the heartbeat. Still normal. I observe the restitution of the head through one eighth of a circle. The presenting shoulder can now be delivered from under the pubic arch.

Another contraction.

"This is it Muriel, you can push now – hard."

I ease the presenting shoulder out with a forward and upward sweep. The other shoulder and arm follow, and the baby's whole body slides out effortlessly.

"It's another little boy," cried the mother. "Thanks be to God. Is he healthy, nurse?"

Muriel was in tears of joy. "Oh, bless him. Here, let me have a look. 'Ow, 'e's loverly."

I am almost as overwhelmed as Muriel, the relief of a safe

delivery is so powerful. I clamp the baby's cord in two places, and cut between; I hold him by the ankles upside down to ensure no mucus is inhaled.

He breathes. The baby is now a separate being.

I wrap him in the towels given to me, and hand him to Muriel, who cradles him, coos over him, kisses him, calls him "beautiful, lovely, an angel". Quite honestly, a baby covered in blood, still slightly blue, eyes screwed up, in the first few minutes after birth, is not an object of beauty. But the mother never sees him that way. To her, he is all perfection.

My job is not done, however. The placenta must be delivered, and it must be delivered whole, with no pieces torn off and left behind in the uterus. If there are, the woman will be in serious trouble: infection, ongoing bleeding, perhaps even a massive haemorrhage, which can be fatal. It is perhaps the trickiest part of any delivery, to get the placenta out whole and intact.

The uterine muscles, having succeeded in the massive task of delivering the baby, often seem to want to take a holiday. Frequently there are no further contractions for ten to fifteen minutes. This is nice for the mother, who only wants to lie back and cuddle her baby, indifferent to what is going on down below, but it can be an anxious time for the midwife. When contractions do start, they are frequently very weak. Successful delivery of the placenta is usually a question of careful timing, judgement and, most of all, experience.

They say it takes seven years of practice to make a good midwife. I was only in my first year, alone, in the middle of the night, with this trusting woman and her family, and no telephone in the house.

Please God, don't let me make a mistake, I prayed.

After clearing the worst of the mess from the bed, I lay Muriel on her back, on warm dry maternity pads, and cover her with a blanket. Her pulse and blood pressure are normal, and the baby lies quietly in her arms. All I have to do was to wait.

I sit on a chair beside the bed, with my hand on the fundus in order to feel and assess. Sometimes the third stage can take twenty to thirty minutes. I muse over the importance of patience, and the possible disasters that can occur from a desire to hasten things. The fundus feels soft and broad, so the placenta is obviously still attached in the upper uterine segment. There are no contractions for a full ten minutes. The cord protrudes from the vagina, and it is my practice to clamp it just below the vulva, so that I can see when the cord lengthens – a sign of the placenta separating and descending into the lower uterine segment. But nothing is happening. It goes through my mind that reports you hear of taxi drivers or bus conductors safely delivering a baby never mention this. Any bus driver can deliver a baby in an emergency, but who would have the faintest idea of how to manage the third stage? I imagine that most uninformed people would want to pull on the cord, thinking that this would help expel the placenta, but it can lead to sheer disaster.

Muriel is cooing and kissing her baby while her mother tidies up. The fire crackles. I sit quietly waiting, pondering.

Why aren't midwives the heroines of society that they should be? Why do they have such a low profile? They ought to be lauded to the skies, by everyone. But they are not. The responsibility they carry is immeasurable. Their skill and knowledge are matchless, yet they are completely taken for granted, and usually overlooked.

All medical students in the 1950s were trained by midwives. They had classroom lectures from an obstetrician, certainly, but without clinical practice lectures are meaningless. So in all teaching hospitals, medical students were attached to a teacher midwife, and would go out with her in the district to learn the skill of practical midwifery. All GPs had been trained by a midwife. But these facts seemed to be barely known.

The fundus tightens and rises a little in the abdomen as a contraction grips the muscles. Perhaps this is it, I think. But no. It doesn't feel right. Too soft after the contraction.

Another wait.

I reflect upon the incredible advance in midwifery practice over the century; the struggle dedicated women have had to obtain a proper training, and to train others. There has been recognised training for less than fifty years. My mother and all her siblings were delivered by an untrained woman, usually called the "goodwife" or the "handywoman". No doctor was present, I was told.

Another contraction coming. The fundus rises under my hand and remains hard. At the same time the forceps that I had clamped to the cord move a little. I test them. Yes, another four to six inches of cord comes out easily. The placenta has separated.

I ask Muriel to hand the baby over to her mother. She knows what I am going to do. I massage the fundus in my hand until it is hard and round and mobile. Then I grasp it firmly, and push downwards and backwards into the pelvis. As I push, the placenta appears at the vulva, and I lift it out with my other hand. The membranes slide out, followed by a gush of fresh blood and some clotted blood.

I feel weak with relief. It is accomplished. I put the kidney dish on the dresser, to await my inspection, and sit beside Muriel for a further ten minutes massaging the fundus, to ensure that it remains hard and round, which will expel residual blood clots.

In later years oxytocics would be routinely given after the birth of the baby, causing immediate and vigorous uterine contraction, so that the placenta is expelled within three to five minutes of the baby's birth. Medical science marches on! But in the 1950s, we had no such aids to delivery.

All that remains is to clean up. While Mrs Hawkin is washing and changing her daughter, I examine the placenta. It seems complete, and the membranes intact. Then I examine the baby, who appears healthy and normal. I bathe and dress him, in clothes that are ridiculously too big, and reflect upon Muriel's joy and happiness, her relaxed easy countenance. She looks tired, I think, but no sign of stress or strain. There never is! There must be an inbuilt system of total forgetfulness in a woman; some chemical or hormone that immediately enters the memory part of the brain after delivery, so that there is absolutely no recall of the agony that has gone before. If this were not so, no woman would ever have a second baby.

When everything is shipshape, the proud father is permitted to enter. These days, most fathers are with their wives throughout labour, and attend the birth. But this is a recent fashion. Throughout history, as far as I know, it was unheard of. Certainly in the 1950s, everyone would have been profoundly shocked at such an idea. Childbirth was considered to be a woman's business. Even the presence of doctors (all men until the late nineteenth century) was resisted, and it was not until obstetrics became recognised as a medical science that men attended childbirth.

Jim is a little man, probably less than thirty but he looks nearer forty. He sidles into the room looking sheepish and confused. Probably my presence makes him tongue-tied, but I doubt if he has ever had a great command of the English language. He mutters, "All right then, girl?" and gives Muriel a peck on the cheek. He looks even tinier beside his buxom wife, who could give him a good five stone in weight. Her flushed pink, newly washed skin makes him look even more grey, pinched and dried out. All the result of a sixty-hour working week in the docks, I think to myself.

Then he looks at the baby, hums a bit – he is obviously thinking deeply about a suitable epithet – clears his throat, and says, "Gaw, he aint 'alf a bit of all right, then." And then he leaves.

I regret that I have not been able to get to know the men of the East End. But it is quite impossible. I belong to the women's world, to the taboo subject of childbirth. The men are polite and respectful to us midwives, but completely withdrawn from any familiarity, let alone friendship. There is a total divide between what is called men's work and women's work. So, like Jane Austen, who in all her writing never recorded a conversation between two men alone, because as a woman she could not know what exclusively male conversation would be like, I cannot record much about the men of Poplar, beyond superficial observation.

I am about ready to leave. It has been a long day and night, but a profound sense of fulfilment and satisfaction lighten my step and lift my heart. Muriel and baby are both asleep as I creep out of the room. The good people downstairs offer me more tea, which again I decline as gracefully as I can, saying that breakfast will be waiting for me at Nonnatus House. I give instructions to call us if there seems to be any cause for worry, but say that I will be back again around lunch time, and again in the evening.

I entered the house in the rain and the dark. There had been a fever of excitement and anticipation, and the anxiety of a woman in labour, on the brink of bringing forth new life. I leave a calm, sleeping household, with the new soul in their midst, and step out into morning sunlight.

I cycled through the dark deserted streets, the silent docks, past the locked gates, the empty ports. Now I cycle through bright early morning, the sun just rising over the river, the gates open or opening, men streaming through the streets, calling to each other; engines beginning to sound, the cranes to move; lorries turning in through the huge gates; the sounds of a ship as it moved. A dockyard is not really a glamorous place, but to a young girl with only three hours sleep on twenty-four hours of work, after the quiet thrill of a safe delivery of a healthy baby, it is intoxicating. I don't even feel tired.

The swing bridge is open now, which means that the road is closed. A great ocean-going cargo boat is slowly and majestically entering the waters, her bows and funnels within inches of the houses on either side. I wait, dreamily watching the pilots and navigators guide her to her berth. I would love to know how they do it. Their skill is immense, taking years to learn, and is passed on from father to son, or uncle to nephew so they say. They are the princes of the docklands, and the casual labourers treat them with the deepest respect.

It takes about fifteen minutes for a boat to go through the bridge. Time to think. Strange how my life has developed, from a childhood disrupted by the war, a passionate love affair when I was only sixteen, and the knowledge three years later that I had to get away. So, for purely pragmatic reasons, my choice was nursing. Do I regret it?

A sharp piercing sound wakes me from my reverie, and the swing bridge begins to close. The road is open again, and the traffic begins to move. I cycle close to the kerb, as the lorries around me are a bit intimidating. A huge man with muscles like steel pulls off his cap and shouts, “Mornin’ narse.”

I shout back, “Morning, lovely day,” and cycle on, exulting in my youth, the morning air, the heady excitement of the docks, but above all in the matchless sensation of having delivered a beautiful baby to a joyful mother.

Why did I ever start? Do I regret it? Never, never, never. I wouldn’t swap my job for anything on earth.

NONNATUS HOUSE

Had anyone told me, two years earlier, that I would be going to a convent for midwifery training, I would have run a mile. I was not that sort of girl. Convents were for Holy Marys, dreary and plain. Not for me. I had thought that Nonnatus House was a small, privately run hospital, of which there were many hundreds in the country at that time.

I arrived with bag and baggage on a damp October evening, having known only the West End of London. The bus from Aldgate brought me to a very different London, with narrow unlit streets, bomb sites, and dirty, grey buildings. With difficulty I found Leyland Street and looked for the hospital. It was not there. Perhaps I had the wrong address.

I stopped a passerby and enquired for the Midwives of St Raymund Nonnatus. The lady put down her string bag and beamed at me cordially, the missing front teeth adding to the geniality of her features. Her metal hair-curlers gleamed in the darkness. She took a cigarette from her mouth and said something that sounded like, "Yer washa nonnatuns arse, eh dearie?"

I stared at her, trying to work it out. I had not mentioned "washing" anything, particularly anyone's arse.

"No. I want the Midwives of St Raymund Nonnatus."

"Yeah. Loike wha' oie sez, duckie. Ve Nonnatuns. Ober dere, dearie. Vat's veir arse."

She patted my arm reassuringly, pointed to a building, stuck the cigarette back in her mouth, and toddled off, her bedroom slippers flapping on the pavement.

At this point in my narrative it would be expedient to refer the bewildered reader to the supplement on the difficulties of writing the Cockney dialect. Pure Cockney is, or was, incomprehensible to an outsider, but the ear grows accustomed to the vowels and consonants, the inflexions and idiom, until after a while, it all becomes perfectly obvious. As I write about the Docklands people, I can hear their voices, but the attempt to reproduce the dialect in writing has proved to be something of a challenge!

But I digress.

I looked at the building dubiously; I saw dirty red brick, Victorian arches and turrets, iron railings, no lights, all next to a bomb site. What on earth have I come to? I thought. That's no hospital.

I pulled the bell handle, and a deep clanging came from within. A few moments later there were footsteps. The door was opened by a lady in strange clothes – not quite a nurse, but not quite a nun. She was tall and thin, and very, very old. She looked at me steadily for at least a minute without speaking, then leaned forward and took my hand. She looked all around her, drew me into the hallway, and whispered conspiratorially, "The poles are diverging, my dear."

Astonishment robbed me of speech, but fortunately she had no need of my reply, and continued, with near-breathless excitement, "Yes, and Mars and Venus are in alignment. You know what that means, of course?"

I shook my head.

"Oh, my dear, the static forces, the convergence of the fluid with the solid, the descent of the hexagon as it passes through the ether. This is a unique time to be alive. So exciting. The little angels clap their wings."

She laughed, clapped her bony hands, and did a little skip.

"But come in, come in, my dear. You must have some tea, and some cake. The cake is very good. Do you like cake?"

I nodded.

"So do I. We shall have some together, my dear, and you must give me your opinion on the theory that the depths in space are forever being pulled by the process of gravitation into heavenly bodies."

She turned and walked swiftly down a stone passage, her white veil floating behind her. I was in some doubt about whether to follow, because I thought I must surely have come to the wrong address, but she seemed to expect me to be right behind her, and talked all the while, asking questions to which she clearly did not expect an answer.

She entered a very large Victorian-looking kitchen with a stone floor, stone sink, wooden draining boards, tables and cupboards. The room contained an old-fashioned gas-stove with wooden plate-racks above it, a large Ascot water heater over the sink, and lead pipes attached to the walls. A large coke-burner stood in one corner, the flue running up to the ceiling.

"Now for the cake," said my companion. "Mrs B. made it this morning. I saw her with my own eyes. Where have they put it? You had better look around, dear."

Entering the wrong house is one thing, but poking around in someone else's kitchen is quite another matter. I spoke for the first time. "Is this Nonnatus House?"

The old lady raised her hands in a theatrical gesture and in clear, ringing tones cried out, "Not born, yet born in death. Born to greatness. Born to lead and inspire." She raised her eyes to the ceiling and lowered her voice to a thrilling whisper, "Born to be sanctified!"

Was she mad? I stared at her in dumb stupefaction, then repeated the question, "Yes, but is this Nonnatus House?"

"Oh, my dear, I knew the moment I saw you that you would understand. The cloud rests unbroken. Youth is freely given, the chimes sing of sad indigos, deep vermilions. Let us make what sense of it we can. Put the kettle on, dear. Don't just stand there."

There seemed to be no point in repeating my question, so I filled the kettle. The pipes all around the kitchen rattled and shook with a most alarming noise as I turned on the tap. The old lady poked around, opening cupboards and tins, chatting all the while about cosmic rays and confluent ethers. Suddenly she gave a cry of delight. "The cake! The cake! I knew I would find it."

She turned to me and whispered, with a naughty gleam in her eye, "They think they can hide things from Sister Monica Joan, but they are not smart enough, my dear. Plodding or swift, laughter or despair, none can hide, all will be revealed. Get two plates and a knife, and don't hang around. Where's the tea?"

We sat down at the huge wooden table. I poured the tea, and Sister Monica Joan cut two large slices of cake. She crumbled her slice into tiny pieces, and pushed them around her plate with long, bony fingers. She ate with murmurs of ecstatic delight, and winked at me as she gobbled morsels down. The cake was excellent, and a fellowship of conspiracy was entered into as we agreed that another slice would be in order.

"They will never know, my dear. They will think that Fred has had it, or that poor fellow who sits on the doorstep eating his sandwiches."

She looked out of the window. "There is a light in the sky. Do you think it is a planet exploding, or an alien landing?"

I thought it was an aeroplane, but I opted for the exploding planet, then said, "How about some more tea?"

"Just what I was about to suggest, and what about another slice of cake? They won't be back before seven o' clock, you know."

She chatted on. I could not make head nor tail of what she was on about, but she was enchanting. The more I looked at her, the more I could see fragile beauty in her high cheekbones, her bright eyes, her wrinkled, pale ivory skin, and the perfect balance of her head on her long, slender neck. The constant movement of her expressive hands, with their long fingers like a ballet of ten dancers, was hypnotic. I felt myself falling under a spell.

We finished the cake with no trouble at all, having agreed that an empty tin would be less conspicuous than a small wedge of cake left on a plate. She winked mischievously, and chuckled. "That tiresome Sister Evangelina will be the first to notice. You should see her, my dear, when she gets cross. Oh, the hideous baggage. Her red face gets even redder, and her nose drips. Yes, it actually drips! I have seen it." She tossed her head haughtily. "But what can it signify for me? The mystery of the evidence of consciousness is a house in a given time, a function and an event combined, and few are the elite, indeed, who can welcome such a realisation. But hush. What is that? Make haste."

She leaped up, scattering cake crumbs all over the table, the floor, and herself, grabbed the tin and hurried with it to the larder. Then she sat down again, assuming an exaggerated expression of innocence.

Footsteps were heard on the stone floor of the hallway, and female voices. Three nuns entered the kitchen, talking about enemas, constipation, and varicose veins. I concluded that I must, against all expectations, be in the right place.

One of them stopped, and addressed me, "You must be Nurse Lee. We were expecting you. Welcome to Nonnatus House. I am Sister Julienne, the Sister-in-Charge. We will have a little chat together in my office after supper. Have you eaten?"

The face and the voice were so open and honest, and the question so artless, that I could not reply. I felt the cake sitting heavily in the bottom of my stomach. I managed to murmur "yes, thank you" and surreptitiously brushed a crumb off my skirt.

"Well, you will excuse us if we have a small meal. We usually prepare our own supper because we all come in at different times."

The Sisters were bustling about, fetching plates, knives, cheese, biscuits and other things from the larder, and laying them on the kitchen table. A cry came from behind the door, and a red-faced nun emerged carrying the cake tin.

"It's gone. The tin's empty. Where is Mrs B.'s cake? She made it only this morning."

This must be Sister Evangelina. Her face was getting redder as she glared around.

No one spoke. The three Sisters looked at each other. Sister Monica Joan sat aloof, beyond all reproach, her eyes closed. The cake was doing something nasty to my intestines, and I knew that the enormity of my crime could not be concealed. My voice was husky as I whispered, "I had a little."

The red face and heavy figure advanced toward Sister Monica Joan. "And she's had the rest of it. Look at her, covered in cake crumbs. It's disgusting. Oh, the greedy thing! She can't keep her hands off anything. That cake was for all of us. You . . . you . . ."

Sister Evangelina was shaking with rage as she towered over Sister Monica Joan, who remained absolutely immobile, her eyes closed, as though she had not heard a word. She looked fragile and aristocratic. I could not bear it, and found my voice. "No, you've got it wrong. Sister Monica Joan had a slice, and I had the rest."

The three nuns stared at me in astonishment. I felt myself blush all over. Had I been a dog caught stealing the Sunday roast, I would have crept under the table with my tail between my legs. To have entered a strange house, and to have consumed the best part of a cake without the knowledge or consent of the lawful owners, was a solecism worthy of severe retribution. I could only mutter, "I'm sorry. I was hungry. I won't do it again."

Sister Evangelina snorted and banged the tin on the table.

Sister Monica Joan, whose eyes were still closed, head turned away, moved for the first time. She took a handkerchief from her pocket and handed it to Sister Evangelina, holding it by a corner with thumb and forefinger, the other fingers arched fastidiously. "Perhaps it is time for a little mopping up, dear," she said sweetly.

Rage boiled even more fiercely. The redness of Sister Evangelina's features turned to purple, and moisture gathered round her nostrils.

"No thank you, dear. I have one of my own," she spat out through clenched teeth.

Sister Monica Joan gave an affected little jump, brushed her face elegantly with the handkerchief, and murmured, as though to herself, "Methinks 'tis raining. I cannot abide the rain. I will retire. Pray excuse me, Sisters. We will meet at Compline."

She smiled graciously at the three Sisters, then turned to me, and gave me the biggest, naughtiest wink I had ever seen in my life. Haughtily, she sailed out of the kitchen.

I felt myself squirm with embarrassment as the door closed and I was left alone with the three nuns. I just wanted to sink through the floor, or run away. Sister Julienne told me to take my case to the top floor, where I would find a room with my name on the door. I had expected a heavy silence and three pairs of eyes following me as I left the kitchen, but Sister Julienne started talking about an old lady she had just visited, whose cat appeared to be stuck up the chimney. They all laughed, and to my intense relief the atmosphere lightened at once.

In the hallway, I seriously wondered whether or not to cut and run. The fact that I was in something like a convent, and not a hospital, was ridiculous, and the whole saga of the cake, humiliating. I could have just picked up my case and vanished into the darkness. It was tempting. In fact I might have done so had the front door not opened at that moment and two laughing young girls appeared. Their faces were pink and freshened by the night air, their hair untidy from the wind. A few spots of rain glistened on their long gaberdine raincoats. They were about my age, and looked happy and full of life.

"Hello!" said a deep, slow voice. "You must be Jenny Lee. How nice. You'll like it here. There are not too many of us. I'm Cynthia, and this is Trixie."

But Trixie had already disappeared down the passage towards the kitchen with the words: "I'm famished. See you later."

Cynthia's voice was astonishing – soft, low, and slightly husky. She also spoke extremely slowly, and with just a touch of laughter in her tone. In another type of girl, it would have been the cultivated, sexy voice of allure. I had met plenty of that type in four years of nursing, but Cynthia was not one of their number. Her voice was completely natural, and she could speak no other way. My discomfort and uncertainty left me, and we grinned at each other, friends already. I decided I would stay.

Later that evening I was called to Sister Julienne's office. I went filled with dread, expecting a severe dressing-down about the cake. Having endured four years of tyranny from hospital nursing hierarchies, I expected the worst, and ground my teeth in anticipation.

Sister Julienne was small and plump. She must have worked about fifteen or sixteen hours that day, but she looked as fresh as a daisy. Her radiant smile reassured me and dispelled my fears. Her first words were, "We will say nothing more about the cake."

I gave a great sigh of relief and sister Julienne burst out laughing, "Strange things happen to us all in the company of Sister Monica

Joan. But I assure you, no one will mention it again. Not even Sister Evangelina."

She said the last words with special emphasis, and I found myself laughing also. I was completely won over, and glad I had not been so rash as to run away.

Her next words were unexpected. "What is your religion, nurse?"

"Well . . . er . . . none . . . er . . . that is, Methodist – I think."

The question seemed astonishing, irrelevant, even slightly silly. To ask about my education, my training and experience in nursing, my plans for the future – all that would have been anticipated and acceptable. But religion? What had religion to do with anything?

She looked very grave, and said gently, "Jesus Christ is our strength and our guidance here. Perhaps you will join us sometimes at Church on a Sunday?"

Sister then went on to explain the training I would receive, and the routine of Nonnatus House. I would be under the supervision of a trained midwife for all visits for about three weeks, and then go out alone for ante- and post-natal work. All deliveries would be supervised by another midwife. Classroom lectures were held once a week in the evening, after work. All study would be done in our spare time.

She sat quietly explaining other details, most of which went over my head. I was not really listening, but wondering about her, and why I felt so comfortable and happy in her company.

A bell rang. She smiled. "It is time for Compline. I must go. We will meet in the morning. I hope you have a restful night."

The impact Sister Julienne made upon me – and, I discovered, most people – was out of all proportion to her words or her appearance. She was not imposing or commanding, nor arresting in any way. She was not even particularly clever. But something radiated from her and, ponder as I might, I could not understand it. It did not occur to me at the time that her radiance had a spiritual dimension, owing nothing to the values of the temporal world.

MORNING VISITS

It was about 6 a.m. when I arrived back at Nonnatus House after Muriel's delivery, and I was ravenous. A night's work, and a six to eight mile cycle ride can sharpen a young appetite like nothing else. The house was quiet when I entered. The nuns were in Chapel, and the lay staff not yet up. I was tired, but I knew that I had to clean my delivery bag, wash and sterilise my instruments, complete my notes and leave them on the office desk before I could eat.

Breakfast was laid out in the dining room, and I would take mine first, then go to bed for a few hours. I raided the larder. A pot of tea, boiled eggs, toast, home-made gooseberry jam, cornflakes, home-made yoghurt and scones. Heaven! Nuns always have a lot of home-made food, I had discovered. The preserves came from the many church bazaars and sales that seemed to go on throughout the year. The delicious cakes and biscuits and crunchy bread were made either by the nuns or by the many local women who came in to work at Nonnatus House. Any staff who had missed a meal through being called out had a free run of the larder. I was deeply grateful for this liberality, which was so unlike hospitals, where you had to plead for a bit of food if you had missed a meal for any reason.

It was a royal feast. I left a note asking to be called at about 11.30 a.m., and persuaded my tired legs to carry me up to my bedroom. I slept like a baby, and when someone roused me with a cup of tea, I couldn't remember where I was. The tea reminded me. Only the kind Sisters would send a cup of tea up to a nurse who had been working all night. In hospital it would be a bang on the door, and that would be that.

Downstairs I looked at the daybook. Only three calls before lunch. One to Muriel, and two visits to patients in the tenements that I would pass on the way. Four hours of sleep had refreshed me completely, and I got out the bike and cycled off in high spirits in the sunshine.

The tenements were always grim looking, whatever the weather. They were constructed as a four-sided building with an opening on one side, all the flats faced inwards. The buildings were about six storeys high, and sunlight seldom reached the inner courtyard, which was the social centre for the tenement dwellers. The courtyard contained all the washing lines and as there were literally hundreds of flats in each block, they were never without loads of washing flapping in the wind. The dustbins were also in the courtyard.

In the times I am writing about, the 1950s, there was a lavatory and running cold water in each flat. Before the introduction of these facilities, the lavatories and water were in the courtyard, and everyone had to go down to use them. Some of the tenements still retained the lavatory sheds, which were now used to house bikes or motor cycles. There did not seem many of them – perhaps three dozen at the most, and I wondered how there could have been enough lavatories for the occupants of about five hundred flats.

I threaded my way through the washing, and reached the stairway that I wanted. All the stairways were external, made of stone steps, and led up to a balcony, facing inwards, which ran the length of the building, going round all the corners, continuously. Each of the flats led off this balcony. Whereas the inner courtyard was the centre of social life, the balconies were the lanes, teeming with life and gossip. The balconies for the tenement women were equivalent to the streets of the terraced house dwellers. So close was the living space, that I doubt if anyone could get away with anything without all the neighbours knowing. The outside world held very little interest for the East Enders, and so other peoples' business was the primary topic of conversation – for most it was the only interest, the only amusement or diversion. It is not surprising that savage fighting frequently broke out in the tenements.

The tenements looked unusually cheerful in the noonday sun when I arrived that day. I picked my way through the litter and dustbins and washing in the courtyard. Small children crowded around. The midwife's delivery bag was an object of intense interest – they thought we carried the baby in it.

I found my entry, and climbed the five storeys to the flat I wanted.

All the flats were more or less the same: two or three rooms leading off each other. A stone sink in one corner of the main room; a gas stove and a cupboard constituting the kitchen. The lavatories, when they were introduced, had to be installed near the water supply, so they were situated in a corner, near to the sink. The installation of lavatories in each flat had been a great leap forward in public hygiene, because it improved the conditions in the courtyard. It also avoided the necessity of chamber pots in every flat which had to be emptied daily, the women carrying them downstairs to the emptying troughs. The ordure in the courtyards used to be disgusting, I was told.

The tenements of London's East End were built around the 1850s, mainly to house the dock workers and their families. In their day, they were probably considered to be adequate housing, quite sufficient for any family. They were certainly an improvement on the mud-floor hovels that they replaced, which barely protected a family from the elements. The tenements were brick built with a slate roof. Rain did not penetrate and they were dry inside. I have no doubt that 150 years ago, they were ever considered to be luxurious. A large family of ten to twelve people in two or three rooms would not have been judged as overcrowding. After all, the vast majority of mankind has lived in such conditions throughout history.

But times change, and by the 1950s the tenements were considered to be slum areas. The rents were a lot cheaper than the terraced houses, and consequently only the poorest families, those least able to cope, entered the tenements. Social law seems to suggest that the poorest families are often the ones that produce the greatest number of children, and the tenements were always teeming with them. Infectious diseases ran through the buildings like wildfire. So did the pests: fleas, body lice, ticks, scabies, crabs, mice, rats, and cockroaches. The pest control men from the council were always busy. The tenements were deemed unfit for human habitation and evacuated in the 1960s, and stood empty for over a decade. They were finally demolished in 1982.

Edith was small and stringy, and as tough as old boots. She looked a good deal older than forty years. She had brought up six children. During the war they had been bombed out of a terraced house, but it had not been a direct hit, and the family had survived. The children were then evacuated. Her husband was a dock labourer, and she was a munitions worker. After the bombing, she and her husband had moved into the tenements, which were cheaper to rent. They both lived there throughout the entire Blitz, and miraculously the tenements, which were the most densely populated dwellings, were not hit. Edith did not see her children for five years, but they were reunited in 1945. The family continued to live in the tenements, because of the rent, and because they had become used to the life. How anyone could manage in two rooms with six growing children was always beyond my understanding. But they did, and thought nothing of it.

She had not been pleased to fall pregnant again, in fact she was furious, but like most women who have a baby late in life, she was besotted with the little thing when he arrived, and cooed over him all the time. The flat was hung with nappies all over the place – there were no disposable nappies in those days – and a pram further reduced the living space in the crowded room.

Edith was up and doing. It was her tenth day after delivery. We kept mothers in bed for a long time after delivery in those days – ten to fourteen days known as the "lying-in" period. Medically speaking, this was not good practice, as it is far better for a woman to get moving as soon as possible, thus reducing the risk of complications such as thrombosis. But this was not known back then, and it had been traditional to keep women in bed after a birth. The great advantage was that it gave the woman a proper, and well-earned, rest. Other people had to do all the household chores, and for a brief period, she could lead a life of idleness. She needed to gather her strength, because once she was on her feet again, everything would devolve to her. When you consider the physical effort required to carry all the shopping up those stairs: coal and wood in the winter, paraffin for stoves, or rubbish carried down to the dustbins in the courtyard; if you consider the fact that to take the baby out, the pram had to be bumped down the stairs, one step at a time, and then bumped up again to get home, often loaded with groceries, as well as the baby, you might begin to understand how tough those women had to be. Almost every time you entered the tenements, you would see a woman bumping a big pram up or down. If they lived at the top, this would mean about seventy steps each way. The prams had big wheels, which made it possible, and were well sprung, which bounced the baby around. The babies loved it, and laughed and shrieked with glee. It was also dangerous if the steps were slippery, because the whole weight of the pram had to be controlled by the handle, and if the mother missed her footing or something happened and she let go, the pram and baby would go cascading down the length of the steps. I always helped when I saw a woman with a pram by taking the other end, therefore half the weight, which was considerable. The whole weight, for a woman alone, must have been tremendous.

Edith was in a grubby dressing gown, down-trodden slippers and hair curlers. She was simultaneously feeding her baby and smoking. The radio was blaring out pop music. She looked perfectly happy. In fact she looked a better colour, and younger than she had a couple of months earlier. The rest had obviously done her good.

"Hello, luvvy. Come on in. How about a nice cup of tea?"

I explained that I had other calls to make and declined the tea. I was able to see how feeding was going. The baby was sucking voraciously, but it struck me that Edith's thin little breasts probably did not contain much milk. However, it was far better for her to continue than to put the baby on to formula milk straight away, so I said nothing. If the baby fails to gain weight, or shows real signs of hunger, we can talk about it then, I thought. It was our practice to visit each day post-natally for a minimum of fourteen days, so we saw a lot of each patient.

It became the fashion about that time to put babies on to formula milk, and to suggest to the mother that this would be best for the baby. The Midwives of St Raymund Nonnatus did not go down this path, however, and all our patients were advised and helped to breastfeed for as long as possible. A fortnight of rest in bed helped to facilitate this, as the mother was not tiring herself by rushing around, and all her physical resources could go into producing milk for the baby.

As I glanced around the crowded room, the minimal kitchen area, and the general lack of facilities, it flashed through my mind that bottle-feeding would be the worst thing for the baby. Where on earth would Edith keep bottles, and tins of formula milk? How would she sterilise them? Would she bother to? Or even bother to keep them clean, never mind sterilising? There was no refrigerator, and I could well imagine bottles of half-consumed milk left lying around the place, to be given a second or third time to the baby, with no thought to the fact that bacteria quickly builds up in milk that has been left to go cold, and then warmed up again. No, breastfeeding would be much safer, even if there was not quite enough milk.

I remember lectures during my Part I midwifery training about the advantages of bottle-feeding, which sounded very convincing. When I first came to work with the Nonnatus Midwives, I thought them very old fashioned in always recommending breastfeeding. I had not taken into account the social conditions in which the Sisters worked. The lecturers were not dealing with real life. They were dealing with classroom situations and ideal young mothers who existed only in the imagination, from educated middle-class backgrounds, women who would remember all the rules, and do everything they were told to do. These classroom pundits were remote from silly young girls who would get the formula mixed up, get the measurements wrong, fail to boil the water, be unable to sterilise the bottles or the teats, fail to wash the bottles. Such theorists could not even imagine a half-empty bottle being left for twenty-four hours, then given to the baby, nor envisage a bottle rolling across the floor, picking up cat hairs, or any other dirt. Our lecturers never mentioned to us the possibility of anything else being added to the formula, such as sugar, honey, rice, treacle, condensed milk, semolina, alcohol, aspirin, Horlicks, Ovaltine. Perhaps such a possibility had never come the way of the writers of these textbooks. But they had been encountered often enough by the Nonnatus nuns.

Edith and her baby looked quite happy, so I did not disturb them, but said we would call the next day to weigh the baby, and to examine her.

I had another visit to make, to Molly Pearce, a girl of nineteen who was expecting her third baby and who had not turned up at the antenatal clinic for the last three months. As she was very near to full term, we needed to assess her.

There was noise coming from inside the door as I approached. It sounded like a row. I've always hated any sort of row or scene, and instinctively shrank away. But I had a job to do, so I knocked on the door. Instantly there was silence inside. It lasted a couple of minutes, and the silence seemed more menacing than the noise. I knocked again. Still silence, then a bolt pulled back, and a key turned – it was one of the few times I had known a door to be locked in the East End.

The unshaven face of a surly looking man stared suspiciously at me through a crack in the door. Then he swore obscenely, and spat on the floor at my feet, and made off down the balcony towards the staircase. The girl came towards me. She looked hot and flushed, and was panting slightly. "Good riddance," she shouted down the balcony, and kicked the doorpost.

She looked about nine months pregnant, and it occurred to me that rows of that sort could put her into labour, especially if violence was involved. But I had no evidence of that, as yet. I asked if I could examine her, as she had not been to antenatal clinic. She reluctantly agreed, and let me into the flat.

The stench inside was overpowering. It was a foul mixture of sweat, urine, faeces, cigarettes, alcohol, paraffin, stale food, sour milk, and unwashed clothes. Obviously Molly was a real slattern. The vast majority of women that I met had a true pride in themselves and their homes, and worked desperately hard. But not Molly. She had no such home-making instincts.

She led me into the bedroom, which was dark. The bed was filthy. There was no bed linen, just the bare mattress and pillows. Some grey army surplus blankets lay on the bed and a wooden cot stood in the corner. This is no place for a delivery, I thought to myself. It had been assessed as adequate by a midwife some months earlier, but quite obviously the domestic conditions had deteriorated since that time. I would have to report back to the Sisters.

I asked Molly to loosen her clothes and lie down. As she did so, I noticed a great black bruise on her chest. I enquired how it had happened. She snarled and tossed her head. " 'Im," she said, and spat on the floor. She offered no other information, and lay down. Perhaps my unexpected arrival has saved her from another blow, I thought.

I examined her. The baby's head was well down, the position seemed to be normal, and I could feel movement. I listened for the foetal heart, which was a steady 126 per minute. She and the baby seemed quite normal and healthy, in spite of everything.

It was only then that I noticed the children. I heard something in the corner of the dark bedroom, and nearly jumped out of my skin. I thought it was a rat. I focused my eyes in that direction, and saw two little faces peering round from behind a chair. Molly heard my gasp, and said, "It's all right. Tom, come 'ere."

But, of course, there must be young children around, I thought. This was her third pregnancy, and she was only nineteen, so they would be under school age. Why hadn't I noticed them before?

Two little boys of about two or three years old came out from behind the chair. They were absolutely silent. Boys of that age usually rush around, making no end of noise, but not these two. Their silence was unnatural. They had big eyes, full of fear, and they took a step or two forward, then clung to each other as though for mutual protection and retreated behind the chair again.

"That's all right, kids, it's only the nurse. She won't hurt you. Come 'ere."

They came out again, two dirty little boys, with snot and tear marks staining their faces. They were wearing only jumpers, a practice I had seen a lot in Poplar, and for some reason I found it particularly repellent. A toddler was dressed only at the top, and left naked from the waist down. It seemed to be especially prevalent among little boys. I was told that the women saved on washing this way. The child, before he was toilet trained, could then just urinate anywhere, and there would be no nappies or clothes to wash. Children would run around the tenement balconies and courtyards all day like this.

Tom and his little brother crept out from the corner, and ran to their mother. They seemed to be losing their fear. She put out an arm affectionately and they cuddled up to her. Well at least she's got some mothering instincts, I thought. I wondered how much time those little children spent behind the chair when their father was at home.

But I was not a health visitor, nor a social worker, and there was no point in speculating on that sort of thing. I resolved to report my observations to the Sisters, and told Molly that we would come back later that week, to ascertain that everything was available for a home delivery.

I still had Muriel to visit, and it was with great relief that I left the foul atmosphere of that flat.

The bright cold air outside and the cycle ride down to the Isle of Dogs refreshed my spirits, and I sped along.

"Hello, luvvy, how's yourself?" was the greeting shouted at me by several women, known and unknown to me. This was always the greeting called out from the pavement. "Lovely, thanks, ah's yerself?" I always replied. It was difficult not to slip into the cockney lingo.

I don't believe it, I said to myself, as I turned into Muriel's street, she can't be here already. Sure enough, Mrs Jenkins was there with her stick and her string bag, her head scarf over her curlers, and the same old long mildew-encrusted coat that she wore summer and winter. She was talking to a woman in the street, hanging intently on to to every word. She saw me slow down and came up to me and grabbed my sleeve with her filthy, long nailed hands.

"How is she, and the little one?" she rasped.

I was impatient, and pulled my arm away. Mrs Jenkins turned up at every delivery. No matter how far the distance, how bad the weather, how early or late in the day, Mrs Jenkins would always be seen hanging around the street. No one knew where she lived, or how she got her information, or how she managed to walk, sometimes three or four miles, to a house where a baby had been born. But she always did.

I was irritated and passed her without speaking. I regarded her as a nosy old busybody. I was young, too young to understand. Too young to see the pain in her eyes, or to hear the tortured urgency in her voice.

"'Ow is she? An' ve li'l one. 'Ow's ve li'l one?"

I went directly into the house without even knocking, and Muriel's mother immediately came forward, busy and smiling. These older generation mothers knew that they were absolutely indispensable at times like these, and it gave them a great sense of fulfilment, an ongoing purpose in life. She was all bustle and information. "She's been asleep since you left. She's been to the toilet and passed water. She's had some tea and now I'm getting her a nice bit of fish. Baby's been to the breast, I've seen to that, but she aint got no milk yet."

I thanked her and went up to the room. It looked clean, fresh and bright, with flowers on the chest of drawers. Compared to the filth and squalor of Molly's flat, it looked like paradise.

Muriel was awake but sleepy. Her first words to me were, "I don't want no fish. Can't you tell mum that? I don't feel like it, but she won't listen to me. She might listen to you."

Clearly there was a difference of opinion between mother and daughter. I did not want to be involved. I checked her pulse and blood pressure – normal. Her vaginal discharge was not excessive;

the uterus felt normal too. I checked her breasts. A little colostrum was coming out but no milk, as her mother had said. I wanted to try to get the baby to feed, in fact that was the main purpose of my visit.

In the cot the baby was sleeping soundly. Gone was the puckered appearance, the discoloration of the skin from the stress and trauma of birth, the cries of alarm and fear at entering this world. He was relaxed and warm and peaceful. Nearly everyone will say that seeing a newborn baby has an effect on them, ranging from awe to astonishment. The helplessness of the newborn human infant has always made an impression on me. All other mammals have a certain amount of autonomy at birth. Many animals, within an hour or two of birth, are up on their feet and running. Others, at the very least, can find the nipple and suck. But the human baby can't even do that. If the nipple or teat is not actually placed in the baby's mouth and sucking encouraged, the baby would die of starvation. I have a theory that all human babies are born prematurely. Given the human life span – three score years and ten – to be comparable with other animals of similar longevity, human gestation should be about two years. But the human head is so big by the age of two that no woman could deliver it. So our babies are born prematurely, in a state of utter helplessness.

I lifted the tiny creature from his cot and brought him to Muriel. She knew what to do, and had started squeezing a little colostrum from the nipple. We tried brushing a little of this over the baby's lips. He was not interested, only squirmed and turned his head away. We tried again, with the same reaction. It took at least a quarter of an hour of patiently trying to encourage the baby, but eventually, we persuaded him to open his mouth sufficiently to insert the nipple. He took about three sucks, and went off to sleep again. Sound asleep, as though exhausted from all his efforts. Muriel and I laughed.

"You would think he'd been doing all the hard work," she said, "not you and me, eh, nurse?"

We agreed to leave it for the time being. I would be back again in the evening, and she could try again during the afternoon, if she wanted to.

As I went downstairs, I smelt cooking. It may not have been to Muriel's liking, but it certainly got my gastric juices going. I was starving, and a delicious lunch awaited me at Nonnatus House. I bade them goodbye, and made for my bicycle. Mrs Jenkins was standing over it, as though she were keeping guard. How am I going to get rid of her? I thought. I didn't want to talk. I just wanted to get back to my lunch, but she was hanging on to the saddle. Clearly she was not going to let me go without some information.

"'Ow is she? An' ve li'l one. 'Ow's ve li'l one?" she hissed at me, her eyes unblinking.

There is something about obsessive behaviour that is off-putting. Mrs Jenkins was more than that. She was repellent. About seventy, she was tiny and bent, and her black eyes penetrated me, shattering any pleasant thoughts of lunch. She was toothless and ugly, in my arrogant opinion, and her filthy claw-like hands were creeping down my sleeve, getting unpleasantly close to my wrists. I pulled myself to my full height, which was nearly twice hers, and said in a cold professional voice, "Mrs Smith has been safely delivered of a little boy. Mother and baby are both well. Now, if you will excuse me, I must go."

"Fank Gawd," she said, and released my coat sleeve and my bicycle. She said nothing else.

Crazy old thing, I thought crossly as I rode off. She ought not to be allowed out.

It was not until about a year later, when I was a general district nurse, that I learned more about Mrs Jenkins . . . and learned a little humility.

CHUMMY

The first time I saw Camilla Fortescue-Cholmeley-Browne ("just call me Chummy"), I thought it was a bloke in drag. Six foot two inches tall, with shoulders like a front-row forward and size eleven feet, her parents had spent a fortune trying to make her more feminine, but to no effect.

Chummy and I were new together, and she arrived the morning after the memorable evening when Sister Monica Joan and I had polished off a cake intended for twelve. Cynthia, Trixie and I were leaving the kitchen after breakfast when the front doorbell rang, and this giant in skirts entered. She blinked short-sightedly down at us from behind thick, steel-rimmed glasses, and said, in the plummiest voice imaginable, "Is this Nonnatus House?"

Trixie, who had a waspish tongue, looked out of the door into the street. "Is there anyone there?" she called, and came back into the hallway, bumping into the stranger.

"Oh, sorry, I didn't notice you," she said, and made off for the clinical room.

Cynthia stepped forward, and greeted the woman with the same exquisite warmth and friendliness that had chased away my thoughts of bolting the night before. "You must be Camilla."

"Oh, just call me Chummy."

"All right then Chummy, come in and we will find Sister Julienne. Have you had breakfast? I'm sure Mrs B. can fix you up with something."

Chummy picked up her case, took two steps, and tripped over the doormat. "Oh lawks, clumsy me," she said with a girlish giggle. She bent down to straighten the mat and collided with the hallstand, knocking two coats and three hats on to the floor.

"Frightfully sorry. I'll soon get them," but Cynthia had already picked them up, fearing the worst.

"Oh thanks, old bean," said Chummy, with a "haw-haw".

Can this be real, or is she putting it on? I thought. But the voice was entirely real, and never changed, nor did the language. It was always "good show", or "good egg", or "what-ho", and, strangely enough, for all her massive size, her voice was soft and sweet. In fact, during the time that I knew her, I realised that everything about Chummy was soft and sweet. Despite her appearance, there was nothing butch about her. She had the nature of a gentle, artless young girl, diffident and shy. She was also pathetically eager to be liked.

The Fortescue-Cholmeley-Brownes were top drawer County types. Her great-great-grandfather had entered the Indian civil service in the 1820s, and the tradition had progressed through the generations. Her father was Governor of Rajasthan (an area the size of Wales), which he still, even in the 1950s, traversed on horseback. All this we learned from the collection of photographs on display in Chummy's room. She was the only girl amongst six brothers. All of them were tall, but unfortunately she was about an inch taller than the rest of the family.

All the children had been educated in England, the boys going to Eton, and Chummy to Roedean. They were placed in the care of guardians in this country, as the mother remained in India with her husband. Apparently Chummy had been at boarding school since she was six years of age, and knew no other life. She clung to her collection of family photographs with touching fervour – perhaps they were the closest she ever got to her family – and particularly loved one taken with her mother when she was about fourteen.

"That was the holiday I had with Mater," she said proudly, completely unaware of the pathos of her remark.

After Roedean came finishing school in Switzerland, then back to London to the Lucy Clayton Charm School to prepare her for presentation at Court. Those were the days of debutantes, when the daughters of the "best" families had to "come out", an expression meaning something quite different today. At that time it meant being presented formally to the monarch at Buckingham Palace. Chummy was presented and two photographs were proof of the event. In the first, an unmistakable Chummy in a ridiculous lacey ball gown, with ribbons and flowers, stood amongst a group of pretty young girls similarly attired, her huge, bony shoulders towering above their heads. The second photo was of her presentation to King George VI. Her great size and angular shape emphasised the petite charm of the Queen and the exquisite beauty of the two princesses, Elizabeth and Margaret. I wondered if Chummy was aware of how absurd she looked in the photos, which she was so pleased and so happy to display.

After the debutante bit came a year at a cordon-bleu school which took a small number of select young ladies on a residential basis. Chummy learned all the arts of the perfect hostess – the perfect hors d'oeuvre, the perfect pâté de foie gras – but remained ungainly, awkward, oversized, and generally unsuited to hostessing in any society. So a course of study at the best needlework school in London was deemed to be the right thing for her. For two years Chummy crocheted, embroidered and tatted, made lace and quilting and broderie anglaise. For two years she machined and set shoulders and double hemmed. All to no avail. While the other girls herringboned and feather-stitched and chatted happily, or sadly, of their boyfriends and lovers, Chummy, liked by all but loved by none, remained silent, always the odd chum out.

She never knew how it happened, but suddenly, unsought, she found her vocation: nursing and God. Chummy was going to be a missionary.

In a fever pitch of excitement, she enrolled at the Nightingale School of Nursing at St Thomas's Hospital in London. She was an instant success, and won the Nightingale Prize three years in succession. She adored the work on the wards, feeling for the first time in her life confident and competent, knowing that she was where she should be. Patients loved her, senior staff respected her, junior staff admired her. In spite of her great size she was gentle, with an intuitive understanding of patients, especially the very old, very sick, or dying. Even her clumsiness – a hallmark of earlier years – left her. On the wards she never dropped or broke a thing, never moved awkwardly or crashed into things. All these traits seemed to beset and torment her only in social life, for which she remained wholly ill-adapted.

Of course, young doctors and medical students, 90 per cent of whom were male and always on the look out for a pretty nurse, made fun of her and passed crude jokes about the difficulty of mounting a carthorse, and which of them had the organ of a stallion suited to the job. Freshmen were told of the ravishingly lovely nurse on North Ward, with whom it would be possible to fix a blind date, but they fled in horror when the blindness was given sight, vowing vengeance upon the jokers. Fortunately, such stories or pranks never reached Chummy's ears and passed straight over her head unnoticed. Had she been informed, it is very likely that she would just not have understood, and would have beamed amiably at her tormentors, shaming them with her innocence.

Chummy's entry into midwifery was less successful, but no less spectacular. It was some days before she could go out on the district. In the first place, no uniform would fit her. "Never mind, I'll make it," she said cheerfully. Sister Julienne doubted if there was a pattern available. "Not to worry, actually I can make it out of newspaper." To everyone's astonishment, she did. Material was obtained, and, in no time at all, a couple of dresses were made.

The bicycle was not so easy. For all the genteel education and ladylike accomplishments, no one had thought it necessary to teach her to ride a bicycle. A horse yes, but a bicycle, no.

"Never mind, I can learn," she said cheerfully. Sister Julienne said it was hard for an adult to acquire the skill. "Not to worry. I can practise," was her equally exuberant response.

Cynthia, Trixie and I went with her to the bicycle shed, and selected the largest – a huge old Raleigh, of about 1910 vintage, made of solid iron with a scooped-out front and high handlebars. The solid tyres were about three inches thick, and there were no gears. The whole contraption weighed about half a ton, and for this reason no one rode it. Trixie oiled the chain and we were ready for the off.

The time was just after lunch. We agreed to push Chummy up and down Leyland Street until she found her balance, after which we would travel in convoy to where the roads were quiet and flat. Most people who have tried to ride a bicycle in adult life for the first time will tell you that it is a terrifying experience. Many will say that it is impossible, and give up. But Chummy was made of sterner stuff. The Makers of the Empire were her forebears, and their blood flowed in her veins. Besides which, she was going to be a missionary, for which it was necessary that she should be a midwife. If she had to ride a bicycle to achieve this, so be it – she would ride the thing.

We pushed her, huge and shaking, shouting "pedal, pedal, up, down, up, down" until we were exhausted. She weighed about twelve stone of solid bone and muscle, and the bike another six stone, but we kept on pushing. At four o'clock the local school ended, and children came pouring out. About ten of them took over, giving us girls a well-earned rest as they ran along beside and behind, pushing and shouting encouragement.

Several times Chummy fell heavily to the ground. She hit her head on the kerb, and said, "Not to worry – no brains to hurt." She cut her leg, and murmured, "Just a scratch." She fell heavily on to one arm, and proclaimed, "I have another." She was indomitable. We began to respect her. Even the Cockney children, who had seen her as a comic turn, changed their tune. A tough-looking cookie of about twelve, who had been openly jeering at first, now looked solemnly at her with admiration.

The time had come to venture further than Leyland Street. Chummy could balance and she could pedal, so we agreed to half an hour cycling together around the streets. Trixie was in front, Cynthia and I on either side of Chummy, the children running behind, shouting.

We got to the top of Leyland Street and no further. It had not occurred to us to show Chummy how to turn a corner. Trixie turned left, calling "just follow me", and rode off. Cynthia and I turned left, but Chummy kept going straight ahead. I saw her fixed expression as she came straight for me, and after that all was confusion. Apparently a policeman had been in the act of crossing the street when the two of us hurtled into him. We came to rest on the opposite pavement. Seeing a representative of the law hit full frontal by a couple of midwives was joy for the children. They screamed with delight, and doors opened all down the street, emitting even more children and curious adults.

I was lying on my back in the gutter, not knowing what had happened. From this position I heard a groan, and then the policeman sat up with the words, "What fool did that?" I saw Chummy sit up. She had lost her glasses, and peered round. Maybe this could account for her next action or maybe she was dazed. She slapped the man heavily on the back with her huge hand and said, "No whingeing, now. Cheer up, old bean. Stiff upper lip and all that, what?" Clearly she was unaware that he was a policeman.

He was a big man, but not as big as Chummy. He fell forward at the blow, his face hitting one of the bicycles, and he cut his lip. Chummy merely said, "Oh, just a little scratch. Nothing to make a fuss about, old sport," and slapped him on the back again.

The policeman was outraged. He took out his notebook, and licked his pencil. The children vanished. The street cleared. He looked at Chummy with menace. "I'll take your name and address. Assaulting a policeman is a serious offence, I'll have you know."

I swear it was Cynthia's sexy voice that got us off. Without her, we would have been up before the magistrate the next day. I never knew how she did it, and she was quite unconscious of her charm. She said little, but the man's anger quickly vanished, and he was eating out of her hand in no time at all. He picked up the bicycles and escorted us down the street to Nonnatus House. He left us with the words, "Nice meeting you young ladies. I hope we meet again sometime."

Chummy had to spend three days in bed. The doctor said she had delayed shock and mild concussion. She slept for the first thirty-six hours, her temperature raised and pulse erratic. On the fourth day she was able to sit up, and asked what had happened. She was horrified when we told here, and deeply remorseful. As soon as she could go out, her first visit was to the police station to find the constable she had injured. She took with her a box of chocolates and a bottle of whisky.

MOLLY

When I called at the Canada Buildings to reassess Molly for a home confinement, she was out. It took three calls before I found her in. On the second attempt, I thought I heard movement in the flat, and knocked several times. There certainly was someone inside, but the door was locked, and no one came to open it.

On the third visit, Molly answered the door. She looked dreadful. She was only nineteen, but she looked pale and haggard. Lank greasy hair hung down her dirty face, and the two filthy little boys clung to her skirt. A week had passed since the first visit when I had interrupted a fight and a glance around the room told me that the domestic situation was worse, not better. I told her that we were reassessing her flat for a home confinement, and that perhaps it would be better if she went into hospital for the delivery. She shrugged, seeming indifferent. I pointed out that she had been to no antenatal clinics, and that this could be dangerous. She shrugged again. I was getting nowhere.

I said, "How is it that four months ago, the Midwives assessed your place as satisfactory for a home confinement, and now it is not?".

She said, "Well, me mum come in, and cleaned up, din't she?"

At last some communication. There was a mother on the scene. I asked for her mother's address. It was in the next block. Good.

A hospital confinement had to be booked in advance by the expectant mother concerned through her doctor. I was not at all sure that Molly would do this; she seemed too slovenly and apathetic to bother about anything. If she won't go to antenatal clinic, she won't bother to change the arrangements for delivery, I thought, and I could imagine a midnight call to Nonnatus House in two or three weeks' time to which we would have to respond. I resolved to see her mother, and report to her doctor.

The Canada Buildings, named Ontario, Baffin, Hudson, Ottawa and so on, were six blocks of densely populated tenements lying between Blackwall Tunnel and Blackwall Stairs. They were about six storeys high, and very primitive, with a tap and a lavatory at the end of each balcony. It was beyond me how anyone could live there, and maintain cleanliness or self-respect. It was said that there five thousand people living in the Canada Buildings.

I found her mother Marjorie's address in the Ontario Buildings, and knocked. A cheery voice called "Come on in luvvy". The usual invitation of an East Ender, whoever you were. The door was unlocked, so I stepped straight into the main room. Marjorie turned round as I entered with a bright smile. The smile vanished as soon as she saw me and her hands dropped to her sides.

"Oh no. No. Not again. You've come about our Moll, 'aven't you?" She sat down on a chair, buried her face in her hands, and sobbed.

I was embarrassed. I didn't know what to do or say. Some people are good at dealing with the problems of others, but not me. In fact, the more emotional people get, the less I am able to cope. I put my bag on a chair and sat down beside her, saying nothing. It gave me the chance to look around the room.

Having seen Molly's squalor, I had expected to see her mother's place in the same sort of condition, but nothing could have been more dissimilar. The room was clean and tidy, and smelt nice. Pretty curtains hung at clean windows. The mats were clean, well brushed and shaken. A kettle was bubbling on the gas stove. Marjorie was wearing a clean dress and pinafore, her hair was brushed and looked nice.

The kettle gave me an idea, and as the sobs lessened I said, "How about making a nice cup of tea for us both? I'm parched."

She brightened up and said, with typical cockney courtesy, "Sorry nurse. Don't mind me. I gets that worked up about Moll, I do."

She got up and made the tea. The activity helped her, and she sniffed away the tears. Over the next twenty minutes, it all came out, her hopes and her heartache.

Molly was the last of five children. She had never known her father, who had been killed at Arnhem during the war. The whole family had been evacuated to Gloucestershire.

Marjorie said, "I don't know if that upset her, or what, but the others turned out all right, they did."

The family returned to London, and settled in Ontario Buildings. Molly seemed to adapt to the new surroundings and her new school, and was reported to be doing well.

"She was that bright," Marjorie said. "Always top o' the class. She could've been a secitary an' worked in an orfice up West, she could. Oh, it breaks my heart, it do, when I thinks on it."

She sniffed and pulled out her handkerchief. "She was about fourteen when she met that turd. His name's Richard, an' I calls 'im Richard the Turd." She giggled at her little joke. "Then she was stopping out late, saying she was down the Youth Club, but I reckoned as how she was telling me lies, so I asks the Rector, an' he tells me Moll wasn't even a member. Then she was stoppin' out all night. Oh, nurse, you can't even know what that does to a mother."

Quiet sobs came from the neat little figure in the flowered apron.

"Night after night I walked the streets, looking for 'er, but I never found 'er. 'Course I never. She'd come home in the morning, an' tell me a pack of lies, as though I was daft, an' go off to school. When she was sixteen, she said she was going to marry her Dick. I reckoned as how she was pregnant anyhow, so I says, 'That's the best thing you can do, my luvvy.'"

They married, and took two rooms in Baffin Buildings. From the start, Molly never did any housework. Marjorie went in and tried to show her daughter how to keep her rooms clean and tidy, but it was no use. The next time she went, the place was as dirty as ever.

"I don't know where she gets her lazy ways from," Marjorie said.

At first Dick and Molly seemed fairly happy, and although Dick did not appear to be in any regular job, Marjorie hoped for the best for her daughter. Their first baby was born, and Molly seemed happy, but quite soon, things began to get worse. Marjorie noticed bruises on her daughter's neck and arms, a cut above her eye, a limp on one occasion. Each time Molly said she had fallen down. Marjorie began to have her suspicions, but relations between her and Dick, never cordial, were breaking down.

"He hates me," she said "and won't never let me come near her or the boys. There's not nuffink I can do. I don't know what's worse, knowing he hits me daughter, or knowing he hits the kids. The best time was when he done six months inside. Then I knew as how they was safe."

She started crying again, and I asked her if social services could do anything to help.

"No, no. She won't say a word against him, she won't. He's got such a hold on her, I don't think she's got a mind of her own any more."

I felt deeply sorry for this poor woman, and her silly daughter. But most of all I felt sorry for the two little boys, whom I had seen in a pitiful state on the occasion when I had interrupted a fight. And now a third child was coming.

I said, "My main reason for coming to see you is about the new baby. Molly is booked for a home confinement, but that, I believe, is only because you had cleaned the place up before our assessment." She nodded. "We think now that a hospital delivery would be best, but she has got to book it, and she must go to antenatal clinics. I don't think she will do either. Can you help?"

Majorie burst into tears again. "I'll do anything in the world for her and the kiddies, but the Turd, he won't let me go near them. What can I do?"

She bit her fingernails and blew her nose.

It was a tricky situation. I thought perhaps we would simply have to refuse a home delivery, and inform the doctors. Molly would then be told that she must go into hospital when labour started. If she refused antenatal treatment, that would be entirely her own fault.

I left poor Marjorie to her sad thoughts, and reported back to the Sisters. A hospital confinement was in fact arranged without

Molly's active consent, and I thought that would be the last we heard of her.

It was not to be. About three weeks later the Midwives received a phone call from Poplar Hospital asking if we could arrange post-natal visits for Molly, who had discharged herself and the baby on the third day after delivery.

This was almost unprecedented. In those days it was accepted by everyone, medical and lay people alike, that a new mother should stay in bed for two weeks. Apparently Molly had walked home, carrying the baby and this was considered to be very dangerous. Sister Bernadette went straight round to Baffin Buildings.

She reported back that Molly was there, looking a good deal cleaner, but as sullen as ever. Dick was not at home. He was supposed to have been looking after the children whilst Molly was in hospital, but whether he had or not was anyone's guess. Majorie had offered to take care of them, but Dick had refused, saying they were his kids, and he wasn't going to let that interfering old bag poke her nose into his family.

There had been no food in the flat. Perhaps Molly had anticipated this, and that was why she'd discharged herself. She had no money on her, but on the way home with the baby, had called in the cooked meat shop, and begged a couple of meat pies on tick. As the butcher knew and respected her mother, he let Molly have them. The two little boys, dressed only in filthy jumpers, were sitting on the floor devouring the pies ravenously when Sister Bernadette had arrived.

Molly hardly spoke, Sister told us. She had submitted to being examined, and the baby, a little girl, to examination, but remained morosely silent all the while. Sister had said she was going to tell Marjorie that her daughter was home.

"Please yerself," was all the reply she got.

Marjorie had had no idea of the turn of events, and ran round to Baffin Buildings straight away. Unfortunately Dick chose the same moment to return, and they met on the landing. He lunged at her drunkenly, and Marjorie ducked. Had he hit her, she would have fallen down the stone staircase. After that, all the poor woman dared to do was to buy food and leave it on the landing outside her daughter's door.

Our custom was to visit twice a day for fourteen days after delivery. Molly and baby were satisfactory, from a purely medical point of view, but the domestic situation was as bad as ever. Sometimes Dick was at home, sometimes not. Poor Marjorie was never seen there. She would have made all the difference in the world to Molly and the little boys. Her cheerfulness alone would have lightened the atmosphere, but she was never allowed in. She had to content herself with coming round to Nonnatus House to ask the Sisters how her daughter and grandchildren were getting on. One day she gave us a bag of baby clothes to take on our next visit. She said she didn't like to leave them on the landing, in case they got damp.

Over the next few days several nurses visited Molly, all reporting the same disquieting condition. One nurse said that she was very nearly sick in the room, and had to rush outside into the fresh air in order to control her stomach. On the eighth evening I called, and there was no reply to my knock. The door was locked, so I knocked again – no response. I thought Molly might be busy with the baby and unable to answer. As it was only 5 p.m., I continued my visits, intending to return later.

It was about 8 p.m. when I got back to Baffin Buildings. I was tired, and it seemed a long climb up to the fifth floor. I was almost tempted to skip it. After all, Molly and baby were medically satisfactory, which was our remit. But something prompted me not to miss this visit, so I wearily climbed the stairs.

I knocked, and there was no reply again. I knocked again, louder – she can't still be busy, I thought. A door opened just down the balcony, and a woman appeared.

"She's out," she said, her fag drooping off her lower lip.

"Out! You can't mean it. She's only just had a baby."

"Well, she's out, I tells yer. Saw 'er go, I did. Tarted up an' all, she was."

"Well where's she gone to?" It flashed through my mind that

she had gone to her mother's. "Has she taken the three children?"

The woman uttered a shriek of laughter, and the fag dropped to the floor. She stooped to pick it up, and her hair curlers clacked together as she bent.

"What! Three kids! You must be joking. Three kids wouldn't do her much good, would it now?"

I didn't like the woman. There was something about the knowing way she grinned at me that was most unpleasant. I turned my back on her, knocked again, and called through the letterbox. "Would you let me in, please, it's the nurse."

There was definitely a movement inside, I heard it quite distinctly. Self-conscious, because I knew that woman was sneering at me, I kneeled down and looked through the letterbox.

Two eyes, close to mine, met my gaze. They were a child's eyes, and they stared at me unblinking for about ten seconds, then vanished. This enabled me to see into the room.

A faint greenish-blue light came from an unguarded paraffin stove. A pram stood nearby, in which I presumed the baby was sleeping. I saw one little boy running across the room. The other was sitting in a corner.

I caught my breath sharply. The woman must have heard it. She said, "Well, do you believe me now? I told you she was out, din't I?"

I felt I must take this woman into my confidence. She might be able to help. "We can't leave the three children alone with that paraffin heater. If one of them knocks it over, they will be burned to death. If Molly's out, where's the father?"

The woman drew closer. She clearly enjoyed being the bearer of bad news. "He's a bad lot, that Dick, he is. You mark my words. You don't wants to 'ave nuffink to do with 'im. He's no good to her, and she's no better than she should be. Oh, it's a shame, I says to our Bette, it's a shame, I says. Them poor little kids. They didn't ask to be born, did they, now? I always says it's a . . . "

I cut her short. "That paraffin heater is a death-trap. I'm going to inform the police. We've got to get in there."

Her eyes gleamed, and she sucked her teeth. She clutched my

arm and said: "You going to call the police, then? Cor!"

She dashed off down the balcony and knocked on another door. I imagined her bearing the news all around Baffin Buildings, even if it took her the entire night. Tiredness had left me, and I sped down the stairs to street level, and just about ran to the nearest phone box. The police listened with concern to my story and said they would come at once. Marjorie had to be informed, I decided, so my next call was Ontario Buildings.

Poor woman. When I told her she crumpled, as though I had hit her in the stomach.

"Oh no, I can't bear any more," she moaned. "I guessed as much. She's gone on the game, then."

So innocent was I, that I didn't know what she meant.

"What game?" I said, thinking she meant darts or billiards or gambling in a local pub.

Marjorie looked at me compassionately. "Never you mind, ducky. You don't need to know about that sort of thing. I must go and see after them kiddies."

We went together in silence. The police were already at the door working on the lock. I had thought that they would bring a locksmith with them, but no – most policemen are expert at picking locks. Do they learn it in College? I wondered.

A crowd had gathered on the balcony. No one wanted to miss a thing. Marjorie stepped forward saying that she was the grandmother, and when the door was opened she was the first to enter. The police and I followed.

The room was suffocatingly hot, and the stench putrid. The children were not to be seen, apart from the baby, who was blissfully asleep. I went over to her, and she looked surprisingly well cared for, clean and well fed. The rest of the room was indescribable. It was full of flies to begin with, and a heap of excrement and dirty nappies in a corner was crawling with maggots.

Marjorie went into the bedroom, gently calling the boys' names. They were behind the chair. She took them in her arms, tears streaming down her face.

"Never mind, my luvvies. Nanna's got you."

The police were taking notes, and I thought perhaps I should leave, as the grandmother would now take charge. But at that moment, there was a commotion outside, and Dick appeared in the doorway. Obviously he had not known that the police were in his flat. As soon as he saw them he turned to run, but his path was barred by the onlookers. They had let him in, but they were not going to let him out again. Perhaps there were several scores to be settled between Dick and his neighbours. He was told that he would be cautioned about the neglect of three children under the age of five.

He swore, spat, and said, "What's wrong with 'em? Kids are all right. Nothing wrong, far as I can see."

"It's a very good thing for you that there is nothing wrong. Leaving them alone with a paraffin heater alight and unguarded would have caused a fire if one of the children had knocked it over."

Dick started to whine. "That's not my fault. I didn't put the heater on. The missus did. I didn't know she'd gone out and left it. The lazy slut. I'll give her what for when I sees her."

The policeman said: "Where is your wife?"

"'Ow should I know?"

Marjorie shouted at him. "Yer villain. Yer know where she is. An' you made her go, didn't you. Yer swine."

Dick was all innocence. "What's the old cow on about now?"

Marjorie was about to scream a reply, but the policeman stopped her. "You can settle your differences when we have gone. We have put it on record that you have been cautioned about leaving your children unattended, and in a dangerous situation. If it occurs again, you will be charged."

Dick was all wheedling charm. "You can take it from me, this will not occur again, officer. I apologise, and will see it never happens again."

The police prepared to leave. Dick said, pointing to Marjorie, "And you can take her with you, and all."

She gave an anguished cry, and held the two little boys closer to her. She appealed to the policemen, "I can't leave them here, the baby, the boys. Can't you see? I can't leave them like this."

Dick said in a soothing, cheery voice, "Don't you worry, old lady. I can look after me kids. There's nuffink to worry about." Then, to the policeman: "Yer can leave 'em safe wiv me. You got my word for it."

Neither of the policemen were fools and they were not taken in for a moment by this display of paternal devotion. But they had no power to do anything but caution him.

One of them turned to Marjorie, "You can only stay here if you are invited, and you certainly cannot take the children away without the father's consent."

Dick was triumphant. "You heard. You've got to have the father's consent. And I'm the father, and I don't consent, see? Now get out."

I spoke for the first time. "Well what about the baby? She is only eight days old, and she is being breastfed. She will wake up hungry soon. Where is Molly?"

I don't think he had noticed me before. He turned, and ogled me up and down. I almost felt him undressing me with his eyes. He was a nauseating specimen, but no doubt he thought he was God's gift to women. He came over to me.

"Don't you worry, nursey. My missus will feed her when she gets back. She's just popped out for a minute."

He took my hand in both of his own, and stroked my wrist. I pulled it sharply away. I wanted to smack his leering face, which he was pushing so close to my own, I could smell his foul breath. I turned my head away in disgust. He drew even closer, his eyes gleaming with mocking interest. He dropped his voice so that no one else could hear,

"Hoity-toity eh? I know how to take you down a peg or two, Miss Hoity-Toity."

I knew how to deal with men like that. Height is a great leveller, and we were level. I didn't need to say a word. I turned my head slowly to look him straight in the eyes, and held his gaze. Slowly his smirk faded, and he turned away. Few men can withstand a woman's look of utter contempt.

Marjorie was kneeling on the floor crying uncontrollably, and hugging the two little boys. The policeman went over to her, took her elbow to help her to her feet, and said gently: "Come on mother, you can't stay here."

Marjorie got up, and the children retreated silently towards the chair in the bedroom. She gave a despairing moan, and allowed the policeman to lead her to the door. She stumbled out, a broken woman, looking twenty years older than when she had entered. She was led through the crowd at the door, and there were many sympathetic voices.

"Oh poor soul."

"Oh it's a shame."

"Don' yer jus' feel for 'er, poor soul."

"'E's a bad'un, an' all."

"It's a shame, oi sez."

She was escorted back to Ontario Buildings, and I returned to Nonnatus House, with much to think about that night.

THE BICYCLE

The hidden steel of a Fortescue-Cholmeley-Browne was revealed to us over the next few weeks as Chummy mastered the skills of riding a bicycle. After the accident Sister Julienne was seriously in doubt as to whether it would be possible, but Chummy was adamant. She could and would learn.

Every spare minute of her time was spent practising. All her district work had to be done on foot in the meantime, and this took far longer than it would have taken on a bicycle. Consequently she had less spare time than anyone else. But she utilised each and every minute of freedom. She would push the old Raleigh up Leyland Street, a slight incline, and then free wheel down; up and down hundreds of times until she acquired her balance. She got up a couple of hours early each morning, and went out every evening from about 8 to 10 p.m., coming back exhausted and breathless. "Well, actually, there's no point in just learning to ride in the daylight," she argued gaily, with irrefutable logic.

These rides in the dark were usually accompanied by crowds of cheering or jeering children. This might have been a menace, had Chummy not gained the respect of an older lad who had joined us on the first day when Cynthia, Trixie and I had been trying to teach her. Jack was a particularly tough specimen of about thirteen, accustomed to fighting for his rights. He soon dispersed the little kids; a few blows, a few kicks, and they were gone. Then he presented himself in front of the bicycle, her champion.

"You gets any more trouble from that lot, Miss, jes' call me. Jack. I'll take care of 'em."

"Oh, that's frightfully good of you, Jack. Actually, I'm most awfully grateful. This old machine's a lively little filly, what?"

Chummy's posh voice must have been as incomprehensible to Jack as his Cockney accent was to her, but nevertheless, they struck a friendship then and there.

After that Chummy learned rapidly. Jack was out early and late, running, pushing, helping her in every way. He developed a particularly ingenious way of teaching her to steer the bike and turn corners; he pedalled whilst she steered! Chummy controlled the handlebars, sitting on the saddle, her legs trailing, whilst he stood on the pedals, doing all the hard work. To propel her twelve stone weight must have been hard work, but Jack was no puny thirteen-year-old, and took pride in his manliness. Early and late he could be heard shouting: "Turn left, Miss; NO, LEF', yer dafty. Easy does it. Not too sharp, now. Aim for that phone box, and keep yer eyes on it."

Neither of them saw defeat as a possibility, and within three weeks they were riding all the way from Bow to the Isle of Dogs in the dark November mornings.

Jack did not own a bicycle, and reluctantly he had to admit that the time had come for Chummy to try on her own. He pushed her off, and she pedalled confidently down the street and round the corner. Sadly he waved as she turned out of sight. He had been useful, and now the fun was all over. He kicked a stone, and slouched off homewards, hands in pockets, one foot in the gutter, the other on the kerb.

But Chummy was not one to let a friendship die, still less to allow kindness and help to pass unnoticed. She discussed it with us at lunch, and we agreed that a gift of some sort would be appropriate. Various were the suggestions – a jar of sweets, a football, a penknife – but Chummy was not happy with any of these ideas. Sister Julienne, ever practical and wise, pointed out that the time, effort and commitment on Jack's part had been very great, so therefore her debt to him was great.

"I don't think the boy should be fobbed off with a trivial token. I feel he should receive something that he really wants and would value. On the other hand, it depends entirely upon what you, the giver, can afford, and only you can know this."

Chummy brightened, and a huge smile lit her features. "Actually, I know what Jack wants more than anything else – a bicycle! And I'm pretty sure Pater would buy one for him if I explained the circumstances, what? He's a sporting old stick, and always coughs up for a good cause. I'll write to him tonight."

Of course Pater coughed up, happy to see his only daughter fulfilled at last. He could no more understand her determination to become a missionary than he could understand her passion for midwifery, but he would support it to the end.

A new bicycle meant a new life for Jack. Very few boys had such a possession in those days. For him, it meant more than status. It meant freedom. He was an adventurous boy, and went miles beyond the East End on his bike. He joined the Dagenham Cycling Club and competed in time trials and road races. He went camping alone in the Essex countryside. He went as far as the coast, and saw the sea for the first time.

Chummy was delighted, and his continued friendship was her greatest joy. He seemed to feel she needed his protection, and so every day after school Jack would turn up at Nonnatus House to escort her on her evening visits. His instinct that the children of the Docks would tease and torment her were right, because on the whole the cockneys did not take to Chummy, and made fun of her behind her back. Her huge size, pedalling steadily along the streets on an ancient solid-wheeled bicycle, brought crowds of children to a standstill, and they lined the pavement shouting things like "what-ho" and "jolly good show, actually" or "steady on, old bean" amid loud-mouthed guffaws. And, to rub salt into the wound, they called her "The Hippo". Poor Chummy treated it with good humour, but we all knew how deeply it hurt her. But when tough, pugnacious, street-wise Jack was with her, the children kept their distance. We all saw him on different occasions, standing in the street or the tenement courtyards, holding two bicycles, his lower jaw thrust forward, his stocky legs slightly apart, coolly looking around him, confident that a look was all that was needed to to protect "Miss".

*

Twenty-five years later, a shy young girl called Lady Diana Spencer became engaged to marry Prince Charles, heir to the throne. I saw several film clips of her arriving at various engagements. Each time when the car stopped, the front nearside door would open, and her bodyguard would step out and open the rear door for Lady Diana. Then he would stand, jaw thrust forward, legs slightly apart, and look coolly around him at the crowds, a mature Jack, still practising the skills he had acquired in childhood, looking after his lady.

ANTENATAL CLINIC

There must be aspects of every job that are disliked. I did not like antenatal work. In fact I would go so far as to say that I hated antenatal clinic, and dreaded the arrival of each Tuesday afternoon. It was not just the hard work – though that was hard enough. The midwives tried to organise the day-book so that we could finish our morning visits by twelve noon. We had an early lunch, and at one-thirty we started to set up the clinic in order to open the doors at 2 p.m. Then we worked through until we were finished, often as late as 6 or 7 p.m. After that, our evening visits began.

That did not bother me – hard work never did. What really got me, I think, was the sheer concentration of unwashed female flesh, the pulsating warmth and humidity, the endless chatter, and above all the smell. However much I bathed and changed afterwards, it was always a couple of days before I could get rid of the nauseating smells of vaginal discharge, urine, stale sweat, unwashed clothes. It all mingled into a hot, clinging vapour that penetrated my clothes, hair, skin – everything. Many times, during the routine antenatal clinics, I had to go out into the fresh air and lean over the rail by the door, heaving, forcing down the urge to be sick.

Yet we are all different, and I did not meet any other midwife who was affected in this way. If I mentioned it, the reaction was one of genuine surprise. "What smell?" or "Well, perhaps it got a bit hot." So I didn't make any further comments about my own reaction. I had to remind myself continuously of the huge importance of antenatal work, which had contributed so greatly to the drop in maternal deaths. Memory of the history of midwifery, and the endless sufferings of women in childbirth, kept me going when I was thinking, I just cannot bring myself to examine another woman.

Total neglect of women in pregnancy and childbirth had been the norm. Among many primitive societies, women menstruating or with child, or in labour or suckling the child, were regarded as unclean, polluted. The woman was isolated and frequently could not be touched, even by another woman. She had to go through the whole ordeal alone. Consequently only the fittest survived, and by the processes of mutation and adaptation, inherited abnormalities, such as disproportion in the size of the pelvis and the foetal head, died out of the race, particularly in remote parts of the world, and labour became easier.

In Western society, which we call civilisation, this did not occur, and a dozen or more complications, some of them deadly, were superimposed on the natural hazards: overcrowding, staphylococcal and streptococcal infection; infectious diseases such as cholera, scarlet fever, typhoid and tuberculosis; venereal disease; rickets; multiple and frequent childbirth; the dangers from infected water. If you add to all this the attitude of indifference and neglect that often surrounded childbirth it is not hard to understand how childbirth came to be known as "the curse of Eve", and how women could often expect to die in order to bring forth new life.

The Midwives of St Raymund Nonnatus held their clinic in a church hall. The idea today of conducting a full-scale antenatal clinic in a converted old church hall is horrifying, and sanitary inspectors, public health inspectors, every inspector you can think of would be there condemning it. But in the 1950s it was by no means condemned, in fact the nuns were highly praised for the initiative and ingenuity they had shown in the conversion. No structural changes had been made, apart from the installation of a lavatory and running cold water. Hot water was obtained from an Ascot water heater fixed to the wall near the tap.

Heating was provided by a large coke fire in the middle of the hall. It was a black cast iron construction which had to be lit earlier in the morning by Fred, the boilerman. Such coke fires were very common in those days, and I have seen them even in hospital wards. (I recall one ward where it was the practice to sterilise our syringes and needles by boiling them in a saucepan placed on the stove). These stoves were very solid, flat topped, and you had to fill them by opening the circular lid and tipping the coke in from a coke-hod. It required quite a bit of muscle power. The stove was situated in the middle of the space, so that heat was radiated all around. The flue went straight up the middle, to the roof.

A few examination couches were available, with movable screens to provide privacy, and wooden desks with chairs, where we wrote up our notes. A long marble-topped surface stood near the sink, upon which we placed our instruments and other equipment. A gas jet stood on this surface, with a box of matches beside it. This single jet of flame was used continuously for boiling up the urine. I can smell it now, more than fifty years later!

The clinic, and those like it all over the country, may sound primitive today but it had saved countless thousands of lives of both mothers and babies. The Midwives' clinic was the only one in the area until 1948, when a small maternity unit of eight beds was opened in Poplar Hospital. Prior to that, the hospital had no maternity unit even though Poplar was said to have a population of fifty thousand people per square mile. When the decision was taken after the war to open a hospital unit, no special provision was made. Quite simply, two small wards were allocated for maternity – one for lying-in, and the other for delivery, doubling-up as an antenatal clinic. This was inadequate, but it was better than nothing at all. Accommodation, equipment, technology, were not really important. What was important was the knowledge, skill and experience of the midwife.

Clinical examination was what I shrank from the most. It can't be as bad as last week, I thought as we prepared to open the doors. I shuddered as I remembered it. Thank God I was wearing gloves, I thought. What would have happened if I had not?

She had been in my mind on and off for the whole of the past week. She had flounced into the clinic at about 6 p.m. in her hair curlers and slippers, a fag hanging from her lower lip, and with her were five children under seven. Her appointment had been for 3 p.m. I was clearing up after a not too stressful afternoon. Two of the other student midwives had left, and the third was still with her last patient. Of the Sisters, only Novice Ruth remained, (a "novice" in the religious life, not in midwifery). She asked me to see Lil Hoskin.

It was Lil's first antenatal visit, even though she had had no periods for five months. This is going to take another half an hour, I sighed to myself as I got out the notes. I scanned through them: thirteenth pregnancy, ten live births; no history of infectious disease; no rheumatic fever or heart disease; no history of tuberculosis; some cystitis but no evidence of nephritis; mastitis after the third and seventh babies, but otherwise all babies breastfed.

Her previous notes gave me most of her obstetric history, but I needed to ask some questions about the present pregnancy.

"Have you had any bleeding?"

"Nope."

"Any vaginal discharge?"

"A bit."

What colour?"

"Mos'ly yellowish."

"Any swelling of the ankles?"

"Nope."

"Any breathlessness?"

"Nope."

"Any vomiting?"

"A bit. Not much though."

"Constipated?"

"Yep, not 'alf!"

"Are you sure you are pregnant? You haven't been examined or tested."

"I should know," she said meaningfully, with a shriek of laughter.

The children by now were rushing around all over the place. The hall, being large and virtually empty, was like a great play area for them. I didn't mind – no healthy child can resist a wide open space, and the urge to run is powerful if you are only five years old. But Lil thought she must exercise some show of authority. She grabbed a passing child by the arm and dragged him to her. She gave him a great blow across the side of the face and ear with a heavy hand, and screamed.

"Shut up and behave yourself, you li'l bleeder. And that goes for the lot of you and all."

The child squealed with pain and the injustice of the blow. He retreated about ten yards from his mother, and screamed and stamped, until he could scarcely breathe. Then he paused, took a deep breath, and started all over again. The other children had stopped running around, and a couple started whimpering. A happy but noisy scene with five little children had been turned in an instant into a battlefield by this stupid woman. I hated her from that moment.

Novice Ruth came up to the child, and tried to comfort him, but he pushed her away, and lay on the floor kicking and screaming. Lil grinned and said to me: "Don't mind him, he'll get over it." Then louder, to the child: "Shu' yer face or yer'll get another."

I couldn't bear it, so to prevent her doing any more harm, I told her that I must examine her urine, gave her a gallipot, and asked her to go into the lavatory to supply a sample for me. After that, I said, I would want to examine her, and would need her undressed below the waist, and lying on one of the couches.

Her slippers slapped across the wooden floor as she went. She came back giggling, and gave me the specimen, then flopped over to one of the couches. I ground my teeth. What has she got to giggle about, I thought. The child was still lying on the floor, but not screaming so much. The other children looked sullen, making no attempt to play.

I went to the work surface to test the urine. The litmus paper turned red, showing normal acidity. The urine was cloudy, and the specific gravity high. I wanted to test for sugar, and lit the gas jet. I half filled a test tube with urine, and added a couple of drops of Fehlings solution, and boiled the contents. No sugar was present. Lastly, I had to test for albumen by refilling the test tube with fresh urine, and boiling the upper half only. It did not turn white or thick, indicating that albumen urea was not present.

This took about five minutes to complete, during which time the child had stopped crying. He was sitting up and Novice Ruth was playing with him with a couple of balls, pushing them back and forth. Her refined, delicate features were offset by her white muslin veil which fell down as she leaned over. The child grabbed it and pulled. The other children laughed. They seemed happy again. No thanks to their rough and brutal mother, I thought as I went over to Lil, who was now lying on the couch.

She was fat, and her flabby skin was dirty and moist with perspiration. A dank, unwashed smell rose from her body. Have I got to touch her? I thought as I approached. I tried to remind myself that she and her husband and all the children probably lived in two or three rooms with no bath, or even hot water, but it did not dispel my feeling of revulsion. Had she not hit her child in that heartless manner, my feelings might have softened towards her.

I put on my surgical gloves, and covered her lower half with a sheet, because I wanted to examine her breasts. I asked her to pull up her jumper. She giggled, and wobbled around, pulling it up. The smell intensified as her armpits were exposed. Two large pendulous breasts flopped down either side of her, prominent veins coursing towards huge, near-black nipples. These veins were a reliable sign of pregnancy. A little fluid could be squeezed from the nipples. Just about diagnostic, I thought. I told her this.

She shrieked with laughter. "Told you so, didn't I?"

I took her blood pressure at that point, and it was fairly high. She will need more rest, I thought, but I doubt if she will get it. The children had recovered their spirits, and were racing about once again.

I pulled her jumper down and uncovered her abdomen, which was large, the skin simply covered with stretch marks. The slightest pressure from my hand showed a fundus above the umbilicus.

"When was your last period?"

"Search me. Las' year, I reckons." She giggled, and her tummy flopped up and down.

"Have you felt any movements yet?"

"Nope."

"I am going to listen for the baby's heart beat."

I reached for the pinard foetal stethoscope. This was a small metal, trumpet-shaped instrument, used by placing the larger end over the abdomen, and then pressing the ear against the flattened smaller end. Normally the steady thud of the heartbeat could be heard quite clearly. I listened at several points, but could hear nothing. I called Novice Ruth, as I felt I needed confirmation, and also an assessment of the duration of pregnancy. She couldn't hear a heartbeat either, but thought that other signs indicated pregnancy. She asked me to do an internal examination to confirm it.

I had been expecting this, and dreading it. I asked Lil to draw her knees upwards and part her legs. As she did so, the odour of stale urine, vaginal discharge, and sweat wafted up to greet me. I struggled to control the nausea. I mustn't be sick, was all I could think of at that moment. Tufts of pubic hair stuck up in clumps, matted together by sticky moisture and dirt. She might have crabs, I thought. Novice Ruth was watching me. Maybe she understood how I was feeling – the nuns were very sensitive, but they spoke little. I dampened a swab with which to clean the moist bluish vulva, and it was whilst I was cleaning her that I noticed that one side was very oedematous, swollen with fluid, whilst the other was not. I started to part the vulva with two fingers, and it was then that my finger encountered a hard, small lump on the oedematous side. I rubbed my finger over it several times. It was easily palpable; hard lumps in soft places make one think of cancer.

I could feel Novice Ruth watching me very closely all the time. I raised my eyes, and looked at her questioningly. She said, "I'll get a pair of gloves. Do not proceed just yet, nurse."

She returned a couple of seconds later, and took my place. She did not say a word until she withdrew her hand, and covered Lil again with the blanket.

"You can put your legs down now, Lil, but stay where you are, please, because we will want to examine you again in a minute. Come with me to the desk, will you, nurse?"

At the desk, which was at the other end of the room, she said to me very quietly: "I think the lump is a syphilitic chancre. I am going to ring Dr Turner straight away and ask him if he can come to examine her while she is still here. If we send her away with instructions to go to a doctor, there is a high chance that she will not go. The spirochaeta pallida of syphilis can cross the placenta and infect the foetus. However, the chancre is the first stage of syphilis, and with early diagnosis and treatment there is a good chance of cure, and the baby will be spared."

I nearly fainted, in fact I remember having to grip the table before I could sit down. I had been touching her – the revolting creature – and her syphilitic chancre. I couldn't speak, but Novice Ruth said to me kindly, "Don't worry. You were wearing gloves. You won't have caught anything."

She left to go to Nonnatus House to ring the doctor. I couldn't move. I sat at the table for a full five minutes, fighting down wave after wave of nausea, and shuddering. The children were playing all around me, perfectly happy. There was no movement from behind the screen, until the low, steady sound of contented snoring penetrated my ears. Lil was asleep.

The doctor arrived about fifteen minutes later, and Novice Ruth asked me to accompany him. I must have looked pale, because she asked, "Are you all right? Will you manage?"

I nodded dumbly. I couldn't say no. After all, I was a trained nurse, accustomed to all sorts of frightful situations. Yet even after five years of hospital work – casualty, theatre, cancer patients, amputations, dying, death – nothing and no one had caused such profound revulsion in me as that woman Lil.

The doctor examined her and took a scrape of tissue from the chancre for the pathology lab. He also took a sample of blood for a Wassermann's test. Then he said to Lil, "I think you have a very early infection of venereal disease. We . . . "

Before he had finished speaking she gave a great baying laugh. "Oh Gawd! Not again! That's a laugh, that is!"

The doctor's face was stony. He said, "We have caught it early. I am going to give you penicillin now, and you must have another injection each day for ten days. We must protect your baby."

"Please yourself," she giggled, "I'm easy," and winked at him.

His face was expressionless as he drew up a massive dose of penicillin and injected it into her thigh. We left her to get dressed, and went over to the desk.

"We will get the results from pathology on the blood and serum," he said to Novice Ruth, "but I don't think there is any doubt about diagnosis. Would you Sisters arrange to visit daily for the injections? I think if we ask her to come to surgery she won't bother, or will forget. If the foetus is still alive, we must do our best."

It was well after seven o'clock. Lil was dressed, and yelling to the children to come with her. She lit another fag, and called out gaily, "Well, tara all."

She looked knowingly at Novice Ruth, and said, with a leer – "Be good" – and shrieked with laughter.

I told her that we would call each day to give her another injection. "Please yerself," she said with a shrug, and left.

I still had all my cleaning up to do. I felt so tired my legs could hardly move. The moral and emotional shock must have contributed to the fatigue.

Novice Ruth grinned at me kindly. "You have to get used to all sorts in this life. Now, do you have any evening visits?"

I nodded. "Three post-natal. One of them up in Bow."

"Then you go and do them. I will clean up here."

As I left the clinic, I thanked her from the bottom of my heart. The fresh air revived me, and the cycle ride dispelled my fatigue.

The following morning, when I looked at the day book, I saw that I had to administer the penicillin injection to Lil Hoskin, Peabody Buildings. I groaned inwardly. I had known it would have to be me. The instruction was that it should be my last call before lunch, and that the syringe and needle should be kept separate from the midwifery case, also, that I should wear gloves. I didn't need telling.

The Peabody Buildings in Stepney were notorious. They had been condemned for demolition about fifteen years before, but were still standing and still housing families. They were the worst type of tenements, because the only water came from a single tap at the end of each balcony, where the only lavatory was situated. There were no facilities in the flats. My attitude towards Lil softened. Perhaps I would be like her if I had to live in such conditions.

The door was open, but I knocked.

"Come on in, luvvy. I'm expecting you. I've got some water ready for you."

How kind. She must have gone to a lot of trouble to get water and heat it up. The flat was filthy and stinking. Hardly a square inch of floor space could be seen, and small children, naked from the waist down, tumbled around all over the place.

Lil seemed different in her own surroundings. Maybe the clinic had intimidated her in some way, so that she had felt the need to assert herself by showing off. She did not seem so loud and brash in her own home. The irritating giggle, I realised, was no more than constant and irrepressible good humour. She pushed the children around, but not unkindly.

"Get out of it, yer li'l bleeder. The nurse can't get in." She turned to me. "Here you are. You can put your things down here."

She had gone to the trouble of clearing a small space on the table, and had put a washing bowl beside it, with soap and a grubby towel.

"Thought you'd need a nice, clean towel, eh ducky?"

Everything is relative.

I put my bag on the table, but took out only the syringe, needle, ampoule, gloves and cotton swab soaked in spirit. The children were fascinated.

"Get back, or I'll clip your ear," Lil said gaily. Then to me, "Do you wants me leg or me arse?"

"Doesn't matter. Whichever you prefer."

She lifted her skirts and bent over. The huge round backside looked like a positive affirmation of solidarity. The children gawped, and crowded in closer. With a shrill scream of laughter Lil kicked backwards, like a horse.

"Garn. Aint you seen this before?"

She roared with laughter, and the bottom wobbled so much it was impossible to inject it.

"Look, hold on to the chair and keep still for a second, will you?" I was laughing now.

She did, and the injection was over in less than a minute. I rubbed the area hard to disperse the fluid, as it was a large dose. I put everything into a brown paper bag to keep it separate. Then I washed my hands and dried them on her towel, just to please her. We carried our own towel, but I thought that to use it would be a conspicuous snub.

She came to the door with me, and out onto the balcony, all the children following. "See you tomorrow, then. I'll look forward to yer comin. I'll 'ave a nice cup of tea for yer."

I cycled off with much to think about. In her own surroundings, Lil was not a disgusting old bag, she was a heroine. She kept the family together, in appalling conditions, and the children looked happy. She was cheerful and uncomplaining. How she had come to pick up syphilis was none of my business. I was there to treat the condition, not to judge.

The next day when I called, I was so pre-occupied with wondering how I could decline the offer of a cup of tea, that when the door opened, I stood staring awkwardly, stupidly, at Lil, who was not Lil. She looked a bit shorter and fatter, the same slippers, the same hair curlers, the same fag – but different.

A familiar screech of laughter revealed toothless gums. She poked me in the stomach. "Yer thinks I'm Lil, don' yer? They all thinks that. I'm 'er mum. We looks like two peas, we does. Lil's had a mis an' gorn to 'ospital. Good riddance, I sez. She's got enough with ten o' them, an' him in an' out all the time."

A few questions elicited the facts. Lil had felt ill shortly after I had left the previous day, and was later sick. She had lain down on the bed, and sent one of the children to fetch Gran. Contractions had started, and she was sick again. Then she must have become unconscious.

Gran said to me, "I'll cope with a mis any time, but not a dead woman. No, sir."

She'd called a doctor, and Lil was taken straight to The London Hospital. We later learned that a macerated foetus was extracted. It had probably been dead for three or four days.

RICKETS

It is hard to imagine today that until the last century no woman had any specialist obstetric care during pregnancy. The first time a woman would see a doctor or midwife was when she went into labour. Therefore, death and disaster, either for mother or child, or both, were commonplace. Such tragedies were looked upon as the will of God, whereas, in fact, they were the inevitable result of neglect and ignorance. Society ladies would have a doctor visiting them during pregnancy, but such visits were not antenatal care and would probably be more like social calls than anything else, because no doctor was trained in antenatal care.

The pioneer in this branch of obstetrics was a Dr J. W. Ballantyne of Edinburgh University. (Indeed some of the greatest discoveries and advances made in medicine seem to come from Edinburgh.) Ballantyne wrote a paper in 1900 deploring the abysmal state of antenatal pathology, and urging that a pre-maternity hospital was necessary. An anonymous gift of £1,000 allowed the first ever bed for antenatal care to be inaugurated, in 1901, at the Simpson Memorial Hospital. (Simpson, another Scot, developed anaesthetics.)

This was the first such bed in the civilised world. It is an incredible thought. Medicine was developing rapidly. The staphylococcus had been isolated; so had the tuberculous bacillus. The heart and circulation were understood. The functions of liver, kidneys, and lungs had been ascertained. Anaesthetics and surgery were advancing apace. But no one, it seems, thought that pre-maternity care might be necessary for the life and safety of a pregnant woman and her child.

It was ten years later, in 1911, before the first antenatal clinic was opened in Boston, USA. Another opened in Sydney, Australia, in 1912. Dr Ballantyne had to wait until 1915, fifteen years after his seminal paper, before he saw an antenatal clinic open in Edinburgh. He, and other far-sighted obstetricians, were faced with bitter opposition from colleagues and politicians who regarded antenatal care as a needless expenditure of public money and medical time.

At the same time the struggle by visionary and dedicated women was in progress to gain properly regulated training in the art of midwifery. If Dr Ballantyne was having a hard time, these women found it harder. You have to imagine what it was like to be on the receiving end of vicious antagonism: sneering, contempt, ridicule, slights about one's intelligence, integrity and motives. In those days, women even ran the risk of dismissal for their opinions. And this treatment came from other women, as well as men. In fact, "in-fighting" between various schools of nurses who had some sort of training in midwifery was particularly nasty. One eminent lady – the matron of St Bartholomew's Hospital – branded the aspiring midwives as "anachronisms, who would in the future be regarded as historical curiosities".

The medical opposition seems to have arisen mainly from the fact that "women are striving to interfere too much in every department of life".* Obstetricians also doubted the female intellectual capacity to grasp the anatomy and physiology of childbirth, and suggested that they could not therefore be trained. But the root fear was – guess what? – you've got it, but no prizes for quickness: money. Most doctors charged a routine one guinea for a delivery. The word got around that trained midwives would undercut them by delivering babies for half a guinea! The knives were out.

In the 1860s the Council of Obstetrics estimated that, out of around 1,250,000 births annually in Britain, about 10 per cent were attended by a doctor. Some researchers put the figure as low as 3 per cent. Therefore, all the rest – well over one million women

* From *Behind the Blue Door in A History of the Royal College of Midwives*, Hansard, p. 23. This is a quote from the proposed Bill for the Registration of Midwives, 1890, from a speech made by Charles Bradlaugh MP.

annually – were attended by women with no training, or by no one at all, other than a friend or relative. In the 1870s Florence Nightingale wrote *Notes on Lying-in Infirmaries*, drawing attention to "the utter absence of any means of training in any existing institution", saying "it is a farce or mockery to call women who attend childbirth, midwives. In France, Germany, and even Russia they consider it woman-slaughter to practice as we do. In these countries everything is regulated by Government – with us, by private enterprise." The guinea earned by doctors for a delivery was a significant part of their income. The threat of being undercut by trained midwives had to be resisted. The fact that thousands of women and babies were dying annually for want of proper attention did not come into it.

However, the courageous, hard-working, dedicated women eventually won. In 1902 the Midwives Act was passed, and in 1903 the Central Midwives Board issued their first certificate to a trained midwife. Fifty years later I was proud to be a successor of these wonderful women, and to be able to offer my trained skills to the long-suffering, cheerful, resilient women of the London Docklands.

At the church hall, the antenatal clinic had been set up again. It was mid-winter, and the coke-stove was burning fiercely. It was well guarded on all four sides for the protection of the numerous little children running around. Lil had been in my mind on and off during the past fortnight – a curious mixture of revulsion and admiration. Whilst I admired the way she coped, I hoped I would not have to meet her again, at least not in the intimate patient/midwife relationship.

The pile of notes on the desk told me it would be a busy afternoon – no time to brood about Lil and her syphilis. There were seven piles of notes, with about ten folders in each pile. Another seven o'clock finish, if we were lucky.

I glanced at the top of the first pile, and saw the name Brenda, a woman of forty-six with rickets. She would be admitted to hospital for a Caesarean, and she was booked with the London

Hospital in Whitechapel, but we were looking after her antenatally. At that moment she hobbled in, punctual to the minute for her two o'clock appointment. As I was at the desk, and the other staff were not available, I took her for examination and check-up.

My heart went out to little Brenda. Rickets showed itself in malformation of the bones. For centuries it was not known what caused the condition. It was thought, perhaps, to be inherited. The child was thought to be "puny" or "sickly" or even just lazy, as rachitic children always stand and walk very late. The bones are shortened and thickened at the ends, and bend under pressure. The spine is deformed, as many vertebrae are crushed. The sternum is bent, and therefore the ribcage is barrelled and frequently twisted in shape. The head is large and square shaped, with a jutting, flattened lower jaw. Frequently, the teeth drop out. As if these deformities were not enough, rachitic children always had a lower immunity to infection, and bronchitis, pneumonia and gastro-enteritis constantly occurred.

The condition was common throughout Northern Europe, especially in cities, and no one knew what caused it, until in the 1930s it was found to be due to the simplest of causes: a lack of Vitamin D in the diet causing deficiency of calcium in the bone.

Such a simple reason for so much suffering! Vitamin D is found abundantly in milk, meat, eggs and especially in meat fat and fish oils. You would think most children would have had an adequate diet of these items, wouldn't you? But no, not poor children from deprived backgrounds. Vitamin D can also be made spontaneously in the body by the effect of ultra-violet rays on the skin. You might think there should be enough sun in Northern Europe to balance things. But no, the sun was not for poor children in industrial cities where the density of buildings virtually blocked out the natural light, and where children had to work long hours in factories and workshops or workhouses.

So these children grew up crippled. All the bones of their bodies were deformed, and the long bones of the legs buckled and bent under the weight of the upper body. During adolescence, when growing ceased, the bones ossified into that position.

Even today, in the twenty-first century, you can still see a few very old people hobbling around who are very short, with legs that bow outwards. These are the brave survivors who have spent a lifetime struggling to overcome the effects of the poverty and deprivation of childhood nearly a century ago.

Brenda beamed at me. Her strange face, with an oddly shaped lower jaw, was alight with eager anticipation. She knew she would have to have a Caesarean section, but that did not bother her. She was going to have a baby, and this time it would live. That was all that mattered to her, and she was intensely grateful to the Sisters, the hospital, the doctors – everyone – but above all to the National Health Service, and the wonderful people who had arranged that everything should be free, that she wouldn't have to pay.

Brenda's obstetric history was tragic. She had married young, and in the 1930s had had four pregnancies. Every baby had died. The tragedy for a woman with rickets is that, along with all the other bones, the pelvis is also deformed, and a flat, or rachitic pelvis develops. The baby therefore cannot be delivered, or at any rate can only be delivered with great difficulty. Brenda had had four long, obstructed labours, and each time the baby had died. She was lucky not to have died herself, as countless numbers of women did in earlier decades all over Europe.

The incidence of rickets had always been slightly higher among little girls than among boys. The reason for this was probably social, and not physiological. Poor mothers of large families tended often (and still do!) to favour the sons, so the boys got more food. Boys have always been more mobile, and go outside to play more. In Poplar, it was always the boys who were down at the water's edge, or in the wharfs or the bomb sites. So they were getting sunlight on their bodies, whilst their sisters were kept at home. Also, many holiday projects were organised by socially aware philanthropists. Summer camps, which took poor boys to the country for a month under canvas, were quite common, and these camps were lifesavers for thousands of boys. But I have yet to hear of summer camps for girls one hundred years ago. Perhaps it was not considered suitable to take girls away from home and put them under canvas. Or perhaps the needs of girls were simply overlooked. Anyway, one way or another, they missed out. The life-giving sun was withheld from them each summer, and rickety little girls grew up to become deformed women who could conceive and carry a child for nine months, but could not deliver the baby.

It will never be known how many women died of exhaustion in the agony of obstructed labour: the poor were expendable, and their numbers not counted. Where was it I had read, in some ancient manual for the *Instruction of Women attending the Lying-in*: "If a woman is in labour for more than ten or twelve days, you should seek a doctor's aid"? Ten or twelve days of obstructed labour, in the hands of an untrained woman! Dear heaven – was there no mercy, no understanding? I had to shut such agonising thoughts out of my mind, and quietly thank God that obstetric practice had moved on. Yet even in my training days, the most up-to-date textbooks taught that a woman with a rachitic pelvis should have a 'trial labour of eight to twelve hours to test the endurance of both mother and foetus'.

Brenda had been subjected to four such trial labours in the 1930s. Why on earth, after the first disaster, it had not been agreed that she should have a Caesarean section for the delivery of subsequent babies, I could not imagine. Possibly she could not afford to pay for it, because, before 1948, all medical treatment had to be paid for.

Brenda's husband had been killed on active service in the war in 1940, so she had not had any more pregnancies. However, at the age of forty-three she had married again, and now she was pregnant once more. Her joy and excitement at the prospect of a living baby seemed to fill the antenatal clinic, and throw everything else into shadow. She called out: "Allo', sis, ah's yerself?" to everyone in sight, and to queries about her health, she responded, "I'm wonderful. Never bin better. On top 'o the world all the time."

I followed her over to the couch, and it stabbed my heart to see her little bow legs struggling to carry her. With each step the right leg in particular bent outwards, and her left hip swung precariously in the opposite direction. I had to arrange two stools and a chair before she could climb on to the couch, but she managed it, with awkward movements. It was painful to see. She was panting, and beaming in triumph when she got up. It seemed that every difficulty in life was a challenge to her, and every one successfully overcome was an occasion for rejoicing. She was not, by any stretch of the imagination, a good-looking woman, but I was not at all surprised that she had found a second husband who, I had no doubt, loved her.

Brenda was only six months pregnant, but her abdomen looked abnormally large, due to her tiny stature, and also to the inward curving of the spine, which pushed the uterus forward and upwards. She could feel movements, and I could hear the foetal heartbeat. Her pulse and blood pressure were normal, but her breathing was laboured. I remarked on it.

"Don't mind me. That's nothing much," she said cheerfully. I did not feel confident about examining Brenda's misshapen body, so I asked Sister Bernadette to confirm, which she did. Brenda was as healthy as could be expected, and was carrying a healthy foetus.

We saw her every week for the next six weeks, and she struggled on with increasing difficulty, using two sticks to help her get about. Her happiness never left her and she never complained. At thirty-seven weeks she was admitted to The London Hospital for bed rest, and a Caesarean section was successfully carried out at thirty-nine weeks.

A fine healthy daughter was delivered, whom she called Grace Miracle.

ECLAMPSIA

Throughout history, and until after the end of the Second World War in 1945, most babies were born at home. Then the drive for hospital delivery started, and it was so successful that by 1975 only one per cent of babies were born at home. The district midwife became very nearly an extinct species.

The fashion, or trend, is reversing slightly today, and the home birth rate is around two per cent. Perhaps this is because hospital delivery presents new and totally unexpected risks for mother and baby, and people are getting wise to this fact.

Sally came to us because she believed her mother more than she believed the doctor, who had advised hospital for her first baby.

Her mother had said, "Nark 'im. You go to the Nonnatuns, luvvy. They'll see yer right."

Gran had stepped in, too, with a wealth of ancient folklore, and hair-raising stories about the lying-in infirmaries, which used to be feared more than death itself by women.

In vain the doctor tried to convince Sally that modern hospitals were not like the old infirmaries, but he was no match for Mum and Gran, so he retired from the ring, and Sally booked with the Midwives of St Raymund Nonnatus.

We saw patients antenatally once a month for the first six months, then fortnightly for six weeks, followed by weekly check-ups for the last six weeks of pregnancy. All went well with Sally for the first seven months. She was a pretty little twenty-year-old, and she and her husband occupied two rooms in her mother's house. She was a telephonist, and her mum, who attended every antenatal visit, was proud of her.

I sat down with her, and went through her notes. Her blood pressure had been quite normal for the first six months. On the previous visit it had been slightly raised. I was concerned to find the BP even higher when I took it. I asked her to go to the scales, and found that she had gained five pounds weight in a fortnight. Warning bells were beginning to ring in my head.

I told Sally that I would like to examine her, and followed her over to the couch. By so doing, I was able to see that her ankles were swollen. A diagnosis was taking shape in my mind. She lay on the couch and I was able to feel, quite certainly, pitting oedema up to the knees – not very pronounced, but palpable to experienced fingers. Water retention – that would account for the weight gain. I examined the rest of her body for oedema, but could find none.

"Are you still getting any sickness?" I asked.

"No."

"Any stomach pains?"

"No."

"Any headaches?"

"Well, yes, now that you mention it, I have. But I puts it down to working on the phones."

"When do you give up work?"

"I gave up las' week."

"And are you still getting headaches?"

"Well, yes, I am that, but Mum says not to worry. It's normal."

I glanced sideways at the mother, Enid, who was beaming and nodding wisely. Thank God the girl had come to antenatal clinic. Mum is not always right!

"Stay there, would you, Sally? I want to test your urine. Have you brought a specimen?"

She had, and Enid produced it after rummaging around in her voluminous handbag.

I went over to the Bunsen burner, which was on the marble slab, and lit it. The urine was quite clear and looked normal as I poured a little into the test tube. I held the upper half of the glass vial over the flame. As it heated the urine turned white, whilst the urine in the lower half of the tube, which was unheated, remained clear.

Albumen urea. A diagnosis of pre-eclampsia. I stood quite still for a moment, thinking.

*

It is strange how you forget things, even momentous things in life. I had forgotten Margaret, but as I stood by the sink looking at that test tube, Margaret and the whole of my first and only horrifying experience of eclampsia flooded into my mind.

Margaret was twenty, and must have been very beautiful, though I never saw her beauty. I saw dozens of photographs of her though, which her adoring and heartbroken husband, David, showed me. All photographs were black and white in those days. They had a particular charm, created by the effects of light and shadow. In some of the photos, Margaret's intelligence and sensitivity claimed your attention, in others her laughing, puckish humour made you want to share the joke. In others, her huge, clear eyes looked fearlessly into the future, and in all of the snaps, her soft brown hair hung curling over her shoulders. One memorable photo was of a laughing young girl standing in a swimsuit beside the sea in Devon, with the spray from the waves leaping up the cliff face, and the wind blowing through her hair. The balance of her body on her long, slim legs and the angle of the shadows from the setting sun made an exquisite photo, by any standards. She looked like the sort of girl I would want to know – but I never did, except through David. She was a musician, a violinist, but I never heard her play.

All these photos David showed me during the two days of watching. When I first met him I'd assumed he must be her father. But no, he was her husband and lover, and worshipped the very ground beneath her feet. He was a scientist, and looked a very reserved, controlled, unapproachable sort of man, perhaps even cold and unemotional. But still waters run deep, and over those two long days the intensity of his passion and pain nearly split the hospital apart. Sometimes he was talking to her, sometimes to himself, occasionally to the staff. Sometimes he muttered prayers, or a few words forced out through sobbing tears. From these fragments, and the case history, I pieced together their story. There was nothing of the cold remote scientist about David.

They had met at a music club, at which Margaret was performing. He couldn't take his eyes off her. All through the interval, and the social afterwards, he followed her every movement with his eyes. He thought he might speak to her, but stammered and couldn't get the words out. He couldn't understand why; he was an articulate man. He did not know what was happening to him. She continued laughing and talking with other people while he retreated to a corner, scarcely able to breathe for the beating of his heart.

In the following days and weeks, he couldn't get her out of his head. Still he didn't understand. He thought it was the music that had affected him so deeply. He felt restless and ill at ease and his comfortable bachelor habits afforded him no comfort. Then he bumped into her in a Lyons Corner House, and amazingly she remembered him, though he couldn't think why. They had lunch together, and this time, far from being tongue-tied, he couldn't stop talking. In fact they talked for hours. They had a thousand things to say to each other, and he had never felt so relaxed and happy with anyone in all his forty-nine years of fairly solitary life. He thought, She can't possibly be interested in a dried-up old fogey like me, smelling of formaldehyde and surgical spirits. But she was. Perhaps she saw the integrity, the spiritual strength and the depths of untapped emotion in that quiet man. She was his first and only love, and he lavished on her all the passion of youth, with the tenderness and consideration of maturity.

Afterwards he said to me, "I am just thankful that I knew her at all. If we had not met, or if we had met and just passed each other by, all the great literature of the world, all the poets, all the great love stories would have been meaningless to me. You cannot understand what you have not experienced."

They had been married for six months, and she was six months pregnant, when she was admitted to the antenatal ward of the City of London Maternity Hospital where I was working. According to her antenatal records, Margaret had been in perfect health throughout the pregnancy. She had been seen at the clinic two days earlier, and everything had been quite normal – weight, pulse, blood pressure, urine sample, no sickness – nothing that would indicate what was to come.

On the day of admission she had awoken early, and was sick, which was unusual as morning sickness had passed about eight weeks earlier. She returned to the bedroom, saying there were spots in front of her eyes. David was concerned, but she said she would lie down again. It was a bit of a headache, and would go if she had another sleep. So off he went to work, saying he would telephone at eleven o'clock, to see how she felt. The telephone rang and rang. He imagined he could hear it echoing through the empty house. She might be out, of course, having woken up refreshed, but a premonition told him to go home.

He found her unconscious on the bedroom floor, with blood smeared all around her mouth, across her cheek, and in her hair. His first thought was that there had been a burglary, during which she had been attacked, but the total absence of any signs of a break-in, and the apparent depth of unconsciousness, the stertorous breathing, the bounding heartbeat that he could feel through her night dress, told him that something serious had happened.

The hospital sent an ambulance straight away, in response to his frantic phone call. A doctor came also, as the implications of David's description were very grave. Margaret was sedated with morphine before the ambulance men were allowed to move her.

We were told to prepare a side-ward to receive a possible case of eclampsia. It was during my first six months of midwifery training, and the ward sister showed me and another student how this should be done. The bed was pushed against the wall, with pillows stuffed down the crack. The head of the bed was padded with more pillows and secured tightly with sheets. Oxygen was brought in: a mouth wedge and airway tube were in readiness, also suction apparatus. The window was covered with a dark cloth to black out most of the light.

Margaret was deeply unconscious on admission. Her blood pressure was so high that the systolic was over 200 and diastolic 190. Her temperature was 104 degrees Fahrenheit and her pulse was 140. A catheter specimen of urine was obtained and tested. So heavy was the deposit of albumen that upon boiling the urine turned solid like the white of an egg. There was no doubt of the diagnosis.

Eclampsia was, and still is, a rare and mysterious condition of pregnancy, with no known cause. Usually there are warning signs before onset known as pre-eclampsia, which responds to treatment, but if untreated may progress to eclampsia. Rarely, very rarely, it occurs with no warning in a perfectly healthy woman, and in the space of a few hours it can develop to convulsion stage. When this stage is reached, the pregnancy is unstable, and the foetus unlikely to survive. The only treatment is immediate delivery of the baby by Caesarean section.

Theatre had been alerted and was ready to receive Margaret. The baby was dead on delivery, and Margaret returned to the ward. She never regained consciousness. She was kept under heavy sedation in a darkened room, but even then she had repeated convulsions that were terrifying to see. A slight twitching was followed by vigorous contractions of all the muscles of the body. Her whole body became rigid, and the muscular spasm bent her body backwards, so that for about twenty seconds only her head and heels rested on the bed. Respiration ceased, and she became blue with asphyxia. Quite quickly, the rigidity passed, followed by violent convulsive movements and spasms of all her limbs. It was hard to keep her from hurling herself on to the floor, and quite impossible to keep a tongue wedge in place. With the violent movements of the jaw she bit her tongue to pieces. She salivated profusely, and foamed at the mouth, which mingled with the blood from her lacerated tongue. Her face was congested and horribly distorted. Then the convulsion subsided, and a deep coma would follow, lasting for an hour or so and followed by another convulsion.

These terrible fits occured repeatedly for a little over thirty-six hours, and on the evening of the second day, she died in her husband's arms.

All this flooded into my mind in the few seconds that I stood at the sink, looking at the sample of Sally's urine. David. What had happened to that poor man? He had staggered out of the hospital half blind, half mad, dumb with shock and grief. Sadly, in nursing, and particularly in hospital nursing, you meet people during some of the most profound moments in their lives, and then they are gone from you for ever. There was no way that David would be hanging around the maternity hospital where his wife had died, just to reassure the nurses. And equally, hospital staff could not go chasing after him to find out how he was coping. I remembered with gratitude what he said to me just after she died, and the words of some great writer (I cannot recall who), came to mind:

> He who loves knows it. He who loves not, knows it not.
> I pity him, and make him no answer.

There was no time to mope. I had to see Sister and report on Sally's condition.

Sister Bernadette was in charge on that day. She listened to my report, looked at the urine sample, and said, "There may be contamination from a vaginal discharge, so we will take a catheter specimen of urine. Could you just get things ready for catheterisation, please, while I go over to Sally and examine her."

When I took the tray over to the couch Sister had already made a full examination, and confirmed everything I had reported.

She said to Sally, "We are going to insert a small tube into your bladder to drain off some urine for testing in path. lab."

Sally protested, but eventually submitted, and I catheterised her. Then Sister said to her, "We think there is a problem with this pregnancy that requires absolute rest, and a special diet, and certain drugs to be administered daily. For this, you must go to hospital."

Sally and her mother were alarmed.

"What's up? I feels all right. Just a bit of a headache, that's all."

Her mother butted in, "If there's anything wrong with our Sal I can look after 'er. She can take it easy at home, like."

Sister was very firm. "It's not just a question of taking it easy and staying in bed some of the time. Sally has to have absolute bed rest, twenty-four hours a day, for the next four to six weeks. She will have to have a special no-salt diet, with low fluid intake. She will need to have certain sedative drugs four times a day. She will need to be watched carefully, and her pulse, temperature and blood pressure will have to be taken several times every day. The baby's progress will also have to be checked daily. You cannot possibly do all this at home. Sally needs immediate hospital treatment, and if she does not get it, the baby will be at risk, and also the health of the mother."

This was a very long speech for Sister Bernadette, who was usually very quiet. It was absolutely effective, though, for it silenced Sally's mum, who gave a squeak, and said nothing.

"I am going now to ring the doctor, to ask him if he can find a bed for you immediately at one of the maternity hospitals. I want you to stay where you are, lying quietly on the couch. I don't want you to go home."

Then she said to Enid: "Perhaps you would go home and get some things for Sally in hospital – nightdresses, toothbrush, things like that, and bring them back here."

Enid scurried off, glad of something to do.

Sally had a couple of hours to wait before an ambulance came, and she was taken into this in a wheel chair. I think she was bewildered by all the fuss and the attention she was getting, especially as she didn't feel ill, had walked to the clinic, and was quite capable of walking out.

Sally was taken to The London Hospital in Mile End Road. She was admitted to the antenatal ward, where there were ten to twelve other young women in just the same stage and condition of pregnancy as herself. She received complete bed-rest, even to the extent of being pushed to the toilet in a wheel chair. She was sedated, and given a specific diet and low fluid intake. Over the next four weeks her blood pressure gradually came down, the oedema subsided, and the headache passed. At thirty-eight weeks of pregnancy, labour was induced. Sally's blood pressure began to rise during the labour, so as soon as she was fully dilated, she was given a light anaesthetic, and a fine healthy baby was delivered by forceps.

Mother and baby both remained well during the post-natal period.

*

Eclampsia is as much a mystery today as it was fifty years ago. It was, and still is, thought to be caused by some defect in the placenta. But nothing has been proven, even though thousands of placentas must have been examined by researchers attempting to isolate this supposed "defect".

Sally's case was typical of pre-eclampsia. Had she not been diagnosed, and received prompt and expert treatment, her condition could have led to eclampsia. But the simple treatment that I have described – total rest and sedation – may have averted its development.

Margaret, who died in that ghastly way, had a very rare onset of sudden, violent eclampsia, with no warning signs, and no pre-eclamptic phase. I have never seen another such case, but they do still occur occasionally.

Pre-eclampsia and eclampsia are still leading causes of maternal and perinatal mortality in the UK, in spite of modern antenatal care. What befell the women with pre-eclampsia when there was no antenatal care? It does not take a great deal of imagination to answer that one. Yet doctors who advocated the study of and provision for proper antenatal care were regarded, one hundred years ago, as eccentrics and time-wasters. The same attitude poured scorn on the idea of a structured and regulated training for midwives.

Let those of us who have borne children thank God that those days are now past.

FRED

A convent is essentially a female establishment. However, of necessity, the male of the species cannot be excluded entirely. Fred was the boiler-man and odd-jobber of Nonnatus House. He was typical of the Cockney of his day and age. Stunted growth, short bowed legs, powerful hairy arms, pugnacious, obstinate, resourceful; all these attributes were combined with endless chat and irrepressible good humour. His most striking characteristic was a spectacular squint. One eye was permanently directed north-east, whilst the other roved in a south-westerly direction. If you add to this the single yellow tooth jutting from his upper jaw, which he generally held over his lower lip and sucked, you would not say he was a beautiful specimen of manhood. However, so delightful was his optimism, good humour and artless self-confidence that the Sisters held him in great affection, and leaned on him heavily for all practical matters. Sister Julienne had a particularly strong line in helpless feminine appeal, "Oh Fred, the window in the upper bathroom won't close. I've tried and tried, but it's no use. Do you think . . .? If you can find time, that is . . .?"

Of course Fred could find time. For Sister Julienne he would have found time to move the Albert Docks. Sister Julienne was deeply grateful, and praised his skill and expertise. The fact that the window in the upstairs bathroom was fixed permanently closed from that time onwards was no inconvenience, and not mentioned by anyone.

The only person who did not respond with delight to Fred's particular brand of Cockney charm was Mrs B., who was a Cockney herself, had seen it all before, and was not impressed. Mrs B. was Queen of the Kitchen. She worked from 8 a.m. to 2 p.m. each day, and produced superb food for us. She was an expert in steak and kidney pies, thick stews, savoury mince, toad-in-the-hole, treacle puddings, jam roly-poly, macaroni puddings and so on, as well as baking the best bread and cakes you could find anywhere. She was a large lady with formidable frontage, and a particular glare as she growled, "Nah then – don' chew mess up my kitchen." As the kitchen was the meeting-point for all staff when we came in, often tired and hungry, this remark was frequently heard. We girls were very docile and respectful, especially as we had learned from experience that flattery usually resulted in a tart or a wedge of cake straight from the oven.

Fred, however, was not so easily tamed. For one thing, the orientation of his eyes being what it was, he genuinely could not see the mess he was making; for another, Fred was not going to kowtow to anyone. He would grin at Mrs B. wickedly, suck his tooth, slap her ample bottom, and chuckle, "Come off it, old girl." Mrs B.'s glare would turn into a shout, "You ge' out of my kitchen you ugly mug, and stay ou'." Unfortunately Fred couldn't stay out, and she knew it. The coke stove was in the kitchen, and he was responsible for stoking it, raking it out, opening and shutting the flues, and generally keeping it in good order. As Mrs B. did much of her cooking, and all of her baking, on that stove, she knew that she was dependent on him. So a strained truce prevailed between them. Only occasionally – about twice a week – a shouting match erupted. I noticed with interest that during these altercations neither of them swore – no doubt this was out of respect for the nuns. Had they been in any other environment, I felt sure the air would have been blue with obscenities.

Fred's duties were morning and evening for boiler stoking and extra time by arrangement for odd jobs. He came in seven days a week for the boiler, and the job suited him very well. It was a steady job, but it also allowed him plenty of time to pursue the other activities he had built up over the years.

Fred lived with his unmarried daughter Dolly in the lower two rooms of a small house backing on to the docks. He had been called up during the war but, due to his eyesight, had been unable to enter the armed services. He was therefore consigned to the Pioneer Corps, where, if Fred is to be believed, he spent six years serving King and Country by cleaning out latrines.

Compassionate leave was granted to him in 1942, when his wife and three of their six children were killed by a direct hit. He was able to spend a little time with his three living children, who were shocked and traumatised, in a hostel in North London before they were evacuated to Somerset, and he was ordered back to the latrines.

After the war, he took two cheap rooms and brought up the remains of his family single-handed. It was never easy for him to find a regular job, because his eyesight was erratic, and because he would not commit himself to be away from home for long hours – he knew that his children needed him. So he had developed a wide range of money-making activities, some of which were legal.

Whilst we, the lay staff, took our breakfast in the kitchen, Fred was generally attending to his boiler, so there was plenty of opportunity to press him for stories, which we did unashamedly, being young and inquisitive. For his part Fred would always oblige, as he clearly loved spinning his yarns, often prefaced by, "You're never going to believe this one." A laughing audience of four young girls was music to his ears. Young girls will laugh at anything!

One of his regular jobs, and the best paid he assured us, as it was highly skilled, was that of a cooper's barrel bottom knocker for Whitbreads the brewer. Trixie, the sceptic, snapped, "I'll knock your bottom for you", but Chummy swallowed it whole and said gravely, "Actually, it sounds frightfully interesting. Do tell us more." Fred liked Chummy, and called her "Lofty".

"Well, these here beer barrels, like, they've gotta be sound, like, and the only way of testin' 'em is by knockin' the bottoms and listening. If it comes up wiv one note, it's sound. If it comes up wiv anover, it's faul'y. See? Easy, bu' I can tell you, it takes years of experience."

We had seen Fred in the market selling onions, but did not know that he grew them. Having the ground floor of a small house gave him a small garden, which was given over to onions. He had tried potatoes – "no money in spuds" – but onions proved to be a money-maker. He also kept chickens and sold the eggs, and the birds as well. He wouldn't sell to a butcher, "I'm not 'aving no one take 'alf the profits", but sold directly to the market. He wouldn't take a stall either, "I'm not paying no bleedin' rent to the council", and laid a blanket on the floor in any space available, selling his onions, eggs and chickens from there.

Chickens led to quails, which he supplied to West End restaurants. Quails are delicate birds, requiring warmth, so he kept them in the house. Being small, they do not need much space, so he bred and reared them in boxes which he kept under the bed. He slaughtered and plucked them in the kitchen.

Chummy, always eager, said, "You know, I think that's frightfully clever, actually. But wouldn't it be a bit whiffy, what?"

Trixi cut her short. "Oh, shut up. We're having our breakfast," and reached for the cornflakes.

Fred's enthusiasm for drains was enough to put anyone off their breakfast. Cleaning out drains was obviously a passion, and his north-east eye gleamed as he poured out the effluvial details. Trixie said, "I'll stuff you down a drain, if you don't watch it," and made for the door, toast in hand. But Fred, a poet with rod and suction, was not to be discouraged. "The best job I ever had was up in Hampstead, see? One of them posh houses. Lady's real la-di-da, toffee-nosed. I lifts up the man'ole cover an' there it is, like, fillin' the whole chamber: a frenchy – a rubber, you know – caught at the inflow end, an' blown up with muck an' water. Huge, it was, huge."

His eyes rolled expressively at their different angles as he expanded his arms. Chummy shared his enthusiasm, but not his meaning.

"You never seen nuffink like it, a yard long, an' a foot wide, strike me dead. Ve lady, ever so posh like, looks at it an' says 'oh dear, whatever can it be?' an' I says 'well if you don't know, lady, you musta bin asleep' an' she says 'don't you be saucy, my good fellow'. Well, I gets the thing out, an' charges her double, an' she pays up like a lamb."

He grinned impishly, rubbed his hands together, and sucked his tooth.

"Oh, jolly well done, Fred, good for you. It was frightfully clever getting double the fee, actually."

Fred's best line, with the highest profit margin, had been fireworks. His unit of the Pioneer Corps had been attached to the Royal Engineers in North Africa for a time. Explosives had been in daily use. Anyone, however humble, working with the REs, is bound to learn something about explosives and Fred had picked up enough to give him confidence to embark on fireworks manufacture in the kitchen of his little house after the war.

"S'easy. You just need a load of the right kind of fertiliser, an' a touch of this an mix it wiv a bi' of that an' bingo, you've got yer bang."

Chummy said, wide-eyed with apprehension: "But isn't it frightfully dangerous, actually, Fred?"

"Nah, nah, not if you knows what you is a-doin', like what I does. Sold like nobody's business, they did, all over Poplar. Everyone was wantin' 'em. I could've made a fortune if they'd left me alone, the bleeders, beggin' yer pardon, miss."

"Who? What happened?"

"Rozzers, police, got 'old of some of me fireworks an' tested 'em, an' sez they was dangerous, an' I was endangering 'uman life. I asks you – I asks you. Would I do anyfing like that, now? Would I?" He looked up from his position on the floor, and spread out his ash-covered hands in innocent appeal.

"Of course not Fred," we all chorused. "What happened?"

"Well, they charged me, din't they, but the magistrate, he lets me off wiv a fine, like, because I 'ad three kids. He was a good bloke, he was, the magistrate, but he says I would go to prison if I does it again, kids or no kids. So I never done it no more."

His most recent economic adventure had been in toffee apples, and very successful it was, too. Dolly made the toffee mixture in the little kitchen, while Fred purchased crates of cheap apples from Covent Garden. All that was needed was a stick to put the apple on, dip it in the toffee, and in no time at all rows of toffee apples were lined up on the draining board. Fred couldn't imagine why he hadn't thought of it before. It was a winner. One-hundred per cent profit margin and assured sales with the large number of children around. He foresaw a rosy future with unlimited sales and profits.

A week or two later, it was clear that something had gone wrong from the silence of the small figure crouched down by the stove, manipulating the flue. No cheerful greeting, no chat, no tuneless whistle – just a heavy silence. He wouldn't even respond to our questions.

Eventually Chummy left the table and went over to him.

"Come on, Fred. What's up? Perhaps we can help. And even if we can't, you will feel better if you tell us." She touched his shoulder with her huge hand.

Fred turned and looked up. His north-east eye drooped, and a little moisture glinted in the south-west. His voice was husky as he spoke.

"Fevvers. Quail's fevvers. Tha's wha's up. Someone complained fevvers was stuck to me toffee apples. So food safety boffins come an' examined 'em an' said fevvers an' bits of fevvers was stuck to all me toffee apples, an' I was endangerin' public 'ealth."

Apparently the health inspector had asked at once to see where the toffee apples were made, and when shown the kitchen, in which the quails were regularly slaughtered and plucked, had immediately ordered that both occupations be discontinued, on pain of prosecution. So great was the disaster to Fred's economy that it seemed nothing could be said to comfort him. Chummy was so kind, and assured him that something else would turn up, something better, but he was not reassured, and it was a glum breakfast that morning. He had lost face, and it hurt.

But Fred's triumph was yet to come.

A CHRISTMAS BABY

Betty Smith's baby was due in early February. As she dashed happily around all December, preparing Christmas for her husband and six children, her parents and in-laws, grandparents on both sides, brothers, sisters and their children, uncles and aunts, and a very ancient great-grandmother, none of the family dreamed that the baby would be born on Christmas Day.

Dave was a wharf manager in the West India Docks. He was in his thirties, clever, competent and he knew his job inside out. He was greatly valued by the Port of London Authority, and he earned a good wage. In consequence, the family was able to live in one of the large Victorian houses just off Commercial Road. Betty never ceased to thank her lucky stars that she had married Dave just after the war, and was able to leave the tenements, with the cramped living conditions and minimal sanitation. She loved her big, roomy house, and that is why she had always been glad to have the family descend on her for Christmas. The children loved it. With about twenty-five little cousins coming from all over Poplar, Stepney, Bow, and Canning Town, they were going to have a high old time.

Uncle Alf was Father Christmas. The house was at the bottom of an incline, and Uncle Alf had a home-made sleigh on wheels. This was taken to the top of the street, loaded with a sack of presents, and at a given signal, pushed off. The children did not know how it was done. All that they saw was Father Christmas trundling gently towards them, with no apparent means of propulsion, and stopping at their house. They were in an ecstasy of delight.

But this year, things were to be rather different. Instead of Father Christmas on a sleigh, a midwife arrived on a bicycle. Instead of a sack full of presents, a baby came, naked and crying.

My Christmas was also very different. For the first time in my life I began to understand that Christmas is a religious festival, and not just an occasion for overeating and drinking. It had all begun in late November with something that I was told was Advent. This meant nothing to me, but for the nuns it meant a time of preparation. Most people prepare for Christmas as Betty had done, buying food, drinks, presents and treats. The nuns prepared rather differently, with prayer and meditation.

The religious life is a hidden life, so I would not see or hear what was going on, but as the four weeks of Advent progressed, I began to feel intuitively that something was in the air. I couldn't put my finger on it, but as children pick up a feeling of excitement from their parents, so I "caught" from the Sisters a real feeling of calm, peace and joyful expectancy, which I found to be strangely disturbing and unwelcome.

It came to a head on Christmas Eve when I returned late from my evening visits. Sister Julienne was around, and said to me, "Come with me to the Chapel, Jennifer, we put up the crib today."

Not wishing to be rude by saying I would rather not, I followed her. The chapel was unlit, except for two candles placed by the crib. Sister Julienne kneeled at the altar rail to pray. Then she said to me, "Our blessed Saviour was born on this day."

I remember looking at the small plaster figures and the straw and things, and thinking, how on earth can an intelligent and well-informed woman take all this seriously? Is she trying to be funny?

I think I murmured something polite about it being very peaceful, and we parted. However, I was not at peace within myself. Something was nagging at me that I was trying to resist. Was it then or was it later that the thought came to me: if God really does exist, and is not just a myth, it must have consequence for the whole of life. It was not a comfortable thought.

For many years I had attended a Christmas midnight Mass somewhere, not for religious reasons, but for the drama and beauty of the ceremony. I was not fussy about denomination. When I was living in Paris, I had been in the habit of attending the Russian Orthodox Church in Rue Darue, for the beauty of the singing. The Christmas mass from 11 p.m. to about 2 a.m. counts as one of the greatest musical experiences of my life. The liturgy, sung by the Russian bass voice of the cantor, rising in quarter-tones, has never left my inner ear, even though more than fifty years have passed.

The Sisters and lay staff attended All Saints Church, East India Dock Road for midnight Mass. I was astonished to find the church absolutely packed. Strong, tough dockers, hard-bitten casual labourers, giggling teenagers in their winkle-pickers, whole families carrying babies, small children, all were there. The crowd was enormous. All Saints is a large Victorian church, and it must have held five hundred people that night. The service was as I had expected – impressive, beautiful, dramatic, but devoid of any spiritual content as far as I was concerned. I wondered why. Why was it the whole meaning of life for these good Sisters, yet just a piece of well executed theatre for me?

We were having lunch around the big table on Christmas Day when the telephone rang. Everyone groaned. We had hoped for a day of rest. The nurse who answered it came back to say that Dave Smith was reporting that his wife seemed to be in labour. The groan turned into a gasp of anxiety.

Sister Bernadette jumped up with the words, "I'll go and talk to him." She came back a few minutes later, and said, "It sounds as though it is labour. At thirty-four weeks this is unfortunate. I have informed Dr Turner, and he will come at once if we need him. Who is on call today?"

I was.

We prepared to go out together. I was a student at the time, and was always accompanied by a trained midwife. From the first moment I had watched Sister Bernadette at work, I knew that she was a gifted midwife. Her knowledge and skill were balanced by her intuition and sensitivity. I would have entrusted my life to her hands, without the slightest hesitation.

Together we left the cosy warmth of an excellent Christmas dinner, and fetched a delivery pack and our midwifery bags from the sterilising room. The pack was a large box, containing pads, sheets, waterproof paper, and so on, which was usually taken to the house a week before the expected delivery. The blue bag contained our instruments and drugs. We fitted them both to our bicycles, and pushed out into a cold windless day.

I had never known London to be so quiet. Nothing seemed to stir, except for two midwives cycling silently along the deserted road. Normally the East India Dock Road is dense with heavy goods lorries going to and from the docks, but on that day the broad thoroughfare looked majestic and beautiful in its solitary silence. Nothing moved on the river or in the docks. Not a sound, but the occasional cry of a seagull. The stillness of the great heart of London was unforgettable.

We arrived at the house, and Dave let us in. Through the window we had seen a big Christmas tree, a fire, and a room crowded with people. About a dozen little faces of curious children were pressed to the window pane as we arrived.

Dave said, "Betty's upstairs. I didn't see no cause to send them home, and she don't want it. She likes a bit of noise, says it will help her."

The sound of lusty singing "Old MacDonald Had a Farm" came from the front room, accompanied by an out-of-tune piano. Full vocal justice was given to the animal noises by various uncles, expert in being the horse, the pig, the cow, the duck. The children screamed with laughter, and shouted for more.

We went upstairs to Betty's room, where the peace and silence contrasted with the noise and clamour below. A fire had been lit and was burning brightly. Hardly any time had been given to Betty's mother to prepare a delivery room, but she had worked miracles. Surfaces had been cleaned, extra linen provided, hot water was available, even the cot had been prepared. Betty's first words were, "This is a turn up for the books, eh, Sister?"

She was a cheerful, down-to-earth sort of woman, who took everything in her stride. No doubt she had the same confidence in Sister Bernadette that I had.

I opened the delivery pack, and covered the bed with brown waterproof paper, then the draw sheets and maternity pads. We gowned and scrubbed up, and Sister examined her. The waters had broken an hour earlier. I saw intense concentration on Sister's face, and then a look of grave concern. She said nothing for a few moments as she slowly took off her gloves, then said gently:

"Betty, your baby seems to be a breech presentation. That means the bottom is coming first, instead of the head. This is a perfectly normal way for the baby to lie until about thirty-five weeks, but then the baby usually turns, and the head is presented first. Your baby has not turned. Now, whilst thousands of babies are born quite safely in breech, there is a greater risk than a head presentation. Perhaps you should consider a hospital delivery."

Betty's reaction was immediate and dogmatic. "No. No hospital. I'll be OK with you, Sister. All me babies have been delivered by the Nonnatuns and born in this room, and I don't want nothing else. What do you say, mum?"

Her mother agreed, and recalled that her ninth had been a breech, and that her neighbour Glad had had no less than four, arse first.

Sister said, "Very well then, we will do our best, but I am going to ask Dr Turner to come." Then to me: "Would you go and ring him, nurse?"

In spite of his comparative affluence, Dave did not have a telephone. There would have been no point, because none of his friends or relatives had a phone, so no one would ever have rung them. The public phone box was sufficient for their needs. As I went downstairs, a stream of shouting children in paper hats, faces alight with excitement rushed past me. A voice from downstairs called out:

"Everyone hide. I'll count twenty, then I'm coming to find you. One, two, three, four . . . "

The children rushed higher in the house, screaming and pushing, hiding in cupboards, behind curtains, anywhere. By the time I got to the front door, all was quiet except: "Seventeen, eighteen, nineteen – cummin'."

I went out into the cold of the deserted street to find the telephone box. Dr Turner was a general practitioner who not only had a surgery in the East End, but also lived there with his wife and children. He was utterly dedicated to his work and his practice, and it seemed to me that he was always on call. Like most GPs of his generation he was a first-class midwife, with a knowledge and skill gained from the experience of his wide ranging practice.

He was expecting my call. I told him the facts. He said, "Thank you, nurse. I will come directly." I imagined his wife sighing, "even on Christmas Day you have to go out."

Back in the house, hide and seek was still going on. The noise was terrific as children were found. As I entered the door, a cheery faced man passed me carrying a crate of empty beer bottles.

"How about joining me for one, then, nurse?" he said. "You and Sister and all. Oops, does she drink, do you think?"

I assured him that the Sisters did drink, but not on duty, and that for the same reason, I would not do so either. A paper streamer shot past my ear, blown by an invisible figure behind a door.

"Oh, sorry, nurse. I thought it was our Pol."

I unravelled the pink and orange thing from my uniform, and went upstairs.

Betty's room was wonderfully quiet and peaceful. The thick old walls and heavy wooden door insulated the sounds and Betty looked calm and content. Sister Bernadette was writing up her notes, and Betty's mother, Ivy, was sitting in a corner knitting. The click of the knitting needles, and the crackle of the fire were all that could be heard.

Sister explained to me that she would not give Betty a sedative, because it might affect the baby. She said it was difficult to tell how long the first stage of labour would last, and at present the foetal heart beat was quite normal.

Dr Turner arrived, looking as though there was nothing in the world he would rather do on Christmas Day than attend a breech delivery. He and Sister conferred, and he examined Betty thoroughly. I expected him to do another vaginal examination, but he did not: he accepted Sister's diagnosis without question. He told Betty that she and her baby seemed very well, and that he would come back at 5 p.m. unless we called him earlier.

We sat down to wait. Much of a midwife's work involves intense, often dramatic activity, but this is balanced by long periods of waiting quietly. Sister sat down and took out her breviary in order to say the office of the day. The nuns lived by the monastic rules of the six offices of the day: lauds; tierce; sext; none; vespers; compline and Holy Communion each morning. In a contemplative community, the offices together occupy about five hours of prayer time. For a working community this is impracticable, so, in the early days of their vocation, the Midwives of St Raymund Nonnatus had had a shortened version devised for them. Thus they were able to maintain their professed religious life, and work full-time as nurses and midwives.

The sight of this fair young face in the firelight, reading the ancient prayers, turning the pages quietly and reverently, her lips moving as she read, was deeply affecting. I sat watching her and marvelled at the depth of a vocation that could make such a pretty young woman renounce life, with all its fun and opportunities, for a religious life bound by the vows of poverty, chastity, and obedience. I could understand the vocation to nursing and midwifery, which to me were fascinating both as a study and a practice, but the calling to a religious life was quite beyond my comprehension.

Betty groaned as a contraction came on. Sister smiled, got up and went over to her. She returned to her breviary, and all that could be heard in the room was the tick of a big clock and the click of Ivy's knitting needles. Beyond the door the sounds of the party continued, but within the room all was calm and prayerful.

I sat in the firelight, and allowed my mind to wander backwards. I had spent many Christmases in hospitals. Contrary to what one might think, it was a happy time. Fifty years ago, hospitals were very much more personal than they are today. The nursing hierarchy was formidable but at least everyone knew or was acquainted with everyone else. Patients stayed in hospital for much longer and, as nurses worked sixty hours per week, we really got to know our patients as people. At Christmas, everyone let their hair down, and even the most draconian old Ward Sister, after a few sherries, would be giggling with the student nurses. It was all rather like schoolgirl fun, but it was good humoured, and the aim was to give a happy time to the patients, many of whom had horrible diseases.

My most abiding Christmas memory was the carol singing on Christmas Eve. Led by Matron, all the nursing staff would go through the wards by candlelight, singing. For someone in a hospital bed it must have been a lovely sight. There may have been over one hundred nurses, twenty or more doctors, and fifty or more ancillary staff. The nurses wore full uniform, and we turned our cloaks inside out showing the scarlet lining. We all carried candles. We walked through each darkened ward, usually containing thirty beds, singing the age-old story of Christmas. All this has long since gone from hospitals, and the memory of it is all that remains, but it was very beautiful, and I know that many patients shed tears of emotion.

The time ticked quietly by. The sounds of "Aye, aye, aye, conga" came from below. They went round and round the sitting room, then the noise got louder and louder as the snake of people started coming up the stairs. They were all shouting at the tops of their voices, and stamping in unison. Sister thought the noise might bother Betty, but she said, "No, no, Sister. I likes to hear it. I wouldn't want this house to be quiet, not on Christmas day, like."

Sister smiled. The last few contractions had seemed stronger and were closer together. She got up, and examined Betty, and said to me, "I think you had better go and call Dr Turner if you please, nurse."

It was four o'clock when I rang him, and Dr Turner arrived within a quarter of an hour. I was excited. This was my first breech delivery. Betty was beginning to feel the urge to push.

Sister Bernadette said to her, "You must try very hard not to push at first, dear. Breathe deeply, and try to relax, but not to push."

We gowned, masked and scrubbed up again. Doctor looked at Sister Bernadette, and said, "You take this delivery, Sister. I'll be here if you need me."

He obviously had complete confidence in her.

She nodded, and told Betty that she wanted her to remain on her back, with her buttocks over the end of the bed, and she asked me and Ivy to hold a leg each. I was learning, and so Sister explained everything that she did clearly and carefully.

I could see something coming, as the perineum expanded, but it did not look like a baby's buttocks. It looked a purplish colour. Sister saw my questioning expression, and told me, "That is the prolapsed cord. It occurs quite commonly in a breech delivery, because the breech is an incomplete sphere, and the cord can easily slip down between the baby's legs. As long as it is pulsating normally, there is nothing to worry about."

The perineum continued to distend, and now I saw the baby's buttocks quite clearly. Sister was kneeling on the floor between Betty's legs because the bed was too low for her to stand. She was explaining everything in a low voice to me, "This is a left sacro-anterior position, which means the left buttock will be born first, from under the pubic bone.

"Now don't push, Betty," she continued, "I want this baby to come slowly. The slower the better.

"The baby's legs will be curled up. I will want to rotate the baby to ensure the best position for delivery, but also the pull of gravity as the baby's body hangs from the vulva will help to maintain flexion of the head. This will be important."

The buttocks were born, and with infinite care Sister inserted a hand and hooked her fingers over the flexed legs.

"Don't push, Betty, whatever you do," said Sister Bernadette.

The legs slid out easily. It was a little girl. A long section of cord also slid out. It was pulsating quite vigorously – one could see it, there was no need to feel it.

"The baby is still fully attached to the placenta," Sister said, "and its life blood is coming through the cord. Even though the body is half born, until the head is born, or, at any rate, until the nose and mouth are clear to breathe, the baby depends upon the placenta and this cord for life."

I found it spooky that this tortuous, pulsating thing was absolutely essential to life, and said, "Shouldn't we push it back?"

"Not necessary. Some midwives do, but I really think there is no advantage to be gained."

Another contraction came, and with it the baby's body slid out as far as the shoulders.

Towels had been placed over the screen by the fire to warm. Sister asked for one and wrapped it firmly around the baby's body, saying as she did so, "The purpose of this is two-fold: firstly the baby must not be allowed to get cold. Most of her body is now exposed, and if the shock of cold air makes her gasp, she will inhale amniotic fluid, which could be fatal. Secondly, the towel gives me something to grip hold of. The baby is slippery, and I have to turn her another one quarter circle so that the occiput will be under the pubic bone. I will do this as I deliver the shoulders."

With the next contraction, the left anterior shoulder impinged upon the pelvic floor, and Sister delivered it by hooking a finger under the arm, and at the same time rotating the body a little clockwise. The right shoulder was delivered in the same manner, and both baby's arms were out. Only the head remained inside the mother.

"You have a little girl," Sister said to Betty, "but from the size of her limbs I don't think she is six weeks premature. I think you got your dates wrong. I want you, Betty, to push now with all your strength and really use every contraction for delivery of the baby's head. Doctor may have to exert some supra-pubic pressure, but I would prefer it if you could push the head out by yourself."

There had been no contractions for a full three minutes, and I was beginning to feel tense and anxious, but Sister was relaxed. The baby was supported by her hands, and then she let go completely, so that it was hanging quite unsupported. I gasped in horror.

"This is the correct thing to do," Sister explained. "The weight of the baby's body will gently pull the head down a little, and will increase the flexion of the head, which is what I want. About thirty seconds like this will be enough. It will not hurt the baby."

Then she took hold of the baby again. I must say I felt relieved. A contraction came on.

"Now push, Betty, as hard as possible."

Betty did, but the head did not descend any more. Sister and Dr Turner agreed that with the next contraction he would exert supra-pubic pressure, and if that did not prove effective, a low forceps delivery of the head would be necessary.

Sister explained to me, "That is because the cord will be compressed between the head and the sacral bones. The baby is all right at the moment, but if it goes on for too long, that is more than a few minutes, there is a definite risk of asphyxia."

I clenched my fingers with shock and anxiety, but Sister

remained completely calm. Another contraction came, and the doctor placed his hands on Betty's abdomen just above the pubic bone and pressed down firmly. Betty groaned with pain, but there was a definite movement of the head.

"I am going to use the Mauriceau-Smellie-Veit method of extraction of the head," Sister explained to me. She was allowing the baby to hang unsupported again, and my heart was in my mouth.

"With the next contraction, all being well, we will have the airways clear, and the baby will be able to breathe. I will want my Sim's vaginal speculum, so be ready to pass it when I need it."

I looked to see where the Sim's was on her delivery tray. My hands were trembling so much that for a ghastly moment I imagined I would knock the whole tray over, or pick up the Sim's only to drop it on the floor.

Another contraction came on, and the doctor exerted the same pressure on Betty's abdomen. Sister placed her right hand over the shoulders of the baby and the fingers of her left hand into the vagina. I could see her gently moving her fingers and feeling for something. The baby was resting on her forearm.

"I am trying to hook my index finger into the mouth of the baby, in order to maintain flexion of the head, so that the mouth and nose will be the first part of the head to encounter the air. It is *not* to exert pressure by pulling. If you ever use this method of delivery, nurse, remember that. If you try pulling, you risk dislocating the jaw."

I felt sick with fear, and just hoped to God that I would never have to deliver a breech. I could see that she was manipulating the back of the skull with her right hand. She explained, "I am simply pushing upwards on the occipital protuberance of the skull to increase flexion. A little more pressure, please doctor, if you can, and I think I shall have the airways clear. That's it. The Sim's now, nurse, please."

I had to grip my wrist with my other hand to stop it trembling. All I could think was, I mustn't drop it, I mustn't drop it. My relief when I handed it over was so great that I almost laughed.

But there was more to see.

The chin of the baby was now on the perineum and Sister carefully inserted the speculum into the vagina, pushing the posterior wall backwards, rather like using a shoe-horn, so that the baby's nose and mouth were exposed. She asked for a swab, which I handed to her, and she wiped the baby's nose and mouth free of mucus.

"Now she will be able to breath, and will no longer be dependent upon the placental blood supply."

It was astonishing to hear a gasp, followed by a tiny cry. The baby's face could not be seen, yet her voice could be heard.

"That's what I like to hear," said Sister. "Did you hear that, Betty?"

"Not 'alf. Is she all right, poor little thing? I reckons as how she's goin' through it as much as what I am."

"Yes. Your baby's quite safe now, and with the next contraction she will be born, I assure you. I think you have a torn perineum, but I can't see it because it's behind the speculum, nor can I do anything about it, because if I remove the speculum your baby will not be able to breathe."

Another contraction was coming. 'This is it,' I thought with some relief. Delivery of the head had so far taken only twelve minutes, but it had seemed like an eternity to me.

The contraction was strong, and doctor was exerting considerable pressure. Sister drew the baby's body downwards until the nose was level with the perineum, and then swiftly upwards over the mother's abdomen. The movement took no more than twenty seconds, and the head was delivered. I nearly sobbed with relief.

The baby was blue.

Sister held her upside down by the ankles.

"This blue tinge is not serious," she said. "It is to be expected. I must make quite sure that the airways are clear. When she starts to breathe strongly and regularly the colour will improve. Pass me the mucus catheter, will you, please?"

I was not trembling any more, so was able to do this without fear of dropping it.

Sister inverted the baby, and held her in her left arm. She then inserted the catheter into the baby's mouth and sucked very gently at the other end to draw any fluid or mucus away. One could hear a bubbling sound as fluid entered the catheter. She then cleared each nostril in the same way. The baby gave two or three big gasps, and coughed, then cried. In fact she let out a tremendous scream. Her colour rapidly changed to pink.

"That's a lovely noise," observed Sister. "A few more screams like that will make me happy."

The baby obliged, and screamed lustily.

The cord was clamped and cut, and the baby wrapped in warm dry towels and handed to Betty.

"Oh she's lovely," exclaimed Betty, "bless 'er li'l heart. She's worth all the pain in the world."

It's a miracle, I thought. The mother literally forgets the agony she has been through the moment she holds her baby.

"It's Christmas Day," remarked Betty. "We must call her Carol."

"That's a lovely name," said Sister. "Now we must get the placenta out, and I think you had better stay where you are because there is a tear, as I thought, and it will be easier for the doctor to stitch you up in this position."

Doctor was drawing up a syringe and said to Sister: "I am going to give ergometrine now, to promote the expulsion of the placenta."

She nodded.

I did not ask why. It was not normal practice to give ergometrine in those days, unless there was undue delay of the third stage, or severe bleeding, or an incomplete placenta. As I noted earlier, oxytocic drugs may be given routinely today, immediately after delivery of the baby.

Within a couple of minutes a contraction came on, and the placenta plopped out into the kidney dish held by the Sister.

"Right, I'll hand over to you, doctor," she said. "You can take my place now.

This was easier said than done though. Sister tried to get up, but couldn't. She gave a gasp of pain.

"My legs! I can't feel them. I've got pins and needles."

Not surprising, poor thing! She had been kneeling on the floor for over half an hour, in the same position, concentrating wholly on the work she was doing.

"I can't move. You'll have to help me, my legs have completely gone to sleep."

The gallant doctor put his arms round her and pulled. She must have been a dead weight, because he made no impression. Ivy and I joined in, pushing and pulling. We were all laughing. Eventually we hoisted Sister to her feet, and got her stamping and moving her legs. Bit by bit the circulation and the nerve supply restored the function, and she was able to stand without help.

The doctor opened his suture case and scrubbed up again. He asked me to hold his torch, so that he had a direct light on to the tear. He anaesthetised the area with a local, and then examined it thoroughly.

"It's not too bad, Betty," he said. "I'll soon have you stitched up, and it will have healed within a couple of weeks. I want to examine you internally, though, to make sure that the cervix is not torn also, because this can sometimes happen in a breech delivery."

He inserted two fingers into the vagina and felt all around. He explained to me, "The breech is smaller in diameter than the head. Therefore the cervix may be sufficiently dilated to allow the passage of the breech, but not relatively open enough to allow the free passage of the head. This will obviously be one of the occasions when the cervix may tear. If that occurs, the mother will have to be transferred to hospital, because I do not have the facilities here to repair a cervix. However," he continued in a confident voice, "you are lucky, Betty, there is nothing torn inside you. I just have to put a few stitches on the outside." He selected his catgut and needle. He pulled the muscle together with forceps, and with a few circular movements of the wrist had made a neat repair. It only took a few minutes.

"There we are. That's that. Now let's get you back into bed, so you will be more comfortable."

Meantime, Sister had been examining the baby. "She weighs

five and a half pounds, Betty. Your little Carol is certainly not six weeks premature. She may be two weeks premature, but you must have been a month out with your dates. You must keep a better record next time."

"Next time!" exclaimed Betty. "That's a good 'un. There won't be a next time. One breech delivery's enough for me."

The baby was out of danger, and the mother comfortable, and so Sister Bernadette and the doctor prepared to leave. I was left to clear up, bath the baby, and write up the notes. On her way downstairs, Sister had to shout through the crowd to get hold of Dave in order to tell him that he had a little daughter. Through the closed doors we in the delivery room heard the shouts of congratulations, and the strains of "For He's a Jolly Good Fellow".

"Who's a jolly good fellah?" said Betty. "Dave? Well, I like the sauce!" She cuddled her baby happily, and laughed.

Dave came up at once. He looked flushed, and only slightly the worse for wear, but he was proud and happy. He took Betty in his arms. I had found many East End men to be barely articulate, but not Dave. He was not a wharf manager for nothing.

"Yer wonderful, Betty, and I'm proud on yer." he said. "A Christmas babe's a miracle, and I reckons as how we can't forget this one's birthday. I reckons we should call her Carol."

He took the baby and then, with alarm, said: "Cor, aint she little! I think I might break her. You'd best have her back, Betty."

Everyone laughed, as Carol had that moment given a little whimper and puckered her face.

I was aware that the sounds from downstairs had changed. The noise of the party had subsided, and we could all hear shuffling and whispers and giggles outside on the landing. Dave said to me: "They are all there, wanting to come and see the baby. When can they come, do you think?"

I could see no good reason why they should not do so; after all, this was not a hospital. So I said, "I will finish cleaning up with Ivy, and when I'm bathing the baby the children can come in. I'm sure they would like that. In the meantime I will need more hot water brought up."

Jugs of hot water arrived, and Ivy and I quickly cleaned up Betty and got her ready for visitors. Then I placed a tin bath on a chair by the fire and prepared water at the right temperature for the baby. Ivy opened the door, and said, "You can come in, now, but you've got to be quiet and good. Anyone who's naughty will be sent straight out."

Clearly grandmother's word was law with small children. I didn't count the number who entered the room, but probably about twenty little ones filed silently in, with big, round, awestruck eyes. It was a good thing the bedroom was large. They stood around me, sat on the bed, stood on chairs, on the windowsill, anywhere, in order to see. I looked around me with delight, for I like children, and this was an enchanting experience. Ivy told them that the baby's name was Carol.

The baby was lying on a towel on my knee, still wrapped in a flannel sheet. I took a damp swab and wiped her face, her ears, her eyes. She wriggled and licked her lips. A little voice said, "Oo, she's got a li'l tongue, look."

The baby's head was messy with blood and mucus, so I said, "I'm going to wash her hair, now."

A little boy on the windowsill said: "I don't like gettin' my hair washed."

"Shut up, you!" said a little girl bossily.

"Shan't. Shut up yourself, bossy-bum!"

"Oo, I aint. You wait . . . "

"Now then," said Ivy with menace in her voice, "one more word from either of you and you'll both go out."

Dead silence!

I said, "Well, I'm not going to use any soap, and it's the soap in your eyes that is nasty."

I held the baby face upwards in my left hand, with her head over the rim of the bath, gently splashed the water over her head, and wiped it with a swab. The main purpose was to get the blood off, and really only to make the baby look more presentable. Most of the vernix or mucus is best left on the skin as a protective covering. I dried her with the towel, and said to the boy on the windowsill, "Now, that wasn't nasty, was it?"

He didn't speak. He just looked at me solemnly, and shook his head.

I loosened the flannel sheet, and the baby lay naked on my knee. There was a united gasp, and several voices cried, "What's that?"

"That is part of the cord," I explained. "When Carol was in her mother's tummy, she had a cord linking her to her mother. Now that she is born, we have cut it off, because she doesn't need it any more. You all used to have a cord where your tummy button is."

Several skirts were pulled up, or trousers down, and several tummy buttons were proudly shown to me.

I took the baby in my left hand, with her head resting on my forearm, and immersed her whole body in the water. She wriggled her tiny limbs, and kicked and splashed. All the children laughed, and wanted to join in.

Ivy said firmly, "Now mind what I says. No noise. You don't want to frighten the baby."

There was instant silence.

I patted the baby dry with a towel, and said, "Now we must put her clothes on."

All the little girls wanted to help, of course. It was just like dressing a doll. But Ivy restrained them, saying they could dress Carol later, when she was a bit bigger. Suddenly, at that moment, there was a piercing scream from a little girl. "It's Percy! It's Percy! He's come to see the baby. He knows, and he wants to say hello."

There were shrieks from the children, and Ivy's discipline ruled no more. They were all pointing in one direction, clamouring round something on the floor.

I followed their gaze and, to my astonishment saw, progressing slowly and in a stately manner from under the bed, an exceedingly large tortoise. He looked one hundred years old or more.

Dave roared with laughter. "Of course he wants to see the baby. He knows all about it. He's a clever one, our Perce." He picked the tortoise up, and the children tickled its wrinkled old skin, and felt its hard toenails.

"Perhaps he wants his Christmas dinner an' all. We'll get 'im some, shall us?" Dave said.

Most of the children were now more interested in the tortoise than in the baby, and Ivy wisely said, "Off you go, downstairs, an' see about Percy's Christmas dinner."

The children left and I was told the reason for this apparition. Percy was kept in a cardboard box under the bed to hibernate for the winter. The bedroom was usually cold. The warmth from the fire, and, perhaps, the movements for several hours, must have woken him up, and, thinking it was spring, he had made his appearance. In theatrical terms, his timing was perfect.

It was seven o' clock by the time I had packed up and was ready to leave. But Dave wouldn't let me go. "Come on, nurse. It's Christmas day. You've got to wet the baby's head."

He pulled me towards the back room where the bar was to be found.

"What's yer poison, then?"

I had to think quickly. I had had only half a Christmas lunch, and nothing to eat since then. Spirits would have knocked me out, so I accepted a Guinness and a mince pie. I didn't really want to hang around. The delivery had been a beautiful Christmas experience, but the party was really not my scene. I had loved hearing it in the background, but to be in the midst of all those buxom, hiccupping aunts with their paper hats and red-faced, sweating uncles, was more than I could take at that moment. I just wanted to be alone.

Out in the street, after the excessive warmth of the delivery room, the cold cut me like a knife. It was a cloudless night, and the stars shone brightly. There was very little street lighting in those days, so starlight was a reality. A heavy frost had descended in all its beauty, covering the black stones of the pavements, the walls, the houses, even my bicycle. I shivered, and decided I must pedal very hard to keep myself warm.

Only a mile or two away from Nonnatus House a sudden impulse made me turn right into West Ferry Road and on to the Isle of Dogs. To go all the way round the Isle before rejoining the East India Dock Road is a seven or eight mile ride, and I can't tell you what prompted me to do it.

No one was about. The docks were closed, and the ships in port were silent. The splash of the water was the only sound as I cycled over the West Ferry Bridge. On the Isle there were no lights, apart from the starlight and the Christmas tree lights in the windows of many houses. The great, majestic Thames was on my right, closely guarding all its secrets. I cycled more slowly, as though afraid to break the spell. As I turned westwards, a low moon started to rise, and a silver path shone across the river from Greenwich to my feet, or so it seemed. I had to stop my bicycle. It looked as though I could have walked on silvered feet from the north to the south bank of the Thames.

My thoughts were fleeting and flickering, like the moonlight on the water. What was happening to me? Why was the work so engrossing? Above all, why were the Sisters affecting me so deeply? I remembered my scornful reaction, only twenty-four hours earlier, to the crib in the Chapel, and then the calm beauty of Sister Bernadette's face as she said her daily office by the soft moving flames. I couldn't match the two up. I couldn't understand. All I knew was that I couldn't dismiss it.

JIMMY

'Is that Jenny Lee? Where the hell have you been hiding all this time? We haven't heard from you in months. I had to get on to your mother to find out where you were. She said you are a midwife in a convent. I had to tell her, gently, that nuns don't do it, so she must be wrong, but she wouldn't listen. What? You are? You must be mad! I've always said you had a screw loose somewhere. What? You can't talk? Why not? The house phone reserved for expectant fathers! Look, that's not funny. All right, all right! I'll hang up, but not till you agree to meet us at the Plasterer's Arms on your evening off. Thursday? OK that's a date. Don't be late."

Dear Jimmy! I had known him all my life. Old friendships are always the best, and childhood friends are very special. You grow up together, and know the best and the worst of each other. We had played together for as long as I could remember, then left home and gone our separate ways, only to meet again in London. Jimmy and his friends came to all the parties and dances organised in the various nurses' homes to which I was attached, and I joined their fraternity in sundry pubs in the West End when I could. It was an excellent arrangement, because they could guarantee meeting lots of new girls, and I could enjoy their company without any commitment.

I had no boyfriends at all when I was young. This was not (I hope) because I was unattractive or boring or sexless, but because I was so in love with a man I couldn't have, and for whom my heart ached more or less all the time. For that reason no other male held the slightest romantic interest for me. I enjoyed the company and conversation of my men friends, and their lively and wide-ranging minds, but the mere idea of a physical relationship with any man other than the one I loved was abhorrent to me. In consequence I had a great many friends, and was in fact very popular with the boys. In my experience nothing arouses a young man's interest more than the challenge of a pretty girl who for some inexplicable reason does not appear to find him the sex symbol of the century!

Thursday evening came. It was nice to be stepping up west for a change. I had found life with the sisters and the work in the East End so unexpectedly absorbing that I hadn't wanted to go anywhere else. However, the chance to dress up couldn't be resisted. Dress was rather formal in the 1950s. Long full skirts that flared outwards at the hem were in vogue; the smaller the waist and the tighter the waistband the better, irrespective of comfort. Nylon stockings were fairly new, and had seams that, *de rigueur*, had to be straight up the back of the leg. "Are my seams straight?" was a girl's constant worried whisper to her friends. Shoes were killers, with five to six inch steel-capped stiletto heels and excruciating pointed toes. It was said that Barbara Goulden, the top fashion model of the day, had had her little toes amputated in order to squeeze her feet into them. Like all the smartest girls of the day, I would totter around London in those crazy shoes, and wouldn't have been seen dead in anything else.

Careful make-up, hat, gloves, handbag, and I was ready.

There was no underground beyond Aldgate then, so I had to take a bus along the East India Dock Road and Commercial Road to pick up the tube. I have always loved the top front seat of a London bus, and to this day I maintain that no transport, however expensive or luxurious, can possibly offer half so much by way of scenery, advantaged viewing point and leisurely locomotion. There is endless time to absorb the passing scenes, perched high above everyone and everything. So my bus ambled along its route, and my mind wandered to Jimmy and his friends, and the occasion when I had very nearly got myself thrown out of nursing, had I been found out.

The hierarchy was very strict in those days, and behaviour, even off-duty, was closely monitored. Except for organised social events, boys were *never* allowed in the nurses' home. I even remember one

Sunday evening, when a young man had called for his girlfriend. He rang the bell and a nurse opened the door. He gave the name of the girl he wanted, and the nurse went off to find her, leaving the front door open. It was raining quite heavily, so the young man stepped inside and stood waiting on the doormat. It so happened that the Home Sister passed at that moment. She stood stock-still, rooted to the spot, and stared at him. She drew herself up to her full 4 foot 11 inches and said, "Young man, how dare you enter the nurses' home! Kindly go outside, at once."

So intimidating were these hospital sisters of the old school, and so absolute was their authority, that the young man meekly went outside and stood in the rain, whereupon the Sister shut the door.

My behaviour over Jimmy and Mike would certainly have merited instant dismissal from the nurses' training school, and very likely the profession altogether. I was working at the City of London Maternity Hospital at the time. Early one evening, after I had come off duty, I was called to the only phone in the building.

"Is that the fascinating Jenny Lee with the fantastic legs?" a smooth voice purred.

"Come off it, Jimmy. What's up? And what do you want?"

"How could you be so cynical, my dear? You grieve me more than I can say. When have you got an evening off? Tonight! What good luck! Could we meet at the Plasterer's Arms?"

Over a convivial pint it all came out. Jimmy and Mike shared a nominal flat in Baker Street, but what with one thing and another, such as girls, beer, clothes, fags, the flicks, the occasional horse, Lady Chatterley (the communal car), and other sundry essentials, there was never quite enough money to pay the rent. The landlady who, of course, was a dragon, was lenient when the rent was two or three weeks in arrears, but when it slipped to six or eight weeks with no money forthcoming, she started breathing fire. One evening the boys returned to find all their clothes gone, and a note stating they would get them back when the arrears had been paid.

They sat down with pencil and paper, and worked out that the replacement value of their clothes would be less than the eight weeks of rent outstanding, so their course of action was obvious. At three o'clock in the morning they slipped quietly out of the house, leaving their keys on the hall table, and spent the rest of the night in Regent's Park. It was a fine September evening, and after a reasonable sleep they stepped jauntily off to work, congratulating each other on an excellent plan well executed. They reckoned they could continue such a *modus vivendi* indefinitely, and thought what fools they had been ever to have paid rent to that dragon of a landlady in the first place.

Jimmy was training to be an architect, while Mike was a structural engineer. They were both attached to the best firms in London (such training in those days was based on the old apprentice system, and students were not college based). Though they could wash and shave in the public lavatories, they could not change their clothes (they had none), and a smart London firm would not tolerate its staff turning up for work day after day covered in autumn leaves! After about a fortnight they began to think that another plan would have to be formulated. Unfortunately, both had an entire wardrobe of clothes still to purchase, so money was very tight.

A third pint was ordered as we discussed the problem. Jimmy asked, "Isn't there perhaps a boiler room or something like that in the nurses' home where we could camp out for a little while?"

Old friends are old friends. I did not even consider the risk I would be taking. I said, "Yes there is, although it's not a boiler room. It's the drying room at the top of the building. All the water tanks are in it, and it's used for drying clothes. I think there's a sink in it too."

Their eyes lit up. A sink! They could wash and shave in comfort!

"As far as I know," I continued "it's only used in the daytime – not at night. There is a fire escape that goes up the back of the building, and presumably there will be a window or door from the drying room on to the fire escape. It's probably locked from the inside, but if I opened it for you, you could get in. Let's go and have a look."

We had another pint or two before leaving for the nurses' home in City Road. The boys went round the back to the fire escape, and I entered the front door. I went straight to the drying room, and found that the slide windows opened easily from the inside. I signalled to my friends below, and each of them in turn climbed the iron ladder. It was not a staircase, just a ladder fixed to the wall, and the drying room was on the sixth floor. Normally, such a climb would be hair-raising but, fortified by several pints, it proved no trouble at all to the boys, and they entered the drying-room jubilantly. They hugged and kissed me, and called me a "brick".

I said, "I don't see why you shouldn't stay here, but don't come before about ten at night, and you must leave before six each morning so that no one sees you. You must keep quiet, too, because I will be in trouble if you are found."

No one ever found out, and they stayed in the drying-room of the nurses' home for about three months. How they managed that terrifying fire-escape in the middle of winter at six o'clock in the morning I shall never know; but when you are young and full of life and vitality, nothing is a problem.

The cry "Aldgate East – all change" broke into my reverie. I found my way to the familiar pub. It was a glorious June evening when the endless daylight lingered on and on – the kind of evening that fills you with gladness. The air was warm, the sun shone, the birds sang. It was good to be alive. By contrast the enclosed atmosphere of the pub seemed dark and gloomy. This was usually our favourite hostelry. This evening the beer was right, the time was right, the friends were right, but, somehow, the venue didn't feel quite right. We chatted a bit, drank a few glasses, but I think we were all feeling a bit restless.

Suddenly someone shouted out, "Hey! Let's all go down to Brighton for a midnight swim!"

There was a chorus of approval.

"I'll go and get Lady Chatterly."

This was the name given to the communal car. Who now

remembers the furore that surrounded the proposed publication of *Lady Chatterley's Lover* by D. H. Lawrence, written in the 1920s, and the court case brought against the publishers for intending to make widely available an "obscene publication"? All that happens in the book is that the lady of the manor has an affair with the gardener, but the case went to the High Court and some pompous QC is on record as having said to a witness, "Is this the sort of book you would allow your servants to read?"

After that Lady Chatterley became synonymous with illicit pleasures and millions of copies of the book were sold, making the publishers' fortune.

Lady Chatterley was not a family car, but an obsolete 1920s London taxi. She was magnificent and huge, and on occasion actually achieved a speed of forty mph. The engine had to be coaxed into life with a starting handle, inserted beneath the elegant radiator. Considerable muscle power was needed, and the boys usually took it in turns to do the cranking. The front bonnet opened like two huge beetle wings when it was required to get at the engine and four majestic coach lamps shone on either side of the fluted radiator. There were running boards from front to back. The wheels were spoked. The capacious interior smelled of the best leather upholstery, polished wood and brass. She was their pride and joy. The boys garaged her somewhere in Marylebone, and spent all their spare time coaxing her frail old engine into life, and titivating her majestic body.

But there was still more to Lady Chatterley. Chimney pots had been added and flower boxes attached. The windows were curtained, which meant that the driver couldn't see out of the rear window, but no one bothered about little things like that. The car also boasted brass door knockers and letter-boxes. Her name was painted in gold across the front, and a notice at the rear read: DON'T LAUGH, MADAM, YOUR DAUGHTER MAY BE INSIDE.

She was brought round to the pub, and everyone turned out to admire her. A few of the original enthusiasts had dropped out, but a crowd of about fifteen climbed into Lady Chatterley and she set off, amid cheers, at a steady twenty-five mph down Marylebone

High Street. The evening was exquisite, warm and windless. The declining sun looked as though it never really would decline altogether, it being already about 9 p.m. The plan included a midnight swim in Brighton, near the West Pier, then back to London with a stop at Dirty Dick's – a transport cafe on the A23 – for bacon and eggs.

Roads in the 1950s were not as they are today. To begin with we had to get out of central London by weaving our way through miles of suburbs – Vauxhall, Wandsworth, the Elephant, Clapham, Balham, and so on. It wasn't quite endless, but it took a couple of hours. Once through the suburbs the driver called out, "We're on the open road now. Nothing to stop us till we get to Brighton."

Nothing, that is, except the temperament of Lady Chatterley, who tended to overheat. Forty mph was her maximum, and she was being driven at that speed for too long. We had to stop at Redhill, Horley (or was it Crawley?), Cuckfield, Henfield and numerous other '-fields' so that she could rest and cool down. Tempers inside the Hackney carriage were becoming as frayed as the upholstery. The sun, which we had thought would never desert us, had relentlessly crept around to the other side of the globe, leaving us girls chilly in our flimsy summer dresses. The boys at the front called out, "Only another couple of miles. I can see the South Downs on the horizon."

Eventually, after a five-hour journey, we crawled into Brighton at about 3 a.m. The sea looked black, and very, very cold.

"Right," cried one of the boys. "Who's for a swim? Don't be chicken. It's lovely once you get in."

The girls were less optimistic. A midnight swim conceived in the warmth and security of a London pub is a very different thing from a 3 a.m. swim in the cold, black reality of the English Channel. I was the only girl who did swim that night. Having come all that way, I was not going to be beaten!

The pebbles of Brighton beach are nasty at the best of times, but if you happen to be wearing six-inch stiletto heels, they are murder. We had planned to swim in the nude, but no one had thought of what we might use for towels. It had been a cold winter and early spring, but nobody had thought about the temperature either.

About six of us stripped off, and with falsely jolly shouts to cheer each other on, we plunged into the sea. Normally, I love swimming, but the cold stabbed like a knife, taking my breath away, and brought on an asthma attack that lasted for the rest of the night. I swam a few strokes, then crawled out of the sea, gasping for breath. I sat on the wet pebbles shivering with cold. I had nothing to dry myself with, nothing to wrap around me. What a fool I had been! Why did I get myself into these crazy situations? I tried to dry my shaking shoulders with a small lace handkerchief. No help. My lungs were on fire, and air just didn't seem to go into them. Some of the boys were really enjoying themselves, tumbling about with one another. I envied their vitality. I hadn't even the strength to crawl back up the beach to the car.

Jimmy came out of the water, laughing and throwing seaweed at someone. He walked towards me. We couldn't really see each other as he threw himself on the pebbles beside me, but at once he sensed that something was wrong. Perhaps he could hear me wheezing. His gaiety left him, and he became kind, concerned, thoughtful, as I had always known him when he was a little boy.

"Jenny! What's up? You're ill. You've got asthma. Oh, my dear, you are frozen. Let me dry you with my trousers."

I couldn't answer. I could only fight for breath. He wrapped his trousers around my back and rubbed hard. He gave me his shirt with which to dry my face and wet hair, and dried my legs with his socks and underpants. He had kept his vest dry, and he put it on me, as I had none of my own. He helped me into my thin cotton dress, then put his shoes on my feet, and helped me walk up the beach to the car. His own clothes were soaking wet, but he seemed impervious to this.

Everyone was sleeping in Lady Chatterley, sprawled about all over the place, and there was nowhere for me even to sit. Jimmy soon dealt with that. He shook a boy. "Wake up, and move over. Jenny's having an asthma attack. She needs somewhere to sit down."

Then, to another: "Wake up there, and take your jacket off. I need it for Jenny."

Within minutes he had procured a corner for me to sit comfortably and a jacket to place around my shoulders. He woke another lad, and took his jacket to put over my legs. He did it all with charm and ease, and everyone liked him so much that no one grumbled. Not for the first time I reflected on what a pity it was that I couldn't love Jimmy. I had always liked him, but no more than that. I had love for only one man, and this had eclipsed the possibility of loving anyone else.

Eventually we started back for London. The boys who had been swimming were in high spirits, invigorated by the swim and bantering with each other. All the girls were sleeping. I sat, leaning forward, elbows on my knees, by an open window, trying to get my lungs working properly again. There were no nebulisers in those days; the only treatment was the breathing exercises I was doing. An asthma attack usually passes in the end. Death from asthma is a new phenomenon related to modern living – indeed we used to say "no one dies from asthma".

A beautiful midsummer dawn was breaking as we left Brighton. We made our slow, majestic way north, several times stopping to let Lady Chatterley cool down. At the foot of the North Downs she refused to go any further.

"Everyone out. We'll have to push," cried the driver, gaily. It was all right for him. He would be sitting at the steering wheel, or so he thought.

The sun was well up, and the summer morning spread over the countryside. We all climbed out of the vehicle. Worried that the physical effort of pushing might bring on another attack of asthma, I said, "I'll take the wheel. You can push. You are stronger than me, and you don't get asthma."

I sat at the wheel of Lady Chatterley while the others pushed her up the North Downs. My heart went out to those poor girls in their stiletto heels pushing all that way, but there was nothing I could do about it, so I simply enjoyed the ride.

The rest must have done the old lady good because, over the crest, as we freewheeled down, she gave a deep cough of contentment, and the engine purred into life. We continued back to London with no further troubles. We were all working that morning, mostly starting at 9 a.m. I was supposed to be on duty at 8 a.m., miles away in the East End. I got back to Nonnatus House just after ten o'clock expecting serious trouble. But, once again, I realised how much more liberal the nuns were than the inflexible hospital hierarchy. When I told Sister Julienne about the night's adventures I thought she would never stop laughing.

"It's a good thing we are not busy," she commented. "You had better go and get a hot bath and a good breakfast. We don't want you down with a cold. You can start your morning's round at eleven o'clock, and sleep this afternoon. I like the sound of your Jimmy, by the way."

A year later Jimmy got a girl into trouble and married her. He could not support a wife and child on his apprentice pay, so he left his training in the fourth year and took a job as a draughtsman with a suburban county council.

About thirty years later, quite by accident, I bumped into Jimmy in a Tesco's car park. He was staggering under the weight of a huge box, walking beside a large, cross-looking woman carrying a potted plant. She was talking incessantly in a rasping voice that assailed my ears before I even noticed them. He had always been slight, but now he looked painfully thin. His shoulders were stooped, and a few grey hairs were brushed across his bald head.

"Jimmy!" I said as we came face to face. His pale blue eyes looked into mine, and a thousand memories of the fun of a carefree youth instantly sparked between us. His eyes lit up, and he smiled.

"Jenny Lee!" he said, "After all these years!"

The woman poked him heavily in the chest with her thumb, and said, "You come along with me, and don't hang about. You know the Turners are coming round tonight."

His pale eyes seemed to lose all their colour. He looked at me despairingly and said, "Yes, dear."

As they left, I heard her say, suspiciously: "Who is that woman, anyway?"

"Oh, just a girl I used to know in the old days. There was nothing between us, dear."

He shuffled off, the epitome of the hen-pecked husband.

LEN AND CONCHITA WARREN

Large families may be the norm, but this is ridiculous, I mused as I ran through my day list. The twenty-fourth baby! There must be some mistake. The first digit is wrong. Not like Sister Julienne to make a mistake. My suspicions were confirmed when I got out the surgery notes. Only forty-two years old. It was impossible. I'm glad someone else can make mistakes as well as me, I thought.

I had to make an antenatal visit to assess the mother and the viability of the house for a home delivery. I never liked doing this. It seemed such an impertinence to ask to see people's bedrooms, the lavatory, the kitchen, the arrangements for providing hot water, the cot and the linen for the baby, but it had to be done. Things could be pretty slummy, and we were used to managing in fairly primitive conditions, but if the domestic arrangements were really quite unviable, we reserved the right to refuse a home delivery, and the mother would have to go to hospital.

Mrs Conchita Warren is an unusual name, I thought as I cycled towards Limehouse. Most local women were Doris, Winnie, Ethel (pronounced Eff) or Gertie. But Conchita! The name breathed "a beaker full of the warm South . . . with beaded bubbles winking at the brim".* What was a Conchita doing in the grey streets of Limehouse, with its pall of grey smoke and the grey sky beyond?

I turned off the main road into the little streets and, with the help of the indispensable map, located the house. It was one of the better, larger houses – on three floors and with a basement. That would mean two rooms on each floor, and one basement room, leading into a garden – seven rooms in all. Promising. I knocked on the door, but no one came. This was usual, but no one called

* from John Keats, 'Ode to a Nightingale'.

out "Come in, luvvy". There seemed to be a good deal of noise inside, so I knocked again, harder. No reply. Nothing for it but to turn the handle and walk in.

The narrow hallway was almost, but not quite, impassable. Two ladders and three large coach prams lined the wall. In one, a baby of about seven or eight months slept serenely. The second was full of what looked like washing. The third contained coal. Prams were very large in those days, with huge wheels and high protective sides and I had to turn sideways to squeeze myself past. Washing flapped overhead, and I pushed it aside. The stairway to the first floor was straight ahead and was also festooned with washing. The sickly smell of soap, dank washing, baby's excreta, milk, all combined with cooking smells was nauseating to me. The sooner I get out of this place the better, I thought.

The noise was coming from the basement, yet I could see no steps down. I entered the first room off the hallway. This was obviously what my grandmother would have called "the best parlour", filled with her best furniture, knick-knacks, china, pictures, lace, and, of course, the piano. It was only used on Sundays and on special occasions.

But if *this* fine room had ever been anyone's best parlour the proud housewife would have wept to see it. About half a dozen washing-lines were attached to the picture rail just below the cornices of a beautifully plastered ceiling. Washing hung from each of them. Light filtered through a single faded curtain that appeared to be nailed across the window, screening this front room from the street. It was obviously impossible to draw this curtain back. The wooden floor was covered with what looked like junk. Broken radios, prams, furniture, toys, a pile of logs, a sack of coal, the remains of a motorcycle, and what seemed to be engineering tools, engine oil and petrol. Apart from all this, there were scores of tins of household paints on a bench, brushes, rollers, cloths, pots of spirit, bottles of thinners, rolls of wallpaper, pots of dried out glue, and another ladder. The curtain was pinned up with a safety pin by about eighteen inches at one corner, allowing sufficient light to reveal a new Singer sewing machine on a long table. Dressmaking patterns, pins, scissors, and cotton were scattered all over the table, and also, quite unbelievably, there was some very fine, expensive silk material. Next to the table stood a dressmaker's model. Also hard to believe, and the only thing that would have resembled my grandmother's front parlour, was a piano that stood against one of the walls. The lid was open, revealing filthy yellow keys, with several of the ivories broken off, but my eyes were riveted by the maker's name – Steinway. I couldn't believe it – a Steinway in a room like this, in a house like this! I wanted to rush over and try it, but I was looking for a way down to the basement, where the noise was coming from. I closed the door, and tried the second room off the hallway.

This room revealed a doorway that led down to the basement. I descended the wooden stairs, making as much clatter and noise as I could, as no one knew I was there and I didn't want to alarm anyone. I called out "Hello" loudly. No reply. "Anyone there?" I called, fatuously. There was obviously someone there. Still no reply. The door was ajar at the bottom, and there was nothing for it but to push it open and walk in.

Immediately there was a dead silence and I was conscious of about a dozen pairs of eyes looking at me. Most of them were the wide innocent eyes of children but amidst them were the coal-black eyes of a handsome woman with black hair hanging in heavy waves past her shoulders. Her skin was beautiful – pale, but slightly tawny. Her shapely arms were wet from the washing tub, and soap clung to her fingers. Although obviously engaged in the endless household chore of washing, she did not look slovenly. Her figure was large, but not over-large. Her breasts were well supported, and her hips were large, but not flabby. A flowered apron covered her plain dress, and the crimson band which held back the dark hair accentuated the exquisite contrast between skin and hair. She was tall, and the poise of her shapely head on a slender neck spoke eloquently of the proud beauty of a Spanish Contessa, with generations of aristocracy behind her.

She did not say a word. Neither did the children. I felt uncomfortable, and started babbling on about being the district midwife, and getting no reply when I knocked, and wanting to see the rooms for a home confinement. She did not reply. So I repeated myself. Still no reply. She just gazed at me with calm composure. I began to wonder if she was deaf. Then two or three of the children began talking to her, all of them at once, in rapid Spanish. An exquisite smile spread across her face. She stepped towards me and said, "*Si. Bebe.*" I asked if I might look at the bedroom. No reply. I looked towards one of the children who had spoken, a girl of about fifteen. She spoke to her mother in Spanish, who said, with gracious courtesy and a slight inclination of her sculptured head, "*Si.*"

It was clear that Mrs Conchita Warren spoke no English. In all the time that I knew her the only words that I heard her speak, apart from dialogue with the children, were "*si*" and "*bebe*".

The impression this woman made upon me was extraordinary. Even in the 1950s that basement would have been described as squalid. It contained, haphazardly, a stone sink, washing, a boiler bubbling away, a mangle, clothes and nappies hanging all over the place, a large table covered with pots and plates and bits of food, a gas stove covered with dirty saucepans and frying pans, and a mixture of unpleasant smells. Yet this proud and beautiful woman was completely in control and commanded respect.

The mother spoke to the girl, who showed me upstairs to the first floor. The front bedroom was perfectly adequate: a large double bed. I felt it – no more sagging than any other. It would do. There were three cots in the room, two wooden dropsided cots, a small crib, two very large chests of drawers and a small wardrobe. The lighting was electric. The floor covering was lino. The girl said, "Mum's got it all ready here," and pulled open a drawer full of snowy white baby clothes. I asked to see the lavatory. There was more than that. There was a bathroom – excellent! That was all I needed to see.

As we left the main bedroom I peered briefly into the room opposite, the door of which was open. Three double beds appeared to be crammed into it, but there was no other furniture at all.

We descended two flights to the kitchen, our feet clattering on the wooden stairs. I thanked Mrs Warren and said that everything was most satisfactory. She smiled. Her daughter spoke to her and she said: "*Sí.*" I needed to examine the woman and take an obstetric history, but obviously I could not do that if we could not understand each other, and I did not feel that I could ask one of the children to interpret. I therefore resolved to make a repeat visit when her husband would be at home. I asked my little guide when this would be, and she told me "in the evening". I asked her to tell her mother I would come back after six o' clock, and left.

I had several other visits that morning, but my mind continually drifted back to Mrs Warren. She was so unusual. Most of our patients were Londoners who had been born in the area, as had their parents and grandparents before them. Foreigners were rare, especially women. All the local women lived a very communal life, endlessly engaged in each other's business. But if Mrs Warren spoke no English, she could not be part of that sorority.

Another thing that intrigued me was her quiet dignity. Most of the women I met in the East End were a bit raucous. Also there was her Latin beauty. Mediterranean women age early, especially after childbirth, and by custom used to wear black from head to foot. Yet this woman was wearing pretty colours, and did not look a day over forty. Perhaps it is the intense sun that makes southern skins age, and the damp northern climate had preserved her skin. I wanted to find out more about her, and intended asking some questions of the Sisters at lunch time. I also wanted to tease Sister Julienne about writing the "twenty-fourth pregnancy", when she really meant the fourteenth.

Lunch at Nonnatus House was the main meal of the day, and a communal meal for the Sisters and lay staff alike. The food was plain, but good. I always looked forward to it because I was always hungry. Twelve to fifteen of us sat down each day at the table. After grace was said I introduced the subject of Mrs Conchita Warren.

She was well known by the Sisters, although not a lot of contact had ever been made because of her lack of English. Apparently she had lived in the East End for most of her life. How was it, then, that she didn't speak the language? The Sisters did not know. It was suggested that perhaps she had no need, or no inclination to learn the language, or perhaps she just wasn't very bright. This last suggestion was a possibility, as I had noticed before that certain people can completely disguise a basic lack of intelligence simply by saying nothing. My mind flitted to the Archdeacon's daughter in Trollope, who had the whole of Barchester society and London at her feet, praising her beauty and bewitching mind, when in fact she was profoundly stupid. She achieved this enviable reputation by sitting around on gilded chairs, looking beautiful and saying not one word.

"How did she come to be in London at all?" I asked. The Sisters knew the answer to this one. Apparently Mr Warren was an East Ender, born into the life of the docks, and destined for the work of his father and uncles. But when he was a young man, something had made him a rebel. He was not going to be cast into any mould. He cut loose, and went off to fight in the Spanish Civil War. It is doubtful if he had the faintest idea of what he was doing, as foreign affairs rarely penetrated the consciousness of working people in the 1930s. Political idealism could have played no part in it and whether he fought for the Republicans or the Royalists would have been immaterial. All he wanted was youthful adventure, and a war in a remote and romantic country was just the stuff.

He was lucky to survive. But survive he did, and came home to London with a beautiful Spanish peasant girl of about eleven or twelve. He returned to his mother's house with the girl, and they obviously lived together. What his relatives or neighbours thought of this shocking occurrence can only be conjectured, but his mother stuck by him, and he was not one to be intimidated by a pack of gossiping neighbours. Anyway, they could hardly send the girl back, because he had forgotten where she came from and she didn't seem to know. Quite apart from this, he loved her.

When it was possible, he married her. This was not easy, because she had no birth certificate and was not sure of her surname, date of birth, or parentage. However, as she had had three or four babies by then and looked about sixteen, and as she was presumably

Roman Catholic, a local priest was persuaded to solemnise the already fecund relationship.

I was fascinated. This was the stuff of high romance. A peasant girl! She certainly didn't look like a peasant. She looked like a princess of the Spanish court, whom the Republicans had dispossessed. Had the brave Englishman rescued her and carried her off? What a story! Everything about it was unusual, and I looked forward to meeting Mr Warren that evening.

Then I remembered the children. I said to Sister Julienne, saucily, "I've caught you out in a mistake at last. You put in the day book the twenty-fourth pregnancy when you must have meant the fourteenth."

Sister Julienne's eyes twinkled. " Oh no," she said, "that was no mistake. Conchita Warren really has had twenty-three babies, and is expecting her twenty-fourth."

I was stunned. The whole story was so preposterous that no one could possibly have made it up.

The door was open when I returned to their home so I stepped in. The house was literally teeming with young people and children. I had seen only very young children and a girl in the morning. Now all the schoolchildren were home, as well as several older teenagers who had presumably returned from work. It seemed like a party, they all looked so happy. Older children were carrying tiny ones around, some of them were playing out in the street, some of them were doing what might have been homework. There was absolutely no discord among them and in all the contact I had with this family no fighting or nasty temper was ever in evidence.

I squeezed past the ladder and the prams in the hallway, and was directed down to the basement kitchen. Len Warren was sitting on a wooden chair by the table, comfortably smoking a roll-up. A baby was on his knee, another crawled along the table, and he had to keep pulling him back by his pants to prevent him falling off. A couple of toddlers sat on his foot and he was jigging them up and down singing, "Horsey, horsey don't you stop". They were screaming with laughter, and so was the father. Laughter lines creased his eyes and nose. He was older than his wife, about fifty-ish, not at all good-looking in the conventional sense, but so frank and open, so downright pleasant-looking, that it did your heart good to see him.

We grinned at each other, and I told him that I wanted to examine his wife and take some notes.

"That's OK. Con's doing the supper, but I spek she can leave it to Win."

Conchita was calm and radiant, standing by the boiler, which in the morning had been doing the washing and was now cooking an enormous quantity of pasta. Copper boilers were common in those days. They were tubs, large enough to contain about twenty gallons, standing on legs, with a gas jet underneath. A tap at the front was the means of emptying them. They were intended for washing, and this was the first time I had seen one used for cooking, but I surmised that this would be the only way of catering for such a huge family. It was sensible and practical, if unusual.

"Here, Win, you tek over the supper, will you, love? Nurse wants a look at yer mum. Tim, come 'ere, lad, you tek the baby, an' keep them two away from the boiler. We don't want no accidents in vis 'ouse, do we now? An' Doris, love, you lends a hand to our Win. I'll tek yer mum and the nurse upstairs."

The girls spoke rapidly to their mother in Spanish, and Conchita came towards me, smiling.

We went upstairs, Len chatting all the time to different children, "Now then Cyril, now then. Let's get that lorry off them stairs, shall we, there's a good lad. We don't want the nurse to break 'er neck, do we nah?

"Good on yer, Pete. Doin yer 'omework. He's a scholar, our Pete. He'll be a professor one of these days, you'll see.

"'Allo, Sue, my love. Got a kiss for yer ol' dad, then?"

He very seldom stopped talking. In fact I would say that in all my acquaintance with Len Warren, he never stopped talking. If occasionally he ran out of something to say, he would whistle or sing – and all executed with a thin roll-up in his mouth. These days health workers would be very disapproving about smoking around babies and a pregnant woman, but in the fifties no connection had been made between smoking and ill health, and nearly everyone smoked.

We went into the bedroom.

"Connie, love, the nurse just wants to have a look at your tum."

He smoothed down the bed, and she lay down. He started to pull up her skirt, and she did the rest.

Her abdomen showed stretch marks, but nothing excessive. From appearances, this could have been her fourth pregnancy, not her twenty-fourth. I palpated the uterus – about five to six months.

"Any movements?" I enquired.

"Oh yeah, yer can feel the li'l soul kickin' an' wrigglin'. He's a right little footballer, that one, 'specially at night when we wants 'a get some sleep."

The head felt uppermost, but that was to be expected. I couldn't locate the foetal heart, but with all the kicking described, it hardly mattered.

I examined the rest of her. Her breasts were full, but firm – no lumps or abnormalities. Her ankles were not swollen. There were a few superficial varicose veins, but nothing serious. The pulse was normal, as was her blood pressure. She seemed to be in perfect condition.

I wanted to try to establish her dates. Merely going on clinical observation can be deceptive. A small baby and a large baby of the same gestation can give the appearance of about four to six weeks' difference, so you need some dates to back up observation. However, with a baby of about seven to eight months old downstairs, it seemed unlikely that Conchita had had a period at all. I was not accustomed to asking such delicate questions of a man. In the 1950s such things were never mentioned in what was called "mixed company", and I felt myself blush scarlet.

"Ah, nah, nuffink like that," he said.

"Could you ask her, please; she might not have mentioned it to you."

"Yer can tek it from me, nurse, she ain't 'ad no periods for years."

I had to leave it at that. If anyone knows, he should, I thought.

I mentioned that we had an antenatal clinic every Tuesday, and we preferred patients to come to the clinic. He looked dubious. "Well, she don't like goin' out, yer know. Not speakin' the lingo an' all, like. And I wouldn't want 'er to get lost or frightened, like. 'Sides, she's got all them babies to look after at home, yer know."

I didn't feel I could insist, so I put her down for home antenatal visits.

In all this time, Conchita hadn't said a word. She just smiled, and submitted passively to being felt and prodded all over, to hearing herself talked about in a foreign language. She got up from the bed with grace and dignity, and moved to the chest of drawers, searching for a hairbrush. Her black hair looked even more beautiful being brushed, and I observed hardly a grey hair. She adjusted the crimson band, and turned with proud confidence to her husband, who took her in his arms and murmured, "There's my Con, my gel. Oh yer looks lovely, my tresher."

She gave a contented little laugh, and nestled in his arms. He kissed her repeatedly.

Such a display of unashamed love between husband and wife was unusual in Poplar. Whatever the relationship in private, the men always kept up a show of rough indifference in front of other people. A good deal of lewd banter often went on between them, which I found very amusing, but they did not openly speak of love. I found the tender, gentle and adoring looks of Len and Conchita Warren very affecting.

I returned many times to the house over the next four months, checking Conchita's progress. I always went in the evenings, in order to speak with Len about the pregnancy. Anyway, I liked his company, liked listening to him talk, enjoyed the atmosphere of this happy family and wanted to find out more about them all. This was not difficult, due to Len's insatiable volubility.

Len was a painter and decorator. He must have been a good one because 90 per cent of his jobs were "up West". "All the nobs' houses" was how he described his work.

Three or four of his elder sons worked with their father in the business, and apparently he was never short of work. With low running costs there must have been quite a bit of money coming into the household. Len worked from home, from his shed in the backyard, where he also kept his barrow.

Workmen in those days didn't have vans or trucks to go around in. They had barrows, usually made of wood, and often home-made. Len's was made out of the chassis of an old pram, with the upholstered pram part removed, and an elongated wooden construction fitted to the highly sprung base. It was perfect. The springs made for lightness of movement, and the huge, well-oiled wheels made it easy to push. When going out to a new job, Len and his sons would load up the barrow with their equipment and push it to the address. They may have had to push for ten miles or more, but that was all part of the job. In that respect, a painter and decorator was lucky, because a job usually lasted a week or so, and they could leave their stuff at the house and go home by tube as far as Aldgate.

Plumbers, plasterers and suchlike were less fortunate. Their jobs usually lasted only a day, so they had to push the tools to the job, and then push them home in the evening. In those days you would see workmen laboriously pushing their barrows all over London. They had to walk on the road, which held up the traffic considerably. But drivers were used to it and just accepted it as part of the London scene.

I once asked Len if he had been called up in the War.

"Nah, 'cos of this Franco-job," he said, pointing to a leg wound that had rendered him unfit for military service.

"Were the family in London all through the war?" I asked.

"Not bleedin' likely, beggin' yer pardon, nurse," he said. "Wouldn' let Jerry get Con an' the kids."

He was shrewd, well informed, and above all enterprising. In 1940 Len had observed the failed strategic bombing of the air bases and ammunition fields. He had seen the Battle of Britain.

"An' I thought to meself, I though', that slippery bugger Hitler, he's not goin' to stop there, he's not. He'll go for the docks next. When the first bomb fell on Millwall in 1940, I knew as how we was in for it, an' I sez to Con, 'I'm gettin' you out of this, my girl, an' the kids an' all.'"

Len didn't wait for any evacuation scheme to come into operation. With typical energy and initiative he took a train from Baker Street out of London to the west, into Buckinghamshire. When he thought he had gone far enough, he got out at what looked to be a promising rural area. It was Amersham, which is almost a London suburb these days, on the Metropolitan Line. But in 1940 it was truly rural, and remote from London. Then he quite simply trudged around the streets, knocking at doors, telling the householders he met that he had a family he wanted to get out of London, and had they got a room they could let to him?

"I must 'ave called at 'undreds of places. I reckons as how they thought I was mad. They all sez no. Some didn't speak, jes' shut the door in my face and said nuffink. But I wasn't goin' to be put off, not by no one. I just reckons as how someone's goin' to say 'yes' some time. You jes' gotta stick with it, Len lad, I says to meself.

"It was gettin' late. I'd spent the whole day trudgin' round, 'aving doors shut in me face. I can tell you, I was feelin' down, an' all. "I was goin' back to the station. I tells you, I was that depressed. I went down a road of shops with flats above 'em. I shan't never forget it. I hadn't knocked at any flats, only houses that looked like what they'd got a lo' of rooms in 'em.

"There was a lady, I shall never forget her, goin' into one o' the doors next to a shop, like, an' I just says to her 'you haven't got a room I could have, have you lady? I'm desperate.' An' I tells her, an' she says 'yes'.

"That lady was an angel," he said reflectively. "Without her, we'd be dead, I reckons."

It had been a Saturday. He had arranged with the lady that he would pack up his household on the Sunday, and move in on the Monday. This they did.

"I told Con and the kids we was goin' on 'oliday to the country."

He simply told their landlord they were moving out. They left all their furniture and only took what they could carry.

The accommodation the lady gave them was called the back kitchen. It was a fairly large stone-floored room on the ground floor leading to a small backyard with access both to the flats above, and to the shop at the side. It contained a sink, running cold water, a boiler, and a gas stove. There was a large cupboard under the stairs, but no heating, and no power point for an electric heater. There was, however, an electric light and an outdoor lavatory. There was no furniture. I don't know what Conchita thought of it all, but she was young and adaptable. She was with her man and her children and that was all that mattered to her.

They lived there for three years. Len made a few trips back to London to collect what furniture and essential bedding he could bring on his barrow. Very soon his mother came to join them.

"Well, I couldn't leave the old gel back there for Jerry to get, could I now?"

Apparently his mother passed most of the day and each night in an armchair in a corner. The older children went to school. Len took a job as a milkman. He had never handled a horse before, but it was a docile old creature that knew the round, and with native quickness Len soon learned, and whistled his way around the roads. The children came with him when they could and felt like King of the Castle sitting up behind the horse.

Conchita looked after her children, and did the lady's washing and cleaning. It was a good arrangement all round. Two more babies were born. It was when they were expecting the ninth baby that the local evacuation authorities decided Len's family needed more room, and they were allocated two rooms, a kitchen and bathroom.

It sounds pretty grim today – just two rooms for three adults and eight children, but in fact they were lucky. The times were hard, and one sees on old newsreels pathetic pictures of train loads of East End children with labels and a small bag being shunted out of London. Thanks to their father, the Warren children were not separated from their parents throughout the entire war.

⋆

Len and Conchita's children were beautiful. Many of them had raven black hair and huge black eyes like their mother. The older girls were stunners, and could easily have been models. They all talked in a curious mixture of Cockney and Spanish when together. With their mother they spoke only Spanish; with their father, or any other English person, pure Cockney. I was very impressed by this bi-lingual facility. I wasn't able to get to know any of them very well, principally because their father never stopped talking, and entertaining me with his chatter. The only girl I did have contact with was Lizzy, who was about twenty and a very skilled dressmaker. I have always loved clothes, and became a regular client of hers. Over several years she made me some beautiful garments.

The house was always crowded, but there was never any discord as far as I could see. If an argument arose among the younger children, the father would say good-humouredly, "Nah ven, nah ven, le's 'ave none of vis," and that would be that. I have seen internecine fighting between siblings, especially in overcrowded conditions, but not between the Warren children.

Where they all slept was a mystery to me. I had seen one bedroom with three double beds in it. Presumably the two bedrooms on the upper storey were the same, and they all slept together.

In the last month of Conchita's pregnancy I visited weekly. One evening Len suggested I had a bit of supper with them. I was delighted. It smelled good and, as usual, I was hungry. I was not at all squeamish about eating food cooked in the boiler that had been used in the morning for washing the baby's nappies, so I accepted with pleasure. Len said, "I reckons as 'ow the nurse would like a plate, like. You get 'er one, will you, Liz love?"

Liz piled some pasta on to a plate for me, and gave me a fork. It was only then that Conchita revealed her peasant origins. All the rest of the family ate from the same dish. Two large shallow bowls, the old-fashioned toilet bowls that used to be found in every bedroom, were filled with pasta and placed on the table. Each member of the family had a fork and ate from the communal bowl. I alone had a separate plate. I had seen this once before when I was living in Paris, and had spent a weekend with an Italian peasant family who had moved to the Paris area to try to find work. They all ate from a single dish in the middle of the table in just the same way.

The time came for Conchita's confinement. There were no dates to go by, and therefore no certainty when she was due, but the baby's head was well down and she looked near the end of term.

"I'll be glad when we gets this baby out. She's getting tired. I won't go to work no more, the lads can do the job. I'll stop here, and look after Con and the kids."

This he did, to my amazement. In those days no self-respecting East Ender would demean himself by doing what he would call "womens' work". Most men would not lift a dirty plate or mug from the table, nor even pick their dirty socks up off the floor. But Len did everything. Conchita lay in bed late in the mornings, or sat in a comfortable chair in the kitchen. Sometimes she played with the little ones, but Len was always watching, and if they got too boisterous, he firmly took them away and amused them elsewhere. Sally, the girl of fifteen, who had left school but not yet gone out to work, was there to help him. Nonetheless, Len could do everything – change nappies, feed toddlers, clear up messes, shopping, cooking, and the endless washing and ironing. And all this was accompanied by singing or whistling and unfailing good humour. Incidentally, he was the only man I have ever met who could roll a fag with one hand and feed a baby with the other.

Conchita's twenty-fourth baby was born at night. A phone call came through at about 11 p.m. that the waters had broken. As fast as I could I pedalled along to Limehouse, because I guessed it would be a quick labour. I was not wrong.

I found everything in perfect readiness. Conchita was lying on clean sheets, with the brown paper and a rubber sheet under her. The room was warm, but not too hot. The baby's crib and baby clothes were all waiting. Hot water was boiling in the kitchen. Len was sitting beside her, massaging her stomach, her thighs, her back, and her breasts. He had a cold flannel with which to wipe her face and neck, and with every contraction he took her in his arms and held her tight. He murmured encouraging noises. "That's my girl. That's my lass. Won't be long now. I've gocher. Jus' hold on to me."

I was startled to see him there. I had expected to see a neighbour, or his mother, or an elder daughter. I had never seen a man at a delivery before, apart from a doctor. But in this, as in everything else, Len was exceptional.

A glance told me Conchita was very near the second stage. I gowned up quickly, and laid out my tray. The foetal heart was steady, and the head barely palpable. It must have been already down on the pelvic floor. As the waters had broken, I did not do a vaginal examination, because any such intrusion could risk infection, and, unless absolutely essential, should be avoided. The contractions were coming about every three minutes.

Conchita was sweating, and moaning slightly, but not excessively. She smiled at her husband between each contraction, and relaxed completely in his arms. She had had no sedation.

We did not have long to wait. A change came over her facial expression, that of intense concentration. She gave a grunt of effort and with the next push, the whole baby slid out at once. It was a small baby, and delivery was so quick I had no time to do anything more than catch the child. The little thing was just lying there on the sheet with no help from me. I cleared the airway, and Len handed me the cord clamps and the scissors. He knew exactly what to do. He could have delivered the baby himself, I thought. The placenta came out fairly quickly also, and there was no excessive bleeding.

Len wrapped the baby tenderly in warm towels, and placed her in the crib. He called downstairs for hot water, and gave the message that a little girl had been born. Then he washed his wife all over, and deftly changed the sheets. He brushed her black hair, and put a white hair band on her, to match her white nightie. He called her his pet, his love, his treasure. She smiled dreamily at him.

He called downstairs for one of his children, "Here, Liz, you take these bloody sheets, and put them in the boiler, will yer, love.

Then we might think about a nice cup of tea, eh?"

Then he turned back to his wife, and took the baby from the cradle, and handed it to her. She smiled contentedly, touching the baby's little head, and kissing its wee face. She didn't say anything, just chuckled with contentment.

Len was ecstatic, and started talking non-stop again. During Conchita's labour he had hardly said a thing. It was the only time I had ever known him to be silent for so long. But now nothing could stop him.

"Oh, look at her. Jes look at 'er, nurse. Isn' she beau'iful? Look at 'er li'l hands. See, she's got fingernails. Oh, she's openin' her li'l mouth. Oh, you li'l swee'heart, you. See, she's got long eyelashes, like 'er mum. She's jes perfick."

He was as excited as a young father with his first baby.

He called all the other children up, and they all sat round their mother, talking in a mixture of Spanish and English. Only the toddlers were asleep. The rest of the house was awake and excited.

I packed up my equipment and slipped silently out of the room, feeling that the unity and happiness of the family would be all the greater if I was not there. Len saw me leave and courteously came out with me. As we left, I noticed that the conversation behind us slipped into Spanish.

He thanked me for all I had done, although I had done virtually nothing. As he carried my bag downstairs, he said: "Let's have a nice cup o' tea together, shall us nurse?".

He chatted happily all the time we had our tea. I told him how much I liked and admired his family. He was a proud father. I told him how impressed I was that they all spoke Spanish so fluently.

"They're a clever lot, my kids, they are. Cleverer than their old dad. I never could pick up the lingo, meself."

Quite suddenly, with blinding insight, the secret of their blissful marriage was revealed to me. She couldn't speak a word of English, and he couldn't speak a word of Spanish.

SISTER MONICA JOAN

"Light is the higher plane – life is the lower – light becomes Life. There is a fiery flash, a vision granted, a golden moment of offering."

I could listen to her all day – the beautiful modulated voice, the moving hands, the hooded eyes, the arch of her haughty eyebrows, the drape of her veil as she turned her long neck. She was over ninety, and her mind was going, but I was utterly captivated.

"Shining questions, infinite response, the astro-mental plane of man lies in the etheric. The outer darkness is a monstrous dragon, with its tail in its mouth. Did you know?"

I sat at her feet, bewitched, and shook my head, not daring to speak in case I broke the spell.

"This is the cosmic body, the critical point, the translation of parallelisms running to the neutral centre of the disappearing point. Have you seen the clouds pass and float and roll as planets do? And so we see Him come, pierced. I am the thorn that pierced His brow. Can you smell burning, my dear?"

"No. Can you?"

"I think that Mrs B.'s ahrimatic unconsciousness has prompted her to make a cake. Let us go with God in all things. I think we should investigate, don't you?"

I would rather have continued listening to her talk, but I knew that once the spell had been broken, there would be no going back – for the time being – and the smell of cake for Sister Monica Joan was irresistible. She smiled appreciatively. "That smells like one of Mrs B.'s honey cakes. Come on, get a move on, don't just sit there."

She jumped up, and with quick, light steps, head held high, back straight, she sped towards the kitchen.

Mrs B. turned as she entered. "Hello, Sister Monica Joan, you're a bit early. They're not done yet. But I've kept the bowl for you to scrape, if you wants to."

Sister Monica Joan pounced on the bowl as though she had not eaten for a fortnight, scraping with the big wooden spoon, and licking both sides with murmurs of delight.

Mrs B. went over to the sink and took a wet cloth. "Nah ven, Sister, you got it all over your habit, an' a bit on your veil, an' all. Wipe your fingers, there's a good girl. You can't go to Tierce like that, can you? And the bell will go any minute."

The bell sounded. Sister Monica Joan looked round quickly, and winked.

"I must go. You can wash the bowl now. Oh the delight in Heaven as the spheres move, and the tiny grains of sand touch the stars. The Phoenix rises from the living flame, and Ceres cries . . . don't forget to keep the crispy ones for me."

She tripped out of the kitchen as Mrs B. fondly opened the door for her.

"She's a caution, she is. You wouldn't fink she'd been in the Docks all through two world wars, and the Depression, would you? She's delivered thousands of our children. In the Blitz she wouldn't leave. She delivered babies in air-raid shelters and church crypts, an' once in what was left of a bombed house. Bless 'er. If she wants the crispy ones, she can 'ave 'em."

I had heard stories like that so often, from so many people – her years of selfless work, her dedication, her commitment. Sister Monica Joan was known and loved throughout Poplar. I had heard that she was the daughter of a very aristocratic English family who were scandalised when she announced in the 1890s that she was going to be a nurse. Wasn't her sister a Countess, and her mother a Lady in her own right? How could she disgrace them so? Ten years later, when she qualified as one of the first midwives in the country, they remained silent in their displeasure. But they cut her off altogether when she joined a religious order and went to work in the East End of London.

Lunch was the one occasion during the day when we all met together. Most monastic orders take their meals in silence, but talking was permitted at Nonnatus House. We stood until Sister Julienne came in and said grace, after which we all sat. Mrs B. would bring in the trolley and usually Sister Julienne would serve, with one other person carrying the plates around. Conversation that day was general: Sister Bernadette's mother's health; the two guests due to arrive at teatime.

Sister Monica Joan was peevish. She couldn't eat a chop, due to her teeth, and she didn't like the mince. Cabbage she could never abide. She would wait for the pudding.

"Do have a little mashed potato, dear, with some onion gravy. You know how you like Mrs B.'s onion gravy. You need the protein, you know."

Sister Monica Joan sighed, as though all the injustice of the world had been heaped upon her,

"'Stop and consider! Life is but a day – A fragile dew-drop on its perilous way.'"

"Yes dear, I know, but a little mashed potato wouldn't go amiss."

Sister Evangelina paused, fork in hand, and snorted, "What's that about a dew drop?"

Sister Monica Joan lost her peevishness, and said, sharply, "Keats, my dear, John Keats. Our greatest poet, though perhaps you don't know. Uh-oh, I shouldn't have said anything about dew-drops. It was a slip of the tongue."

She took out a fine lawn handkerchief, and held it delicately to her nose. Sister Evangelina was beginning to turn red around the neck.

"Your tongue slips a great deal too often, if you ask me, dear."

"No one was asking you, dear," Sister Monica Joan addressed the wall, very, very quietly.

Sister Julienne intervened. "I've put a few fresh carrots on your plate also. I know you like carrots. Did you know that the Rector has seventy-two young people from the youth club in his confirmation class this year? Just imagine! That, on top of all their other work, will keep the curates busy."

Everyone murmured interest and approval of the size of the confirmation class, and I watched Sister Monica Joan push the carrots around her plate with her forefinger. Such compelling hands, all bones and veins covered with transparent skin. Her nails were usually long, because she couldn't be bothered to cut them, and resisted anyone else doing so. The forefingers on both hands were astonishing. She could bend the first joint, keeping the rest of the finger quite straight. I sat quietly watching, and tried to do it myself, but couldn't. She got some gravy on her fingertip, and licked it off. She seemed to like it and brightened a little. She dipped her finger again. Meanwhile, conversation had turned to the forthcoming jumble sale.

Sister Monica Joan took up her fork, and ate all the potato and gravy, but not the carrots, then pushed her plate away from her with a hard-done-by sigh. She had obviously been thinking. She turned to Sister Evangelina and said loudly, but in the sweetest tone, "Keats may not be your cup of tea, but do you admire Lear, dear?"

Sister Evangelina looked at her with justifiable suspicion. Instinct told her there was a trap, but she had neither verbal skill nor wit, only a heavy, ponderous sort of honesty. She walked straight into the trap. "Who?"

It was the worst thing she could have said.

"Edward Lear, dear, one of our greatest comic poets, 'The Owl and the Pussy Cat', you know. I thought perhaps you might particularly admire 'the Dong with the Luminous Nose', dear."

There was a gasp around the table at this piece of effrontery. Sister Evangelina's face turned red all over, and the moisture began to glisten. Someone said "Pass the salt, please", and Sister Julienne asked quickly if anyone would like another chop. Sister Monica Joan looked archly at Sister Evangelina, and murmured to herself, "Oh dear, now we are back to Keats and dewdrops." She took out her handkerchief and started to sing "Ding Dong Bell, Pussy's in the Well", as though to herself.

Sister Evangelina nearly exploded with impotent rage, and scraped back her chair. "I think I can hear the telephone; I will go and answer it," she said, and left the refectory.

The atmosphere was tense. I glanced sideways at Sister Julienne, wondering what she would do. She looked exceedingly cross, but could say nothing to Sister Monica Joan in front of us all. The other Sisters looked down at their plates, discomfited. Sister Monica Joan sat erect and haughty, her hooded eyes closed. Not a muscle moved.

I had often wondered about her. Her mind was obviously going, but how much was senility, and how much downright naughtiness? This gratuitous, unprovoked attack on Sister Evangelina was a piece of premeditated malice. Why did she do it? Her history of selfless dedication in over fifty years of nursing the poorest of the poor would imply saintliness. Yet here she was, deliberately humiliating her Sister in God in front of the entire staff, including Mrs B., who had just brought in the pudding.

Sister Julienne rose, and took the tray. Serving the pudding caused the diversion she needed. Sister Monica Joan knew that disapproval was in the air. Generally she was served first with pudding, and given a choice, but on that occasion she was served last. She sat aloof, seeming not to notice. On any other occasion she would have complained bitterly, gobbled up her pudding, and asked for more. But not today. Sister Julienne took up the last bowl, placed some rice pudding in it, and quietly said, "Hand that to Sister Monica Joan, if you please." Then she said, "I will go and see Sister Evangelina, if you will all excuse me. Sister Bernadette, would you please say the closing grace?"

She rose, said a private grace, crossed herself, and left the room.

There were a few desultory remarks about the prunes being a little tough, and would it, or would it not rain for the evening visits, but we all felt a little uncomfortable, and were glad when the meal was over. Sister Monica Joan stood up with a regal toss of her head, and crossed herself elaborately as grace was said.

Poor Sister Evangelina! She was not a bad sort, and certainly did not deserve the torment she got from Sister Monica Joan. Her nose was a trifle red, admittedly, but by no stretch of the imagination could it be described as "luminous". She was heavy and plodding, both in mind and body. Her big flat feet clumped about. She banged things down on the table, rather than putting them down. She flopped down into a chair, rather than sitting down. I had seen Sister Monica Joan observing all these characteristics with pursed lips, drawing in her skirts as the heavy feet passed. She, so light, so dainty, who moved with such grace, seemed unable to tolerate the other's physical shortcomings, and called her the washerwoman, or the butcher's wife.

Nor was Sister Evangelina any match for the quicksilver mind of Sister Monica Joan. She thought slowly and pedantically, entirely concerned with practical matters. She was a careful, hardworking midwife, and an honest and devout nun; I doubt if she had ever had an original idea in her life. Sister Monica Joan's flashing wit and wisdom, her mental gymnastics, leaping from Christianity to cosmology, to astrology, to mythology, all of them thrown together in poetry and prose, and muddled in a mind on the verge of decay, was too much for Sister Evangelina. She just stood with her mouth open, looking stupid, or snorted her incomprehension and stomped off out of the room.

There was no doubt that Sister Evangelina had her cross to bear, and perched on the top was Sister Monica Joan, giggling and winking, kicking her heels in delight as she made such catty remarks as, "I think there's thunder coming – oh no, it's only you, dear. The weather is a little unsettled, isn't it, dear?"

Sister Evangelina could only grind her teeth and plod on. She never got the better of these altercations, try as she might. Had she possessed a sense of humour, she could have defused the situation with laughter – but I never saw Sister Evangelina laugh spontaneously, whatever fun was going on in the house. She would watch other people, to make sure it was funny, and then laugh when others did. Sister Monica Joan would mock this also, "The tinkling bells chime, and the stars laugh with joy. The little cherubs clap their wings and laugh with heavenly harmony. Sister Evangelina is a little cherub, and the tinkling sounds of her laughter ring the changing universe into eternal changelessness. Don't they, dear?"

Poor Sister Evangelina could only say, with solemn emphasis, "I don't know what you mean."

"Ah, so far, so far, the never star, the fruition of Joy, the husk of Despair."

Sister Julienne tried her best to keep the peace between the two Sisters, but not very successfully. How can you reprimand a nonagenarian whose mind is wandering? And would it do any good? I am sure she wondered, as I did, how much of it was due to senility, and how much was calculated mischief-making; but she could never be sure, and in any case Sister Monica Joan's wit had always flashed and gone before she could do anything about it. So Sister Evangelina's suffering continued.

The monastic vows of poverty, chastity and obedience are hard, very hard. But harder still is the task of living, day in, day out, with your Sisters in God.

MARY

She must have planned it, and picked me out as I got off the bus at the Blackwall Tunnel. It was about 10.30 p.m. and I had been to the newly opened Festival Hall. Perhaps I looked smarter than most of the other travellers that night, which she assumed meant more affluent. She came up to me, and said quietly, in a lilting Irish voice: "Could you change a five pound note for me?"

I was staggered. Change for five pounds! I doubt if I had three shillings to last the rest of the week. It would be like someone stopping you in the street today and asking if you had change for a five hundred-pound note.

"No, I haven't," I said brusquely. My head was full of music, I was replaying the performance over and over again in my mind. I didn't want to be bothered with total strangers asking silly questions.

It was something about her despairing sigh that made me look at her again. She was very small and thin, with a perfect oval face, rather like a pre-Raphaelite painting. She could have been anywhere between fourteen and twenty years of age. She wore no coat, only a thin jacket that was quite inadequate for the cold evening. She had no stockings or gloves, and her hands trembled. She looked a very poor, ill-nourished girl – yet she obviously had five pounds.

"Why don't you go into that café and change it?"

She looked furtive, "I dare not. Someone would see me and tell. Then they would bash me up, or kill me."

It occurred to me that she had probably stolen the money. Stolen goods are of no value unless you can get rid of them. Sterling can usually be passed on without much trouble, but this girl was obviously too afraid to attempt it. Something made me say: "Are you hungry?"

"I haven't eaten today, nor yesterday."

No food for forty-eight hours, and five pounds in her pocket. Curiouser and curiouser, as Alice said to the caterpillar.

"Well look, let's go into that café and get you a meal. I will pay with your five pounds, and then anyone who sees will think it's mine. How's that for a scheme?"

The girl's face brightened with a joyful smile. "You had better take it now, so no one will see me giving it to you."

She looked around her, and then thrust the huge white crackling bank note into my hand. She is very trusting, I thought. She is afraid of someone, but she's not afraid that I will pocket the five pounds and run off.

In the café we ordered steak and two eggs and chips and peas for her. She took her jacket off and sat down. It was then that I saw she was pregnant. She wore no wedding ring. Pregnancy outside marriage in those days was a terrible disgrace. It was not as bad as it had been twenty or thirty years previously. Nonetheless, she would have a hard time ahead of her, I reflected.

She ate in hungry concentration, whilst I sipped a coffee, looking at her. Her name was Mary and was an Irish beauty, with tawny brown hair, delicate bone structure, and pale skin. She could have been a Celtic Princess, or the spawn of a drunken Irish navvy, it was hard to tell – perhaps there is not much difference, I thought.

The first of her hunger was assuaged, and she looked up at me with a smile.

"Where do you come from?" I asked.

"County Mayo."

"Have you ever been away from home before?"

She shook her head.

"Does your mother know you are pregnant?"

Fear, guilt and resentment came into her pretty eyes. Her lips tightened.

"Look, I'm a midwife. I notice these things. I'm trained to do so. I don't suppose anyone else has noticed yet, though."

Her face relaxed, so I said again, "Does your mother know?"

She shook her head.

"What are you going to do?" I asked.

"I don't know."

"You will have to go back home," I said. "London is a big and scary place. You can't bring up a child by yourself here. You need your mother's help. You will have to tell her. She will understand. Mothers hardly ever let their daughters down, you know."

"I can't go back home. It's impossible," she said.

She wouldn't answer any more questions on that subject, so I said, "How did you get to London, and why did you come, anyway?"

She was more relaxed now, and looked more inclined to talk. I ordered apple pie and ice cream for her. Slowly, and in bits and pieces, the story came out. I was so charmed by the lilting music of her voice, that I could have listened all night, regardless of whether she was reading a laundry list or telling me the age-old pathos of her life.

She was the eldest of five living children. Eight of her brothers and sisters had died. Her father was a farm worker and peat cutter. They lived in what she called a sheelin'. Her mother did washing for "the big house", she told me. When she was fourteen her father caught pneumonia in the west Irish winter, and died. The family was left with no protector. The sheelin' was tied to the lands worked by the father and, as none of the sons was old enough to take over the labour, the family was evicted. They moved to Dublin. The mother, a country woman who had never travelled more than walking distance from the mountains and meadows where she had been brought up, was quite unable to cope with the alien environment. They found lodgings in a tenement, and at first the mother took in washing, or tried to, but there was so much poverty and competition from other women similarly placed that she soon gave up the struggle. They couldn't pay the rent, and were again evicted. Mary took a job in a factory, working sixty hours a week for a pittance. Mick, her brother of thirteen, lied about his age and left school, taking a job in a tannery. For both of them it was child slave labour.

The combined efforts of these two might have been just enough to keep the family afloat, had it not been for their mother.

"Me poor mam! I hate her for what she did to us, yet I can't hate her really. She never could get herself away from the hills and the broad sky, from the sound of the curlew and the skylark, the sea, and the silence of the night."

Her voice was like the sad, plaintive cry of an oboe rising from an orchestra.

"At first she just drank Guinness 'because it does me good" she said. Then she took to any old sour stout that she could get. Then it was poteen, which the knife-sharpener man distilled. I don't know what she drinks now. Most likely it's meths and cold tea."

The schoolmistress reported that the three younger children were playing truant, and that when they did come to school, they were half-starving and half-naked. They were taken away from their mother, and put into an orphanage. The mother didn't seem to notice that they had gone. She had already hitched up with another man.

"It's probably a good thing that they were taken away, because I have two little sisters, and I wouldn't want what happened to me to happen to them."

I shuddered. I had heard from Child Care Officers that if a mother takes another man into the house this can frequently be the death sentence for the children.

"He was a big man. I had never seen him sober. There was nothing I could do. I never knew that anything could be so awful. He did it again and again, until I got used to it. It was when he started hitting me and my mam with anything he could get hold of that I knew I had to leave. Me mam didn't seem to notice the wallops, I think she was too drunk to feel anything. But I wasn't. I thought he would kill me."

She had slept in the streets of Dublin for a few nights, with her possessions in a string bag, but her thoughts were on London. She said, "Do you know the story of Dick Whittington and his black cat? Me mam used to tell us that story, and I always thought London must be a beautiful place."

She went to the docks, and enquired about the cost of the

fare to England. It was equivalent to three weeks' wages, so she continued at the factory, and slept in a store room at night.

"I was as quiet as a mouse, and as secret as a shadow, and no one knew I was there. Even the caretaker didn't find me when he did his rounds at night, or I would have been thrown out," she said with a mischievous grin.

She spent nothing on food, scrounging what she could from other girls in the factory, and at the end of the third week, she took her wages and left, saying she wasn't coming back.

There were many cargo boats going daily from Dublin to Liverpool in those days, but nonetheless, she had to wait until the Monday before she could get a passage.

"I spent the whole of Sunday wandering around the docks. It was beautiful, with the great ships, and the water splashing, and the seagulls crying. And I was that excited about going to London, that I didn't notice I was hungry."

After another night spent in the open, she paid all her money apart from a few shillings, on a one-way ticket and boarded the vessel.

"It was the most exciting moment of my life, and as I said goodbye to Ireland, I crossed myself and prayed for the soul of me dad, and asked our Holy Mother Mary to look after me poor mam, and me brothers and sisters."

She arrived in Liverpool docks at about 7 p.m. on Monday evening. They did not seem to be quite as different as she had expected. In fact, they looked exactly like Dublin docks, only bigger. She did not know what to do. She enquired where London was, and was told three hundred miles away.

"Three hundred miles," she said. "I nearly fainted. I'd thought it was just around the corner. Can you believe I was so silly?"

She'd spent another night in the open, and found some bread that had been thrown out for the seagulls. It was stale and dirty, but satisfied the worst of her hunger. In the morning, as the sun rose, her spirits and youthful optimism rose also, and she enquired how she could get to London without any money. She was told that 95 per cent of the transport lorries leaving that day would be going to London, and all that was necessary was to ask the driver if he would take her.

"You shouldn't have any difficulties, a pretty girl like you," her informant had said.

I know this to be true from my own experience. From the age of about seventeen, I had hitch-hiked all over England and Wales, always thumbing down long distance lorries and reaching my destination safely. I was always alone. I knew it was said that lorry drivers pick up girls for one purpose only, but this had not been my experience. All the lorry drivers I met were sober, hard-working men, who knew the road, had a load to deliver, and had a schedule to fulfil. Furthermore they were in a named company lorry, and any complaint would identify them immediately, not only to the boss, but also to the wife back home!

Mary found her lorry driver, and told me, "He was such a nice man. It was a long journey and we talked all the way. I sang him songs me dad taught me when I was a child, and he said I had a pretty voice. In some ways he was like me dad. You know, he even took me into a transport café and bought me a meal, and he wouldn't take anything for it. He said 'you keep that, lassie, because I think you are going to need it.' I thought to myself, I'm going to like it in England if all the Englishmen are like this". She paused, and looked down at her plate. Her voice was barely audible when she said, "He was the last good man I have met in this country."

There was silence between us for quite some moments. I did not want to force her confidence, and in any case I am not by nature nosy about other people's affairs, so I said, "How about another ice cream? I'm sure you could manage it. And I wouldn't mind another coffee, if you think you can afford it."

She laughed, and said, "I can afford a hundred cups of coffee."

The proprietor brought our order, and said it was 11.15 and he was closing his till, so could we pay now. But we were welcome to sit at the table until midnight.

The bill was two shillings and ninepence, including coffee. That is equivalent to about twelve pence today. I drew myself to my full height, and with a grand gesture drew out the five pound note.

He jumped and spluttered, "Look 'ere, ain't you got nuffink smaller'n that? How do you expect me to change five pounds?"

I said coldly and firmly, "I'm sorry, but I have nothing smaller. If I had, I would have given it to you. My friend has no money on her at all. If you can't change the note, I am afraid we cannot pay for this meal."

I folded the note and put it back into my handbag. That did it. He said, "All right, all right, Miss Toffee-nose. You win."

He went and scratched through the till, then had to go out to the back to unlock the safe. He came back to the table, muttering and grumbling, and counted out four pounds, seventeen shillings and three pence change, whereupon I handed over the five pound note.

Mary was giggling like a schoolgirl at all this. I winked at her, and put the change into my bag. She remained just as trusting, because I could have got up and walked out with all her money.

It was getting late. Although it was my night off, I had had a very busy day, and I was on duty at 8 a.m. the next morning, with the likelihood of another busy day ahead. I was tempted to say, "Look I must get off now" but something drew me to this lonely girl, and I said, "Have you any plans for the baby?"

She shook her head.

"When is it due?"

"I don't know."

"Who are you booked with for confinement?"

She said nothing, so I repeated the question.

"I'm not booked with anyone," she said.

I was concerned. She looked about six months' pregnant, but if she had been half starved it might be a small baby, in which case she could be nearer to full term. I said: "Look Mary, you must be booked for a confinement. Who is your doctor?"

"I haven't got one."

"Where do you live?"

She didn't answer, so I asked again, still no answer. She looked angry, and a hard suspicious tone came into her voice:

"It's none of your business," she said. I think if I hadn't had her four pounds, seventeen shillings and three pence in my handbag, she would have got up and walked out.

"Mary, you might as well tell me, because you need a doctor, and antenatal care for your baby. I am a midwife and can probably arrange it for you."

She bit her lip, and picked her fingernails, then said, "I've been living at the Full Moon Café in Cable Street. But I can't go back there any more."

"Why not?" I said. "Is it because you stole five pounds from the till?"

She nodded.

"They'll kill me if they find me. And they *will* find me, somehow, I'm sure of that. Then they will kill me."

She said these last words in a flat matter of fact voice, as though she had faced and accepted the inevitable.

It was my turn to be silent. I knew that the East End was a violent place. The midwives did not see it because we were deeply respected, and on the whole only dealt with the respectable families. But this girl could easily have been in potentially violent company and if she had stolen from them that undercurrent of violence could erupt into reality. Her life might well be in danger. I had not yet heard about the notorious cafés of Cable Street.

I said, "Have you got anywhere to sleep tonight?"

She shook her head.

I sighed. The responsibility was beginning to dawn on me.

"Let's go and see if the YWCA is open. It's very late, and I am not sure what time they close, but it's worth a try."

We thanked the proprietor, and left. In the street I gave Mary her money, and we walked the mile to the YWCA. It had closed at 10 p.m.

I was weary and tired. My stiletto heels were killing me. I had another mile to walk back to Nonnatus House, and a heavy day's work to come. I cursed myself for getting involved at all. I could so easily have said at the bus stop, "No, I do not have change for five pounds", and walked away.

But I looked at Mary standing outside the closed door. She

looked so small and vulnerable, and somehow utterly docile in my hands. How could I leave her in the street with, possibly, men looking for her who might kill her? Who would notice if she disappeared? I thought, There, but for the grace of God, go I, and that solemn thought was truer than you might suppose.

She shivered in the cold night air, and pulled her thin jacket around her neck. I was wearing a warm camel hair coat with a beautiful fur collar of which I was very proud. The collar was detachable, so I took it off and put it round her thin little neck. She gave a sigh of joy and snuggled into the warm fur.

"Ooh! that's lovely," she said, smiling.

"Come on," I said. "You had better come back with me."

ZAKIR

The mile walk from the YWCA to Nonnatus House seemed endless. I was too tired to want to talk any more, so we walked in silence. At first all I could think about was my feet and those infernal shoes, designed for elegance, not for hiking. Suddenly the bright idea came to me to take the damned things off! So I did, and my stockings too. The cold pavement felt lovely, and cheered me up.

What was I going to do with Mary? There were only ten bedrooms at Nonnatus House, all of which were occupied. I decided to put her in the staff sitting room, and to find some blankets from the general storeroom. I knew I would have to be up before 5.30 a.m. to tell Sister Julienne as she came out of chapel. I could not risk anyone finding the girl without my first having informed the Sister-in-Charge. The nuns did not and could not take in every down-and-out who turned up at their door. If they did, they would be inundated, and the ten bedrooms would soon have ten sleeping in every bed! The nuns had a specific job to do – district nursing and midwifery – and their calling had to be directed to this end.

As I trudged along in my bare feet, I pondered Mary's words about the lorry driver, "He was the last good man I have met in this country." How tragic. There are millions of good men – the vast majority, in fact. How was it that she, a sweet and pretty girl, had never met them? How had she come to this destitute state? Was it all, perhaps, due to love? Or the absence of love? Would I have been in Mary's position, had it not been for love? My thoughts went, as they always did, to the man I loved. We had met when I was only fifteen. He could quite easily have used and abused me, but he didn't, he respected me. He loved me to distraction, and wanted only my ultimate good. He had educated me, protected me, guided my teenage years. Had I met the wrong man at the age of fifteen, I reflected, I would probably be in the same position as Mary now.

We trudged on in silence. I didn't know what Mary was thinking about, but my soul was longing for the sight, the sound and the touch of the man I loved so much. Poor little thing. What sort of touch had she known if the lorry driver was the only good man she had met?

We arrived at Nonnatus House. It was getting on for 2 a.m. I fixed Mary up in the sitting room with some blankets, and said, "The lavatory is down the end of this corridor, dear. Sleep well, and I will see you in the morning."

I went wearily to bed, and set my alarm for 5.15 a.m.

The Sisters were surprised to see me as they came out of chapel. It was still the time of the Greater Silence of their monastic vows, so there was no speech. I went up to Sister Julienne and told her exactly what had happened. She did not speak, but her eyes spoke their understanding. The nuns passed me in silent procession, and I went back to bed, resetting my alarm for 7.30 a.m.

At 8 a.m. I went to Sister Julienne's office.

"I have spoken to Father Joe at Church House, Wellclose Square," she said. "They can take the girl, and will look after her. I have peeped into the sitting room. She is sound asleep, and will probably sleep until midday. We will bring her some breakfast when she wakes up, and then take her along to Church House. You go and have your breakfast now, and then start your morning's work."

Her eyes smiled at me, and she added: "You could not have done otherwise my dear."

Once again, I was struck by the kindness and flexibility of the Sisters, compared with the rigid inflexibility of the hospital systems under which I had worked. Had I taken anyone into a nurses' home without permission for a night, there would have been hell to pay, simply because it was against the rules.

Mary did not wake up until four o'clock in the afternoon. It was our teatime, just before we started the evening work, so I did not have long to see her before I had to go out. Sister Julienne had taken her some tea and bread and butter, which she was eating when I went into the sitting room. Sister was explaining to Mary that she could not stay at Nonnatus House, but could go to a house where she would be welcome to stay. Antenatal care would be provided, and arrangements made for delivery. Mary looked at me with big solemn eyes, and I nodded and said that I would come to see her.

And that is how I got into the world of pimps and prostitutes, the foul brothels, masquerading as all-night cafés, that lined Cable Street and the surrounding area of Stepney. It is a hidden world. The same goes on in every town and city the world over, and always has done, but few people know anything about the business, nor indeed do they want to.

There are two sorts of prostitutes: the high class ones, and the rest. The French courtesans were probably the top of the market, and we read about their salons, their lavish entertainments, their artistic and political influence with amazement.

In London, the smart West End call girls today normally work within a very expensive establishment with a few select clients, and can command enormous fees. These are usually very intelligent women who have worked it all out, planned it, studied it, and entered prostitution with a true professionalism. One such girl said to me: "You have to go into it at the top. This is not a job where you start at the bottom and work your way up. If you start at the bottom, you just sink lower."

The vast majority of prostitutes start at the bottom, and their life is pitiable. Historically, prostitution has been the only means of earning a living for a woman who is destitute, particularly if she has children to feed. What woman worthy of the name Mother would stand on a high moral platform about selling her body if her child were dying of hunger and exposure? Not I.

Today – and indeed in the 1950s – such starvation is not seen in Western societies, but there is a different type of hunger which feeds the prostitution trade. It is starvation of love. Thousands run away from desperate circumstances, and find themselves alone and friendless in a big city. They are craving affection, and will attach themselves to anyone who appears to offer it. This is where the pimps and madams score. They offer the child food and lodgings and apparent kindness, and within days, prostitution is forced upon them. The only difference between the twenty-first century and the 1950s is that back then, the children procured for soliciting were around fourteen years of age. Today the age has dropped to as low as ten.

Mary's lorry driver was heading for the Royal Albert Docks, and so he had dropped her off in Commercial Road. She told me, "I felt so terribly alone, more alone than I had ever felt before. In Ireland, when I was making my plans to come to London, I was all excited. The journey was thrilling, because I was going to the beautiful city of London, and I didn't feel alone, because my thoughts were full of dreams. But when I got here I didn't know what I was going to do."

Who was it that said "'Tis better to travel hopefully than to arrive?" I daresay we have all experienced this in one way or another.

Mary went into a confectioner tobacconist, bought a bar of chocolate, and ate it as she wandered down the busy road. At the time, Commercial Road and East India Dock Road were said to be the busiest roads in Europe, because the Port of London was the busiest port in Europe. The continuous stream of lorries bewildered and frightened her. By contrast, Dublin had been as quiet as a country village. The shrill blast of a siren nearly gave her a heart attack, and then she saw thousands of men pouring out of the dock gates. She flattened herself against a doorway as they passed, chatting, laughing, squabbling, shouting and talking to each other. But not one of them spoke to the shy, small figure in the doorway. In fact it is doubtful if any of them even noticed her. She said, "I nearly cried with loneliness. I wanted to shout out 'I'm here, just beside you. Come and say hello to me. I've come a long way just to be here.'"

She didn't like Commercial Road much, so she turned off into a side street where she saw children playing. She was scarcely more than a child herself, but they didn't want her to join in the game. She continued on until she came to what was known as the Cuts – the canal that went under Stinkhouse Bridge on its way to the Docks. It was pleasant standing by the bridge, looking down at the moving water, and she stood there a long time watching a water rat pop in and out of his hole and seeing the shadows lengthen.

"I just didn't know what I was going to do. I wasn't cold, 'cause it was summer, and I wasn't hungry, 'cause that nice lorry driver had given me sausage and chips. But I felt so empty inside, and sick with longing for someone to talk to me."

Night came, and she had nowhere to sleep, nor the money to purchase a night's lodgings. She had already spent many nights in the open, and the prospect did not bother her. There were bomb sites all over the East End at the time, and she found one that looked as though it might do. However, it was a bad choice.

"I was woken in the night by the most terrible noise. Men screaming and fighting and cursing and swearing. In the moonlight I saw knives and flashing things. I crawled deeper into the hole I was in, and hid under some foul-smelling sacks. I just kept quite, quite still, and didn't breathe. Then I heard the police whistles and dogs barking. I was frightened the dogs would smell me, but they didn't. Perhaps the sacks I was under smelt so bad they couldn't smell anything else."

She giggled. I didn't. My heart was too full for laughter.

Apparently she had stumbled into a bomb site regularly used by the meths drinkers. After the police had cleared the place, Mary crept out, and spent the rest of the night by the Cuts.

The next day was spent in much the same way as the first, just wandering around the Stepney end of Commercial Road with nothing to do.

"There were a lot of buses around, and I wondered if I should get on one and go somewhere else, because I didn't really like it where I was. But they all said places like Wapping and Barking, Mile End, and Kings Cross, on the front, and I didn't know where these places were. I had wanted to come to London, and the lorry driver said it was London when he put me down, so I didn't get on a bus, because I wouldn't know where I was going to."

Two more days were spent like this. Completely alone, talking to no one, sleeping in the Cuts at night. On the third evening Mary spent the last of her pennies on a sausage roll.

The fourth day in London would have been without food, had she not seen an old lady in a churchyard feeding the sparrows with breadcrumbs.

"I waited until the old lady had gone, then I shooed the birds away, and crawled around scooping up the breadcrumbs and putting them in my skirt. The sun was shining, and the trees were nice. I saw a little squirrel. I sat on the grass and ate a whole lap full of breadcrumbs. They tasted all right. The next day I went to the churchyard again, thinking that the old lady would come to feed the birds. But she didn't come. I waited the whole day but she still didn't come."

In the evening she scavenged some bits of food from a dustbin.

As she was talking, I wondered why it was that a bright young girl, who had had the initiative and enterprise to plan her journey all the way from Dublin, could not have been more resourceful and forward thinking when she arrived in London. There were places she could have gone – the police, a Catholic Church, the Salvation Army, the YWCA – where people would have helped her, sheltered her, and probably found her a job. But such a course of action did not seem to have occurred to her. Perhaps it would have done, given a little more time. But instead she met Zakir.

"I was looking in a baker's window, sniffing the bread and thinking what I wouldn't give to have some. He came and stood beside me, and said, 'Do you want a cigarette?'

"He was the first person who had spoken to me since the lorry driver. It was so nice just to hear someone say something to me, but I didn't smoke. Then he said, 'Do you want something to eat, then?' and I said: 'I'll say I do.'

"He looked down at me and smiled, such a lovely smile. His teeth were gleaming white, and his eyes were kind. He had beautiful eyes, a dark black-brown colour. I loved his eyes the moment I looked into them. He said, 'Come on, let's get some of their nice filled rolls. I'm hungry too. Then we'll go and sit by the Cuts and eat them.'

"We went into the shop, and he bought lots of rolls with different fillings, and some fruit pies, and some chocolate cake. I felt very scruffy beside him, because I hadn't washed or changed my clothes for days, and he looked so smart and well dressed, and had a gold chain on."

They sat on the grass of the towpath, leaning their backs against the wall, watching the barges go by. Mary said she was tongue tied. She felt overwhelmed by this kind, handsome youth who seemed to like her, and she couldn't think of a thing to say, even though for four or five days she had been longing for someone to talk to.

"He talked all the time, and laughed, and threw bits of bread to the sparrows and pigeons, and called them 'my friends'. I thought someone who is friends with the birds must be very nice. Sometimes I couldn't understand quite what he was saying, but the English accent is different to the Irish accent, you know. He told me he was a buyer for his uncle, who had a nice café in Cable Street and who sold the best food in London. We had such a lovely meal sitting there on the towpath in the sunshine. The rolls were delicious, the apple pies were delicious, and the chocolate cake was out of this world."

She leaned back on the stone wall, and sighed with contentment. When she woke up the sun was behind the warehouse, and his jacket was over her. She found that she was leaning on his shoulder.

"I woke up with his strong arm around me, and his beautiful brown eyes looking down at me. He stroked my cheek, and said, 'You've had a nice big sleep. Come on, it's getting late. I had better take you home. Your mother and father will wonder what has happened to you.'

"I didn't know what to say then, and he didn't talk either. After a bit, he said: 'We must get going. What will your mother think, you being out with a stranger all this time?'

"Me mam's a long way off in Ireland.'

"Well, your dad then.'

"Me dad's dead.'

"You poor little thing. I suppose you are living with an auntie in London?'

"He stroked my cheek again when he said 'you poor little thing', and I thought I would melt with happiness. So I snuggled up in his arms, and told him the whole story – but I didn't tell him about me mam's man and what he'd done to me, because I was ashamed, and didn't want him to think badly of me."

"He didn't say anything. For a long while he just stroked my cheek and my hair. Then he said: 'Poor little Mary. What are we going to do with you? I can't leave you here by the Cuts all night. I feel responsible for you now. I think you had better come back with me to my uncle's place. It's a nice café. My uncle is very kind. We can have a good meal and then we can plan your future.'"

CABLE STREET

Pre-war Stepney, just east of the City, with Commercial Road to the north, the Tower and Royal Mint to the West, Wapping and the Docks to the South, and Poplar to the east, was the home of thousands of respectable, hard-working, but often poor East End families. Much of the area was filled with crowded tenements, narrow unlit alleyways and lanes and old multi-occupant houses. Often the old houses had only one tap, and one lavatory in the yard, to serve between eight and a dozen families, and sometimes a whole family of ten or more might occupy one or two rooms. The people had lived like this for generations, and were still doing so in the 1950s.

This was their inheritance and their accepted lifestyle, but after the war, things changed dramatically, for the worse. The area was scheduled for demolition, which did not actually take place for another twenty years. In the meantime, the area became a breeding ground for vice of every description. The condemned houses, which were privately owned, could not be sold on the open market to responsible landlords, so they were bought up by unscrupulous profiteers of all nationalities, who let out single, derelict, rooms for fantastically low rents. The shops were bought up in the same way and turned into all night cafés, with their 'street waitresses'. They were, in fact, brothels, making life hell for the decent people who had to live in the area, and bring their children up in the midst of it all.

Overcrowding had always been part of the East Ender's life, but the war made it far worse. Many homes had been destroyed by the bombing and not replaced, so people lived anywhere they could find. On top of this, in the 1950s, thousands of commonwealth immigrants poured into the country with no provision made for where they were going to live. It was not uncommon to see groups of ten or more West Indians, say, going from door to door, begging for a room to let. If they did find one, in no time at all it would be filled with twenty to twenty-five people, all living together.

This sort of thing the East Enders had seen before, and could absorb. But when it came to the blatant widespread use of their streets, their alleys and closes, their shops and houses, as brothels, it was a very different matter. Life became sheer hell, and women were terrified to go out of doors, or to let their children out. The tough, resilient East Enders, who had lived through two world wars, lived through the Great Depression of the 1930s, survived the Blitz of the 1940s, and come up smiling, were to be crushed by the vice and prostitution that descended in their midst in the 1950s and '60s.

Try to imagine, if you can, living in a derelict building, renting two rooms on the second floor, with six children to bring up. And then try to imagine that there is a new landlord, and through threats, intimidation, fear, or genuine rehousing, one by one, all the families you have known since childhood have moved out. All the rooms of the house in which you live have been divided up and filled with prostitutes, as many as four or five to each room. The general store, which used to be the ground floor of the building, has been turned into an all-night café with noise and loud music, parties, swearing, fights, going on all night. The trade of prostitution goes on all night and all day, with men tramping up and down the stairs, and hanging around on the stairways or landings, waiting their turn. Imagine it, if you can, and imagine the poor woman who has to take her toddlers out shopping, or get the children off to school, or go down to the basement alone to get a couple of buckets of water with which to do her washing.

Many such families were on the council waiting list for rehousing for as much as ten years, and the biggest families had the least chance of getting other accommodation because the council (under the Housing Act) was not allowed to put a family of ten into a four-room flat, even though the two room conditions under which they were living had been condemned for human habitation.

Into this environment came Father Joe Williamson, who was

appointed Vicar of St Paul's in Dock Street in the 1950s. He devoted the rest of his life, his considerable energies, his powerful mind and above all his Godliness, to cleaning up the area and helping the East End families who had to live there. Later, he began his work of helping and protecting the young prostitutes, whom he loved and pitied with all his heart. It was he who opened the doors of Church House, Wellclose Square, as a home for prostitutes, and this was the place Mary went the day after I had picked her up at the bus stop. I visited her there several times, and it was during these visits that she told me her story.

"Zakir put his coat around my shoulders, because it was getting chilly, and he carried my bag. He put his arm round me, and led me through the crowds of men leaving the docks. He escorted me over the road like a real gentleman, and I can tell you I felt like the greatest lady in London by the side of such a handsome young man."

He took her down a side street off Commercial Road, which led into other side streets, each one narrower and dirtier than the last. Many windows were boarded up, others broken, others so dirty that it would have been impossible to see through them. There were very few people around, and no children played in the streets. She looked up the height of the black buildings. Pigeons flew from ledge to ledge. A few of the windows looked as if someone had tried to clean them, and had curtains. One or two even had washing hanging out on a little balcony. It looked as though the sun never penetrated these narrow streets and alleys. Filth and litter were everywhere; in the corners, the gutters, piled up against railings, blocking doorways, half filling the little alleys. Zakir carefully led Mary through all this dirt, telling her to be careful, or to step over this or that. The few other people they met were all men, and he protectively drew her closer to him as they passed. One or two of them he obviously knew, and they spoke to each other in a foreign language.

Mary said, "I thought he must be so clever and educated to speak a foreign language. He must have been to a very expensive school to have learned it, I thought."

They came to a wider, longer street, which was Cable Street and Zakir said to her, "My uncle's café is just up there. It's the best and the busiest one in the street. We can have a meal together, just you and me. Won't that be fun? My uncle also owns the whole building and he lets out rooms, so I'm sure he would find one for you. That way you won't have to sleep by the Cuts any more. Perhaps he could find a job for you in the café, washing up, or peeling the vegetables. Or he could put you in charge of the coffee machine. Would you like to work the coffee machine?"

Mary was enchanted. Working the coffee machine in a busy London café was about the height of her dreams. She clung to Zakir in gratitude and adoration, and he squeezed her hand.

"Everything's going to be all right for you from now on," he said. "I've got that feeling."

Mary was too overcome to speak. She loved him with all her heart. They entered the café. It was dark inside because the windows were so filthy, and the net curtains that hung from halfway down were nearly black with filth. A few men sat at formica tables, smoking and drinking. One or two of them sat with a woman, and a group of women and girls sat together at a bigger table smoking. No one spoke. The silence in the place was quite eerie, and somehow threatening. Everyone looked up as Zakir and Mary walked in, but still no one spoke. Mary must have contrasted sharply with the other girls and women in the café, who all seemed pale. Some of them looked sullen, some were scowling, and all looked haggard. By contrast, Mary's eyes were shining with expectation. Her skin was glowing with the fresh air, first from the boat trip, then from sleeping by the Cuts for four nights. Above all, the soft, sensuous glow of love filled her, irradiated her whole being.

Zakir told her to sit down while he went to speak with his uncle. He took her string bag with him. She sat at a table by the window. Several of the people in the café stared at her, but did not speak to her. She didn't mind, she smiled quietly to herself; she didn't really want to talk to anyone, now that she had Zakir. A rough-looking man came over and sat opposite her at the table, but she turned her head away haughtily. The man got up and left.

She heard some sniggering from the girls in the corner, so she turned to them and smiled, but no one smiled back.

After about ten minutes Zakir came back. He said, "I have spoken to my uncle. He is a good man, and he will look after you. We will have a meal together later. It is only seven o'clock now. The fun starts at about nine o'clock. You will enjoy the evening. This café is famous for its entertainment, and for its food: my uncle employs the best chef in London. You can have whatever you want. My uncle is a very generous man, and he says you can choose whatever you fancy from the menu and the wine list. He only says this because you are a special friend of mine, and I am his favourite nephew. I am the meat buyer, and I have to travel a lot to find the best. A good café must have good meat, and I am the best meat buyer in London."

Certainly the meat in Mary's dinner was very good. She chose meat pie and beans and chips. Zakir had the same, because there was nothing else on the menu that evening. But to Mary, who had been brought up in the poverty of rural Ireland, mainly on potatoes and swede, and then the destitution of Dublin, the meat pie was the finest thing she had ever tasted, and she sighed with contentment.

They sat in the corner by the window. From his seat Zakir could see the whole of the café and his eyes roamed around it continuously, even when he was talking to Mary. From her seat, she could see about half the café, but she didn't look around, nor did she want to. She had eyes only for Zakir.

He said, "Now let us choose our wine. You must always be careful with the wine, because a good wine is essential to a good dinner. I think we will have Chateau Marseilles 1948. It is an excellent wine, full bodied, yet not too heavy, with a tantalising piquancy that lingers on the palate and suggests the warmth and brilliance of the grape. I am an expert in wines."

Mary was impressed, in fact overwhelmed by his polish and urbanity. She had never tasted wine before, and did not like it. She had expected something delicious from the dark-red liquid in her tumbler, but thought it was bitter and sour. However, as Zakir was

The author in uniform.

ABOVE: Millwall Docks 1955. The romance and beauty of the great docks was our background. *Photo courtesy of Museum in Docklands, PLA Collection.*

BELOW: West India Docks, East India Docks, Millwall Docks and Canary Wharf. *Photo courtesy of Simmons Aerofilms.*

LEFT: Bombsites were the home of the meths drinkers. *Photo by Frank Rust, courtesy of The Wellclose Trust.*

BELOW: The sites also served as playgrounds. *Photo by Frank Rust, courtesy of The Wellclose Trust.*

TOP: Chrisp Street, Poplar. *Courtesy of Tower Hamlets Local History Library and Archives.*

ABOVE: The corner of Cable Street and Ensign Street, Stepney, in the 1950s. A community destroyed by prostitution. *Photo by Frank Rust. Courtesy of The Wellclose Institute.*

Father Joe in his parish. *Photo by Frank Rust. Courtesy of The Wellclose Trust.*

RIGHT: A communal tap. Water often had to be brought in from outside for the midwife's use. *Photo by Frank Rust. Courtesy of The Wellclose Trust.*

BELOW: Slum conditions in the 1950s. In spite of their surroundings, the family is happy and not short of food. *Photo by Frank Rust. Courtesy of The Wellclose Trust.*

Cable Street 1950s. Prostitutes and their customers leaving. Children who live there in the foreground. *Photo by Frank Rust. Courtesy of The Wellclose Trust.*

Mothers watch children playing in a happy street scene in the Docklands.
Photo courtesy of The Island History Trust.

drinking his with delight, murmuring things like "an excellent vintage, drink up, you won't find anything better than this in all of London" or "ah, what a bouquet – quite exquisite – I assure you this is a rare treat", and as she did not want to hurt his feelings by saying she didn't really like it, she swallowed the whole tumbler full in one gulp, and said, "Delicious."

He refilled her glass. All the while his eyes were roving around the café. When he spoke to Mary he smiled, but as he looked around the café neither his eyes nor his mouth smiled. Mary could not see the table where the girls and women were sitting, but they were directly opposite Zakir. Frequently he stared over towards them with cold unblinking eyes, nodded slightly, and moved his head momentarily in another direction, then back again towards the table. Each time, Mary could hear the scrape of a chair as one of the girls got up. About half a dozen times during the meal he got up and went over to the table. Mary followed him with her eyes, not because she was suspicious, but because she just couldn't take her eyes off him. She noted with satisfaction that he did not seem to like the girls very much, because he never smiled at them, but seemed to be talking with his teeth closed and his eyes fixed and hard. Once she saw him clench his fist, and push it up against a girl's face in a menacing fashion. The girl got up and went out.

Mary thought, "He likes me the best. He doesn't like those girls. They look a nasty bunch anyway. But I am his special friend," and a warm glow flooded over her.

Each time Zakir returned, he showered Mary with smiles, his beautiful white teeth flashing and his dark eyes gleaming.

"Drink up," he said. "You can't have too much of this excellent wine. Would you like some fruit or some gateau? My uncle says you can have anything you want. Soon the entertainment will begin. It is the best in London. The night clubs of London, Paris and New York are famous all over the world, and this one is the best in London."

Mary drank up, and ate a piece of sticky, sweet cake which Zakir said was Black Forest gateau with morello cherries marinated in chartreuse. Although Mary could not find the cherries it tasted delicious, but unfortunately the wine now tasted even worse than before and the sourness made her tongue feel all furry and her lips and mouth rough.

She was vaguely aware, in a hazy sort of way, that the café was filling up. Men were coming in continuously. Zakir said, "This is our busy time. You will enjoy the entertainment, won't you?"

Mary smiled and nodded, anxious to please. In reality her eyes were hurting, because the air was getting more and more smoky, and her head was beginning to ache. She felt deeply tired after the meal, and would rather have gone to sleep, but she thought that she must stay awake to enjoy the entertainment that Zakir had so kindly brought her to see. She drank some more wine, and tried to keep her eyes open. She was not aware that shutters had been put up at the windows, the doors locked, and the lights dimmed.

Quite suddenly the most deafening noise shattered her fuddled senses. She nearly fell off her chair in fright, and had to grip the edge of the table to keep herself upright. It was louder than anything she had ever heard in her life, louder even than the dock yard siren that had frightened her in Commercial Road. And it went on and on. It was a jukebox, and the noise was rhythm music.

Zakir shouted: "The entertainment. Turn your chair and watch. It is the best in London."

All the men in the room had turned their chairs, and were silently facing a table in the centre.

A girl leapt up on to the table and started dancing. The table was only about three foot wide, so she could not really dance for fear of falling off, but she moved her body, her hips, her shoulders, her arms and neck in rhythm with the music. Her hair flew about her. The men cheered. Then she threw off a shawl that was round her shoulders. The men cheered again and scrambled to get it. Slowly, suggestively, she undid the buttons of her blouse and threw it off, revealing a crimson bra. She undid the band which kept her skirt on, and it dropped to her feet. Beneath it, she wore only a crimson string that ran round her waist and between her legs. Her bottom was enormous. She turned to face the wall, shaking her bottom and thighs then bent over with her legs apart.

Mary was stunned. All sleepiness had left her and she couldn't believe her eyes. She couldn't believe it was happening.

Zakir flashed his beautiful teeth at her and shouted: "It is good, no? I told you we have the best entertainment in London."

The girl straightened up and turned to face her audience. She stared around her in an insolent fashion, and slowly began to undo the fastenings of her bra. The men cheered and screamed and stamped as two huge breasts fell out, with crimson tassels attached to each nipple. With a skill that must have taken much practice, she began to make her breasts gyrate faster and faster, and the tassels flew round and round with ever increasing speed. Mary's eyes were hypnotised by these tassels. She was numb with amazement until gradually the gyrations slowed down, and the tassels drooped to the floor, swinging slightly. The girl undid the string around her waist, and threw it to the audience, who scrambled to get it.

Now the serious part of her dance started. She shook and moved her pelvis slowly back and forwards. Her eyes were fixed on her audience, and her tongue was hanging out. She did this for quite a long time, sometimes moving her upper body as well, sometimes swinging her breasts from side to side. The jukebox was turned down a bit, so that just the beat of the drums was heard, and all the time her pelvis moved back and forwards to the rhythm.

Mary was quite mesmerised. As suddenly as it had started, and with a scream, the girl stopped, and lay down on the table. There was not a lot of space, but she lay with her back and head on the table, and her legs high in the air, heels touching. The jukebox went up loud, louder, louder again, as she slowly opened her legs until they were almost horizontal, revealing her vast fleshy, hairy vulva. Then, with even more skill, and to the screams of delight from her audience, she started to produce ping-pong balls from her vagina, and throw them at the audience. The speed and the number were bewildering. There must be some magic in this, Mary thought, no woman can have so many ping-pong balls inside her. The balls were flying around the room, the men throwing them at each other, at the girls, at the walls, in a frenzy of excitement.

The other girls had now left their table and joined the men, some sitting on their knees and fondling them or being fondled, some going out the back in pairs, some just sitting, smoking and drinking. Two older women came up to the girl lying on the table, and each took hold of a leg. Then they beckoned to the men. There was a rush towards her, but two thickset, middle-aged men wearing knuckledusters barred the way. They snarled at the advancing men, and said something. Mary could not hear what was said because of the noise of the jukebox, but several of the men turned and went back to their seats. Some remained standing, however, and Mary saw a lot of money being handed to the knuckledusters. Then one by one, the men undid their trousers and penetrated the girl on the table. Some, whilst waiting their turn, came up the sides and rubbed her breasts with their hands. After more money was pressed into the knuckledustered hands, one went up to her head, undid his trousers, and pressed his penis into her mouth, while the girl contentedly sucked. After that, several other men did the same, one at a time.

Mary felt sick. Her experience of the Irishman had been enough to tell her what was going on, and the sight of the money passing hands told her the rest. She did not need to ask any questions. She shuddered, and crossed herself. "Holy Mary, mother of God, pray for me," she whispered.

Mary told me all this over cups of coffee and digestive biscuits as we sat in the kitchen of Church House in Wellclose Square. I visited her often. I was not a social worker, nor even a voluntary church worker. I just liked the girl, and the circumstances of our meeting gave us a bond; and she trusted me and was clearly able to talk to me. As I wanted to find out more about prostitutes and their way of life, I encouraged her to talk.

I said, "After that, why did you not just leave? You were free to do so. No one could have stopped you. Why didn't you just go?"

She was quiet, and nibbled the edge of a biscuit.

"I should have done, I know, but I couldn't leave Zakir. He took my hand and squeezed it and said, 'Is this not good entertainment? You will find nothing better in London. All the night-clubs in London are trying to get that dancer for their shows, but

I found her and brought her to my uncle and he pays her well, so she will not go to another café. She performs each night for us, and makes the café famous. But my dear little Mary, you are looking tired. You need to go to bed. Come. My uncle has a room ready for you.'"

He tenderly took her hand, and led her through the crowd of men and girls, pushing them aside, putting his arm protectively around her.

She said to me, "I knew he cared for me then, because he treated me differently to all the others. He was looking after me and protecting me from all those rough men, wasn't he?"

I sighed. With the wisdom of my twenty-three years, I wondered if it was really possible that a girl of fourteen or fifteen could be so taken in by a smooth-talking scoundrel. I felt that I could not have been. But now I am not so sure.

He led her out the back to the kitchen area, and said, "This is the stairway to the upper rooms. They are very fine and beautiful. You will see. If you want the lavatory, it is over there, in the yard."

He pointed to a wood and asbestos shack.

Mary did need to go and after whispering, "Don't go away," she went over to it. It was revolting and evil smelling, but in the dark Mary could not see the magnitude of the ordure covering the wet and slippery floor.

She returned to Zakir, who led her through the kitchen and up to the first floor. He produced a key, opened a door and switched on the light.

Mary found herself in a room the like of which she had never seen, nor even imagined, in all her life. Lights shone from the walls, not the ceiling, and some even shone from the curtains. There were mirrors on the walls reflecting the lights. She gasped at the gold and silver that seemed to be everywhere although it was, in fact, just chrome. In the centre of the room stood a huge brass bed, with what looked to her like a silk covering. After the dark, dingy interior of the café below, it seemed like paradise.

She murmured, "Oh, it's beautiful Zakir, just beautiful. Is this really the room your uncle will let me have?"

He laughed, and replied, "It is the most beautiful room in London. You will not find a finer room anywhere. You are a lucky girl Mary, I hope you know that."

"Oh I do, I do, Zakir," she sighed, "and I am grateful with all my heart."

He had seduced her with practised ease. She did not want to talk about it, and I did not want to press her. I felt that the memory of that one night was sacred to her. She did, however, say, "I am sure he loved me, because no one else has ever touched me in the way that he did. All the other men were rough and horrible. But Zakir was gentle and beautiful. I thought I would die with happiness that night. It would have been best if I had died," she added quietly.

As they lay in each other's arms, watching the daylight banish the soft darkness, he whispered, "There, my little Mary, did you enjoy that? Did you think anything like that could come to you? There are many other things that I can show you also."

"Then I made a terrible mistake," she said to me. "If I had not made that mistake, he would love me still. But I thought I should tell him all the truth about myself, so that there would be no secrets between us. I told him about me mam's man in Dublin, and what he did to me."

"Zakir pushed me away from him then, and jumped up, shouting, 'Why do I waste my time with you, you little slut. I am a busy man. I have better things to do with my time. Get up, and get yourself dressed.'

"He slapped me in the face and threw my clothes at me. I was crying, and he slapped me again, and said, 'Stop snivelling. Get your clothes on, and hurry up.'

"I got dressed as quickly as I could, and he pushed me out of the door on to the landing. Then his mood changed again, and he smiled at me. He wiped my eyes with his handkerchief and said, 'There, there, my little Mary. Don't cry. It will be all right. I am quick tempered, but it is soon over. If you are a good girl, I will always look after you.'

"He put his arm around me, and I felt happy again. I knew it had been my fault for telling him about the Irishman. You see, I had hurt his feelings. He had wanted to be the first."

Her gullibility astonished me. After all that she had been through and witnessed, did she really cling to the dream that Zakir had loved her, and prized her virginity so much that his love ceased when he knew that she had been raped by a drunken Irishman?

"He took me down to the café area, and called over to one of the women I had seen holding the leg of the girl on the table the night before. He said to her, 'This is Mary. She'll be all right. Tell Uncle when he gets up.'

"Then he said to me: 'I have to go out now. I am a busy man. You stay with Gloria and she will look after you. Do what Uncle tells you. If you do what Uncle tells you, and are a good girl, I will be pleased with you. If you do not, I will be cross with you.'"

Mary whispered: "When are you coming back?"

He said, "Don't worry, I will come back. Stay here and be a good girl, and do what Uncle tells you."

CAFÉ LIFE

During my time at Nonnatus House, I took many walks around Stepney to see what it was like. It was simply appalling. The slums were worse than I could ever have imagined. I could not believe that it was only three miles from Poplar where, although poor, badly housed and overcrowded, the people were cheerful and neighbourly. In Poplar everyone would call out to a nurse: " 'Allo luvvy. 'Ow's yerself? 'Ow you doin' then?" In Stepney no one spoke to me at all. I walked down Cable Street, Graces Alley, Dock Street, Sanders Street, Backhouse Lane and Leman Street, and the atmosphere was menacing. Girls hung around in doorways, and men walked up and down the streets, often in groups, or hung around the doors of cafés smoking or chewing tobacco and spitting. I always wore my full nurse's uniform, because I did not want to be propositioned. I knew that I was being watched, and that my presence was deeply resented.

The condemned buildings were still standing, nearly twenty years after they had been scheduled for demolition, and were still being lived in. A few families and old people who could not get away remained, but mostly the occupants were prostitutes, homeless immigrants, drunks or meths drinkers, and drug addicts. There were no general shops selling food and household necessities as the shops had been turned into all-night cafés, which in fact meant they were brothels. The only shops I saw were tobacconists.

Many of the buildings apparently had no roofs. Father Joe, the vicar of St Paul's, told me he knew of a family of twelve who lived in three upper rooms, with tarpaulins to shelter them. Most of the upper storeys were quite derelict, but the lower storeys, protected by the floor above that had not yet collapsed, were teeming with humanity.

In Wellclose Square (now demolished) there was a Primary

School that backed on to Cable Street. I was told that every kind of filth was thrown over the railings, so I spoke to the caretaker. He was a Stepney man born and bred, a cheerful East Ender, but he looked grim when I spoke to him. He told me that he came in early every morning to clean up before the children came to school: filthy, blood-and wine-sodden mattresses were thrown over into the school playground; sanitary towels, underwear, blood-stained sheets, condoms, bottles, syringes – just about everything. The caretaker said he burned the rubbish each morning.

Opposite the school in Graces Alley was a bomb site where the same sort of filth was thrown by the café owners every night. This was never cleaned up or burned; it just accumulated, and stank to high heaven. I could not bear to go past it – the smell from fifty yards away was enough for me – so I never did visit Graces Alley, although I was told that a few Stepney families still lived there.

The brothels, ponces and prostitutes dominated the area and the squalid derelict buildings seemed to stand gloating over the sordid trade, and evil, cruel practices. The more Cable Street became known for its cafés, the more the customers flocked there, and so the trade fed itself. The local people could do nothing. Their voice was silenced by the noise of the jukeboxes. In any case, they lived, I was told, in deadly fear of complaining and were crushed by the magnitude of the problem.

There had always been brothels in the East End. Of course there had; it was a dock land. What else would you expect? But they were always absorbed and tolerated. It was when hundreds of brothels sprang up in a small area that life became intolerable for the local inhabitants.

I could well understand the fear felt by local people, and that to complain, or in any way interfere with the profits of the café owners, would mark you out for retribution. A knifing or a beating would be all that you would get for your courage. I was glad that I walked down Sander Street in broad daylight. Through the dirty windows the haggard, painted faces of girls could be seen leaning on the windowsill, looking out, openly touting for men. As Sander Street led directly off Commercial Road, men were constantly looking into it, and going down it. These houses used to be a neat little terrace only ten or fifteen years before, a place where families lived and children played. The day I went, it looked like something from a horror film. The girls in the windows did not pester me, of course, but there were a lot of big, sinister-looking men around, who glared at me as if to say, "You get out of here." Did any Stepney family really live amid all this? Apparently yes. I saw two or three little houses with clean windows and net curtains, and a well-scrubbed doorstep. I saw one old lady shuffling along close to the wall, eyes down, till she came to her door. She looked around furtively, then opened the door with her key and shut it quickly after her. I heard two bolts slamming shut.

There is a saying amongst the masters of working dogs, be they sheep dogs, guard dogs, police dogs or huskies, 'Don't treat them with kindness, or they won't work for you.'

It is the same with pimps and prostitutes. The girls are treated like dogs, but usually far, far worse. Dogs have to be bought or bred, and in consequence are usually well looked after. They are expensive assets, and the loss of a valuable dog is a serious matter. But girls on the game are utterly expendable. They do not have to be bought, like a dog or a slave, yet they live a life of slavery, subject to the will and the whims of their masters. Most girls enter the trade voluntarily, not really aware of what they are doing, and within a very short time they find that they cannot get out of it. They are trapped.

Zakir had left Mary with the words, "Be a good girl, and do what you are told, and I will be pleased with you." Mary lived on this promise for months. Just for a smile from Zakir she would, and did, do anything.

He left her at about 8 a.m. with Gloria, a hardened old pro of about fifty who occasionally worked, but whose main job was to keep the girls up to scratch. She stared at Mary unsmiling, and said, "You 'eard what he said. You 'ave to do as you are told. You'd better get on wiv cleaning up the café and the kitchen before Uncle comes down."

Mary didn't know what to do. The whole area looked so big, and was in such a mess, that she didn't know where to begin. In the sheelin' back in Ireland, cleaning was a simple business – a bed, a table, a mat, a bench; that was all. But the café looked enormous. She stared around in bewilderment. A heavy foot landed in the small of her back, and she was flung forward a yard or two.

"Get on wiv it, you lazy bitch, don't just stand there starin'."

Mary jumped to it. She remembered what Zakir had said about a job in the café washing up, and she ran round collecting dirty glasses, mugs, spittoons, and a few dirty plates. She hurried with them into the kitchen, which was filthy, and over to the greasy sink. There was only cold water in the tap, but she washed everything up as best she could, and then dried the things on a filthy bit of old sheet. Gloria, in the meantime, was putting chairs up on the tables.

"Clean the floor when you've done," she called.

There wasn't a broom, but there was a wet mop, and Mary rubbed it all over the floor, in reality just pushing the dirt around.

"That's better," said Gloria. "Go and clean the kazi now."

Mary looked blank.

"The gerry, the lav, the bog, stupid."

Mary went out to the yard. It stank. The lavatory had probably been used by over a hundred men during the night, and each night before, and had not been cleaned properly for years. Most of the men peed on the ground around the shack, so the cobblestones were always wet and slippery. There was no toilet paper, only the torn up newspaper that littered the place. Some of the men had been sick, and as it was a warm summer morning, the stench was rising. This was also the only lavatory available for the girls to use, and as there was no bin, used sanitary towels lay scattered all over the yard.

Mary stared at it in horror, but fearing another kick in the back, she quickly got to work. There was a broom in the yard, so she swept up most of the more solid filth into a pile in a corner. Then she got a bucket of water, and swilled it over the yard. It seemed to be effective, so she fetched several other buckets of water, and did the same.

Gloria came out, and stared around silently. She took the fag from her mouth. "You done a good job 'ere, Mary. Zakir'll be pleased wiv you. An' Uncle an' all."

Mary glowed with pleasure. To please Zakir was her keenest desire. She said, timidly, pointing to the pile of filth in the corner, "What shall I do with that?"

"Take it over to the bomb site in Graces Alley. I'll show you where it is."

There was no other way of picking the mess up but with her hands. Mary was not happy about it, but did so nonetheless. She had to make four trips to the bomb site to get rid of it all.

Mary felt filthy. Her last wash had been in the Cuts, and she hadn't changed her clothes for days. She went into the kitchen and washed her face and arms under the cold tap, then her feet and legs, which made her feel better. She tried to remember what had happened to the string bag, that contained her clean blouse. She remembered Zakir had carried it the night before, and she had not seen it since. She asked Gloria where he might have put it.

Gloria laughed: "You won't see that again," she said. And indeed Mary didn't.

At that moment a man entered the café. He was one of the knuckledustered pair Mary had seen the night before taking money from the men. He was thickset, with a large stomach, which hung over the belt of his trousers. Dirty slippers scraped across the floor and tattoo marks covered his arms. His face was terrifying, and robbed Mary of the power of speech. She slunk away out into the yard. The man was Uncle.

"Come back here," he shouted.

Mary was powerless to disobey. She stood before him trembling. He just stared at her with hard black eyes and sucked at his fag end. He put out a podgy hand, grabbed her shoulder, pushed her head sideways, then said, "You good girl, obey me. I look after you. You bad girl. . ." He didn't finish the sentence, just curled his lips and held a threatening fist up to Mary's face.

He said to Gloria, "Take her," then he walked out.

*

The old building consisted of the shop and back yard, two rooms in the basement, and about eight rooms on the upper storeys. All the rooms were divided into three or four small cubicles by thin boarding. In each cubicle was a narrow bed, or, in some, as many as four to six bunk beds. All the beds were filthy, grey, ex-army blankets the only cover.

Mary was taken upstairs, past the gold and silver room where she had spent the night with Zakir, to the top of the house. In the attic were about twenty girls, lying on the floor or on bunk beds. Most were asleep.

Gloria said, "You stop here. We'll want you later."

Mary sat down on the floor in a corner. She had known nothing but poverty all her life, and, since her Dublin days, had slept only in makeshift slum dwellings or outdoors, so she was not surprised or dismayed. It was hot in the attic, and she soon fell asleep.

She was woken at about 2 p.m. by movement. Most of the girls were going out. She stood up, but was told to stay where she was. She remained in the hot attic all afternoon accompanied by the heavy snores of the girl she had seen dancing on the table. She had had no food or drink, and spent the afternoon dreaming of Zakir.

In the early evening, the girl woke up. She was called Dolores, and was about twenty; a cheerful buxom wench who had been a prostitute since childhood. She knew no other life, and could not imagine any other way of earning a living. She sat up sleepily, and saw Mary, "You new?" she enquired.

Mary nodded.

"Poor little thing," she said. "Never mind, you'll get used to the game. It's all right when you get used to it. What you need is a gimmick, like me. I'm a stripper. But not one of your regular strippers. I'm an *artiste*." She said the word artiste with great pride.

"Come on, we'd better go down to the café before Gloria comes up. You need a clean blouse, here, have one of mine. And you need a bit of make up. I'll do it for you."

She chatted all the time as she dressed, doing her hair and Mary's, and making them both up. Mary liked her. Her buoyant cheerfulness was infectious.

"There now, you look lovely."

In fact, Mary looked grotesque, but she couldn't see it. The sight of her painted face in the mirror thrilled her.

"Will Zakir be there tonight?" she said.

"Yes, you'll be seeing him, don't worry."

Mary was overjoyed, and followed Dolores into the café for the evening's entertainment.

They went to the large table, where a number of girls already sat. Zakir was at the corner table, and Mary's heart leapt. She took a step towards him, but he waved her away without speaking, and she sat down sadly with the other girls. They were not talking much, and they all stared at her. One or two gave a thin smile, others openly scowled. One rough, dirty-looking girl said, "Look at her. Zakir's latest. Who does she think she is. We'll soon cut her down. You'll see, Mary, Mary, quite contrary."

Mary told me that she hadn't really liked it, and wanted to leave.

"Well, why didn't you?" I asked.

"Because Zakir was sitting in the corner, and nothing in the world could have dragged me away from him."

I supposed that was how he got and kept most of his girls.

I said, "If you had known what kind of life he was dragging you into, would you have left?"

She thought, and said: "I don't think so, at first. It was not until I saw him bring in several other young girls, and sit at the corner table with them, that I began to understand what he meant when he said he was 'the meat buyer'. I wanted to run over to the girl and warn her, but I couldn't, and anyway, it would have done no good."

That night Mary had her first clients. She was auctioned as a virgin, and the highest bidder got her first, with eight others following after. The next day Zakir put his arm around her, and told her that he was very pleased with her. He flashed his smile at her and her heart melted.

She lived off this smile, and the others he condescended to give her, for months.

For the first week, the clients were arranged for her from the men who came to the café, and they paid Uncle. She hated it, and found the men revolting, but as Dolores and many of the others said, "You get used to it."

When she was pushed out on to the street, and told to find her own clients, the real horror began.

"I had to bring back one pound each day," she said. "If I didn't, Uncle would hit me in the face, or knock me down and kick me. At first I asked for two shillings [10p] but there were so many other girls on the game, asking sixpence or one shilling, that I had to cut my price too. Sometimes I would bring the men back to the café, but sometimes we just did it in alleyways or doorways, up against a wall, anywhere – even the bomb sites. I hated myself. There were dreadful fights between girls about whose pitch was whose, and fights between the men. If a girl tried to go to another protector, she might get her throat cut. You just don't know the dreadful things that go on."

"I was out all the time. I got some sleep in the mornings, but I had to go out every afternoon until about five or six the next morning. I hardly got any food, except some chips at the café, if I was lucky. I hated it, but I couldn't seem to stop. I'm filthy, I'm bad, I'm . . . "

I cut her short, not wanting her to dwell on self-reproval: "Well, you left in the end. What made you do that?"

"The baby," she said quietly, "and Nelly. I liked Nelly," she continued. "She was the only girl who was always kind to all the other girls. She never quarrelled and was never spiteful. She came from an orphanage in Glasgow and never knew who her father and mother were, nor if she had any brothers and sisters. She was always lonely, I think, because deep down inside, she was always looking for someone who belonged to her. She was two years older than me."

Then Mary told me the terrible truth.

"Gloria found out that Nelly was expecting a baby. It had happened before, other girls had fallen pregnant, but I hadn't been involved, because I wasn't friends with them. Gloria made arrangements, and a woman came in. I don't know who she was, but the girls said she always did it. It was a morning, and I was asleep after my night out. I heard terrible screaming, and I knew at once that it was Nelly's voice. I ran downstairs and found her in a little room. She was lying on a bed screaming, and Gloria and two other girls were holding her legs open while this woman stuck what looked like steel knitting needles inside her. I rushed in and took Nelly in my arms, and told them to stop, but of course they wouldn't. I couldn't stop the pain for Nelly, either, so I just held her tight in my arms."

I asked Mary to tell me more about Nelly.

"It was dreadful. The woman went on and on poking and scraping. Then suddenly there was blood everywhere. All over the bed, and the floor, and the woman. She said, 'That's all she needs. Just keep her in bed for a few days. She'll be all right.' They cleaned up, and threw the mess into the bomb site, while I stayed with Nelly. She was dead white, and still in dreadful pain. I didn't know what to do, so I just stayed with her, and gave her water, and tried to make her comfortable. Gloria looked in sometimes, and told me to sit with her, and not to go out that night."

Mary started to cry.

"Sometimes she knew who I was, sometimes she didn't. She got terribly hot. Her skin was burning up. I wiped her with cold water, but it didn't help. All the time she was bleeding, till the mattress was soaked with blood. I sat with her all day and all night, and the pain never left her. In the early morning, she died in my arms."

She was silent – then said bitterly:

"I don't know what they did with her body. There was no funeral, and no police came. I suppose they just got rid of her, and told no one about it."

I pondered, was it really possible to dispose of a body? If the girl had no relatives or friends, who would enquire about her if she disappeared? The other girls at the café knew her, but it seemed that they all lived in so much fear of Uncle, that they would say nothing. If Gloria or the abortionist were caught, it would probably have meant a charge of murder or at the very least manslaughter, so a web of protection was woven around them. I had little doubt that many other prostitutes had disappeared and no one ever missed them because they were usually homeless, unwanted girls.

A couple of months later, Mary realised that she, too, was pregnant but fear made her conceal the fact. She continued to go out soliciting, even though she was sick most of the time. She told me that she wanted to get away but was too afraid to try. The baby didn't mean anything to her, until she felt it moving inside her, and then a rush of maternal love swept over her. Some time later, as she was dressing in the attic one day, another girl screamed out:

"Look at Mary. There's a bun in the oven."

And then everyone knew.

Mary was frantic, and knew she had to get away. She said, "I didn't mind if they were going to kill me. But they weren't going to kill me baby."

That evening she came in with a customer, and as she went upstairs, she saw that the door of the gold and silver room was open. She told the man to undress in a cubicle, and slipped into the room. There was a lot of money on a table. She grabbed five pounds and ran like mad, out into the street and away.

FLIGHT

Mary ran for her life, and the life of her baby. She hadn't the faintest idea of where she was going, so she just ran, driven by fear. It was night-time, and in her heightened imagination, she thought that someone was pursuing her with every step. She mainly kept to the unlit side streets, because under the lights of the main roads, she thought she would be recognised.

"I turned corner after corner, and hid in doorways, then doubled back and ran down another dark street, always avoiding the lights of the big roads. I spent nearly the whole night running."

In fact, Mary must have run round in circles, because she described the river and the docks and boats, and a church where she rested in the porch, which sounded very like the famous Bow Bells church. She did not get very far. After her sleep in the church porch, the terrors of the night departed, and she thought she would take a bus, to get a long way away, to a place where no one would look for her. It was not until she had actually boarded the platform of a bus and saw the bus conductor clipping tickets and taking one and two penny fares, that she realised her predicament with the five pounds. She could not possibly use it. She leapt off the bus just as it started to move, and fell into the gutter. Several people came over to help her up, but she was so terrified that she brushed them aside, and ran, hiding her face in her hands.

Mary spent the whole day hiding. It did not seem rational. I asked her, "Why did you not go to a police station and claim protection?"

Her reply was interesting.

"I couldn't. I was a thief. They would have locked me up, or taken me back to the café, and made me give the money back to Uncle."

Her terror of Uncle was almost tangible, so she spent the whole day wandering, and hiding from people. She must have headed south again from Bow towards the river as it was in the East India Dock Road that she finally had the idea of asking someone, a lady who did not look as though she could possibly be mixed up in prostitution, to change the five pound note. As I stepped off the bus that evening she had approached me and I had taken her back to Nonnatus House where she had had the first good meal, and the first night's sleep in a secure, warm environment that she had had since leaving the sheelin' back in County Mayo.

It was Sister Julienne who made the arrangements for Mary to go to Church House in Wellclose Square. This house had been set up, and staffed by volunteers as a refuge for prostitutes by Father Joe Williamson.

Father Joe was a saint. Saints come in all sorts of shapes and sizes – they don't have to wear halos. Father Joe was born and bred in the slums of Poplar in the 1890s. Somehow he survived cold, hunger, neglect, and four years at the front during the First World War. He was a rough, tough East End street kid, crude and loud mouthed, yet when he was no more than a child, he had a vision that God was calling him to be a priest. He overcame a lack of proper education, a thick Cockney accent that no one else could understand, the inability to express himself, and class prejudice. He was ordained in the 1920s, and many years later, after serving as a parish priest in Norfolk, returned to the East End, to St Paul's parish in Stepney, right in the heart of the red-light district. He saw at first hand the appalling life these girls led. From then on, he devoted the rest of his life to helping prostitutes who wanted to escape. The Wellclose Trust still exists in the twenty-first century, and is still engaged in the same work.

At Church House Mary was given a bath, clean warm clothes and good food. She was with about six other girls who, with varying degrees of success, were trying to kick the habit of prostitution. Mary was too frightened to go out, but gradually her fears about being found and murdered subsided, colour returned to her pale cheeks, and her Irish eyes began to sparkle.

I visited her several times during this period of calm, because she always seemed to want me to, and also because I wanted to learn more about prostitutes. It was during these visits that I learned the harrowing details of her life in London. I think she was relatively happy during this brief period, but it could not last. For one thing her pregnancy was advancing, and whilst she could receive antenatal care at Church House, they were not equipped to cope with a mother and baby. But more important was the fact that Church House was perilously close to Cable Street and the Full Moon Café. Whilst she did not leave the house there was no danger, but at some stage, she would want to venture out – Church House was not a prison. When she did, the chances of her being recognised, Father Joe speculated, were very real, and Mary's fears of abduction or murder were not a fantasy.

In her eighth month of pregnancy, and still only fifteen years old, she was transferred to a home for mothers and babies run by the Roman Catholic Church. It was in Kent, and I went there once, about a fortnight before the baby was born. Mary was full of excitement and happiness. She enjoyed the company and friendship of the other women and girls, who were not prostitutes, but were from the poorest and most vulnerable sections of society. Many of them had babies, and Mary was able to indulge her instincts in the gentlest and happiest of all feminine activities. The nuns held classes in baby care, and she happily bathed and dressed dolls, and listened to talks on colic, nappy rash and breastfeeding, counting the days until her baby would be born.

The staff at Church House received a postcard the same morning as one arrived for me, telling of the birth of a little girl, Kathleen. I thought one of the nuns must have written it, because I knew that Mary could read a little, but could barely write. However, her name was written in big letters across the bottom, with a row of kisses. I was deeply touched by these straggly X's, about twenty-five of them, and I wondered who else she had communicated her wonderful news to with so many kisses. Her mother? Her brothers and sisters? Did she know where her drunken mother was, or her sisters in the orphanage in Dublin? If a postcard had been sent to the old address as she remembered it, had it been received, or had the family moved on? Did anyone else know? Did anyone else care? Tears came to my eyes as I looked at the row of X's, kisses showered with such lavish affection on someone she had merely picked up at a bus stop.

A few days later, it being my day off, I went to see Mary in Kent, feeling that someone must rejoice with her over this miraculous event. On the journey, I pondered that it might be the making of her. Motherhood brings out the best in most women, and flighty, giddy young girls often become responsible, reliable mothers, as soon as the baby is born. I had not the slightest doubt that she was a sweet and loving young girl, who was too trusting by half. I reflected that it had been her gentle, trusting nature, combined with the poverty and physical hardships of her life, that had led her to prostitution in the first place. There was no doubt that she hated it, and had been virtually a slave. Now she was liberated.

The train jogged along through the countryside, and I felt a quiet wave of satisfaction and pleasure. I had not reflected upon how she was going to support herself and the baby.

I found Mary radiant with happiness. The soft glow of early motherhood emanated from her, and seemed to embrace me with its warmth as I entered the door. Two months' rest, good food and good antenatal care, had worked miracles on her. Gone was the pale, pinched look, gone the nervous hand movements; above all, the fear had disappeared from her eyes. She was completely unconscious of her beauty, which made her all the more appealing. And the baby? Well of course, every baby is the most beautiful in the world, and this little one surpassed all others without even trying! Kathleen was ten days old, and Mary told me all about her excellence: how well she slept, how well she fed, how she gurgled and laughed and kicked. She prattled on joyously, totally absorbed by her own all-consuming love. I left thinking that this was the best thing that could possibly have happened to her, and that a new life was opening up for Mary.

★

A fortnight or so later a postcard arrived:

NERS JENY
NONATUN HOSE
POPLER LUNDUN

It is a tribute to our postal service that it arrived at all, for, apart from the address, it had no stamp. On the back was scrawled:

BABY GON. CUM TOO SEE MEE. MARY XXXXXX.

I showed the card to Sister Julienne, feeling concerned.

"Does GON mean gone? If so where? Surely it cannot mean the baby has died?" I asked.

Sister turned the card over in her hand several times, before saying: "No, I think if the baby had died, she would have written DED. You had better go to see her on your day off, which is obviously what she wants."

The train journey to Kent seemed longer and more tiresome than the previous one. I had no happy thoughts to make the time fly past. My mind was puzzled, and an unpleasant feeling of foreboding would not go away.

The mother and baby home looked much the same as before, pleasant open grounds, prams dotted about the gardens, smiling young women, nuns going about their work. I entered, and was taken to a sitting room.

I was stunned when I saw Mary. She looked absolutely ghastly: her face was swollen, red and blotchy, with great rings under her eyes. She stared at me, unseeing. Her hair was dishevelled, her clothes were torn. I stood in the doorway looking at her, but she did not see me; instead she leapt up, rushed to the window, and began to hammer the glass with her fists, moaning all the while. Then she ran to the opposite side of the room and beat her forehead on the wall. It was hard to believe what I was seeing.

I went over to her and said "Mary" quite loudly. I repeated her name several times. She turned, eventually recognising me, and gave a cry. She grabbed me and tried to speak, but words wouldn't come.

I led her to a sofa, and sat her down.

"What is it?" I asked "What has happened?"

"They have taken my baby."

"Where?"

"I don't know. They won't tell me."

"When?"

"I don't know. But she's gone. She wasn't there in the morning."

I didn't know what to say. What can one say to such terrible news? We stared at one another in mute horror, then she winced with pain, a pain that seemed to suffuse her entire body. She threw her arms outwards and fell back against the cushions. I saw at once what the trouble was. She had been breastfeeding, and now, with no milk being drawn off, her breasts were horribly engorged. I leaned forward and opened her blouse. Both breasts were enormous, as hard as stone, and the left side was bright red and hot to touch. 'She could get a breast abscess,' I thought. 'In fact she probably has one already.'

She moaned: "It hurts," and gritted her teeth together to stop herself from screaming.

My mind was in turmoil. What on earth had happened? I couldn't believe that Mary's baby had been taken away. When the worst spasm of pain had passed, I said, "I am going to see the Reverend Mother."

She grasped my hand. "Oh yes, I knew you would get my baby back."

She smiled, and as she did so, tears flooded her eyes, and she turned her head into the cushion, sobbing pitifully.

I left, and enquired my way to the Reverend Mother's office.

The room was bare and sparsely furnished: a desk, two wooden chairs, and a cupboard. The walls were white, and only a bare crucifix broke the smooth surface. The Reverend Mother's habit was entirely black, with a white veil. She looked middle-aged, and very handsome. Her expression was serene and open. I felt at once that I could talk to her.

"Where is Mary's baby?" I demanded aggressively.

The Reverend Mother looked at me steadily, before replying, "The baby has been placed for adoption."

"Without the mother's consent?"

"Consent is not necessary. The child is only fourteen."

"Fifteen," I said.

"Fourteen or fifteen, it makes no difference. She is still legally a child, and consent is neither valid nor invalid."

"But how dare you take her baby away without her knowledge. It is killing her."

The Reverend Mother sighed. She sat perfectly straight, not resting against the back of the chair, her hands folded beneath her scapular. She looked timeless, ageless, pitiless. Only the cross on her breast moved to the rhythm of her breathing. She said evenly, "The baby is being adopted into a good Roman Catholic family who have one child. The mother, due to an illness, can have no more. Mary's baby will have a good upbringing and a good education. She will have all the advantages of a good Christian home."

"Good Christian home be bothered," I said, my anger rising. "Nothing can replace a mother's love, and Mary loves her baby. She will die, or go mad, from the grief."

The Reverend Mother sat for a moment, quietly looking at the branch of a tree that was moving just outside the window. Then she turned her head slowly, and looked straight into my eyes. This slow, deliberate movement of her head, first towards the window, and then back towards me, helped to check my anger. Her face was sad. Perhaps she is not pitiless, I thought.

"We have done all we can to trace Mary's family. We have spent three months searching parish and civil records in Ireland, with no success. Mary's mother is a drunk, and cannot be traced. There are no living uncles or aunts. The father is dead. The younger siblings are in care. If we could have found any relative or guardian who would take Mary and her baby, and pledge responsibility for them, there is no doubt at all that she would have been able to keep her baby. However, we could find no one. In the wider interests of the baby, the decision was taken for adoption."

"But it will kill Mary," I said.

The Reverend Mother did not answer this, but said: "How can a girl of fifteen, with no literacy, no home, no trade beyond that of prostitution, support and care for a growing child?"

It was my turn not to answer the question.

"She has left prostitution," I said.

The Reverend Mother sighed again, and paused for quite a long time before speaking. "You are young, my dear, and full of righteous indignation, which our Lord loves. But you must understand that it is very, very rare for a prostitute to leave the trade. It is too easy to make money. A girl is hard up, and the opportunity is always there. Why slave away all day in a factory for five shillings, when you can earn ten or fifteen shillings in half an hour? We know from experience that few things are more damaging to a growing child than to watch mother working on the streets."

"But you cannot condemn her for what she has not yet done."

"No, we do not condemn, nor blame. The Church forgives. In any case, it is quite clear that Mary was more sinned against than sinning. Our main concern is for the protection and upbringing of the baby. Mary has nowhere to go when she leaves here. Who will take her in? We endeavoured to find a residential post in service for Mary to go to, but with a baby no such post could be found."

I was silent. The Reverend Mother's logic was irrefutable. I repeated my earlier point, "But it will kill her. She already looks half mad."

The Reverend Mother sat perfectly still, the leaves fluttering outside the window. She did not speak for about half a minute. Then she said: "We are born into suffering, uncertainty, and death. My mother had fifteen children. Only four survived childhood. Eleven times my mother suffered the agonies that Mary is going through. Countless millions of women throughout history have buried most of the children they have borne, and endured the sorrows of child bereavement. They have lived through it, as Mary will, and they have borne more children, as I hope Mary will."

I could say nothing. Perhaps I should have ranted and railed about the arrogance and presumption of taking the decision out of Mary's control; I could have sneered at the wealth of the Roman Catholic Church; I could have asked why could the Church not support Mary and her baby for a few years? I could, perhaps should, have said many things, but I was silenced by my own knowledge of the statistics of child mortality, by the depth of understanding in her words, and by the sadness in her eyes.

I merely said, "Will Mary ever know who has adopted her baby?"

The Reverend Mother shook her head.

"No. Even I do not know the actual name. None of the Sisters are ever told. The adoption is completely anonymous, but you can assure Mary that her baby has gone to a good Catholic family, and that she will have a good home."

There was nothing more to be said, and the Reverend Mother rose from her seat. This was the signal that the interview was over. She withdrew her right hand from behind her scapular and held it out to me. Long, slender, sensitive fingers. It is not often that you see such a beautiful hand, and as I took it, her grasp was firm and warm. Our eyes met, with sadness and, I think, mutual respect.

I returned to the sitting room. Mary leapt from the sofa as I entered, her face alight with expectancy. But she read my features in an instant and, with a cry of despair, she fell back on to the sofa and buried her head in the cushions again. I sat beside her, trying to console her, but consolation was impossible. I told her the baby would go to a good home, where she would be well looked after. I tried to tell her how impossible it would be for her to work, and live, and support a growing child. I don't think she heard or understood anything I said. Her face remained hidden in the cushions. I told her I had to leave soon, but she did not respond at all. I tried to stroke her hair, but she pushed my hand away angrily. I crept out of the room, and shut the door quietly, too sad even to say goodbye.

I did not see Mary again. I wrote to her once, but received no reply. A month later, I wrote to Reverend Mother, enquiring, and was informed that Mary had accepted a residential post as a ward maid in a hospital in Birmingham. I wrote to her there but again, no reply.

Circumstances bring people together, and take them apart. One cannot keep up with everyone in a lifetime. In any event, was there any true friendship between myself and Mary? Probably not. It was mainly a friendship of dependence on her part, with pity and (I'm almost ashamed to confess it) curiosity, on my part. I was intrigued to find out more about the hidden world of prostitution. That is no basis for a meeting of minds, and true affection, so I let the contact drop.

Some years later – by which time I was very happily married with two children – front page headlines in all the papers carried the story that a baby had been snatched from a pram in a suburb of Manchester. Desperate and tearful parents were interviewed on television, begging for the return of their baby. A nationwide police hunt was launched, and sightings of the possible kidnapper were reported from all over the country. All of them proved to be red herrings. Twelve days passed, and the story receded from public attention.

On the fourteenth day, I read that a woman had been apprehended in Liverpool, boarding a boat for Ireland. She was carrying a six-week-old baby, and was being held for questioning. A few days later, a larger report carried the story that the woman questioned had been charged with the unlawful abduction of a baby two weeks earlier. The photograph was of Mary.

She was held in custody for five months awaiting trial. During all that time, I wondered if I should go to see her, but did not do so. Part of my hesitation was because I wondered what on earth we would talk about, but also, with two children under three, a home to care for, and a part-time night sister's post, a trip to Liverpool and back – to what end? – was an intimidating prospect.

I followed the trial in the newspapers. Mitigating circumstances of the loss of her own baby were raised. Her counsel emphasised the fact that the baby had been well cared for, and stressed that no harm was intended. But the prosecution dwelt upon the suffering of the parents and the vagrant, unstable life that Mary had always led. Twenty-six other offences of soliciting and petty larceny were taken into consideration.

The jury found Mary guilty, with a plea for mercy. Nonetheless, the judge sent her down for three years, with a recommendation that psychiatric treatment should be given whilst the prisoner was in Her Majesty's custody.

Mary commenced her sentence in Manchester Prison for Women in her twenty-first year.

SISTER EVANGELINA

Due to a broken shoulder I was unable to take the final midwifery exam, and had to wait several months for the next sitting. Sister Julienne suggested I might join the General District practice for added experience. Thus, I had the privilege of working with old people who had been born in the nineteenth century.

Sister Evangelina was in charge of General District nursing. Whilst I was eager to undertake the nursing, I was not at all keen to work with Sister Evangelina, whom I found ponderous and humourless. Also, she gave me to understand, subtly but unmistakably, that she did not at all approve of me. She was constantly finding fault: a door banged; a window left open; untidiness; day-dreaming ("wool-gathering" she called it); boisterousness; singing in the clinical room; forgetfulness, the list was endless. I could do nothing right for Sister Evangelina. When Sister Julienne informed her that I was to work with her, she stared at me, her heavy features set in a dour expression, then said "Humph!" and turned and stomped away. Not a word more!

We worked together for several months and, whilst I never grew close to her, I certainly grew to understand her better, and to realise that all nuns, by the very fact of their monastic profession, are exceptional people. No ordinary woman could live such a life. There must inevitably be something, or many things, that are oustanding about a nun.

To me, Sister Evangelina looked about forty-five; an unimaginable age when you are twenty-three. But nuns always look years younger than they really are, and she had, in fact, been a nurse in the First World War, so therefore must have been over sixty at the time of which I am writing.

The first morning did not start well. The clinical room boiler had gone out, and her instruments and syringes were therefore not sterile. She called loudly and crossly to Fred to come and attend to it, and grumbled about "that useless man" as he whistled his tuneless way downstairs with his shovels and rakes and pokers. She ordered me to "go to the kitchen, and boil these things up on the gas stove, whilst I sort out the dressings, and look sharp about it". On the way to the door, a glass syringe fell out of the overflowing kidney dish and broke on the stone floor. She shouted at me about carelessness and clumsiness and what she has to put up with these days. When she got to the bit about "flighty young girls" I fled, leaving the broken glass behind me. In the kitchen, Mrs B. was at the gas stove with half a dozen saucepans boiling away merrily, and she did not receive me amicably. Consequently it took quite a long time to sterilise the things, and I could hear Sister Evangelina shouting before I had even left the kitchen. She took the equipment from me to pack the bags, commenting on my "dawdling around, and wool-gathering, as usual, and didn't I realise we had twenty-three insulin injections, and four sterile dressings, and two leg ulcers, and three post-operative hernias, as well as two catheterisations, two bed-baths and three enemas to get through before lunch?".

All the midwives had gone, and we were the last to leave that morning. The bicycle shed was nearly empty. Sister Evangelina's favourite bicycle had been taken, inadvertently, by someone else. Her nose grew red, her eyes bulged, and she muttered under her breath about how she "didn't like this one, and that old Triumph was too small, and the Sunbeam was too high", and she supposed she would have to make do with the Raleigh, but it wasn't the one she liked.

Respectfully, I pulled the Raleigh out for her, fixed the black bag on the back, and watched the tyres sag as her large, heavy body clambered onto it. I think I realised then that she was not in her forties. Her square, bulky frame had no agility, and it was only by sheer determination and will power that she got herself pedalling at all.

Once out on the road her mood seemed to lighten, and she turned to me with something that resembled a smile. Along the streets numerous voices called out "Mornin', Sister Evie." She smiled brightly – I hadn't seen her smile like that before – and called gaily back. Once she tried a wave, but the bike wobbled perilously, so she didn't try again. I began to think that she was popular and well known in the area.

In the houses she was bluff and gruff, and not at all polite (I thought), but nonetheless everyone seemed to take it in good part.

"Now then, Mr Thomas, have you got your sample ready? Don't keep me waiting; I've got to test it, and I haven't all day to hang around waiting for you. Right, hold still for the injection. Hold still, I said. Now, I'm off. If you start eating sweets, they'll kill you. Not that I would care, and I dare say your missus would be glad to see the back of you, but the dog would miss you."

I was shocked. This was no way to talk to patients, according to the nursing textbooks. But the old man and his missus roared with laughter, and he said: "If I goes first, I'll keep a place warm for yer, eh, Sis Evie? An' we can share the ol' toasting fork."

I thought she would be furious at such effrontery, but she stomped downstairs in good humour, with "Out of my way, boy" to a child we met in the passage.

Her good humour, and her rough badinage with all the patients, continued throughout the morning. I ceased to be startled, because I realised that this was what the patients liked about her. She approached them all without a trace of sentimentality or condescension. The older Docklanders were accustomed to meeting middle-class do-gooders, who deigned to act graciously to inferiors. The Cockneys despised these people, used them for what they could get, and made fun of them behind their backs, but Sister Evangelina had no patronising airs and graces. She would have been incapable of them. Imagination was not her strong point, and she could not have contrived nor invented anything. She was unswervingly honest, and reacted to every person and every situation without guile or affectation.

As the months passed I began to understand why Sister Evangelina was so popular. It was because she was one of them. She was not a Cockney, but had been born into a very poor working-class family from Reading. She never told me this (she hardly ever spoke to me) but, from remarks made to the patients, it became perfectly clear. For example, "These young housewives, they don't know they're born. What! A lavatory in every flat? Remember the old middens, do you, Dad, and the newspaper on the seat, and queueing up in the frost when you're bursting?" This was usually followed by laughter, and some coarse lavatorial humour, ending up with the old chestnut about the chap who fell in a midden and came up with a gold watch. Lavatory humour was not considered vulgar or in bad taste amongst the working class during the early part of the last century, because the natural bodily functions were a conspicuous event. There was no privacy. A dozen or more families shared one midden, which had only half a door, the upper and lower portions being missing. So everyone knew who was in it, could hear everything and, above all, could smell everything. "She's a stinker" was not a moral observation, but a statement of fact.

Sister Evangelina shared this robust humour. Before an enema: "Now then, Dad, we're going to put a squib up your arse, shake your insides about a bit. Got the jerry ready, Mother, and the clothes pegs to clip on our noses." Laughter would continue about how he hadn't "been" for a fortnight, and there must be a turd inside as big as an elephant's. And no one was the slightest bit embarrassed, least of all the patient.

No, indeed, Sister Evangelina was not humourless. The only trouble was that at Nonnatus House her humour was different from everyone else's. She was surrounded by middle-class values, and the safety-valve of humour, which was common to all the nuns, was perpetually closed to her. She simply couldn't understand their jokes, so she always had to watch to see when everyone else was laughing and then joined in, somewhat half-heartedly.

Equally, her own brand of humour would definitely not have been appreciated in the convent. In fact it would have been greeted with severe disapprobation. Perhaps she had tried in the past, and been required by the Reverend Mother to do penance for loose or unguarded speech, so the young novice had simply buttoned herself up, and outwardly appeared solemn and heavily serious. It was only with her patients in the docklands that she could truly be herself.

Even her speech slipped from the middle-class pronunciation that she had acquired over the years into an approximation of the Cockney dialect. She never spoke broad Cockney – that would have been an affectation of which she was incapable – but certain phrases and idioms came naturally to her. She would talk freely about "Mystic Spec", which puzzled me greatly, until I discovered it was Cockney slang for Mist. Expect., "Mist." being medical Latin, short for "mixture", and "expect.", short for "expectorant". This meant Ipecacuanha, which could be bought at any chemist's, and was the sovereign remedy for just about everything. She also talked about "pew-monica" for pneumonia, and "the screws" for rheumatism, "Uncle Dick" for a bit sick, or "a touch of the inkey blue", meaning flu. She had a variety of expressions for an intestinal disorder – the runs, the squitters, the gripes, the cramps, the needles – all of which were greeted with howls of laughter. She obviously understood a lot of Cockney rhyming slang, although she did not use it much. Having said that, I remember being flummoxed when she told me to get her "weasel", and just stared at her, not daring to ask what she meant. Someone else fetched her coat.

She shared the older people's fear of hospitals, a fear which was widely expressed through scorn and derision. Most hospitals in England, even in the 1950s, were converted workhouses, so the buildings alone had an aura of degradation and death for people who had lived all their lives with the terror of being sent to the workhouse. Sister Evangelina did nothing to dispel this fear of hospitals; in fact she actively encouraged it, an attitude that would have been heavily censored by the Royal College of Nursing, had they known about it. She would say things like, "You don't want to go into hospital to be messed about by a lot of students", or "They only make out they treat the poor for the benefit of the rich", both statements implying that the hospitals liked to experiment on their poor patients. She proclaimed, from experience, that women who went into hospital with complications after a back-street abortion were deliberately given a rough time. That Sister Evangelina was incapable of inventing, or even exaggerating, anything, spoke to the truth of her statement. Whether or not such treatment was widespread in England in the early part of this century I am unable to say. However, in the mid 1950s, I had witnessed the appalling truth of her remark in a Paris hospital, an experience I have been unable to forget to this day.

Sister Evangelina had plenty of homespun advice to offer her patients: "Where-ere you be, let your wind go free", to which the reply was always chanted: "In Church and Chapel let it rattle". Once an old man followed this by "Oops! sorry, Sister, no disrespect", and she replied, "None taken – I'm sure the Rector does it an' all." Constipation, diarrhoea, leeks and greens, gripes and pipes, flutes and fluffs provided more hilarity than any other subject, and Sister Evangelina was always in the thick of it. After recovering from my initial shock, I realised that it was not considered to be vulgar or obscene. If the Kings of France had been able to defecate daily before his entire Court, so could the Cockneys! On the other hand, sexual obscenities and blasphemy were strictly taboo in respectable Poplar families, and sexual morality was expected and enforced.

But I digress. Sister Evangelina interested me greatly because of her background: the slums of Reading in the nineteenth century, and the fact that she had raised herself from abject poverty and semi-literacy to become a trained nurse and midwife. It would have been hard enough for a young man, but for a girl to break free from ignorance and poverty and become accepted in a middle-class profession was exceptional. Only a very strong character could have achieved it.

I discovered that the First World War had been her key to freedom. She was sixteen when war broke out, and had been working in the Huntley and Palmer's Biscuit Factory in Reading since the age of eleven. In 1914, posters appeared all over the town calling on people to join the war effort. She hated Huntley and Palmer's and with youthful optimism decided that a munitions factory could only be an improvement. She had to leave home as the factory was seven miles away – too far to walk when working hours were from 6 a.m. to 8 p.m. Accommodation was provided for the girls and women in dormitories that slept sixty or seventy females on narrow iron bedsteads with horsehair mattresses. The young Evie had never slept in a bed all by herself before, and thought this really must be an example of superior living. A uniform and shoes were provided for the workers, and as she had only worn rags and no shoes before, this was also a real luxury, even though the shoes hurt her poor young feet. Food from the factory kitchens, though plain and meagre, was better than anything she had ever had, and she lost the pale, pinched, half-starved look. She became, not a beauty, but passably pretty.

At the factory bench, where she stood all day putting nuts into military machinery, a girl talked about her sister who was a nurse, and told stories about the young men who were wounded, diseased and dying. Something stirred in young Evie's soul, and she knew that she must become a nurse. She found out where the girl's sister worked, and applied to the Matron. She was only sixteen, but was accepted as a VAD, which really meant, for a girl of her class, a skivvy in the hospital wards. She didn't mind. It was the sort of menial work she had been doing all her life, with no promise of anything else. But this time the horizons were broader and clearer. She watched the trained nurses with admiration, and decided that, however long it took, she would be one of them.

Sister Evangelina and her ageing Poplar patients spoke frequently about the First World War, and shared memories and experiences. It was from these conversations overheard during a bed bath or a surgical dressing that I was able to piece together her history. Occasionally she would speak to me directly, or answer a question, but not very often. She never unbuttoned with me much.

She spoke only once about her soldier patients. She said, "They were so young, so very young. A whole generation of young men died, leaving a whole generation of young women to weep." I looked across the bed at her – she did not know I was looking – and saw tears gathering in the corners of her eyes. She sniffed loudly, and stamped her foot, then continued bandaging up the dressing somewhat roughly, with: "There you are, Dad, that's that. We'll see you in three days. Keep 'em open," and stomped off.

She was twenty when she volunteered to go behind enemy lines. She and a patient were talking about the air force of those days, the tiny bi-planes, only invented about twenty years previously. She said, "It was after the German spring offensive in 1918. Our men were wounded, stranded behind the line with no medical help. None could be sent to them by road, so an airlift was arranged. I parachuted down."

The patient said, "You've got guts, Sister. Didn't you know that 50 per cent of all those early parachutes never opened at all?"

"Of course I knew," she said, bluntly. "It was all explained to us. No one was pressed. I volunteered."

I looked at her with new eyes. To volunteer to jump from an aeroplane, knowing full well that there was a 50 per cent chance of it being your last step, would take more than guts. It would take an inner heroism of a rare quality.

One day we were returning from the Isle of Dogs to Poplar. West Ferry Road, Manchester Road, and Preston Road were, as they are today, a continuous thoroughfare following the course of the Thames. In those days, however, the road was cut by bridges in several places. This allowed the cargo boats to enter the docks, which were a mass of canals and berths and basins and jetties. Just as we approached the Preston Road Bridge, the traffic lights turned red, the gates closed, and the swing bridge rotated. This could mean as much as half an hour's closure of the road. Sister Evangelina cursed and fumed under her breath. (That was another thing, incidentally, that the Poplar people liked about her; she was not too holy to swear quietly to herself!) An alternative was open to us: we could retrace our steps, and cycle all the way round the Isle of Dogs to rejoin the West India Dock Road in the Limehouse area, a distance of about seven miles. Sister Evangelina would have none of that. Pushing her bike, she strode purposefully through the NO ENTRY, KEEP OUT gate, past DANGER signs, over the cobbles to the water's edge. Fascinated, I followed; what on earth was she up to? She stomped over towards the massed barges, calling to any dockers in sight to come and help us. Several came forward, grinning and pulling off their caps. One of them was known to her.

"Morning, Harry. How's your mother? I hope her chilblains have cleared up now the weather's better. Give her my regards. Take this bike, will you, there's a good lad, and lend us a hand."

Pulling her long skirts up and tucking them into her belt, she strode towards the nearest barge. "Give me your arm, lad," she said to a huge man of about forty. Grabbing him, she cocked up a leg, giving us a glimpse of thick black stockings and long bloomers elasticated just above the knees, and stepped on to the nearest barge. I realised what she was going to do: she was planning to cross the water as the dockers did, by jumping from barge to barge until she reached the other side.

There were eight or nine moored barges to be traversed in that way. The men, bless them, gathered round. Across the deck of the first barge there was no trouble. But then there were the two adjoining sides of the boats to be clambered over, before she could reach the second deck, and the barges were moving. It took all the strength of the big man, and two or three others besides, to get her over. I heard "gi's a leg up, there's a good lad" and "heave" and "hold me" and "push" and "good for you, Sis". I followed nimbly enough, and couldn't take my eyes off this game old nun, her veil blowing in the wind, rosary and crucifix swinging wildly from side to side, her nose growing redder with the exertion. Two men carried the bicycles, high above their heads, and she turned round and reprimanded them sharply: "Just you look after our bags. This is no laughing matter."

The second and third barges were traversed without mishap, but there was a gap of about eighteen inches before the fourth one. She looked at the water between and said "humph". She pulled her skirts even higher, rubbed a dewdrop off her nose with the flat of her hand, and said to the big man: "You go over there first and be ready to catch me." Three young men got hold of her – she was no lightweight – and she stepped up on to the side. She stood on the narrow edge of the moving barge, her two flat feet firmly planted, and looked resolutely at the big man on the other side. She was panting. She sniffed again loudly, and said: "Right, if I can put my weight on your shoulders, I'll be OK." He nodded, and raised his arms. Gingerly she leaned forward and placed her hands on his shoulders, and he caught her under the arms while the younger men steadied her from behind. My heart was in my mouth. If the barge moved at that moment, or if she slipped, there would have been nothing anyone could have done to prevent her from falling into the water. Could she swim? What if she went under the barge? It didn't bear thinking about. Slowly, carefully, she lifted one foot, brought it forward, and put it on the edge of the next barge. She waited a second, gaining her balance, and then swiftly brought the other leg over, and jumped into the arms of the big man. Cheers went up all round, and I nearly collapsed with relief. She sniffed again.

"Well, that wasn't too bad. No worse than a fart in a colander. Let's carry on." The remaining barges all adjoined each other, and she reached the other side, red faced and triumphant. She pulled her skirts down, took her bicycle, smiled at them all, and said, "Thanks, lads, you've been great. We'll be off now." And with her usual parting comment to dockers, "Keep 'em open and you won't need a doctor," she cycled out of the harbour.

MRS JENKINS

Mrs Jenkins was an enigmatic figure. For years she had been tramping all over the Docklands, from Bow to Cubitt Town, from Stepney to Blackwall, yet no one knew anything about her. The reason for her ceaseless tramping was an obsession with babies, specifically newborn babies. She seemed to know, God knows how, just when and where a home confinement would take place, and nine times out of ten would be found hanging around in the street outside the house. She never said much, and her enquiries about "'Ow's ve baby? Ow's ve li'le one?" were invariably the same. On being told the baby was alive and healthy, she often seemed satisfied and shuffled away. She was always seen on a Tuesday afternoon hanging around outside the antenatal clinic, and most of the young mothers brushed past her impatiently, or pulled their young toddlers away from her, as though she were contaminated or would put an evil spell on the child. We had all heard the muttered comments, "She's an ol' witch, she is, she gives the evil eye," and no doubt some of the mothers believed it.

Mrs Jenkins was never welcome, never wanted, often feared, yet this did not deter her from going out, at any time of the day or night, often in atrocious weather, to stand in the street outside the house where a baby was born, asking "Ow's ve baby? Ow's ve li'l one, ven?"

She was a tiny woman, as thin as a rake, with birdlike features, and a long pointed nose that stretched sharply between hollow sunken cheeks. Her skin was a yellowish grey, criss-crossed with a thousand wrinkles, and she appeared to have no lips because they were drawn in over her toothless gums, and she chewed and sucked them all the time. A faded black hat, greasy and shapeless, was pulled down low over her head, from which tufts of wispy grey hair escaped now and then. Summer and winter she wore the same long grey coat of indeterminate age, from beneath which protruded enormous feet. For such a tiny woman the huge feet were not only improbable, but absurd, and I am sure she received much ridicule as she shuffled her endless way around the neighbourhood.

Where she lived, no one knew. This was as much a mystery to the Sisters as it was to everyone else. The clergy had no idea. She didn't appear to go to church or belong to any parish, which was unusual among the older women. The doctors did not know, as she did not seem to be registered with any doctor. Perhaps she did not know that there was now a National Health Service and that everyone could have medical treatment free of charge. Even Mrs B., who always had her ear close to the ground as far as local gossip and information were concerned, didn't know anything about her. No one had ever seen her going into a Post Office to collect her pension.

I had always found her interesting but repugnant. My contact with her was frequent, but was always confined to her questions about the baby, and my cold reply, "Mother and baby are well", to which she invariably replied "Fank Gaud, fank Gaud fer vat." I never tried to initiate conversation, because I didn't want to get involved, but once when I was with Sister Julienne, she went straight up to the woman, took both her hands in her own and, with her all-embracing smile, said, "Hello Mrs Jenkins, how nice to see you. What a lovely day it is. How are you getting on?"

Mrs Jenkins shrank back, a half-afraid, half-suspicious look in her dull grey eyes, and pulled her hands away.

"Ow's ve baby?" she said. Her voice was rasping.

"The baby's lovely. A beautiful little girl, strong and healthy. Do you like babies, Mrs Jenkins?"

Mrs Jenkins shrank away still further, and pulled the collar of her coat up over her chin.

"A baby girl, yer say, doin' nicely. Fank Gaud."

"Yes, thank God indeed. Would you like to see her? I'm sure I could get the mother's permission and bring the baby out for a few moments."

But Mrs Jenkins had already turned, and was hobbling away in her large, man-size boots.

An expression of infinite love and compassion spread over Sister Julienne's face. She stood quite still for several minutes, watching the bent old figure shuffling along the pavement. I watched Mrs Jenkins too, and noticed that she shuffled because she hadn't the strength to lift the boots off the ground. Then I looked again at Sister Julienne, and felt ashamed. Sister wasn't looking at the boots. She was looking, I felt, at seventy years of pain and suffering and endurance, and holding Mrs Jenkins before God in her silent prayers.

I had always been repelled by Mrs Jenkins, mainly because she was so dirty. Her hands and fingernails were filthy, and the only reason I spoke to her, reporting on the baby just born, was to avoid her grabbing my arm, which she would do with surprising strength if her questions were not answered. It was easier to answer briefly, and at a safe distance, and then to escape.

On one occasion while I was on my rounds, I saw Mrs Jenkins step off the pavement into the road. She stood with legs wide apart, and peed into the gutter like a horse. There were a lot of people around at the time, and none of them looked surprised as a torrent of urine streamed into the gutter and down the drain. Once I saw her in a little alley between two buildings. She picked up a piece of newspaper from the ground, then lifted up her coat and started rubbing the newspaper around her private parts, intent on her task, grunting all the while. Then she let the coat fall and started examining the contents of the newspaper, poking it with her fingernail, sniffing it, peering at it closely. Finally she folded it up and put it in her pocket. I shuddered with revulsion.

Another unpleasant thing about Mrs Jenkins was a brown stain on her face that extended from her nose to her upper lip, and was ingrained in the lines at the corners of her mouth. Having seen and observed her lavatorial habits, it is not hard to imagine what I assumed this brown stain to be. But I was wrong. As I got to know her better, I discovered that Mrs Jenkins took snuff (her "comfort", she called it) and the brown stain was caused by the snuff dropping out of her nose.

Not surprisingly, shopkeepers would not serve her. One greengrocer told me he would serve her outside the shop, but wouldn't allow her in.

"She picks over all me fruit. She squeezes me plums an' me tomatoes, then puts 'em back. Then no one'll buy 'em. I got a business to run, I can't have 'er in 'ere."

Mrs Jenkins was a local "character", known by name only, avoided, feared, ridiculed, but a complete mystery.

The Sisters received a request from a locum doctor in Limehouse to visit a house in the Cable Street area of Stepney. This was the notorious prostitutes' area which I had explored during my brief friendship with Mary, the young Irish girl. The doctor reported that an elderly lady with mild angina was living in appalling conditions, and probably suffering from malnutrition. The patient's name was Mrs Jenkins.

I turned off Commercial Road, heading towards the river, and found the street. Only half a dozen buildings remained standing; the rest were just bomb sites with a jagged wall sticking up here and there. I found the door and knocked. Silence. I turned the door handle, expecting to find it open, but it was locked. I went round the side, which was littered with filth, but a thick layer of dirt covered the windows and I could not see through. A cat rolled sensuously on its back, whilst another sniffed at a pile of garbage. I returned to the front door, and knocked louder several times, feeling glad that it was daylight. This was not the sort of area to be alone in after dark. A window opened in a house opposite, and a female voice called out: "What you want?"

"I'm the district nurse, and I have come to see Mrs Jenkins."

"Throw a stone up a' ve second floor winder," was the advice given.

There were plenty of stones lying around, and I felt a perfect fool standing in nurse's uniform, with my black bag at my feet, throwing stones up at the second floor. "How on earth did the doctor get in?" I wondered.

Eventually, after about twenty stones, some of which missed, the window opened, and a man's voice called out in a thick foreign accent, "You see old woman? I come."

Bolts were pulled back, and the man stood well behind the door as it opened so that I could not see him. He pointed along the passage to a door at the end, saying: "She live there."

Victorian tiles flagged the passageway which passed a staircase with a fine carved oak banister. This was still in beautiful condition, although the stairs were crumbling and looked highly dangerous. I was glad that I did not have to walk up them. The house had obviously been part of a fine old Regency terrace once, but was now in the last stages of decay. It had been classed as "unfit for human habitation" twenty years previously, yet people were still living there, hidden away amongst the rats.

No sound came when I rapped on the door, so I turned the handle and walked in. The room had been the back scullery and wash house of the premises. It was a single storey extension with a stone-flagged floor. A large copper boiler was attached to an outside wall, and next to it was a coke stove with an asbestos flue running up the wall and out of the ceiling through a huge and jagged hole open to the sky. A large wood and iron framed mangle and a stone sink were the only other objects that caught my eye. The room appeared empty and abandoned and smelled powerfully of cats and urine. It was very dark, because the windows were so black with dirt that no light could penetrate. In fact, most of the light in the room came from the hole in the roof.

As my eyes became accustomed to the gloom I discerned a few other things: several saucers lying around on the floor with bits of food and milk in them; a small wooden chair and table with a tin mug and teapot on it; a chamber pot; a wooden cupboard with no door. There was no bed, no sign of a light, nor of gas or electricity.

In the corner furthest away from the hole in the ceiling was a decrepit-looking armchair in which an old woman sat, silent, watchful, her eyes filled with fear. She shrank back in the chair as far as she could go, her old coat pulled tight round her, a woollen scarf over her head and covering half her face. Only her eyes showed, and they penetrated mine as our gaze met.

"Mrs Jenkins, the doctor tells us you are not well and need home nursing. I am the district nurse. Can I have a look at you, please?"

She pulled her coat closer round her chin and stared at me silently.

"Doctor says your heart's fluttering a bit. Can I feel your pulse, please?"

I put out my hand to feel her wrist pulse, but she pulled the arm away from me with a terrified intake of breath.

I was nonplussed, and felt a bit helpless. I didn't want to frighten her, but I had a job to do. I went over to the unlit stove to read the notes by the light coming through the ceiling: there had been evidence of a mild attack of angina pectoris when the patient had fallen in the street outside the house, and an unnamed resident had carried her back to her own room. The same man had called a doctor and admitted him. The woman had obviously been in pain, but this seemed to pass fairly quickly. The doctor had been unable to examine the patient, due to her violent resistance, but as her pulse was fairly steady, and her breathing had improved rapidly, the doctor had advised a nursing visit twice a day to monitor the situation, and suggested that the Social Services department might improve the woman's living conditions. Amyl nitrite had been prescribed in the event of another attack. Rest, warmth, and good food were advised.

I tried again to feel Mrs Jenkins' pulse, with the same result. I enquired if she'd had any more pain, and got no reply. I asked if she was comfortable, and again there was no reply. I realised that I was getting nowhere, and would have to report back to Sister Evangelina, who was in charge of general district nursing.

I was not too keen on reporting my total failure to Sister Evangelina because she still seemed to think me a bit of a fool. She called me 'Dolly Daydream', and spoke to me as though I needed to be directed in the most rudimentary points of nursing procedure, even though she knew I had about five years of nurse's training and experience behind me. This, of course, made me nervous, and so I dropped or spilled things, and then she called me "butter-fingers", which made it worse. We did not have to go out together very often, which was a relief, but if I reported, as I would have to, that I could not manage a patient, inevitably she would have to accompany me on the next visit.

Her reaction was predictable. She listened to my report in heavy silence, glancing up at me from time to time from under thick grey eyebrows. When I had finished, she sighed noisily, as though I were the biggest fool ever to carry the black bag.

"This evening I have twenty-one insulin injections, four penicillin, an ear to syringe, bunions to dress, piles to compress, a cannula to drain, and now I suppose I have to show you how to take a pulse?"

I was stung by the injustice. "I know perfectly well how to take a pulse, but the patient wouldn't let me, and I couldn't persuade her."

"Couldn't persuade her! Couldn't persuade her! You young girls can't do anything. Too much bookwork, that's your trouble. Sitting in classrooms all day, filling your heads with a lot of codswallop, and then you can't do a simple thing like taking a pulse."

She gave a contemptuous snort and shook her head, spraying the bead of moisture that balanced on the end of her nose all over her desk and patients' notes that she was writing up. She drew a large man's handkerchief from beneath her scapular and wiped up the fluid, which caused the ink to smudge, and so she humphed again, "There now, look what you have made me do."

The further injustice made my blood boil, and I had to bite my lips to prevent a sharp reply, which would only have made things worse.

"Well then, Miss Can't-take-a-pulse, I suppose I will have to go with you at 4 p.m. We will make it our first evening visit, after which we can both go our separate ways. We will leave here at 3.30 p.m. sharp, and don't be a minute late. I won't be kept hanging around, and I shall want my supper at seven o' clock as usual."

With that, she pushed her chair back noisily, and stomped out of the office, with another pointed "humph" as she passed me.

Half past three came round all too quickly. We pulled the bicycles out of the shed, and the nun's silence was more eloquent than her grumbling had been. We reached the house without a word, and knocked. Again no reply. I knew what to do, so told Sister about the man on the second floor.

"Well, get hold of him then, don't stand around talking, chatterbox."

I ground my teeth and started throwing stones up at the window in a fury. It was surprising I didn't break the glass.

The man shouted out, "I come", and hid behind the door again as we passed. However, he then added "I come no more. You go round back, see? I not answer no more."

In the dim light of Mrs Jenkins' room a cat came towards us, mewing. The wind made a curious sound as it hit the hole in the roof. Mrs Jenkins was huddled in her chair, just as I had left her in the morning.

Sister Evangelina called her name. No reply. I was beginning to feel justified – she would see that I had not been exaggerating. Sister walked over to the armchair. She spoke gently, "Come on, mother. This won't do. Doctor says there's something up with your ticker. Don't you believe a word of it. Your heart is as good as mine, but we've got to have a look at you. No one's going to hurt you."

The bundle of clothes in the chair didn't move. Sister leaned forward to feel her pulse. The arm was pulled away. I was delighted. "Let's see how Sister Know-all copes," I thought.

"It's cold in here. Haven't you got a fire?"

No reply.

"It's dark, too. What about a light for us?"

No reply.

"When did you first feel bad?"

No reply.

"Do you feel a bit better now?"

Again, total silence. I was feeling very smug; Sister Evangelina appeared as incapable of examining the patient as I had been. What would happen next?

What in fact did happen next was so utterly unexpected that, to this day, more than fifty years later, I blush to remember it.

Sister Evangelina muttered, "You're a tiresome old lady. We'll see what this does."

Slowly she leaned over Mrs Jenkins and as she bent down she let out the most enormous fart. It rumbled on and on and just as I thought it had stopped it started all over again, in a higher key. I had never been so shocked in all my life.

Mrs Jenkins sat upright in her chair. Sister Evangelina called out: "Which way did it go, nurse? Don't let it get out. It's over there by the door – catch it. Now it's by the window – get hold of it, quick."

A throaty chuckle came from the armchair.

"Cor, that's better," said Sister Evangelina happily; "Nothing like a good fart to clear the system. Makes you feel ten years younger, eh, Mother Jenkins?"

The bundle of clothes shook, and the throaty chuckle developed into a real belly laugh. Mrs Jenkins, who had never been heard to speak apart from obsessive questions about babies, laughed until the tears ran down her face.

"Quick! Under the chair. The cat's go' it. Ge' it off him quick, e'll be sick."

Sister Evangelina sat down beside her, and the two old ladies (Sister Evie was no spring chicken) rocked with laughter about farts and bums and turds and stinks and messes, swapping stories, true or false, I couldn't tell. I was deeply shocked. I knew that Sister Evie could be crude, but I had no idea that she possessed such an extensive and varied repertoire of stories.

I retreated to a corner and watched them. They looked like two old hags from a Bruegel painting, one in rags, one in a monastic habit, sharing lewd laughter with the happiness of children. I was completely out of the joke, and had time to ponder many things, not least of which was how on earth Sister Evangelina had been able to produce such a spectacular fart at that precise moment.

Could she command one at will? I had heard of a performer at the Comédie-Francaise, immortalised by Toulouse-Lautrec, who would entertain the Parisian audiences of the 1880s with a rich variety of sounds emitting from his backside, but I had never heard of, still less encountered, anyone who could actually do it. Was Sister Evangelina gifted, or had she acquired the skill through hours of practice? My mind dwelled with pleasure on the possibility. Was it her party piece? I wondered how it would go down at the convent on festive occasions, such as Christmas and Easter. Would the Reverend Mother and her Sisters in Christ be amused by such a singular talent?

The two old girls were so innocently happy that my initial reaction of disapproval seemed to be churlish and mean-spirited. What was wrong with it, anyway? All children laugh endlessly about bottoms and farts. The works of Chaucer, Rabelais, Fielding, and many others are full of lavatorial humour.

There was no doubt about it. Sister Evangelina's action had been brilliant. A masterstroke. To say that a fart cleared the air may seem a contradiction in terms, but life is full of contradictions. From that moment on, Mrs Jenkins lost her fear of us. We were able to examine her, to treat her, to communicate with her. And I was able to learn her tragic history.

ROSIE

"Rosie? Tha' you, Rosie?"

The old lady lifted her head and called out as the front door banged. Footsteps were heard in the passage, but Rosie did not enter the room. Things were happening fast to improve Mrs Jenkins' living conditions. The Social Services had been called, and some cleaning had been carried out. The old armchair had been removed because it was full of fleas, and another donated. A bed had also been provided, but had never been slept in. Mrs Jenkins was so accustomed to sleeping in an armchair that she could not be persuaded to try the bed, so the cats slept on it. Sister Evangelina commented wryly that the new government must have more money than sense to provide Social Services for cats.

The most remarkable change was the repair of the hole in the roof which Sister Evangelina achieved through single-handed combat with the landlord. I was with her when she mounted the rickety stairs to the second floor. I would not have been surprised if they had given way under her considerable weight and warned her accordingly, but she glared at me, and strode up them to put the fear of God into the landlord.

She banged hard on the door several times. It opened a crack, and I heard, "What you want?"

She demanded that he come out and speak with her.

"You go away."

"I will not. If I go away, it will be to set the police on you. Now come out and talk to me."

I heard words like "disgrace", "prosecute", "prison", and whining pleas of poverty and ignorance, but the net result was that the hole in the roof was patched up with a heavy tarpaulin, weighted down with bricks. Mrs Jenkins was delighted, and grinned and giggled with Sister Evie as they shared a cup of strong sweet tea and a piece of Mrs B.'s homemade cake that Sister Evie invariably brought with her when she visited Mrs Jenkins.

A tarpaulin to mend a hole in the roof may seem inadequate, but there was no chance of getting anything better or more durable. The building was condemned for demolition, and the fact that it was still lived in at all was due to the acute housing shortage caused by the bombing of London in the war. People were glad to live anywhere they could find.

The coke stove was usable, but furred up, and Fred, boilerman extraordinaire of Nonnatus House, cleaned and serviced it. Sister Evangelina was determined that Mrs Jenkins should stay in her own home.

"If the Social Services had their way they would put her in an old people's home tomorrow. I'm not having that. It would kill her."

When we first examined Mrs Jenkins we had found her heart to be quite fair. Angina is common amongst the elderly, and with a quiet life, warmth, and rest, it can be kept under control. Her main problems were chronic malnutrition and her mental state. She was clearly a very strange old lady, but was she mad? Would she do any harm to herself or others? We wondered if she needed to see a psychiatrist but we could not tell without assessing her over a period of weeks.

The other problems were dirt, fleas and lice. It was my job to clean her up.

A tin bath was brought from Nonnatus House, and I boiled up water on the coke stove. Mrs Jenkins was dubious about all this, but I only had to mention that Sister Evangelina wanted her to have a bath, and she relaxed and chuckled, champing her jaws.

"She's a good 'un, she is. I tells my Rosie an' all. We 'as a good laugh, we 'as. Rose an' me."

I had quite a job persuading her to undress, and she was very apprehensive. Under the old coat she wore a rough wool skirt and jumper, but no vest or knickers. Her frail little body was pathetic to behold. There was no flesh on her, and all her bones stuck out at sharp angles. Her skin hung loose, and I could count every rib.

The revulsion she had hitherto inspired in me turned to pity when I beheld her frail, skeletal body.

Pity is one thing, shock another. Shock was waiting for me when I took her boots off. I had noticed her huge man-sized boots before, and wondered why she wore them. With difficulty I untied the greasy knots and undid the laces. She wore no socks or stockings, and the boot would not budge. It seemed stuck to her skin. I eased a finger down the side, and she winced. "Leave it be. Leave it."

"I've got to get them off to put you in the bath."

"Leave it," she whimpered; "my Rosie'll do it by an' by."

"But Rosie's not here to help. If you will let me, I can get them off. Sister Evangelina says your boots have got to come off before you have your bath."

It would be a long job, so I wrapped a blanket over her and knelt down on the floor. Some of the skin was indeed stuck to the leather, and tore as I eased the boot back and forth. God knows when they had last come off. Eventually I eased the boot over her heel and pulled. To my horror there was a sort of scratching, metallic sound. What was it? What had I done? As the boot came off, an extraordinary sight met my eyes. Her toenails were about eight to twelve inches long, and up to one inch thick. They were twisted and bent, curling over and under each other, and many of the toes were bleeding and suppurating at the nail-bed. The smell was horrible. Her feet were in a terrible condition. How had she managed to tramp all over Poplar for so many years with feet like that?

She didn't even murmur as I was taking the boots off, though it must have hurt, and she looked down at her bare feet with no surprise – perhaps she thought everyone's toenails were like that. I helped her over to the bath, and it was surprisingly difficult because, without her boots, she had lost her balance and the toenails kept getting in the way, nearly tripping her up.

She stepped over the edge of the big tin bath and sat down in the water with delight, splashing and giggling like a little girl. She picked up the flannel and sucked the water noisily, looking up at me with smiling eyes. The room was warm because I had stoked up the fire, and a cat strolled up and looked curiously over the edge of the bath. She splashed him in the face with a giggle, and he retreated, offended. The front door banged, and she looked up sharply. "Rosie, that you? Come 'ere, girl, an' look a' yer ol' mum. It's a rare sight."

But the footsteps went upstairs, and Rosie didn't come.

I washed Mrs Jenkins all over, and wrapped her in the big towels provided by the Sisters. I had washed her hair and wrapped it in a turban. I had not seen too many fleas, but I applied a sassafras compress to kill any nits. The only thing I could not cope with were her toenails – a good chiropodist would have to be called in for such monsters. (I am reliably informed, incidentally, that Mrs Jenkins' toenails are to this day displayed in a glass case in the main hall of the British Chiropody Association.)

The nuns always kept a store of second-hand clothes, rescued from many jumble sales, and Sister Evangelina and I had sorted out some garments which I had brought with me. Mrs Jenkins looked at the vest and knickers and stroked the soft material with wonder.

"Is this for me? Oh, it's too good. You keep 'em fer yourself, duckie, they're too good for the likes o' me."

I had difficulty in persuading her to put them on, and when she did, she rubbed her hands up and down her thin body with amazement, as though she couldn't get over her new underwear. I dressed her in the jumble-sale clothes, which were all too big, and quietly put her old clothes out the back door.

She settled comfortably in the armchair, stroking her new clothes. A cat jumped on to her knee, and she tickled him gently.

"What'll Rosie say when she sees all this finery, eh, puss? She won' know 'er ol' mum, she won', dressed up like a queen."

I left her with the happy feeling that we were doing a great deal to improve her intolerable conditions. Outside, I put her flea-ridden clothes into a bag, and looked for a dustbin. There were none to be seen. There was no provision for waste disposal in the area because no one was supposed to be living in the condemned buildings, so no public services were provided. The fact that people *were* living there and everyone, including the Council, knew about it, made no difference to official policy. I left the bag of clothes in the street amongst the piles of rubbish already lying around.

A feeling of decay and menace hovered over the whole area like an evil vapour. The craters left by the bombs were filled with rubbish and smelled horrible. Jagged bits of wall, rose starkly towards the sky. No one was around: mornings in a red-light district are generally slow for business. The quietness had an oppressive quality about it, and I would be glad to get away.

I had barely turned the corner of the house when the sound started. I froze to the spot, the hair prickling on the back of my neck as a sort of terror gripped me. It was like the howl of a wolf, or an animal in dreadful pain. The sound seemed to come from everywhere, echoing off the few buildings, and filling the bombsites with an unearthly pain. The noise stopped, but I literally couldn't move. Then it started again, and the window in the house opposite opened. The woman who had told me to throw stones to attract the landlord leaned out, shouting, "It's that mad old hag. Yer lookin' after 'er. Tell 'er to shu' up, or I'll come and kill 'er, I will. You tell 'er from me."

The window banged shut. My mind raced.

Mad old hag? Mrs Jenkins? It couldn't be! She couldn't be making that anguished noise. I'd left her contented and happy only a few minutes ago.

The noise stopped and, trembling, I went back into the house, down the passage to her door and turned the handle.

"Rosie? That you, Rosie?"

I opened the door. Mrs Jenkins was sitting just as I had left her, with a cat on her knee and another preening itself beside her chair. She looked up brightly.

"If you see Rosie, tell 'er I'm coming. Tell 'er not to lose 'eart. Tell 'er I'm comin', an' the li'l ones, an' all. I'll scrub an' scrub all day, an' they'll let me come this time, they will. You tell my Rosie."

I was bewildered. She couldn't have made that howling noise; it was impossible. I took her pulse, which was normal, and enquired if she felt all right, to which she did not reply but smacked her lips together and looked steadily at me.

There seemed no point in my staying, but I left with misgivings that morning.

Sister Evangelina took the morning report, and I told her that Mrs Jenkins seemed to enjoy her bath. I reported on the toenails and the fleas. I reported that her mental condition seemed fairly stable – she loved her new clothes, was chatting companionably to the cats, and was not at all withdrawn and defensive. I hesitated to report the unearthly noise I had heard in the street; after all it might not have come from Mrs Jenkins. It was only the woman opposite who had suggested it had.

Sister Evangelina looked up at me, her heavy features expressionless.

"And?" she said.

"And what?" I faltered.

"And what else? What have you not reported?"

Was she a mind reader? There was clearly no way out. I told her of the ghastly cry I had heard from the street, adding that I couldn't be sure it was Mrs Jenkins.

"No, but you cannot be sure that it was *not* Mrs Jenkins, can you? Describe the cry."

Again I hesitated, as it was so difficult to describe, but I ended by likening it to the howl of a wolf.

Sister looked down at her notes, not moving, and when she spoke her voice was different, subdued and low. "Those who have heard that sound can never forget it. It makes your blood run cold. I think the cry you heard probably did come from Mrs Jenkins, and it was what used to be called 'the workhouse howl'."

"What is that?" I enquired.

She did not reply straight away, but sat tapping her pen with impatience. Then, "Humph. You young girls know nothing of recent history. You've had it too easy, that's your trouble. I will come with you on your next visit, and I will also see if we can get hold of any medical or parish records about Mrs Jenkins. Proceed with your report."

I completed the report and had time to wash and change before lunch. At table, it was hard to join in the general conversation. I was hearing in my mind that horrible wolf-howl, thinking of Sister Evangelina's explanation, and remembering. Her words brought to mind something my grandfather had told me years before, about a man he knew well who had fallen on hard times. The man had applied to the Board of Guardians for temporary relief, and had been told that he could not have it, but would be sent to the workhouse. The man replied, "I would rather die" and went away and hanged himself.

When I was a child the local workhouse had been pointed out to me with hushed and terrified whispers. Even the empty building seemed to evoke fear and loathing. People would not go down the road in which it stood, or would pass on the other side with faces averted. The dread even affected me, a little child who knew nothing about the history of the workhouses. All my life I have looked on those buildings with a shudder.

Sister Evangelina frequently accompanied me on my visits to Mrs Jenkins, and I had marvelled at the way in which she got the old lady talking. Reminiscing was obviously good therapy for her, as she relived the pain of the past with a loving and sympathetic person.

The Council supplied Sister with the old records of the Board of Guardians of Poplar Workhouse. Mrs Jenkins had been a pauper inmate from 1916 to 1935. "Enough to drive anyone mad," Sister Evie commented wryly. She had been admitted as a widow with five children, unable to support herself. She was described as an "able-bodied adult". The records stated that Mrs Jenkins was discharged in 1935, with the gift of a sewing machine, the use of which would enable her to support herself, and twenty-four pounds, which was her accumulated earnings after nineteen years in the workhouse. No further mention was made of the children.

The records were dry and scant. Mrs Jenkins herself filled in the missing details in her conversations with Sister Evie. Little bits of the story came out here and there, relived with a complete lack of emotion or melodrama as though her story were nothing unusual.

I felt that she had seen and experienced so much suffering for so long that she had accepted it as inevitable. A happy life seemed unthinkable to her.

She had been born in Millwall, and like most girls had gone to work in a factory at the age of thirteen, and then married a local boy when she was eighteen. They rented two rooms over a tailor's shop in Commercial Road, and six children were born to them over the next ten years. Then her young husband developed a cough that did not get better. Six months later he was spitting blood. "He jus' wasted away," she said in a matter-of-fact tone. Three months later he was dead.

Mrs Jenkins was strong and less than thirty years of age at the time. She left the two rooms and took a small back room for herself and her children. She returned to work in the shirt-making factory, working from 8 a.m. to 6 p.m. Her baby was only three months old, but Rosie – her eldest daughter – was already ten and left school in order to look after the younger children. Extra hand-sewing was taken in, and she often sat half the night sewing by candlelight. Rosie learned to sew too and became a good needlewoman, often sitting up with her mother into the night hours. These silent hours of female labour brought in a little extra money – enough to feed the family – after the rent was paid.

Then catastrophe struck. The machinery of the factory was completely unguarded, and the sleeve of Mrs Jenkins' dress caught in a wheel, dragging her right arm towards the cutting blades. Her arm was badly injured, she lost a lot of blood, and tendons were severed before the machine was stopped. She was lucky not to lose her arm. She showed us the six inch scar. The lacerations were never stitched because she could not afford to pay a doctor, and the scar, though healed, was wide, deep red, and irregular. Her arm was slightly withered because the tendons had not been sutured. It was surprising that she could use her hand at all.

She looked at the scar without emotion. "This is wha' done fer us," she said.

The family moved out of the back room, and found shelter in a basement with no window. It was close to the river's edge, and at high tide, when the water level rose, moisture seeped through the brickwork and ran down the walls. For this hovel, the landlord demanded one shilling a week, but with the mother not earning, how was this to be found?

She went out begging, but was driven off the streets by the police who saw her as an undesirable vagrant. She pawned her coat, and with the money bought matches, then went out into the streets as a match seller. The profits from her sales brought in a little money, but not enough to pay the rent as well as feed the children.

Bit by bit she pawned everything they had – the furniture, pots, saucepans, the plates and mugs, clothes, linen. Last to go was the bed in which they all slept. She constructed a platform out of orange boxes to raise them off the damp floor, and on this the family slept. Finally the blankets had to go in to be pawned, and mother and children clung to each other for warmth at night.

She asked the Board of Guardians for outdoor relief, but the chairman said she was obviously lazy and workshy, and when she told them of the accident in the factory, and showed them her right arm, she was told not to be impertinent, or it would count against her. The gentlemen debated amongst themselves, and offered to take two of her children off her hands. She refused, and returned to the basement with six hungry mouths to feed.

With no light, no heat, constant damp and mildew, and virtually no food, the children became sickly. The family struggled on for six months like this, and still the mother could not work. She sold her hair; she sold her teeth, but it was never enough. The baby became lethargic and ceased to thrive. She called it "wasting fever".

When the baby died no money could be spared for burial, so she sealed him in an orange box weighed down with stones, and slipped him into the river.

That furtive journey in the middle of the night with her dead baby was the moment when she finally accepted defeat, and knew that the inevitable had come. She and the children would have to go to the workhouse.

THE WORKHOUSE

The Poor Law Act of 1834 started the workhouse system. The Act was repealed in 1929, but the system lingered on for several decades because there was nowhere else for the inmates to go, and long-term residents had lost the capacity to make any decisions or look after themselves in the outside world.

It was intended as a humane and charitable Act, because hitherto the poor or destitute could be hounded from place to place, never finding shelter, and could lawfully be beaten to death by their pursuers. To the chronically poor of the 1830s the workhouse system must have seemed like heaven: a shelter each night; a bed or communal bed to sleep in; clothing; food – not lavish, but enough, and, in return, work to pay for your keep. The system must have seemed like an act of pure Christian goodness and charity. But, like so many good intentions, it quickly turned sour.

Mrs Jenkins and her children left the basement with three weeks' rent owing. The landlord had threatened to put the whip to her back if she did not pay the following day, so they had left during the night. The family had nothing to take with them; neither she nor the children wore any shoes, their clothes were just rags thrown over their thin bodies. Dirty, hungry, and shivering they stood in the unlit street, ringing the great bell outside the workhouse.

The children, were not particularly unhappy as yet; in fact, it seemed something of an adventure to them, creeping out in the dead of night and making their way along dark roads. Only their mother was crying, because only she knew the dreadful truth: that the family would be separated once they entered the workhouse gates. She could not bring herself to tell the children, and hesitated before ringing that fateful bell. But her youngest child, a boy of nearly three, started coughing, so she pulled the handle resolutely.

The sound echoed through the stone building, and the door

was opened by a thin, grey man who demanded, "What do you want?"

"Shelter, and food for the little ones."

"You'll have to come to the Reception Room. You can sleep there till morning, unless, of course, you're 'casuals' and go to the Casual Centre. There's no food until morning."

"No, we are not casuals," she said wearily.

They were the only people in the reception room that night. The sleeping platform, a raised wooden construction, was covered with fresh straw and looked inviting. They cuddled up together in the sweet-smelling hay, and the children fell asleep at once. Only the mother lay awake, her arms around her children, until dawn. Her heart was breaking. She knew it would be the last time she would be allowed to sleep with her children.

Morning sounds, keys clanking, and doors opening, were heard long before anyone unlocked the door of the reception room. Finally, the Mistress entered. She was a resolute looking woman, not unkind, but one who had seen too many paupers to be swayed by emotion. She took their names, and briefly told them to follow her to the washhouse, where they were stripped, and made to wash all over with cold water in shallow stone troughs. Their clothes, such as they were, were removed, and workhouse uniforms provided. These were of coarse grey serge, cut to fit almost any size of person. There were a variety of odd shoes. No undergarments were provided, but that did not matter, because none of them were accustomed to vests or pants, even in the coldest weather. Then their heads were shaved. The boys thought this was great fun, and giggled and pointed at the girls, cramming their fists into their mouths to stop themselves from laughing aloud. Mrs Jenkins did not have to be shaved because she had no hair, having sold it some weeks previously; she was given a bonnet to cover her bare head. She timidly asked if there would be any food for the little ones, and was told that it was too late for breakfast, but that lunch would be served at 12 noon.

They were taken to the Master's office for segregation. Everyone dreaded this moment, including the Master and Mistress, and four strong pauper inmates were brought in to take the children away. Mrs Jenkins had persuaded herself that it would not be too bad for the younger ones, because they would all be with Rosie, who had looked after them while she was at work. But this was not to be.

The Master looked at the little ones. "Ages?" he demanded.

"Two, four, and five," she whispered.

"Take them to the children's ward. And the older boy? What age is he?"

"Nine."

"He'll go to the boys' ward. The girl?" he demanded, pointing at Rosie.

"Ten."

"Take her to the girls' ward," he ordered.

Rough hands were laid on the children. The Master turned and walked out. He was not going to stay to watch the scene. As he left, he barked to the helpers, "Mind you do as you are bidden. You know the rules."

Mrs Jenkins could not give Sister Evangelina or me the details of the parting. It was too terrible to talk about. The children were dragged away screaming, and she was pushed into the women's quarters. Great doors were shut behind her, and keys were turned. She heard the sounds of screaming children and doors banging. Then she heard no more. She was told much later by a friendly woman who worked in the kitchens that there was a little boy who cried all the time, and whose eyes never left the great door of the children's quarters, watching every person who came in. He never said a single word except "mummy" from the day he entered to the day he died. Was it her little boy? She never knew, but it might have been.

I asked Sister Evangelina about this segregation, which seemed so utterly inhuman that it could not be true, but she assured me that it was. Segregation was the first rule of all workhouses throughout the country, and the one most rigorously applied. Husbands and wives were separated, parents and children, brothers and sisters. Usually, they never saw each other again.

If Mrs Jenkins was odd, it was not surprising.

One evening I visited her quite late. It was dark and, down the side passage leading to her back door, I heard a strange, subdued human voice that was chanting in a rhythmic way. I peered through the window and saw Mrs Jenkins on her hands and knees on the floor, scrubbing. An oil-lamp stood beside her, throwing a huge and ghostly shadow of her small figure on to the wall. She had a pail of water beside her, and a scrubbing brush, and she was scrubbing the same square of floor obsessively. All the while she seemed to be repeating a rythmic pattern of words that I could not distinguish but she did not change her position.

I rapped on the door and entered. She lifted her head, but did not turn round.

"Rosie? Come 'ere, Rosie. Look a' this, girl. Look 'ow clean it is. Master'll be pleased when 'e sees how clean I scrubbed it."

She looked up at the great shadow of herself on the wall.

"Come an' see here, Master. It's so clean, an' I done it all. It's clean, an' I done it to please you, Master. They says I can see my li'l ones if I please you, Master. Can I? Can I? Oh, let me, just once."

Her cry lifted, and her tiny body fell forwards. Her head hit the bucket, and she gave a whimper of pain. I went over to her.

"It's me, the nurse. I'm just doing my evening visit. Are you all right, Mrs Jenkins?"

She looked up at me, but didn't say a word. She sucked her lips, and gazed at me steadily as I helped her to her feet and led her to the armchair.

On the bare table was a cooked lunch, left for her by the Meals on Wheels ladies. It was untouched, and quite cold.

I moved the plate, and said, "Didn't you fancy your lunch, then?"

She grabbed my wrist with unexpected strength and pushed my arm away. "For Rosie," she said in a hoarse whisper.

I checked her physical condition, and asked a few questions, none of which she replied to. She just gazed at me unblinkingly, and continued sucking her lips.

On another occasion when I called, she was chuckling to herself as she played with a piece of elastic. She was stretching and releasing it and twisting it round her fingers. She said to me, as I entered, "My Rosie brought me a bit of elastic las' night. Look 'ow it stretches. It's good an' strong. She's a clever girl, my Rose. She can always get hold of a bi' of elastic for you, if you wants it."

I was beginning to get irritated with Rosie. She wasn't much help to her old mother. A bit of elastic, indeed! Was that the best she could do?

But then I saw the tenderness and happiness on the old face, and the warmth and love in her voice as she fiddled with the elastic. "My Rosie give it me, she did. She go' it fer me, she did. She's a dear girl, my Rose."

My heart softened. Perhaps Rosie was as simple as her mother, her mind also unhinged by her early life in the workhouse. I wondered how long she had spent there, and what had happened to her brothers and sisters.

Life in the workhouse was terrible. All inmates were locked into their quarters, which consisted of a day room, a sleeping room and an airing yard. They were confined to the dormitory from 8 p.m. to 6 a.m., and there was a drain or channel running down the centre, into which they relieved themselves at night. The day room was their dining room, where they sat at long benches to eat. All windows were above eye level so that no one could see out of them, and the window sills sloped downwards, so that no one could climb up and sit on them. The airing yard was an enclosed gravel square, from which no door or gate issued. It was, effectively, a prison.

Misery and monotony blurred days into weeks, and weeks into months. The women worked all day, mostly rough work: in the laundry, washing for the entire workhouse; scrubbing – the Master was fanatical about scrubbing; cooking poor quality food for all the inmates; heavy sewing, such as sacks, sails, matting; and, strangest of all, picking oakum. This was old rope, usually tarred, which had to be untwisted and unpicked into strands, which were then used for caulking the seams of wooden ships. This sounds easy; but it was not. The rope, especially if caked in oil or tar or salt, could be as hard as steel, and unpicking it tore the hands and left the fingers raw and bleeding.

Yet the working hours were less terrible than the hours of rest. Mrs Jenkins found herself among about one hundred other women of all ages, including the sick and infirm. Many of them appeared to be mad or demented. Tired from their physical work, there was nowhere to sit down, except on benches in the middle of the day room or the airing yard. In order to rest themselves, the women sat back to back on a bench, each supporting the other. There was nothing to do, nothing to look at or listen to, no books, nothing with which to exercise the mind. Many of the women just walked up and down, or round and round in circles. Most of them talked to themselves, or rocked backwards and forwards continuously. Some moaned aloud, or howled into the night air.

"I will ge' like tha' meself," thought Mrs Jenkins.

They were ushered into the airing yard twice a day for half an hour of exercise. From the yard, Mrs Jenkins could hear the sounds of children's voices, but the walls were fifteen feet high, and she could not see over them. She tried calling the names of her children, but was ordered to stop, or she wouldn't be allowed out into the yard again. So she just stood by the wall where she thought the sounds came from, whispering their names, and straining her ears to catch the sound of a voice she would know to be her child's own.

"I didn' know wha' I done wrong to be in there. I jus' cried all the time. An' I didn' know wha' they done wiv the li'l ones."

When the spring came, and the days grew warmer and longer, and new life was surging all around in the world that she could not see beyond the workhouse walls, Mrs Jenkins was informed that her youngest child, a boy aged three, had died. She asked why, and was told that he had always been sickly, and that no one had expected him to live. She asked if she might attend the funeral, and was told that he had already been buried.

The little boy was the first to go. Mrs Jenkins never saw any of her children again. Over the next four years, one by one, they all died. The mother was merely informed of each death, she was given no cause. She did not attend any of the funerals. The last to die was a girl of fourteen. Her name was Rosie.

THE BOTTOM DROPPED OUT OF PIGS

Always expect the unexpected, and you will never go wrong. Fred had suffered a severe setback from the enforced closure of his quail and toffee-apple empire, and was looking round for something new. The unexpected came from a chance remark from Mrs B. as she came bustling into the kitchen muttering, "I don' know what fings is comin' to. The price o' bacon these days! I've never seen nuffink like it."

Fred slapped his shovel down on the floor, raising a cloud of ash, and shouted: "Pigs! That's the answer. Pigs. They was doin' it in the war, an' it can be done again."

Mrs B. rushed over to him, broom in hand. "You messy bugger, messin' up my kitchen."

She held the broom aggressively, ready to strike. But Fred neither heard nor saw. He grabbed her round the waist, and twirled her round and round in a frenzied dance.

"You got it, old girl, you 'as. Why didn't I think on it. Pigs."

He made snorting, honking noises, supposed to represent a pig, which did not improve his looks at all. Mrs B. extricated herself from his embrace, and poked him in the chest with the broom handle.

"You crazy . . ." she started shouting, and he yelled back. When two Cockneys are engaged in a shouting match it is impossible to understand the lingo.

Breakfast was over, and we heard the Sisters' footsteps. They appeared in the doorway, and the slanging match stopped.

In high excitement, Fred explained that he had just had a brilliant idea. He would keep a pig. It could live in the chicken run, which he could easily convert into a pigsty, and in no time at all the pig would be ready for the bacon factory, and his fortune would be made.

Sister Julienne was enchanted. She loved pigs. She had been brought up on a farm, and knew a lot about them. She said that Fred could have all the peelings and waste from Nonnatus House, and advised him to go round the local cafés begging similar favours. Shyly she asked if she might come to see the pig when it was installed in the hen/pig house.

Fred wasn't one to hang around. Within a matter of days the pigsty was complete. He and Dolly pooled their resources and a pink, squealing little creature was soon purchased. Sister Julienne was profuse in her praise.

"You've got a fine pig, there, Fred. A real beauty. You can tell by the width of the shoulders. You've made a good choice."

She gave him one of her sparkling smiles and Fred turned as pink as the pig.

Fred yielded to Sister Julienne for advice about bran mash and nut mix, as well as supplies of food waste from local cafés and greengrocers. They were frequently seen in deep and earnest conversation, Fred sucking his tooth and whistling inwardly as he concentrated on the detail. Sister also advised him on hay and water and mucking out, and she impressed us all with her knowledge in the art of pig rearing.

It was a busy and happy time for Fred. Each day at breakfast we heard details of the pig's progress, her lusty appetite and rapid growth. As the weeks passed, mucking out consumed more of Fred's time and labour. However, this proved to be a money-maker. Most small houses had tiny back gardens, no more than a yard in most cases, but quite sufficient to grow a few things. Tomatoes were popular, and so, surprisingly, were grapevines, which grew exceedingly well in Poplar and produced succulent fruit. Word soon got round, and Fred's pigshit was in great demand. He concluded that there was no losing with pigs. The more he fed her, the more thick, black stuff she excreted, and the more money he made. Within a few weeks the sale of manure had covered the initial cost of the piglet.

The whole of Nonnatus House, Sisters and lay staff alike, took a deep interest in the pig and Fred's financial aspirations. We read in the papers that the price of meat was rising, and concluded that Fred had been very shrewd.

However, the vagaries and vicissitudes of the market are notorious. Demand fell. The bottom dropped out of pigs.

The blow was heavy. Fred was glum. All that feeding and mucking and raking. All the plans and hopes. And now the pig was hardly worth the cost of slaughter. No wonder the bounce had gone out of Fred's bent little legs. No wonder his North-East eye drooped.

Sunday was a day of rest in Nonnatus House. After church we were all gathered in the kitchen, having coffee and cakes left by Mrs B. from her Saturday bake. Fred was packing up to leave, but Sister Julienne invited him to join us at the big table. Conversation turned to the pig; his fag drooped.

"What'm I goin' to do wiv 'er? She's costin' me money to feed 'er an' I can't ge' nuffink for 'er."

Everyone sympathised and muttered "hard luck" and "shame", but Sister Julienne was silent. She stared at him intently, and then said, clearly and positively, "Breed from her, Fred. You could keep her as a breeding sow. There will always be a market for good healthy piglets, and when prices pick up, as they will, you could get a good price for them. And don't forget, a sow always delivers between twelve and eighteen piglets."

Such advice – so obvious, so simple, yet so unexpected! Fred's mouth fell open, and his fag dropped on to the table. Picking it up with an apology, he stubbed it out in the ashtray. Unfortunately it was not an ashtray; it was Sister Evangelina's meringue, which she had been on the point of eating. She remonstrated with characteristic vigour.

Fred was abashed and apologetic. He picked up the meringue, brushed off the ash, picked the fag end out of the cream, and handed it back to Sister Evangelina. "Piglets. Tha's the answer. I'll be a pig breeder. I'll be the best pig breeder on the Isle."

Sister Evangelina snorted, and pushed the meringue away from her with disgust. But Fred noticed none of this. He was in a trance, muttering, "Piglets, piglets, I'll breed pigs, that's what I'll do, I will."

Sister Julienne, practical and tactful, handed another meringue to Sister Evangelina, and said, "You will have to take the *Pig Breeders' Guide*, Fred, and find a good stud boar. I can help you, if you need help in the first instance. My brother is a farmer so I can ask him to send a copy."

And that was how it all started. *The Pig Breeders' Guide* arrived, and Fred and Sister Julienne were soon poring over it. It was disconcerting to see Fred attempting to read, because he had to hold the page to the left of his South-West eye in order to read anything at all. Even when he could make out a sentence or two, the language of pig breeders was completely foreign to him, and he could not have managed without Sister Julienne, who translated the strange jargon into comprehensible Cockney.

A good stud boar was selected, a telephone call made, an agreement reached, and a small open truck arrived from Essex.

Sister Julienne could hardly contain her excitement. Instructing Sister Bernadette to take charge of the House in her absence, she put on her outdoor veil and cloak, pulled a bicycle out of the shed, and cycled off to Fred's house.

The Essex farmer was a rural gentleman of settled habits. He had scarcely ventured beyond the peaceful confines of Strayling Strawless to Market Sodbury. His thoughts, as he drove his open truck with his stud boar into the heart of London's Docklands, have not been revealed to us. The boar, resting his head contentedly on the side of the truck, jogged along for several miles without arousing much interest, but once in the more densely populated streets of London it was a different story. All the way through Dagenham, Barking, East Ham, West Ham, and down to Cubitt Town on the Isle of Dogs, the pig drew crowds. He was a large animal whose only exercise was that of copulation. His nature was comparatively docile, but in ten years his tusks had never been cut, and in consequence he looked more ferocious than he really was.

As the truck turned in at the end of the street Sister Julienne arrived on her bicycle and met Fred. Together they approached the farmer, who stared at them without saying a word. Sister Julienne stood on tiptoe, looking over the edge of the truck, and brushed back her veil which had been blowing towards the pig's tusks.

"Oh, he's a beautiful fellow," she whispered excitedly.

The farmer looked at her, sucked his pipe, and said, "I don't believe this."

He asked to see the sow. The entry to Fred's yard was via a side passage that ran between the houses, at the end of which was the boundary wall to the docks. The Thames ran behind it. The farmer was thus confronted with the towering sides of ocean-going cargo vessels.

"They are never going to believe this. Never," he muttered, as he stooped to pick up his pipe and the keys that had fallen from his hands.

He was directed into Fred's yard.

"There she is, an' lookin' for a bi' of fun from that there big bugger o' your'n."

"Fun!" growled the farmer, "This bit of fun will cost you one pound, cash in hand."

Fred knew the cost, and had the money ready, but grumbled nonetheless. "Cor – pound a poke – that's more'n they gets up West, that is."

Sister Julienne remonstrated: "It's no good grumbling, Fred. A pound is the going rate, so you had better pay up."

The farmer eyed the nun strangely, but Fred handed over the money without another word.

The farmer pocketed the cash, and said, "Right! We'll bring him round."

But that was easier said than done.

A crowd had gathered, and was growing all the time – word travels fast on the Isle. The farmer backed his truck up against the passage, lowered the rear trailer board, and leaped into the truck to drive the boar down, but the boar refused to budge. A pig's eyesight is poor, and, to a creature accustomed to the open countryside of Essex, the passage must have looked like the black hole into hell.

"Get up and help me," shouted the farmer to Fred.

Together they pushed and walloped and shouted at the boar, which got nasty, and looked as if it might be tempted to use its tusks after all. The crowd in the street gasped, and mothers pulled their children back as the boar slowly and tentatively, descended the ramp on its tiny trotters and entered the passage. Even then it was not plain sailing. The alley was narrow, and the boar very nearly got stuck. The two men pushed from behind. Sister Julienne ran through the house, through the pig yard and the outside gate, and into the passage with turnip tops in her hand, which she said would entice the pig forward. She held them under its nose, but still it would not move.

Fred had an idea, "Wha' we needs is a red hot poker to stick up his arse, like wha' they do with camels in the desert when they wants 'em to go over a bridge. Camels won' go over water, you know."

"You stick a red hot poker up his arse, and I'll stick one up yours, mate," the farmer threatened, and continued pushing.

Eventually the boar was coaxed down the passage into Fred's yard. A crowd of children followed, and more went into neighbouring gardens and hung over the fence.

The farmer got cross. He spoke with slow emphasis.

"You'll have to clear this crowd away. Pigs are shy animals, they won't do anything in front of an audience."

Again, Sister Julienne took charge. She spoke with quiet authority to the children, and they crept away. She, Fred, and the farmer went into the house and shut the door. But Sister could not resist the temptation to peep out through the curtains to see how the sow took to her "husband", as she insisted on calling the boar.

"Oh Fred, I don't think she likes him – look, she's pushing him away. He's definitely interested, do you see?"

Fred stood by the window, sucking his tooth.

"No, no, not like that!" cried Sister Julienne, wringing her hands in anguish. "You mustn't bite him. That's not the way. Now she's running. Fred, I'm afraid she might not accept him. What do you think?"

Fred didn't know what to think.

"That's better. There's a good girl. She's getting more interested, do you see, Fred? Isn't it wonderful?"

Fred grew alarmed.

"He'll kill 'er, he will. Look at 'im, the big bugger. He's biting her. Look 'ere, I'm not standin' fer this, not no 'ow. He'll kill 'er, he will, or break 'er legs or somefink. I'm gonna put a stop to this, I am. It's barbaric, I tells yer."

Sister had to restrain him.

"It's all perfectly natural. That's the way they do it, Fred."

Fred was not easily pacified. Sister and the farmer had to hold him back until it was all over.

The Nuns were assembled in the Chapel, kneeling in private prayer. The bell for Vespers sounded just as Sister Julienne entered Nonnatus House. Flushed and excited, she raced along the corridor, leaving behind footsteps of a sticky and highly pungent substance on the tiled floor. In haste, she composed herself, took her place at the lectern, and read:

> *"Sisters, be sober, be vigilant, for your adversary*
> *the Devil roareth around like a raging lion, seeking*
> *whom he may devour."*

One or two of the Sisters looked up from their prayers and glanced sideways at her. A few sniffed suspiciously.

She continued:

> *"Thine adversary roareth in the midst of thy congregation.*
> *Thine enemy hath defiled thy holy place."*

The sniffs got louder, and the Sisters glanced at each other.

> *"But as for me, I walk with the godly."*

The sacristan filled the censer with an unusually large quantity of incense and swung it vigorously.

> *"In my prosperity I said I shall never be cast down."*

Smoke filled the air.

> *"But thou, oh Lord, hath seen my pride*
> *and sent my misfortune to humble me."*

There was unrest amongst the Sisters. Those kneeling closest to Sister Julienne shuffled a little distance from her. It cannot be easy to shuffle sideways whilst on your knees and wearing monastic habit, but in extremis it can be managed.

> *"But thou dost turn thy face from me,*
> *and I was troubled, and I gat me to my*
> *Lord, right humbly."*

The incense swung furiously, smoke billowing out.

> *"And I will say unto my Lord, I am*
> *unclean. I am unfit to dwell in Thy Holy Place."*

Coughing broke out.

> *"And I cried aloud What profit is there in me?*
> *I am undone. I shall go down into the Pit.*
> *Oh Lord, hear my prayer. Let my cry*
> *come unto Thee."*

Eventually, and not before time, Vespers concluded. The Sisters, red-eyed, choking and spluttering, filed out of the chapel.

It took a long time for Sister Julienne to live down the opprobrium of having filled the chapel with the odour of pigshit, and I am sure that God forgave her long before her Sisters did.

OF MIXED DESCENT I

In the 1950s the African and West Indian population in London was very small. The ports of London, like those of any nation, had always been a melting pot for immigrants. Different nationalities, languages, and cultures were flung together and intermingled, usually bound to each other by poverty. The East End was no exception, and over the centuries just about every race had been absorbed and propagated. Tolerant warm-heartedness has always been a hallmark of the Cockney way of life, and strangers, though they may have been regarded with distrust and suspicion at first, were not resisted for long.

Most of the immigrants were young, single men. Men have always been mobile, but not so women. In those days it would have been virtually impossible for a young, poor woman to go jaunting around the world by herself. Girls had to stay at home. However bad the home, however great the hardships and poverty, however much their spirits longed for freedom, they were trapped. This indeed is still the fate of the vast majority of the women of the world today.

Men have always been luckier, and a footloose young man in a foreign place, once his stomach is full, is after one thing – girls. The East End families were very protective of their daughters and, until recently, pregnancy out of wedlock was the ultimate disgrace and a catastrophe from which the poor girl never recovered. However, it did occur quite frequently. If the girl was lucky, her mother stood by her and brought up the baby. Occasionally the father of the child was forced to marry her, but this was a mixed blessing, as many a girl found to her cost. Whatever the social hardship for the girl, it did mean a continuous infusion of new blood – or new genes, as we would say today – into the community. This may, in fact, account for the distinctive energy, vitality, and boundless good humour of the Cockney.

Whilst daughters were protected, married women were in a different situation altogether. A young unmarried girl who became pregnant could not hide from anyone the fact that she was unmarried. A married woman could bear anyone's child, and no one would be any the wiser. I have often felt that the situation is loaded against men. Until recently, when genetic blood tests became possible, how could any man know that his wife was carrying his child? The poor man had no other assurance of paternity than his wife's word. Unless she is virtually locked up, he can have no control over her activities during the day while he is at work. All this does not matter very much in the broad spectrum of life, because most men are quite happy with a new baby, and if a husband happens to be fathering another man's child, he is not likely to know, and, as they say, "what the eye does not see, the heart does not grieve over". But what happens when his wife brings forth a black man's child?

The East Enders had hardly faced this before, but after the Second World War the potential was there.

Bella was a lovely young redhead of about twenty-two. She was well named. Her pale skin, slightly freckled, her cornflower blue eyes would captivate any man, and her red curls would bind him to her for ever. Tom was the happiest and proudest young husband in the East India Docks. He talked about her incessantly. She came from one of the 'best' families (the East Enders could be incredibly snobbish and class-conscious in their social gradings) and they had married after four years of courtship, when Tom was finally able to support her.

They had a slap-up wedding. She was the only daughter and her family were determined to do her proud. No expense was spared: a wedding gown with a train that reached halfway down the church; six bridesmaids and four pageboys; enough flowers to give you hayfever for a week; choir; bells; a sermon – the lot! That was just to show the neighbours what could be done. The reception was designed to prove the unrivalled superiority of the family to all the friends and relations. A fleet of Rolls Royces, eighteen in all, drove the most important people from the church a hundred yards down the road to the church hall hired for the occasion. The rest had to walk – and got there first! The long trestle tables had been spread with white cloths, and nearly collapsed under the weight of hams, turkeys, pheasants, beef, fish, eels, oysters, cheeses, pickles, chutneys, pies, puddings, jellies, blancmanges, custard, cakes, fruit drinks and, of course, the wedding cake. Had he seen the wedding cake after he had constructed St Paul's Cathedral, Sir Christopher Wren would have broken down and wept! It was seven storeys high, each layer supported on Grecian columns, with towers and balustrades and flutings and minarets. It boasted a domed roof bearing a coy-looking bride and bridegroom surrounded by lovebirds.

Tom was a bit abashed by all this, and didn't quite know what to say but, as he had said the all-important words "I do", none of the family really cared whether he said anything else. Bella was quietly enjoying being the centre of attention. She was not a loud or showy girl, but her enjoyment of being the occasion for such extravagance was notable. Her mother was in her element, and bursting with pride. She was also just about bursting out of her tight-fitting purple taffeta suit. (Why is it that women always dress so outrageously for weddings? Look around you, and you will see middle-aged women in things that should have been left behind with their twenties, drawn tightly across expanding backsides, pulled in at the waist, emphasising folds of flesh that would be better covered; ridiculous hairdos; ludicrous hats; kamikaze shoes.) Bella's mother and several of her aunts had fashionable veils to their hats, which made eating rather difficult, so they pushed their veils up, and pinned them to the tops of their heads, which made the hats look even more absurd.

Bella's father held the floor for forty-five minutes whilst he gave his wedding speech. He spoke at length of Bella's babyhood, her first tooth, her first word, her first step. He went on to discuss her brilliant school career, and how she had got a school certificate which was now framed and hanging on the wall. No doubt he would have gone on to the swimming certificate and the cycling test had Bella's mother not said, "Ow gi' on wiv it, Ern."

So he turned his attention to Tom, and told him what a lucky chap he was, and how all the other chaps had been after her, but that he (Ern) had reckoned that he (Tom) was the best of the bunch, and would look after his little Bella, because he was a good hard-working lad, and would remember that success in life and marriage depends upon "early to bed and up with the cock".

The uncles guffawed and winked, and the aunts affected to look shocked and said to each other, "Ow, 'e is a one, 'e is."

Tom turned pink and smiled because everyone else was laughing. It was possible that he didn't understand. Bella kept her eyes firmly on her jelly, it being prudent that she shouldn't be seen to understand.

After the delights of the honeymoon spent in one of the best boarding houses in Clacton, they returned to a small flat, near to Bella's mum. Flo was determined that her daughter should have the best of everything, and had purchased fitted carpets in their absence. Such a luxury was virtually unknown in the East End in those days. Tom was bemused and kept rubbing his toes up and down the soft pile to see how it moved. Bella was enchanted, and it triggered an orgy of spending on household items, most of them relatively new and unheard of among her neighbours: an upholstered three-piece suite; electric wall lights; a television; a telephone; a refrigerator; a toaster; and an electric kettle. Tom found them all very novel, and was glad that his Bella was so happy playing the little housewife. He had to take on more and more overtime to keep up the payments, but he was young and strong, and didn't mind, as long as she was content.

Bella booked with the Nonnatus Midwives for her first pregnancy, because her mother advised it. She attended antenatal clinic each Tuesday afternoon, and was perfectly healthy. She was about thirty-two weeks pregnant when Flo came to see us one evening. It was outside our routine hours, but she seemed agitated. "I'm worrit about our Bell, I am. She's depressed or summat. I can see it, an' Tom can see it an' all, 'e can. She won't talk, she won't look at no one, she won't do nuffink. Tom says, 'e says, often the dishes aren't even washed up when he gits in, an' the place is a real pigsty. Somefinks up, I tells you."

We said that clinically Bella was quite healthy, and the pregnancy was normal. We also said that we would visit her at home, in addition to her Tuesday antenatal clinic.

Bella was certainly depressed. Several of us visited, and we all observed the same symptoms – lethargy, inattention, disinterest. We called in her doctor. Flo made heroic efforts to try to get her out of it, by taking her out to buy piles of baby clothes and various paraphernalia considered necessary. Tom was very worried, and fussed and fretted over her whenever he was at home; but as he worked such long hours, even longer now in order to pay for all the baby things, most of the burden fell on Flo, who was a solicitous and devoted mother.

Bella went into labour at full term. She was neither early nor late according to her dates. Her mother called us around lunchtime to say that the pains were coming every ten minutes, and that she had had a show. I finished my lunch, and stocked up on two helpings of pudding as a precaution against missing my tea. A primigravida with contractions every ten minutes is not an emergency.

I cycled in a leisurely manner round to Bella's house. Flo was waiting on the doorstep to greet me. It was a sunny afternoon, but she looked worried. "She's like I says, no change, but I'm not 'appy. Somefink's up. She's not 'erself. It's not normal, it's not."

Like most women of her generation, Flo was an experienced amateur midwife.

Bella was in the sitting room on the new settee, digging her fingernails into the upholstery. She was pulling out bits of stuffing. She stared at me dully as I entered and ground her teeth. She continued grinding her teeth for some time after she had withdrawn her attention from me. She didn't say a word.

I said, "I must examine you, Bella, if you are going into labour. I need to know how far on you are, and what the baby's position is, and listen to its heartbeat. Could you come into the bedroom, please?"

She didn't move. More stuffing came out of the sofa. Flo tried to coax her along. "Come on, luvvy, it won't be long now. We all has to go through it, but it's over in next to no time. Yer'll see. Come on, now. Into ve bedroom."

She made to help her daughter up, but was pushed roughly away. Flo almost lost her balance and fell. I had to be firm.

"Bella, get up at once and come with me into the bedroom. I have to examine you."

She looked like a child who knows the voice of command, and came quietly.

She was two to three fingers dilated, foetal head down, a normal anterior presentation, as far as I could assess, and waters unbroken. The foetal heart was a steady 120. Bella's pulse and blood pressure were good. Everything seemed perfectly normal, except this curious mental state, which I could not understand. The tooth-grinding continued all through the examination, and was getting on my nerves.

I said, "I'm going to give you a sedative, and it would be better if you stayed in bed and slept for a few hours. Labour will continue while you are asleep, and you will be refreshed for later on."

Flo nodded wisely in approval.

I laid out my delivery things, and told Flo to ring Nonnatus House when contractions were every five minutes, or sooner if she was worried. I noted with satisfaction that there was a telephone in the flat. We might need it, I thought, in view of Bella's mental state. Post-partum delirium is a rare and frightening complication of labour, requiring swift and skilled medical attention.

The phone rang about 8 p.m., and Tom's voice asked me to come. I was there within ten minutes, and he let me in. He seemed anxious but excited.

"This is it, then, nurse. Cor, I hopes as 'ow she'll be all right, her an' the baby. I can't wait to see my li'l baby, yer know, nurse. It's somefink special, like. Bell's bin a bit down of lates, but she'll perk up when she sees the baby, won't she, now?"

I went into the bedroom just as Bella was starting a contraction. It was powerful, and she was moaning in pain. Her mother was wiping her face with a cold flannel. We waited for and timed the next contraction. Every five minutes. I thought, I doubt if it will be long now. The girl looked drowsy and lethargic between contractions, and I did not want to give more sedative or analgesic if delivery was close.

"How is she?" I said to Flo, slightly tapping my head to indicate my real meaning.

She replied: "She hasn't said a word since you lef', not a word she 'asn't. She wouldn't even look at Tom when 'e comes 'ome, nor say nothin' to 'im neither. No' a word, nuffink. Poor lad, 'e feels it, 'e do."

She patted her heart to indicate the feeling.

With the next contraction the waters broke, and Bella's breathing became more rapid. She grabbed her mother's hand.

"There, there, my pet. It won' be long."

The contraction had passed, but Bella still clung to her mother's hand with a vice-like grip. Her eyes were staring wildly.

Bella gave a low scream – "No!" then, with her voice rising with every reiteration, "No! No! No! Stop it. You gotta stop it."

Then she emitted horrible high-pitched gurgling sounds. She threw herself around the bed, making this dreadful noise, something between a scream and a laugh. It was not a cry of pain, because she was not having a contraction. It was hysteria.

I said, "I must ask Tom to ring for the doctor at once."

Bella cried out, "No! I don' want no doctor. Oh Gawd! Don' chew understand? The baby's goin' to be black. He'll kill me, Tom will, when 'e sees it."

I don't think Flo understood what she had said. So uncommon were black people in the East End at that time that her daughter's words didn't make any sense to her.

Bella was still screaming. Then she swore at her mother and yelled at her, "Can' chew understand, you silly ol' cow. Ve baby's goin' ter be black!"

This time Flo understood. She leaped away from her daughter, and stared at her in horror. "Black? Yer jokin'. Yer must be. You mean it's not Tom's baby?"

Bella nodded.

"You filthy slut, you. Is this what I brings you up for, is it? To disgrace me and yer dad!"

Her hand flew to her face, and she drew in breath with a horrified gasp.

"Oh my Gawd," she whispered to herself. "They've got a big knees-up planned for yer dad at the Club, an' they was keepin' it a surprise. He's President this year, an' the lads wanted a real old knees-up when 'is first gran'child's born. It'll be the joke of all Poplar, it will. He'll never live it down. They won't let 'im."

She wrung her hands silently, then screamed at her daughter. "Oh, I wish you'd never been born, I do. I 'opes as how you dies now, you an' that bastard inside yer an' all, I 'opes."

Another contraction came on, and Bella screamed with pain. "Stop it. Don't let it come. Stop it some'ow."

"I'll give you 'don't let it come'," screamed Flo. "I'll kill you afore it comes, yer filthy bitch, you."

They were both screaming at each other. A terrified Tom appeared in the doorway. Flo turned on him, her face red with passion. "Get out of here," she said. "Vis is no place for a man. Just get out. Go for a walk, or somefink. An don't come back 'til termorrer mornin'."

Tom withdrew with speed. Men were accustomed to being ordered about in that way when it came to childbirth.

His appearance must have made Flo think more clearly. She became practical. "We've gotta get rid of it," she said. "No one mus' know, least of all 'im. When it's born I'll take it away and put it in an institution. No one will know."

Bella grabbed her hand, her eyes alight. "Oh mum, will yer? Will yer do that fer me?"

My head was spinning. Up to that moment I had been flattened morally and emotionally, by all the noise, and the high drama going on between mother and daughter. But this was a new turn of events.

"You can't possibly do that," I said. "What are you going to tell Tom when he gets home tomorrow?"

"We'll tell 'im it's dead," said Flo confidently.

"But you can't do that in this day and age. You can't spirit away a living baby and announce that it died. You would never get away with it. Tom thinks he's the father. He would ask to see the baby. He would ask why it died."

"He can't see ve baby," said Flo with less confidence. " He's got to think it's dead and buried."

"This is ridiculous," I said. "We are not living in the 1850s. If I deliver a living baby, I have to make my report, and that has to go to the health authorities. The baby can't just die or disappear. Someone will have to account for it."

Just then another contraction came on, and the dialogue had to be suspended. My head was racing. They were mad, both of them, beyond all reason.

The contraction passed. Flo had also been thinking furiously and making her plans. "Well you go away, then. Say you 'ad to go to another patient, or summat. I can deliver the baby myself, an' I don't 'ave to make no bleedin' report to no bleedin' authority. I can just take the baby away when it's born, an' no one'll know where it's gorn to, they won't. An' Tom'll never see it."

I reeled under the impact of this suggestion. "I can't possibly do that. I'm a professional midwife, trained and registered. Bella is my patient. I can't walk out on her in the first stage of labour, and leave her in the hands of an untrained woman. I still have to make my report. What am I to tell the Sisters? How am I to account for my actions?"

Another contraction came on. Bella was screaming. "Oh, stop it. Don' let it come. Let me die. What'll 'e say? 'e'll kill me!"

Her mother, defiant, said, "Don't you fret, my luvvy. He'll never see it. Yer mum'll get rid of it for yer."

"But you can't," I shouted. I felt myself getting hysterical, too. "If a living baby is born, it can't just be 'got rid of'. If you try anything like that, you will have the police after you. You will be committing a crime, and then your situation will be worse than ever."

Flo sobered up a bit. "It'll have to be adopted, then."

"That's more like it," I said. "But even then the baby has to be registered, and adoption papers have to be drawn up and signed by both parents to give consent. Tom thinks it is his baby. You can't hide it from him and then tell him he's got to sign his baby away for adoption. He wouldn't agree to that."

Bella started screaming again. Dear God, what's her blood pressure doing, I thought. Maybe, with all this second stage trauma, the grandmother will get her way after all and the baby will die! I got out my foetal stethoscope to listen to the heartbeat. Bella must have read my thoughts. She pushed the stethoscope away.

"Leave it alone. I wants it to die, can't you see that?"

"I must ring for the doctor," I said. "Anything could happen, and I need help."

"Don't you dare," Flo snarled at me. "No one mus' know – no doctors. I've got to get rid of it somehow."

"Don't let's start on that again," I shouted. "I need a doctor, and I'm going to ring for one now."

Quick as a flash, Flo was in front of me. She grabbed my surgical scissors from the delivery tray, rushed into the other room, and cut the wire of the telephone. She glared at me in triumph.

"There now. Yer can go down ve road an' telephone ve doctor."

I didn't dare do such a thing. The second stage was imminent. The baby might be born in my absence, and I might return to find it had been "got rid of".

There was another contraction. Bella seemed to be bearing down. She was still crying hysterically, but definitely giving a push. Flo started wailing.

"Shut up," I said in a cold, hard voice. "Shut up, and get out of this room."

She looked startled, but stopped her noise.

"Now, leave this room at once. I have a baby to deliver, and I cannot do it with you present. Go."

She gasped, and opened her mouth to say something, but

thought better of it and left, shutting the door quietly behind her.

I turned to Bella. "Now roll over on to your left side, and do exactly as I tell you. This baby will be born within the next few minutes. I don't want you to have a tear or a haemorrhage, so just do as I say."

She was quiet and cooperative. It was a perfect delivery.

The baby was pure white and looked just like Tom. She was the apple of her father's eye, and was doted upon by her proud grandfather. Her wise grandmother kept the secrets of the delivery room to herself.

I was the only person outside the family to know, and until this moment, I have never told a soul.

OF MIXED DESCENT II

The Smiths were an average, respectable East End family, with a rub-along sort of marriage. Cyril was a skilled pilot in the docks, and Doris worked in a hairdressers, as her five children were now of school age. They were not hard up, but took their holidays in the hop-picking fields of Kent. Both Cyril and Doris had enjoyed such holidays all through their childhood. Their own children enjoyed the healthy country air, the camaraderie of the other children, the open spaces to run around in, and the chance to earn some pocket money if they filled their baskets with hops. The family met the same people, year after year, who came from other areas of London, and friendships were formed and renewed every year.

Each family had to take their own bedding, primus stove, and cooking equipment. They were allocated a space considered sufficient for the size of each family in sheds or barns, where they dwelt for a fortnight. Food was bought from the farm shop. Some took tents and camped. The adults worked all day in the fields, picking the hops for which they were paid, and most of the children joined in. In the 1950s, poverty was not as extreme as it had been for earlier generations, so the necessity to earn the pittance which was euphemistically called a wage had largely passed. In days gone by, children had had to work from morning to dusk to earn a few pennies which, added to their parents' money, would help the family through the winter. The hop-picking holidays had also been lifesavers for many East End children, because they were exposed to the sunshine, which prevented rickets.

By the 1950s, the children were mostly free to play, and to join in the picking only if they wanted to. Many farms had a stream or river running through them, which was the centre of childhood fun. The evenings were a great time for the whole temporary community, as they would light fires in the open air, sing songs, flirt and tell stories, and generally make believe that they were country folk and not city-dwellers at all.

Before the war the annual hop-pickers consisted almost exclusively of East Enders, Romany gypsies, and tramps. After the war, with increased mobility of population worldwide, a more varied group of people turned up at the farms each year. (Mechanisation of hop-picking put an end to this annual activity for so many people.)

Doris and Cyril settled with their children in the shed, occupying the seven-foot square space that had been chalked on the floor for them. They were given a straw palliasse to sleep on, and with the primus stove and a hurricane lamp, it was all considered very comfortable. There were a lot of new people at the farm that year, and several families from the West Indies, which was quite a surprise. At first Doris was stand-offish. She had never met or spoken to a black person before, much less slept in the same barn as a group of them, but the children immediately made friends, as children always do. The women were laughing and friendly, and Doris quickly found her inhibitions breaking down.

In fact the holiday proved to be a real eye-opener for Doris and Cyril. They had never before realised that West Indian people could be so much fun. It is said that East Enders are good-humoured. Well, beside the West Indians, Cockneys look positively dour. Doris and Cyril laughed from morning to night, and the hard work of hop-picking was barely felt. Tired but elated in the evenings, Doris would leave the fields to prepare a meal for her family, and then join the groups sitting around the fires. The songs were new this year. She had never heard West Indian singing before, with its blend of beauty and tragedy, and it stirred deep and nameless longings in her heart. She joined in the choruses and the round songs with an ear for music that she never knew she possessed. Cyril didn't think much of the music, and nothing on earth would have induced him to open his mouth and sing, so he joined one of the other groups around another fire where the blokes were more to his liking.

Time passes all too quickly when you are enjoying yourself, and no one wanted to leave at the end of the fortnight. But their time was up, and they all declared it was the best holiday of their life, and that they would meet again next year. The children cried at parting.

The humdrum life of work and school and neighbours and gossip started again, and gradually the memory of the Kentish holiday faded into a dream.

No one was surprised when Doris announced at the Christmas party that she was pregnant again. She was only thirty-eight, and five children was not considered to be a large family. Cyril was told that he "wasn't 'alf a lad", and they were both given everyone's good wishes.

She went into labour early one morning. Cyril rang us on his way to work. Doris was able to get the children up and off to school, and a neighbour came in to be with her for a while. I arrived around 9.30 a.m. to find everything in good order. The house was clean and tidy. The baby things were ready and immaculate. All the requirements we asked for, such as hot water, soap, and so on, were ready. Doris was calm and cheerful. The neighbour left as I arrived, and said that she would pop in later. Labour was uneventful, and fairly quick.

At twelve noon she delivered a baby boy, who was quite obviously black.

I, of course, was the first to see him, and didn't know what to say or do. After I had cut the cord, I wrapped him in a towel, and placed him in the cot whilst I attended to the third stage. This allowed me a little time to think: should I say something? If so, what? Or should I just hand her the baby, and let her see for herself? I decided upon the second course.

The third stage of labour usually takes at least fifteen to twenty minutes, so during that time I simply picked the baby up, and put him in Doris's arms.

She was silent for a long time, and then said, "He's beau'iful. He's so lovely, 'e makes me wanna cry."

Tears silently came to her eyes and coursed down her cheeks.

She sobbed inwardly to herself as she clung to the baby.

"Oh he's so beau'iful. I never meant to, but wha' could I do? An' now wha' am I goin' to do? He's the lovelies' baby I ever seed."

She could speak no more for crying.

I was shaken by the unexpected turn of events, but had to attend to my job. I said, "Look, I think the placenta will come soon. Let me put the baby back in the cot, only for a few minutes, so that we can complete your delivery safely, and clean you up. We can talk after that."

She allowed me to take the baby, and within ten minutes everything was complete.

I put the baby back in her arms, and silently attended to my clearing up. I felt it better not to initiate any conversation.

She held him quietly for a long time, kissing him, and rubbing her face against his. She held his hand, and flexed his arm, and said, "His fingernails is white, yer know."

Was this a cry of hope? Then she continued, "Wha' am I goin' to do? Wha' can I do, nurse?"

She sobbed in broken-hearted anguish, and clung to the baby with all the fervour and passion of a mother's love. She couldn't speak; she could only groan, and rock him in her arms.

I couldn't reply to her question. What could I say?

I finished what I was doing, and checked the placenta, which was intact. Then I said, "I would like to bath the baby, and weigh him, is that all right?"

She gave the baby to me quietly, and watched every move as I bathed him, as though she was afraid that I might take him away. I think she knew in her heart what was going to happen.

I weighed and measured him. He was a big baby: 9lb 4oz, twenty two inches long, and perfect in every way. He certainly was beautiful; his skin was a dusky tawny colour, fine, dark curly hair already showed on his head. The slightly depressed bridge of his nose, and splayed nostrils accentuated his high, broad forehead. His skin was smooth and unwrinkled.

I gave him back to his mother, and said, "He is the loveliest baby I have ever seen in my life, Doris. You can be proud of him."

She looked at me with bleak despair. "Wha' am I goin' to do?"

"I don't know. I really don't. Your husband will be coming home from work this evening, thinking he is the father of a new baby. He will ask to see him, and you cannot hide him. I don't think you should be alone when he comes home. Can your mother come round to be with you?"

"No. That would make fings worse. He hates my mum. Can you be 'ere wiv me, nurse? You're right. I'm frightened of Cyril seeing 'im."

And she clutched the baby to her, in a desperate gesture of protection.

"I'm not sure that I would be the right person", I replied. "I'm a midwife. Perhaps you need a social worker to be here. I definitely think you need someone for your own protection, and that of the baby."

I promised to look into it, and left.

I imagine she had one happy afternoon with her baby, dozing, cuddling, kissing him, forging with him that unbreakable bond that is a mother's love for her baby, which is every baby's birthright. Perhaps she knew what was coming, and tried to cram a lifetime of love into a few short hours. Perhaps she crooned to him the West Indian spirituals that she had learned around the camp fire.

I reported to Sister Julienne, and expressed my fears. She said, "You are right that someone must be there when her husband sees the baby. However, I think it would be better for a man to be present. All the social workers in this area are women. I will speak to the Rector."

In the event, the Rector sent a young curate to be at the house from five o'clock onwards. He did not go himself, because he thought it would look too portentous if he arrived at the house.

The curate reported that events had transpired very much as I had expected. Cyril took one silent, horrified look at the baby, and made a great swipe at his wife with his fist. The blow was deflected by the curate. Then he made to grab the baby and hurl it against the wall, and was only prevented from doing so by the curate. He said to his wife, "If this bastard stays in the 'ouse one single night, I'll kill 'im, an' you an' all."

The savage gleam in his eye showed that he meant it. "You jest wait, yer bitch."

An hour later the curate left carrying the baby in a small wicker basket, with a bundle of baby clothes in a paper bag. He brought the baby to Nonnatus House, and we cared for him overnight. He was received into a children's home the next morning. His mother never saw him again.

OF MIXED DESCENT III

Ted was fifty-eight when his wife died. She developed cancer and he nursed her tenderly for eighteen months. He gave up his job in order to do so, and they lived on his savings during her illness. They had a happy marriage, and were very close. No children had been born to them, and they had depended entirely on each other for companionship, neither of them being particularly extrovert or sociable. After her death, he was very lonely. He had few real friends, and his mates at work had largely forgotten him since his leaving. He had never cared for pubs and clubs, and was not going to start trying to be the clubby sort at the age of nearly sixty. He tidied the house but couldn't bring himself to clear his wife's room. He cooked scrappy meals for himself, went for long walks, frequented the cinema and the public library, and listened to the radio. He was a Methodist, and attended church each Sunday, and although he tried joining the men's social club, he couldn't get on with it, so he joined the Bible class instead, which was more to his liking.

It seems to be a law of life that a lonely widower will always find a woman to console and comfort him. If he is left with young children he is even more favourably placed. Women are queueing up to look after both him and the children. On the other hand, a lonely widow or divorcee has no such natural advantages. If not exactly shunned by society, she is usually made to feel decidedly spare. A lonely widow will usually not find men crowding around anxious to give her love and companionship. If she has children, the men will usually run a mile. She will be left alone to struggle on and support herself and her children, and usually her life will be one of unremitting hard work.

Winnie had been alone for longer than she cared to remember. Her young husband had been killed early in the war, leaving her with three children. A meagre pension from the State barely covered the rent, let alone compensated for the loss of her husband. She took a job in a paper shop. The hours were long and hard – from 5 a.m. to 5.30 p.m. She got up each morning at 4.30 a.m. to get down to the newsagents to receive, sort, pack, and put out the newspapers. Her mother came in each day at 8 a.m. to get the children up and off to school. It meant that they were alone for about four hours, but it was a risk that she had to take. Winnie's mum suggested that they should all come and live with her, but Win valued her independence, and refused unless, as she said, "I jes' can't cope any more". That day never came. Winnie was the coping sort.

They met in the paper shop. She had served him for many years, but never noticed him particularly amongst all her other customers. It was when he started hanging around in the shop for longer than necessary to buy a morning paper that she, and the other staff, began to take note. He would buy his paper, then look at another, then look at the magazine shelves, sometimes buying one. Then he would pick up a bar of chocolate and turn it over in his hand, sigh, and put it back, and buy a packet of Woodbines instead. The staff said to each other, "Somethink's up with that old geezer".

One day, when Ted was holding a bar of chocolate, Winnie went up to him and asked kindly if she could help.

He said, "No, dearie. There's nothing you can do for me. My wife used to like this chocolate. I used to get it for 'er. She died last year. Thank you for asking, dear".

And their eyes met with sympathy and understanding.

After that Winnie always made a point of serving him. One day Ted said, "I was finkin' o' goin' to the flicks tonight. How about comin' wiv me – if yer 'usband don't object".

She said, "I aint got no 'usband, an' I don't mind if I do".

One thing led to another, and within a year he asked her to marry him.

Winnie thought about it for a week. There were over twenty years between them; she was fond of him, but not really in love with him. He was kind and good, though not wildly exciting. She consulted her mother, and the outcome of the female deliberations was that she accepted his offer of marriage.

Ted was overjoyed, and they had a Methodist Church wedding. He did not want to take his new bride to the house which he had shared for so long with his first wife, so he gave up the rental and took another terraced property. Winnie was able to give up the tiny cheap flat where she had brought up her children, so the terraced cottage was just for her and Ted. It seemed like a palace to her. As the weeks and months passed after the marriage her happiness grew, and she told her mother that she had not done the wrong thing.

When he was young Ted had prudently taken out an insurance policy that matured when he was sixty. He now did not have to go out to work ever again. Winnie, on the other hand, did not want to give up the paper shop. She was so used to hard work that idleness would have bored her to tears but, as Ted wanted her at home more, she agreed to cut down her hours. Their life was very happy.

Winnie was forty-four when her periods stopped. She thought it was the menopause. She felt a bit odd, but her mother told her that all women feel a bit funny during the change, and not to worry. She continued in the paper shop, and brushed aside any feelings of queasiness. It wasn't until six months later that she noticed she was putting on weight. Another month passed, and Ted noticed a hard lump in her tummy. Having experienced his first wife dying of cancer, hard lumps were a source of deep anxiety for him. He insisted that she should see the doctor, and went with her to the surgery.

Examination showed her to be in an advanced stage of pregnancy. The couple were shattered. Why this obvious explanation had not occurred to either of them before is impossible to conjecture, but it hadn't, and they were both knocked sideways by the news.

There wasn't much time to prepare for a new baby. Winnie left the paper shop that day, and booked with the Sisters for her confinement. Hastily, the bedroom was prepared, and baby equipment bought. Perhaps it was buying the pram and little white sheets that affected Ted so profoundly. Overnight he changed from a bemused and bewildered elderly man to an intensely excited and fiercely proud father-to-be. Suddenly he looked ten years younger.

A fortnight later Winnie went into labour. We had arranged for a doctor to be present at the delivery, because there had been so little time for antenatal preparation, and because Winnie, now forty-five, was decidedly old for having a baby.

Ted had taken note of our requirements and advice about preparation. He couldn't have planned it more carefully or thoroughly. He had told Win's mother not to come but that Ted would inform her when the baby was born. He had obtained books on childbirth and babycare, which he read all the time. When she went into labour he called us, full of joy and anticipation, tinged only with a little anxiety.

The doctor and I arrived at almost the same time. It was early first stage, and it had been agreed that I should stay with her throughout labour, from the time of arrival to the third stage completion. The doctor examined her and said he would leave and call back just before evening surgery to assess progress.

I sat down to watch and wait. I advised that she should not lie down, but walk about a bit. Ted took Win's arm and gently and carefully led her up and down the garden path. She could quite easily have walked it by herself, but he wanted and needed to be protective, quite forgetful of the fact that only two weeks earlier she had been dashing off to the paper shop. I suggested she should have a bath. The house boasted a bathroom, and so he heated up the water, and gently helped her in. He washed her, carefully helped her out and then dried her. I advised a light meal, so he poached an egg. He couldn't have done more.

I looked at his library books: Grantley Dick Read's *Natural Childbirth*; *Margaret Myles's Midwifery*; *The New Baby*; *Positive Parents*; *The Growing Child*; *From Birth to Teens*. He had been doing his homework.

The doctor returned just before 6 p.m., and there was no real change in the early labour pattern. We agreed that, in view of her age, if the first stage continued for longer than twelve hours, Winnie should be transferred to the hospital. Both Ted and Winnie agreed to this, but hoped it would not be necessary.

Between 9 and 10 p.m. I observed a change in the labour pattern. Contractions were more frequent and stronger. I started her on the gas and air machine, and asked Ted to go out and phone for the doctor.

When he arrived the doctor gave her a mild analgesic, and we both sat down and waited. Ted courteously offered us a meal, or tea, or drinks, whatever we wanted.

We did not have long to wait. Just after midnight the second stage of labour commenced, and within twenty minutes the baby was born.

It was a little boy, with unmistakably ethnic features.

The doctor and I looked at each other, and the mother, in stunned silence. No one said a word. I have never known such an unnerving silence at a delivery. What each of us was thinking the others never knew, but our thoughts must all have been about the same question: "What on earth is Ted going to say when he sees the baby?"

The third stage had to be dealt with, and this was conducted in dead silence. While the doctor was busy with the mother, I bathed, checked, and weighed the baby. He certainly was a beautiful little thing, of average weight, clear dusky skin, soft curly brown hair. A picture perfect baby – if you are expecting to see a baby of mixed racial origins. But Ted wasn't. He was expecting to see his own child. I shut my eyes in a futile attempt to obliterate the scene to come.

Everything was finished and tidied up. The mother looked fresh in a white nightgown; the baby looked beautiful in a white shawl.

The doctor said, "I think we had better ask your husband to come up now."

They were the first words to be spoken since the delivery.

Winnie said, "I reckons as 'ow we'd best get it over wiv".

I went downstairs and told Ted that a baby boy had been safely born, and would he like to come up.

He shouted, "A boy!" and leaped to his feet like a youngster of twenty-two, not a man of over sixty. He bounded up the stairs two at a time, entered the bedroom and took both his wife and the baby in his arms. He kissed them both and said, "This is the proudest and happiest day of my life."

The doctor and I exchanged glances. He hadn't noticed yet. He said to his wife, "You don't know what vis means to me, Win. Can I 'old ve baby?"

She silently handed him over.

Ted sat on the edge of the bed, and cradled the baby awkwardly in his arms (all new fathers look awkward with a baby!) He looked long at his little face, and stroked his hair and ears. He undid the shawl, and looked at the tiny body. He touched his legs, and moved his arms, and took his hand. The baby's face puckered up and he gave a little mewing cry.

Ted gazed at him silently for a long time. Then he looked up with a beatific smile, "Well, I don't reckon to know much about babies, but I can see as how this is the most beautiful in the world. What's we going to call him, luv?"

The doctor and I looked at each other in silent amazement. Was it really possible he hadn't noticed? Winnie, who had seemed unable to breathe, took a large shuddering breath, and said, "You choose, Ted, luv. He's yourn."

"We'll call 'im Edward, then. It's a good ol' family name. Me dad's an' gran'dad's. He's my son Ted."

The doctor and I left the three of them sitting happily together. Outside, the doctor said, "It is possible that he just hasn't noticed yet. Black skin is pale at birth, and this child is obviously only half-black, or even less than that, because his father may have been of mixed racial descent. However, pigmentation usually becomes more marked as the child ages, and at some stage Ted is certainly going to notice and start asking questions."

Time went by, and Ted didn't notice or, in any event, didn't appear to notice. Win must have had a word with her mother and other female relatives to say nothing to Ted about the baby's appearance, and indeed nothing was said.

Win went back to work part-time at the paper shop after about six weeks. Ted had longer each day with the baby and assumed most of the parenting. He bathed and fed him, and proudly took him out in the pram, greeting passersby and inviting them all to look at "my son Ted". As the baby grew older, he played with him all the time, inventing learning games and toys. In consequence, by the age of eighteen months, little Ted was very bright and advanced for his age. The relationship between father and son was lovely to see.

By the time the child reached school age, his features were noticeably black. Yet still Ted did not appear to notice. He had made a wider circle of friends than he had ever had in his life before, largely due to the fact that he took the child everywhere, and people responded to this bright, handsome little boy, whom Ted introduced proudly as "my son Ted". The child was just as proud, in his own way, of his father and as he clung to his big protective hand, gazed up adoringly with his huge black eyes. At school he always spoke of "my dad" as though he were the king himself.

Ted, approaching seventy, had no inhibitions about waiting outside the school gates along with young mothers nearly half a century his junior. Only two or three little black or mixed race children would come running out of school, to black mothers, but one of them would fling himself into Ted's arms with the cry, "Daddy."

"Lets go down the docks today, son," he would say, kissing him. "There's a big German vessel jes' come in vis mornin' wiv three funnels. Yer don' see 'em very often. An' yer mum will 'ave tea ready when we gits back."

Yet still he didn't seem to notice.

Of course there were whisperings and gossip amongst neighbours and acquaintances, but none of them actually said anything to Ted. The more unkind would snigger and say, "There's no fool like an old fool." And the rest would laugh and agree, "Yer can say tha' again".

I have a different theory.

In the Russian Orthodox Church there is the concept of the Holy Fool. It means someone who is a fool to the ways of the world, but wise to the ways of God.

I think that Ted, from the moment he saw the baby, knew that he could not possibly be the father. It must have been a shock, but he had controlled himself, and sat thinking for a long time as he held the baby. Perhaps he saw ahead.

Perhaps he understood in that moment that if he so much as questioned the baby's fatherhood, it would mean humiliation for the child, and might jeopardise his entire future. Perhaps, as he held the baby, he realised that any such suggestion could shatter his whole happiness. Perhaps he understood that he could not reasonably expect an independent and energetic spirit like Winnie to find him sexually exciting and fulfilling. Perhaps an angel's voice told him that any questions were best left unasked and unanswered.

And so he decided upon the most unexpected, and yet the simplest course of all. He chose to be such a Fool that he couldn't see the obvious.

THE LUNCHEON PARTY

"No Jimmy, not this time. You and Mike are *not* camping out in the boiler room at Nonnatus House. I may have deceived the Home Sister at the Hospital, but I am not going to deceive Sister Julienne. Besides, I don't trust you. I don't believe for a moment that there is *another* emergency. I think you just want to be able to boast to the boys that you have slept in a convent!"

Jimmy and Mike looked a trifle crestfallen. They had been plying me with beer and soft talk, in the confident expectation that I would swallow a load of rubbish about them being down on their luck and out of their digs, and would I smuggle them in the back door of Nonnatus House? The male of the species is sweetly naive.

The evening had been fun – a change and relaxation from the rigours of daily work. The beer had been pleasant, and the conversation exuberant, but it was time to go. It was a long way back to the East End, buses were not plentiful after 11 p.m., and I would have to be up at 6.30 a.m. the next morning for a full day's work. I stood up. An idea had come to mind. It seemed a pity to disappoint them altogether.

"But how would you like to come to lunch one Sunday?"

Their enthusiastic agreement was immediate.

"OK. I will ask Sister Julienne, and will ring you to fix a date. I must be off now."

I spoke to Sister Julienne next day. She had heard about Jimmy before, on the occasion when I had taken a 3 a.m. swim in the sea at Brighton and arrived for work at ten in the morning. She agreed at once to a luncheon party for the boys.

"It would be delightful. We usually entertain retired missionaries, or visiting preachers. A couple of lively young men would be a pleasure for us all."

She fixed a date for three weeks ahead, when there were no other guests for Sunday lunch, and I telephoned Jimmy to firm up the arrangements.

"Do you think the nuns could run to three of us for lunch? Alan wants to come. He thinks he might get a story."

Alan was a reporter, scraping a modest living on his first job in Fleet Street. I thought it highly likely that Sister Julienne could find one more chair at the refectory table, but was not at all sure that Alan would get much of a story out of the lunch. However, hope always runs high in a young reporter's heart – until the iron enters his soul, that is.

The girls were in a flutter of excitement about three young men coming to Sunday lunch. We were all single nurses with a seemingly endless working week and were often hard put to meet eligible young men. Expectations ran high.

I wondered, with a good deal of amusement, how the meal would go. What would the boys make of us? How would they react to the nuns, particularly to Sister Monica Joan? And it would be interesting to see Alan's "story".

The day arrived, warm and bright, and none of our patients was expected to go into labour, which would have disrupted the luncheon party. Everyone was in a flurry of excitement. Had the boys known the flutter they were causing in so many female hearts, they would have been deeply flattered. Or perhaps not. Perhaps they would have regarded it as no more than their devastating charms were due.

They arrived at about 12.30 p.m., just after the Sisters had entered chapel for Tierce, the midday Office.

I opened the door. They certainly looked very spruce, in grey suits, newly washed shirts, and highly polished shoes. I had never before seen them look like that on a Sunday morning. Obviously lunch in a convent was a novel experience for such dedicated young men-about-town. They looked a little unsure of themselves, though.

We kissed, but slightly more formally than usual – no hugs, no laughter, no badinage about nothing much – just a formal kiss, a polite "How are you?", and "Did you have a good journey?"

I felt a trifle uncomfortable, having never found conversation easy. We all know people in a certain context, and outside the familiar, often find them to be completely different. I had known Jimmy since childhood, but normally met up with the others in London pubs. I didn't know what to say, and just stood around looking awkward, thinking the whole thing was not such a good idea after all. The boys could find nothing to say either.

Cynthia saved the day. She always did, without knowing how or what she had done. She stepped forward, her soft smile dispelling the tension and filling the rather strained atmosphere with warmth. When she spoke, the slow sexy voice just knocked them over. All she said was: "You must be Jimmy and Mike and Alan. How lovely – we've been looking forward to this. Now which of you is which?"

Was it the way she said it, or the wide smiling eyes, or the unaffected warmth of her welcome? The boys must have met scores of girls who were more beautiful, with more self-conscious allure, but they could seldom, if ever, have met a girl with a voice quite like that. They were absolutely bowled over and all three stepped forward at the same time, crashing into each other. She laughed. The ice was broken.

"The Sisters will be here soon, but come into the kitchen and have a coffee, and we can have a chat."

Coffee, nectar, ambrosia? They followed eagerly; anything with this glorious girl would be heaven. I, thankfully, was forgotten and I breathed a sigh of relief. The luncheon would be a success.

Mrs B. had neither sex appeal nor an alluring voice, "Now don' you make a mess in 'ere. I've got lunch to serve."

Jimmy smiled confidently at her. "Don't you worry, madam; we won't mess up this beautiful kitchen, will we boys? What a magnificent kitchen, and what glorious smells! All your own home cooking, I take it, madam?"

Mrs B. sniffed, and eyed him suspiciously. She had grown-up sons of her own, and was not susceptible to their particular charms. "You jes' watch it, tha's all I'm sayin'."

"Oh, watch it we certainly will," said Mike, whose eyes had not left Cynthia as she filled the kettle. The water pipes all around the kitchen rattled and shook as she opened the tap. She laughed and said, "That's just our plumbing system. You'll get used to it."

"Oh, I'd like to get used to it", said Mike with enthusiasm.

Cynthia laughed and blushed a little, brushing back the hair that had fallen over her face.

"Allow me," said Mike gallantly, taking the kettle from her and carrying it over to the gas stove.

Chummy appeared in the doorway, her head buried in *The Times*.

"I say, gels, did you know that Binkie Bingham-Binghouse is getting spliced at last? Jolly good show, what? Actually, her Mater will be frightfully chuffed, don't you know. They thought she was on the shelf. Good old Binkie, haw haw!"

She looked up and saw the boys. At once she went red, and jerked the arm holding the newspaper. It crashed into the dresser, setting the cups rattling and shaking. The paper caught behind a couple of plates and sent them crashing to the floor, smashing them into a dozen pieces.

Mrs B. rushed forward, snarling:

"You clumsy great . . . you – you – jest get out o' my kitchen, you clumsy . . . you!"

Poor Chummy! It always happened that way. Social situations were a nightmare for her, particularly when men were around. She just didn't know what to say to a man, nor how to behave.

Cynthia again saved the day. She grabbed a dustpan and brush, saying, "Never mind, Mrs B. Luckily it was the plate with the crack in it. It needed throwing out, anyway."

Deftly she swept up the bits, Mike appreciatively studying her neat little bottom as she bent down.

Chummy stood in the doorway, abashed and tongue-tied. I tried to get her to come over and join us for a cup of coffee, but she flushed scarlet and muttered something about going upstairs to wash her hands before lunch.

The boys looked at each other in wonder. Lunch in a convent

was an unknown, but a female giant hurling plates around was the last thing they had expected. Alan took out his notebook and started scribbling furiously.

We heard the bell sound from the chapel and a little later the Sisters' footsteps. Sister Julienne walked briskly into the kitchen, small, plump, and motherly. She looked at the boys with true affection, and held out both hands.

"I've heard so much about you, and this is a real treat for us all to have you here. Mrs B. has prepared roast beef and Yorkshire pudding, followed by apple pie. Will you like that, do you think?"

Three cool, sophisticated young men responded like three small boys taking sweets from a favourite auntie.

We entered the refectory. After grace, during which the boys eyed each other with amusement, and muttered a self-conscious "Amen", we sat at the large square table and Mrs B. brought in the luncheon trolley. Sister Julienne served as usual, and Trixie took around the plates.

Alan was outrageously handsome. He had perfect, regular features, clear skin, dark curly hair, and soft dark eyes fringed with eyelashes that any girl would kill for. I had met him a couple of times, and when the girls flocked around him in droves, trying to win a glance from his bright eyes, I had noticed that he treated them as pleasing but inconsequential toys. He regarded himself as a "leader of opinion". With a degree in philosophy from Cambridge University, he had already formed conclusions about life which he had picked up secondhand, without having lived much of it himself. The troubles and turmoils that befall most of us had yet to disturb his assumption of superiority. He had a huge regard for his own intelligence which, I had concluded, was adequate but not outstanding. He placed his notebook and pencil beside him on the dining table, which was rude, but Alan was not troubled by propriety; he was on a job, not a guest at a luncheon party.

He had been placed next to Sister Monica Joan and was slightly annoyed about this, probably regarding her as being too old to be of interest to his readership. He had wanted to sit next to Sister Bernadette and talk about the impact of the new National Health

Service upon the older style of medicine. However, he was not one to be deflected from his purpose and called across the table to Sister Bernadette.

"As nuns are the servants of God, and the State has now taken over your midwifery service, do you now see your role as servants of the State?"

He had planned this carefully, as he wanted to portray the futility of religion in his story. This would appeal to his editor.

Sister Bernadette was contemplating her Yorkshire pudding with pleasure, and was unprepared such a question. In the ten seconds that it took for her to think of a suitable reply, Sister Monica Joan addressed him.

"In the puny compass of our wit the Silver Cord is loosed. The State is the servant of the Orb. The servant is wiser than the organic process of growth differentiated by truth at the fountain head. Do you see your role as one of the forty-two Assessors of the Dead?"

"What?"

Alan stopped eating, mouth open, fork raised.

"Eh, that is . . . I mean . . . pardon?"

"Kindly don't wave your fork at me like that, young man. Put it down," said Sister Monica Joan sharply. She eyed him imperiously. "We were discussing the role of the free spirit, released by the confluence of the several centres, until you so rudely poked your fork in my ear. But what is that to me? Let us go with God, and accept the unacceptable. It is a lonely walk into the mind's retreat. Is there another roast potato? A soft one, and a little more onion gravy, if you please."

She passed her plate, and looked sideways at Alan, with a certain amount of distaste. But she was prepared to continue the conversation.

"Do you regard your role as a new form of sanctity without precedent, or an equivalent revelation of the universe, also without precedent?" she enquired politely.

The whole table was looking at Alan as he struggled for words. I was quietly killing myself. This was better than expected.

"I really don't know. I hadn't thought about it."

"Oh, come now. A young man of your genius must surely consider the impact of your thought as the exertion of energy released by the activities of your several centres. Your thought is the vibration of the horizontal, the centralisation of the polarities of positive and negative. I cannot believe that you have not thought about your thought. It is the duty of every great man to reflect upon the excellence of the intellect or, to put it more simply, the auditory impact of the divine consciousness, within the limits of fragmentation. Wouldn't you agree?"

Mike spluttered, and Cynthia quietly nudged him. Trixie nearly choked, and sent a shower of peas across the table. Jimmy and I looked at each other with secret delight. Poor Alan, aware that all eyes were upon him, had the grace to blush.

Sister Monica Joan murmured, as though to herself, but loud enough to be heard by all, "How sweet. Old enough to know it all, and young enough to blush. Perfectly charming."

Having neatly disposed of Alan, she turned her attention to the roast potato.

Sister Julienne looked brightly round the table. "Who would like some more roast beef? And I'm sure Mrs B. has another Yorkshire pudding in the oven. Mike, you look like a good carver. How about you carving for those who want seconds?"

Mike took up the carving knife, sharpened it with a flourish, and sliced generous helpings. Mrs B. came in with another Yorkshire pudding, piping hot. The boys had brought wine with them, and glasses were found. We were not accustomed to wine with lunch at Nonnatus House, but Sister Julienne said that on such a special occasion, all rules would be waived. The nuns giggled like schoolgirls drinking their wine, murmuring "Ooh, what a treat – delicious – you must come again".

Jimmy and Mike were in sparkling form. It had to be owned that they had great charm and *savoir faire* and the luncheon was a huge success. Even Sister Evangelina was relaxed and laughing with Jimmy; but then it's not hard to laugh with dear Jimmy, I reflected. Only Chummy was quiet. She didn't look unhappy, just cautious, aware that at any moment she might knock over a glass of wine, or send a tureen flying. She did not dare to join in the fun. But she smiled all the while, and seemed to enjoy herself in her own way.

The only person who did not look happy was Alan. In fact he looked downright furious. Sister Julienne tried several times to draw him into the conversation, but he would have none of it. He had been made to look a fool by a nun of ninety, and he wasn't going to forgive her, or any of them for that matter. He never did produce his story, I was told.

To my great alarm Mike told the story of when they had lived in the drying room of the nurses' home for three months, and how they had climbed that treacherous fire escape twice a day, in the dark of winter. I had long since left the hospital involved, so could not be sacked, but I felt alarmed about what the Sisters would think of my sins. One glance at Sister Julienne's face, a little flushed with wine, reassured me. She looked towards me and laughed.

"You were taking a chance. I remember when a young man was caught in a nurse's bedroom at St. Thomas's. The girl was immediately dismissed. She was a good nurse, too. It was a pity. However, a few months later, four young men were found in the broom cupboard – or was it the laundry room, I forget – and no one ever discovered who was responsible. It's just as well, because goodness knows how many nurses would have been lost to the profession if they had been found out. That was just before the war, when we needed all the trained nurses we could get."

Puddings arrived, and Sister Julienne rose to serve them. A strange noise from across the table caught my attention, and I looked in that direction. To my astonishment, it was Sister Evangelina, laughing! In fact she was laughing so much, she was spluttering into her napkin. Her neighbour Jimmy, kind and gentlemanly, patted her on the back and handed her a glass of water. She gulped it down, and sat, dabbing her eyes and nose, muttering through chokes and giggles.

"Oh dear. This is too much for me . . . it takes me back to the time when . . . oh, I shall never forget . . . "

Jimmy set to work seriously slapping her back, which seemed to help, but it caused her veil to slip sideways.

We were all determined to get to the bottom of this. Never before had Sister Evangelina been seen laughing convulsively in the Convent, and it obviously had something to do with young men in nurses' bedrooms.

"What happened? Tell us."

"Come on, now. Be a sport."

Sister Julienne paused, serving spoon in hand.

"Oh come on, Sister. You can't leave us in suspense like this. What's the story? Jimmy, give her another glass of wine."

But Sister Evangelina couldn't, or wouldn't, tell. She blew her nose, and wiped her eyes. She spluttered and gurgled and coughed. But she wouldn't say any more. She just grinned mischievously at everyone. A grin from Sister Evangelina was unheard of, never mind a mischievous one!

Sister Monica Joan had been watching this little exhibition with half-closed eyes, and a tiny smile playing round her lips. I wondered what she was thinking. Sister Evangelina certainly looked a mess, with her veil askew, her face bright red, moisture seeping from every orifice. I feared an icy comment and so, I think, did Sister Evangelina, for she looked at her tormentor with apprehension. But we were both wrong.

Sister Monica Joan waited until the laughter had subsided, and with the timing of an instinctive actress recited slowly and dramatically, " 'Oh – I shall remember the hours that we spent, In age I'll remember, and not to repent.' "

She paused for effect, then leaned across the table towards Sister Evangelina, and winked. In a stage whisper that could be heard by all, she said confidentially, "Don't say another word, my dear, not another word. The nosy lot. They clamour and clatter. They chatter and natter. Don't feed their idle expectations, my dear, 'twill only debase your memories!"

She looked Sister Evangelina straight in the eyes, and winked again, with warmth and understanding. Was it possible? Did I imagine it? Was it a trick of the light? Did Sister Evangelina, or did she not, wink back?

Sister Evangelina never told. I daresay she went to her grave with the story locked in her heart.

The puddings were a masterpiece of Mrs B.'s creative skills. Sister Monica Joan had two helpings of ice cream with chocolate fudge sauce and a little apple pie. She was in brilliant form.

"I remember a young man shut in a wardrobe at Queen Charlotte's Hospital," she recalled. "He was locked in for three hours. It would have been perfectly all right, and no one would have found out, but the foolish fellow had borrowed his father's horse, and tied it to the hospital railings. Now you can hide a young man in a wardrobe or under a bed. But how, I ask, can you hide a horse?"

With a gasp I realised that these memories dated back to the 1890s! What happened? But she wouldn't remember.

"I only remember the horse tied to the railings."

What a pity! Life is so fleeting, and the past so rich. I wanted to hear more. Her mind was perfectly clear at that moment, and knowing how it could cloud over, I asked if she had not found the discipline and petty restrictions of nursing to be intolerable.

"Not a bit of it. After the confinement and restraints of family life, nursing was freedom and adventure. We did not have the licence you young people enjoy today. It was the same for all of us. I recall my cousin Barney. His mother, my aunt, had a French maid. One day – in the middle of the day, my dears – she, my aunt, stepped out on to the terrace to find the French maid seated on a chair, and Barney on his knees placing the shoe on to the foot of the gel. The shoe."

She paused and looked around her.

"Not the petticoat, or anything like that. Just the shoe. My aunt screamed and fainted, I was told. The maid was immediately dismissed, and the family was so scandalised that Barney was given a ten pound note, and a one-way ticket to Canada. He was never seen or heard of again."

Mike speculated that being sent off to Canada was probably the best thing that could have happened to him. Sister Monica Joan looked very thoughtful before replying, "I would like to think that. But it is just as likely that poor Barney died of hunger or disease in the Canadian winter."

It was a sobering thought. I asked for more stories. She smiled at me indulgently.

"I am not here for your entertainment, my dear. I am here by the grace of God. Four score years and ten, it has been. A score too long . . . too long."

She fell silent for a minute, and no one dared speak. She had seen so much, done so much in life – fighting for independence in her youth; entering a religious order in middle age, wartime nursing and midwifery in the London Docks when she was nearly eighty years old. Who could match such experience?

With a slightly amused, slightly quizzical expression in her fine eyes, she looked around at us, so young, so frivolous, so superficial. Her elbow was resting on the table, her slender fingers supporting her chin. We were spellbound by her presence.

"You are all so young," she mused reflectively. "Youth is the first fair flower of spring."

Lifting her head, she spread out her eloquent hands towards us. Her face was radiant, her eyes shining, her voice joyful and triumphant.

"Therefore . . . 'Sing, my darlings, sing, Before your petals fade, To feed the flowers of another spring.'"

SMOG

Conchita Warren was expecting her twenty-fifth baby. I had seen quite a lot of the family during the past year because Liz Warren was the dressmaker of my dreams. She was the oldest daughter, twenty-two years old, and had been making clothes since she first had a doll. It was all she had ever wanted to do, she told me. On leaving school at fourteen, she went straight into an apprenticeship with a firm of high-class dressmakers, with whom she still worked. She did not usually take private clients at home because she said the mess was such that she couldn't ask ladies to come to the house for fittings. However, as I was accustomed to the house, it did not bother either of us. She was an expert in her trade, and enjoyed making garments for me over many years.

I had always loved clothes, and took a good deal of time and trouble over them. My clothes were specially made for me, and I turned my nose up at ready-to-wear stuff. Today this would be unusual and terribly expensive, but it was not the case in the 1950s. In fact it was cheaper. Really good quality clothes could be made for a fraction of what they cost in the best shops. Beautiful materials could be found in the street markets, going for a song. I usually designed my own things, or adapted styles. When I lived in Paris, I would attend the catwalk shows of the great French couturiers – Dior, Chanel, Schiaparelli. The opening of the season was, of course, reserved for the press and the very rich, but after about two or three weeks, when the excitement had settled down, the fashion shows continued, perhaps twice weekly, and anyone could attend. I loved them, and made careful notes and sketches of what I knew would suit me, in order to have them made for me later.

The only trouble was finding a dressmaker skilled enough to make her own paper patterns. Liz was perfection. She not only made up her own patterns, but she had a real stylish flair, and often suggested or adapted things to suit the cloth or the cut. We were about the same age, and it was a happy collaboration.

During one of these visits Liz told me, with a wry smile, that her mother was expecting again. Together we speculated on how many more Conchita was likely to have. Her precise age was not known, but she was probably about forty-two, so she could have another six to eight babies. Going on past form, we put our money on a total of thirty babies.

Conchita booked again with the Sisters for another home confinement, and requested antenatal visits at home. For continuity's sake, I was asked to take the case. She was in perfect condition again. She looked radiant, and did not really look pregnant until about twenty-four weeks, although once again her dates were uncertain. The youngest little girl was one year old. Len was all excitement and anticipation, as though this were only his second or third baby.

It was winter, and very cold and icy. Heavy snow clouds hung over the city, trapping the smoke fumes from all the coal fires, steam trains, and steam engines, the profuse smoke from the ocean-going vessels, and above all the factories, which were largely fuelled by coal. A thick London smog developed. One can have no conception these days of what they were like. The air would be heavy, foul-smelling, and a thick yellowish-grey colour. It was impossible to see more than a yard ahead, even at midday. Traffic was virtually at a standstill. The only way a vehicle could move would be for a man to walk ahead of it, carrying two bright lights – one to shine ahead of him, so that he could find his way, and the other shining behind him for the vehicle to follow. These smogs were a feature of many winters in London at the time, and lasted until the atmospheric pressure lifted, allowing the trapped fumes to escape.

Conchita must have gone into the backyard for something. She either slipped on the ice, or tripped over something she could not see. She must have fallen heavily and lay partly concussed on the freezing concrete for some time. The only children in the house were the little ones under five. She was found by the other children when they came home from school. Apparently she was sufficiently conscious to crawl and with the help of her children, all under eleven, she got back into the house. There was evidence that she had tried to do so before but, being unable to see through the smog, had actually crawled away from the house. It is a miracle that she did not die of exposure. She was in a bad way. A small child went to get a neighbour, who wrapped her in blankets and gave her hot brandy and water. Older children began returning home after 4 p.m. and learned of their mother's accident. Len and the oldest boys were last to return, because they had been on a job in Knightsbridge and the journey home had taken two and a half hours.

That night Conchita went into labour.

The phone rang at about 11.30 p.m. I was called to the phone, as it was my case. I was aghast – firstly because of the premature labour, and secondly because of the weather conditions. How on earth was I to find my way to Limehouse? I was speaking to one of the elder sons, who briefly explained the circumstances. My first question was, "Have you called the doctor?" Yes, he had, but the doctor was out. "Well, you must keep on trying," I said, "because your mother may be ill. If she was concussed, and her temperature dropped a lot, she may need medical treatment, quite apart from the pregnancy. Ring the doctor again now. He may have difficulty getting to you, but so will I."

I replaced the telephone, and looked out of the window. I couldn't see a thing. Thick grey swirls of fog seemed to be circling the window panes, trying to get in. I shivered, as much with apprehension for Conchita's awful plight as reluctance to go out at all. The sirens from the river boats, and those in the docks, moaned a hollow call.

We had hardly been out of the house for three days, hoping and praying that no one would go into labour before the smog lifted. It was a situation I could not, should not, handle alone.

I went up to the Sisters' floor to call Sister Julienne. Nuns go to bed at about nine o'clock because they get up before 4 a.m. for the first Office of the day, so eleven-thirty would be the middle of the night for them. Nonetheless, with the first light tap on the door, Sister was awake.

"Who is it?," she called out.

I said my name, and that Conchita Warren was in premature labour.

"Wait a minute."

I waited thirty seconds, and Sister joined me in the corridor, shutting the door of her cell behind her. She was wearing a coarse brown wool dressing gown, and, amazingly, her veil. The question, does she go to bed in the thing? flashed through my mind. It must be damned uncomfortable.

But there was no time to reflect upon the habit of a nun. I told her briefly the story that had been given to me over the telephone.

She thought for a moment and said, "Limehouse is over three miles away. You might not get there. There is no point in me, or any of the midwives, coming with you, because two people can get lost just as easily as one. You must have a police escort. Go now and ring the police, and God be with you, my dear. I will pray for Conchita Warren and her unborn baby."

The knowledge that Sister Julienne would be praying for us had an extraordinary effect. All the tension and anxiety left me, and I felt calm and confident. I had learned to respect the power of prayer. What change had come over the headstrong young girl who, only a year earlier, had found the whole idea of prayer to be a joke?

I spoke to the police and told them it was an emergency. I was told that the safest way to get there would be to walk, but the quickest would be by bicycle. The policeman said: "There is no point in sending a car, because you can't see further than the bonnet, and we would have to have a man walking ahead. We will send a bicycle escort."

I said I would be ready within ten minutes. My delivery bag was already packed and ready. All my thoughts were with Conchita – I did not think that the baby was likely to survive at around twenty-eight weeks gestation. Finding the bicycle shed in the smog and loading up my bike was a tricky business, but I was at the front of Nonnatus House in less than ten minutes.

Two policemen arrived shortly after on bicycles with very powerful lights, front and rear, which illuminated about two yards ahead. One rode ahead of me, and I was instructed to follow him. The other rode beside me, I being on the kerb side. Thus we progressed with surprising speed, because there was no other traffic around.

Looking back over nearly half a century it seems absurd to be racing to an emergency labour on bicycles at about ten miles per hour. But even today I can think of no better way. What would be the advantage of the most powerful police car with nil visibility?

We arrived at the Warren household in less than fifteen minutes. I could not have done it alone. The men said they would wait, in case I needed them further, and a couple of the Warren girls took them down to the kitchen for a cup of tea.

I went upstairs to Conchita. She looked ghastly, deathly white, with bright pink splodges under her eyes. She moaned. I took her temperature, which was 103°F. At first I could not feel her pulse, but, on careful counting, I found it to be 120, and intermittent. Her blood pressure was barely perceptible. Her breathing was shallow and rapid, at around forty breaths per minute. I watched her in silence for a couple of minutes, as a contraction came on. It was powerful, and her features distorted in pain, a high-pitched groan emanating from her throat. Her eyes were open, but I don't think she could see anyone.

Len was cradling her in his arms. The suffering on his face was enough to break your heart. He was stroking her hair, and murmuring to her, neither of which she seemed to feel or hear. Liz was in the room.

I enquired if the doctor had been called. He had, but was still out on a call. The call had been put through to another doctor, who was also out with a patient. All doctors worked terribly hard at these times. The London smogs were notorious killers.

I said that we should arrange for a hospital admission as soon as possible.

"Is she tha' bad?" Len asked.

It is astonishing how people do not see what they don't want to see. To me it was obvious that Conchita could easily die, especially if complications arose from labour and delivery. But Len couldn't see this.

I went and spoke to the policemen. One said he would telephone the hospital. The other one undertook to try to find one of the local GPs and escort him to the house, if possible. How an ambulance would get there and back was an open question.

I returned to Conchita, and started to lay out my delivery things. It was possible that I would be alone with a premature delivery, and a sick and possibly dying woman.

Suddenly I remembered that Sister Julienne was praying for us. Again, the relief was overwhelming. All my fears vanished, and the calm certainty that all would be well flooded my mind and body. I remembered the words of Mother Julian of Norwich:

"All shall be well, and all will be well
and all manner of things shall be well."

I must have given a great sigh of relief, which Len picked up. He said, "You reckons as how she'll be all right then, do you?"

Should I tell him that Sister Julienne was praying for us? It seemed so silly, almost irrelevant. But I did; I felt I knew him well enough. He didn't dismiss it.

"Well, I reckons as 'ow its goin' to be all righ', then, too."

His face was brighter than it had been since I entered the room.

It would have been advisable to examine Conchita vaginally to see how far she was in labour, but I couldn't get her into the right position. She wouldn't allow Len or me to move her. Liz explained to her in Spanish what was required, but she didn't understand or respond in any way. I could only assess the progress of labour from the strength and frequency of contractions, which were approximately every five minutes. I listened for the foetal heart, but couldn't hear a thing.

"Is the baby alive, then?" asked Len.

I didn't like to say a straight "No," so I hedged my bets.

"It's unlikely. Remember your wife got very, very cold today, and has been unconscious. Now she has a fever. All this will affect the baby. I cannot hear a heartbeat."

One of the real problems of premature delivery at the stage of pregnancy Conchita had reached is that the foetus is often lying transversely across the uterus. A human baby ideally should be born head first. A breech delivery is possible, but difficult. A transverse or shoulder delivery is impossible. The head does not normally descend into the pelvis until after thirty-six weeks. A foetus of around twenty-eight weeks is quite large enough to block the cervix completely if contractions push it downwards in the transverse position. In that event, without surgical intervention, the death of the baby is inevitable. I palpated the uterus trying to find out the baby's position, but it was no use, I could not tell. A vaginal examination might have enlightened me, but there was no way that we could persuade Conchita to cooperate.

All I could do was wait. The minutes between contractions ticked by slowly. They were coming every three minutes now. Her pulse was more rapid, 150 per minute; and her breathing seemed to be more shallow. Her blood pressure was quite imperceptible. I prayed for a knock on the door to announce the arrival of a doctor or the ambulance, but none came. The house was silent, save for the low moaning of Conchita as each contraction came and went.

Inevitably the contractions became stronger, and it was then that Conchita began to scream. I have never in my life, before or since, heard such terrifying sounds. They came from the depths of her suffering body with a force and power that I would have thought impossible, given her fevered, debilitated state. She screamed on and on, wild terror in her unseeing eyes, the sound reverberating wave after wave against the walls and ceiling of the room. She clung to her husband, tore at him, until his face and chest and arms were bleeding. He tried to hold her, to comfort her, but she was quite beyond comfort.

I felt helpless. I did not dare to give her an analgesic to lessen the pain and quieten her, because her pulse and blood pressure were so abnormal, and I knew that any drugs would probably kill her. I thought that if it was a normal delivery she had a chance of living; if it was a transverse presentation she would die, unless an ambulance were to arrive quickly. I could not get near her to feel the uterus, or even to hold a leg, as she was throwing herself around the bed with the strength of a wild animal in a trap.

Poor Liz looked terrified. Len, with unconditional love, was still trying to hold her in his arms and console her. She sank her teeth into his hand with the strength of a bulldog, and hung on. He didn't cry out, but winced with pain, sweat and tears falling from his forehead and eyes. He didn't even try to force her jaw open or to pull away. With alarm, I thought that she would sever a tendon. Eventually she loosed the hand, and flung herself to the other side of the bed.

Then, as suddenly as it had started, it was all over. She gave a terrible cry, and a massive push, and water, blood, foetus, placenta – everything – was delivered on to the bed sheets at once. She fell back exhausted.

I could feel no pulse at all. Her breathing seemed to have stopped. But I could feel a flutter of a heartbeat, so I listened with my stethoscope. It was faint and irregular, but it was there. The foetus was blue, and looked quite dead. I snatched a large kidney dish from the dresser, scooped everything into it, and dumped it on the dresser.

"Now we must quickly get her warm," I said, "cleaned up and comfortable, if she is to stand a chance. You help me, Liz – clean warm sheets, a couple of hot water bottles. I will check the placenta in a minute to see if it is complete. If we can get her to drink something hot it will help. Hot water and honey would do; a teaspoon of brandy in it would be even better. The main thing is to treat the shock. And let us all hope and pray that the bleeding won't get worse."

Len went out to issue some instructions, and to pacify the terrified family gathered around the door. Liz and I started to clean the dirty sheets and linen from under Conchita. Len soon returned with clean sheets and hot water bottles, and Liz and I started to make the inert body comfortable.

Len must have gone over to the dresser. Liz and I had our backs to it, busy with Conchita. We heard a gasp.

"It's alive!"

"What!" I cried.

"It's alive, I sez. Ve baby's alive. It's movin'."

I rushed over to the dresser, and looked at the gory mess in the kidney dish. It moved. The blood actually moved. My heart stood still. Then I saw the tiny creature in the pool of blood, and its leg moved.

Oh, dear God, I could have drowned it! I thought.

I lifted the tiny body out with one hand and tilted it upside down. It seemed to weigh nothing. I have held a new born puppy of about the same size. My head raced.

"We must clamp and cut the cord quickly. Then we must get him warm."

It was a little boy.

I felt desperately guilty. The cord should have been clamped five minutes earlier. If he dies now, it will be all my fault, I thought. I had discarded this tiny living soul to drown in a dish of blood and water. I should have looked more closely. I should have thought.

But wallowing in self-reproach gets us nowhere. I clamped and cut the cord. I felt the fragile rib cage. He was breathing. He was a survivor. Len had warmed a small towel on a hot water bottle, and we wrapped him in the cloth. He moved his head and arms a little. All three of us were stunned by the life in the baby. None of us had seen a human child quite so tiny. A baby that is two months premature usually weighs about four pounds, and seems tiny enough. This baby was about one and a half pounds and looked like a tiny doll. His arms and legs were much smaller than my little finger, yet a miniscule nail completed each digit. His head was smaller than a ping-pong ball, and looked disproportionately large. His rib cage looked like fish-bones. He had tiny ears, and his nostrils were the size of a pin-head. I had never imagined that a baby of around twenty-eight weeks could be so lovely. I felt I ought to suck the mucus from his throat, but was terrified of hurting him. Anyway, when I got the catheter, it was far too large, and would never have gone into his mouth. To force a hosepipe into a normal baby's mouth would have been just as inappropriate. So I just held him nearly upside down with one hand, and gently rubbed his back with one finger.

I had no experience of caring for a premature baby, and did not know what to do. All my instincts told me that he must be kept warm and quiet, preferably in the dark, and with frequent feeding. No cot was ready. Where could we put him? Just then Conchita, who was lying quietly, spoke.

"*Niño. Mi niño. Dónde está mi niño?*" (Baby. My baby. Where is my baby?)

We looked at each other. We had all thought she was semi-conscious or asleep, but obviously she knew exactly what had happened, and wanted to see her baby.

"We've gotta give 'im to 'er. Liz, you tell her he's very little and we've gotta be very careful with him."

Liz spoke to her mother, who smiled slightly and sighed with weariness. Len took the baby from me and sat down beside his wife. He held the baby in one hand so that the child lay within her gaze. Her eyes had been vacant and unfocused for several moments and I don't think she saw or understood at first; she had expected to take a full term baby into her arms. Liz spoke to her again, and I heard the words.

"*El niño es muy pequeño.*" (The baby is very small.)

Conchita struggled to adjust her vision to the minute scrap held in Len's hand. You could almost see the struggle and the effort it cost her. Gradually she became aware, and with a sharp intake of breath put out a shaking hand to touch the child. She smiled, and murmured "*Mi niño. Mi querido niño,*" (my baby, my darling baby) and drifted off to sleep, her hand resting on Len's hand and the baby.

Just then, the Flying Squad arrived.

THE FLYING SQUAD

An Obstetric Flying Squad was provided by most big London hospitals, and I believe by all regional hospitals, as an emergency backup for domiciliary midwifery. The service must have saved thousands of lives, because before the 1940s, when no service existed, a midwife could find herself entirely alone with any obstetric emergency – such as a mal-presentation, haemorrhage, cord prolapse, or placenta previa – and all she could do would be to call in the local GP who might or might not be skilled in midwifery.

It was the proud boast of the Flying Squad of the London Hospital that it could reach any obstetric emergency in twenty minutes. But that was reckoning without a London smog. When the policeman contacted the hospital about Conchita no ambulance had been available to bring the Flying Squad. The smog caused acute and deadly respiratory failure in thousands of old people each year, and every doctor and ambulance was out on these cases. When one finally did return to the depot, the driver, who had been working non-stop for sixteen hours, was sent off duty, and another had to be found. Even then, a policeman had to cycle in front of the ambulance to guide it – hence the delay of nearly three hours. However, a registrar, a houseman, and a nurse from the obstetrics department had been sent by the hospital.

Everything happens at once, so they say, and within minutes a GP also arrived on foot. God bless him, I thought. He looked exhausted. He had been working all day and all night, and very likely most of the night before, yet he had the professionalism and the courtesy to apologise for being late.

With so much medical know-how in the house, it was necessary to have a case conference to decide the best course of action for mother and baby. We went down to the kitchen for this, and I asked Len to accompany me. Liz was left with her mother and the baby. The two ambulance men and the policemen joined us too – they couldn't be asked to sit outside in the cold, and there was nowhere else for them to sit in the house. Sue, one of the older girls, made tea all round.

I gave my case history, and handed over the recorded notes. All doctors were agreed that mother and baby must be transferred to hospital at once. Len was alarmed.

"Does she 'ave to go? She won't like it. She's never been away from home before, she hasn't. She'd be lost an' frightened. I knows as 'ow she would. We can look after 'er. I'll stop at home, an' the girls can muck in an all, till she's better."

The doctors looked at one another and sighed. Fear of hospital was commonplace. Among the older generation, it arose mainly from the fact that most of the hospital buildings were converted workhouses, which had been feared more than death itself. The doctors agreed that as Conchita was now safely delivered, if no post-natal complications arose, she probably could be treated at home. A course of antibiotics would clear the infection that was causing fever. The head injury, causing concussion and delirium, would heal with rest and quiet. They tried to point out that she would get more rest in hospital than at home, surrounded by children, but Len would have none of it, so they capitulated.

However, the baby was another matter. He hadn't been weighed, but my guess of between one and a half and two pounds was accepted. They all said twenty-eight weeks was barely viable, and that a living baby of that gestation must have hospital treatment, with the latest technological equipment, and twenty-four hour expert nursing and medical care. They suggested that he should be transferred at once to Great Ormond Street Hospital for Sick Children. Len looked dubious, but when they told him that without such care the baby would die, he readily agreed.

We all went upstairs to the bedroom. I don't know what these hospital doctors thought of having to squeeze past all the prams in the hallway and parting the washing flapping around their heads as they climbed the wooden stairs. Nor did I ask. But I smiled to myself.

Conchita was sleeping, the tiny baby lying on her chest. One hand was protectively over it, the other lay limp by her side. She was smiling, and her breathing, although shallow, was regular and less rapid. I approached the bed and felt her pulse. It was slightly stronger, and regular, but still rapid. I counted 120 per minute, which, though abnormal, was an improvement. Liz was cleaning up quietly and efficiently, and the whole scene was peaceful.

The baby looked even smaller now that the entire hand of the mother covered it. Only its head was visible. It did not really look as if it were alive, although its colour did not suggest death.

The registrar wanted to examine Conchita. I told him that I had not yet examined the placenta, as I had not had time between delivery and the arrival of the ambulance. We examined it together; it was very ragged. "Not hopeful," he muttered, "and it all came out at once, you tell me? I must have a look at her."

He pulled back the bedclothes to examine her abdomen and see the vaginal discharge. Conchita seemed quite unconscious and didn't move as he palpated the uterus. Some blood rushed out.

"Another pad," he said, and, to the houseman, "Draw me up 0.5 cc of ergometrine for injection."

He sank the needle deep into her gluteus muscle, but she didn't move. He covered her and said to Len: "I think part of the placenta has been left behind. She may have to go to hospital for a D and C. It would only be for a few days but we cannot risk a haemorrhage occurring at home. In her condition it would be very serious."

I saw Len turn white and he had to grab the back of a chair to prevent himself from falling.

"However," continued the registrar kindly, "it may not be necessary. The next five minutes will tell if the injection is going to be effective."

He then took Conchita's blood pressure.

"I can hear nothing," he said, and the three doctors exchanged significant glances. Len groaned and had to sit down. His daughter put her hand on his shoulder, and he squeezed it.

We all waited. The registrar said, "There is no point in examining the baby. It is obviously alive, but we are none of us paediatricians. Examination must wait for the experts."

He asked for the telephone, to ring Great Ormond Street Hospital, but there was no telephone in the house. He cursed silently under his breath and asked where he could find the nearest phone box. It was two hundred yards down the road, on the other side. The long-suffering houseman was dispatched out into the freezing fog and icy roads with a pocket full of pennies gleaned from us all, to ring the hospital and make the necessary arrangements.

We continued waiting. There was no sign of an abdominal contraction. Five minutes slipped by. The houseman returned to say that Great Ormond Street would send a paediatrician and a nurse with an incubator and special equipment to collect the baby at once, although the time of their arrival depended on visibility.

Another five minutes passed. There was steady vaginal bleeding, but no contractions.

"Draw up another 0.5cc," the registrar said. "We must give it intra-venously. There is something in there that has to come out. If we can't get it this way," he said to Len, "we will have to take her back with us for a scrape. And if you value her life, you must agree to this."

Len groaned, and nodded dumbly.

I clamped the upper arm and endeavoured to pump up a vein for injection, but nothing showed. Her blood pressure was so low that the venous return could not be found. The registrar tried, with a couple of stabs, to locate the vein and on the third attempt blood showed in the syringe. He emptied the 0.5cc into her vein, and I released the arm.

Within a minute Conchita winced in pain and moved her legs. A large quantity of fresh blood spurted from her vagina, and then, mercifully, several large, darker lumps. There was a pause, then a second contraction. The registrar grasped the fundus and pressed the uterus hard, downwards and backwards. More blood and placenta were evacuated.

All this time Conchita was inert, but I thought I saw her hand tighten over her baby.

"That might be it," said the registrar, "but we must wait a bit longer to see."

He was more relaxed now and started chatting with anyone who would listen about the excellent golf down at Greenwich and the house he was buying at Dulwich, and his holiday in Scotland.

Over the next ten minutes there was no further blood loss, and no more contractions. Thanks to modern obstetrics, the danger of post-partum haemorrhage had been overcome for Conchita. But she still looked very ill indeed. Her breathing and pulse were rapid, her blood pressure abnormally low, and her temperature high. She did not appear to be conscious, although as her eyes were now closed, she might have been asleep. Nonetheless, her hand was still firmly placed over the baby, and any attempt to remove it was resisted.

With difficulty Liz and I cleaned up the bed again, and the houseman was given the messy job of checking the bits of placenta against the larger piece that had first been delivered, and measuring the blood that we had managed to contain.

"Placenta seems to be all here, sir, and I measure one and a half pints of blood. Add to that about eight ounces lost in the bed, and you could say around two pints of blood loss."

The registrar muttered to himself, then said aloud, "She really needs a transfusion. Her blood pressure is already low. Can we do it here?" he added, turning to the GP.

"Yes, I'll take a sample now for cross-matching."

I had wondered why the GP had remained all the while, when he could have left. Now it became clear to me. He anticipated having ongoing responsibility for Conchita if she was to be cared for at home, and he wanted full cognisance of the facts.

At that moment the ambulance arrived from Great Ormond Street to collect the baby.

A PREMATURE BABY

It was a thousand pities, I thought, from the point of view of the good gossips of Limehouse, that all this had been carried out in a London smog. Had it been a clear night, every move would have been witnessed and reported – a midwife, police, teams of doctors, ambulances, each with a police escort. Such a sensation would have kept the gossips in business for a year at least. As it was, not even the next-door neighbour would have been able to see the two ambulances parked outside the Warren house, and police coming and going throughout the night. Their only consolation might have been that the whole street was wakened by the blood-curdling screams that lasted for about twenty minutes.

The paraphernalia and personnel that emerged from the second ambulance was overwhelming. A doctor came hurrying past, carrying an incubator. Another followed with a ventilating machine. A nurse followed with a huge box. Two ambulance men and the policeman came last, each carrying oxygen cylinders. All this equipment had to be manoeuvred past the three coach prams and two ladders lining the hallway. The washing hanging overhead didn't help, because it got caught up on the equipment and several small, dainty items, personal to the young ladies of the house were transported upstairs. The children, who had been in and out of bed all night, hung over the banisters, and hid in doorways, to get the full impact of the procession.

On reaching the bedroom, the medical staff entered whilst the policeman and the ambulance men were directed down to the kitchen to join their colleagues for tea. Nevertheless, the bedroom, of average size, now contained five doctors, two nurses, a midwife, and Len and Liz. There was equipment everywhere. My delivery instruments still covered the dresser. The obstetrician's was on the chest of drawers. The paediatrician's had to be left on the floor, whilst we hastily cleared space.

"I think we'll push off, now," said the registrar to his colleague." I'm very glad to see you. The mother is to be nursed at home. Good luck with the baby."

They left, but the GP remained.

The paediatrician looked at the baby and gasped.

"Think he'll make it, sir?" asked the young doctor.

"We'll have a damn good try," said the paediatric registrar. "Fix up the oxygen, and the suction, and heat up the incubator."

The team got busy.

The paediatrician leaned over Conchita to take the baby. You could not tell whether she was asleep or semi-conscious, but the muscles of her arm tightened, and she held the baby fast.

He said to Len, "Would you tell her to let me have the baby, please? I've got to examine him, before we can transport him."

Len leaned over his wife and murmured to her, trying to loosen her hand. It tightened, and her other hand came up to cover the first.

"Liz, luv, you tell yer mum we've got to 'ave the baby, to take to hospital."

He shook her gently, trying to waken her. Her eyes flickered, and opened a little.

Liz bent over her and spoke to her in Spanish. None of us could tell what she said. Conchita opened her eyes more, and tried to focus on the little creature lying on her chest.

"No," she said.

Liz spoke to her again, more persuasively and urgently this time.

"No," said her mother.

Liz tried a third time.

"*Morirá! Morirá!*" (He will die.)

The effect on Cochita was dramatic and immediate. She opened her eyes wide, desperately trying to focus on the people around her. She saw the equipment and the white coats. I think her clouded brain took it all in and she struggled to sit up. Liz and Len helped her. She looked wildly round at everyone, thrust the baby down between her breasts, and folded her arms over him.

"No", she said. Then repeated louder, "No."

"Mama, you must," said Liz softly. "*Si no lo haces, morirá.*" (If you don't, he will die.)

Conchita's face was blank with anguish, but something was going on in her mind. One could almost see her struggling to get her thoughts under her command. Struggling to think, to remember, she held her breasts and the tiny baby fast, and glanced down at his head. The sight of it must have been the catalyst that brought it all together for her. Her mind seemed to clear, and a fierce, determined look came into her huge black eyes.

She looked round at each of the people in the room, her eyes finally clear and focused, and said with perfect confidence: "*No. Se queda conmigo.*" (He stays with me). "*No morirá.*" Then, with more emphasis: "*No morirá.*" (He will not die.)

The doctors didn't know what to do. Short of tearing her arms apart with brute force, which Len would not have allowed, and grabbing the baby, there was nothing they could do.

The paediatrician said to Liz, "Tell her that she can't look after it. She hasn't got the equipment or the know-how. Tell her the baby will be taken to the finest children's hospital in the world, and will have expert treatment. Tell her he cannot live without an incubator."

Liz started to speak, but Len stepped in, and showed his true strength and manliness. He turned to the doctors and nurse.

"This is all my fault, an' I must apologise. I said the baby could go to hospital without consultin' my wife. I shouldn't 'ave done that. When it comes to the kiddies she must always 'ave the last word, she must. An' she don't agree to it. You can see she don't. An' so the baby's not goin' nowhere. He'll stop 'ere with us, and he'll be christened, an' if he dies, he'll have a Christian burial. But he's not goin' nowhere without 'is mother's consent."

He looked at his wife, and she smiled and stroked the baby's head. She seemed to understand that he was on her side, and the battle was over. She looked at him with confident love, and said quietly, "*No morirá.*"

"There you are," said Len buoyantly, "he won' die. If my Connie says that, then he won't die. You can take it from me."

And that was that. The doctors knew they were defeated, and started to pack up their equipment.

Len graciously apologised a second time, thanked them for the trouble they had taken, and said again that it was all his fault. He offered to pay for the expense of the ambulance, and the time of the medical and nursing staff. He offered them a cup of tea in the kitchen. They declined. He gave them one of his winning smiles and said:

"Go on, 'ave a cup. Yer got a long journey and it'll warm yer."

He had such an engaging way about him, that everyone agreed to accept the hospitality, even though they were cross about the wasted journey.

He and Liz helped the team downstairs with all their equipment, and the GP and I were left alone. He had hardly spoken during the past three hours or so, and I liked him for this. We knew that we had a huge responsibility, and that both mother and baby could still die. Conchita's condition had been serious, but now, with the loss of two pints of blood, it was critical.

"She must have blood," said the GP. "I have taken a sample for cross-matching, and as soon as the blood bank can supply it, I will set up an I.V. We will need a district nurse to stay with her while it is going in. Can you Sisters provide one?"

I told him I was sure of it. He said, "I'm going to start antibiotics at once, because she is breathing only into the upper lobes. I would like to listen to her chest, but I doubt if she will let me, because of the baby."

He was right – she wouldn't. So he drew up an ampoule of penicillin and injected it into the thigh.

"She must have one ampoule I.M. for seven days b.d.," he said, as he entered it on the notes, and wrote out a prescription.

"Now I'm going to try to see about this blood. That's as much as I can do at present. Frankly, nurse, I don't know what to do about the baby. I think I will have to leave it to you and the Sisters. They are sure to have more experience than I have."

"Or me," I said. "I have never handled a premature baby before."

We looked at each other with shared helplessness, and he left. Bless him, I thought. He hadn't had any sleep for God knows how long; it was about 5 a.m., it was a filthy morning; and now he was leaving, on foot in thick fog, to try to get the blood sorted out. No doubt he had a surgery at 9 a.m. and a full day's work after that.

I was so tired I could scarcely think. The adrenalin had been pumping all night, and now my body was drained. Conchita was sleeping; the baby could have been alive or dead for all I knew. I tried to think if there was anything I could do, but my brain wouldn't work. Should I go back to Nonnatus House? How could I get there? The policemen had gone, and I couldn't face the prospect of cycling alone in the fog.

Just then Liz came in with a cup of tea.

"Sit yerself down, luvvy, and 'ave a rest," she said.

I sat down in the armchair. I remembered drinking half a cup of tea, and then the next moment it was daylight. Len was in the room, sitting on the bed, brushing Conchita's hair and murmuring sweet nothings to her. She was smiling at him and the baby. He saw me waken and said, "Feel better now, nurse? It's ten o'clock, an' it said on ve news tha' the fog'll start to lift today."

I looked at Conchita who was sitting up in bed, the baby still between her breasts. She was stroking his little head and cooing to him. She looked pathetically weak, but her skin colour and her breathing had improved. Above all, her eyes were still focusing and she looked collected. The delirium from concussion had quite gone.

From then on she improved rapidly. No doubt the penicillin helped, but alone it could not have effected the astonishing transformation, within a few hours, from someone close to death who didn't even know her own husband, to a calm competent woman who knew exactly what she was doing and why.

I have a theory that it was the living baby that cured her, and that the crisis had occurred when she thought that they were going to take him away. In that moment, her powerful maternal instincts had kicked in, and told her that she was the protector, the provider. She didn't have time to be ill. She couldn't afford to be woolly minded. His life depended on her.

Had the baby died at birth, or had he been taken away to hospital, I think Conchita would have died also. The animal world is full of such stories. I have heard that a sheep or an elephant will die if the baby dies, and live if the baby lives.

The level of consciousness or unconsciousness is also deeply interesting. Having sat with many dying patients over the years, I am not at all convinced that what we call "unconscious" is anything like the state of unknowingness we think it to be. Unconsciousness can be profoundly knowing, and intuitive. Conchita had seemed quite unconscious, yet her hand tightened over her baby when the paediatrician tried to take him. She could not have seen who was in the room, because her eyes were not focusing, nor known what had been said, because she did not understand the language. Yet somehow she understood that they were planning to take her baby away, and she fought back with every ounce of her strength. This had cured her.

Douglas Bader, the Battle of Britain flying ace, tells a similar story. After an air crash and bi-lateral mid-thigh amputations, he heard a voice say, "Hush, a young airman is dying in that room." The words focused his mind, and he thought, "Die? Me? I'll bloody well show you." The rest is history.

Conchita reached for a saucer at the side of her and began to squeeze her nipples, pressing out a few drops of colostrum, which fell into the saucer. Then she took a fine glass rod which was used by one of her daughters for icing cakes. She held the little baby in her left hand and, having suspended a drop of colostrum on the glass rod, touched his lips with it. I watched, fascinated. His lips were no bigger than a couple of daisy petals. A tiny tongue came out and licked the fluid. She repeated this about six or eight times, then tucked him back between her breasts.

Len said: "She's bin doin' this every 'alf 'our since six o'clock.

Then they both 'ave a little sleep, an' she does it agen. She said 'e won't die, and 'e won't, yer know. She knows 'ow to look after 'im."

I checked that she was not bleeding unduly, and left. I had to get back to Nonnatus House to report, and to request a district nurse to monitor the blood transfusion when it arrived. The smog was beginning to lift, and one could just about see across the road. It felt as though the world was filling with new life as the foul smog cleared, and I cycled back with a light heart.

Sister Julienne herself prepared a huge breakfast of double bacon and eggs for me "to keep the wolf from the door", as she put it, and then took my report in the dining room whilst I was eating. She said, "I have never cared for such a premature baby myself, but a Sister in one of our other Houses has experience. We will consult her. Conchita will have to be watched very carefully for further blood loss."

She found the whole story astonishing, and said, quietly, "God's will be done." She then went away to make arrangements for covering the blood transfusion.

Conchita didn't lose any more blood. After the transfusion colour returned to her cheeks, and also to Len's. She was weak, but all danger had passed. The baby lay on her breast, day and night, fed in the manner that I have described about every half hour. All the lay staff and Sisters from Nonnatus House came to see the two of them, it was such a beautiful and unusual sight. On the fourth day I weighed the baby in a handkerchief. He was 1 lb. 10 oz.

After three weeks, Conchita began to get up for short periods. I had thought ahead, and had wondered what would happen to the baby. Obviously Conchita had also been thinking ahead, and knew exactly what was to be done. She had asked Liz to acquire from the dressmakers several lengths of the finest unbleached silk. With the help of her skilled eldest daughter, she fixed a kind of sling or firm blouse around her shoulders and breasts, tight underneath, but loose above. The baby was carried in this for five months, between his mother's breasts, never leaving her.

Who had taught her this? I have never before or since, in any literature, heard of such a way of caring for a premature baby. Was it purely maternal instinct? I remembered back to the delivery, and to her monumental struggle when they tried to take the baby. I had the impression then that she was trying to think, trying to remember something; and the sudden clarity and conviction with which she said, " *No morirá*."

Had she remembered seeing a peasant or gypsy woman carrying a tiny premature baby like this when she was a child in Southern Spain? Had this fleeting memory of times half forgotten been the cause of her conviction that her baby would not die?

Some years later, when I was night sister at the Elizabeth Garrett Anderson Hospital in Euston, I cared for several premature babies of about the same gestation and weight. They were all nursed in incubators, and I do not remember any fatalities. The hospital staff prided themselves on the excellent modern care which preserved the life of the baby. The hospital way, and Conchita's way, are poles apart. Incubator babies are alone, day and night, lying flat on a firm surface, usually in strong light. Only hands and clinical equipment touch the baby. Food usually comes as formula cow's milk. Conchita's baby was never alone. He had the warmth, the touch, the softness, the smell, the moisture of his mother. He heard her heartbeat and her voice. He had her milk. Above all, he had her love.

Possibly today, her decision to refuse hospitalisation for the baby would have been over-ruled by Court Order, the assumption being that only trained staff and advanced technology can adequately care for a premature child. In the 1950s we were less intrusive into family life, and parental responsibility was respected. I am forced to the conclusion that modern medicine does not know it all.

Admittedly Conchita was lucky. The speed of delivery might have caused brain damage to the baby, but this did not occur. Apart from that, the great danger for a premature baby arises from immature vital organs, especially lungs and liver. The baby did indeed become very jaundiced, more than once, in the first few months, but each time it passed. It was a miracle, after I had heedlessly left the baby in a kidney dish, that his lungs were not wholly, or even partly collapsed from birth. I can take no credit for that. However, the fact is, he breathed. I like to think that by holding him upside down, and tapping his fragile back with a finger, I facilitated his first breath. His mother was advised to do the same after each feed, because, if fluid enters the trachea, a premature baby cannot cough as a full-term baby would. She was also given a very fine suction tube, and shown how to use it.

Apart from that, which was very little, the baby received no medical treatment. The constant temperature of his mother's skin kept his body temperature stable. Possibly the constant rise and fall of her breathing helped him over the first critical weeks. I am sure that her feeding policy – a few drops of breast milk placed on the lips at frequent intervals – was the right one. She even did this all through the night, I was told. Conchita took no precautions about sterilising her feeding equipment. I doubt if she had ever heard of such a thing. The saucer and the glass rod were simply wiped clean after each use, ready for the next time. The baby survived. Either he is the ultimate survivor, or we put far too much emphasis on technology and techniques, I thought.

We visited three times a day every day for six weeks, then twice a day for a further six weeks. Domiciliary care was good in those days. At four months he weighed six and a half pounds and was responding with smiles, and turning his head. He reached out a tiny hand to grasp a finger. He gurgled and chuckled to himself. I was told he hardly ever cried.

Several times in those post-natal months I thought of that dreadful night when he was born, and remembered Sister Julienne's words to me as I left. "God be with you, my dear. I will pray for Conchita Warren and her unborn baby." She had not just said that she would pray for Conchita. Nor had she assumed that the foetus would be born dead. She had said, with equal emphasis, that she would pray for them both. In fact, she prayed for us all.

One happy day in midsummer I made a routine call to check the weight of the baby. Laughter was coming from the downstairs kitchen as I descended the stairs. The baby was lying in a cot with his brothers and sisters around him. They were all laughing. A delicious smell wafted towards me. Conchita, smiling and in full command, was standing over the steaming copper boiler making plum jam. The copper boiled ferociously as she stirred with a huge wooden spoon. Thank God she had had the wisdom and the strength not to let the baby go, I thought. Had she done so, I felt sure that she would have died, and all the happiness of the household would have died with her.

OLD, OLD AGE

Whilst I was fascinated and captivated by Sister Monica Joan, I could not for the life of me decide if she really was verging on senility or not. I could not avoid the suspicion that she might craftily be manipulating us all, in order to get her own way – an old lady's prerogative down the ages! Without doubt she was highly intelligent, well informed, and in some ways deeply learned, though it was often hard to disentangle the muddled strands of her discourse. In view of her history, fifty years professed nun, nurse and midwife in the East End of London, there could be no doubt of her Christian vocation. Yet her behaviour was often far from Christian. She was often selfish and inconsiderate. Flashes of brilliance and flashes of senility crossed and recrossed each other in lightning streaks; goodness and cruelty rubbed shoulders; memory and forgetfulness were intertwined. The old are deeply interesting and I watched her often. Which was the real Sister Monica Joan? I could not tell.

No doubt she had always been eccentric. Even the manner in which she went to church was singular. She would leave Nonnatus House, walk swiftly down Leyland Street, round the corner and straight across the East India Dock Road, without so much as glancing to right or left. Lorry drivers would slam on their brakes, tyres would scream, lorries would come to a shuddering halt, whilst this elderly nun, gown and veil billowing out behind her, crossed the busiest road in London.

One day a mounted policeman on a jet black horse was proceeding sedately down the centre of the road. He wore a magnificent white helmet and long white gauntlets, which gave him a kind of Ruritarian, operatic appearance. He saw Sister Monica Joan and, anticipating what would happen, turned his horse sideways in the road, raised his gloved hands to halt the traffic in both directions and indicated that she could cross. As she passed, Sister turned, looked up at the horse and rider, and said, quite clearly and loudly, "Thank you, young man, that is very kind. But you need not trouble yourself. I am perfectly safe. The angels will take care of me." She tossed her head and walked swiftly on.

That incident occurred years before I knew her, so clearly her idiosyncrasies had always been there although perhaps they had become more accentuated as she grew older. Sometimes I wondered, though, if her celebrated eccentricity was not an affectation, assumed for the childish delight of drawing attention to herself. Like the incident with the cellist. Poor fellow, it must have shattered him, and I tremble to think what it did must have done to the pianist.

All Saints, East India Dock Road, was and still is a prestigious church, commanding a favoured position in the diocese. Built in classical Regency style, and beautifully proportioned, the interior is a gem and the acoustics beyond reproach, making it an excellent place for concerts.

The Rector had managed to persuade a world famous cellist to perform. Cynthia and I were given the evening off in order to attend the concert. At the last minute we thought how nice it would be to take Sister Monica Joan. Never again!

To begin with, she insisted on taking her knitting. Neither Cynthia nor I remonstrated as we should have done, but that was only with the wisdom of hindsight. We entered the church, which was full, and Sister Monica Joan wanted to sit in the front row. Like a dowager duchess she sailed down the central aisle, with Cynthia and me trotting after her like a couple of lady's maids. She sat down middle centre, directly opposite the chair placed in readiness for the cellist, and we sat on either side. Everyone knew Sister Monica Joan, and from the outset I felt conspicuous and uncomfortable.

The chairs were too hard. Sister Monica Joan fidgeted and grumbled, trying to adjust her bony bottom to the wooden chair. We offered her a kneeling pad, but that was no good. Cushions had to be found. Curates ran hither and thither poking into sacristy cupboards, but with no luck. Church paraphernalia contains everything but soft cushions. The nearest thing was a length of velvet curtaining. This was folded up, and placed under her bony prominences. She sighed at the young curate, who was new and eager to please.

"If that's the best you can do, I suppose it will have to do." Her sharp tone erased the smile from his face.

The Rector stepped forward to welcome the audience, and said that coffee would be served in the interval.

"And now it is my great pleasure to welcome—"

He was cut short.

"Do you have decaffeinated for those who do not drink coffee?"

The Rector stopped. The cellist, one foot on stage, paused.

"Decaffeinated? I really don't know, Sister."

"Perhaps you would be good enough to find out?"

"Yes, of course Sister."

He signalled to a curate to go and find out. I had not seen the Rector look uncertain before; it was a new experience.

"May I continue, Sister?"

"Yes, of course." Very graciously she inclined her head.

" . . . my pleasure to welcome to All Saints the renowned cellist and pianist . . . "

They bowed to the audience. The pianist seated herself at the piano. The cellist adjusted his stool. Silence fell on the audience.

"She's wearing brocade, my dear."

Sister Monica Joan's articulation was faultless, and, as I have said, the acoustics at All Saints are superb. Her stage whisper, which at its best could penetrate a railway station at rush hour, reached every corner of the church.

"We used to do that in the 1890s; cut down some old curtains, and make a second best dress out of them. I wonder whose curtains she got hold of?"

The pianist glared, but the cellist, being a man, had noticed no insult, and started tuning up. Sister Monica Joan was fidgeting beside me, trying to get comfortable.

Satisfied, the cellist smiled confidently at his audience and raised his bow.

"It's no good. I can't sit like this. I shall have to have a cushion at my back."

The cellist let his arm fall. The Rector gazed helplessly at his curates. A lady from the back came forward. She had providently brought a cushion for herself, and Sister Monica Joan was welcome to use it.

"How very kind. It is greatly appreciated. So kind."

Her regal graciousness could have out-queened the Queen Mother. She felt the cushion, and decided she would sit on the cushion and have the cloth at her back. Cynthia and the Rector adjusted all this, whilst the cellist and pianist sat quietly looking at their instruments. I was squirming, trying in vain not to be noticed.

The recital started and Sister Monica Joan, comfortable at last, took out her knitting.

Knitting during a recital is not common. In fact I have never seen anyone do it. But Sister Monica Joan was not concerned with what other people did or did not do. She always did exactly as she chose. Nor is knitting generally considered to be a noisy occupation. I had frequently seen Sister Monica Joan knitting in absolute serenity and silence. But not on this occasion. The knitting was of a lacy pattern, requiring three needles, and this produced absolute mayhem.

She dropped the needles repeatedly. They were steel knitting needles, and each time they fell they clattered on to the wooden floor. Cynthia or I had to retrieve them, depending on which side the needle had dropped. The ball of wool fell and rolled under several chairs. Someone about four chairs down kicked it back towards her, but the trailing piece of wool caught around the leg of a chair and pulled tight, thus pulling several stitches off the work in Sister Monica Joan's hands. "Be careful," she hissed at us as the cellist approached a particularly difficult cadenza, his eyes closed in rapture. He opened his eyes sharply, and an unexpected bum note sounded from the strings. Seeing Sister Monica Joan fumbling after the wool, the cellist, with true professionalism, launched into his cadenza. He finished the movement in masterly fashion.

The slow movement started very quietly and peacefully, but the ball of wool was not so easily dealt with. The person four chairs down tried to retrieve it and push it back the way it had come, without success. The ball rolled backwards, and got tangled around the feet of someone sitting behind, who picked it up, causing the trailing end to pull tight again, pulling several more stitches off Sister Monica Joan's needle.

"You are ruining it," she spat out to the man behind.

The pianist was playing a hauntingly tender passage. She turned from the piano and looked daggers at the first row.

As the final cadence approached another needle dropped to the floor with a resounding clatter, destroying the plaintive cry of the cello in the dying fall of the movement.

The Rector, with a desperate look on his face, came forward and whispered to Sister Monica Joan to be quiet. "What did you say, Rector?" she said loudly, as though she were deaf – which she wasn't. He backed off in alarm, fearing that he might make things worse.

The third movement was an *allegro con fuoco*, and the duo played it faster and with more fire than I have ever heard.

Cynthia and I, who were just about dying with mortification, were counting the minutes until the interval when we could take Sister home. I was grinding my teeth in fury, and plotting murder in my heart. Cynthia, who has a sweeter nature than mine, was patient and understanding. But worse was to come.

The musicians brought the third movement to a triumphant close. With a magnificent gesture the cellist swept the bow upwards, and raised his arm aloft, smiling confidently at the audience.

Only a few seconds were to elapse before the applause began, but it was time enough for Sister Monica Joan to make her exit. She stood up abruptly.

"This is too painful. I cannot put up with this a moment longer. I must go."

With knitting needles dropping all around her she passed the musicians and, in full view of the entire audience, swept down the central aisle towards the door.

Tumultuous applause broke out from the Poplar audience. Stamping, cheering, whistling – no musicians could have asked for a greater ovation. But they knew, and we knew, and they knew that we knew, that the applause was not for them or their music. They bowed stiffly, faces set in a grim smile, and left the platform.

Black fury took possession of me. I greatly respect musicians, knowing their years of intensive training, and I could not excuse this last gratuitous insult, which I saw as deliberate. I could have hit Sister Monica Joan, hard, in front of a couple of hundred people. I must have been shaking with rage, because Cynthia looked at me in alarm.

"I'll take her home. You stay and find a chair at the back somewhere, and enjoy the second half."

"I can't enjoy anything after that," I hissed through clenched teeth; my voice must have sounded strange.

She laughed her soft, warm laugh. "Of course you can. Get yourself a cup of coffee. They are playing the Brahms Cello Sonata next."

She gathered up the knitting needles, extricated the wool from around the chair legs, put it all into the knitting bag, blew a kiss with a whispered "cheerio", and ran off after Sister Monica Joan.

For many days, or perhaps it was weeks, I could not bring myself to speak to Sister Monica Joan. I was convinced that she had deliberately set out to wreck the recital, and to humiliate the musicians. I remembered her petulance when she did not get her own way, her sulks when she was thwarted, and above all her relentless torment of Sister Evangelina. I made up my mind that the apparent senility was no more than an elaborate game she was playing for her own amusement. I decided that I wanted nothing more to do with her. I could be as haughty as Sister Monica Joan if I chose to be, and whenever we met, I turned my head away and said not one word.

But later an incident occurred that left me in no doubt at all about the reality of her mental condition.

It was about 8.30 in the morning. The Sisters and other staff had all left for their morning visits. Chummy and I were the last to leave, and were just stepping out when the telephone rang.

"Is that Nonnatus 'ouse? Sid ve Fish 'ere. I thought you ought'a know Sister Monica Joan has jus' gone past me shop in 'er nightie. I've sent ve lad after 'er, so she won't come to no 'arm."

I gasped in horror, and quickly told Chummy. We dropped our midwifery bags, grabbed a Sister's cloak from the hall-stand, and sprinted down towards Sid's fish shop. Sure enough, weaving a zig-zag line down the East India Dock Road, the fish boy a couple of paces behind, was Sister Monica Joan. She was wearing only a long white nightie with long sleeves. Her bony shoulders and elbows stuck out under the thin cloth. You could have counted every vertebra in her spine. She wore no dressing gown, no slippers, no veil, and the wind blew thin white strands of hair upwards from a head that was nearly bald. It was a cold morning, and her feet and ankles were blue-black with cold and bleeding. From behind I saw these sad old feet, like skeleton's bones, clad only in mottled blue skin, doggedly, determinedly trudging on to a destination known only to her clouded mind.

Without her veil and habit she was almost unrecognisable, and looked vaguely grotesque. Her rheumy, red-rimmed eyes were watering. Her nose was bright red, and a dew-drop hung on the tip. My heart gave a lurch, and I realised how much I loved her.

We caught up and spoke to her. She looked at us as though we were strangers, and tried to push us aside.

"Mind, out of my way. I must get to them. The waters have broken. That brute will kill the baby. He killed the last one, I swear it. I must get there. Out of my way."

She took another few steps on bleeding feet. Chummy threw the warm woollen cloak around her shoulders, and I took off my cap and put it on her head. The sudden warmth seemed to bring her to her senses. Her eyes focused, and she looked at us in recognition. I leaned towards her and said slowly, "Sister Monica

Joan, it's breakfast time. Mrs B. has made some nice hot porridge for you, with honey in it. It will be getting cold if you don't come now."

She looked at me eagerly and said, "Porridge! With honey! Ooh, lovely. Come along, then. What are you standing there for? Did you say porridge? With honey?"

She took two steps, and cried out in pain. Obviously she had not been aware of her cut and bleeding feet. Thank God for Chummy, her size and strength. She picked Sister Monica Joan up in her arms as though she were a child, and carried her all the way back to Nonnatus House. A crowd of curious children followed.

We alerted Mrs B., who was full of concern.

"Oh, the poor lamb. Get her up to bed. She mus' be froze, poor dear. She'll catch 'er death o' cold. I'll get a couple of 'ot water bottles, and make her some porridge, an' some 'ot chocolate. I knows as wha' she likes."

We got her to bed and left her in Mrs B.'s capable hands. We both had a morning's work to attend to, and had to go.

I attended my morning visits as though in a dream. Now and then in life, love catches you unawares, illuminating the dark corners of your mind, and filling them with radiance. Once in a while you are faced with a beauty and a joy that takes your soul, all unprepared, by assault. As I cycled around that morning, I knew that I loved not only Sister Monica Joan, but all that she represented: her religion, her vocation, her monastic profession, the bells, the constant prayers within the convent, the quietness, and the selfless work in the service of God. Was it perhaps – and I nearly fell off my bike with shock – could it be the love of God?

IN THE BEGINNING

Sister Monica Joan developed pneumonia. She fell deeply asleep when Chummy, Mrs B. and I placed her into bed that cold morning, and remained apparently unconscious for the whole day. Her temperature was high, her pulse full and throbbing, and her breathing laboured. Nonnatus House was sad and subdued. The chapel bell, calling the Office of the day, sounded like the portent of a funeral bell. We all thought that she would die. However, we had not taken into account two significant factors: antibiotics, and her own phenomenal stamina.

Today, antibiotics are as common as a cup of coffee. In the 1950s they were relatively new. Today, over-use has reduced their efficacy but in the 1950s they really were a miracle drug. Sister Monica Joan had never had penicillin before, and responded immediately. Within a couple of shots her temperature dropped, her pulse returned to normal, the murmur in her chest vanished, and she opened her eyes. She looked around. "I really don't know why you are all standing there doing nothing. Haven't you got any work to do? I suppose you think I am going to die. Well, you are wrong. I'm not. You can tell Mrs B. that I will have a boiled egg for breakfast."

Her stamina and physical strength became apparent during the next few weeks. Had she led a life of luxury and idleness, as her aristocratic birth would have allowed, I am quite sure that she would have died, in spite of the penicillin. However, a life of intense hard work had rendered her as tough as old boots. A mere touch of pneumonia could not kill her. She recovered quickly, and became very peevish about being kept in bed, which the doctor insisted upon. She thought she had a slight cold, and had no memory of the incident that had brought her to bed in the first place. She did not actually call the doctor a fool, but she looked at him in such a way that left no doubt in his, or anyone else's mind.

"I do not pretend to understand your superior wisdom, doctor, but we will go with God in all things. Am I to understand that I can have visitors?"

Yes indeed, Sister Monica Joan could have visitors (as long as they did not tire her), whatever she wanted to read (provided it did not strain her eyes), and whatever she wanted to eat (provided it did not upset her digestion).

Sister Monica Joan settled back on her pillows, contented. Books were provided and Mrs B. was instructed to attend to her every wish.

A nun's bedroom is properly called a cell and is small, bare, and plain, without comfort. However, since her retirement from active midwifery, Sister Monica Joan had managed to wangle things so that her cell was comparatively large, comfortably furnished, and pretty: an elegant bedsitting-room would be the more appropriate description. Lay people are not normally admitted to a nun's cell, but Sister Monica Joan had just extracted the doctor's assurance that she could have visitors, and thus began a very happy period of my life.

Every day I visited her, and as I entered the room, an almost tangible feeling of peace and tranquillity surrounded me. She was always sitting up in bed, with no outward signs of illness or fatigue, her veil perfectly adjusted, her white nightie high in the neck, her soft skin opaque, and her large eyes clear and penetrating. Her bed was always covered in books, and she had a number of notebooks in which she wrote voluminously in a firm stylish hand.

I discovered that she was a poet. I suppose it should not have surprised me, but it did. All her life she had written poetry, and had in her notebooks a collection of several hundred poems dating from the 1890s.

I am no judge of poetry – I do not have an ear for it. But the consistency of her output impressed me and I asked if I might have a look. She shrugged negligently.

"Take it. I have no secrets, my dear. I am but a spark in the divine fire."

Over many long evenings I studied these poems. I had expected them all to be religious poetry, having been written by a nun, but they were not. Many were love poems, many satirical, and many were humorous, as:

One of the sweetest things in life to see
Is a calm, settled fly,
Cleansing its fastidious face
On my chosen reading place;
He twines his legs around his arse
And takes his time,
As Beauty with her glass.

or:

Lyric of an Obese Dachshund Bitch

They are equally pretty,
My toes or my tittie,
To ramble or gallop upon;

Whatever will happen
When I must re-cap'em
The days that my nipples wear out
And are gone?

This is my favourite:

It's OK to be tight on
The seafront at Brighton
But I say, by Jove
Watch out if it's Hove.

It may not be great poetry, but I thought it had charm. Or perhaps it was the charm of Sister Monica Joan that coloured my assessment.

I found a revealing poem about her father, which told a lot about her early life:

Fretful, unloving, mannerless Papa,
What a crustaceous old boy you are –
How you do go it!
Blowing your bugle, like a ham stage-star,
How you do blow it!
And where does it get you, Papa?
Or is it wasted breath?
"Leave everything to me"
Vainly the old man saith.

With an arrogant, domineering father her struggle to assert herself and to leave home must have been monumental. A weaker character would have been crushed.

For a lovesick young girl, her love poems spoke to my heart, and brought tears to my eyes. As:

To an Unknown God

I sang to you
In the day of my bliss
And you were near

I thought of you
In my lover's kiss
And felt you there

I turned to you
When our love was too brief
And found your strength.

I needed you
In the years of my grief
And knew you, at length.

"Our love was too brief." Oh, I knew all about that. Does one have to suffer so dreadfully in order to know the unknown God? Who, when, what was the story of Sister Monica Joan's lost love? I longed to know, but dared not ask. Did he die, or did her parents object? Why was he unobtainable? Was he already married, or did he just cease to care, and leave her? I longed to know, but could not ask. Any intrusive questions would deserve, and receive, a caustic comment from that barbed tongue.

Her religious poetry was surprisingly slender, and as I was eager to know more about her religion, I asked her about this aspect of her poetry. She replied with these lines from Keats' *Ode to a Grecian Urn*:

> "Beauty is truth, truth beauty" – that is all
> Ye know on earth, and all ye need to know.

"Do not ask me to immortalise the great Mystery of Life. I am just a humble worker. For beauty, look to the Psalms, to Isaiah, to St John of the Cross. How could my poor pen scan such verse? For truth, look to the Gospels – four short accounts of God made Man. There is nothing more to say."

She looked unusually tired that day and, as she lay back on the pillows, the wintry light from the window accentuating her pale, aristocratic features, my heart filled with tenderness. I had come to a convent by mistake, an irreligious girl. I would not have described myself as a committed atheist for whom all spirituality was nonsense, but as an agnostic in whom large areas of doubt and uncertainty resided. I had never met nuns before, and regarded them at first as a bit of a joke; later, with astonishment bordering on incredulity. Finally this was replaced by respect, and then deep love.

What had impelled Sister Monica Joan to abandon a privileged life for one of hardship, working in the slums of London's Docklands? "Was it love of people?" I asked her.

"Of course not," she snapped sharply. "How can you love ignorant, brutish people whom you don't even know? Can anyone love filth and squalor? Or lice and rats? Who can love aching weariness, and carry on working, in spite of it? One cannot love these things. One can only love God, and through His grace come to love His people."

I asked her how she had heard her calling, and come to be professed. She quoted lines from *The Hound of Heaven* by Francis Thompson.

> I fled Him, down the nights and down the days;
> I fled Him down the arches of the years;
> I fled Him down the labyrinthine ways
> Of my own mind; and in the midst of tears
> I hid from Him.

I asked her what was meant by "I fled Him", and she became cross.

"Questions, questions – you wear me out with your questions, child. Find out for yourself – we all have to in the end. No one can give you faith. It is a gift from God alone. Seek and ye shall find. Read the Gospels. There is no other way. Do not pester me with your everlasting questions. Go with God, child; just go with God."

She was obviously tired. I kissed her and slipped away.

Her constant phrase, "Go with God", had puzzled me a good deal. Suddenly it became clear. It was a revelation – acceptance. It filled me with joy. Accept life, the world, Spirit, God, call it what you will, and all else will follow. I had been groping for years to understand, or at least to come to terms with the meaning of life. These three small words, "Go with God", were for me the beginning of faith.

That evening, I started to read the Gospels.

APPENDIX

On the difficulties of writing the Cockney dialect

London Cockney is as distinct and as clearly defined a dialect as Scottish or Yorkshire or any other. Its origins can be traced back to Kentish, East Anglian, Mercian and Saxon speech forms. Certain idioms of colloquial Cockney language appear in Chaucer.

I have never understood why Cockney speech is said to be lazy English. It is the opposite. Cockneys love language, and use it continually, with a rich mixture of puns, slang, spoonerisms and rhymes. They carry a verbal library of anecdotes, ditties and yarns in their heads, which can be improvised to suit any occasion. They love long, colourful words. They can throw in description and simile with lightning speed, with a sure instinct for effect. Rhythm is important, and the compelling rhythm of a cockney dialogue is equal to that of a Mozart opera. Cockneys have a verbal mastery second to none in my opinion. The only trouble is, it is so fast and so idiomatic that it goes straight over the heads of most people.

To listen to a group of Cockneys talking together, when they do not suspect they are being overheard, is like listening to another language. Most people will only be able to understand the odd word here and there. The speed of speech goes like an express train. Half a dozen words are slurred, condensed, abbreviated, swallowed whole, and the end result is one word, understandable to another Cockney, but to nobody else, for example *Wachoofinkovisen?* (What do you think of this, then?)

To achieve this rapid delivery of speech, an essential device has been developed to a high degree of perfection – the glottal stop. This is a consonant sound, easier to execute than to explain. Most consonants are produced by the tongue, teeth and hard palette. The glottal stop is produced by rapid opening and shutting of the glottis (the entrance to the windpipe). It is a conscious action, but with continued use becomes unconscious. Cockney babies, in my experience, used to produce this sound before they could speak.

Singers use the glottal stop to prefix a vowel. It is used a great deal in the German language. In English it is used to separate two vowels in words like 'pre-empt', 're-enforce', 'co-opt', 're-enter', and a few others. Most people saying these words will place a glottal stop between the vowels, and the movement can be felt in the throat.

Cockneys use the glottal stop to replace 't' and several short words. Phonetically, the glottal stop is represented by two dots ':' like a colon. The words 'water' or 'little', written with a glottal stop, become wa:er, li:le. Thousands of English words contain 't' and to replace them all with a glottal stop sign makes the written word look ridiculous. Consider: *'eedin:aw::oo 'ave 'i:i:* (he didn't ought to have hit it.)

This rapid succession of vowels would be unintelligible in speech without the use of the glottal stop.

't' can come in for other changes. Sometimes it becomes a 'd', e.g. *bidda budder* (bit of butter), *arkadim* (hark at him), *all ober da place* (all over the place).

't' followed by 'r' becomes 'ch', e.g. *chrees* (trees), *chrains* (trains).

't' followed by another word beginning with a vowel again becomes 'ch', e.g. *whachouadoin'ov?* (what are you doing?), *doncha loike i:?* (don't you like it?).

Sometimes 't' is heavily emphasised, becoming 'ter', e.g. *gichaw coa-ter, we're goin'ah-ter* (get your coat, we're going out).

'th' is nearly always replaced by 'f' or 'v,' e.g. *vis*, *va'*, *vese* and *vose* (this, that, these and those); and *fink*, *fings*, *fanks*, *frough* (think, things, thanks, through).

'f' and 'v' were so common in the 1950s and the sound was so impressed into my aural memory that I have found it very difficult to write the Cockney speech without using them. *Ve baby*, *ve midwife*, and so on, came more naturally than Standard English. The widespread use of 'f' and 'v' may have arisen early in the twentieth century because practically all men, and not a few women, usually had a limp, wet Woodbine hanging off the lower lip. The articulation of an 'f' or 'v' would leave the soggy appendage undisturbed, but the fricative 'th' might result in it being spat out!

Over decades speech changes, and I believe that the 'f' and 'v' are dying out. Perhaps this is because cigarettes are filter tipped and thrown away! The succulent remains of a Woodbine are not preserved and cherished and rolled around the lips as they used to be.

On the subject of change, the Dickensian reversal of 'v' and 'w' seems to have dropped out of Cockney speech altogether, e.g. *vater* (water) and *wery* (very). Occasionally an old-fashioned shopkeeper (are there any left?) can be heard to say *welly good, sir*, but not welly often!

As speed is all important, 'h' is seldom used. However, the suggestion (which is a sort of tasteless joke) that Cockneys trying to 'talk proper' put 'h' in the wrong places is not quite correct. I have listened very carefully, and only noticed an aspirated 'h' used for special emphasis, often with a glottal stop thrown in as well, e.g. *oie was :henraged* (I was enraged); *bleedin' ca:s :heverywhere* (bleeding cats everywhere).

'L' in the middle or end of a word is usually lost and replaced by 'oo' or 'w'. This is just about impossible to write convincingly. Consider: *li:oo* (little); *bo:oo* (bottle); *vere's a sayoo of too-oos darn Mioowaoo* (there is a sale of tools down Millwall).

'N' and 'm' seem to be virtually interchangeable; a patient of mine had an *emforced rest due to an emflamed leg*. Another found *aoo vose en:y bo:oos ah:side ve 'ahse enbarrussin'*. (all those empty bottles outside the house embarrassing). In Poplar people used to *eat bre:m bu:er* (bread and butter).

There are many other consonant changes, which vary from family to family and from street to street. 'Sh', 'ch', 'zh' (as in treasure) and 'j' replace almost anything, e.g. *we're garn :a shea-shoide* (we're going to the seaside). *Ve doctor, 'e shpozhezh, vish fing wazh a washp shting azh wha: 'azh shwelled up loike* (the doctor he supposes, this thing was a wasp sting that has swelled up).

Wocha is the most common of all Cockney greetings, which has passed into Standard English. It is a very old form of "What are you (doing)?" The 'ch' in *wocha* replaces two or three words.

'J' can replace 'd'. *Jury Lane's a jraugh:y ole plashe.* (Drury Lane's a draughty old place.)

'J' and 'zh' frequently join words together, e.g. *Izee comin', djou fink?* (Is he coming, do you think?) *'Azhye mum?* (How is your Mum?).

The softening of fricatives may have arisen from the fag-end already mentioned. In fact to speak the dialect, one only has to purse the lips, imagine a Woodbine stuck somewhere on the lower lip, and let the words roll out with the minimum of mouth movement, and you've got it!

If you think representing consonants in written Cockney speech is hard, that is only because you haven't tried the vowels! There are five vowels in the alphabet, plus 'y' and 'w', and no possible combination of these seven sounds can convey the complexity of Cockney vowels, which are washed and soaped and rinsed and put through the wringer, then stretched and twisted beyond anything that any phonetician can imagine. Italian is the language of pure vowels (the singer's delight). English has diphthongs and a few triphthongs. Cockney has quadraphthongs and quinquaphthongs, septaphthongs and octophthongs, and God knows how many more. They all differ from person to person, from time to time, from place to place, and from meaning to meaning. Vowels are the vehicle by which voice inflexion is carried, and singers spend years studying the tone, colour and meaning that can be placed on vowels. The Cockney does it from birth.

Many Cockney vowels are elongated and made unnecessarily complex, e.g. *loiedy*, *lahoiedy* (lady). Others are reduced to almost nothing, e.g. *fawna* (foreigner).

Diphthongs in Standard English can become a single pure vowel in Cockney, e.g. *par* (power), *sar* (sour).

In writing, to render 'I' as 'oi' gives the wrong impression, because Cockneys do not say 'oi', as in oil or joy. They say something like *aoiee.*

'Ow' becomes an approximation of 'aehr', e.g. *aehr naehr braehn caehr* (how now brown cow).

'O' (as in go) is 'eao' (or something like it), e.g. *'e breaok 'is leig, feoo off of a waoo, 'e did* (he broke his leg, fell off of the wall, he did); *'e niver aw: :oo 'ave bin up vere, aoiee teoozh'im* (he never ought to have been up there, I tells him).

I was struggling to express the Cockney accent in written form, until a professor of English Literature said to me, "You will not succeed, because it cannot be done. People have been trying since the fifteenth century, but it has never been successful."

What a relief! I will struggle no more.

Grammar, Syntax and Idiom

In all countries at all times in history, the poorest of the poor have tended to live around the docks. Trapped by poverty, they have become isolated, and remained more or less static. This may be why Poplar of the 1950s existed in a sort of time warp, with habits, customs and family life being somewhat behind the times. With the closure of the docks, this changed.

Speech is a living entity, changing with the people. But Cockney language changes have lagged far behind those of middle-class English. Many Cockney speech forms – idioms, grammar and syntax – which today are considered flawed, are, in fact, very ancient speech forms that can be traced back to Tudor times.

Here are some typical examples:

Possessive (conjugated)

myern	mine (my one)
yourn	yours (your one)
hisn, hern	his, hers
ourn	ours
yourn	yours
theirn	theirs

The '-self' form becomes:

Meself	myself
Yerself	yourself
his-self, herself	himself, herself
usselves	ourselves
yerselves	yourselves
vemselves	themselves

Verbs frequently take the third person singular for the whole conjugation:

I was	*I tells*	*I says*
you was	*you tells*	*you says*
he/she was	*he/she tells*	*he/she says*
we was	*we tells*	*we says*
you was	*you tells*	*you says*
vey was	*vey tells*	*vey says*

Some expressions in the past tense use the past participle on its own, without the auxiliary (have, did):

I done	I have done	*I gone*	I went
you done	you have done	*you gone*	you went
he/she done	he/she has done	*he/she gone*	he/she went

we done	we have done	*we gone*	we went
you done	you have done	*you gone*	you went
vey done	they have done	*vey gone*	they went

I bin	I have been
you bin	you have been
he/she bin	he/she has been
we bin	we have been
you bin	you have been
they bin	they have been

The form of the past participle may itself be changed:

I seed	I saw
you seed	you saw
he/she seed	he/she saw
we seed	we saw
you seed	you saw
vey seed	they saw

The demonstrative adjectives 'these' and 'those' are usually replaced by 'them', pronounced with a 'v', e.g. *vem sosjis* (these sausages), *vem cabjis* (those cabbages).

The relative pronouns 'who', 'which', and 'that' are replaced by 'as' and 'what', or sometimes both, e.g. *a bloke wha: oie knows*, or *ve bloke as wha: oie knows* (the bloke that I know).

'So' is often replaced by 'that', e.g. *moei col's va: bad, oei can: smeoo nuffink* (my cold's so bad, I can't smell anything).

'Here' and 'there' are often used for emphasis, e.g. *vish 'ere ca:s a good mahsher* (this cat's a good mouser) *va: vere kid's a roei: 'an'foo* (that kid's a right handful).

Auxiliary verbs are frequently duplicated, e.g. *oei woon: 'arf 'a towd 'im orf, oei woon:* (I wouldn't half have told him off, I wouldn't); *'e don: 'arf maihk yer laugh, 'e do.* (he doesn't half make you laugh, he does).

No: 'alf (not half) is an emphatic positive in Cockney dialect.

'Off of' nearly always replaces 'from': *oei go: i: off of 'Arry. 'E give i: :a me* (I got it from Harry. He gave it to me).

Adverbs frequently become adjectives: *'e done famous a: schoo-oo, vish term loeik* (He did famously at school this term); *ve job's go:a be done proper, loeik* (The job's got to be done properly).

To end a sentence with 'like' is typical Cockney dialect.

'The' is frequently omitted altogether and replaced with a glottal stop, *fetch : tea* (fetch the tea), *go : pichers* (go to the pictures).

A double glottal stop, executed with lightning speed, can sometimes be detected in such sentences.

The conjunction 'that' is usually replaced by 'as how', pronounced 'azhow' – *oei knowed azhow i: was vem as wa: done i:* (I knew that it was them who had done it).

The relative pronouns 'who' and 'which' are frequently rendered 'as what': *ve ca: as wa: 'as brough: in a mahsh* (The cat which has brought in a mouse).

Plural pronouns are split into singulars, sometimes repeating the plural for emphasis: *me an' 'er, we goes : pichers* (me and her, we went to the pictures); *vem an' uzh, we 'azh a good foie:* (them and us, we had a good fight).

Comparisons are subject to many enhancements, and can go clean over the top: 'better' and 'best' become *betterer, bestest*, or *more betterer, most bestest*, or *even bestestest. Vat wozh ve beshteshtish fing wha: 'e ever done.* (That was the best thing he ever did.) Good is often kept the same, although I have heard *gooderer* and *goodist*.

'worse', 'worst' become *worser, worsest*, or *worserer, worsesest*. Bad also, may be kept the same but can be *baderer, baddest*.

Things can go even further on the lips of a Cockney wordsmith: *ve mos' worsestest fing wha: 'e ever done was more be:erer van 'er wickidniss* (The worst thing he ever did was better than her wickedness). And that's about the most worsestest bit of grammar I have ever heard – but I love it!

'A-' prefixes the participles of many common verbs and this is a survival of the 'y-' prefix that was used in the Middle Ages:

"Wha: chew sh'poash :a be a-doin' of, eh?" (What are you supposed to be doing?)

"Oei wus a-ge:in me mum's errins" (I was getting my mum's errands [shopping])

"Weoo, your mum's a-comin' rahnd : corner nah an' a-callin' for yer" (well, your mum's coming round the corner now, and calling for you).

These are all typical examples of Cockney speech, and are of great antiquity. If Henry VIII had used similar grammatical forms it would have been the King's English, and pockets of the Docklands people retained this speech form in the 1950s.

Shakespeare wrote, not for the instruction of the intelligentsia, but for the entertainment of the London people. Double negatives occur in his plays and so, presumably, they were acceptable. Cockneys make generous use of such negatives: *she ain: nahbody, va: cah, oei'm a-tellin' ya; she ain: no: go: nuffink* (triple negative!) *on 'er back wha:s no: cast-offs, oei teoozhya* (she isn't anybody, that cow; she hasn't got anything on her back which isn't a cast-off, I tell you). We are taught at school that a double negative makes an affirmative, but when, in Cockney, three, four or five negatives are used, the rule ceases to bind!

'Never' is nearly always used for 'did not':

"You broke ve cup."

"No, oei niver. Straigh: up, oei niver." (You broke the cup. No I didn't. Honestly I didn't.)

'To' is usually dropped after the prepositions 'up', 'down', and 'round' and replaced by a glottal stop: *up : Aooga*' (up to Aldgate); *dahn : Dilly* (down to Piccadilly); *rahn' : Pop* (round to the pawnbroker).

Cockneys generally seem to need to 'have been and gone' before they can do or say anything: *she been an' gawn an' got sploeiced* (she has got married) *oei been an' gawn an' done it nah!* (I've done it now!). A Cockney boy of my acquaintance had to 'turn round' before he could say or do anything:

> *An' I* (pronounced *oie*) *turns rahn' an' I says "'ah abah: goin' darn Steps?" An' 'e turns rahn' an' says "you're on". So we offs, an' we gi:s 'alf-way vere an' 'e turns rahn an' says, 'e says "'ah abah: some fishin'?" So I turns rahn' an' says "Fishin! Why didn: you say va: afore? We're 'alf-way vere nah. We ain: go: no gear." So 'e turns rahn' an' 'e says "oh come on, won: take long." So we turns rahn an' goes 'ome for : gear, loike.*

Such circumlocution would make all but the coolest head dizzy, but to those accustomed from early childhood to being, linguistically, in a perpetual state of revolution it is all perfectly clear and logical.

The present tense is nearly always used to depict a fast-moving series of past events, and this gives particular strength and vitality to a story:

> *Oie'm tellin yer, last nigh: vey 'as a set-to. She clocks 'im one on : snout, an' 'e grabs 'er an' pushes 'er 'gainst : fender, an' she 'its 'er 'ead, an' vat's 'ow she gi:s a black eye, see? Oei'm tellin' yer.*

A particularly charming idiom in narrated gossip is the continuous use of 'I said', 'she/he said' – but used in the present tense. (In all the following I is pronounced oie.):

I says to 'er, I says, "look 'ere" I says, "I've just abou: 'ad it up to 'ere" I says "an' you be:er watch it" I says "or else". an' she says, she says "wha:" she says, "you fre:enin' me?" she says, an' I says "I am va: you ge: narky wiv me", I says, "an' I'll give yer a proper mahfoo-oo (mouthful). *I'm tellin' yer, nah jes watch i:, 'cos I'm tellin' yer."*

This last phrase I'm tellin' yer is intensely Cockney, and is always spoken with determination, and sometimes anger. It is also a guarantee of veracity: *oei teoozhya vis 'ere nag's a winner, oei'm a-tellin' yer* (I tell you, this horse is a winner, I'm telling you.); *oei teoozhya, 'e's va: mean 'e wouldn: give the pickins ah: 'is shnah:* (I tell you, he's that mean, he wouldn't give you the pickings out of his snout [nose]).

"Don't talk to me about . . . " or "you can't tell me nothing about . . . " are both used as an opening gambit to attract attention. They both imply unrivalled personal experience and specialist knowledge of a subject already under discussion:

Dandruff! You can't tell me nuffink abah: dandruff, you can't. Cor, we all go: i:. I goddi:, me mum's goddi:, me dad's goddi:, me free sisters an' me nan's goddi:. An' know what? Bleedin' dawg's goddi:. Cor! Dandruff all over : bleedin' place; on : table, on : dresser, on : mantlepiece, all over : floor. Everywhere. Me mum she shweeps up bucki:s of i: every day. Gor blimey, don: talk :a me 'bah: dandruff, ma:e.

Subordinate clauses take on a life of their own; overheard in All Saints between two church workers, one of whom had been asked to join the roster of flower-arrangers:

"'oo asked yer to be a flarh-loeidy (flower-lady) *ven?"*
"Ve loeidy wiv ve long teef."
"Oh yers. Ve loeidy wiv ve long teef an' ve boss-oiyes (boss-eyes)*."*
"Nah, nah, no: 'er. Ve loeidy wha: asked me :o be a flarh-loeidy's teef are more longerer'n 'erens.

The foregoing is just a taste of the rich vernacular that goes to make up the Cockney dialect. A comprehensive study would be a full-time job for any writer, but it would be rewarding.

Slang

Slang, rhyming slang and backslang were so much a part of Cockney speech in the 1950s that many children starting school at the age of five had to learn a whole new vocabulary.

Backslang has largely disappeared from the vernacular. It used to be the language of the Costers, and was used between themselves for trading and bargaining, e.g *yennep* (penny). The street coster lingered almost to the end of the twentieth century, but has just about disappeared now.

The slang I heard in the 1950s was rich, varied, colourful, obscene, racy, and widely used. It has been said that rhyming Cockney slang was originally developed to outwit authority and nosy parkers. If this was the case, it was entirely successful, because no one but the initiated could follow it. Whatever the origins of this closed language, the humour of it is too good to be missed.

The following is taken from Jack Jones's *Rhyming Cockney Slang*, published by Abson Books in 1971:

Almond Rocks	Socks	*Me almonds need darning*
Biscuits and Cheese	Knees	*She ain't 'arf got knobbly biscuits*
Bristol Cities	Titties	*A fine pair of Bristols*
Butcher's Hook	Look	*Let's 'ave a butchers at it*
China Plate	Mate	*'e's me best China*
Greengages	Wages	*I'll pay you when I get me greens*
Khyber Pass	Arse	*'e can stick that up his Khyber!*
Mince Pies	Eyes	*She's got lovely minces*
Pen and Ink	Stink	*It pens a bit*
Rabbit and Pork	Talk	*She can't 'arf rabbit*
Uncle Bert	Shirt	*Why 'aven't you washed me uncle?*
Weasel and Stoat	Coat	*I'll put on me weasel*

This evocative and often elusive language was widely used until the 1970s, but with the closure of the docks and the disintegration of family life, Cockney speech is changing, and this fascinating heritage of rhyming slang is falling into disuse. It was once a vital, living, idiomatic form of speech, but I predict that during the first quarter of the twenty-first century it will become a mere relic, found only in dictionaries to be studied and reproduced in soap operas for the amusement of the masses.

The following books can be recommended:

The Muvver Tongue, by Robert Balthrop and Jim Woolveridge, The Journeyman Press, 1980
The Cockney, by Julian Franklyn, Andre Deutsch, 1953
Dictionary of Rhyming Slang, by Julian Franklyn, Routledge, 1975

An unrivalled record of Cockney speech is to be found in *Mayhew's London* and the other following books can be recommended:

Balthrop, Robert and Jim Woolveridge, *The Muvver Tongue* (The Journeyman Press, London, 1980).
Franklyn, Julian, *The Cockney* (Andre Deutsch, 1953).
Franklyn, Julian, *Dictionary of Rhyming Slang* (Andre Deutsch, 1961).
Harris, Charles, *Three Ha'Pence to the Angel* (Phoenix House, London, 1950).
Jones, Jack, *Rhyming Cockney Slang* (Abson Books, London, 1971).
Lewey, F., *Cockney Campaign* (Heffer, 1944).
Matthews, Professor William, *Cockney Past and Present* (Routledge, London, 1940).
O'London, Jack (Wilfred Whitten), *London Stories* (TC & EC Jack Ltd, Bristol, 1948).
Quennell, Peter, ed., *Mayhew's London* (Hamlyn, London, 1969).

Robbins, G., *Fleet Street Blitzkrieg Diary* (Ernest Benn Ltd, London, 1942).
Upton, Clive and David Parry, *The Dictionary of English Grammar: Survey of English Dialects* (Routledge, London, 1994).

GLOSSARY

Glossary by Terri Coates MSc, RN, RM, ADM, Dip Ed

albumenuria: Now called proteinuria. Testing of urine for the presence of protein is still a part of normal antenatal care. Urine is no longer boiled to diagnose the presence of protein in urine. The midwife now dips a strip of reactive paper into a sample of urine. The resulting colour of the strip gives an indication of the amount of protein present in the urine.
amniotic fluid: The fluid that surrounds and protects the baby in the womb. Amniotic fluid is also known as the "waters".
antenatal: Before birth.
anterior presentation: The back of the baby's head in labour will normally be in the front or anterior part of the mother's pelvis. This anterior presentation is the most favourable for the baby to adopt for a normal delivery.
asphyxia: Insufficient oxygen supply to the vital organs, particularly the brain, sometimes resulting in death or permanent damage.

bd: Medical shorthand used as an instruction on prescriptions to mean twice a day.
BP: Medical shorthand for blood pressure.
breech: A baby that is positioned bottom down rather than the usual head down.
breech delivery: The description of the breech delivery has changed little over the decades though breech delivery at home is now a very unusual occurrence. A breech delivery is slower than a head-first delivery as the baby's body negotiates the pelvis first and the widest diameter, the head, is delivered last. When the baby's head enters the pelvis it is maintained in a flexed position by the weight of its own body hanging down outside the mother's body. This ensures that the head is delivered slowly and safely.

Caesarean section: An operation to deliver a baby through an incision in the mother's abdomen.
cervix: The neck of the womb.
chancre: The initial lesion of a syphilis infection.
chloral hydrate: A mild sedative and analgesic used in the early stages of labour. The drug was given as a drink with either water and glucose or fruit juice. Chloral hydrate is an irritant to the stomach which often causes vomiting so is no longer used.
colostrum: The first breast milk. Mature breast milk is produced from the third or fourth day after the birth of the baby.
contraction: The intermittent tightening of the muscles of the uterus (womb), which are painful during labour.
cord: The umbilical cord attaches the baby to the placenta before birth.
crown: The crown refers to the top of the baby's head, usually the first part of the baby's head to emerge. When it emerges it is said to "crown".
cystitis: Inflammation or infection of the bladder.

D and C: Dilatation and curettage (D and C) is an operation to remove any pieces of placenta or membrane from the uterus after delivery to prevent further bleeding or infection.
delivery techniques: Placing the heel of the hand behind the anus is no longer undertaken as part of delivery. It is now considered to be unnecessary and invasive.

eclampsia: A rare and severe consequence of pre-eclampsia which is characterised by convulsions. Eclampsia is an infrequent cause of death of a mother and unborn baby. The old term used for eclampsia was toxaemia.
enema: A preparation used to empty the lower bowel. It used to be given to all women at the start of labour, administered in the belief that it would stimulate contractions and make space for the baby to descend. Research has shown that an enema is not a labour stimulant and is no longer used.

episiotomy: A cut made to enlarge the opening of the vagina during delivery.
ergometrine: An oxytocic drug which makes the muscle of the uterus contract after delivery. The oxytocic drugs of choice now are either syntometrine or syntocinon.

Fehlings solution: A chemical used for testing for the presence of sugar in urine. The chemical is now used in a tablet form (clinitest), added to 5 drops urine and 10 of water. The colour of resulting solution is compared to a chart for a result.
first stage of labour: From the start of regular painful contractions until the cervix (neck of the womb) is fully open.
forceps delivery: If a baby becomes stuck in the mother's pelvis during labour then forceps would be used to assist the delivery. Forceps are applied in two halves, one either side of the baby's head, and the operator pulls gently on the forceps to deliver the baby. A low forceps delivery refers to the baby being low in the mother's pelvis.
full term: The duration of a pregnancy is (nine months) forty weeks. Full term is considered to be between thirty-eight and forty-two weeks of pregnancy.
fundus: The top of the uterus.

gallipot: A small glass or ceramic bowl for medicines or lotion.
gas and air machine: Gas and air was a popular form of pain relief for labour. The air has now been exchanged for oxygen but is still usually called "gas and air". The "gas" in current use is nitrous oxide.
gestation: The number of weeks of pregnancy.
gluteus muscle: Gluteus or gluteus maximus muscle is the large muscle in the bottom.

IM: Intra muscular or into the muscle.
IV: Intra Venous (IV) or intra venous infusion may be more commonly known as a drip.

kidney dish: A kidney-shaped bowl available in various sizes to hold medical equipment.

left side: Positioning women on their left side for delivery was popular for a while. Women are now encouraged to choose the position for delivery that is most comfortable for them; the left side or left lateral position is rarely used.

lying in: A period of ten to fourteen days when a woman was confined to bed and was not expected to get up for *any* reason. This enforced bed rest created problems rather than encouraging recovery. Women are now expected to be up and out of bed very soon after the birth of the baby.

macerated foetus: A baby that has been dead in the womb for a while and the skin has started to break down.

mastitis: Inflammation or infection of the breast.

Mauriceau-Smellie-Veit: A series of manoeuvres to deliver a breech baby. This method of breech delivery is still used by some midwives and obstetricians.

mucus catheter: Mucus is now sucked from the baby's mouth using gentle electrical suction rather than oral suction to prevent the spread of infection.

multigravida: A woman who has had more than one pregnancy.

nephritis: Kidney infection.

nurse: The title of nurse is now rarely used for or by midwives. Midwifery is an entirely separate profession. Many midwives were trained as nurses but this dual qualification is now less common.

occipital protuberance (or occiput): The back of the baby's head.

oedema: Swelling caused by fluid retained in the tissues.

oxytocic drugs: See ergometrine.

paediatrician: A doctor who specialises in the care of babies and children.

path. or path lab: A shortened term for a pathology laboratory where samples of blood would be sent for confirmation of infection.

pelvic floor: The layer of muscle that lies across the lower part of the pelvis.

perineum: The area between the vaginal opening and the anus. The perineum is often damaged in childbirth. A tear or cut (episiotomy) in the perineum may require stitches, but usually heals quickly.

pinard: A pinard or foetal stethoscope is shaped like a listening trumpet and is placed on the abdomen of the woman so that the midwife can hear the foetal heartbeat.

pitting oedema: Swollen skin will stay dented if pressure has been applied.

placenta: Also known as the afterbirth. The placenta is attached to the wall of the uterus during pregnancy and separates after the birth of the baby.

placenta praevia: When the placenta forms partly or wholly over the opening of the uterus. Severe bleeding can occur. Delivery is usually by Caesarean section.

post-natal or post-partum: The six weeks following birth.

post-partum delirium: Is now called puerperal psychosis; the less severe form is called post-natal depression.

pre-eclampsia: A disease that is peculiar to pregnancy. The symptoms are high blood pressure, protein in the urine and oedema (swelling).

premature baby (care of): Skin to skin care is now widely used for the care of premature babies. Separation of the mother and baby in modern neonatal intensive care units is kept to a minimum and contact between the mother and her baby is encouraged. Skin to skin care is also known as Kangaroo Care. The modern history of its use goes back to the early 1980s in Bogota, Columbia, where it was developed out of medical need as there were not enough incubators to keep the premature babies warm. The success of Kangaroo Care has now spread all over the world. Kangaroo Care works because the baby is kept warm so uses fewer calories, needs less oxygen and has a better breathing rate. Babies receiving this

form of care have also been found to cry less and sleep better than those cared for in an incubator.
primigravida: A woman pregnant with her first baby.
pubic bone: The centre and front part of the pelvis.

sacro anterior position (left or right): Positions that a breech baby could be in immediately before delivery. The baby's sacrum (bone at the base of the spine) lies at the front of the mother's pelvis.
scrape: Another name for D and C (see above).
second stage: The time when the neck of the womb or uterus is fully open until the delivery of the baby.
shave: The perineum was shaved for labour until the 1980s. It was thought to make the skin cleaner for delivery. Research has shown that shaving does not improve the cleanliness of the perineum either before or after delivery.
sim's speculum: An instrument that looks like a double ended shoe horn bent into a gently curved M shape used to stretch the vaginal walls.
spirochaeta: A type of organism such as *treponema pallidum*, the cause of syphilis.
suprapubic: Above the pubic bone.

third stage: The time from the birth of the baby to the complete delivery of the placenta.

uterus: Also known as the womb.

vagina: Birth canal.
vernix caseosa: The sticky white substance that is on the baby's skin at birth, usually seen in the skin folds.
vulva: A woman's genital organs.

waters: A protective bag of water surrounds the baby in the womb. The bag breaks during labour and the water drains away.

References

Cowell B., and Wainwright D., *Behind the Blue Door*, Cassells Ltd, London 1981.

Morton, L. T., *A Medical Bibliography* (3rd edn, The Trinity Press, London, 1970).

Myles, Margaret F., *Text Book for Midwives*. V. Ruth Bennett and L. K. Brown, eds (Churchill Livingstone, Edinburgh, 1999).

Richardson H., 'Kangaroo Care: why does it work?', *Midwifery Today*, 44 (1997), 50–51.

Stables D., *Physiology in Childbearing with Anatomy and Related Biosciences* (Balliere Tindall, Edinburgh, 1999).

FRANK

'Give me a boy for the first five years
of his life, and I will make the man.'
Rousseau

Frank had but a dim recollection of his father. He remembered a tall, strong man, whom he held in awe. He remembered his big voice and huge, rough hands. He could remember once tracing the veins on the back of this vast hand with his little fingers, and looking at his own smooth white skin and wondering if he would ever have hands like that. To be like his father was his only ambition and he worshipped him. In the later, sadder years of his childhood he tried desperately to remember what his father had been like, but a phantom that comes and goes could not have been more elusive and only the dimmest memory remained.

He remembered his mother much more clearly; his sweet, gentle mother who was never strong because she was always coughing. He remembered the sound of her voice as she sang songs to him and played with him. Above all, he remembered her cuddles as she put him to bed and lay down beside him.

In the winter his mother hardly went out of doors because of her weak chest and his father would say, as he went off to work, 'Now you look after your mother while I'm away, Frank lad. I'm relying on you to take care of her for me.' And Frank would look up at his god with big solemn eyes and accept the task as a sacred duty.

When a tiny baby was born – so tiny that everyone said she would not live – Frank was four years old. He had been an only child all his life and could not conceive of any other child entering his world. Many boys of that age become very jealous of a new-born baby, but not Frank. He was mesmerized by this tiny creature, hardly bigger than a teacup, who could move and cry, and who needed so much care. Not for a moment did he resent the hours of attention given to the baby. In fact, he liked to help. The most fascinating thing of all was to watch his mother breast-feeding the baby, and he tried never to be far away when this mysterious and beautiful ritual was going on. He kept very quiet, crept close to his mother, and watched, spellbound, as the baby sucked and the milk oozed from the nipple.

The baby was premature and sickly, and for a long time her life hung in the balance. His father said to him, many times: 'You've got a special job to do, young man. You've got to look after your little sister. That's your job now, lad.'

So Frank watched over her, and hardly went out to play with the other boys in the court, because he was so busy looking after his little sister.

The baby didn't die. She gained strength and became quite robust although she always remained small. She was christened Margaret but was called Peggy, because Margaret seemed too long a name for such a small baby. After the christening Frank's father said, 'You done a good job there, son, I'm proud of yer.'

Then catastrophe struck. In those years typhoid was raging through East London. His huge, strong father, who had never known a day of illness in his life, was hit by the epidemic and died within a few days. His mother, who had never been strong, was spared and so was the baby. His mother went out to work, cleaning offices. She left home in the early hours each morning, and again each evening, leaving Frank to look after Peggy, who was by now a toddler.

One day Frank ran home from school (he didn't think much of school, regarding it as a waste of time) to take over the domestic responsibilities from his mother, so that she could go out to her job. It was cold and she was coughing badly, but she went nonetheless. Money had to be earned, or they would be homeless. Frank did as he had so often done before: he put some wood that he had found on his way home onto the fire, made some tea for himself and

Peggy, played with her and as the fire was dying, he undressed her and put her to bed, creeping in beside her for warmth.

In the middle of the night he woke up, aware that something was wrong. It was pitch black, and the quiet was terrifying. He could hear Peggy breathing, but that was all. Something was missing. Nausea seized him as he realised that his mother was not there. In a panic, he felt all over the bed, but the side where his mother usually slept was empty. He called out in a small voice so as not to wake Peggy, but there was no reply. He crept out of bed and found the matches. He struck one and the flame leapt up, lighting the whole room momentarily. His mother was not there. Blinded by tears, he crept back into bed and held Peggy in his arms.

The cold had badly affected his mother as soon as she stepped outside. She was asthmatic and bronchitic, and had been fighting down a chest infection for several weeks. She had a mile to walk to the bus, and the freezing mist rising off the river had got into her lungs. She was thankful for the brief respite of sitting in the bus, but by the time she got to the building where she was employed, she felt more dead than alive. She went to the cleaning cupboard to get out her things, but the bucket felt so heavy that she could hardly move it. She asked permission to make herself a cup of tea, saying she would feel better with something warm inside her. The tea was indeed comforting, but the building was cold and she sat shivering in the basement, pulling her shawl around her shoulders and coughing. One by one the office workers left and she found herself alone.

Normally, this office took her about three hours, but after one hour, she had scarcely cleaned one tenth of it. She felt so weak she could scarcely drag herself around, and there was still the scrubbing to do. She returned to the basement to get the bucket – the one that had felt impossibly heavy when empty – and filled it with water. She pushed it along the floor with her feet and then lifted it up the stairs one by one, resting it on each stair as she did so. She reached the second storey this way, and then her failing strength must have given out. She fell down the stairs that she had climbed so laboriously, knocking the bucket over as she fell. She was drenched with water and lay on the stone floor all night. In the morning they found her dead at the bottom of the stairs.

Frank had never spent a night away from his mother. There was only one bed, so they had all slept together even when his father was alive. He had never even contemplated a time without the comforting warmth of her body beside him. Now, in the dark and cold of the room, the bed felt like a hostile and alien territory, and he wanted to run away from it, run to the next-door neighbours, screaming. But there was Peggy to think of. She was quietly sleeping, unaware that anything was wrong. So he bit his lips, rubbed his fists into his eyes and cuddled up close to her.

He was six years old.

He must have slept, because it was daylight when he was awoken by Peggy crying. There was some milk and water left from the night before but it was cold and she pushed it away. He did not know what to do. He took a wet nappy off her, as he had seen his mother do, but then he didn't know what to do with it, so hid it under the bed. There was no more wood for the fire. He drank the cold milk himself and crept back into bed. They fell asleep again.

He awoke as a crowd of neighbouring women entered the room.

'Oh, it's a shame, oie tells ya.'

'Poor li'l kids. Vey didn' ask 'a be born.'

'Both dead in six months.'

'It makes yer wanna cry, don' it?'

Frank looked around him in bewilderment and held Peggy defensively, pulling the blanket up higher.

A man entered the room.

'Are these the children of the deceased?' he enquired.

A chorus of voices answered.

'Yeah, more's the pity.'

'Poor li'l lambs.'

'Vey don' know wha's 'appened.'

'And is there no relative to look after them?'

'No' as 'ow I knows on, do you, Lil?'

'Nah, no one.'

'They will have to come with me, and the effects sold to contribute to the Guardians' expenses.'

He looked around the room at the meagre furniture – one bed, one table, and two chairs, a small cupboard, a washing bowl, a chamber pot, a candlestick, some tin plates and cups – all back-breakingly acquired by the father, to provide for his family.

'Will someone get them ready while I take an inventory?'

Two women stepped forward, and Frank grabbed the back of the bed, clutching Peggy.

'Where's Mummy?' he asked plaintively.

'Yer mum's dead, luvvy, more's the pity.'

'No, my dad's dead,' he insisted.

'An so's yer mum, dearie. Found dead vis momin' in ve office.'

'Blue, she was,' chorused the women to each other.

'Froze stiff, vey say, an' soakin' wet.'

'Wet froo, an' all, and 'er wiv her weak chest.'

'No' surprisin' ain't it.

Frank looked from one to another, and horror struck his heart. Was his mother dead? He had promised his father that he would look after her! What had gone wrong? Peggy was beginning to whimper again. Kind hands were placed on him. He clung to the bars of the bedstead with all his strength and turned his back on the women, holding Peggy, who was beginning to scream now, between his body and the head of the bed.

'You will have to get him free,' said the man. 'They cannot stay here alone.'

It took four women to loosen his fingers from the bars. A child's fingers can be incredibly strong if they are curled around something. Eventually two women were holding him and Peggy in their arms. He was biting and scratching and kicking in an hysteria of fear and rage. He shouted at the woman holding Peggy, 'Give her to me. She's my sister. Don't take her away.' Tears were streaming down his face.

'We will have to go. Does anyone know where the key is kept?' said the man.

The door of the room was locked, and they made their way downstairs. The woman holding Frank was badly bruised. They walked through the streets, collecting a crowd of onlookers as they went.

Frank and Peggy were admitted to the infants' section of the workhouse, where boys and girls under seven years of age were housed. They were undressed and bathed and treated not unkindly. In fact, Peggy's tiny stature and wispy blonde hair evoked a stream of sympathy from the women who received them. Frank had exhausted his fury, and sullenly allowed himself to be washed and his hair examined for fleas.

'We'll have to cut it off. You know the rules.'

He submitted to having his head shaved, but when he saw a large woman doing the same to Peggy, he rushed at her and butted her in the stomach with his head. She collapsed onto a chair winded, then grabbed the boy and thrashed him soundly, whilst another officer shaved Peggy.

'It's a shame, cutting this pretty hair. But it will soon grow again.'

Poor little Peggy looked like a tiny Martian when they had finished, and Frank sobbed with impotent rage.

The children were dressed in workhouse clothes and taken to the playroom to meet the other children. We would not call it a playroom today, because there was nothing to play with. It was just a large, bare room, about forty feet long by twenty feet wide, with high, uncurtained windows, and rough floorboards.

'Now you play quietly with the others until tea time.'

The door was shut, and the officer left.

They stood shyly in the doorway, looking at about forty other children, all wearing the same clothes. Frank, acutely self-conscious that he and Peggy had no hair, tried to hide her under his jacket. A boy of about his age ran up to them, shouting 'You're new. You're new. Where've you come from? What's your name, baldy? An' who's this little squirt, then?'

He pulled at Peggy's arm and tickled her scalp. Frank flung himself at the boy, fighting with savage fury. All the rage that had been building up during the day was concentrated in his attack. The other children stood back to watch the fun. The other boy was no slouch when it came to fighting and the two were evenly matched. There were no adults in the room to stop them.

Peggy was terrified and ran screaming to a corner, where she crouched down, hiding her head. A little girl with dark hair left the others, came over to her, and put her small arms around the sobbing child.

'Don't cry, please don't cry. They're only fighting. Boys are always fighting. Boys are awful. Here, sit on my knee.'

The girl sat down on the floor and Peggy climbed on to her knees. She played with a long, dark ringlet hanging down near her face, and laughed when she pulled it and it bounced back up again.

The girl smiled happily.

'You're like a little doll. I've never had a doll, but I've seen them. And you're better than a doll, because you're real, and dolls are only pretend. Will you be my friend? My name's Jane, and I'm three. What's yours?'

Peggy didn't say anything, but her tears stopped. Jane sat quietly, cuddling Peggy, and laughing to herself as she watched the fight.

The boys were roughly the same age and weight, but Frank had the advantage of cold, calculated fury and his desire to defend his sister. He glanced at the other boys who were egging them on, and knew instinctively that if he lost this fight, Peggy would never be safe from their tormentors. After a few minutes Frank's adversary was on the floor in a corner.

'Truce. Give in. Hold 'im off,' he called out.

Frank turned to face the others. He raised his fists defiantly.

'Anyone else want a go?'

No one stepped forward.

Frank swaggered over to the corner where Peggy sat on Jane's knee.

'Thanks,' he said. 'She's only two, and she's scared. Her name's Peggy and I'm Frank.'

The girl had a merry laugh, open features and piercing blue eyes. Frank liked her, he liked the way she was nursing Peggy, and he saw the contentment with which the little girl responded to the older one. He knew that he could trust her.

'Let's be friends,' he said.

Over the next few weeks, the reality of his mother's death dawned upon Frank. He would never see her again and pain inside reduced him to tears. Other boys laughed and jeered at him, but he only had to stick out his jaw and raise his fists aggressively, and they quickly backed off. Peggy did not seem as unhappy, because Frank was always there for her. Also, Jane had taken to her and petted and fussed over her, calling her 'my little doll'. Jane was indisputably the leader among the girls, so her protection meant a good deal.

Jane was good for Frank also. He liked her with the instinctive affection that recognizes a kindred spirit. He approved of her gentle ways with Peggy, and he also liked her naughtiness. She was always playing tricks and pranks, making everyone laugh. She would jump out from behind a door when the officer opened it, shouting 'boo', and then run away laughing. She was always caught and smacked, but nothing seemed to quench her high spirits. The day she climbed the waterpipe in the playground and sat on the gutter and wouldn't come down was one of the funniest things Frank could ever remember. Fat old officer Hawkins had been on duty that day and got onto a ladder, then lumbered up it, with all the boys crowding around underneath, trying to see her knickers. When she finally got Jane down, she thrashed her soundly in the playground, and then again in the evening before bedtime, but Jane just rubbed her bottom, shook her curls defiantly, and did not seem to care.

The night times were the worst for Frank. Alone in a small hard bed, with darkness all around, he sobbed silently for his sweet mother. He missed the warmth of her body, he missed the smell of her skin, the touch of her hand, the sound of her breathing. He would creep over to Peggy's bed and get in beside her, and the smell of her hair would numb his pain. This became their one comfort in the first months of their life in the workhouse.

A year passed. After breakfast one morning, Frank and two other boys were taken to the Matron's office. She said abruptly, 'You are big boys now that you are seven, and we are taking you to the boys' section today. Wait in the hallway, and the van will come for you at nine o'clock.'

The boys did not know what she meant, and the three of them sat on the bench, engaged in mock fights and ribaldry.

At nine o'clock, a man entered the front door and enquired, 'Are these three to go?'

They were taken outside to a green van and told to climb in the back. It was all very exciting. They had never been in a van before, so they clambered in willingly, ready for adventure. The van started with a jerk, and they were thrown off the bench onto the floor. They shrieked with laughter. This was going to be a good day. A ride in a van! You wait till we get back and tell the others. The van stopped twice, and other boys of their own age climbed in. Soon there were eight boys, all shouting and skidding around the floor of the van as they turned corners, or pressing against each other to see out of the small back window in order to wave at people as they passed. Everyone turned to look, because motorised transport was comparatively unusual in those days. The boys felt very privileged, and infinitely superior to the people walking.

Eventually the van stopped and the back door opened. Frank saw a very large, grey, stone building in front of him, and he did not much like the look of it.

'Where am I?' he asked.

'This is the boys' section. You come here when you are seven and stay until you are fourteen,' said a tough looking man, who was a workhouse officer.

'And where's Peggy?' he demanded.

'I don't know who Peggy is, but she's not here.'

'Peggy is my sister and I look after her. My dad told me to.'

The officer laughed.

'Well, someone else will have to look after her. There's no girls allowed in here.'

Still Frank did not understand. He was unsure, uncertain and he felt like crying, but he wasn't going to let the other boys see him, so he squared his shoulders, clenched his fists and put on a swagger as they were taken to the Master's office.

The interview was brief. They were told that they must obey the rules, obey the officers at all times, and that if they did not do so they would be punished. The Master then said, 'You will be given your duties and lunch is at one o'clock. You will start school tomorrow.'

Frank had wanted to ask about Peggy, but the Master so terrified him that he did not dare speak. He followed the officer to the dining hall with a feeling of panic in his heart that he had not known since the night when he had awoken to find his mother's side of the bed empty.

Lunch in a huge refectory with about one hundred and fifty other boys, some of them very big, was terrifying and he could not eat. He ate half a potato and drank some water, but it nearly choked him, and he could not stop his tears from falling. Some of the bigger boys pointed at him and sniggered. None of the male officers showed any sympathy. The eight new boys who had come together were all considerably more sober now. The fun and high spirits of the van ride evaporated as the reality of the situation began to dawn upon them. They had left the small world and comparative kindness of the nursery, where there were women officers and nurses, for the harsh, often brutal world of the workhouse proper where, for the next seven years, they would encounter only male officers.

Back in the nursery, Peggy looked around for Frank, but could not find him. She looked in the lavatory and the washroom, but he was not there. She looked in the classroom and under the stairs, but he was not in those places either. Bewildered and frightened, she stood on the bottom stair hugging the banister, and stamped her feet. An officer came up to her, but she screamed and stamped her little feet even faster.

'Poor little thing,' remarked the officer to a colleague, 'she's going to miss her brother, they were very close. She'll just have to get over it in her own time. There's nothing we can do.'

Peggy was three years old and Frank had been with her all her life. She had not noticed the loss of her father when she was eighteen months old, and had only the vaguest memory of her mother. But Frank was her world, her life, her security and she was utterly devastated. All day she stood on the bottom step, hugging the smooth, round balustrade, sometimes silent, sometimes sobbing. Sometimes she kicked the stairs and hurt her toe. Twice she wet herself, but still she wouldn't move. Jane tried to talk to her, but Peggy shook her shoulders and screamed, 'Go away.'

'Leave her alone,' said an officer to Jane, 'she'll get over it in a day or two.'

Towards evening Peggy started to bang her head on the balustrade. It hurt, but she wanted it to. Perhaps Frank would come when he knew she had hurt herself. When he didn't come, she sobbed uncontrollably then slipped down onto the stairs in a deep sleep. A nurse picked her up, carried her to the dormitory and put her to bed.

For the next three months, Peggy hunted for Frank every day. She always expected to find him, but never did. She asked everyone: 'Where's Frank?' and was told that he had been transferred to the big boys' section, but she did not understand. She developed the habit of sitting alone in a corner and rocking herself. A nurse, who knew that this was a particularly frightening development in a lonely, insecure child, tried to comfort her. But Peggy would not be comforted. Each lonely night, she sucked her thumb and rocked herself and cried for Frank to come to her. But he didn't come.

As time passed, she stopped looking for Frank and asked for him less, until eventually she stopped asking. It was assumed that she had forgotten all about him.

It was to be nine years before brother and sister saw each other again, and by that time they did not recognise each other.

Farewell to the East End

JENNIFER WORTH

CLINICAL EDITOR

Terri Coates MSc. RN. RM. ADM. Dip Ed

PHOENIX

This edition published for
Index Books Ltd

A PHOENIX PAPERBACK

First published in Great Britain in 2009
by Weidenfeld & Nicolson
This paperback edition published in 2009
by Phoenix,
an imprint of Orion Books Ltd,
Orion House, 5 Upper St Martin's Lane,
London WC2H 9EA

An Hachette UK company

15 17 19 20 18 16 14

This is the third work of non-fiction, of which the first two were published by Merton Books. The events it recounts are true. However, certain names and identifying characteristics of some of the people who appear in its pages have been changed. The views expressed in this book are the author's.

A CIP catalogue record for this book
is available from the British Library.

Typeset by Input Data Services Ltd, Bridgwater, Somerset

Printed and bound in Great Britain by Clays Ltd, St Ives plc

www.orionbooks.co.uk

Praise for Jennifer Worth

'These are powerful stories delivered with sweet charm and controlled outrage' *Times Literary Supplement*

'Worth is indeed a natural storyteller – in the best sense of the term, with apparent artlessness in fact concealing high art – and her detailed account of being a midwife in London's East End is gripping, moving and convincing from beginning to end ... *Call the Midwife* is also a powerful evocation of a long-gone world ... and in Worth it has surely found one of its best chroniclers' *Literary Review*

'A chilling insight into life for the average mother [in the 1950s]'
Sunday Express

'Sheer magic' *The Lady*

'Worth's book made me cry in a railway carriage' Matthew Parris, *Spectator*

'Worth is a vivid writer with a talent for the sting in the tail ... a highly readable book – and a must for social planners' *Evening Standard*

'Jennifer Worth has a gift for storytelling and a keen eye for the evocative' BBC TV's *Who Do You Think You Are?*

'Jennifer Worth's entertaining and moving account of her experiences among the Docklands people balances sentiment with gritty realism'
Docklands News

'A candid, poignant memoir ... this gripping narrative includes breech babies, adulterous relationships, urban pig-breeding and a surreal strip show in a brothel' *Townswoman*

'Worth's talent shines from every page' *Sainsbury's Magazine*

'In her marvellous new book ... [t]here are desperately sad stories here, but tales of great hope too. Of ordinary people living, giving birth and building their families despite enormous hardship and poor sanitation. And of midwives delivering superb care in the toughest conditions'
East End Life

'Nobody who reads *Call the Midwife* will ever forget it' *The Woman Writer*

'The Docklands in London's East End in the 1950s seems more like the nineteenth century than 50 years ago' *Good Book Guide*

Jennifer Worth trained as a nurse at the Royal Berkshire Hospital in Reading. She then moved to London to train as a midwife. She later became a staff nurse at the Royal London Hospital, Whitechapel, then ward sister and later night sister at the Elizabeth Garrett Anderson Hospital in Euston. Music had always been her passion, and in 1973 Jennifer left nursing in order to study music intensively. She gained the Licentiate of the London College of Music in 1974 and was awarded a Fellowship ten years later. Jennifer married Philip Worth in 1963 and they live together in Hertfordshire. They have two daughters and three grandchildren.

By Jennifer Worth

Call the Midwife
Shadows of the Workhouse
Farewell to the East End
Eczema and Food Allergy: The Hidden Cause – My Story

Dedicated to Cynthia
for a lifetime of friendship

ACKNOWLEDGEMENTS

My thanks and gratitude to:

Terri Coates, the midwife who inspired me to write these books, Kirsty Dunseath for her editing skills, Dr Michael Boyes, Douglas May, Jenny Whitefield, Joan Hands, Helen Whitehorn, Philip and Suzannah, Ena Robinson, Mary Riches, Janet Salter, Maureen Dring, Peggy Sayer, Mike Birch, Sally Neville, the Marie Stopes Society.

Special thanks to Patricia Schooling of Merton Books for first bringing my writing to an audience.

All names have been changed. 'The Sisters of St Raymund Nonnatus' is a pseudonym.

CONTENTS

In 1855 Queen Victoria wrote to her daughter Vicky, the Crown Princess of Prussia, who was expecting a baby:

What you say about the pride of giving life to an immortal soul is very fine, but I own I cannot enter into all that. I think very much more of our being like a cow or a dog at such moments, when our poor nature becomes so very animal and unecstatic.

'YOUTH'S A STUFF WILL NOT ENDURE'

Someone once said that youth is wasted on the young.* Not a bit of it. Only the young have the impulsive energy to tackle the impossible and enjoy it; the courage to follow their instincts and brave the new; the stamina to work all day, all night and all the next day without tiring. For the young everything is possible. None of us, twenty years later, could do the things we did in our youth. Though the vision burns still bright, the energy has gone.

In the heady days of my early twenties I went to work in the East End of bomb-damaged London as a district midwife. I did it out of a yearning for adventure, not from a sense of vocation. I wanted to experience something different from my middle-class background, something tough and challenging that would stretch me. I wanted a new slant on life. I went to a place called Nonnatus House,† which I thought was a small private hospital, but which turned out to be a convent run by the Sisters of St Raymund Nonnatus. When I discovered my mistake I nearly ran away without unpacking my bags. Nuns were not my style. I couldn't be doing with that sort of thing, I thought. I wanted adventure, not religion. I did not know it at the time, but my soul was yearning for both.

* 'Youth is such a wonderful thing. What a crime to waste it on children.' George Bernard Shaw. The quote in the chapter title is from Shakespeare, *Twelfth Night*, act 2, scene 3.

† The Midwives of St Raymund Nonnatus is a pseudonym. I have taken the name from St Raymund Nonnatus, the patron saint of midwives, obstetricians, pregnant women, childbirth and newborn babies. He was delivered by Caesarean section ('*non natus*' is the Latin for 'not born') in Catalonia, Spain, in 1204. His mother, not surprisingly, died at his birth. He became a priest and died in 1240.

The nuns generated adventure. They plunged headlong into anything, fearlessly: unlit streets and courtyards, dark, sinister stairways, the docks, brothels; they would tackle rogue landlords, abusive parents – nothing was outside their scope. Sparky, saintly Sister Julienne with her wisdom and humour inspired us all to dare the impossible. Calm Novice Ruth and clever Sister Bernadette inspired respect, even awe, with their vast knowledge and experience of midwifery. Gruff and grumpy Sister Evangelina shocked and amused us with her vulgarity. And naughty Sister Monica Joan! What can be said of this wilful old lady of fey and fascinating charm who was once prosecuted for shoplifting (but found not guilty!)? 'Just a small oversight,' she said. 'Best forgotten.'

We took our lead from the Sisters, and feared nothing, not even getting our bikes out in the middle of the night and cycling alone through some of the toughest areas of London, which even the police patrolled in pairs. Through unlit streets and alleyways, past bomb sites where the meths drinkers hung out, past the docks where all was silent at night but for the creaks and moans as the ships stirred in their moorings, past the great river, dark and silent, past the brothels of Cable Street and the sinister pimps who controlled the area. Past – no, not past – into a small house or flat that was warm, bright and expectant, awaiting the birth of a new baby.

My colleagues and I loved every minute of it. Cynthia, who had a voice like music, and a slow, sweet smile that could calm any situation, however fraught. Trixie, with her sharp mind and waspish tongue. Chummy, a misfit in her colonial family because she was too big, too awkward, to fit into society, and who totally lacked self-confidence until she started nursing and proved herself a hero.

Youth, wasted on the young? Certainly not for us. Let those who waste their youth regret the passing of the years. We had experience, risk, and adventure enough to fill a lifetime. And to remember in old age is sweet; remember the shaft of sunlight piercing the black tenements, or the gleaming funnels of a ship as it left the docks; remember the warmth and fun of the Cockney people, or the grim reality of too little sleep and yet another call out into the night; remember the bicycle puncture and a policeman fixing it, or jumping barges with Sister Evangelina when the road was closed; remember the London smog, yellow-grey and choking thick, when Conchita's premature baby was born, or Christmas day, when a breech baby, undiagnosed, was delivered; remember the brothels of Cable Street, into which the child Mary was lured, and where old Mrs Jenkins lived, haunted by hallucinations of life in the workhouse.

I remember the days of my youth when everything was new and bright; when the mind was always questing, searching, absorbing; when the pain of love was so acute it could suffocate. And the days when joy was delirious.

THREE MEN WENT INTO A RESTAURANT . . .

Carters used to say that a working horse knew the way back to his stable and would pick up his feet and pull his cart with a lively step at the close of day, knowing that soft hay, food and water were at the end of the journey. That was how we midwives felt as we headed home after evening visits.

A cold but kindly west wind blew me all the way down Commercial Road and the East India Dock Road towards the welcome of Nonnatus House, the warmth of the big kitchen and – most important of all – food. I was young, healthy and hungry, and the day had been long. As I pedalled along, Mrs B's home-made bread was foremost in my mind. She had a magic touch with bread, that woman, and I knew she had been baking that morning. Also in my mind was the puzzle Fred had presented us with at breakfast. I couldn't work it out – three nines are twenty-seven, plus two makes twenty-nine – so where was the other shilling? It was nonsense, didn't make sense, it must be somewhere. A shilling can't vanish into thin air! I wondered what the girls had made of it. Had they got any closer to solving the riddle? Perhaps Trixie had worked out the answer; Trixie was pretty sharp.

With the wind behind me the ride was easy, and I arrived at the convent glowing. But Trixie had come from the east, had cycled two miles into a strong head wind, and was consequently a bit ratty. We put our bikes away and carried our bags to the clinical room. The rule was that equipment must be cleaned, sterilised, checked and the bag repacked for immediate use in the middle of the night, should it be needed. Chummy – or Camilla Fortescue-Cholmeley-Browne – was ahead of us.

'What-ho, you jolly swags,' she called out cheerily.

'Oh no, spare me!' groaned Trixie, 'I really can't stand it just now. I'm not "jolly", and I'm not "what-hoing" anyone. I'm cold, my knees ache, and I'm famished. And I've got to clean my bag before I get a bite.'

Chummy was all solicitude.

'Sorry, old bean, didn't mean to sound a wrong note, what? Here, I've just finished folding these swabs. You have them; I can quickly do some more. And the autoclave is at 180 degrees; I put it on twenty minutes ago when I came in. We'll get these bally bags done in a jiff. Did you see Mrs B making bread this morning?'

We had. Mrs B not only made the best bread north of the Thames, she made jams and chutneys, cheesy scones and cakes to die for.

Our bags packed, we emerged from the clinical room and headed towards the kitchen, hungry for supper, which was a casual meal that we prepared ourselves. Lunch was the main meal of the day, when we all gathered around the big dining table, usually about twelve or fifteen people including visitors. Sister Julienne presided, and in the presence of the nuns and, frequently, visiting clergy, it was a more formal affair, and we girls were always on our best behaviour. Supper was different; we all came in at different times, including the Sisters, so we took what we wanted and ate in the kitchen. Standards were relaxed and so was conversation.

The kitchen was large, probably Victorian, and had been modernised in Edwardian days, with bits and pieces added on later. Two large stone sinks stood against the wall beneath windows that were set so high no one could see out of them, not even Chummy, who was well over six feet tall. The taps were large and stiff, fed by lead pipes that ran all the way round the kitchen and were attached to the wall with metal fixtures. Whenever you turned a tap on, the pipes gurgled and shook as the water made its way along its course, sometimes coming out in a trickle, sometimes in vicious spurts – you had to stand well back to avoid a soaking. Wooden plate racks were fixed above each sink which was flanked on either side by a marble-topped surface. This was where Mrs B did all her mixing and kneading of dough, covering the mixture with a cloth for it to rise, and all the other magic rituals necessary for making bread.

Against the second outside wall stood a double-sized gas stove, and the coke stove, which had an oven attached and a flue which ran up the wall and disappeared somewhere near the ceiling about fifteen feet above. The hot water for the whole convent was dependent upon this boiler, and so Fred, the boiler- and odd-job man, was a very important person indeed, a fact even Mrs B was obliged to concede. Fred and Mrs B were both Cockneys, and a guarded but fragile truce existed between them, which now and then erupted into a slanging match, usually when Fred had made a mess of Mrs B's nice clean kitchen, and she would go for him hammer and tongs. She was a large lady of formidable frontage, and Fred was undersized even by Cockney standards, but he stood his ground and fought his corner manfully. The exchanges between them were rich, but Mrs B knew that the Sisters couldn't do without him, so reluctantly they settled down to another period of truce.

Mrs B certainly had a point. Fred certainly was messy. The main problem was his squint, the most spectacular you have ever seen. One eye pointed north-east, the other south-west, so he could see in both directions at once, but not in the middle. Not infrequently, when he was shovelling his ash, or tipping his coke, it would go in the wrong direction, but he would sweep it up willy-nilly, and often whatever he was sweeping, particularly the ash, would go the wrong way also. Ash could be flying all over the place, at which point Mrs B . . . well, I need not go on!

We settled down to our bread with cheese and chutney, and dates and apples, with a few pots of lemon curd, jam or marmalade. We really appreciated our food because we had all been war-time children, brought up amid strict rationing. None of us had seen a banana or chocolate until we were in our mid to late teens, and had been brought up on one egg and a tiny bit of cheese that was to last a whole week. Bread, along with everything else, had been strictly rationed, so Mrs B's delectable provender brought murmurs of delight.

'Bagsie the crust.'

'Not fair, you had it last time.'

'Well, we'll split it, then.'

'How about cutting the crust off the other end, as well?'

'No, it would go stale in the middle.'

'Let's toss for it.'

I can't remember who won the toss, but we settled down.

'What do you make of Fred's puzzle?' I asked.

'Don't know,' said Chummy, her mouth full. She sighed with contentment.

'It's a load of rubbish if you ask me,' said Trixie.

'It can't be rubbish, it's a question of arithmetic,' I replied, cutting another wedge of cheese.

'Well, you can think of arithmetic, old sport, I've got better things to think about. Pass the chutney.' Chummy had a large frame to fill.

'Leave some for Cynthia,' I said. 'She'll be coming in any minute, and that's her favourite.'

'Whoops, sorry,' said Chummy, spooning half back into the jar. 'Greedy of me. Where is she, by the way? She should have been back an hour ago.'

'Must have been held up somewhere,' said Trixie. 'No, it's not arithmetic. I passed my School Certificate with merit, and I can assure you it's not arithmetic.'

'It is. Three nines are twenty-seven – that's what they taught me at school – plus two makes twenty-nine.'

'Correct. So what?'

'So where's the other shilling?'

Trixie looked dubious. She didn't have a quick answer, and she was a girl who liked quick-fire repartee. Eventually she said,

'It's a trick, that's what it is. One of Fred's low-down, wide-boy Cockney tricks.'

'Nah ven, nah ven, oo's callin' me a low-down Cockney wide-boy, I wants to know?'

Fred entered the kitchen, coke-hod in one hand, ash bucket in the other. His voice was friendly, and his toothless grin cheerful (well, not quite toothless, because he had one tooth, a huge yellow fang right in the centre). From his lower lip hung the remains of a soggy Woodbine.

Trixie didn't look abashed at having insulted the good fellow; she looked indignant.

'Well, it *is* a trick. It must be. You and your "three men went into a restaurant" yarn.'

Fred looked at her with his north-east eye and rubbed the side of his nose. He rolled the Woodbine from one side of his mouth to the other and sucked his tooth, then gave a sly wink.

'Oh yeah? You reckons as 'ow it's a trick. Well you work i' ou' Miss Trick – see? You jest work it out.'

Fred slowly kneeled down at the stove and opened the flue. Trixie was furious, but Chummy came to the rescue.

'I say, old sport, go and look in the big tin, see if there's any of that cake left. She's a gem, that woman Mrs B, a jewel. I wasted two years at the Cordon Bleu School of Cookery, fiddling about stuffing prunes with bacon and filling figs with fish, soppy things like that. But no one there could come up with a fruit cake like Mrs B's.'

Trixie calmed down as we tackled the cake.

'Leave some for Cynthia,' said Chummy. 'She'll be here in a minute.'

'Aint she come back yet? Ve quiet one? She should be 'ere by now.'

Fred, as well as being a tease, frequently showed a protective instinct towards us girls. He rattled the rake in the flue.

I still wasn't satisfied that Trixie was right about Fred's story being a trick. I had been puzzling about it on and off all day, and now that Fred was here I wanted to get to the bottom of it.

'Look here, Fred. Let's get this straight. Three men went into a restaurant. Right?'

'Right.'

'And they bought a meal costing thirty shillings?'

'Straight up.'

'So they paid ten shillings each. Correct?'

'You're a smart one, you are.'

I ignored the sarcasm.

'And the waiter took the thirty shillings to the cashier – yes?'

'Yes.'

'. . . who said the men had been overcharged. The bill should have been twenty-five shillings. Have I got it?'

'You 'ave. Wha' 'appened next?'

'The cashier gave five shillings change to the waiter.'

'No flies on you, eh? Musta been top of ve class a' school.'

'Oh, give over. The waiter thought, "The customers won't know," so he trousered two shillings and gave the men three shillings.'

'Naugh'y naugh'y. We all done it, we 'as.'

'Speak for yourself.'

'Ooh, 'ark at 'er. Miss 'oity-toity.'

Trixie intervened.

'That's where I don't get it. Each man took a shilling change, so that means each one had paid nine shillings instead of ten.'

We all chorused, 'And three nines are twenty-seven plus two in the waiter's pocket makes twenty-nine. So what happened to the other shilling?'

We all looked at each other blankly. Fred carried on raking and shovelling and whistling his tuneless whistle.

'Well, what happened to it, Fred?' shouted Trixie.

'Search me,' said Fred, 'I ain't got it, copper.'

'Don't be silly' – Trixie was getting irritated again – 'You've got to tell us.'

'You work i' ou',' said Fred provocatively as he gathered up his ash bucket. 'I'm goin' to empty vis, and you three smart girls'll 'ave an answer 'afore I gets back.'

Novice Ruth and Sister Bernadette entered at that moment.

'An answer to what, Fred?'

'Vem girls'll tell yer. They're workin' it ou'.'

While the Sisters attended to their supper, we told them the conundrum. Novice Ruth was a thoughtful girl, and she paused, knife in hand. 'But that's crazy,' she said, 'it doesn't work. Where's Cynthia, by the way?'

'She's not in yet.'

'Well she should be by now, if she had only her evening visits to do.'

'She must have been delayed.'

'I suppose so. This is delicious bread. Mrs B does have a magic touch when it comes to bread. The secret's in the kneading, I think. Knowing just when to stop.'

Trixie had got out pencil and paper.

'We've got to work this out. A shilling can't vanish.'

She started writing down figures, but it got her nowhere, and she began to get cross again. Then she had a bright idea. 'Let's use matches instead of shillings.' She took the box from the gas stove and emptied it out. 'We three will be the three men, and Novice Ruth can be the dishonest waiter, and you, Sister Bernadette, can be the cashier.'

She pushed a pile of matches towards Chummy and me.

'Now you, Novice Ruth, you're the waiter – put a tea towel over your arm. Come up to us with the bill, that bit of paper will do, and ask us for thirty shillings.'

Novice Ruth joined in with the spirit of things. We each counted out ten matches and gave them to her, and she collected them up.

Sister Bernadette had made herself a sandwich and was watching us quizzically.

'Now you're the cashier, Sister. Go and sit over there.'

Sister Bernadette gave Trixie an old-fashioned look and moved her chair to the end of the table.

'No. That's not far enough – go and sit by the sink.'

Sister picked up her sandwich and moved her chair to the sink.

'Now,' said the stage director, 'waiter, you must take the bill and the money to the cashier.'

The waiter did as she was told.

'Cashier, you must add up the bill and find it is wrong, and say to the waiter . . . go on, say it . . .'

Sister Bernadette said, 'This is wrong. The bill comes to twenty-five shillings, not thirty. Here is five shillings change. Give it to the men,' and she handed five matches to Novice Ruth.

'Good,' said the director condescendingly, 'very good.'

Trixie turned to Novice Ruth.

'Now what do you do, waiter?'

'I see the chance to earn a bit on the side,' said the pious novice slyly as she tucked two matches into her pocket.

'Yes, that's correct. Proceed.'

Novice Ruth returned to the table and gave us three matches. We each took one.

'Good show,' cried Chummy. 'I've only paid nine shillings for my meal.'

'And so have I,' I said. 'What have you paid, Trix?'

'Well, I've paid nine shillings. I must have done, because, because . . . oh dear, that's where it all goes pear-shaped,' cried Trixie in real anguish, because usually she had an answer for everything. 'Three nines are twenty-seven and . . . look, we must have gone wrong somewhere. Let's start again.'

Once more we shook out a random pile of matches. 'You be the dishonest waiter again, Novice Ruth.'

At that moment Sister Julienne entered.

'What on earth are you doing with all those matches? And what did I hear about Novice Ruth being a dishonest waiter?

As Novice Mistress of Nonnatus House I cannot approve of that,' she said, laughing.

We sorted out the second lot of matches and told her Fred's riddle.

'Oh, that old chestnut! Fred comes out with that one for all the girls. He's just doing it to stir you up. No one's worked it out yet, so I doubt if you will be able to. I came here to see Cynthia. Has she gone upstairs?'

'She's not in yet.'

'Not in! Well where is she? It's nearly nine o'clock. She should have finished her evening visits by six thirty or seven at the latest. Where is she?'

We didn't know, and suddenly we felt guilty. We had been stuffing our faces and worrying over a silly old riddle, when really we should have been worrying over the fact that Cynthia was not with us, time was passing, and no one knew where she was.

Fred had come back into the kitchen and heard this last bit of conversation. He went over to the stove as we all looked anxiously at one another. His voice was reassuring.

'Don't choo worry, Sister. She'll be safe as 'ouses. Somefinks made 'er late, but she won't 'ave come to no 'arm, you'll see. You know ve old Cockney sayin', "A nurse is safe among us." Nuffink will 'appen to 'er. She'll turn up.'

Novice Ruth spoke. 'I think it's very likely that she was delayed at the Jessops, Sister. The baby is a fortnight old, and Mrs Jessop went for Churching today. The women always have a party afterwards, and I expect Cynthia was invited to join them.'

Sister Julienne looked somewhat relieved but nonetheless said, 'I feel sure you are right, but the bell for compline will sound any minute now, and it would ease my mind if you, Nurse Lee, would cycle round to Mrs Jessop's whilst we are saying our evening office.'

*

It was only a ten minute ride to the Jessops, and on the way I thought about this curious business of Churching. I had never heard of it before my stay at Nonnatus House. My grandmother, mother and aunts had never gone in for it, as far as I was aware, but many of the Poplar ladies would not go out after a child was born until they had been properly 'Churched' by the vicar. Perhaps it was a service of thanksgiving for a new baby, or more likely thanks for having survived the ordeal of childbirth, dating back to a time when giving birth was frequently attended by death. It occurred to me, though, that the origins of Churching could be even more ancient, stemming from the times when women were considered to be unclean after childbirth and needed to be ritually cleansed. As with many other pagan rituals the Church had merely adopted the practice and incorporated it into the liturgy.

There certainly was a party going on at the Jessop household – screams of female laughter could be heard all the way down the street (men were excluded from these occasions), and it took me some time to make myself heard. When the door finally opened I was all but dragged in and a glass was forced into my hand. I had to extricate myself and make my enquiry. Cynthia was not there. She had visited at 6.30 but, in spite of being pressed to stay, she had left at 6.45.

The Sisters were leaving the chapel after Compline as I arrived back at Nonnatus House. Normally this is the time of the Greater Silence, which is the monastic observance of quiet until after the Eucharist the following morning. But there would be no Silence that evening. Sister Julienne immediately rang the police, but no accident had been reported, and a nurse had not requested help for any other reason. She then instructed each of us, including three nuns, to go out on our bikes searching the streets. She marked out which areas, relating to the addresses of Cynthia's evening visits we were to search, on a plan and instructed us to enquire at each house what time Cynthia had arrived and left. Sister Evangelina, who was well over sixty, and had had a long working day, got her bike out and doggedly pedalled against the wind, searching for the missing girl. Fred, who couldn't ride a bike, went out on foot to search the streets nearest to Nonnatus House. Only Sister Julienne remained behind, along with Sister Monica Joan, because the House could not be left empty. We were a midwifery practice, and someone had to be on call at all times.

Subdued and anxious, we left Nonnatus House, each going in different directions, with instructions to ring Sister Julienne if we had any positive news. I do not know what was going through the minds of the others as we went around; I only know that I was fearful for Cynthia. The streets were narrow and unlit, filled with half-destroyed, boarded-up houses and areas marked for demolition. Bomb sites, in which the meths drinkers slept, were round every other corner. The possibility of danger was everywhere, yet I doubt if any one of us had ever felt under threat. Fred's reminder of the Cockney saying 'A nurse is safe among us' was perfectly true. We all knew that we were protected by our uniform, and that the Sisters were respected and even revered for their dedication to three generations of Cockney women. No man would attack a nurse – if he did it would be the worse for him, because the other men would make him pay for it.

And yet . . . and yet . . . Cynthia was missing, and as I cycled around looking for her the knowledge that this was a rough district which, in some areas, had been made virtually lawless by the Kray brothers, could not be shifted from my mind. A couple of policemen were approaching. Now why, I thought, do the police always go around in pairs, whilst we nurses go out alone, even in the middle of the night? I stopped and spoke to them, but no, they had not seen another nurse that evening, nor heard of one in trouble, but they would keep their eyes open. I called at a couple of houses that had been on Cynthia's list, but she had left them some three hours before.

The ride back to Nonnatus House was not pleasant. I went

through many side roads and back streets, even calling her name from time to time. But she was not to be found.

It was nearly ten o'clock and I was returning to the convent when I saw coming from the approach way to the Blackwall Tunnel two figures – a man with a distinctive hobble-de-hoi gait pushing a bicycle, and a female figure walking beside him. My heart leaped, and I quickened my pace, calling out, 'Cynthia, Cynthia, is that you?' It was, and I almost cried with joy.

'Oh, thank God you are safe. Where have you been?'

Fred answered for her.

'She's been froo ve Blackwall Tunnel – twice. Vat's where she's bin.'

'Through the Tunnel? On a bike? You can't have.'

Cynthia nodded dumbly.

'But you could have been run over.'

'I know,' she gasped, 'I nearly was.'

'How did you get there?'

She couldn't answer, so Fred did.

'I dunno as 'ow she got in. All I knows is I found 'er comin' out lookin' 'alf done for.'

'Oh Fred, I'm so glad you found her.'

'I ain't done much, really, all I done was push 'er bike.'

'Thank you, Fred,' murmured Cynthia gratefully.

We got her back to the convent. Most of the others had already returned with the bad news that she had not been found, so when she emerged the relief was almost overwhelming. In the light, we could see the state she was in. She was filthy, covered in oil and thick, greasy mud, and she stank of petrol.

When she had had a cup of tea she was able to answer some questions.

'I don't know how it happened, but somehow I got in the wrong lane of traffic, and then was forced into the entrance to the tunnel, and once I was there I couldn't stop and turn round, and then the tunnel closed over me, and started to go downhill, and I just went faster and faster, because the lorries kept me going on.'

Fred, who saw himself as the hero of the hour, finished off the story. None of us had been through the tunnel, but he told us that it was a mile long and zig-zagged all the way under the Thames from Poplar to Greenwich. It was narrow, having been built for Victorian traffic, and was far too narrow for twentieth-century freight vehicles. Two lorries going in opposite directions could only just pass each other if each of them drove as close as possible to the wall, sometimes scraping it. Cynthia could easily have been crushed. She could not have got off her bike because there was nowhere to stand; a concrete barrier about twelve inches high and the same deep was all that separated the road from the tunnel wall. She just had to keep cycling amid the noise, the dazzle of headlights, and the exhaust fumes. As she approached the other side, the tunnel started to ascend, and so she had to pedal uphill. To make matters worse, with the wind in a certain direction, the Blackwall acted as a wind funnel, as it had on that night. So poor Cynthia was forced to cycle uphill against a strong head wind – the worst possible combination.

And then, of course, she had to come back . . .

It is often surprising how quickly the young can recover from a nasty experience. Cynthia was not injured – she had been badly frightened and was physically exhausted, but she was not hurt. We made a big fuss of her. We sat her down near the stove, and Fred opened the vent and raked some hot coals onto the hearth to warm her. Novice Ruth boiled some water and poured it into a tin bowl, into which she put a spoonful of mustard, and instructed Cynthia to take off her shoes and stockings and soak her feet. The heat brought the colour back into her cheeks. Chummy cut the crust off the other end of the loaf and added a wedge of cheese with the last of Mrs B's chutney. Trixie brought out the cake. Sister Julienne made a large mug of steaming cocoa.

Cynthia leaned back in her chair and sighed.

'I don't know how it happened, I really don't, but once I had got into the situation I couldn't get out of it. It was a nightmare. But it's all over now, thank God, and Mrs B's bread is delicious.'

She sank her teeth into the buttered crust and giggled.

'I don't know if the police knew I was there. I'm sure I shouldn't have been.'

Sister Julienne said, 'It is probably illegal. I don't think even motor bikes are allowed through the tunnel, never mind a bicycle! I will have to inform the police you have been found, but I won't tell them where you have been.'

Fred interrupted. 'Best not tell the police nuffink. Wha' vey don't know vey can't do nuffink abaht.'

Cynthia looked steadily at him. 'Fred,' she said, 'I've been thinking on and off all day about that story you told us at breakfast and I can't work it out. Three men went into a restaurant . . .'

'Oh no, not that again,' wailed Sister Julienne. 'I'm going to bed.'

TRUST A SAILOR

Novice Ruth had the face of a Botticelli angel. None of the men of Poplar had the courage to speak to her as she passed by; they seemed to be in awe of her beauty, her clear white skin, her wide grey eyes, her perfect teeth and gentle smile. It wasn't that they were afraid of talking to a nun – they talked to the others. Perhaps it was her distinction, her quiet lady-like ways and above all her loveliness that left them tongue-tied. If any of them thought, 'a nun! What a pity, what a waste!' they would never have dared to say so.

She was about twenty-five, closer to the age of us young girls than to the other Sisters, but she was not one of us. No, she was firmly of the monastic order and, as she was still in her Noviciate, the rule was probably stricter for her than it was for her fully professed Sisters. Her profession filled her with a joy that was well-nigh tangible, and this happiness lent radiance to her beauty. She was also a fully trained nurse and midwife. After her training she had tested her calling to the religious life as an Aspirant and then a Postulant, before going on to the two years of her Noviciate. Yet still the monastic rule would require three more years of training, with solemn vows to be taken at the end of the first and second years, and final vows at the end of the third year. It was not a path to embark upon lightly, yet it seemed no burden to Novice Ruth. Holiness appeared to be her natural milieu.

But there was another side to Novice Ruth that I am not sure anyone, apart from we girls, knew about. Certainly the people of Poplar never saw it, and I doubt if her older Sisters did. She had a tendency to a giggly girlishness that was most unexpected and therefore all the more endearing. She would laugh at almost anything. This side of her came out mostly around the big kitchen table when we were sorting out our supper, especially if two or three of us were there before the Sisters came in. This was the time when we swapped yarns about the doings of the day. Anything would set Novice Ruth off: the simplest thing like a chain or a pedal coming off a bike, or losing your cap in the wind. She would literally curl up giggling and have to hold her sides as tears streamed from her eyes. Her laughter was most infectious, and we all enjoyed supper when Novice Ruth was around.

She was also a serious mimic and could take off anyone to perfection. Sister Monica Joan was one of her favourites: 'I see the shifting shades of the etheric ether descending into the slime of Planet Earth and illuminating . . . oooh, jam *and* butter on these scones, how delicious.' And she'd have us all in stitches.

One evening we were in the kitchen enjoying cheese and chutney sandwiches with crumpets and honey to follow when the heavy tread of Sister Evangelina was heard. I was always nervous of Sister Evangelina as she had made it quite clear that she did not approve of me and, for her, I could do nothing right. The characteristic 'humph' assailed my ears, then the humourless voice: 'Nurse Lee, Nurse Scatterbrain, I want a word with you.' Every muscle in my body tensed, and I leaped to my feet, knocking over a pot of runny honey. 'Yes, Sister,' I said smartly and turned round, to find Novice Ruth. I got nasty indigestion from that one.

No one could mimic the Cockney dialect and accent better than Novice Ruth. Whether it was the whining of a child or the scolding of a mother or the raucous shout of a coster, she had them all down to perfection. After a hard day she was particularly fond of 'Nah ven, nah ven, le's 'ave a cup o' tea an' a bi' o' cake, ducky. Nice bi' o' sailor's cake, eh ducks?' And we would split our sides with laughter, though I am not at all sure that, if Novice Ruth knew what the last phrase meant, she would have repeated it so often. We had heard that remark many times in the homes around the docks, and I doubt that any of us knew what it meant. I suspect we all thought sailor's cake was a rich fruit cake with rum in it.*

The telephone rang at 1.30 a.m. Novice Ruth answered it.

'Nonnatus House. Can I help you?'

A soft Irish voice replied.

'I was given your number, and told to call you when I was in labour.'

'What is your name and address, please?'

'Kathleen O'Brian, 144 Mellish Street, the Isle of Dogs."

Ruth did not recognise either the name or the address from antenatal visits. Neither could she recall any expectant mother with an Irish accent.

'Are you booked with us?'

'I don't know.'

'Well, you must be booked with someone.'

'What does that mean?'

'It means that you have registered for antenatal care and delivery of the baby, and for postnatal care.'

'Oh.'

There was a long pause.

'Well, I'm not sure what that means, but I think I'm in labour, and I was told to call you. Can you come? The pains are getting quite strong, an' all.'

'How often are they?'

'Well. I don't rightly know, I don't have a clock, but quite often, and quite strong, and . . . oh, there's the click. The pennies are running out and I don't have any more . . . 144 Mellish Street, Isle of Dogs . . .'

The phone went dead.

Ruth put on her habit and went to the office to search through

* The meaning is too rude to print, but those interested can consult *Rude Cockney Rhyming Slang* by Jade Janes, published by Abson Books, London, 1971.

the antenatal notes. She could find no Kathleen O'Brian. The woman must have booked elsewhere, but she would have to go to Mellish Street to see the woman and get the address of the correct midwifery service before she could refer her on. Ruth went to the shed and got out her bicycle. She was just about to cycle off, when she paused. Perhaps she ought to take her delivery bag. You never knew! She went back to the clinical room and fetched it.

The cold night air woke her up as she cycled through the quiet streets. She found Mellish Street without any trouble; it ran at right angles to the river. The houses were drab and tall, the street unlit, and she could see no house numbers. So she got off her bike and detached the lamp, shining it on the buildings in the hope that it would illuminate a number. It shone on number 20. She pedalled on, the cobbles making it a slow and painful ride.

Suddenly a female voice called out in the still night: 'Is that the nurse?'

'Yes, and I'm trying to find number 144.'

'It's me you are wantin', me darlin', and right glad I am to see you.'

The soft Irish accent was unmistakable, but the voice trailed away into a groan of pain, and the girl leaned against the wall, her head thrown back and her face contorted with agony. She suppressed the scream rising in her throat, giving a high strangulated sound, even though she pressed both hands to her mouth. The midwife took her body in both hands to support her – she was just a slip of a girl, barely more than eighteen, small and thin and heavily pregnant. The contraction was powerful and long, but eventually it subsided. The girl relaxed and laughed.

'Oh, that was a nasty one. Me mammy didn't ever tell me it could be as bad as that.'

'You shouldn't be standing out here in the street.'

'I didn't want you to miss the house.'

'Well, someone else could have looked out for me.'

'There is no one else.'

'What! You mean you are alone here, in labour?'

'What else could I be doing!'

'Oh, never mind. We've got to get you to your bedroom before the next contraction comes on.'

'I've got a room on the third floor, and I'm feelin' fine now.'

Ruth removed her delivery bag from the bike, took the girl's thin arm, and together they entered the house. It was completely dark inside, so she ran back to her bike to detach the cycle lamp. The torchlight illuminated the narrow stairway. They passed several closed doors, but there was not a sign of another human being. On the second-floor landing the girl started groaning and breathing heavily, doubled up with pain. Ruth was alarmed; it was possible that the girl was entering the second stage of labour. She took hold of the girl again to support her, and then suddenly felt a rush of warm fluid at her feet. The waters had broken.

'Quickly,' she said, 'upstairs. Only one more flight. You have to get to your room. We can't have the baby born on the landing.'

The contraction passed, and the girl smiled.

'I can get there. Don't trouble yourself, nursey. I feel fine now the pain's gone.'

With surprising agility the girl mounted the stairs, followed by Ruth, and they entered a pitch-dark room, cold as a coffin. She looked around her and said cheerfully, 'I'm so glad you brought a light with you, because the meter ran out, and I only had enough pennies either for the telephone or for the meter. I think it was the angels told me to use them for the telephone.'

The torch light revealed a bleak, barren room, devoid of any comfort. A rough wooden bedstead stood against one wall. A dirty, stained mattress and pillow lay on the worn-out springs. There were no sheets or pillow-cases; two grey army blankets were the only coverings. A small table and chair and a chest of drawers were the only other furniture in the room. There were no curtains, no rug or mat. An enamel bowl and a jug half full of cold water stood on the table. The electric meter was high on the wall near to the door. In those days the majority of houses and flats received gas and electricity through payment into a coin meter. When the coin ran out, the power supply cut off. Every midwife carried a shilling in her pocket, because meters running out were a constant hazard in our work. Ruth climbed onto the chair, inserted a shilling and turned the key. A dim electric light bulb hanging from the middle of the ceiling cast a gloomy light over the room, and now Ruth could see the girl more clearly. Her small face was delicately boned, and her mouth was beautifully shaped. Her eyes were cornflower blue, and her hair a glorious autumn brown. She sat on the edge of the bed, holding her stomach. Her eyes were laughing.

'Trust a sailor! This is what happens to a girl when she trusts a sailor! What's your name, nurse?'

'Novice Ruth.'

'Ruth. That's me mam's name. She always says . . .'

'Look here, Kathy, we haven't got time to chatter. You can tell me what your mother says after your baby is born. It won't be long now because I can see you are in advanced labour, and your waters have broken. Undress and get onto the bed. I must examine you. Where is your maternity pack?

'What's that? I don't know.'

'Every expectant mother is given a box for her home birth containing sheets to protect the mattress, cotton wool for the baby, sanitary towels, that sort of thing. Where are they? Have you got them?'

'No.'

'You should have been given a maternity pack. Who did you book with?'

'I was just told to call you when I went into labour.'

'You've told me that. But which clinic did you go to for antenatal care?'

'None.'

'None! You mean you have had no antenatal care?'

'I didn't tell anyone I was pregnant. Me mam and me grandma, they would have killed me, they would. Never trust a sailor, they always say. And I did, silly me, and now look at me.'

The girl cheerfully patted her stomach. But then her face changed. 'It's coming again . . .'

She threw her head back as pain seared her body. Beads of sweat stood out on her forehead, and her whole expression seemed to be turning inwards as her mind and body focused on the tremendous force of the contraction.

There was no time to lose. Ruth took her stethoscope, gown, gloves and mask from the outer compartment of her delivery pack. She opened the box, and the sterile lid formed a tray on which she placed in readiness her kidney dishes, gallipots, sterile water, antiseptics, scissors, hypodermic syringe, needles, sterile cotton wool and gauze swabs, catheters and blunt forceps. She also carried chloral hydrate, potassium bromide, tincture of opium and pethidine for relief of pain. Cord clamps and cord dressings, powder for the baby and gentian violet or silver nitrate for sterilisation of the cord stump completed her equipment.

All her training and experience told her that a primigravida* who had had no antenatal care should be transferred immediately to hospital. But to arrange this, she would have had to go down the road to a phone box, and birth was imminent. While she was gone the baby would probably be born. She looked at the thin, horsehair mattress on sagging springs. There were no sheets, no waterproofing, no brown paper, no absorbent pads. There was no cot, no baby clothes, nor any apparent provision for a baby. There was no fire, nor heating of any kind, and the room was cold. There was a jug of cold water, but she had no means of heating it. The light was quite inadequate for

* A full glossary of obstetric terms is included at the back of the book.

delivery, and the only means of supplementing it was the bicycle lamp. But her midwife's training had been strict and uncompromising; whatever the circumstances, she must improvise, and cope.

The contraction passed, and the girl sighed with relief.

'Oh, that's better. I feel all right when the pain has gone.'

'I want to listen to your baby's heartbeat, and then to examine you. I need to know how near you are to delivery. Would you lie down, please?'

She palpated the girl's abdomen to determine which way the baby was lying. She listened for the heartbeat and heard it quite clearly. Satisfied that the baby was safe, she prepared to do a vaginal examination, saying as she gowned and gloved: 'You don't seem to be prepared for having a baby. There isn't even a cot or baby clothes here.'

'Well, I haven't really been here long enough to get anything. I only came over from Ireland yesterday.'

'What! You came on the ferry yesterday!'

'Yes.'

'But you might have gone into labour on the boat.'

'I might have, but I didn't. The angels must have been looking after me.'

'When you got to Liverpool, how did you get to London?'

'I got a lift with an overnight lorry driver.'

'I can't believe it! You might have had the baby on the lorry!'

'The angels again.' The girl shrugged cheerfully.

'When did you arrive?'

'This morning. I had been given this address and the landlord's name. That was the only good thing my charming sailor-boy did for me.'

She looked around the room and smiled contentedly.

'Just draw up your knees for me, please, and let your legs fall apart. I want to examine you internally. The waters have broken, and I want to feel how far you are dilated, and in what position the baby is lying.'

But there was no time for a vaginal examination. Another contraction was coming, and the girl winced in pain, throwing herself around the bed in an effort to escape it. The pain intensified as the uterine contraction became more fierce. Ruth admired the way the girl was coping with labour – she had already had a lot of physical exertion getting to London during the past twenty-four hours. She must have been tired and hungry, and there were no signs of food in the room. She had had no sedation or analgesic, yet she made no fuss nor complaint. The contraction became even more powerful, and suddenly Kathy spontaneously pulled her legs up, gave a prolonged grunt and pushed with all her strength. Ruth only got there just in time, pressing the palm of her hand firmly over the emerging head of the baby and holding it back to prevent an uncontrolled delivery.

'Kathy, don't push, not now, do *not* push. The baby mustn't be born too quickly. Pant, my dear, quick breaths: in, out, in, out. Don't push, just pant quickly, in, out, in, out.'

The girl did exactly as she was told, and Ruth breathed a sigh of relief as the contraction passed.

'With the next contraction your baby will be born. I know you feel as though you want to push, but don't, not until I tell you. I want the baby's head to be born slowly. If you push too soon, it will come too fast. Do you understand me Kathy?'

The girl smiled weakly and nodded.

'Is it possible for you to turn onto your left side to face the wall? It will make it easier for both of us.'

The girl nodded and turned over, and as she moved another contraction started.

Ruth was on her knees beside the low bed with its sagging mattress. The light was terrible, but she had no time to get her torch. The girl gave a low scream and buried her pretty face into the filthy pillow in order to stifle the sound. The baby's head was emerging fast, too fast. Again Ruth held it back.

'Don't push, Kathy, just pant in and out quickly. Keep panting – like that. Good girl.'

As the contraction subsided she eased the pressure on the presenting part and allowed the head to slide out a little, until it crowned. The perineum was stretched, but was still holding it back.

'Only one more contraction, and your baby will be born. Try not to push. Your stomach muscles are pushing hard enough. They don't need any help. The baby will come anyway.'

Kathy nodded, but was unable to speak because another contraction came almost immediately. Ruth slowly edged the perineum around the broadest part of the baby's head – 'Now you can push, Kathy.' The girl did so, and the head was born.

'That is the hardest part over, my dear. There will be a minute of rest, then another contraction.'

Ruth watched the head move about ten degrees clockwise as it aligned with the rest of the body. Another contraction came quickly.

'You can push now, Kathy – as hard as you like.'

Deftly she hooked her forefinger under the presenting shoulder. The baby's whole body slid out easily, Ruth guiding it upwards between the mother's legs, and over the pubic bone.

'You can turn over now, Kathy, onto your back, and look at your baby. It's a little boy.'

The girl rolled over and raised her head.

'Oh, bless him. A sailor's son. Isn't he tiny, nurse?'

The baby was indeed tiny, smaller than Ruth had expected from her admittedly brief abdominal examination. From appearances, he seemed to weigh no more than four pounds. 'No doubt due to malnutrition and overwork in the mother during pregnancy,' she thought bitterly. It was not uncommon. She clamped the cord in two places, and cut between the clamps. The baby was now a separate being.

But where should she put him? There was no cot, no blankets, he was small, and the room was cold. He must be kept warm.

She pressed him firmly under his mother's arm.

'Keep him warm with your body. Haven't you got anything I can wrap him in?'

The girl was contentedly cuddling her naked baby and paid no attention to what was being said. Ruth opened the chest of drawers. There was a towel in the top drawer. She opened the second drawer. There were a couple of jumpers in it. She opened the third drawer, which was empty. 'This will have to do,' she thought, taking up the towel and jumpers. They were all cold, but thankfully did not feel damp.

'Just lift your head and shoulders a minute, will you, Kathy? I want to put these things under your body to warm them, before I wrap your baby in them.'

She pulled the dirty grey blankets over the girl and baby to keep them warm and sat on the chair beside the girl to await the third stage of labour. A few minutes passed. She placed her hand on the abdomen to assess progress. 'Something's not right here,' she thought. The uterus felt hard and bulky, and a strong contraction was developing. Kathy grit her teeth and started to bear down. Ruth leaped into action.

'There's another baby coming! Don't push, whatever you do, don't push – just pant, like you did before.'

Kathy was tensing all her muscles, and the baby lying under her arm was in danger of being crushed. Ruth grabbed the towel and jumpers and pulled them sharply from under the girl's body, then took the baby from her. She wrapped him up quickly, and put him in the top drawer of the chest.

She returned to the bedside, pulled back the blankets and saw the head of the second baby emerging. She was just in time to control a rapid delivery.

With a twin birth, if the lie of the second baby is in a normal head-down position, if the uterine activity is normal, and especially if the baby is small, the birth can be fairly quick, because the birth canal has stretched, and there will be little resistance. Two or three good strong contractions may be sufficient to complete the birth. Kathy's second delivery was swift and easy, and within a few minutes the baby was lying on his mother's abdomen. She stretched out a hand to touch him. Her voice sounded incredulous. 'Another baby! It can't be true.'

'It is true, Kathy. You have another little boy.'

Kathy stroked his head. 'Another little boy,' she repeated vaguely. Her blue eyes were wide and dreamy, and her body was limp after the exertion. Her voice sounded far away.

'Another little sailor boy. Oh, you poor wet little thing. And where's your daddy, little sailor, where's your daddy? He sailed away on the deep blue sea. Sailed far away.'

Ruth took Kathy's pulse and blood pressure, which were slightly lowered, but not too much. She knew that she had been lucky in having no complications for which medical assistance, or at least another midwife, would have been necessary.

'You are a healthy girl,' she said aloud. "How did you get yourself into this pickle?'

Kathy smiled dreamily. "Oh, that sailor boy. His curling hair, his night-black eyes, and oh, his saucy smile! Somehow I knew he wouldn't be true. Never trust a sailor, they said, and silly me, I did. Now I've got two little sailor boys. What's me mammy going to say? And me grandma? She's the one I'm frightened of. A real terror, she is. If you knew her, you'd be frightened too, nurse.'

Kathy sighed sleepily, and closed her eyes. 'I feel so tired now,' she murmured, and fell fast asleep.

Ruth had many practical duties to attend to, not least of which was to separate the baby from his mother – and she had only one set of cord clamps in her bag, which she had used for the first baby. So she cut a gauze swab in half, tied each piece firmly to the cord, and cut between the knots. 'Always improvise,' her midwifery tutor had taught.

The baby was small, but looked perfectly formed and healthy. Ruth picked him up, and he whimpered. She held him upside down, and he cried lustily. 'That's what I like to hear,' she thought, 'cry some more, little baby. Your lungs are only small, and this is the best way of inflating them.' The baby obliged by screaming. She nodded in satisfaction and laid him with his mother to keep him warm.

Then she began wondering what to do with him. Ideally both he and his brother should have been bathed, examined thoroughly, weighed and measured, and put into a clean cot near to a fire. But she had no hot water, no soap, no clean towels, and the room temperature was far too cold to expose his naked body. To wrap him up warm was the immediate challenge. She looked around the room for something – anything she might use. She saw a cupboard in the corner and opened it, hopefully, but all she found was a lot of broken mechanical equipment. Then she saw the clothes that Kathy had taken off – a skirt, a jumper and a thin, cheap jacket. 'That will do,' she thought, 'better than nothing, anyway.' The garments were still quite warm, so she wrapped the baby up in them, and tucked him into the second drawer. 'Phew!' she thought, 'this has been a night. What next?'

What happened next was more than she, or anyone else for that matter, could have imagined in their wildest dreams.

Ruth sat down once more on the chair beside the mother, to await the third stage of labour. She had time to reflect on the situation. After a twin birth the uterine muscles are stretched and tired and can take up to half an hour to contract again for the expulsion of the placenta. Kathy lay sleeping, her fragile yet strong young body exhausted from a twin birth, and soothed by the blessed relief from pain. Ruth sat beside her and leaned her head on the wall. She glanced at her watch. What had happened to the time? Less than an hour had passed since she had got out of bed to answer the telephone. She tried to recall the sequence of events: the cycle ride through the night, the girl standing out in the street, the race to get upstairs, the waters breaking on the landing, and the birth of one baby, then two. It had been like a speeded-up film. What did time mean, anyway? There were some who said that time does not exist, others who said that past, present and future are one and the same. What did anyone know about time? Least of all herself. And Kathy was sleeping, blissfully sleeping.

Ruth placed her hand on the fundus of the uterus to assess progress of the third stage and stiffened with shock. The uterus still felt full, hard and bulky. 'There's something wrong here,' she thought, 'this doesn't feel like a placenta.'

She carefully palpated the abdomen. 'It's definitely not a placenta. It can't be . . . It's not possible . . .'

She picked up her foetal stethoscope, applied it to the abdomen in several places and heard a rapid, regular heartbeat. Her mouth went dry, and she had to sit down again. Another baby! Undiagnosed triplets, no antenatal care, no assistance available, and apparently no one else in the building to summon help. She shivered as much from shock and fear as from the cold. Thoughts were racing through her mind. Would the delivery be normal? She had been lucky twice, but the third baby might be lying in any position. He might be a transverse lie, or a shoulder or a brow presentation . . . or anything. She palpated the abdomen but could not feel a head or a breech. The foetal heartbeat was a steady 150 beats per minute, which was undoubtedly high, but might be normal for a third baby. She had never delivered triplets, nor even seen a triple birth. She felt numb with fear. Would he be healthy, like the others? There might be breathing problems, or other life-threatening difficulties derived from immature internal organs. Perhaps the placenta might come away first, leaving the baby with no maternal blood supply, or the cord might prolapse. She didn't know if there would be one, two or three placentae. She couldn't see inside, and she could not tell from external palpation.

Nearly half an hour had passed since the second birth, and there was no contraction. Kathy still slept quietly, but Ruth was trembling with anxiety. 'If this is uterine inertia, it is a serious condition, and the baby will die. Dare I risk leaving Kathy alone for ten or fifteen minutes while I go to a telephone to call the hospital?' she asked herself. She dithered. Should I? Shouldn't I? Which course of action would be the least dangerous?

The situation resolved itself. In her sleep Kathy groaned in pain, and in the same instant there was a click from the electric meter and the light went out. The room was in total darkness. Ruth knew the bicycle torch was on the chest of drawers, but in trying to locate it she knocked it onto the floor, and then had to crawl around trying to find it. She could hear Kathy groaning and straining and pushing, but there was nothing she could do until she had light. She found the torch and switched it on. Kathy now lay calm and apparently asleep. Ruth went over to the bed and pulled back the blankets. A baby lay in a pool of blood, between his mother's legs. She propped the torch on the end of the bed and picked up the baby. He was small, like the other two, but seemed perfectly formed, and even gave a little cry. She held him upside down, and he cried more loudly. 'This is a miracle,' Ruth thought. She cut another gauze swab into two pieces and ligated the cord, then cut the baby free from his mother. She lay him on his mother's abdomen and covered them both to keep them warm. There was no other clothing available in the room, so she took one of the grey army blankets off the mother, cut it into pieces, wrapped a piece round the baby, and tucked him into the bottom drawer. The other pieces of blanket she tucked under and around all three babies to ensure that they were warm. Then she closed, or rather nearly closed, the drawers to keep out any draughts.

Meanwhile, Kathy was sound asleep, her body exhausted. Ruth sat beside her and tentatively palpated the uterus – would there be another one inside? But no; the abdominal muscles and the uterus felt soft. Ruth breathed a sigh of relief, but at the same time reminded herself that labour was far from over. The third stage had to be completed, and she knew that this was frequently the most difficult and the most dangerous part of delivery. She leaned back in the chair and closed her eyes. Was this a dream? Could it really be happening? She had been out the night before, followed by a busy day, and had enjoyed very little sleep in the past twenty-four hours. She very nearly dozed off, but a warning bell sounded in her brain, and she jumped up and splashed her face with cold water from the enamel jug. The shock soon focused her mind again.

About twenty minutes had been spent wrapping and settling the babies, during which time there had been no contractions. Something had to be done. Ruth picked up the torch and shone the beam of light into the bed. The mess was quite indescribable; a great pool of blood and amniotic fluid was seeping into the uncovered mattress – and she could do nothing about it. Normally a midwife would have covered the mattress with brown paper, absorbent sheets, a rubber sheet, and on top of that more absorbents, which could be changed frequently – but she had none of these. The mess would have to stay where it was. She shone the beam of light onto Kathy's vulva. Three cords were showing. But how many placentae would she have to deal with? It could be as many as three, if the babies had developed from three separate ova. She did not know, and there was no way she could find out.

Ruth knew the risk of post-partum infection and in other circumstances she would have removed all soiled padding from beneath Kathy, washed her, cleaned the vulva with antiseptic, replaced the bedding with clean absorbent sheets and covered her legs with more clean sheeting. She would also have scrubbed her hands thoroughly, and put on sterile gloves. But none of this was possible. She also knew that warmth was essential, because a woman sweats during labour, losing a lot of body heat, and can become cold and shivery. Yet there was only one thin army blanket available.

She shone the torch despairingly around the empty room and saw her coat hanging on the back of the door. That would do. She took it off the hook and covered the girl with it for extra warmth. Kathy's breathing was deep and regular, her pulse and blood pressure were on the low side, which was a good sign, and her colour was fine. There had been no contractions, and the uterus felt as it should feel.

In those days the management of the third stage of labour was left entirely to nature, and midwives were taught not to meddle or interfere with the process which separates the placenta from the uterine wall and controls bleeding. Today an oxytocic drug may be injected immediately after the baby is born, and a powerful contraction develops, separating the placenta, so that the third stage is over in a few minutes. We did not have that advantage. Patience, experience, observation and masterly inactivity were our guides. We were taught that meddling with the uterus or attempting to hurry the third stage would usually give rise to partial separation of the placenta, causing haemorrhage. We were taught never, never to pull on the cord, and only to knead or massage the fundus after uterine contractions had already developed, and only then if it became absolutely necessary.

Ruth sat quietly beside the bed, her left hand guarding the uterus, which she could clearly feel. The torchlight was growing fainter, so to save the battery she switched it off and sat in total darkness. Twenty-five minutes had passed with no sign of a contraction, and she was beginning to grow anxious. She might have to leave the girl alone while she summoned medical aid. But then she felt a distinct hardening of the uterus, and the fundus rose under her hand. Kathy moaned with pain and moved awkwardly.

'This is it.' Ruth stood up, switched on her torch and shook Kathy. 'Wake up. I want you to push as hard as you can. Wake up and push down. Draw your knees up to your chest so that you can push as hard as possible, as though you were going to open your bowels – go on, push – harder.'

Kathy did as she was told, and Ruth assessed from the feel of the uterus that the placenta had separated and was lying in the lower segment. The fundus had risen higher in the abdomen and was still hard and firm.

'Now relax, Kathy. Put your legs down and breathe in and out deeply. Relax as much as you can. I am going to press on your tummy. It will be uncomfortable, but it won't hurt.'

Using the fundus as a piston, and with firm but gentle pressure, she pressed her left hand in a downward and backwards direction. Her right hand took hold of the cords and lifted the emerging placenta from the vault of the vagina. Two cords were attached. One remained hanging from the vagina, indicating that one placenta remained in utero.

At this point Ruth massaged and kneaded the fundus vigorously, and another contraction developed. 'Start pushing again, Kathy, like you did before. We have to get this out with this contraction.'

'What's going on?' moaned poor Kathy.

'I'll tell you later. Just push with all your strength.' Kathy did so, and a few seconds later the other placenta slid out onto the mattress.

A huge gory mass of placentae lay on the bed. Ruth scooped them up into kidney dishes and placed them on the table. She had not the slightest chance of examining them, because the torchlight was dim and growing dimmer by the minute as the battery failed.

Kathy was wide awake now. 'What's been happening?' she asked. 'I've got twins. Where are they?' She looked around her.

'No. You're wrong. You've got triplets, and they are in the chest of drawers.'

'Triplets! You mean three babies?'

'Yes.'

'How?'

'Well, you were exhausted and fell asleep after the second baby was born, so the third baby must have slid out with hardly any pain worth speaking of. Not enough to wake you up, anyway. I didn't see it, because the meter had run out, and I'd dropped my torch.'

'And I've got three babies?'

'Yes. Three little boys.'

Kathy leaned back with an incredulous sigh.

'Holy Mary, Mother of God – what's me mam going to say? Oh be-Jesus, illegitimate triplets. Trust a sailor!'

Ruth cleared up and returned to the convent, where arrangements were made for Kathy and the babies to be admitted to the London Hospital. The girl had no one to look after her, and she was quite unable to look after the babies in the room where she was lodging. She had no money, no clothing, no heating, no food even, and the babies were small and vulnerable.

We did not find out what happened to them after they left hospital. If the sailor could not be traced and persuaded to marry Kathy and support his children, the prospects for them were bleak. Returning to the family in Ireland would have been the best thing, but in rural Ireland in the 1950s poverty and the shame of illegitimacy drove many families to reject their grandchildren. Places in a children's nursery in London would have been offered, with access for the mother, but she would have had to live separately and support herself. It is unlikely that she would ever have earned enough money to have the boys with her and to support them. Adoption would have been possible, if Kathy had agreed, but the chances of anyone wanting to adopt all three babies were slender, so the boys would probably have been separated and would have grown up not knowing they had brothers.

Whilst I cannot record a happy ending, Kathy was buoyant, cheerful and resourceful, and we cannot be sure that life treated her harshly. It might have been quite the opposite. So often in medicine we see and become deeply involved with people at the most intimate and dramatic time of their lives. But then, like ships, they pass in the night; they are gone and we see them no more.

CYNTHIA

I was cycling back to the convent after a morning's work, weaving my way in and out of the lorries on the East India Dock Road, singing to myself as I pedalled the old Raleigh, which was as heavy as lead with two of its three gears not working, and perfecting my no-hands-steer-with-knees-and-bodyweight technique, when I saw Cynthia ahead of me. She was cycling more slowly than me, and her bike was wobbling about on the road. I called out, 'Hi, there!' as I drew level; but my high spirits quickly changed to concern. She was crying.

'What's up? Oh, Cynthia dear, what's happened?'

She looked round, tears streaming down her face. A lorry screeched past, hooting noisily, its driver gesticulating obscenely.

'Here, we had better pull into the kerb, or we'll have an accident. Now what's up? Tell me. I've never seen you like this before.'

Cynthia was the peace-maker amongst us, a wise and mature influence. To see her crying in the street was a real shock. I gave her my handkerchief because hers was wet.

'The baby's dead,' she whispered.

'What? It can't be,' I gasped incredulously.

I knew she had been out all night. She had come into breakfast tired but happy, telling us of the delivery of a baby boy – a normal delivery, a healthy baby, and a contented mother. She had left them at 6 a.m., everything satisfactory. We were required to make a return visit within four hours. I had left to make my morning visits at 8.30, and Cynthia had remained behind to clean and sterilise her equipment and write up her notes before returning to the newly delivered mother and baby at 10 a.m.

'What happened?' I asked when I had recovered from the shock.

'I went back to the house as usual,' Cynthia explained. 'I never thought anything would have happened. The door was open, and I went in. Everyone was crying. They said the baby was dead. I couldn't believe them. I went and saw the baby. It was quite dead and cold.'

'But how? Why?'

'I don't know.'

She blew her nose and wiped her eyes. 'I don't know. I just don't know,' she whispered and started crying again.

'Look here, we'd better get back, but don't try riding that bike. You'll only fall off. I'll push it for you.'

We started walking along the pavement, with me pushing both bikes – a noble but futile gesture. Have you ever tried pushing two bikes along a pavement crowded with people and prams and children running around? Soon Cynthia's tears were mixed with tears of laughter.

'I'll take mine, or you'll do someone a nasty injury.'

We walked along without speaking for a while. I didn't know whether to ask more questions or to keep silent, but she said: 'They've taken him away.'

'Who? The doctors?'

'No. The police.'

'Police? Why? What for?'

'Post-mortem examination. The parents didn't want them to, but the police insisted, saying it was the law with a sudden, unexplained death.' Her voice faltered and she started crying again.

'I don't know if I did anything wrong. I've been going over and over it in my mind. I did everything we were taught to do. The baby cried soon after birth. I cleared the airways. I cut the cord aseptically. All his limbs moved independently. His spine was straight, his breathing was normal, and the sucking reflex was there. He was a perfect baby, I thought. I don't know why he died, or if I did something that might have caused his death.'

She shuddered and could hardly walk straight. The front wheel of her bike hit a bus stop, and the handlebars twisted and poked into her chest, making her groan with pain. We straightened out her bike.

'Of course you've done nothing wrong. You are the best of midwives. I just *know* it wasn't your fault in any way.'

'You can't be sure,' she whispered. 'That's why the police took him away.'

We continued for a while in silence. I did not like to intrude on Cynthia's thoughts but felt compelled to ask, 'What did you do?'

'Well, I tried mouth-to-mouth resuscitation, but it was hopeless. The baby was quite cold and stiff.'

She was shaking, and her voice was barely audible above the noise of the street.

'Let's get off this main road into a quieter one,' I said. 'All this noise is getting on my nerves. Then you can tell me more.'

We pushed our bikes round a corner and continued in a more peaceful environment. Children were playing in the street, women were scrubbing their doorsteps or shaking mats. Several greeted us.

'I went down the street to the phone box,' Cynthia continued, 'and rang Nonnatus House and spoke to Sister Julienne. She came straight away. It was wonderfully reassuring to see her. She christened the baby, even though he was dead, and prayed with the family and me, and then she went to inform the doctor and the police. I had to remain in the house with the baby's body.'

She started crying again. I leaned over and squeezed her hand.

'We didn't have to wait long. The doctor came. He examined the little body and said he could see nothing to suggest the cause of death, but that a post mortem would be necessary before a death certificate could be issued. The family were terribly upset at this, saying they didn't want to see their baby cut up, they just wanted him to have a quiet Christian burial. The doctor was ever so kind with them, but explained that a PM was unavoidable under the circumstances.'

We continued plodding along, circling around a group of little girls playing hop-scotch.

'Two policemen arrived. They took notes and spoke with the doctor. Then they questioned me. It was awful. They weren't nasty or bullying or anything like that . . . it was just being questioned about a death, and seeing them write down everything I said that was so awful. I must have looked as white as a sheet, because the doctor was very kind and assured me that I was in no way at fault. I had been asked to tell them everything I knew, you see. They asked to see my records, and took my notes away with them. I think I had filled in everything correctly. I don't know. It's like a bad dream.'

She looked ill.

'You need a good hot cup of tea,' I said, 'We're nearly at the convent – good thing too. You look just about finished.'

'It's the shock, I suppose.'

'I'll say it is!'

'I'm cold, too.'

'Not surprising. You had no sleep last night?'

'A couple of hours, then I had to go out.'

By now we had reached Nonnatus House. I took both the bikes to put them away. Cynthia said she had to report to Sister Julienne as soon as she got in.

In the bicycle shed Sister Bernadette was putting her bike away.

'Ah, Nurse Lee. Just the person I wanted to speak to. Did I see you cycling with no hands down the East India Dock Road?'

Sister Bernadette was a midwife whom I both respected and admired, but she could be very sharp.

'Me? Oh, er, well perhaps . . .'

'I am sure it was you. I can't think of any other midwife who would cycle in that nonchalant fashion down the main road. And were you whistling by any chance?'

'Whistling? Well, I'm not sure. I can't quite remember, but I suppose I might have been.'

'You certainly were. Now look here, Nurse Lee, you are not one of the local lads. You are a professional woman. They can do that sort of thing, but you can't. It's too casual, too lackadaisical. It gives the wrong impression. It simply won't do.'

'I'm sorry, Sister.'

'Don't do it again, Nurse.'

'No, Sister. I won't, Sister.'

But I did, and I'm sure she knew that I did!

Cynthia did not come in for lunch. She had been sent to bed with a couple of aspirins and some hot chocolate. Sister Julienne said grace and when we were seated told everyone what had happened.

'Humph,' grunted Sister Evangelina, 'alive and healthy at six o'clock. Dead at ten. Sounds like smothering to me.'

'Oh no, Sister. I am sure you are wrong. They are a nice family. They wanted the baby. They wouldn't do a thing like that.' Sister Julienne was shocked.

'Can't be sure. No one can. These secrets are well kept. There have been more unwanted babies smothered than I've had hot dinners. Desperation drives people to do it.'

'But these people are not desperate,' Sister Julienne replied. 'I agree with you that desperation might lead a starving family to smother a newborn baby, but those days are past.'

Chummy, Trixie and I were wide-eyed with interest. We had heard nothing like this before, coming as we did from middle-class backgrounds. But Sister Evangelina had been born into the slums of Reading in the 1890s and had experienced more poverty and deprivation than we could ever dream of.

'But wouldn't they be caught?' asked Chummy.

'Probably not.' Sister Evangelina glared at Chummy, and then at Trixie and me. 'You young girls! Ignorant! Don't know anything of the past! So many babies were born, and so many died, that the authorities would never have noticed a few smothered here or there – especially if a relative had assisted at the birth, and no one else. The family could just say the baby was still-born.'

'But why?' asked Trixie.

'I've told you: desperation. Poverty, starvation, homelessness, that's what drove people to do it. Read your history books!'

Sister Evangelina was a formidable lady. Her temper was irascible, and the fuse short. We dared not press her.

Aristocratic Sister Monica Joan, who was in her nineties and whose mind was not entirely reliable, had eaten very little. She picked at the mashed potato and onion gravy which Mrs B had lovingly prepared for her, pushed her plate aside and sat fingering her spoon, turning it this way and that as she held it between thumb and forefinger, with the other three fingers arched fan-like. She was watching the changing light in the bowl of the spoon and the reflections of those around her. She giggled.

'Now you are upside down. Now the right way up, but your face is all fat . . . hee, hee, hee! Now it's thin. This is such fun. You should have a look.'

She appeared to be completely absorbed in the spoon and her own thoughts, and I doubted whether she had taken in a word of the previous conversation. How wrong one can be.

Sister Monica Joan had the instincts of an actress, and her timing was impeccable. She dropped the spoon onto the table with a clatter. Everyone jumped and looked at her. She was now the focus of attention, which she relished. She looked coolly around the table at each of us, and said unhurriedly: 'I have seen several cases of smothered babies, or perhaps I should say, where I have strongly suspected smothering, but could not prove it.'

She looked around to judge the effect of her words.

'We had a young maid at the convent – not this House, the one that was bombed out – she was a sweet girl from a respectable family. After a few months, it became clear that she was pregnant.

She was only a girl of fourteen. We were quite shocked, but kept her on, with her mother's approval, until her time. Then we delivered her baby in their little house. One of our Sisters delivered it, and everything appeared to be satisfactory, if an illegitimate baby in a respectable family can be described as satisfactory. At any rate, mother and baby were alive and well when the Sister left them. A few hours later a note was brought to the convent saying that the baby had passed away. The Sister went to the house and found the baby dead, and the child-mother deeply asleep. She could not be roused. It looked like a sleep induced by laudanum. An inquest was held, but nothing was proved.'

Sister Monica Joan picked up the spoon again and turned it in the light, gazing intently at the changing shapes.

'Everything looks so different from varying angles, doesn't it? We see things one way and assume it is correct. But then, move the light just a fraction . . .', she turned the spoon slightly, 'and you see it quite differently. Very often the death of a baby was seen as a blessing, not as a tragedy.'

'Very true,' grunted Sister Evangelina, 'if a family already had half a dozen mouths to feed, and no food and no work, it *would* be a blessing.'

'Poverty. Grinding, abject poverty with no end.' Sister Monica Joan turned the spoon again, gazing at it. 'We were the greatest empire the world had ever seen. We were the richest nation in the world. Yet turn the light just a little and you see destitution so terrible that men and women were driven to kill their own babies.'

'Surely you exaggerate, Sister?' said Sister Julienne in a shocked voice.

Sister Monica Joan turned her elegant head and raised an eyebrow. No one could have looked less like a champion of the poor!

'I do not say it happened all the time, nor that every family was guilty. But it happened. You are too young to have seen the conditions in which working people lived. A thousand people crowded into a slum street of decaying buildings with no lavatories, no furniture, no heating, no blankets, no water except the rainwater that seeped through the rotten roofs and walls and basements. And above all, never enough to eat. In this I do not exaggerate. I have *seen* it. And not just one street, but hundreds of them. An endless warren of slums, housing hundreds of thousands of people. Read General Booth or Henry Mayhew, if you don't believe me! Of course babies died all the time, and of course some were helped on their way by a desperate parent. What else would you expect?'

Trixie, Chummy and I could not speak. Her words and her appearance were so compelling that nothing further could be said. But Sister Julienne spoke.

'Let us thank God that those days are past. Such poverty will never be seen again in this country, though it exists in many parts of the world, especially since the last war, and we must pray for those people.'

At that moment Mrs B came in with pudding, which she took over to Sister Julienne. Mrs B was Queen of the Kitchen – an excellent and valued cook.

'I've made a nice junket 'ere for Sister Monica Joan. A strawberry one. I knows as 'ow she likes strawberry best.'

'Junket! Ooh yummy. And strawberry too!'

In an instant Sister Monica Joan changed into a little girl at a birthday party, contemplating the feast with gleaming eyes. She said no more about the sinister disappearance of babies, but quietly I resolved to read General Booth and Mayhew on the subject.

Cynthia was rested, but subdued and sad, when she came down for tea at four o'clock. She carried out her evening visits as usual, and over the subsequent days she continued her duties. But we could all see that the baby's death was weighing on her mind.

The post-mortem report was received a week later. The baby had died of atelectasis.

Atelectasis means a non-expansion of the lungs. It is not a disease or malfunctioning of the lungs. During foetal life the lungs are airless and collapsed (i.e. in a state of atelectasis). When the baby is born, with the first intake of breath, the lungs expand. However, small patches of atelectasis, or non-expansion could (and still can) remain for a few hours or even days, and these patches could go undetected. If the baby's general condition was good there would be no cause to suspect a collapsed or unexpanded area of lung.

Cynthia's baby was full-term and breathed vigorously at birth with perhaps only three-quarters of the lung capacity; he had a good colour and a good heartbeat and cried and kicked lustily, so there was no cause for alarm. However, a newborn baby is very delicate. As he lay still and sleeping, the effort to breathe with a reduced lung capacity may have been too much for him. Breaths would have become shallower and shallower until the lower lobes of the lungs were not expanding at all. They would then collapse, causing a larger area of atelectasis to develop. Shallow breaths drawn only into the upper lobes of the lungs cannot feed sufficient oxygen into the body to sustain life. The baby would simply have breathed more slowly and more feebly, until even the upper lobes collapsed, and the baby died.

Cynthia was completely exonerated by the post-mortem report. It confirmed that with the baby's first breaths the greater part of the lungs had expanded but had subsequently collapsed during the four hours when the baby was alone with his mother. The question of why the mother did not notice anything unusual (for example, difficulty in breathing, change of skin colour from pink to blue to pallid white, with limpness of muscle tone) and raise the alarm was left unanswered.

No blame was attached to Cynthia, and no fault was found in her delivery or her immediate postnatal care. However, the whole experience had a deeply depressing effect on a sensitive young girl who kept asking herself, 'Could I, should I have done something differently?' and the trauma did not easily go away.

LOST BABIES

How could a baby be born and then disappear? It seems impossible, but in fact it was not so very difficult. It would depend on who knew about the pregnancy in the first place, who knew about the birth, and whether the birth was registered or not.

Family births have always been recorded in parish registers, but this was not obligatory. Since 1837 parents have been required to register a birth with the General Register Office, but it took nearly a century for this law to be enforced. Scarcity of medical care, the high expense of that provision, and vast numbers of births caused thousands of babies to be born and to die unregistered. Still-born babies were not registered until 1929. This made it easy for families to describe babies who had lived for a short time and subsequently died as 'still-born'.

In the 1870s it was estimated that, out of approximately 1.25 million births annually in the UK, only 10 per cent of women had any medical attention (another survey put the figure as low as 3 per cent). Therefore each year over a million women must have given birth with no medical attention. The death rate was enormous. In the 1870s it was estimated that in some of the poorest areas, maternal deaths were around 25–30 per cent and infant deaths around 50–60 per cent. These figures were estimated and collected by the pioneers calling for the training and registration of midwives.*

The first Midwives Act was passed in 1902. Prior to that, midwifery was largely an untrained profession. Any woman could call herself a midwife and go around delivering babies

* I have drawn on several sources for this chapter. For more information a full list is given in the bibliography.

for a fee. She was also called 'the handy-woman' in many communities. She had many roles and dwelled in the shadowland of respectability and the law. She was a solo private practitioner, answerable to no one. At the turn of the nineteenth century it was estimated that around 40,000 handy-women were practising in Great Britain, many of them calling themselves 'midwives'. Some of these women had acquired a knowledge of childbirth handed down through generations, and they were good and conscientious practitioners. However, others were slatternly and often illiterate. Many women could not afford even a handy-woman, and delivered themselves, with just the help of a friend or older relative. No woman had any antenatal care, not even if she was rich, so the fact of pregnancy was not recorded.

With this lack of medical attention it would have been easy for a baby to be born and to die without anyone knowing, apart from the immediate family, who may have had any number of reasons for wanting to conceal the birth.

Illegitimacy was the main reason for hiding a birth. Young people today cannot imagine the disgrace that was once attached to a birth out of wedlock. So great was it that sometimes a young girl would commit suicide rather than reveal she was pregnant. Many a poor woman would conceal the pregnancy beneath her skirts, work until the day she went into labour, deliver the baby herself, and go straight back to work. If she did not register the birth, who would be any the wiser? If the baby died, as many did, who would know? The rich had a more subtle way of dealing with an errant daughter – she could be certified 'insane' and confined to a mental asylum for the rest of her life. The baby would then be removed and placed in a private home or orphanage, with no stain attached to the family.

Another reason for concealing a dead baby was the expense of a funeral. A burial cost money, and every respectable working-class mother spent a few pennies each week on insurance to cover family deaths. A pauper's grave was the ultimate disgrace, and to be thus shamed in front of her neighbours was every self-respecting woman's dread. But many could ill-afford burial insurance, so it would be better for women caught in this trap to pretend it had never occurred and slip the little body into the river. In the 1950s I nursed a woman who had done just that thirty years earlier.*

If the respectable poor were driven to conceal the birth and death of a baby because of the cost of registration and burial, what of the abject poor?

In 1880 nine dead babies were found in a box on the steps of an undertaker in Long Lane, Bermondsey, East London. This was reported in all the newspapers. Would a doctor or midwife have attended the birth of these babies? Would these infants have been registered by parish or state? Could the parents, or at least the mothers, be traced? Not a chance. These nine babies would have been but a few of the nameless children thrown into an unmarked grave, the offspring of the abject poor who were destitute and starving, who were outside any census and beyond enumeration, and whom Charles Booth (1844–1916), the first social statistician, numbered at 255,000 for all London and at 1.95 million for Great Britain as a whole.† Later surveys considered this estimate to be conservative, stating that the figure was nearer to 3 million.

Obvious mental or physical disability was another reason for concealing a birth. Fear was the catalyst – fear, amongst the poor, of having to support a sickly child who could contribute nothing to the family income. There was also fear of the stigma attached to having a disabled child. It was widely supposed that congenital defects were due to something vaguely sinister 'in the blood', which would mark the family out from its neighbours. The baby could be left to die (probably with the connivance of the mother, or the women who had helped with

* See *Call the Midwife*, p. 221.

† Charles Booth, *The Life and Labour of the People of London*, Vols. I to IX, The Journals of the Royal Statistical Society, 1887.

the birth) and then described as still-born. The father would probably have been unaware of any impairment, because men rarely had anything to do with birth in those days. 'Women's matters' were taboo, a silence enforced as much by women as by men.

The upper classes – aristocracy and royalty – were particularly fearful of the stigma of a disabled child in the family. It could lead to ostracism because of so-called 'tainted blood', and the upper classes were not above smothering their own babies at birth.

Poverty led to the abandoning of babies. How much of this really went on I don't know, but we midwives were always being told about it. The women of Poplar would say 'Gor! You don' wanna go dahn Lime'ouse [or Bow or Millwall or wherever]. Dreadful people vey are. Leaves ver babies on doorsteps, vey do.' And women of Limehouse would say exactly the same about the women of Poplar! We got the impression that babies were being left in droves on the doorsteps of every other parish. However, we never saw it, and no baby was left on the convent steps during the 1950s. I personally know a lady who comes from Manchester, and was born in 1940. She tells me that she was an abandoned baby. She was found on a doorstep one morning along with the milk bottles. The baby was very sickly, but although the couple who found her were poor, they arranged for her to go into hospital and paid for the specialist baby care. Then they fostered her for the rest of her childhood.

There are many reliable records of babies being left on workhouse steps, or at the door of one of the state-run orphanages in earlier years. These babies would be named by the workhouse and registered as 'parents unknown'.

General Booth, in his volume *In Darkest England*, records that the Salvation Army 'lasses' frequently had newborn babies thrust into their arms by desperate young mothers, with heartbreaking words such as 'You take him, dearie, he'll have a better life with you. I can't give him anything.' Then the mother would disappear into the crowd, leaving no trace of her identity or address.

Infanticide – that's an ugly word. Did deliberate infanticide go on before pregnancy and birth had to be attended by a registered midwife? It would have been a hanging matter, so the secret would have been well kept. I doubt if any mother would kill her newborn babe in cold blood, but desperate poverty could well drive a grandmother to do such a thing. History is full of grim realities. I recall reading in the national press some years ago of a Scottish woman in the remote highlands who had died at the age of ninety-three. After her death it was revealed that she had drowned seven babies born to her daughter, who was unmarried and of very limited intelligence. Forensic investigation uncovered the remains buried around the croft. What could go on undetected in the remote highlands of Scotland could well go on in the overcrowded slums of any great city, especially in centuries past. It must have happened times beyond number, and nobody knew.

Did fathers kill babies? Who knows? One of our elderly Sisters certainly thought so. I am not of the school that thinks men are the root of all evil, but it is certainly a possibility that some fathers may have been driven to it. Accident is more likely than murder, in my opinion. A newborn baby is very delicate. In overcrowded conditions someone or something falling on the baby could cause death; suffocation in the family bed could occur – there are many possibilities. It must also be remembered that domestic violence was an accepted part of life in some families. Women and children expected to be beaten up, and in such a scene a misdirected blow could easily kill a baby. If such a thing happened the mother would have done everything possible to conceal the death, and if the baby was unregistered she would probably get away with it. If her husband, the wage earner, was convicted of murder, it would be the gallows for him, or transportation if the judge was lenient. Either way, the family would be deprived of financial support.

Not all missing babies died, however. The more prosperous the family, the more reason for concealing an unwanted birth. A wealthy girl's mother could keep her confined to the house, conduct the delivery herself, perhaps with the aid of a handywoman, dispose of the baby, and no one would know. But how? A respectable matron could not go hawking a newborn baby around the workhouses and orphanages because, firstly, the baby would be refused admission, and, secondly, the neighbours would quickly find out. So an arrangement for private fostering, or 'boarding' as it was called, had to be found. Many handywomen had an 'understanding' with women who boarded babies, acting as intermediary, and taking a fee from both parties.

I knew a woman whose daughter, then aged twenty-four, had an illegitimate baby in 1949, which is not so very long ago. The woman said to me, smugly, 'I took it away at birth, of course. My daughter was not allowed to see it. The baby went to an orphanage.' It must have been a private commercial establishment, because the baby was not an orphan. Both parents were known and living.

A decade later, I delivered the baby of a young girl in Poplar. Throughout the delivery her mother shouted repeatedly that she would 'get rid of the baby and put it in a home or institution'. At one stage she ordered me – the midwife – to 'clear off'. She could deliver the baby herself and then get rid of it. I don't know what she had in mind, but obviously she knew of some lawful way of disposing of an unwanted baby.*

The standard of care in these private 'homes' for babies would depend entirely on the person in charge. One of my friends was an illegitimate child seventy-five years ago. She was sent from one private boarding or foster parent to another, and eventually went to live with a single lady who loved and cared for her and became a lifelong guardian and friend. By way of contrast a

* If you want to know why the mother took that attitude, and how the story ended, you will have to read *Call the Midwife*!

woman in Clapham was prosecuted in the 1920s for having eight babies (each of which she was paid to care for) in five cots in the basement of her house. The babies ranged from newborn to three years old. The toddlers could not walk. They had never been out of their cots. They could not talk; they had not heard enough language.

Traffic in children has been going on for as long as mankind has been sinning and suffering. Josephine Butler (1828–1907) writes in her journals, pamphlets and diaries of the second half of the nineteenth century about seeing thousands (yes, *thousands*) of little girls, some as young as four or five, in the illegal brothels of London, Paris, Brussels and Geneva. It broke her heart to see them. The children had a life expectany of two years, yet the brothel owners, frequently women, seemed to have an unlimited supply of little girls for their rich clients. 'Clean' children, who were free from venereal disease, commanded a high price. All this is well documented, but strangely Mrs Butler never mentions little boys, though this branch of the trade must have been going on.*

Where did all these children come from? It could certainly not have been from the Salvation Army or the workhouses or state orphanages, nor from the established management orphanages such as Coram, Barnardo or Spurgeon. So from where, then?

A basic law of economics is that supply will meet demand. If brothel keepers wanted 'clean' children, unscrupulous women who boarded unwanted babies would supply them, for a price. No questions asked. Many children were not named or registered, and for those who were, a false birth certificate was provided. The parents or relatives probably never knew what had happened to their children. They just vanished as though they had never been born.

* Jane Jordan, *Josephine Butler*, John Murray, 2000.

Baby selling – the last resort of a starving mother – was rife throughout the population explosion of the nineteeth century. This led to the terrible evil whereby traders, usually women, secured the custody of unwanted little ones, took out an insurance policy on their lives and then by neglect, cold and starvation ensured the death of the child and claimed the insurance. There are many recorded instances of this practice. Dr Barnardo is on record as having thwarted the murderous designs of a ruthless old harridan who had acquired three babies, insured them all, pawned their clothes, covered them in rags and left them without heat or food.

This must make terrible reading for anyone who is seriously studying family history. But life is made of happiness and tragedy in equal proportions, and we will never change that.

SOOT

Within the midwifery practice it was noticed that several babies had developed various infections: sticky eyes, pustules, aural discharge, diarrhoea, an infected umbilical stump. Not all babies were affected, but of those that were, one became quite ill. Swabs were taken for analysis, and the report came back from the pathology lab. All the infections were caused by the same strain of staphylococcus aureus. Where was it coming from?

All Sisters and nurses had to be screened, and the analysis proved that Cynthia was carrying a staphylococcus aureus infection, which she was passing on to the babies. Gentle Cynthia was horrified that she was the cause, especially as she did not look or feel ill in any way. But the report from the lab was incontrovertible. She was taken off work straight away and treated with antibiotics, and the infection cleared.

All the babies were also treated with penicillin, and they recovered. In previous decades, before the advent of antibiotics, some of the babies affected might have died. Certainly one or two would have developed chronic otitis media, or pink eye, or a lung infection, which could lead to something worse. But antibiotics, being new in those days, were more effective.

Cynthia was off work for two weeks, and returned to the district with confidence. No more infections occurred amongst the babies.

The first case Cynthia went to on returning to work was in a comfortable little house in Bow. It was a nice sort of home to be working in and everything was going well: the young mother having her fifth baby was progressing in labour; her mother was looking after the four young children downstairs; her grandmother, an experienced matriarch for whom childbirth was less alarming than a visit to the dentist, was competently helping Cynthia. She – the grandmother – was looking at the fire.

'Sulky ole fire, that. Needs a bi' of life in it afore this baby's born. We wants a nice warm room for ve new baby, eh, nurse?'

She picked up the poker, stirred the sluggish embers and opened the air vent. Flames leaped up the chimney. There was a rumbling from somewhere near the roof and a cascade of soot fell, completely dousing the fire. The grandmother screamed and rushed forward with a sheet of newspaper in an attempt to contain the soot in the grate. But there was a second rumble, louder than the first, and another fall of soot came rushing down the chimney, smothering the poor woman and flying all over the room. Cynthia's sterile delivery equipment, carefully laid out on the chest of drawers, was covered in soot; the white bed linen was black; the lovingly prepared crib with its white lace and bows was black; Cynthia, aseptically prepared for delivery in a sterile white gown, cap, mask and gloves, was black; and the woman lying on the bed was black, although she was past caring – the second stage of labour was approaching and she was suffering a massive contraction prior to full dilation of the cervix. Cynthia gazed at the scene and raised her gloved hands in horror. Her first instinct was to wash them, and she rushed over to where the washing bowl stood. But a film of soot was floating on the water, and soot clung to the sticky wet soap. She tore off her gloves and was relieved to see clean hands.

'Oh my Gawd,' moaned the grandmother, 'I never seed nuffink like it. What's you goin' 'a do, nurse?'

'There is nothing I can do. If a baby is going to be born, no power in the world will stop it. We will have to continue like this. You go downstairs for some more hot water, and take this bowl with you and get it washed. You can also ask if there is any more clean linen in the house. I don't think there will be time to get another sterile delivery pack from Nonnatus House, but you could try.'

With the last contraction the waters had broken, and viscous amniotic fluid was flowing over the absorbent mattress coverings. Falling particles of soot were rapidly sticking to it.

As Cynthia spoke particles of soot blew off her mask, so she tore the thing off. She would be better without it. The upper part of her face and eyes were black, her mouth, nose and chin were white. She looked like a comic turn.

Poor Janet, sweating profusely from the pain and pressure of advanced labour, had soot sticking to her entire body. It had even managed to penetrate beneath her nightdress. She raised her legs and vaguely rubbed her hands down her thighs, perhaps to wipe the soot away, but it only served to make thick, slimy black streaks.

'Oh Gawd, wha' a mess,' she moaned, beginning to pant. 'Vere's anuvver contraction comin', I can feel it. Aaah . . .' she groaned in agony.

Cynthia did not need to make a vaginal examination. She could see the head descending.

'Don't push, Janet, whatever you do. Just pant, quickly, like a little dog. In, out, in, out – quick, shallow breaths. That's right, keep panting. I need to turn you over onto your left side in order to deliver the baby.' (We were taught, in those days, to deliver on the side.)

In the meantime the grandmother had taken the washing bowl away and returned with clean hot water. She also had some clean towels and sheets.

'We can take 'er into anuvver room, nurse.'

'That would be nice, but I doubt if it will be possible. The baby might drop out on the landing! See here, I'm holding the head back as it is. Another contraction and it will be born.'

'Oh Lor, vis is awful. Jim's gone down the road to ring ve Sisters, but he's not goin' 'a be in time, is he?'

'No. Just keep panting, Janet. Everything is all right. A bit of soot isn't going to do you or the baby any harm.'

Cynthia's warm, soft voice had a reassuring effect on the two women. The contraction was passing. Janet looked up and relaxed. She giggled, and then began to laugh uncontrollably.

'You do look funny, you two. If only you could see yourselves . . . oh no, not again . . . aaah . . .'

Another contraction came within seconds of the last.

'This is it,' she gasped, holding her breath.

'Yes it is. Now you have to turn over quickly.' Cynthia beckoned to the grandmother. 'Bring me those clean towels. Can we get this dirty maternity pad out of the way and put the towels under her, so that there is a clean surface for the baby to be born onto?'

They changed the linen, but it was not so easy to contain the soot. Their hands were filthy, and touching anything made matters worse. Cynthia turned the pillow over, so that there was a clean surface on which Janet could lay her head, but even that soon got dirty as her hair streaked across it. Her grandmother tried washing Janet's forehead in cold water, which helped a little.

The delivery was not complicated, but childbirth is sometimes a gory business and blood and amniotic fluid can get everywhere. Mixed with soot, the mess was quite indescribable. The baby, a little girl, wet and sticky, was covered in black slime, and clumps of soot. With swabs and clean water Cynthia washed it away and held the baby upside down in order to drain mucus from her throat (this procedure was thought to be helpful in those days, and we were taught to do it). The baby screamed lustily. Cynthia looked at her sterile delivery tray in despair. At this stage she would normally have cut the cord, but the scissors, clamps, swabs and sterile water were filthy.

At that moment she heard heavy footsteps on the stairs and the sound of Sister Evangelina's voice grumbling.

'What is all this about needing a new delivery bag? Calling me out to bring one! I've had to cycle half a mile to bring it. The impertinence! I suppose the nurse messed up the first one. These young midwives! Can't be trusted to do anything properly.'

The door opened. Sister Evangelina entered, stared at the scene in disbelief, and exclaimed 'What the devil have you been up to?' Then she laughed. She laughed so much it shook the house. She fell against the door frame holding her stomach, then sat down on a chair and threw her head back, knocking her wimple askew.

Sister Evangelina was a large and impressive lady. She was what is usually described as a 'rough diamond'. Born into a large family in the slums of Reading at the turn of the last century, she had grown up in desperate poverty. The First World War offered her the chance of escape from the treadmill of inherited penury. She had left school at twelve to work in a biscuit factory and at the age of fifteen had gone to work in a munitions factory. Later she had moved to a military hospital, where she trained as a nurse, and where the one romance of her life had occurred, though she never spoke of it. She joined the Sisters of St Raymund Nonnatus, becoming fully professed as a nursing nun, and had worked in Poplar for thirty years, including during the Blitz. She was a great favourite of the people of Poplar, largely because of her down-to-earth, no-nonsense approach to their ailments, her rough-and-ready ways and her crude language. Of course, she had a completely different vocabulary and use of language within the convent. In fact, with us she could be extremely dour and grumpy, and not easily given to laughter. Yet on this occasion she could not stop. Her face, which was red and mottled at the best of times, turned a deep crimson, and her nose shone like a beacon. She slapped her hand on the mantelshelf to steady herself and took out a giant-sized handkerchief with which to wipe her streaming eyes and nose. 'Ooh, I'm peeing me drawers. You don't know what you look like, you three – you've made me pee me drawers, you have.' And off she went into paroxysms of laughter again.

Sister Evangelina also enjoyed earthy vulgarity. In fact basic bodily functions were an endless source of amusement to her. This predilection for lavatorial humour was something she shared only with her Cockney patients. Within the convent she was very prim and proper, and I doubt her Sisters in God ever saw the crude side of Sister Evangelina.

She slapped her ample thighs and leaned forwards, nearly choking. In alarm Cynthia thumped her back. When she could speak, Sister gasped, 'Talk about the Black and White Minstrel Show – this is the Black and White Midwives' Show!'

Sister Evangelina did not possess a subtle wit, and her jokes were heavy, but she was delighted with her pun, and kept repeating 'Black and White Midwives – have you got it? Black and White . . . Oh dear, now I'm doing it again – I'll have to have one of your sanitary towels before I can get home.'

By now, the children had come running upstairs to see what all the laughter was about. They had been alarmed when their granny had appeared, all black, demanding clean water and soap and clean sheets. They had heard rapid conversation which they did not understand, and then seen their father rushing down the road to make a telephone call. When a very large and cross-looking nun had entered the little front room, stamping and grumbling, they had hidden behind the sofa. It was all very intimidating. But then they heard guffaws of female laughter descending the stairs and brightened considerably, rushing upstairs before anyone could stop them.

The children burst in through the door, and stood stock-still for a second or two whilst they took in the scene, scarcely able to believe that grown-ups could get into such a state. Everyone was black. Everyone was laughing. The big nun, her white veil streaked with soot, was rocking backwards and forwards with her face so red she looked as though she might burst. Somewhere in the mess a baby was screaming. The children positively let rip. They jumped up and down and bounced on their mother's bed, to the alarm of Cynthia, because the baby was still attached to its mother. They rolled on the floor, getting as much soot on themselves as they could and smearing it on each other's faces. Their grandmother tried to establish order and keep control, but she didn't stand a chance.

The big red nun laughed so much she was wheezing and coughing. 'Oh dear oh dear, this is going to finish me. Pass me that towel. I can't contain myself.' She stuffed the towel up her skirts and wiped it around her legs. The children couldn't believe their luck, and crowded around, lying on the floor trying to get a look at a nun's knickers.

Meanwhile, all the laughter must have been good for labour, because the third stage was progressing rapidly. The third stage of labour can be an anxious time for a midwife, and requires a great deal of knowledge, experience and care to enable the placenta to be delivered complete. But Cynthia hardly had to do anything. Janet couldn't stop laughing and the placenta just slid out in one piece. It was a revolting sight, bloody and slimy and covered in soot, but at least it was out. Placenta and baby, of course, were still attached!

'Sister, I shall need clean scissors and clamps and swabs,' said Cynthia quietly.

Sister Evangelina was not just a comedy act for the children's entertainment. She was a professional nurse and midwife, and her mood changed instantly.

'We will have to take the baby into another room and scrub up thoroughly. We cannot cut the cord in these conditions. As it is, the soot is not going to harm the baby. But I am not sure what would happen if it got into the bloodstream.'

Disappointed children were shooed away and taken downstairs. The baby, with the placenta still attached, was carried into another bedroom, and with sterile equipment the cord was cut.

The job of cleaning up fell to the grandmother. It took her about four days, and she needed a holiday to recover.

NANCY

The harlot's curse from street to street
Shall weave old England's winding sheet.
William Blake (1757–1827)

Sister Monica Joan had fascinated me from the first time I met her on a cold November evening in Nonnatus House, when we had devoured an entire cake between us, and she had rambled on about poles diverging and saucers flying and etheric ethers converging and goodness knows what else. She has continued to fascinate me over the years, and I have never been able to resolve the enigma that was she. How could a young woman of beauty, talent, intellect and wealth reject the privileges of the Victorian upper class to work in squalor amongst the poorest of the poor at the end of the nineteenth century? How could she reject offers of love and marriage and children to become a nun? I was never able to answer these questions. A religious-minded woman who has nothing to lose by embracing the monastic life, I could understand. But Sister Monica Joan had everything to lose. Yet she gave it all up. In fact, she had given up her position in society ten years before entering the convent, by becoming a nurse – a lowly and almost despised occupation in the 1890s. She was not, however, a saint! She was wilful, haughty, sarcastic; she could be cruel and unfeeling, arrogant and demanding. All these faults I was aware of – and loved her still.

I liked nothing better than to go to her room when work permitted and listen to her talking. Sometimes her mind wandered through a muddle of various religions – Christian, pagan, oriental philosophies, occultism, theosophy, astrology; she embraced them all with uncritical enthusiasm, whilst still observing the strict monastic disciplines of her order.

*

One day I asked Sister why she had given up her life of wealth and privilege for the humble life of a nurse, a midwife and a nun.

She winked at me.

'So you think our life "humble", do you? Nonsense. Fiddlesticks. Ours is a life of adventure, of daring, of high romance.'

'I agree with you there,' I said. 'Almost every day comes as a surprise. But I started nursing when I was eighteen, because there was no other choice. But why did you? You had plenty of choices.'

'You are wrong, my dear. The choice of which pretty dresses to wear? Pooh! The choice to spend each afternoon "visiting", and talking about nothing? Pooh! Pooh! The choice to spend hours embroidering or making lace? Oh, I couldn't stand it – when nine-tenths of the women of Britain were toiling with their half-starved, stunted broods of children. I could not leave my father's house and start nursing, or lead any sort of useful life until I was over thirty.'

She was in good form. I was on to a streak of luck, because it was always a lottery talking with Sister Monica Joan. At any moment she might say no more. I said nothing, but waited.

'When Nancy died, I had an almighty row with my father, who wanted to control me. I hated the shallow, empty life I was leading, and wanted to throw myself into the struggle. I left home to become a nurse. It was the least I could do in her memory.'

'Who was Nancy?'

'My maid. She had been surgically raped.'

'What! Surgically raped? What on earth does that mean?'

'Exactly what it says. Josephine Butler had rescued the child and she asked me if I could take her on as my lady's maid. I was eighteen at the time, and my mother permitted me to have a lady's maid of my choice. Nancy was thirteen.'

'Who was Josephine Butler?'

'An unknown saint. You are ignorant, child! I cannot waste

my time with such ignorance. Go, fetch my tea, if your mind cannot rise to higher thoughts.'

Sister Monica Joan closed her fine, hooded eyes, and haughtily turned her head on her long neck, to signify that she was offended, and that the conversation was over.

Humiliated by her cruel tongue and furious with her (not for the first or last time), I retreated to the kitchen. But that same evening I asked Sister Julienne about Josephine Butler.

Josephine Butler, born in 1828, was the daughter of a wealthy landowner in Northumberland.* The whole family of seven children were highly educated and brought up to think deeply about class inequality and the conditions of the poor. In those days, this was considered to be radical, unconventional and dangerous. Her grandfather had worked with Wilberforce for the abolition of the slave trade, and Josephine had listened to adult discussions about slavery, child labour, factory work and related subjects throughout her childhood. In later life she said, 'From an early age I mourned about the condition of the oppressed.' She was particularly drawn to the condition of women whose abject poverty drove them into prostitution, through which they would frequently become pregnant, and then both the woman and child would be destitute.

In 1852, at the age of twenty-four, Josephine married George Butler, an academic and professor at Oxford University. He was ten years older than her and was a reformer and radical thinker, just as her father had been. It proved to be a perfect meeting of minds. After the marriage Josephine moved with her husband to Liverpool. It was not difficult to find poverty in Liverpool in the 1850s. The workhouse alone housed 5,000 souls. She visited and worked in the oakum sheds: 'vast underground cellars, unfurnished, with damp

* For this account of the life of Josephine Butler, I have referred to several sources, all of which are detailed in the Bibliography.

floors and oozing walls, where women sat on the floor all day picking their allotted portion of oakum. Yet they came voluntarily, driven by hunger and destitution, begging for a few nights' shelter and a piece of bread.'

In 1864 their little daughter Eva, aged five, fell downstairs and was killed. Josephine was paralysed with grief. She had always been deeply religious, but now she turned in on herself, rejecting all comfort, all consolation.

Unknown to Josephine, and indeed to most people in Britain, 1864 was the year in which the Contagious Diseases (Women) Act was passed in Parliament. When she did learn about it two years later it came as a shock and was the catharsis needed to rouse her from deepening depression.

The Contagious Diseases (Women) Act of 1864, intended 'for the prevention of contagious diseases at certain naval and military stations', was profoundly immoral. Venereal disease was spreading rapidly among the armed forces and was thought likely to undermine military strength. It was widely assumed in those days that women spread the diseases, and that to curtail the spread of infection prostitution must be controlled. So far, so good – in theory. But there were not, and never had been, legalised brothels in England. Women touted for their customers in the streets, and so the Act empowered the police to find their victims in the streets.

The Contagious Diseases Act was administered by a special unit of volunteers from the Metropolitan Police who were known as 'the Spy Police'. These men had the power to arrest *on suspicion only* any woman found alone in the streets whom they thought might be soliciting, confine her in a cell and call a doctor to examine her vaginally for evidence of venereal disease (Josephine Butler called this 'surgical rape'). There were no female police officers or doctors in those days so the women were handled entirely by men *who had volunteered for the job in the first place*, and no witnesses were required. If evidence of venereal disease was found the woman would be confined to a lock hospital* for treatment. If no evidence was found, she would be given a certificate saying that she was 'clean', but her name would be kept on a special police register and she could be arrested and re-examined at any time. In theory the woman had to give written consent for the first examination, but this was a cynical farce because the Act stated that a woman who refused to sign should be confined indefinitely until she did consent to be examined.

Any woman of any age could be subjected to this horrifying treatment. At the time the age of consent was thirteen, so a child of that age could legally be regarded as a woman. The Contagious Diseases Act affected only working-class women, because upper-class women never walked in the streets alone, but would be accompanied or in a carriage. Men of any age or class were exempt from arrest and examination, even if caught in the act of soliciting, because the Act of 1864 was specifically designed for the control of women.

Josephine was stirred to the depths of her soul by the injustice and the immorality of the Act. She saw at once that the floodgate had been opened for the police to abuse women with impunity, and she vowed to God, and to her husband, that she would devote all her strength to getting it repealed. George was the perfect husband for her. In those days men controlled their wives absolutely. A respectable woman was not supposed to know about things like prostitution and syphilis, still less to talk about them publicly. George could have forbidden Josephine to take any action; instead he supported her.

Josephine addressed meetings all over the country, she wrote articles and pamphlets, she lobbied Parliament. She shocked and scandalised Victorian Society with her outspoken language at public meetings, describing 'the surgical violation of women'. She not only insisted that the medical examination

* A lock hospital was the official term for a hospital treating venereal disease. The infected patients could not leave and were locked in. It was effectively a prison.

of women by the speculum was a form of rape, but also made public accusations against the police, doctors, magistrates and Members of Parliament, saying, in the strongest language, 'There is such a thing as the medical lust of indecently handling women, as well as the legislative desire to rule women with an iron hand for the purpose of gratifying vicious propensities in men.'

Such speeches from the lips of an educated middle-class lady were deeply shocking, but they were enough to stir the conscience of the nation, and in 1883 the Contagious Diseases (Women) Act was removed from the statute books of Great Britain.

Nancy's misfortune was that she was the daughter of a poor woman who lived in Southampton, a naval dock town. She was the eldest of five children whose father had died. Their mother took in washing from the garrison, and Nancy carried it back and forth. She was thirteen at the time of her arrest.

One of the volunteer police had observed her coming and going and lusted after her. He had unlimited power. One evening he accosted her.

'What do you go to the Docks for?'

'Please, sir, I take the washing.'

'And what else?'

'I collect the money, if you please, sir.'

'What money?'

'For the washing, sir.'

'Is that all?'

'Yes, sir.' Nancy was beginning to feel frightened.

'You're a bad girl. You're telling me lies.'

'I'm not, sir. I'm a good girl,' she whispered.

'You're a wicked girl. Come with me.'

He grabbed her arm and hustled her along the dark street. She was sobbing now.

'My mum's expecting me. I must go home.'

'If your mum knew what you'd been up to, she wouldn't want you home, ever.'

'I'm a good girl. I haven't been up to anything. And I've got threepence in my pocket for the washing, and my mum needs it.'

'Your mum would be ashamed to touch the money you've been earning if she knew how you'd earned it, you wicked girl.'

They reached the police station, and he pushed the terrified child into a cell.

'Wait there,' he ordered, going out and locking the door.

The Act required that a doctor should carry out the examination, so the police officer sent a message boy to call the doctor, who came quickly. They were hand in glove: two men, lustful and eager to discharge their duties to the letter of the law, and well beyond it, if they were sufficiently aroused. There were no witnesses, and none were required.

The doctor barked at Nancy, 'Can you write your name?' She nodded, too terrified to speak. 'Then write it here.' He thrust a piece of paper and a pen at her. She signed. Unknowingly, she had consented to be examined.

Swiftly the policeman picked her up and laid her on the half-length couch, pulling her skirts above her head and tying the ends under the table, effectively blinding and gagging her. The doctor grabbed her legs, pushed her knees towards her chest, and fixed her heels in the leather straps that were attached to metal stirrups. Her thighs were forced wide apart, and her bloomers were ripped off. Nancy thrashed around in terror, and, even though her legs were secured, she succeeded in throwing the upper half of her body off the table.

As she fell backwards, hanging by her legs, one of her lower vertebrae was crushed against the metal edge of the couch. It was an injury from which she never recovered. The policeman swore and yanked her back on the couch, securing her arms and body with a leather strap, so that she was unable to move at all.

Then the examination began. The Act required that the examining surgeon should first assess if a gonorrhoeal discharge or warts, or a syphilitic chancre was present on the external labia. If necessary, he could explore the vagina with his fingers, to feel for a chancre or other signs of venereal disease. If he was in any doubt he could use a vaginal speculum and forceps with which to examine the cervix. The doctor and the police officer took full advantage of all their legal rights. It took them forty-five minutes to conduct an examination that should only have taken two or three minutes.

Today a clear plastic vaginal speculum is still used for clinical examination. Then it was a heavy metal instrument about five or six inches long made of two halves. When closed, it is roughly circular, about one and a half inches in diameter. This is inserted into the vagina. The jaws then open to about three or four inches, and a central ratchet holds it open so the cervix is visible. In the nineteenth century, the speculum would have been made of rough, unpolished metal, and I doubt if anyone would have taken the trouble to lubricate it.

The surgeon and policeman thrust the speculum repeatedly into Nancy, twisting and turning it. They thrust their hands into her young body. Then they introduced other instruments, including long-handled forceps, with which they were able to grab hold of the cervix, pulling and turning it, ostensibly to examine for signs of venereal disease. Can you imagine the pain for a thirteen-year-old virgin? Whether they raped her phallically as well is not known. When they were satisfied they untied her. 'She is clean. No sign of venereal disease. We can give her the certificate. Get up, girl, you can have your certificate to say that you are clean. Your mother will be pleased.'

The distraught mother was powerless. There was no one to complain to. If she had been so bold as to complain to the police, she would probably have been victimised herself. In any case the men had acted within the requirements of the law. If they had raped the girl it was of no consequence because the speculum had opened up the vagina. Josephine Butler coined the phrase 'surgical rape', and thousands of innocent women were subjected to it.

Nancy's mother wrote to the Association for Repeal of the Contagious Diseases (Women) Act and received a visit from Mrs Butler herself, who advised her that Nancy must leave Southampton at once, because she could be seized again at any time and re-examined. Mrs Butler promised to find a position for the child, and that is how Nancy came to be the lady's maid to young Monica Joan, the rebel daughter of a baronet.

Sister said, 'Her back was badly injured, she could hardly walk. She was cringing and terrified. She was with me for eleven years, and then she died of tuberculosis of the spine.'

She said no more about Nancy. Perhaps it would have been too poignant, too troubling, after all those years, for Sister Monica Joan to recall.

MEGAN'MAVE

Megan'mave were identical twins and masters in the art of grumbling. They must have spent their time in the womb grumbling to each other about cramped living conditions, a damp environment, too dark, smelly, and wet. And when they emerged into the world kicking and screaming they would have started to complain about too much light, noise, fuss and bustle. Their cot would have been too hard or too soft; their clothes too tight or too loose; their milk too hot or too cold; and the breast (if they ever had suckled a breast) would have been grabbed by relentless baby hands as they each sucked a nipple voraciously, each fixing black unblinking eyes on the mirror image of herself across the soft and yielding body of the mother. After feeding they would have grumbled to each other about excesses of wind and gripe; they would surely have grumbled about the paucity of the milk, or the lack of proper nourishment to which they were daily subjected, and which would be the cause of untold suffering as they grew up. Over the years they honed their chosen art to an unprecedented level, finding fault with everything and everyone.

Megan'mave kept a fruit and vegetable stall in Chrisp Street market. From Wednesday to Saturday each week they could be heard shouting more loudly and more aggressively than any other coster. They had an intimidating way of glaring at a potential customer and demanding, 'Well?' If the unwary buyer, perhaps through nervousness, were to hesitate, they would lean forward menacingly, black gypsy eyes gleaming, and repeat, 'Well? What do you want?' even more loudly. Should the innocent buyer have supposed that the customer was always right, that error would soon be rectified. Megan'mave were always right, and the customer was always wrong.

It was surprising that they sold anything at all, but, strange to say, they were very successful, and their stall was easily the most popular. Women in curlers, wearing headscarves and carpet slippers, with Woodbines and babies appended, crowded forward with their shopping bags to be bullied and insulted as they acquired their bargains. Perhaps that was the secret of Megan'mave's success – everything was a penny or a halfpenny cheaper than it was on other stalls. But I have watched them at work, and wonder if the bargains were not more apparent than real. The two women moved about with lightning speed and ferocious energy. They could weigh a pound of carrots or turnips, throw them in a bag, twist the corners, add the cost to the last item, glare at the customer, and demand 'that will be three shillings and sevenpence halfpenny' before the average person could draw breath. Mental arithmetic was their genius – and their prodigious memory. They would rattle off, with machine-gun precision, a list of about fifteen different items, together with the prices, adding it all up in complicated shillings and pence (there were twelve pence to a shilling, not ten), and no one dared to question them. Once I saw a bold woman look at her change and say, 'I gave you a ten shilling note. I should have three and fourpence change, not two and elevenpence!' The two women behind the stall drew together. They grabbed the shopping basket, tipped everything out, weighed it again, shouted out the prices, tossed figures back and forward to each other, and came up with the magic total of seven and a penny. They pushed the bag at the woman: 'There you are, and there's yer change, two and eleven. An' don' come back 'ere. We don' wan' your sort. Next?' The poor woman wandered off, bewildered, counting her pennies.

Perhaps most of their customers were too mesmerized by the speed of delivery and the confidence of their joint attack. No one could be as quick as they were. Singly, each was as sharp as a razor, but together they resembled a double-edged sword. To

Megan'mave all customers were there to be manipulated, to be squeezed of a couple of pence here and there, to be bullied into buying more than they wanted, and to be hypnotized into thinking they had got a bargain.

The physical appearance of Megan'mave was singular, to say the very least. They looked like something out of another century, and another country. They had fine features, high cheek bones and clear but slightly swarthy skin. I have mentioned their black, flashing eyes, which undoubtedly had an unnerving effect on their customers. They were both very thin, almost skeletal, but strong and muscular; their hands were large and bony, and their fingers long. Their clothes – how on earth can one describe their clothes? To begin with, they were identical, like their wearers, and excessively plain, yet would have stood out in any crowd. Megan'mave always wore garments of dark brown or fusty black, long in the skirt and shapeless in the body, pulled tightly into their waists by heavy leather belts, from which hung two or three rings of keys. Their stockings were thick lisle, and their shoes were old, shapeless, and unpolished. Their head-gear, without which they were never seen, was distinctive. Each wore a headscarf, an ordinary headscarf that any woman could buy, but it was the way they wore them that arrested attention. The scarves were pulled down low over their foreheads, so that barely the eyebrows were visible, and tied very tightly at the nape of the neck, so that not a wisp of hair could be seen. So tight were the knots that the scarves were strained almost to splitting. I sometimes wondered if the two women were bald, as the result of some rare disease, but this proved not to be the case. What with their clothes and their headscarves they looked rather like Buddhist nuns, but without the smile. I was reminded of a Hogarth etching of very poor women from the back streets of eighteenth-century London transported to the life and vitality of Chrisp Street market, Poplar.

Megan'mave were married. It was said that the banns had been read out on three successive Sundays for Margaret, spinster of this parish, but that Mavis had signed the register, or perhaps it was the other way round – hearsay can be notoriously unreliable. To be sure, both of them answered to the title of Mrs M. Carter. Which of them had stood at the altar and vowed to love, honour and obey, no one was quite sure, least of all Sid, the man of their choice. If he had ever had any illusions about the reality of these ancient marriage vows, Megan'mave soon relieved him of such fantasies. Megan'mave were the boss, and Sid had to honour and obey! In his romantic younger days Sid may have thought that he was getting a bargain – two women for the price of one – but life taught him that Megan'mave were the ones who got all the bargains, while everyone else paid the price. He was a little wisp of a Cockney, about five and a half feet tall and seven stone in weight, who was always seen in the market carrying boxes of apples and pears, cabbages and turnips, to the stall where his wives were doing their strident stuff. Unlike other Cockneys he never laughed and joked, never went for a drink with the other costers, never joined in when dirty yarns were being spun, could never see the funny side of life. He never even smiled. He just doggedly carried on, humping the boxes and crates, his thin frame sometimes trembling under the weight, his cap pulled well down over his eyes and his lips fixed in a tight, straight line. He spoke to no one, and invited no one to speak to him. When the market was over, he vanished. If he had a favourite pub, or a favoured walk or haunt by the river edge, no one knew what or where it was.

When Mave became pregnant it was a shock to the three of them. They had been married for several years with no issue, to use the old biblical term, and life without children was comfortable enough. They were thirty-eight, and Mavis assumed a saintly, martyred expression. Poor Sid got the rough end. The wives grumbled and nagged at him mercilessly, until he lost another stone in weight and looked as if he might disappear altogether.

Mave's pregnancy brought out the warrior in Meg. Mave

became rather docile and quiet, whilst Meg doubled her energy and aggression. She had found a new meaning to life. It would be no exaggeration to say that her whole life had hitherto been leading up to this point. She suddenly discovered that Mavis had been suffering for years from numerous diseases and infirmities caused by neglect, hardship, ignorance (other people's) but most seriously by medical error. The catalogue of ailments could easily be traced to babyhood, when Mave, the second twin, had had her arm pulled by a stupid and ignorant midwife, who ought to have been strung up, Meg reckoned. Everyone could see that there was nothing wrong with Mave's arm; she had been heaving fruit and veg around the markets for twenty years, but Meg was unimpressed by the evidence. 'An' look at her constitooshun! It's 'er constitooshun, see! No proper nourishment when she was a baby – ooh, terrible it was, I tells yer. Dad – he drank, an' Mum – no good she was, couldn't stand up to 'im. No proper nourishment – vat's what started it – an' look at 'er now – can't expect 'er to go through wiv bein' pregnant. She ain't got no constitooshun, see?'

Long-standing complaints and grudges against the medical profession were remembered, dragged up and exploited for all they were worth. 'Medical blunders' became her pet phrase.

'Welliclose weins. She 'ad welliclose weins, see? Right mess they made of 'em. Stripped 'em, they did. Well, they shouldn't 'ave done it. I've been readin' up about it, an' it was done all wrong. Medical blunder! Made 'er 'alf lame. Look at 'er. It wasn't done right. Them weins is all swellin' up. Show 'em yer legs, Mave.'

Mave pulled down her stockings. 'Well, vat's not right. If them weins 'ad been done proper in ve first place, they wouldn't be swellin' up now. Doctors! I could teach 'em a thing or two. Don't know nuffink, vey don't.'

Another day it was 'golf stones'.

'Look at 'er. Gone yeller she 'as. I tells ve doctor, I sez, look 'ere, she's gone yeller – it's golf stones, see? You wan's 'a do somefink about it, or I'll call the Medical Council. But 'e wouldn't do nuffink. Too busy playin' golf, if you ask me.'

Meg became a voracious reader. She plundered all the second-hand bookstalls and book fairs from Portobello Road to Poplar, searching for ancient medical text-books. Most of the stall holders were glad to get rid of the old rubbish, out of date medically by a century or two, but Meg was delighted with her purchases and bore them home triumphantly. 'Ancient wisdom,' she called it. Megan'mave devoured the faded print and agreed that everything the doctors said about Mave's pregnancy was based on error, ignorance, stupidity, or downright malevolence, and was not to be trusted.

Because of her age – thirty-eight years – Mavis was told by her doctor that she must have a hospital confinement for the delivery of her first baby. Meg immediately came in, all guns firing. ''ospital! Don't make me laugh. Charnel 'ouse, you mean. I know vese infirmaries, I do. You can't pull the wool over my eyes, you can't. Women die like flies in them infirmaries!'

In vain the doctor protested that modern hospitals were not like the old infirmaries, but Megan'mave were adamant. With cold and crafty eye, Meg produced from her bag a book, yellow with age and disfigured with damp marks, and gave him a knowing look.

'What do you say to this, ven? "Pregnancy is a natural process, requiring little mechanical assistance. No man should act as accoucheur, but women should be instructed to do all that is required." What do you say to that, Dr Clever Dick? It's 'ere, in ve book.' Triumphantly Meg pushed the book towards him. 'Read it.'

'But this is Dr A. I. Coffin, *Treatise on Midwifery*, published in 1866. Medical and midwifery practice have moved on since then.'

'Don't come vat one on me. You doctors is all the same. I know your sort. Medical neglect, vat's what you get in 'ospitals. She needs special treatment. Look at 'er. Weak constitooshun, she's got.' Mave put on her martyred expression. 'An' all from medical blunders years ago.'

Mave pursed her lips. 'Terrible, it was.'

Meg did the same, and echoed, 'Terrible.'

They both rolled their eyes and sucked in their breath: 'Shocking!'

The doctor could hardly refrain from laughing.

'What do you want, then, if you don't want to go into hospital?'

'Special treatment, that's what, the best.'

'I'll speak to Sister Julienne, the Sister-in-Charge of the Midwives of St Raymund Nonnatus. They are a very old established order of midwives who have been practising in the area since the time when Dr Coffin wrote his book. Sister Julienne might agree to accept Mavis.'

Sister Julienne accepted Mavis for antenatal care and for delivery at home, but she would require a doctor present at the birth because of the age of the mother having her first baby.

Meg rapidly became an expert in pregnancy, antenatal care and childbirth. She studied Nicholas Culpeper, a seventeenth-century apothecary famous for his herbal remedies, and his *A Guide to Having Lusty Children*, published in 1651. She applied all his remedies to Mavis. She found on a stall a copy of Culpeper's *Directory for Midwives*, published in 1656, which greatly impressed her, because the burden of the text was the castigation of all other manuals on midwifery – an easy approach that suited Meg's turn of mind precisely. However, she failed to notice the confession made by Culpeper that the book contained no practical advice as he, the author, knew nothing about midwifery.

Then she discovered Jane Sharp's *The Whole Art of Midwifery* of 1671 and started talking about lily, hyacinth, columbine, jasmine and cyclamen, to hasten delivery and ease the pains of childbirth; cinnamon and aniseed to nourish the child in the womb; poultices of fennel and parsley to lay over the abdomen; caraway and cumin seeds to increase the breast milk. 'Ancient wisdom,' Meg said, with a knowing air.

In the 1950s the rules of the Central Midwives Board required women to be seen at antenatal clinic once a month for the first six months; once a fortnight from six to eight months pregnancy; and each week during the final month. This was not good enough for Megan'mave. They came in to clinic every week, and sometimes twice a week, because we held two clinics, one in Poplar and the other in Millwall. Each visit they reported another serious illness which must be examined at once, and every new complaint was accompanied by a new book, or a new chapter in an old book that had suddenly revealed there was something wrong with Mavis, which the ignorant and neglectful doctors and midwives had failed to notice. The consequences would have been calamitous had it not been for the untiring vigilance of Meg.

It had been an exhausting Tuesday afternoon clinic in the converted church hall next to Nonnatus House – hot, sticky, smelly, sweaty. I was just about at the end of my tether, having examined dozens of women, some of them none too clean, and boiled up dozens of urine samples to test for albumen, nearly being sick at the stench every time, when Megan'mave entered the clinic door. Four midwives were on duty, and one of the nuns. We all looked sideways at each other and groaned inwardly. My table was nearest to the door, and unfortunately no one was with me. Megan'mave sat down, and without a word of introduction Meg barked, 'Well, what 'ave you got to say to vis?' She pushed a book towards me.

Wearily I looked up at the four black eyes staring at me accusingly. The headscarves were pulled down low, identical features wore the same expression of mistrust, four hands rested on the table, four solid feet were planted firmly on the floor. They had come to do battle.

'But Megan, I don't know . . .'

'Me name's not Megan!'

'Oh, I'm sorry.' I fumbled with my notes to gain time.

'My name is Meg, short for Margaret, see, an' I'll thank you to get it right, young lady.'

'Oh, I see. Certainly. Now what is the trouble?'

'The fillipin toobs is crossed.'

'The what?'

'Fillipin toobs. Don't you listen?'

'Yes, I heard you. But what are fillipin toobs?'

'Call yerself a midwife, an' you don't know?'

'I'm sorry, but I've never heard of them.'

Both women drew in their breath and rolled their eyes backwards and sideways in an exaggerated expression of disbelief. 'Shocking!' 'Sheer ignorance!' 'Never 'eard of 'em?' 'Medical incompetence!' They shook their heads, groaned, rolled their eyes and tut-tutted to each other. One of them behaving in such a way would have raised a smile, but the two of them with identical body language doing it was indescribably funny. This is going to be rich, I thought to myself and perked up no end.

'You will have to enlighten me,' I said sweetly.

'We've got to teach ve midwives, 'ave we?'

'I'm only a student,' I murmured humbly.

'Shockin. An' vey call this the National 'ealth Service.'

They showed the whites of their eyes again and sucked in their breath, and I had to dig my fingernails into my skin to prevent myself from laughing.

'Well, young lady, since you don't know, I'll 'ave to tell you. The fillipin toobs is 'ere in vis book.' She opened a grimy old book at what seemed to be a very primitive sketch of the female genital tract. Meg pointed with a dirty fingernail.

'Vat's the toobs, an' Mave's, they're crossed, see?'

Mave put on her martyred look, and groaned again. Meg took her hand.

'Vat's what's doin' it. Makin' 'er feel bad.'

'I'm not sure that I understand you.'

'No, you don't know nuffink, you don't. I'm tellin' yer, the fillipin toobs is crossed, an' it's makin' her bad. Now d'you understand?'

'I understand the Fallopian tubes. But they can't be crossed. It's not possible.'

'Course it's possible. Don't try no cover-ups. You can't fool me, you can't. They've tried that afore, but I'm too smart for 'em. Medical blunders, an' medical cover-ups. Mave, she 'ad 'er 'pendix out when she was fourteen – show 'em yer scar, Mave.' Mave obligingly lifted her skirts. 'an' vey sewed 'er up wrong an' got the toobs crossed, an' she's bin sufferin' ever since, see? Oooh, I could write a book on the sufferin' she's 'ad. Write a book, I could.'

Both women started rolling their eyes again, and I had to stand up to control myself. Trixie had finished her afternoon's work, and she sauntered over, sensing a bit of fun. 'What's up?' she enquired.

Meg described for her the whole saga of the 'pendix and the fillipin toobs, and the medical blunders that Mavis had suffered, starting with the withered arm caused by a midwife who should have known better, and welliclose weins stripped by a surgeon as didn't know what 'e was doin', and golf stones the doctor wouldn't do nuffink abaht, and the fact that now Mave was pregnant she was sufferin' because the toobs was all crossed.

Trixie was an outspoken girl, short on tact.

'Don't be daft,' she said bluntly.

Meg leaped to her feet and clenched her fists. She would possibly have struck Trixie full in the face, had not the gentle Novice Ruth come up at that moment.

'Ladies, ladies, please, what is the matter?'

'Matter? She called me daft, vat's what's the matter.'

Novice Ruth looked disapprovingly at Trixie, who shrugged. 'You haven't heard the story yet.'

The nun turned to Megan'mave.

'I apologise if one of our nurses has been rude to you. I assure you it will not happen again. Now, please tell me your troubles. I'm sure we can help.'

The opportunity was too good to miss, and the two women jointly, with mirrored body language, moans and groans, rolling eyes and hissing breath, recalled every misfortune that Mavis had suffered at the hands of an incompetent and hostile medical profession.

Novice Ruth was very sympathetic, but she looked a bit vague.

'What can we do to help?' she enquired.

'It's the fillipin toobs what's crossed. They wants uncrossin,' said Meg emphatically.

Novice Ruth looked as though she was losing the plot.

'Fallopian tubes,' I whispered.

'Oh, I see. But how can they be crossed?' she enquired innocently.

'I'm tellin' yer. Ve surgeon, 'e sewed 'er up wrong wiv her 'pendix an' got ve toobs crossed. Vat's why she's sufferin'. Bin sufferin' for years, she 'as.'

Novice Ruth looked down at her crucifix, and I saw a flicker of a smile play at the corners of her mouth.

'I will examine Mavis,' she said quietly. 'Please follow me to the examination room.'

Meg gave me a triumphant glance and shot a look of pure venom at Trixie. Mave undressed as requested and lay down on the couch. Novice Ruth, an expert and experienced midwife, examined Mavis, asked several questions which Meg answered, and when she had finished the examination said, 'Both you and your baby seem to be in perfect condition for thirty-two weeks of pregnancy. The baby is developing normally, and the heart-beat is good. You, Mavis, are perfectly fit. I have examined everything possible – heart, blood pressure, urine. I can find nothing wrong with you. If you are suffering discomfort, I think it is probably heartburn, or wind, which afflicts a lot of pregnant women.'

'Heartburn? Wind? What about ve toobs?' shouted Meg.

'I was coming to the toobs,' lied the saintly Novice Ruth convincingly. 'I have examined them carefully, and can assure you that although they may have been crossed at the time of the unfortunate appendicitis operation, they have now uncrossed themselves. Nature is a wonderful healer. You have nothing more to fear from the Fallopian tubes.'

MEG THE GYPSY

The practice was extremely busy. Every midwife will tell you the same story. You can tick over comfortably for weeks, and then suddenly there are more women in labour than midwives to cope with them. Some say it is the phases of the moon, others say it is the local beer.

Trixie had been working all night. A delivery at 10 p.m. and another at 4 a.m. had left her exhausted, and she still had a day's work to get through. An hour of sleep after lunch had helped, though the evening visits were heavy. At nine, a long luxuriant bath with her favourite salts had eased her mind, and she was looking forward to the bliss of sleep.

The telephone rang. Not me, thought Trixie. Someone else is on first call, and she sank deeper into the water, turning on the hot tap with her toes.

A moment later there was a bang on the door.

'Trixie, old sport. You in there?' Chummy's voice sounded through the door.

'Yes.'

'I've got to go out. You're on first call now.'

'What! You're joking. I can't be.'

'Sorry and all that. But Cynthia is already out on a delivery, and Jennifer has a day off. It's up to you.'

'I just don't believe it.' Trixie groaned and felt sleep enveloping her.

'What did you say? Never mind, I can't hang around.'

Chummy's footsteps retreated down the corridor.

Trixie's tired mind refused to take in the reality of the situation. She felt she might doze off in the bath, but forced herself to get out, dried and into bed, where she immediately fell into a deep and dreamless sleep.

At 11.30 the phone rang. Usually a midwife on first call will hear it instantly, be out of bed and alert within seconds. The subconscious will keep the mind half-awake, ready for action. But Trixie slept on. Eventually the persistent ringing penetrated her ears, and she awoke confused – someone had better answer that damned phone, she thought. Then she remembered Chummy's bang on the bathroom door.

Horrified, she struggled out of bed and picked up the phone.

'Yes. Nonnatus House here. Who is it?'

'And about time, too! What d'you fink yer playing at? She coulda died afore you answered the telephone,' a harsh female voice barked.

Trixie shook her head vigorously, trying to focus her thoughts.

'Who is dying? What is the trouble?'

'Trouble? The trouble is you. You lazy good-for-nothing.'

Trixie groaned and sank onto the wooden bench beside the telephone, but her training came to the rescue. Mechanically she heard herself say, 'Please give me your name and address and tell me, as clearly as you can, what is the matter.'

'It's Meg, from Mile End, and it's Mave, see. Mave's in labour, and you gotta come quick.'

The clouds were lifting from Trixie's tired brain.

'But Mave is not due yet. Not for another month.'

'Don't you come vat one over me. You just get 'ere at the double, or I'll report yer to the authorities for negligence, refusin' to come to a woman in labour.'

Trixie was wide awake now. Mave was thirty-six weeks pregnant. A premature labour would be a serious matter, and dangerous for the baby.

'I'll come straight away,' she said and put down the phone.

Trixie hastened into her uniform. But before going to the clinical room for her bag, she went to the Sisters' corridor and knocked on Sister Bernadette's door to tell her that, according to Meg, Mavis was in premature labour.

'Go and assess the situation and inform me. If premature labour is established, she must be transferred immediately to hospital,' were the instructions.

Trixie collected her bag and attached it to her bicycle. She had a three-mile ride, and a fine drizzle was falling, the sort that gets you damp all over. Her legs were heavy, and turning the pedals seemed like one of the twelve labours of Hercules.

She reached the Mile End Road, which is broad and straight, and cycled along it looking for the turning, but missed it, and had to go back. This can't be happening to me, she thought. Once in the narrow street of identical terraced houses, the only light in a window led her to the correct address. She was met at the door by Meg.

'Call vis straight away, do yer? More like a snail's pace, I call it. You bin twenty minutes gettin' 'ere.'

If Meg thought she could intimidate Trixie, she was in for a shock.

'If you can get here any quicker on a bicycle, you are welcome to try. Now, cut the criticism and take me to your sister.'

In the bedroom it was hot and stuffy. A big fire was burning, and the windows were closed tight. Mave was lying on the bed moaning pathetically, clutching her stomach with both hands.

'See, she's sufferin' somefink wicked. Bin like vis for a couple of hours, she 'as. Somefink wicked.'

Mave moaned and whimpered. 'When's ve baby comin? I can't stand much more of vis. They'll 'ave to take it away. Cut me open.'

Meg echoed, 'She can't stand no more. It's 'orrible. Too much for 'er, with 'er weak constitooshun.'

Trixie took off her coat and sat down beside the bed.

'Ainchoo goin' a do nuffink?' demanded Meg.

'I am doing something,' said Trixie, 'I'm assessing the progress of labour.'

''Sessin'? Wha'choo mean, 'sessin'? She needs treatment. Dr Smellie in 'is book, 'e says the midwife should put ve woman on a birfin' stool.'

'Birthing stool! Where do you get that rubbish from?'

'It's 'ere in 'is book. You read it. You're supposed to know about vese fings.'

Trixie glanced at the aged book.

'That is two hundred years out of date. Don't cram your head with a lot of stuff you don't understand. No one uses birthing stools any more.'

Meg stared hard at Trixie, and recognition dawned.

'Ain't you ve one what called me daft?'

'Perhaps I did, and I wouldn't have been far wrong. Now be quiet with all your mumbo-jumbo, and let me get on with my job.'

'Look 'ere, I'm not 'avin' you. You can send for someone what knows what to do.'

'There's no one else on call. I should be delighted to go back to bed, but there is no one else who could come. You're stuck with me, and if you don't like it you can lump it. Now be quiet. I want to examine Mave.'

Trixie pulled back the bedclothes and palpated the uterus. The head was above the symphysis pubis, but she could not feel anything else definitive. There seemed to be lumps all over the place. She stood still, thinking, head on one side.

'Well, Miss Stoopid, what you goin' a do now?'

'I'm going to listen to the baby's heartbeat,' replied Trixie coldly, trying hard to ignore the woman's insults. She took out her Pinards and applied it to the abdomen.

'You better get on wiv this and stop messin' abaht. My sister's in labour, I tells yer.'

'Be quiet, will you? I can't hear a thing with you making all that noise.'

Meg rolled her eyes to the ceiling and sucked in her breath, indicating her total lack of confidence in the procedure.

Trixie listened carefully and counted a steady 120 beats per minute. She stood up, satisfied.

'Well, the baby is quite healthy. Now I must ask you some questions. When did you first feel contractions, Mave?'

Meg answered, 'About ten o'clock. Came on sudden. Terrible it was.'

'Will you be quiet. I'm asking Mave. Not you.'

Trixie was too tired to be patient. She turned to Mave.

'And how frequent are the contractions?'

Meg answered regardless: 'All ve time. Can'choo see? She's sufferin'.'

Trixie's slender reserves of patience snapped.

'Will you shut up and get out of here? Either you go or I will go. I'm not prepared to carry on like this.'

Trixie was taking a risk and she knew it. If she deserted a woman in labour the consequences would be severe. But the gamble paid off. Meg left.

Trixie could now devote her attention to Mave. She was puzzled because, although she had been observing Mave for at least twenty minutes, and although Mave looked and sounded as if she were in advanced labour, there appeared to be no contractions.

'When did this start?'

'About ten o'clock,' Mave groaned.

'And how frequent were the contractions? Did you time them?'

Mave looked pained.

'They was all ve time. Never stoppin'. Meg says Dr Smellie says . . .'

'Never mind what Dr Smellie says. Contractions don't just start and never stop. It's not possible.'

Mave assumed her martyr's expression.

'You don't understand. I'm dyin'. You don't care.'

She hung onto her belly and rolled onto her side.

'Stop all this fuss,' barked Trixie. 'You are no more dying

than I am. I haven't seen a contraction since I came into this house.'

'That's 'cause you don't know nuffink. Meg, she says . . .'

'I won't hear any more about Meg. Now tell me, when did you last open your bowels?'

'What?' Mave jerked round to face Trixie.

'You heard. When?'

'I'm not sure. Couple of weeks ago, p'raps.'

'You are constipated. And what did you have for supper?'

'Gooseberry pie and custard.'

'Green gooseberries?'

'Yes. Two 'elpin's.'

'Well, that's the trouble, then. You've got gut ache. You're not in labour at all, you old fraud. Getting me out of bed for a stomach ache!' Trixie was furious. 'Do you realise I have been working for forty hours with no sleep, and you wake me up for nothing. I will give you some castor oil and an enema, and then I am going back to my bed and leaving you to get on with it.'

That was the first of many false labours. During the next four weeks, twice a week, Meg called us out. Several times she sent Sid, their husband, with a message of impending disaster. Poor man! He stood cap in hand, his sheep eyes watering with embarrassment, muttering something quite unintelligible. Wearily we had to attend the call to assess the situation, but we knew that we were being led up the garden path. Meg was never grateful, nor even polite. She continued to tell us that we didn't know our job, and we should read some of the books she had been readin', an' Mave should be confined in a darkened room, with a binding on her belly, an' 'ad we got ve muvver's caudle an' ve birfin' stool, an' smellin' salts an' salt candle, an' she 'ad jest got a book by Dr Jacob Rueff which was written in Latin in 1554, but she'd got an English translation, called *The Expert Midwife*, which says that ve baby's cord must be cut with a special knife which was blessed by the Bishop an' if it's a baby boy ve cord must be cut long, because as 'e grew up it would make 'is penis long, see, an' did we know all vis, wha' she knewed? It was difficult to answer without giggling, and what with Doctors Smellie, Rueff and Coffin, the whole saga became an on-going joke around the big dining table each lunchtime, when we were all assembled together.

However, quite inadvertently, Meg did us a service, and I, for one, learned a great deal about the horrifying conditions in which women had given birth in previous centuries.

Sid stood at the convent door again. The market had just closed, and he was in his workman's clothes. He was too conscious of his appearance to step into the hallway. Meekly he handed Trixie a note and muttered, 'Meg, she says ...' He shook his head sorrowfully, raised his eyes appealingly and left.

It was just after lunch, morning visits were done, the practice was reasonably quiet, and we had settled down in our sitting room for a nice, peaceful afternoon. Trixie burst in, note in hand.

'I won't go. It's that infernal woman again.'

Cynthia looked up from her book.

'Try telling that to Sister Julienne.'

'But it will be another false labour.'

'Very probably. But you are on first call, and you can't refuse to go.'

Trixie sighed noisily, defeated by the facts.

'Well, I won't stay long, that's all.'

Grimly she cycled the well-worn path to Mile End. Meg was at the door.

'Oh, it's you, is it?'

'Yes. I'm sorry to say it is.'

'Well, I 'ope as 'ow you knows what yer doin' vis time, because Mave's in labour an' we don't want no bunglers.'

'Speak for yourself,' said Trixie drily.

She went upstairs to the bedroom. It was pitch dark inside,

so she went straight to the curtains and drew them back. Daylight flooded in.

'Don't do that,' shouted Meg.

'I must see what I am doing.'

'It's dangerous.'

'Yes, it will be dangerous if I can't see.'

'I mean, a woman in labour must be confined in a dark room.'

'Rubbish.'

'Don't you rubbish me.'

'I will if you talk rubbish. Now I've come to look at Mave, not to talk to you.'

She went over to the bed. Mave was sitting up, looking quite comfortable.

'Meg gets worried. I 'ad a few pains an hour ago, but they've gone, an' I reckons as 'ow you can go home now.'

Trixie ground her teeth crossly.

'You'll cry wolf once too often.'

'Wha'choo mean?'

'I mean if you carry on like this, you'll call when you really need us, we won't believe you, and we won't come.'

'That's negligence,' shouted Meg.

'It'll be your own fault.'

Both women sucked in their breath – 'shockin', a disgrace, I tells yer. Vey don't care, vey don't. Can't trust no one.'

Trixie ignored them and sat down beside Mave.

'I must examine you, and then I shall go. Lie flat, please.'

She palpated the uterus, and could feel a head low down, which satisfied her that the woman was close to full term, but not necessarily in labour. The foetal heart was very vigorous and could be heard in several places. Just then, the uterus tightened, and Mave gave a slight moan. Trixie sat still with her hand on the uterus, and took out her watch, counting about fifty seconds before the tightening relaxed.

Meg opened her mouth to speak, but Trixie silenced her.

'Would you go and make a cup of tea, please? Mave looks thirsty and needs a drink.'

Meg, grumbling about not being anyone's servant, left the room.

Trixie sat quietly. Ten minutes later she felt another contraction, slightly stronger than the first.

'You are in labour, Mave. And this time it is not a false alarm. Your baby will be born today.'

Meg came in with the tea.

'I'm in labour, Meg. Our baby'll be born soon.'

Mave looked unusually cheerful, but Meg turned white, and the teacups rattled in the saucers so much that they nearly fell out of her shaking hands.

'I must go to the telephone on the corner to ring Sister Bernadette,' said Trixie.

'You're not leavin' 'er. That's negligence, that is,' shouted Meg.

'It would be negligence if I didn't go. I'll be back before the next contraction comes. You two have your tea, and you can discuss my negligence while I'm gone.'

Sister Bernadette said she would come straight away. A primigravida of thirty-eight years requires careful treatment. Mave had been told quite categorically that she should have her baby delivered in hospital, but she had refused. The fear of hospitalisation was so entrenched in working-class women of limited education in those days that nothing could shift it. They associated hospitals with the old infirmaries that were converted workhouses. Very likely if she had been taken into hospital, Mave would have been so tense and terrified that the psychological strain would have had a damaging effect on labour. So a home delivery, with an experienced midwife and if possible a doctor present, was the best compromise.

Trixie returned to the bedroom, which was in darkness again. She went over to the curtains to draw them back, but Meg stopped her.

'She's gotta be in a dark room.'

'She has not.'

'She must. Ve book, it says . . .'

'I don't care what your old book says. I'm in charge here, not you.'

Quite a tussle ensued, but the curtains were finally drawn back, filling the room with daylight. Mave was sitting up in bed looking quite fit and cheerful, but Meg was hovering around, grumbling under her breath and throwing nasty looks at Trixie.

'If you two have finished your tea,' said Trixie, 'you can take the cups away. I want to prepare my equipment for a delivery.'

Meg took the cup and saucer from Mave and stared into it. She gasped, and stared harder, then went deathly pale and trembled all over. The cup fell from her hand and shattered into pieces on the floor. She moaned, 'Oh no, no, no,' and fell against the wardrobe, half fainting. Trixie grabbed her arm.

'Hold on! Steady. What's the matter with you?'

Meg seemed unable to speak.

'You had better get out of here.'

Trixie led her to the door. The woman looked stricken and clung to her arm for support.

Finally Meg found her voice. 'It's an omen, an evil omen.'

'What is?'

'Ve tea leaves. An' then ve cup breakin'. It's bad. Bad. I ain't seen worse.'

'What are you talking about?'

'Vey never lie. Never.'

'Who don't?'

'It's an omen. Bad, I tells yer. Ve tea leaves never lie.'

Sister Bernadette arrived, required to see Mave at once, and said that the doctor would come as soon as he had finished his surgery. She examined Mave vaginally and assessed an os two fingers dilated with a foetal head low down, anterior presentation. The foetal heart was strong, the mother relaxed and cheerful. Mave looked happier than she had been throughout pregnancy.

By contrast, Meg was going to pieces. She hovered in the doorway, whimpering and moaning. Her face was the colour of one of her old books. Whenever Mave had a contraction, Meg groaned and rolled her eyes and many times looked near to collapsing. She moaned 'Vis is goin' to kill 'er, vis is. She can't stand it. She's got a weak constitooshun. You gotta do somefink – it can't go on like vis. The omens are bad.'

Quietly but firmly Sister Bernadette ordered her to leave the delivery room. Meg wailed and whined, but just for once Mave did not agree with her. She looked at Sister Bernadette and nodded. Then she said, 'You go, Meg. I'll be all right without you.'

Labour was progressing normally. Sister Bernadette and Trixie settled down to waiting and watching. Sister took out her breviary and said her evening office. Time ticked by. The doctor came, saw that things were going well and said that he had a few evening visits to make, but would return after they were completed. Trixie showed him to the door.

Returning through the living room, she heard strange sounds coming from the kitchen, so she looked round the door. The kitchen was filled with a weird greenish-yellow light. Smoke was coming from a burner and she spied Meg dressed from head to foot in a long green robe. A green scarf covered her head, pulled down low over her brow. Her face was white, and dark circles surrounded black, black eyes. She did not see Trixie, so engrossed was she in her activity.

Meg the gypsy was dealing out cards. She was cutting the pack methodically, laying down four cards face upwards, slowly and deliberately, then cutting the pack again. She was muttering, 'Death! I see it. Mortuary. Coffin. Grave.' Then she would shuffle the cards and cut again. 'Ve same. Always ve same. Them cards never lie.' She shuffled again, and laid down four different cards, and lastly, slowly, fearfully, cut the pack once more. Her skin shone with a ghastly greenish light. 'Ve same. First, ve teacup, now ve cards, vey cannot lie. Death. Death.' Her head fell forwards onto her arms, and the cards slithered across the floor.

MAVE THE MOTHER

The atmosphere in the delivery room was quiet and cheerful. Sister Bernadette had a presence. She was a young woman of about thirty to thirty-five, deeply religious, and her monastic vocation filled her with happiness. She was also a highly professional nurse and midwife. She radiated control, confidence and calm, which had a soothing effect on any woman with whom she was working. Mave looked quite different. Her martyred air had gone, her eyes were bright, and she seemed excited. Contractions were regular, every ten minutes. Sister had given Mavis a dose of castor oil, and Trixie had shaved her and given her an enema (the required practice in those days).

The doctor returned at 9 p.m. and agreed that he would stay. General practitioners, although they were not trained obstetricians, were the first point of call for a midwife. In fact, a medical student's training involved 50 per cent clinical experience in hospital under an obstetrician and 50 per cent district midwifery under a midwife. Consequently the general practitioner, unless he had a great deal of experience, frequently knew less about childbirth than the midwife. This could sometimes lead to a strained situation, particularly if the midwife did not trust the doctor's judgement. But we were fortunate. The Sisters of St Raymund Nonnatus had been practising for so long in the East End of London, with such a good record, that all the local doctors respected their judgement.

Mave was sleeping lightly between contractions, having had a dose of chloral hydrate. At 11 p.m. the waters broke. Sister prepared to do a vaginal examination, but with the next contraction the head was visible. She told Trixie to scrub up and to take the delivery.

The second stage of labour was surprisingly quick. Mave was nearly forty, and this was her first pregnancy, but she was relaxed and comfortable, the uterine muscles were strong, and her perineum stretched without difficulty. Only two more contractions were necessary and the head crowned. Sister Bernadette smiled at Mave, who looked up at her trustingly.

'Now, with the next contraction I don't want you to push. Just pant and concentrate on your breathing, because we want the baby's head to be born slowly.'

Mave was wonderful. We had all expected her to create a terrible fuss during labour and refuse to cooperate, but not at all. With the next contraction the head was born. Trixie waited for restitution of the head, and after only a few moments the shoulder slid under the pubic arch and the baby was born.

'She's a little girl.'

'Oh, thank God. I don't like boys,' said Mave.

The baby gave a lusty scream, and Meg put her head round the door. She was still wearing her strange green outfit, and her black eyes devoured us all, her gloomy features contrasting with Mave's radiant smile.

'We wan'ed a li'le girl, Meg, and we got one.'

'She'll die. I seed it all.'

'Don't talk like that.' Sister Bernadette was angry.

'Worms an' coffins. It's in ve cards.'

'Will you go away. I won't have you in here,' the nun said.

'Vey never lie.'

'I never heard such nonsense. Now go away this minute.'

Meg rolled her eyes, making herself look weirder than ever.

'It's all worms an' coffins,' she muttered as she left, shaking her head mournfully.

If Mavis heard these words of doom she did not seem to take any notice, as she cuddled her baby in a state of exhausted euphoria.

The cord was clamped and cut, and Sister took the baby to examine and weigh her. She was a very small baby, weighing only 4 lb 12 oz, but was not premature and appeared to be normal and healthy in every way. Trixie left the baby to Sister, and concentrated on the management of the third stage of labour. There were no contractions, so Trixie waited. After ten minutes she decided to massage the fundus to stimulate another contraction. The uterus felt bulky, and then she saw a movement, like a kick, as the wall of the uterus rose and fell briefly. She put her hand over the place, and it happened again.

'Sister, I think there is another baby in here,' she said.

Midwife and doctor were at the bedside in an instant.

'That would account for a small first baby,' Sister said as she palpated the uterus. 'You are quite right, nurse, and I think it is a transverse lie. Pass me the Pinards, please.'

She listened carefully. The heartbeat could be heard low down, just over the pubic bone. It was rapid but regular. Sister counted 140 beats per minute. She asked the doctor to confirm the lie of the baby. He said that he could not tell and would rely on Sister's judgement, but whatever the lie of the baby he advised we call the Flying Squad, and immediately transfer Mavis to hospital.

Until that moment Mavis had appeared unconcerned and relaxed, but at the word 'hospital' she wailed in anguish. Meg rushed into the room.

'Wha'choo doin' to 'er?' Her voice was harsh and aggressive.

'Vey're goin' 'a put me away. In an infirmary.'

'Over my dead body.'

'It's not an infirmary,' said the doctor, 'it's a modern hospital, where Mavis will get the best treatment.'

'She'll never come out alive. Or never come out a' all. I know wha' goes on in them places. Vey keeps the likes of Mave an' me, an' never lets 'em out. Uses 'em for sperimnents, that's wha' vey do.'

Mavis became almost hysterical, shrieking and sobbing, 'I won't go,' and Meg threw her arms protectively around her. Sister felt Mave's pulse, which had been normal until that moment, but had now risen to an alarming 110 beats per minute.

'If this goes on, the baby will be in serious distress,' remarked Sister. 'We must prepare for a twin birth at home. You will not be sent to hospital, Mavis. But Meg, you must go. I am not prepared to deliver the second baby with you in the room.'

Meg rolled her eyes. 'I told yer, didn't I? It was an evil omen wiv the tea leaves. An' ve cards. Vey'll die. You mark my words.'

Sister pushed her out of the room. Then she scrubbed up. She was calm and controlled.

'There have been no contractions since the birth of the first baby. If the foetus is lying transversely this will help me. First I must make quite sure of the lie of the baby, and secondly ascertain whether or not the waters have broken. If the uterus is inert, and the membranes intact, it is usually possible to turn the baby to the correct position for delivery. I want you to monitor the foetal heart every few minutes, nurse.'

Trixie listened and said the heartbeat remained at 140. Sister carried out a vaginal examination.

'Yes. I can feel the amniotic sac bulging through the dilated os – splendid – but I cannot identify the presenting part. It is certainly not a head. It might be a breech, I suppose, but I cannot be sure. I'm not going to do too much . . . remember, that, nurse. Never try poking around too much in a twin birth. You might rupture the membranes, and if an arm or a shoulder is presenting and descends into the birth canal, you will then have an impacted foetus which cannot be delivered vaginally.'

Sister withdrew her hand and removed her gloves.

'I am going to attempt an external version – unless you want to do it, doctor?'

The doctor shook his head.

'It would be better if you did it, Sister.'

Sister nodded.

'What is the foetal heartbeat, nurse?'

'One hundred and fifty; a little raised, Sister.'

'Yes. Now Mavis, lie quite still and relax. You are not in any pain, are you?'

'Nope.'

'I have to turn your baby. I am going to exert a lot of pressure. I want you to breathe deeply all the time and concentrate on relaxing.'

Mavis nodded and smiled. Since the threat of hospitalisation had been removed, she had been quite relaxed, and her pulse had dropped to a steady seventy-two beats per minute.

'I want you to watch me carefully, nurse, so that you will know how to do it another time.' Trixie fervently hoped that would never happen.

'Here in the right iliac fossa is the head . . . feel it, nurse . . . I'm correct, am I not?' Trixie nodded, though she could feel no identifiable head. 'And over here is the breech . . . can you feel that?'

Trixie nodded vaguely. 'I think so, Sister.'

'Good. Now what I cannot tell is whether the foetus is lying dorso-anterior or dorso-posterior. You said that you saw and felt a kick. Where? Point to the spot.'

Trixie did so.

'Hmmm – not much help. Now what I want to do is to flex the foetus into a ball as much as I can, which will enable me to turn it more readily.'

Sister grasped what she had identified as the head and the breech and slowly closed her hands together.

'Yes . . . it is moving . . . the foetus is definitely flexing. The head is closing towards the breech, and the back is curved under the fundus. Splendid! Feel it now, nurse. Can you feel the difference?'

Trixie felt but could not truthfully say she noticed anything different. The doctor felt also and nodded approvingly.

'You must have X-ray hands, Sister,' he murmured.

'I must turn the foetus now, and I want to turn it so that it follows its nose. About a quarter circle will be sufficient, and the head will be presenting. This is going to hurt, Mave, but only for a minute. I want you to relax as much as you can.'

Sister Bernadette, the expert midwife, with the ball of her right thumb behind the head, and with the fingers of the left hand beneath the breech, firmly and slowly, her two hands working together, feeling her way, successfully achieved external cephalic version of the foetus. She turned the baby.

'The head is now lying just above the pubic arch . . . can you feel it, nurse?'

To her surprise, Trixie could and she nodded enthusiastically.

'To ensure that it remains in that position I am going to ask you to hold it there . . . grasp it firmly . . . and hold the breech with the other hand. After version a foetus can slip back into its former position. I am going to puncture the membranes to permit the head to engage. This can usually be done quite easily with blunt forceps.'

Sister scrubbed up again and punctured the membranes. Amniotic fluid flowed over the bed.

'While I am here I will want to feel the foetal skull to find the position of the fontanelle, which will tell me if it is an anterior or a posterior presentation . . . ah, marvellous! The head is well down in the pelvis. Couldn't be better. Now all we need are some good contractions and your other baby will be born.' She smiled at Mavis, who responded warmly.

They waited, but still a contraction did not come. Trixie listened to the foetal heart again. It was 160. Sister and doctor looked at each other without speaking.

Minutes ticked by. Sister looked at her watch.

'Twenty-five minutes have passed since the birth of the first baby, and no contraction. The foetal heartbeat is going up. We cannot allow this to go on beyond thirty minutes. Why do I say that, nurse?'

Trixie was startled by the sudden question. She hadn't a clue! She mumbled something about 'The mother needs to rest'.

'Nonsense!' snapped Sister Bernadette. 'Didn't they teach

you anything in the classroom? You'd better pay attention, because there is no teacher like experience. One day you may find yourself in a similar situation, with no one to help you.'

Trixie was terrified at the thought, but muttered, 'Yes, Sister.'

'We cannot allow the uterus to rest for too long because of the risk to the mother and baby. We do not know the condition of the placenta, which is the life blood of the foetus. If the twins are uniovular . . . and what does that mean, nurse?'

'It means that they have developed from one ovum.'

'Correct. That would mean that, after the birth of the first baby, there is the possibility of the placenta separating from the uterine wall while the second twin is still in utero. I need not continue.'

Sister indicated that Mavis was listening to the viva voce, but her unfinished sentence protected Mavis from hearing that if the placenta of uniovular twins separated after the birth of the first baby and before the second was born, the second twin would be robbed of its blood supply and would die in utero. If that were not bad enough, the risk of haemorrhage might kill the mother also, because contraction and retraction of the uterine muscle controls bleeding during the third stage of labour. If a second foetus is still in the uterus, its presence will interfere with the third stage, and the raw placental site will bleed freely.

Sister asked Trixie to record the foetal heart again. It was still 160.

'Satisfactory. Now I want to stimulate the uterus. There are three simple ways in which we can do this. What are they, nurse?'

Trixie's mind went blank.

'Really! I sometimes wonder what they taught you in the classroom. You did have lectures on twin births?'

'Yes. I think so, Sister.'

'You only think so! I trust you were not asleep during the lectures, nurse.'

'Oh no, Sister. Never,' said Trixie untruthfully.

'I hope not! Well, we can stimulate uterine contractions by puncturing the amniotic sac. This I have already done, and I did it to make the head engage after cephalic version. However, it has not stimulated uterine contractions. Secondly, we can massage the fundus, just as we do to stimulate the third stage of labour.'

Sister massaged the fundus vigorously, but it did not have the desired effect.

'If these two methods fail, we can put the first baby to the breast. And how will this help, nurse?'

Trixie was dreading another question, and this was the worst. She swallowed, and shook her head.

'As you will doubtless be aware, nurse, the posterior lobe of the pituitary gland produces a hormone we call pituitrin.'

Trixie nodded her head, and tried to look as if she already knew what Sister was talking about.

'Pituitrin, as you will know, plays a part in lactation.'

'Oh yes, of course, Sister.'

'Can you describe to me, please, the role of pituitrin in lactation?'

Me and my big mouth, thought Trixie, ruefully.

'Well, as you do not seem to know, I will tell you. The stimulation of the nipple by the infant activates the posterior lobe of the pituitary gland to secrete pituitrin, which acts on the unstriped muscle surrounding the breast lobules and ducts, producing a flow of milk. But also – and this is the important point – pituitrin stimulates contraction of the muscles of the uterus.'

Sister Bernadette put the baby to the breast, but she was too sleepy and would not suck.

'It is now thirty minutes since the birth of the first baby. Uterine inertia can go on for hours, and all the time the risk to mother and baby increases. This is where medical assistance is needed.'

The doctor was unpacking his case, laying out several drugs, syringes and instruments, including Haig Ferguson's obstetric forceps.

'What will be the first line of medical intervention, nurse?'

Trixie was on the spot again so she glanced at the doctor's equipment.

'Well, forceps, I suppose.'

'Nonsense. Forceps will be the *last* thing we use. First we must get the uterus to contract. In the past I have known quinine to be used, but it is not advisable. As you may remember, a synthetic preparation of pituitrin is now available, called Pitocin, which is much more reliable and safe, and which I am sure Doctor is planning to use.'

She looked towards the doctor.

'Quite right, Sister. I am preparing a small dose – 0.25 ml – to be injected intramuscularly. If the uterine muscles do not respond, the procedure can be repeated every half hour for two hours. But hopefully after the first injection we will see some action.'

'Pitocin is usually effective,' continued Sister, 'but there are certain specific contra-indications to its use. What are they, nurse?'

Again Trixie was under interrogation. She tried desperately to think back to her lectures, but was tired and couldn't remember a thing.

'Come now, nurse. This won't do at all. Pitocin should not be given if there is any risk to the mother or baby by stimulating the uterus. Firstly, disproportion; if it is apparent that a foetus cannot descend into a narrow or misshapen pelvis, as we see with a rachitic pelvis, giving Pitocin would be disastrous. Secondly, malpresentation: this baby was lying transverse or obliquely. If Pitocin had been given too early, before I carried out an external version, an impacted foetus would have been the result. Lastly, the condition of the foetus. What should be a contra-indication for the use of Pitocin, nurse?'

Finally something stirred at the back of Trixie's mind. 'The foetal heart.'

'Excellent. Foetal distress can be determined from the heartbeat. And I shall want another recording, please, before the injection is given.'

Trixie listened again. 'One hundred and seventy, Sister, and quite regular.'

'That is satisfactory because it is regular. It is when the heartbeat is swinging wildly that we should worry about foetal distress. I think we are ready, doctor.'

The doctor injected 0.25 ml, and they all waited in silence. Mavis, warm and comfortable, had fallen asleep. Her three attendants were tense and anxious. Sister sat with her hand resting on the fundus, but no contractions came. She listened to the foetal heart a couple of times. It was 170 and rising. Half an hour had passed. She looked at the doctor, who said, 'I think I will inject 0.30 ml this time, Sister.' She nodded in agreement.

More waiting. The foetal heart remained rapid, far too rapid, and Sister was biting her lip with anxiety. Another twenty minutes, and still no contractions came. Sister Bernadette and the doctor exchanged glances every so often, and Trixie could feel the mounting tension in the room.

It all happened at once, Trixie said later. A powerful movement of the uterus, and immediately a violent rush of blood from the vagina, a pint or more.

'The placenta has separated. Quick. Give me the foetal stethoscope,' cried Sister in alarm. Mavis was awake and the foetal heart was racing so fast that Sister could not count it.

'We have to get this baby out immediately. Mavis – you must come to the bottom of the bed – never mind about the blood, just slither down – now raise your legs to your chest. Nurse, hold the legs steady in the lithotomy position.'

There was no anaesthetic available. It was far too late even to give a Pethidine injection. Mavis had to bear the pain. The gas and air machine might have helped her a little, but no one would claim that it was a full anaesthetic.

Sister reached again for the Pinards. The heartbeat had dropped to a dangerously low eighty beats per minute. 'We haven't a moment to lose,' she whispered.

The doctor placed two fingers into the vagina and hooked them behind the perineum, pulling it as taut as possible. With sharp episiotomy scissors he then cut the perineum diagonally. Mavis let out a piercing scream, and Meg rushed into the room. Seeing Mavis in a lithotomy position surrounded by blood she yelled, 'Murder!' and rushed over to the bed. She attempted to fight the doctor, but Sister pulled her back by the shoulders. Meg turned on her like a tigress and slapped her face so hard that the poor Sister fell against the wall. But she stood up again quickly, her face burning.

'If you interfere, Mavis will die. There *is* no alternative. You may not believe it, but we know what we are doing. And we are doing it to save the life of mother and baby.' She repeated more emphatically: 'If you interfere, your sister will die.'

Meg stared at her blankly. The shock of Sister's words reduced her to silence.

'Now, if you want to help, and I am sure you do, you will hold this gas and air mask over your sister's face . . . keep it firm over her nose and mouth . . . turn the knob up to maximum and talk to Mavis quietly, try to keep her calm. This is going to hurt, but you can help a great deal if you do as I say. Mavis needs you. Her life depends on it.'

Meg calmed down. She administered the gas and air. Giving her something to do was the best thing that Sister could have suggested.

Sister Bernadette listened to the foetal heartbeat. It had dropped to sixty beats per minute, and was weak and irregular. The doctor inserted the first blade of the forceps into the vagina, muttering to Trixie, 'Whatever you do keep her legs in that position. Don't let her move.' Trixie, who was trembling and felt sick, put all her weight on the two legs.

'Sister, the os is still fully dilated, thank God, but the head is above the rim. Can you apply steady pressure on the fundus to try to force the baby down an inch or two? There's not a moment to lose.'

Sister grasped the fundus with both hands and pressed down as hard as she could. There was a massive spurt of blood and meconium from the vagina, splattering the doctor all over. He hardly noticed it.

'Quickly. The head is down a little. But more.'

Sister applied more pressure, and a contraction developed.

'That's better. It's coming. Now I can get hold of it.'

The doctor inserted the second blade of the forceps around the head of the baby. Muffled screams were heard from Mavis, behind the gas and air mask, and Meg was looking grim, but held the mask in place.

Slowly, steadily, the doctor pulled the forceps, with Sister applying pressure from above.

'Keep those legs still,' muttered Sister to Trixie. 'She must not move at this stage.' It took all of Trixie's strength to prevent Mavis from throwing herself off the bed.

Within half a minute the head was born. The baby's face had no colour. Sister immediately left the bedside, took a couple of swabs and a fine catheter, and tried to clean the airways, but the baby did not move or attempt to breathe.

The doctor hooked a finger under the presenting shoulder and with one swift movement pulled the baby upwards towards the mother's abdomen. It was another little girl, completely white and limp. She looked dead.

A mere ninety seconds had elapsed between the first haemorrhage and the birth of the baby, yet Trixie told us later that it had seemed like ninety minutes. Time had stretched unnaturally. Even the steady tick, tick, tick of the clock seemed to slow down, as if time itself were suspended.

The baby was separated from the mother. She was like a rag doll and seemed to be quite dead. Sister carried her near to the fire. The doctor stretched out his hand and touched a tiny arm that swung lifelessly. He looked at Sister.

'Do what you can,' he said sadly, 'we might have to . . .'

But there was no time to speculate. There was another spurt of fresh blood, and the cord, which was protruding from the vagina, lengthened.

'The placenta is coming. Quick, nurse, fetch a kidney dish,' he said.

Trixie tried to get one, but her legs were shaking and she could not move. The placenta slid out onto the floor.

'We will examine it later,' said the doctor, pushing it aside with his foot. 'First, I must control the haemorrhage.'

Blood continued to seep out, then another spurt of fresh blood. The prognosis for Mavis was not looking good. She was no longer in pain, but was extremely weak and sweating from shock. Meg's know-all arrogance had burst like a bubble. The speed and drama of events had shaken her. She sat quietly at Mave's head, stroking her hair, whispering words of love and comfort.

The doctor massaged the uterus vigorously and squeezed out clots by further kneading and fundal pressure. Mavis groaned and weakly moved a leg.

'I think that is all the residual blood clots. I need to administer intravenous Ergometrine, but I want you, nurse, to exert external bi-manual compression of the uterus while I am preparing the injection. Have you ever done it before?'

Trixie shook her head.

'This is what you do, then. It will be only for a minute or two, but we cannot allow the uterus to relax. If it does we might get another haemorrhage.'

'Right, then, stand here . . . press the left hand into the abdomen just above the umbilicus, like this. Now, clench your right hand into a fist and press down as far as possible behind the symphysis pubis . . . that's it . . . now push the ball of the uterus upwards and compress it between the two hands as hard as you can . . . harder . . . that's it. Keep it there.'

The doctor went over to his medical kit to draw up the injection. He returned to the bedside and bound the upper arm tightly in order to inject into a vein at the bend of the elbow. But he could not find a vein. Mavis had lost so much blood that her veins were flat and slippery. He made several attempts with no success. He swore under his breath.

'Keep that compression going, nurse. Another haemorrhage could be fatal. I must get an intramuscular injection. They take longer to work, but if I can't get a vein it will have to be an IM.'

Trixie continued exerting bi-manual compression of the uterus. She was feeling sick and faint, but the sight of Mavis looking so ill and the thought of another haemorrhage and its consequences kept her strength up.

The doctor returned and swiftly plunged the needle into Mavis's thigh. 'That'll do the trick.' Then, to Trixie: 'I'll take over now. I want you to go and ring the hospital.'

Meg interrupted. 'No. I won' let 'em take 'er.'

The doctor turned on her savagely.

'Will you be quiet, woman, and stop interfering. If Mavis had gone into hospital, as I advised in the first place six months ago, all this might never have happened.'

Meg held her peace.

Sister Bernadette had carried the baby closer to the fire and had wrapped a roll of soft cotton wool around her. She cleared the airways with a fine mucus catheter. Blood, mucus and meconium were sucked out of the nose, mouth and throat. She held the tongue forwards with fine baby forceps, because if the tongue is without muscle tone and flaccid, it can fall backwards into the throat, blocking the airways. She held the baby completely upside down for a few seconds, and then sucked out the airways again. She turned the baby face downwards and massaged the back from base of spine upwards, then cleared the airways once more. Next she undertook a procedure known as Eve's Rocking – that is, alternately raising the head and feet of the baby by about forty-five degrees. The baby did not respond. Sister administered mouth to mouth resuscitation by filling her cheeks with air and puffing three puffs into the tiny white lips, then twenty seconds of Eve's Rocking again, then three more puffs. After about two minutes of this procedure she listened to the baby's heartbeat.

Her face became radiant. 'I can hear a faint heartbeat – around eighty per minute. Praise the Lord.' And she continued her efforts. Suddenly the baby gave a short, convulsive gasp, sucking air into its lungs and then lay quite still again, making no further attempt to breathe. But a baby can take shallow breaths that are almost imperceptible to the observer. Sister could still hear a faint heartbeat, so she continued. A couple of minutes later the baby gave another convulsive gasp, repeated thirty seconds later, and this pattern continued for nearly half an hour, during which time the heartbeat increased to a healthy 120 per minute.

Sister Bernadette had no drugs, no oxygen, no incubator or modern equipment for resuscitating an infant with asphyxia pallida. She had only the methods described above, and the baby did not die.

The intramuscular injection of Ergometrine given to Mave by the doctor worked within five minutes. The uterus contracted into a firm hard ball, and all fears of further haemorrhage were removed. Mavis looked terribly ill, however. Her skin was white, cold and clammy, caused by pain and blood loss. She was in a state of obstetric shock, but her condition was stable. Sleep would benefit her, so the doctor gave an injection of morphine, which he could not have done while the baby was in utero. She dozed off in Meg's arms.

The doctor prepared for suturing. There was now no hurry, so he gave Mavis a local anaesthetic around the perineum and the vaginal wall, and sat back, waiting for it to take effect. Once the local anaesthetic had numbed the perineum, the doctor was able to repair the episiotomy. He was relieved to find that the cervix was not torn.

Meanwhile Trixie was down the road ringing the Flying Squad. She had taken off her gown and cap but had forgotten to take off her mask. There was blood on her hands and arms, and smeared down her uniform and legs. As she ran down the road she did not notice that people were looking at her rather strangely. It was not until she was inside the telephone box that she realised she did not have the three pennies on her with which to make a telephone call, so she stopped a passer-by. 'Can you let me have threepence for an urgent telephone call?' Only then did she notice the mask, so she pulled it off. Her hand was trembling, and she noticed the blood on it for the first time.

'I must have threepence. I forgot to bring it. I must ring the hospital.' Trixie's voice was shrill. Dubiously the man dug into his pocket and produced three pennies. 'Thanks.' She dived into the box, but her hand was shaking so much that she could not dial the number or put the pennies in the slot, so she called the man back.

'You're in a bad way, nurse,' he said.

Trixie felt too weak to answer, so she merely handed him a bit of paper.

'Ring that number for me, please.'

The phone rang, and a voice answered immediately. Briefly Trixie explained the situation and gave the address. 'We will send the Flying Squad immediately,' the voice said.

'Do you need any help getting back to the house?' asked the man kindly.

'I'll be all right. Thanks for your help.'

When Trixie returned to the house, Meg was shouting at the doctor and Sister.

'You murderers! Look wha' you done. You've hurt 'er. I'll

report you to ve authorities, I will. Look at ve blood. You nearly killed 'er, you did.'

The doctor tried to defend himself

'The placenta separated prematurely. That was the cause of the blood loss. I did not cause it.'

'Liar! Tell vat to the judge. Medical blunderers.'

She turned on Sister. 'An' you, yer no better. You'll kill vat baby afore you're finished. An' it'll be your fault if she dies. I'll not forget vis, I'll not.'

Bewildered, the doctor looked at Sister.

'Can you explain?' he asked plaintively.

'I doubt it,' said Sister wearily. Her eye was swelling up, from the blow she had received from Meg. 'We've been trying for six months with no success. I doubt if any explanation will get through.'

'I'll not forget vis. You jest wait. You'll pay fer vis an' all, the pair of you.' Meg rolled her eyes and spat on the floor.

The Obstetric Flying Squad arrived. This was an emergency service held in readiness by all big hospitals for the support of domiciliary midwives. It was their proud boast that they could get to any emergency in twenty minutes, and they seldom failed to do so. An obstetrician, a paediatrician, and a nurse came, armed with an incubator, oxygen, drip, drugs, anaesthetics and all the other equipment used for obstetric surgery and infant resuscitation. They entered a small, hot and stuffy room that looked like a battle scene. Blood was literally everywhere. The doctor, covered in blood, was suturing the patient. The placenta still lay on the floor. Sister Bernadette, who was tending the baby, looked as though she had been in the front line. The skin around her eye was now blue, her face red and swollen, and her veil streaked with blood. A weird-looking woman in green glared at the hospital team with accusing eyes. 'More murderers. I'll see you don't get 'er,' she hissed venomously.

The doctor and the obstetrician consulted. Mavis was sleeping peacefully because of the morphine given half an hour earlier by the doctor. But she had lost a lot of blood, and the shock was severe. An intravenous infusion of blood plasma by drip was installed.

The placenta was scooped up off the floor, and the two doctors examined it. It was large, but appeared to be complete. The consultant palpated the woman's abdomen. The uterus was firm and hard, about the size of a grapefruit, as it should be. He looked around the small, stuffy room that contained not a vestige of clinical apparatus; at the woman in a state of primary obstetric shock; at the volume of blood loss; at the first baby sleeping peacefully in the crib; at Sister Bernadette tending the asphyxiated twin.

'In circumstances like these, undiagnosed twins, a transverse lie, premature separation of the placenta and haemorrhage could spell certain death. You have done really well, old chap.'

'Thanks,' said the doctor wearily. He seemed to be in a state of exhaustion. 'We do our best.'

'You done yer best!' shouted Meg. 'You wants lockin' up, I say. If you'd done like what I said an' put 'er on a birfin' stool in ve first place, vis would never 'ave 'appened.'

The consultant looked at Meg in astonishment.

'Take no notice, we've had this the whole time,' whispered the doctor. 'Nothing will convince her.'

The nurse took the baby from Sister Bernadette and placed the child in the incubator, warmed to 95 degrees F, and humidified to avoid drying of the respiratory mucous membranes. The baby was breathing, but her breaths were shallow. Her muscle tone was flaccid, and her skin tone bluish. Her heartbeat was regular, but faint. The paediatrician, after examining the baby, injected 1 cc of Lobeline into the umbilical vein in the cord and milked it towards the abdomen. Oxygen was attached to the incubator, and the oxygen input adjusted to 30 per cent.

The paediatrician advised immediate transfer to Great Ormond Street Hospital. Paradoxically, Meg, who had so violently opposed hospital for Mavis, did not object. The baby was kept in Great Ormond Street for six weeks until her weight was over five pounds, and then she returned home. Both babies thrived. They grew up to be strong, healthy girls, brought up entirely by their mother and aunt. They were a regular sight in Chrisp Street market, helping on the fruit and veg stall, and they became great favourites with the locals.

Thirty years later I was visiting Trixie, who had recently moved to Basildon in Essex. We went shopping, and she insisted we call at the market. It was a large and lively market, with open stalls and old-fashioned costers crying out their wares. I heard the strident voice of a woman calling out, 'Best apples, only thirty pence a pound. You won't find cheaper anywhere. Best bananas. Melons. Grapefruits.'

We approached the stall.

'Well? Wha'choo want?' demanded the female.

I gasped, staring at two identical women in drab brown dresses, leather belts at the waist, men's boots, and tight headscarves pulled down low over the forehead. I could not speak.

'If you don't know wha'choo want, I can't hang about. Next.'

The years rolled back. 'Megan'mave,' I exclaimed.

'What?' The two women drew together. Black eyes flashed a challenge.

'Megan'mave! But you can't be – it's not possible!'

'Mave's our mum, an' Meg's our aunt. D'you wanna make somefink of it?'

No, I didn't. Trixie grinned at me, and we slipped quietly away, chuckling.

MADONNA OF THE PAVEMENT

I saw them in High Holborn. They stood out from the tense, jostling crowd because they seemed to have no object in life, nowhere to go, nothing to do; they were aimless, lost. They stood out also because they were so poor. Poverty is such a relative thing; but no man is really poor till life becomes a desert island that gives him neither food nor shelter nor hope. They were such obvious failures at this game of getting and keeping called success. If they had suddenly shouted in pain above the thunder of the passing wheels they could hardly have been more spectacular in their misery, this man, this woman, this child.

He slouched along a few yards in advance of the woman. He looked as though Life had been knocking him down for a long time, then waiting for him to get up so that it might knock him down again. His bent body was clothed in greenish rags and his naked feet were exposed in gashed boots. He was not entirely pathetic. He was the kind of man to whom you would gladly give half a crown to salve your conscience; but you would never allow him out of sight with your suit-case!

She carried her baby against her breast in a ragged old brown cloth knotted round her shoulders. Perhaps she was twenty-five, but she looked fifty because no one had ever taken care of her, or had given her that pride in herself which is necessary to a woman's existence. She had not even the happiness of being wanted or necessary – a condition in which the altruistic soul of woman thrives. This man of hers would obviously be better off without her. She had once been pretty.

The shame of it! To parade her woman's body draped in rags through streets full of other women in their neat clothes, to meet the pitying eyes of other wives and mothers, and to drag on, tied like a slave, behind this shambling, shifty man. Is there a crucifixion for a woman worse than this?

He walked ahead so that she had plenty of time to wonder why she

front door, always shut. The only thing that might at one time have distinguished the pub from its neighbours was its sign; but it was so old that it hung from only one hinge, and most of the paint had worn off.

Sister Evangelina and I entered by the pub door, which was the only entry to the landlord's living accommodation upstairs. The public bar was about twenty feet square, high-ceilinged with a wooden floor. A few cheap wooden tables and chairs stood around the place, with the bar itself to one side. An unshaded electric light bulb, around which flies buzzed continuously, hung from the centre of the ceiling. The walls and ceiling were a dirty yellowish brown and were spotted all over with fly-stains. A single picture hung on a wall, but it was so dingy and faded that one would have been hard pressed to say whether it was a seascape or a hunting scene.

It was 12.30 p.m. when we arrived – opening time – and the pub, which at that time of day should have been humming with life, had only one customer: a solitary man of indeterminate age staring at the wall and sieving a pint of beer through his moustaches. The silence was oppressive.

A woman stood behind the bar, half-heartedly wiping a few glasses with a grimy cloth. She was old, far too old to be a barmaid. Her grey hair was scooped into an untidy bun at the back of her head, and wisps hung across her face, which was lined and grey. Her eyes seemed dull and lifeless, and her lips lacked any colour. She was small and thin and had no teeth. She looked up as we entered.

'You wants 'a see Mr Lacey, I s'pose? I'll take you to 'im.'

She turned towards the man with the moustaches.

'Look to ve bar a bit, will yer, Mr 'arris? If anyone comes in, call me, will yer?'

She had an apologetic, deferential air about her, and her voice echoed bleakly in the bare room. The man grunted and continued sieving his beer, as he watched us over the rim of his glass.

We followed the woman up a dark, uncarpeted stairway. 'Vere's no light,' she said. 'Watch yer step.'

We entered the rooms above the bar, and she led us to the bedroom. A large, fat, pink man lay on a bed in a fair-sized room also swarming with flies. A bar-table covered in fag-ends and a rough wooden cupboard were the only other furniture. It was summer time, and a thin army blanket was thrown over the man's stomach, apart from which he was naked. The light was dim, because the sunlight struggled to penetrate the dirt on the windows.

'Is that my beer, Annie?'

'No, John, it's ve Sister's.'

'You idle, useless, woman, I told you 'a get me a beer. I don't want no bloody Sisters.'

Sister Evangelina strode across the room.

'Don't you call me a "bloody Sister", and I'll thank you to keep a civil tongue in your head. What are you doing in bed at this time of day? Sit up.'

'Who the hell are you?'

'I'm the "bloody Sister", now sit up. Go on.'

The man looked at her in astonishment and struggled to a sitting position, keeping the grey blanket carefully over his middle. The woman crept into a corner and stood there, meekly fingering her apron.

'That's better. Now what's wrong with you that a good dose of salts wouldn't clear?'

'I'm ill.' He groaned and raised his eyes to Heaven.

'Rubbish. You're fat. That's what's wrong with you. When did you last open your bowels? What you need is a good clear-out.'

'No, I'm ill. I'm in agony.' He groaned again and rubbed his hands over his chest and stomach. 'It's no use. You're too late. I'm dying.' He leaned back on the pillows and sighed weakly.

'Good riddance, if you ask me.'

The man jerked his eyes open. 'What?'

'You old fraud. You're no more dying than this young nurse here. Now what's wrong with you?'

'I got die-betes.'

'Is that all? Millions of people have cancer.'

'I'm dying, I tells ya.'

'Rubbish. Now get up. I want some of your pee to test for sugar.'

'I can't get up. I tells ya, I got DIE-betes. I'm dying yer see?'

'You'll do as you're told, and no arguments. Is there a lavatory in the flat? Right, go and fill a pot of pee. I don't want the stinking stuff, but I have to test it for sugar. Now off you go, quick. I haven't got all day.'

More from astonishment than compliance the man struggled to his feet, pulled the blanket across his middle and shuffled out of the room, his bare buttocks wobbling with every step. When he had gone Sister turned to the woman.

'Is he always like this?'

'Not never no different.'

'Never gets up?'

'No.'

'Humph. A good dose of salts and an enema up the arse is what he needs.'

''e wont like vat, 'e wont.'

'Clear his system, it would. He's all clogged up, that's the trouble with him. I don't hold with all this new-fangled medical clap-trap. Staphluses and coccuses and viruses and what have you. A good strong dose of salts and a good hot soap and water enema is all he needs to clear his system. Then there wouldn't be any more of this nonsense about being ill and dying.'

The man shuffled back into the room, groaning and rolling his eyes in a touching affectation of exhaustion. He put the chamber pot on the table and flopped into the bed.

Sister took the blood-sugar-testing equipment from her bag. With a pipette she counted ten drops of water and five drops of urine into a test tube and dropped a tablet into it. The tablet fizzed and bubbled, and the liquid turned bright orange.

'It's high in sugar, not surprising. You'll have to stop the beer and have an injection every day, twice a day.'

The man gave a howl of anguish.

'Not ve needle, oh no! I couldn't stand no needle. Never could stomach needles. I shall faint. Faint, I tells yer.'

'Well, you faint, then. Every day if you like.'

'You're 'ard,' he murmured, weakly.

Sister drew up a syringe and came towards him. The man screamed, leaped out of bed with the agility of a mountain goat and stood stark naked in the corner, whimpering. Sister advanced on him, and as he could not retreat any further, she plunged the needle into his leg and the injection was over in a second.

I heard a stifled sound from the other corner and turned. For the first time the woman's features relaxed and she giggled. I caught her eye and winked.

The man was whingeing and rubbing his leg.

'You're 'ard, I tells yer, 'ard. No pity on a man wha's never done you no 'arm.'

Sister Evangelina was unmoved.

'Cover up your balls and bits, get dressed and get on with your work in the pub.'

'I can't. I'm ill. Annie, get me a beer. I've 'ad a nasty shock.'

'Oh no, you don't. You've got to cut out the beer.'

He gave her a sly, shifty look.

'If I cuts out ve beer, will you cut out ve needle?'

'Perhaps, in time, when your blood sugar is lower.'

'Then p'raps, in time, I'll cut out ve beer.'

'You old weasle. You may be lazy, but you're not daft. Have it your own way. Kill yourself, if you want to, but don't expect any pity from me.'

With that, Sister stomped out of the room. At the door, she said, 'Expect the nurse, every morning and evening, for the needle.'

*

Bullies are always cowards. Sister Evangelina had, as usual, struck exactly the right note with her patient on the first visit. I had the thankless task of injecting Mr Lacey twice daily with insulin, and although he whined and whinged every time, he did not resist. In fact, after a few days, he assumed a heroic stance, telling me that not many men could bear such pain, and he ought to be in the medical books. With each injection, he screwed up his face into an expression of noble endurance, and when it was done he sank back on the pillows, a heap of exhausted suffering. He took himself absolutely seriously. He was both comic and contemptible.

Daily visits to the pub enabled me to get to know Mrs Lacey. Whatever time of day I called, she was always working. She did everything necessary to keep the pub running. She received the barrels of beer on delivery days, when they were rolled down the hatch into the cellar, then single-handed she rolled them across the floor and fixed them to the pumps going up to the bar. She carried crates of bottles up and down the narrow stone stairs from cellar to bar, and the crates of empties into the street for collection. She cleaned the bar room, scrubbed the tables, washed the glasses. She emptied the spitoons and cleaned the outside lavatory. She served behind the bar during opening hours when a few men sat sullenly, drinking beer. She did it all with a slow, methodical dullness as though she expected nothing else. She always looked tired, she always looked spiritless, she seldom spoke. She just carried on working, eighteen hours a day, seven days a week, 365 days a year.

The only time Mrs Lacey left the pub was to go shopping. Then she would cook a meal and take it up to her husband in bed. I had seen her cooking and told her that he must have no sweet things.

'I daren't cross 'im,' she whimpered. ''e must 'ave 'is puddings. Won't do wivout 'em.'

It was pointless trying to reason with her. The poor woman clearly lived in fear of her husband.

The same applied to his beer consumption. Visiting twice a day enabled me to see just what went on. He would thump on the floor and scream out, 'Fetch us a beer and look lively,' and she would run upstairs with a pint. The doctor, Sister Evangelina and I all told him it was making him worse, but he sneered. 'If I gets worse it's all your fault. You're supposed to get me better.' I tested his urine twice daily and kept a careful chart of his blood-sugar levels, but they were always high, and sometimes dangerously high.

Mrs Lacey looked at least twenty years older than she was. She had a cringing, apologetic way of talking, quite unlike so many Poplar women who were full of breezy self-confidence. She called me 'madam' and 'lady nurse' and asked if she could carry my bag upstairs. When I refused she said, 'But it's too heavy for a lady like you. I'll take it.' And she did. When I thanked her she looked surprised and said, 'It's good of you, madam, real kind. I don't expect no thanks. Real kind, I says. I 'preciate it, I do.' Up in the bedroom her husband shouted to her 'Put ve bag on ve table, you lazy slut, an' ge' out. I'm the one who's got to suffer ve needle to keep me from dying. Now ge' ou'.' If I had been carrying a 4-inch intramuscular needle with me that day, I would have rammed it deep into his fat buttocks and been glad to do so!

Down in the bar I said to her: 'You shouldn't let him talk to you like that.'

'Like wha', madam?'

'Calling you lazy. Telling you to get out.'

'I don' notice nuffink.'

Poor woman. She did not notice all the insults, but she had noticed a word of thanks.

The next time I called she was in the cellar, struggling to get a great barrel of beer across the floor to the pump taps. I went down to give her a hand. She was deeply troubled.

'Oh, no, no. A lady like you can't be movin' barrels o' beer. It's not righ', not fittin' like. I can do it by meself.'

I ignored her.

'You take one side, I'll take the other. We'll have the job done in no time.'

And we did. She sat down on the barrel sweating.

'It takes me twen'y minutes 'a get a barrel fixed up by meself. An' we done it in two. Oh, madam, I'm vat grateful, I am. I wish I 'ad a daughter. Every woman needs a daugh'er as she gets on.'

'Have you any children?'

'I got a boy. A lovely boy, 'e is. Bob. 'e's in Americky. 'e's doin' well, doin' nicely. I'm proud on 'im. Loves 'is ol' mum, 'e do.' She gave me a bleak smile.

We climbed the treacherous stone steps from cellar to bar and immediately heard continuous banging on the ceiling. Upstairs in the bedroom Mr Lacey was in a frenzy of rage.

'You idle, useless woman,' he shouted. 'What 'ave you been doin' all vis time, eh? Sitting around, drinkin' tea an' gossipin', that's wha'! When me, your lawful 'usband, wha's sufferin' an' dyin', wants yer. Now listen 'ere, you stupid wench, them letters you brought up. Well one of 'em is from Bob. 'e's comin' 'ome. In three weeks. Sailin' from New York, 'e is. Says 'e's got a surprise for us.'

Mrs Lacey gave a faint moan and clung to the table.

'Bob? My Bobby? Comin' 'ome? An' got a su-prise for us?'

'Yes. Three weeks. Now I shall want a new shirt an' a new pair o' trousies, an' some new socks, if you're not too idle to ge' yerself round shops an' buy me some. Now ge' on with it. I gotta suffer ve needle, an' I'm goin' 'a need all me strength to bear ve pain.'

After the injection Mr Lacey moaned, 'Bob's goin' to see wha' 'is poor old dad 'as to suffer. His poor ole dad wha' was good to 'im and sacrificed everyfing to bring 'im up proper an' give 'im a good ejication, wha's dyin' now with no one to care for 'im.' Tears of self-pity rolled down his fat cheeks.

Each time I called that week and the next, Mrs Lacey was in a flurry of excitement. Her usual slow, listless behaviour was replaced by smiling activity. She was decorating his bedroom. Paints and brushes, wallpaper, new curtains, a light shade – everything had to be perfect for her Bob. I couldn't imagine how she found the time to do it, as well as all the work of running the pub, but she did, and gladly.

One morning when I entered the private bar she was emerging from the cellar, carrying a crate of bottles. The weight was obviously as much as her strength could bear, and she let the crate down with an exhausted sigh. I was indignant.

'You shouldn't have to work so hard,' I said.

'It's better'n no work.'

She was panting and perspiring, so she wiped her face with the dirty glass cloth. She sat down on the bar stool for a moment.

'It's better'n draggin' yerself through ve streets wiv nowhere 'a go, no place to rest yer 'ead, nowhere to rest ve baby.'

I looked at her silently, wondering what she had suffered during the great depression, when there was no work for men, even those who were eager to work – and I doubted Lacey had ever been eager. She looked up, and a rare smile lit her tired features.

'An' Bobby was my baby. Bob wha's comin' 'ome next week. Comin' 'ome to 'is mum. He's a lovely boy, 'e is. Doin' well, vey say. Doin' nicely. His letter's a treat, 'e's got a good 'and. Writes real nice, 'e do. I'm vat proud, I can tell yer.'

By the beginning of the third week the room was decorated, and she wanted to show it to me. She was doubtful about the choice of curtains. Did I think he would like them? Did they match the room?

In contrast to the rest of the dreary pub, the room was bright and cheerful, and I gasped with genuine admiration when I entered and saw all that she had achieved in a fortnight. She saw my face and giggled with pleasure.

'An' ve curtains. Will 'e like 'em?'

'The curtains are lovely. I'm sure he'll be thrilled.'

'I bin sewing 'em every day sittin' behind ve bar.'

Two days later she said shyly, 'I got meself a new blouse. I mus' look me best when 'e comes. Bu' now I got it 'ome, I'm not sure. If I puts it on, will you tell me if it suits me?'

When I came down after seeing Mr Lacey, his wife was in the bar, wearing a pink blouse. It was not what is described as 'shocking pink', but any colour in that dingy brown and puce room would have been a shock. She stood nervously, biting her lip with her toothless gums.

'Is it too bright?'

I couldn't say 'yes', could I?

'It is lovely. Bob will be proud of you. You look really pretty.'

She glowed with pleasure. Had anyone ever paid her a compliment before?

'We 'ad a letter vis morning from Southampton. Ve boat come in yesterday. 'e's comin' tomorrow or ve next day, an' he'll be 'ere for three weeks. Three weeks! My Bob.'

Her voice trailed away in emotion.

'I'll 'ave to ge' vis blouse off, keep it clean. Can' 'ave it grubby afore 'e comes. An' you really like it?' She looked up wistfully. 'Really?'

For two days Mrs Lacey stood in the bar in her pink blouse, wiping the tables, serving her customers. Mr Lacey came downstairs, dressed in his new shirt and trousers, and sat at a table drinking beer and smoking Woodbines. Both of them were on edge. Many times she went out into the street and ran to the corner just to have a look. But no Bob. 'Somefink musta delayed 'im, he'll be 'ere by an' by,' she kept saying.

At eleven o'clock on the second evening, she wearily called, 'Time. Finish yer glasses. Time please,' and shut the bar. Mr

Lacey shouted, 'Fine son you got,' and went to bed. She sat at a table, her head on her arms, and wept bitterly.

On the evening of the third day the door of the bar opened, and a young man entered. He was good-looking and well dressed in a style not common in Poplar. The bar was empty.

'Hello. Anyone there?' he shouted. He was well spoken, with a slight American accent.

'Fine sort of homecoming this is – anyone there? Jeepers, what a hole! Sorry about this,' he said to his companion, a tall shapely girl with blonde hair, cut in the pageboy style. Her clothes were tight-fitting and well cut. The neckline of her jacket plunged low enough to reveal an enticing cleavage. Her shoes were high and pointed, and fine nylon stockings covered her shapely legs. Her lips were vivid red, her eyes deeply blackened, and her perfume was subtle and exotic. She was smoking, and she used a long cigarette holder.

She looked around the grimy, desolate beer-den. She looked at the flies buzzing round the light bulb. She looked at the yellowing ceiling, and at the filthy windows, and said, 'Jeez, what a dump! Is this where you were brought up?'

Bob coloured.

'Oh no, no. They've only been here eight years. They moved here after I left home. They've come down in the world, I'm sorry to say. I was brought up in a fine house in the country. We had a maid and a gardener in those days. But look, we don't have to stay if you don't want to. We could easily slip away. No one knows we're here.'

The American girl was about to speak when the door leading from the cellar was kicked open. Mrs Lacey entered the room, struggling to carry a great crate of bottles. Her attention was entirely focused on getting the crate to the bar without dropping it. She loosed her hold, and stood trembling, leaning on the bar. She was dishevelled and the dirt on her face was streaked with tears. The girl stared at her in amazement and whispered, 'Who's that?' He whispered, 'Ssshhh. Let's get out,' and made a move towards the door. But the girl's high heels made a sharp clicking sound on the floor, and the woman turned. She gave a strangled cry.

'Bob, my Bob. You've come, then. I knowed as 'ow you would. Come 'ome to yer ole muvver. My boy.'

She ran across the room and laid her dirty grey head on his clean white shirt.

'Steady on, ol' girl. Don't make a show of yourself. I said I'd come, didn't I?'

He untangled her arms from around him, and took a couple of steps backwards. She sat down on one of the chairs, leaning her arms on the table. Tears were streaming down her face, and she wiped them away with a hand covered in dust from the cellar.

'My Bobby. It's my Bob. My lad. Come 'ome.' She had not noticed the girl.

'Yes, it's me. Now pull yourself together, Mum. I said in my letter I had a surprise for you. I want to introduce you to Trudie. We are going to get married and she wanted to meet you.'

The two women stared at each other as though they were from different planets. It would be hard to say which received the greater shock. Neither spoke.

Bob said, 'Where's Dad?'

Mrs Lacey roused herself. 'Of course. Yer dad. I'll get 'im,' and she ran off upstairs.

'Is she really your mother, Bob?' enquired the girl.

''fraid so.'

He kicked the leg of a table.

'We shouldn't have come. It was a mistake.'

Footsteps were heard on the stairs, and Mr Lacey lurched into the bar. He had not shaved for two days, and his new shirt and trousers were covered in cigarette ash and beer stains. He staggered towards them and held out a hand.

'Great ter see yer, son. Welcome 'ome.'

Bob winced and took another step backwards.

'Good to see you, Dad. This is Trudie, my fiancée. I wanted you to meet her.'

The older man ogled the girl, then reeled towards her.

'Cor, not 'alf. Nice bi' of crumpet.'

He attempted to kiss her, but she jumped aside. He did not notice the expression on her face, but Bob did.

'Take a seat. Take a seat.'

Mr Lacey waved his arm, the jovial, expansive landlord.

'We'll 'ave beer'n whisky. We'll 'ave a chat, catch up on yer news, son. Sit down. This is a celebration.'

He sat down himself.

'Annie' he yelled, thumping the table. 'Annie! Where is tha' idle, stupid woman. Never there when she's wanted. Come 'ere, can'cher. We wants a drink.'

Mrs Lacey re-entered the bar. She was wearing her pink blouse, and had washed her face. She was trembling with excitement.

'Do somefink useful for a change, you lazy slu', an' ge' us some drinks, an' a packet o' crisps.'

He turned towards the girl.

'I got die-betees. I aint goin'ter live long. 'as to have a needle every day. Agony, it is. Dyin', vat's me.'

He leaned over the table and looked down her cleavage. She drew back. Bob nearly hit his father.

Mrs Lacey brought some beer and some whisky to the table.

'We don' 'ave much call fer anyfink else 'ere. Bu' I can get some rum if you prefer.'

She sat down next to Bob and shyly touched his jacket.

'My boy. My dear boy,' she whispered, gazing at him with adoring eyes.

'Well, wha' 'ave you been up to, Bob? Apart from touchin' up ve girls?'

The father leered at Trudie suggestively.

'I'm in insurance,' said Bob coldly, 'doing well. Lots of room for promotion.'

His mother stroked his arm and echoed, 'Insurance. My boy. Jes' fancy. Insurance. Yer doin' nicely, ven. I'm vat proud on yer, I am.'

Her face glowed with happiness.

The door opened, and a couple of down-at-heel men entered. Both were dirty, and a powerful smell of unwashed body odour entered with them. They stared at the four people round the table and went to sit at the far end of the room. Mrs Lacey jumped up to serve them and then came back and sat down beside Bob. She took his hand and with her forefinger traced little circles on his wrist.

'It's bin a long time. Eight years you bin in Americky. An' yer doin' nicely. Insurance. Cor, my boy in insurance. Wha'choo fink o' va', eh, Dad?'

'Oh, give over, Muvver. Yer daft. Bob don't wan'cher maulin' 'im. Do you, son?'

Bob couldn't answer, but he moved his hand away and looked at Trudie.

'Well, we'd better be on our way. I'm showing Trudie the old country, and we've got a tight schedule.'

'I'll cook a meal for us all. Yer room's ready. I done it special for yer,' said his mother eagerly.

'Oh no. We're not stopping. We've booked into an hotel up West, and I have dinner reservations for us tonight.'

'Not stoppin'?' Her face was blank with sorrow.

'No. There's a lot I want to show Trudie. She's never been to England before and she wants to see so much.'

'Of course. I understand.' Mrs Lacey's voice was barely audible. She spoke to Trudie. 'You're a lucky girl. You got a good man. He's my Bob, an' he'll be a good husband. There's somefink I wanna give you, if you can wait a moment.'

She slipped upstairs.

The three round the table looked uncomfortable. The young

people looked at each other and squeezed hands under the table. The father leaned forward.

'Did I tell you I got die-betees? Killin' me, it is. Injections every day. Agony, real agony, an' I can't get no 'elp from 'er.' He jerked his thumb towards the door whence his wife had departed. He made a scornful hissing sound. 'Useless, I tells yer straight. Useless.' He coughed and retched in his throat, leaned across, pulled the spittoon towards him and spat messily into it. Trudie looked as though she was going to be sick.

Mrs Lacey returned to the table. In her hand she held a folded envelope of tissue paper. She sat down beside Trudie and opened it for the girl to see inside.

'It's for you, dear. It were Bob's, when he was a baby. I kep' it all vese years, an treasured it. Bu' now it's for you.'

She opened the paper and revealed a baby's bonnet, yellow with age, cheap lace half torn off and ribbons frayed and crumbling.

'Take it, dear. It's yourn now.'

The girl looked bewildered and muttered a quick 'Thank you'.

The young people stood up.

'Well, we must be on our way,' said Bob with forced cheerfulness. 'Nice seeing you both. Don't forget you'll always be welcome in America. It's a big country. Lots of space. There will always be a welcome for you.' And they left.

An hour or so later, Mrs Lacey was putting some crates in the street. There, in the gutter, lay the precious bonnet. She went upstairs and took off the pink blouse. She never wore it again.

THE FIGHT

A district midwife in Poplar, East London, in the 1950s could find herself in many strange and unexpected situations. It was about 7 o'clock when I reached the tenements on a cold, wet night, and a menacing sound greeted me. Two women were fighting. I had never seen such a thing before and crept closer to listen to the comments of bystanders.

The fight, apparently, was over a man. Well of course, I thought, what else would two women fight about?

It was dark, but light from some of the windows illuminated the scene sufficiently to show that both women's blouses had been torn off, and they were clawing, hitting, punching, biting and kicking each other. One had long hair, which was a great disadvantage to her, as it gave her adversary something to grab hold of. Literally hundreds of people were in the courtyard – men, women and children – shouting, jeering, cheering, egging them on. The woman with the long hair had now been forced to the ground, and the other was on top of her, banging her head against the cobblestones.

Just as I was thinking, Dear God, someone's got to stop this, I heard the piercing sound of police whistles, and two policemen rushed into the yard, wielding their truncheons to show that they meant business. Had they not come when they did, the woman on her back might have been seriously concussed, if not killed. The police were everywhere in the East End in those days, always on the beat – on foot, of course, as there were very few police cars. Within minutes at least another ten policemen had arrived, summoned by the shrill and distinctive sound of the whistle – there were no short-wave radios to connect members of the force, and the whistle was the only means of summoning help. If they heard it, police would run from every direction towards the source of the sound. Now, at the sight of the Law, the crowd disappeared.

Within less than two minutes I was alone in the courtyard with the police and the two women, who had by now been separated. The injured one was shivering and moaning in pain. The other was standing over her, held back by a young policeman; but that didn't stop her snarling and swearing and spitting at the woman on the ground.

'You'll be charged for this,' warned the officer.

'Fuck you, see if I care,' she screamed and attempted to kick him. Another prevented her, saying, 'If you attack a policeman it will be the worse for you. And if this woman dies it will be a hanging matter.'

That brought her to her senses. It had not been many years before that Ruth Ellis had been hanged for murdering her lover. The episode had shaken the nation, and memories were still very much alive. Even in the dark and rain, with filth streaked over her face, the woman seemed to turn pale.

I kneeled down on the wet cobbles to examine the other female, who lay quite still. She was soaking wet, and her long, sodden hair hung down over her face and shoulders. I examined her as best I could in the dark and said, 'The first thing we have to do is get some blankets. She is in a state of shock, and the cold will do her as much harm as the head injury. Then we must get her to hospital for an X-ray.'

She moaned, 'Nah, nah, I don' wan' no 'ospital. I'll be all right.'

It seemed terribly quiet after all the noise. There was not a soul in sight. A policeman shouted out into the night air, 'Anyone who can hear me, bring a couple of blankets.' His voice echoed around the four walls of the tenement courtyard.

A few minutes later several doors opened, and women came out carrying blankets. They gave them to us and retreated silently back to their flats, shutting the doors behind them. All

Earnest 'collectors' swapping cards on the pavement – a not unusual scene in the East End of fifty years ago. Boys collected marbles, bottle tops and cigarette cards; girls collected buttons, ribbons and cotton reels. Swapping and bargaining was a serious business © Allen Young

Men trundled barrels like this all over London in the 1950s © Allen Young

It was a sad day for the local lads when the water sprinklers were taken out of service © Tower Hamlets Local History Library and Archives

Right: A vigorous public health programme to limit the spread of tuberculosis was started around 1910 © The Stroke Association

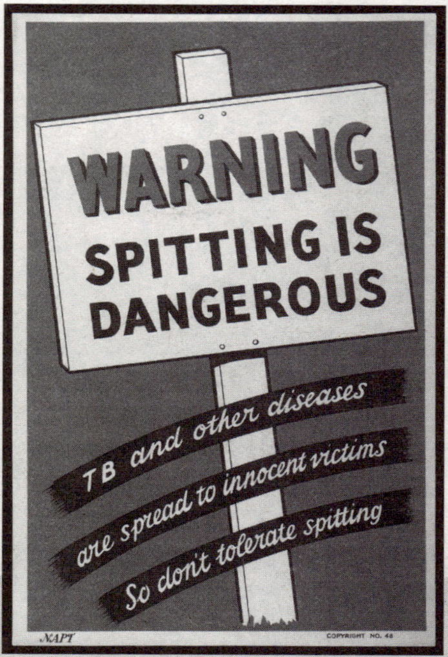

Below: Cows were herded down Stepney High Street as late as the 1940s. Testing cattle for TB was not compulsory until 1945, and 'our own cows' probably contributed to outbreaks in the East End © Tower Hamlets Local History Library and Archives

Left: A market scene from the 1950s with a rather intriguing sign © Allen Young

Below: Preparations for war – grim days © Tower Hamlets Local History Library and Archives

Grovesnor Buildings, corner of Cotton Street. Of the Canada Buildings, only one was destroyed. The others remained, three of them completely untouched by bombs © Tower Hamlets Local History Library and Archives

A boat under construction jutting out onto Manchester Road, Isle of Dogs, around 1920 © Tower Hamlets Local History Library and Archives

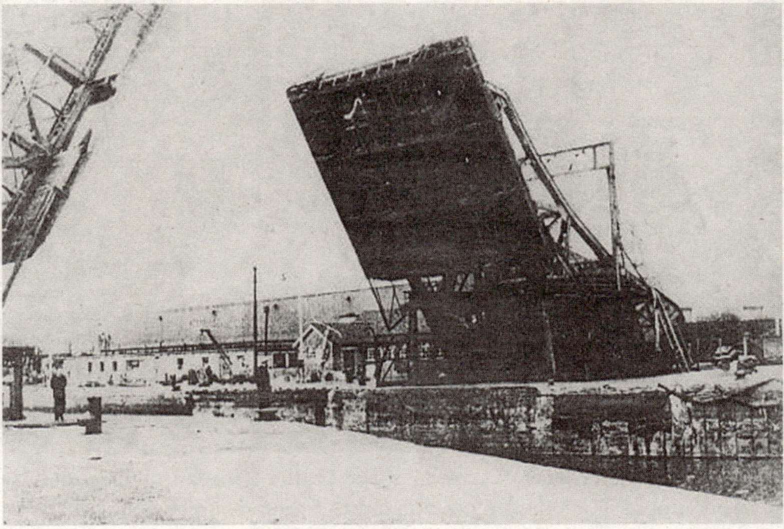

Entrance lock to West India Docks, looking towards the Wood Wharves from the river side. Chummy would have entered at this point, in the dark and wind © Museum of London Port of London Authorities Collection

Children getting a treat from an old-fashioned ice-cream vendor © Tower Hamlets Local History Library and Archives

Men were still unloading timber like this in the 1950s. They were tough, lean and very strong © Museum of London Port of London Authorities Collection

Jenny Lee at the wedding, 1959

the lights were off by this time, and faces that we could feel but not see were pressed against every window.

I rubbed the prostrate woman's limbs with a blanket to try to warm her, and we wrapped another one around her. Finally she sat up.

Her assailant perked up no end.

'Garn, she's all righ', the cow, she deserves more'n she got, more's the pi'y. I'd like to see 'er in 'ell.'

'We're taking you to the station,' said the young policeman.

'She started it, the fuckin' bitch.'

Then suddenly she changed her tune. Perhaps in the heat of the moment she hadn't realised that she was half-naked and surrounded by men – or maybe, in her state of undress, the idea of a police station seemed an attractive one. She sidled up to the young officer and rubbed her bare breast against his arm, giving him a lewd wink. Her shrill voice dropped about an octave and a half, and she said huskily, 'Is tha' an invitation, dearie?'

I, and most of the policemen, laughed. This dirty, rain-soaked woman trying to play Delilah looked so ridiculous. But the funniest part of all was the young policeman's reaction. He could not have been a day over nineteen, young enough to be her son. He looked pink and clean and high-minded. He glanced down at the substantial breast rubbing his arm and jumped like a scalded cat. We roared with laughter. All the faces watching at the windows must have been laughing too. The young man was covered with confusion and turned scarlet.

'Where are your clothes?' he spluttered in a prim Scottish accent. I don't suppose he meant to sound pompous and priggish, but he did.

It was a fair question, too. Where indeed were her clothes? They were scattered around the place, trodden by the crowd into the puddles. She advanced on the confused young man and with each hand lifted a huge, pendulous breast, waving her nipples in his face.

'Your guess is as good as mine, dearie.'

With a cry of alarm the young policeman leaped away. None of his colleagues was going to help him out; the scene was too good to miss. He knew he was beaten, so he grabbed a spare blanket that was lying on the ground and gave it to his tormentor.

'In the name of Heaven, woman, cover your nakedness,' he appealed to her in desperation. The other men fell about laughing. But things were getting out of hand, and the dignity of the Law had to be preserved. An older officer stepped forward.

'We are not going to charge you,' he said. 'Go to your flat, but I want your name and flat number.'

She turned sullen again. Her moment of exhibitionism over, she reluctantly gave her details.

'Now off you go, and don't let's have any more of this, or you'll be in real trouble. This is a caution.'

Then he turned to his men.

'Now all of you, back to your duties. You two stay here with the nurse and the injured woman. Report back if you need help.'

They left, suppressing their mirth and as they walked away I could hear voices saying, 'Coverr yourr nakedness, woman!' The young Scot bit his lip and looked to be on the verge of tears. He wouldn't live this moment down and he knew it.

The injured woman was sitting on the wet ground throughout this scene. As the other left, she screamed out, 'Look at 'er, the filthy slut. She's always like that, throwin 'erself around. She's no be'er than a whore. Trollop! Filth! Garbage!'

She screamed the words at the retreating figure, who made to come back and attack her again, but the second policeman barred the way.

'Now get off!' he said. 'If there's any more trouble you will be charged.'

Finally she left. The injured woman had obviously got her verbal energy back, but I was concerned about her head, having seen and heard several terrible blows as it was banged against the stones. She could easily have sustained a fracture and needed medical treatment.

I said, 'We've got to get her to hospital for an X-ray.'

'Nah! Nah!' she cried; 'I won' go to no 'ospital. Yer can't make me. I'll be all right. Jes leave me alone.'

We couldn't possibly just leave her there in the rain, so we agreed that we would take her back to her flat and then depart. She was still shaky and weak. She pulled the blanket around her, shivering. The young Scot was very kind.

'You can lean on me,' he said. 'Just show us the way, and we'll get you home.'

There were four flights of stairs to climb, and she could scarcely walk, but she managed it, grim determination forcing her on. She kept muttering 'no 'ospital, no 'ospital.' I think it was the dread of hospitals, and the fear that if she stumbled and fell she would be forcibly carried to one, that kept her going.

The long walk around the balconies seemed interminable. I could see faces pressed against the windows which vanished as we drew close. One little boy's face remained as we passed, and a hand shot out and snatched him back. I heard a curse, a heavy slap and a yelp of pain. I winced for the child. He was only being curious.

When we got to her door, the woman refused to let us come in with her.

'Nah, get orf,' she said, 'bleed orf. I'll be all right.'

We left, and I never saw her again. Women were tough in those days, really tough. Perhaps this woman was so used to violence that it had become part of life. Perhaps some kind neighbour took care of her for a few days. If she did have a hairline fracture of the skull, it mended in its own time and with no assistance from the doctors.

A charge was not brought against either woman. For one thing the injured woman made no official complaint, and for another personal fights in those days were common. Police just separated the adversaries and, unless some other crime was involved, charges were seldom made.

Such scenes were no surprise to the Sisters, I discovered, when, full of the importance of my story, I related it at luncheon the following day. The nuns had seen it all before, and sometimes a great deal worse. It was a violent area. However – and we all agreed on this – overall we saw far more goodness and kindness and open-handed generosity than the opposite.

On reflection it was surprising there was not more violence in the tenements, because people lived so close to each other. There was no privacy, no chance of solitude, seldom even quiet. Nerves must frequently have been stretched to breaking point within the family and between neighbours. Domestic violence was regarded as a fact of life. Even in the 1950s it was accepted that men beat their wives. We often saw women with bruises or black eyes, or limping. They never complained to the police: 'keep out o' the way o' coppers' was the rule. They may have talked about it among themselves, but in an attitude of resignation, rather than complaint. Times were changing, however, and the younger women, those of the post-war generation, were certainly developing more independence. But the older women accepted it all. The saying was 'If 'e don't beat yer, 'e don't love yer.' Twisted logic if ever there was some, but it was a belief widely held on to.

Life was not easy for the men either. They worked desperately hard and were accustomed to harsh treatment from their employers – it was just accepted as an aspect of their employment. The majority of Poplar men were dockers, and traditionally dockers were treated as beasts of burden, and expendable at that. Such treatment would brutalise any man. Yet the vast majority were not brutes; they were decent hardworking blokes who brought home most of their money to their wives and tried to live as good husbands and fathers. But, for all their hard work, they did not seem to get much peace or comfort in their homes, because of the overcrowding and too many children. What man, after ten or twelve hours of hard manual labour, would look forward to returning home to two or three small rooms with half a dozen kids running around? It was a matriarchal society, and 'home' was for women and children. The men were often made to feel like outsiders in their own homes.

Consequently the men spent most of their time in each other's company – all day at work and in the evenings meeting their mates at the Working Men's Clubs, the numerous Seamen's Clubs, the dog races, football, speedway and pubs. Pub life was convivial and provided the welcome and good cheer that home so frequently did not. Pubs also provided alcohol, which relaxed tired muscles, soothed frayed tempers and consoled the yearning for hopes and dreams long since abandoned.

THE MASTER'S ARMS

Oh what can ail thee, knight-at-arms,
Alone and palely loitering?
The sedge has withered from the lake,
And no birds sing.

I see a lily on thy brow,
With anguish moist and fever-dew,
And on thy cheek a fading rose
Fast withereth too.
'La Belle Dame Sans Merci', by John Keats

The Master's Arms in Poplar had seen much history in its hundred years. It was a freehold, started by old Ben Masterton in 1850, and passed from father to son over four generations. Many of the big breweries had tried to buy the family out, but they were a stubborn lot, the Mastertons, and in spite of the difficulties of running a freehold, not to mention the financial insecurity, they had always refused to sell, preferring shaky independence to safe wage earning. It was said that old Ben, with his one sound leg and one wooden one, had fallen off a trading vessel when drunk, and the ship had sailed away without him. He had nothing else to do but indulge his favourite activity, so he started a drinking house, which became a firm favourite among the seamen. He married a local girl who enjoyed the bawdy life, and she bore fourteen children, six of whom survived childhood. Old Ben ultimately expired in an alcoholic stupor, as everyone had said he would, and two of his sons took over the business, at the time of the economic depression in the 1880s, when it was nearly impossible to get work in the docks, and thousands starved as a result. In times of hardship pubs always flourish, and people will always drink, whatever the suffering of their families.

When the Jack the Ripper furore broke out in 1888, and the area became the centre for ghoulish visitors, the two brothers decided to expand their cramped premises, smarten up the dingy interior and put a few macabre pictures and posters on the walls proclaiming: 'This is where it all happened.' The visitors flocked in, and one of the two brothers led a guided tour of all the murder spots, with grisly details of how the killings were done, embellished for the shivering delight of the crowd, who then returned to the pub for suitable refreshment. Business was looking good.

The pub took on a life of its own after that and became well known for its landlords, its warmth and hospitality and its easy-going atmosphere. Every pub was easy-going in those days, but there were limits to how easy the going should be, and the brothers set the tone. There was to be no fighting, no child prostitution, no illegal gambling, or money handling and no opium smoking. Again the Masterton brothers were successful, and the pub flourished.

In the year that Queen Victoria died, one of the brothers died also. His funeral was less spectacular than the Queen's but lavish enough by Poplar standards, and was enjoyed by all. There's nothing like a good East End funeral to raise the spirits, and the Master's Arms opened its generous doors to patrons after the church solemnities. The surviving brother decided to hang up his boots and pass the freehold on to his son, who ran the pub efficiently for twenty-five years throughout the Edwardian period, the disaster of the 1914-18 War and the chaos of the years that followed. It was he who bought a piano, found a piano-player and introduced the communal sing-songs. He did so because of the misery of the times, with the hope that it would cheer people up to have a good sing – or a good cry if need be. The sing-songs and dancing became a feature of the Master's Arms, and, try as they might, no other pub in the area could rival the Arms for their Saturday night entertainment.

In 1926, the year of the great General Strike, when most

industry in Britain was forced to close, Bill Masterton's father died, and he, fourth generation, took over the Master's Arms. He was a thick-set man, a little above average height, with great strength and phenomenal energy. He could work any other man into the ground without breaking sweat. He had a good, practical intelligence, ideal for running a small business, and was known by all as the Master. He was married to an Essex girl, who had not expected a pub life when she married a self-employed carter, and she never really settled down in Poplar or took to the life. Bill once persuaded her to act as barmaid, but she hated it so much that he said she would drive the customers away with her miserable face. Relieved, she devoted her time to her children.

Oliver, her eldest, was the joy of her heart, resembling his good-looking father in appearance, but with a more loving nature. Julia, her second, was a bit of a mystery; she was a solemn little girl who never said much, and children who don't talk always make grown-ups feel uneasy. But Mrs Masterton had plenty to do with the three younger boys, who tumbled and romped all over the place. Then she found herself pregnant again, and a little girl was born, as pretty a baby as you could wish for. They called her Gillian. Her husband seemed to like the last baby, which was a surprise to the newly delivered mother. He had not taken much notice of the others, always saying, 'The children are your concern. You look after them – I'll look after the money. Can't say fairer than that.'

And indeed he couldn't. He worked hard, and the pub was profitable. Mrs Masterton was never short of money, unlike so many Poplar women. She did not want to see her children growing up like the Cockney kids and with a Cockney accent, so, when the time came, they all went to a small private school outside the borough. Her husband grumbled, but paid the term's fees for each child, saying, 'You know best when it comes to the kids. Let's hope it's worth the money.' Husband and wife rubbed along together, each with their own role, but with little communication or understanding. 'You're more interested in your pub than your children,' grumbled Mrs Masterton sometimes. 'Don't be daft,' her husband remarked, 'what do you expect me to do – change nappies? Ha, ha, I should think! Anyway they're all right, aren't they? Doing nicely. What more do you want?'

Julia was nine when her older brother started coughing. 'It's a winter cold,' said his mother and rubbed his chest with Vick. But the cough continued. 'It will go in the spring,' said the mother and applied a flannel jerkin under his school clothes. But the cough did not go away.

Oliver wanted to be chosen for the school football team. He practised his kicking and passing skills resolutely; the cough was a nuisance. He didn't really feel ill, and he didn't see why it should interfere with his soccer career. When he started coughing up thick, yellowish phlegm, he spat into a bit of paper and put it in the dustbin. He didn't tell his mother. Mothers fussed so, and he wasn't going to be fussed. Not him. He was going to be captain of the team.

When his mother found blood on his pillow one morning, she was very alarmed. She questioned him about his health, but he said he felt all right. Nonetheless she called the doctor, who on examining the child suspected tuberculosis and advised an X-ray and a pathology lab analysis of his sputum. Both results confirmed the presence of tuberculosis. As a precaution, the doctor arranged for all other members of the family to be X-rayed, but they were all pronounced clear. He also arranged for Oliver to be removed immediately from school because, he told the parents, the boy would probably infect other children. He would be sent to a special school attached to Colindale Sanatorium in North London. He would have to reside there, and he would have the latest and best medical treatment available.

Oliver was deeply distressed. What about his football, and the athletics team he had joined? The doctor tried to explain that sports were played at the new school, but nothing would console the child. His mother was distressed for other reasons. Her adored eldest son, her pride and joy, was being sent away, and although she could visit him, it was small consolation.

Oliver stayed for about six months at Colindale. He settled down and began to enjoy himself. The country air suited him, and all summer he played games and appeared to improve greatly. His mother was delighted, and was given permission by the doctors to take him away for a summer holiday by the sea. 'It will do him good,' they all said. Hope is so important during illness. But he never got as far as the sea. He never left Colindale. 'Le Belle Dame Sans Merci' had him in thrall.

Oliver died, and the family was thrown into a state of shock. The poor mother nearly went demented with grief, and it seemed as though she would never raise herself again. The father became very quiet and withdrawn, but opened the pub as usual.

Whenever Julia thought of that first death – her big brother, whom she had idolised – she was filled with anger and disgust. The family rooms were over the pub, and the child was lying in an open coffin for family and neighbours to come in and pay their respects. The children, aged from two to nine, were subdued and sad, their mother was weeping all the time, while their father said nothing. Women, some known to the children, some strangers, came in with flowers and small gifts. They laid their posies on the young body and sniffed. 'You'll have to bear up, Amy. Think of the others,' they said. Her mother wept and could not answer. The women crept downstairs, leaving the family with their loss. And all the time the noise from the pub was rending the quiet. The piano was pounding out popular songs, raucous voices were singing 'Pack up yer troubles in yer old kit bag and smile, smile, smile'. The stamp of feet shook the table on which the coffin was laid. The shrieks and screams of half-drunken voices continued until late evening, after which there came peace, which the poor mother yearned for. One night Julia went into the room and sat with her mother in the blessed quiet. They fell asleep together in the armchair. 'You are my comfort,' said her mother and stroked her hair.

The day of the funeral was a nightmare. It took place on Whitsun Bank Holiday. Julia's mother had begged her father not to open the pub that day, but he refused. There was a terrible row, and the children cowered in the attic, terrified. Their mother and grandmother and aunts all went at him, telling him to show some respect, but still he would not change his mind. 'Business must go on,' he shouted, as he ran downstairs to open up. On bank holidays, pubs could be open from 10 a.m. until the small hours of the morning and always did good business.

The hearse drew up at the back of the pub while crowds of excited holiday-makers were pouring in the front. The mother had wanted a horse-drawn funeral cortège for her eldest son, but it turned out to be a fiasco. The coffin was reverently carried downstairs and placed in the carriage, but at that moment a group of excited youths emerged from the pub and staggered round the corner, closely chased by four shrieking girls. The high-pitched voices frightened the horses, one of them reared, and this was the signal for panic among the other three. They bucked and lunged in all directions. The funeral directors lost their solemn demeanour and started shouting and pulling on reins and bridles in a desperate effort to prevent the carriage overturning. The coffin could be heard crashing against the wooden panels of the carriage. The group of mourners wearing black, the women veiled and the children carrying flowers, were distressed and terrified.

The horses eventually calmed down and the funeral was conducted calmly, but with frozen silence between Julia's mother and father. Neither tried to comfort the other for the loss of their first-born. Immediately after the ceremony, her father said, 'I must get back to the Arms; it's going to be a busy day. Are you coming, Amy?' She shook her head, 'I can't go back to that noise, not feeling as I do.' 'Please yourself,' he replied and walked off. The family stayed out all day, and most of the evening, but finally they had to return because the little children were tired and crying. The noise from the pub was deafening as they drew near, and a crowd of half-drunk holiday-makers grabbed Mrs Masterton and tried to get her to join in the dancing. With difficulty she tore herself away and shepherded her children upstairs, then slammed and bolted the door. The singing reached a crescendo at about eleven o'clock with 'Hands, knees and boompsey-daisy, let's make the party a wow, wow-wow'. Men and women clapped, slapped their knees and then banged their bottoms together to shrieks of laughter and cat-calls and lewd whistles. As it was a Bank Holiday, the grieving family had to endure several hours more of the high jinks.

That was just the first death. Even though they had been screened and pronounced clear, one after another the three younger boys contracted the disease. The distraught mother nursed them. Two went to Colindale Sanatorium, but came home to die when the doctors said that there was nothing more that could be done. Julia could never forget the years spent with the hush of death upstairs and the din of drunkenness downstairs. Her mother seemed to be numb with grief, and her father increasingly morose and silent, but each time he said, 'Business as usual,' and opened the pub. This caused tension between husband and wife, giving rise to terrible quarrels as each vented their anger and frustration on the other.

The last remaining boy was nine when he first showed signs of weight loss, fainting and sweating. He did not cough, but the doctor advised Mrs Masterton to take him away to the country to get more fresh air. They went to Skegness, where the sea air is bracing, so they say.

Mrs Masterton took Gillian with them also. 'Just to be on the safe side,' she told her family and friends. She did not consult her husband. By then, husband and wife were barely on speaking terms. Gillian was the youngest, and her father's favourite. She was a pretty, affectionate child, and she adored her father, who spoiled her shamefully. He had paid six months' advance rental on a cottage by the sea and had assumed that just his wife and youngest son were going. They left during pub hours whilst Mr Masterton was working, and it was not until later in the day, when Gillian did not return from school, that he realized with a shock that she had gone.

The impact was terrible. He had not reckoned that women could be so devious. He was filled with rage and his first instinct was to take the next train to Skegness and bring the girl back. But he was an intelligent man. After closing the pub that night he sat in his office to brood, head in hands. He felt hot tears coming, so he locked the door – he didn't want anyone to see signs of weakness. Perhaps she was right. They had lost three boys, and now the fourth was showing signs of illness. He slumped over his desk and bit his lip until he tasted blood. If his Gillian, his pretty little girl, died, he felt he would die also. She was better off by the sea, away from the foul London air. She would be back in six months, and her chatter and laughter would fill his heart again.

Julia stayed at home with her father. She was sixteen and doing well at school, coming up to her School Certificate, which her teachers were confident she would pass with Matriculation. Father and daughter were left alone together.

The relationship was tricky. Julia had never liked her father and felt that he did not like her. In reality they had both suffered from the fact that they were too similar in temperament. In particular, neither of them could talk much, which was a great disadvantage. Both of them imagined that the other was looking at them with some sort of malign thought, whereas each one was actually trying desperately to think of something meaningful to say. So long periods of silence existed between them, each wanting to break the ice, but not knowing how to do so.

They were both intelligent, but the gulf widened because they each had a different type of mind. His was entirely practical and instinctive, whilst hers was becoming increasingly academic. She would be doing her homework, and he would pick up a book and say 'What's this?'

'Algebra.'

'What's that?'

'A branch of mathematics.'

'You mean arithmetic?'

'Yes, if you like.'

'Looks like a load of rubbish.'

'Well it's not. It's beautiful.'

'Beautiful! What do you mean?'

And so it went on. The publican spent just about all his time immersed in his business, and Julia spent all her time at school, in the public library, or doing her homework. Each of them, father and daughter, were locked into their own worlds of loneliness and unhappiness.

But the young can be perceptive beyond their years. Although she said little, or perhaps *because* she spoke little, Julia observed, absorbed and interpreted everything. She began to think that her father was not as indifferent as he appeared to be. She and her mother wrote to each other every week. Mrs Masterton never wrote to her husband, but every time a letter arrived from Skegness her father was eager to know the news.

'How are the children, are they doin' all right?' and he grunted with satisfaction at the weekly good news. Once he shyly handed to Julia some pretty hair ribbons and a child's bolero. 'It's Gillian's birthday. Send this to her, will you? I hope it's the right size.' He kept on repeating, 'I hope I got the size right. The woman in the shop said it would fit. It's pretty, don't you think? Do you think she'll like it?' Nervously he repeated the doubts and questions several times. When a picture done with coloured crayons and a letter in childish print arrived for him he seemed happier than Julia had ever seen him. She was surprised and saw her father with new eyes, but still she could not speak openly to him. Neither of them had ever shown any affection towards the other, and it was impossible now that he was so completely turned in on himself and his business, and she was verging on adulthood, expanding her mind and emotions to the world beyond the Master's Arms.

Six months passed, and the boy seemed to be completely better after the summer at the seaside. The family returned home, and Mr Masterton had his little girl again.

Julia watched them together and was amazed at the liberties he allowed. Gillian would sit on his knee at breakfast and dip bread-and-butter soldiers into his boiled egg – something it would have been unthinkable for any of the other children to do. He brushed her hair and tied a ribbon in it. He seemed to notice the little boy more too, and was kind to him. 'You did right,' he said to his wife with grudging respect. 'They are glowing with health.'

But tuberculosis is cruel. A person can contract the disease, and the bacillus will lie dormant for years, sometimes for a whole lifetime, and the host will not even know it is there. At other times it can strike and kill within months or even weeks – that sort used to be called galloping consumption. The little boy came home from school with a temperature. His mother put him straight to bed and called the doctor. He was transferred to the sanatorium and given all the treatment known at the time. But, three months later, the doctors advised that there was nothing more that could be done for him, and he would be happier if he came home to die.

Grief again gripped the family with cold, grey hands. The boy was laid out in the parlour, like his brothers before him, and family and friends came to pay their respects. 'You've got your girls to comfort you,' they said to the weeping mother. 'It always strikes the boys first. It's their constitution, see.' Mrs Masterton did not ask her husband to close the pub; she knew it would be useless. 'I'll come to the funeral,' he said, 'In the meantime, business as usual.' Daytimes were quiet enough, but each evening the racket started. 'I hate the pub,' said Mrs Masterton, who looked more like sixty than forty. 'So do I,' said Julia. 'With all my heart, I hate it.'

Julia passed her School Certificate with Matriculation. She had but one longing – to leave home. But it was not easy for young girls in the 1930s. Britain was in the grip of the Great Depression, opportunities for girls were few, and wages were very low. She wanted to continue her studies, but could not do so without money. It should have been possible; the pub was profitable and her father was not hard up, but she did not feel she could ask him to finance a college course. She discussed it with her mother, who said, 'You must ask your father,' but so wide was the gulf between father and daughter that she could not bring herself to say a word. So, in the end, she applied to the Post Office for telegrapher's training. She went to Leytonstone, which was more genteel than Poplar but less interesting, and lived in a hostel for girls.

She was lonely, very lonely. She never felt herself to be one of the girls. She always felt apart from them, separated by something inside her that she could not understand. She developed the habits of an observer, sitting on the outside of a group of giggling girls, watching, but quite unable to join in their light-hearted chatter. This was not popular. At different times several girls demanded, 'What are you looking at us for?' to which she had no answer. They proclaimed her stuck-up. She was friendly, in a superficial way, with several of the girls, but had no real friends. Once she did venture out with a crowd of girls, and afterwards vowed never again! The greatest part of her time, when she was not working, she spent in the public library, and she read everything available – history, novels, theology, travel, science fiction, poetry – literally anything she could lay her hands on. The world of books extended her mind and compensated for the dull routine of the telephone exchange. She dared not leave her job because in the depression of the 1930s she was lucky to have a job at all.

She did not really enjoy the work, either. She applied herself, but knew in her heart that, intellectually, it was beneath her. The superintendent was a bitch, and seemed to pick on Julia, perhaps because she was different, and tried to make her life a misery. It was not a happy time, but at least she was away from the foul atmosphere at home between her mother and father, away from the riotous revelry of the pub, and away from the figure of death that seemed to stalk every room. She would put up with anything rather than go back.

Each week mother and daughter corresponded. Neither of them had much to say in their letters, but it kept them in touch. The best news was always that Gillian was well, doing nicely at school, was friends with the vicar's daughter, was going on a Sunday School outing, and so on. The mother said little about herself, and nothing about her husband.

Then came the terrible news that Gillian was unwell. The vicar was praying for her. The doctor had been called. A sanatorium was advised. The mother went with the child, and the husband rented a small cottage for his wife so that she could be near. The sanatorium came highly recommended, but then they heard that the air in Switzerland would be better. Santa Limogue in the Alps achieved a very good cure rate, it was said. So a place was booked, and Gillian and her mother crossed the Channel in the middle of winter by sea, then were conducted by train to the haven of miracle cures for tuberculosis. But the journey, lasting two days and nights, was too much for the child, and she died shortly after arrival.

Julia wept. Her family was cursed. She hid her tears under the bedclothes in the dormitory where she slept with twenty other girls, and during the day she was more silent than ever. She wrote a long, grieving letter to her mother, for the first time opening her heart to her, which to her surprise she found liberating. She wrote a brief letter to her father but could not think what to say. She remembered him with little Gillian on his knee, as she dipped soldiers into his boiled egg; she remembered the present of hair ribbons and a bolero. But still she could not think of what to say to him. So in the end she sent a few words on half a sheet of notepaper, to which he sent no reply.

The funeral took place in Switzerland. The mother returned home, but after a few months she left her husband to live with a sister in Essex. Correspondence continued between mother and daughter, and they met every so often and had a day out together. The father continued to run the pub, but they never corresponded, and Julia never visited. In spite of loneliness, which had become a way of life for Julia, she did not regret leaving home. The memories of drunken revelry repelled her, and thoughts of death haunted her.

No, she would never, she vowed, never go back to the Master's Arms.

TUBERCULOSIS

Youth grows pale, and sceptre-thin, and dies.
'Ode to a Nightingale', by John Keats

Tuberculosis is as old as mankind. Evidence of the disease has been found in a Neolithic burial ground near Heidelberg, Germany and in mummies from Egyptian tombs 1000 years BC; and Hindu writings refer to 'a consumption'. Hippocrates used the word *phthisis* to describe the cough, wasting, and ultimate destruction of the lungs. The disease is universal, and bears no relation to climate. It has been found in native tribes of North America, in primitive African tribes and amongst the Inuits of Alaska; China, Japan, Australia, Russia, Corsica, Malaya, Persia have all known it. There is probably no tribe or nation on earth that has been free from tuberculosis.

The disease has waxed and waned throughout recorded history, usually starting unnoticed, then reaching epidemic proportions, then waning as the population acquires collective immunity to the tubercle bacillus, over approximately a 200-year cycle. In Europe and North America it reached epidemic proportions between around 1650 to 1850 (varying somewhat from nation to nation), and it has been confidently concluded by medical scientists and historians that at the height of an epidemic 90 per cent of any population would have been infected. Of this number 10 per cent would have died. The lungs are the main focus of the bacillus, but they are not the only target; the meninges, bones, kidneys, liver, spine, skin, intestines, eyes – practically all human tissue and organs can be and have been destroyed by tuberculosis. It was called 'the Great White Plague of Europe'.

Historically, the highest morbidity from tuberculosis occurred between the ages of fifteen and thirty. Throughout European literature of the eighteenth and nineteenth centuries the tremendous creative outburst of the 'Sturm and Drang' writers and poets of the Romantic movement dominated the public imagination. Today we look back on their sickly characters, amazed at apparently healthy young women fainting and going into a terminal decline, or languorous youths too weak to do anything much except sit around looking pale and interesting and writing poetry. But this was no morbid fantasy. Lassitude, weakness, weariness, loss of weight and colour were common amongst the young, and they were early signs of infection, unrecognised by most people. By the time coughing, fever and lung haemorrhage occurred the condition was called consumption, and it was too late for effective treatment. The flower of youth was gathered in its prime.

From ancient times there has been a belief that some relationship exists between tuberculosis and genius. The intellectually gifted are the more likely to contract the disease, and the fire which consumes the body makes the mind burn more brightly. Throughout Europe in the eighteenth and nineteenth centuries, the idea was fostered in the public imagination that consumption was the product of a sensitive nature and a creative imagination. Did not famous musicians, poets, painters and authors die from consumption? The tenuous connection was widely accepted with gratitude by those grieving the death of an only son or a beloved daughter. Grief needs an outward expression, and if a mother can interpret a few morbid poems written by her dying son as evidence of a genius snatched too soon from the world, she is somewhat comforted.

Indeed the immense creativity of this period of European history might have been an indirect product of tuberculosis. Opium was widely prescribed for the control of coughing, and it has been said that many consumptives who could afford it were addicted to opium. Many drugs are hallucinogenic, but not all arouse creativity as opium does.

*

Dwellers in the cold North assumed that grey skies, foggy winters and biting winds caused tuberculosis. Therefore the consumptive rich flocked in droves to Southern climates, trying to escape the cold North, but to little avail. They carried the seed of death with them and spread it amongst their hosts. In the South of France, Nice, once a pretty fishing village, suddenly became fashionable. Hotels were built, and filled with cadaverous consumptives, ghostly pale, with sunken features and haunted eyes. It was said that performances at the Opera House could not be heard above the sound of coughing and spitting! Rich Americans fled south to Florida and New Mexico to beg of the sun a last ray of hope. But the sun had no healing powers to cure advanced galloping consumption; in fact, exposure to the sun could have a negative effect.

Medical advice changed. Mountain air was prescribed – desert air, sea air, tropical air, moist air, dry air, gentle winds, fierce winds, no wind. Consumptives who could afford to do so journeyed hither and thither in vain. By the end of the eighteenth century it was obvious to everyone that tuberculosis did not respond to any climatic conditions, and respected no geographical boundaries.

Medical science was in its infancy, and treatments were rudimentary. The unpredictability of the course and outcome of tuberculosis had always baffled doctors – some consumptives died within months of contracting the disease, others recovered spontaneously with no treatment, whilst some lived a long and active life with intermittent bouts of debility. The sick begged for treatment; anything that might offer a glimmer of hope was clutched with shaking hands. But the outcome of the treatment was as unpredictable as the disease itself, and probably had little effect upon the course of the illness anyway. Despite that, one fashionable treatment followed another. Bleeding and blistering were common, as were leeches, plasters and poultices, cuppings and inhalations. Lifestyle was tackled, and various courses advised: vigorous exercise, such as skiing, riding, walking, or sea bathing sometimes helped. Deep breathing was advocated, also flute playing and singing. Other physicians insisted that rest was essential – total bed rest for months or years on end, often in an enclosed, heated room in which it was forbidden to open a window. Elizabeth Barrett lay in bed for years until Robert Browning romantically carried her off to Italy, where she spontaneously recovered!

Diet is important in any illness, and dietary fads followed each other with bewildering speed. Some physicians advised extreme abstention – a starvation diet we would call it today – and the Brontë sisters almost certainly suffered from malnutrition, imposed by their father and his medical advisers. Others went for diets rich in meat, offal, warm animal blood, fat, cream, fish, eggs and milk – asses' milk, goat's milk, camel milk, sheep's milk and human milk (still favoured in the United States in 1900). All have had their day.

Drug therapy was almost non-existent. Ancient herbal remedies existed in every culture or tribe from time immemorial, some of which would ease symptoms, but none of which could destroy the tubercle bacillus. In the eighteenth and nineteenth centuries digitalis, quinine and mercury were used, although the universal balm and comforter was opium.

The great flaw in all treatments was the fact that the highly contagious nature of tuberculosis was not recognised. No special precautions in the care of a dying consumptive were advised by physicians. Quite the contrary, a hot stuffy room, with windows never opened, was favoured. Many are the testimonies of a loving parent or sibling who spent whole days and nights in the same room, and often in the same bed, as the sufferer. Millions of people who showed no signs of disease were carriers.

If all the money in the world could not protect the rich from the ravages of tuberculosis, what became of the labouring poor? Not for them the luxury of hotels in southern France or Alpine Switzerland, or even the cost of a doctor. They could barely afford an aspirin, or a day off work. Loss of work could spell destitution, so they laboured on until they died.

In industrial cities, firstly in England and later throughout Europe and America, crowded into factories and workshops, cold, half-starved men, women and children laboured for twelve or more hours a day in enclosed, foetid conditions and returned at night to tenement dwellings the sanitary conditions of which were beyond our imaginings. Infection would have passed with rampant speed from one sad individual to another, made more livid and virulent by the physical debility of the victim, caused by overwork and malnutrition.

In previous centuries all over Europe, child labour was the norm. From 1750 onwards, in industrial Europe, children were confined in closed, ill-ventilated rooms, working up to twelve hours a day. The Royal Commission on Child Labour in Manufacture of 1843 described children of seven and eight years as ... 'stunted in growth, pale and sickly; the diseases most prevalent are disorders of the nutritive system, curvature of the spine, deformity of the limbs, and diseases of the lungs, ending in consumption'. The number of deaths from tuberculosis amongst these children may not even have been recorded. They were child paupers, frequently gleaned from workhouses, unwanted, unprotected, endlessly expendable.

In the enclosed workhouses of Britain, where inmates were confined and not allowed out, contagion would have been a continuous fact of life. The only record I have been able to find of the incidence of tuberculosis in a workhouse was from one in Kent, where in 1884 it was recorded that *all* of the seventy-eight boy inmates suffered from tuberculosis, and that amongst ninety-four girls only three could be found who were not infected. It has not been recorded how many of these workhouse children died, but many would have. Undoubtedly the worse the living conditions, the worse the effects of the tuberculosis bacillus. In the Jewish ghetto of Vienna, at the height of the epidemic, it was recorded that 100 per cent of the dwellers were affected, of whom 20 per cent died. The rich Viennese were terrified to go anywhere near the area.

For the poor, consumption was not the romantic image of pale, wasting youth. It was not the occasion to lie in bed for months on end, writing long, sad poems. It did not lead to extended travel abroad. No, indeed; for the labouring poor consumption was the great killer, the breeder of destitution, the father of orphaned children.

While the highest mortality from tuberculosis occurred in young adults, children also died. In the graveyard of Burton on the Welsh Borders, where my father and grandparents are buried, can be found the tragic memorial to ten children from one family who died between the ages of six months and twelve years from 'wasting consumption'. The composer Gustav Mahler was one of fourteen children, seven of whom died of tuberculosis. The Masterton family, whose tragic story I tell, were not the only ones with such a history. In the tenements of Poplar lived the parents of six children, all of whom, I was told, had died of consumption. The prevalent sadness of the parents is, to this day, alive in my memory.

Contagion – the possibility of the spread of disease from one person to another by some unseen agent, but especially by breath – was not part of medical thinking at the time. Consumption was considered to be an hereditary malformation of the lungs, and the fact that so many families were consumptive lent weight to this theory. Strangely, the equally observable fact that, inside closed religious orders, where monks and nuns were not related, up to 100 per cent could be found to be infected, did not prompt physicians to pursue another line of thought.

However, in 1722 an English physician, Benjamin Marten, published a paper postulating that 'a species of animalculae, or wonderfully minute living creatures, capable of subsisting in our bodies, may be fretting and gnawing at the vessels of the lungs'. The idea was considered so preposterous that the medical thinkers of the time refused to believe it. Had Marten's hypothesis been accepted, and proper isolation and decontamination procedures been adopted, the Great White Plague of Europe might never have occurred.

In 1882, the German scientist Robert Koch, in a home-made laboratory, isolated the tuberculous bacillus for the first time and demonstrated by animal experiments that the bacillus was responsible for the disease that had baffled generations of researchers and medical thinkers. He also demonstrated that the bacillus could cross from man to animals and vice versa, thus proving that milk from tuberculous cows could infect human beings, especially children.

From that time onwards, massive public health programmes were ordered in all European countries and in America. The public were instructed in the facts of infection and contagion, which were completely new concepts for them to grasp. The strange and novel process of sterilisation had to be taught. Limiting the spread of infection was the order of the day, and this continued for nearly eighty years.

Pasteurisation of milk was started in the 1920s. This was nearly forty years after Koch had demonstrated the cross-infection from animals to humans, but even then a great many people would not believe it and refused to buy pasteurised milk. TB testing of cattle was at first voluntary for farmers, but became obligatory in the 1930s. In the 1920s large notices saying 'SPITTING PROHIBITED' were displayed in all public buildings, meeting places, and on public transport – and these notices were still displayed in the 1950s and '60s. All pubs and private bars, such as those in golf and tennis clubs, had a spittoon in the bar.

Consumptives were removed from the workplace; even the idle rich were no longer free to wander around the South of France infecting others; they had to be treated in isolated sanatoria. Medical and nursing staff were specialists. Strict barrier nursing of TB patients was undertaken, and TB nurses did not enter general hospitals. A consumptive parent was removed from his or her children. A consumptive child was removed from school. Due to these measures tuberculosis, which had terrorised Europe, began to lose its grip.

The possibility of vaccination was considered. Vaccination against infectious disease was first developed in 1796 by Edward Jenner, who had observed the link between cow-pox and human smallpox. In the 1880s, when Robert Koch discovered the tuberculous bacillus, he held out great hopes that a vaccine could be prepared from dead tuberculous bacilli. This should have gone well, but, in the early use of the treatment, tragedy struck. A batch of the vaccine had been improperly prepared, and living bacilli were injected into a large group of children, all of whom contracted tuberculosis, and many of whom died. This disaster halted the use of a vaccine for over sixty years, and a safe and effective treatment had to wait until the 1950s, when the BCG (Bacillus-Calmette-Guerin) strain became available for the prevention of tuberculosis.

But a vaccine is preventative, not curative for those already infected. In the first half of the twentieth century many curative drugs were developed and used. In the 1930s sulphanilamide was tried; in the 1940s para-animo-salicylic acid; in the 1950s streptomycin was the first of the antibiotics to be introduced, and this one saved millions of lives.

X-rays were invented as long ago as 1895, and could determine the extent of the disease. Surgery was attempted, and by the 1930s was relatively well advanced, from removal of a whole lung to removal of one or more diseased lobes of the lungs. Thoracoplasty and artificial pneumo-thorax, aimed at resting the lungs, was attempted in the 1890s and developed throughout the early part of the twentieth century.

But it was the public health programmes carried out over eighty years that were chiefly responsible for success, and by the end of the 1960s tuberculosis was no longer a major cause of death in European countries and America.

*

We, the favoured few of the twenty-first century, do not, cannot know the dreadful impact that tuberculosis had in days gone by. Let us be thankful for the advance in medical knowledge, and let us strive to extend it worldwide.*

* This essay is not intended as a medical analysis of tuberculosis. I am not a doctor and did not train as a tuberculin nurse. It is merely intended to provide an historical background to the story of the Masterton family, for those who may be interested. My main source of information has been the book *The White Plague* by René and Jean Dubois, published in 1953 by Victor Gollancz Ltd.

THE MASTER

And there she lulled me asleep
And there I dreamed – Ah! Woe betide! –
The latest dream I ever dreamt
On the cold hill side.
'La Belle Dame Sans Merci', by John Keats

They were having tea in Lyon's Corner House in The Strand. They usually met there. Mrs Masterton liked the atmosphere. Refined, she called it. It was their usual afternoon out, once a month. Mrs Masterton poured the tea.

'They tell me your father's ill,' she said abruptly.

'Dad? Ill? I didn't know.'

'I heard it from our milkman, whose brother is a cab driver. Cabbies get to know everything. He said the Master of the Master's Arms in Poplar is ill. That's all I know.'

'What's wrong?'

'I don't know.'

'Have you seen him?'

'No. That's why I wanted to talk to you, Julia. When did you last see him?'

'Some years ago. I'm not sure.'

'There was no rift, or anything, between you? No harsh words, nothing like that?'

'No. We never quarrelled. We just barely spoke. I never knew what he was thinking. I always thought he was giving me funny looks. I don't know why. Perhaps he wasn't. I don't know. He loved Gillian, but he never loved me, I'm sure of that. Did he love the boys?'

'I think he did, in his way.' The bereaved mother sighed. 'He's a funny man. Never could show his feelings, but I think he loved the boys. And yes, he loved Gillian. She was the apple of his eye.'

Mrs Masterton screwed up her table napkin and forced back her tears.

'Life can be so hard. All gone, and only you, my comfort, left.'

Mother and daughter squeezed hands across the table, as the afternoon pianist enjoyed his runs and trills. Both women were lost in memories. Julia broke the silence.

'I ought to go and see him.'

'I was hoping you would say that, dear.'

'I'll go on my day off.'

'That's my girl.'

Mrs Masterton paused, fumbling for her lipstick, then said hesitantly, 'Ask him if he wants to see me, will you, dear? I won't push myself on him, but if he wants, I'll come. Poor old Dad. I don't like to think of him alone and ill. He wasn't a bad husband. I'm sure he meant well. But we never got on, and the pub always came first.'

Julia went to Poplar early in the morning. She wanted to get there before the Master's Arms opened. The tram rattled on its rails to an area she had not visited for more than six years. She couldn't get away fast enough when she was seventeen. Now at the age of twenty-three it filled her with interest, and she eagerly watched for landmarks she had known since childhood. She felt strangely excited, almost exhilarated, which was the opposite of what she had expected after so long an absence.

She got off a stop before the Master's Arms, in order to walk the last quarter mile, and she noted all the shops she had known: the general store on the corner which sold sweets – she and her brothers had haunted it; the baker's that always gave off lovely smells; the pawnbrokers, with their three brass balls and ever-open door; the Jewish tailor. She knew them all and felt comforted by the familiarity.

A man was sweeping the pavement outside the Master's Arms. She accosted him, and asked if Mr Masterton was at home. He was, but he was ill, and not receiving visitors, the man informed her. Julia said 'He will see me. Can you let me in, please? I'm his daughter.'

The man stopped sweeping, leaned on his broom and stared at her.

'His daughter! I never knew 'e 'ad a daughter. Said 'is family was all dead.'

The daughter that never was, thought Julia sadly. He doesn't even mention me. But then, to be fair, she had never mentioned her father to the girls at the telephone exchange; so why would he, who was equally reserved, be likely to talk about her to his employees?

'I am his only living daughter. Can you let me in?'

The man was immediately respectful.

'No, ma'am, but Terry 'as a key. 'e was 'ead barman, but 'e's been manager since ve boss got ill. I'll take yer to him.'

Terry was equally surprised at the news of a daughter and muttered something about 'Me mum looks after ve old boy.' Julia did not like the familiarity.

'If you mean my father, then please refer to him as Mr Masterton,' she said coldly. 'Now please, let me in to the family quarters.'

She ascended the wooden stairs that she knew so well. All was quiet, save for her footsteps. She entered the big rooms where the family had lived together in happier days, where the children had laughed and played before Death spread its dark shadow over them. She saw the door of the room where her brothers had been laid out before burial, but she did not open it. Instead she went into the kitchen – it was clean but cold and appeared to be unused. Was no one there at all? She called out, 'Dad, are you here?' A voice answered 'Who's there? Is that Mrs Weston?' She went towards the sound of the voice. 'No, it's not Mrs Weston. It's me, Julia.'

She went into a bedroom. In a single bed by the window lay a man she did not recognise. His face was thin and shrunken, his eyes sunk deep into the eye-sockets. His breathing was fast, difficult and noisy and his neck was so thin it looked as though it might snap. His skin was grey, but two patches of bright red colouring under the eyes made him look as if he had been painted like a clown. Thin hands rested on the sheets, and bony fingers with long nails were plucking at the bedclothes. 'Is that you, Mrs Weston?' he croaked. He turned his head, and his dull eyes grew wider as he recognised her.

'Julia! What are you doing here?' His voice was husky.

'I heard you were ill, Dad.'

'It's nothing much. Just a passing fancy. The doctor's been. He says I'm getting along nicely. I'll be up and doing in a few days. Nice to see you, girl. Sit down.'

She took a chair and sat next to the bed.

'Why didn't you let me know you were ill?'

'No need to bother anyone. You've got your own life to lead. I do all right here. Mrs Weston comes in and does for me. I thought you were her just now when you called. I didn't think for a moment it would be you.'

Julia felt herself choking with emotion.

'I'm sorry, Dad. I should have come earlier, long ago.'

'No, no, girl. 'course not. You've got your own life. And you're doing all right, I dare say. Is it still the Telephone Exchange?' She nodded. 'A good job, good prospects. You'll be doing all right – your own life, your own friends – you can't be looking backwards over your shoulder all the time.'

Julia compared the imaginary contentment his words implied with the bleak reality of her life. She did not know what to say.

'Do you get enough food?'

'Mrs Weston comes in and cooks for me, but I don't want much. Can't seem to get it down.'

'Oh, Dad. What can I do?' Julia felt close to tears.

'Nothing, girl, nothing. You get on and enjoy your own life. You're only young once; make the most of it.'

'But Dad, I must do something.'

'Don't take on, girl. I want for nothing. Mrs Weston gets me all I need, and I've appointed her son Terry as manager. He'll keep the pub going until I'm up and doing myself.'

He sank back on the pillows. The effort of speaking had exhausted him. Julia sat quietly, engulfed in remorse, regret and self-reproach. Her own father, whom she had not seen for six years, and he looked to be on the point of death. His eyes were closed, but he stretched out a limp hand towards her and whispered rather than spoke.

'It's nice to see you, lass. Good of you to come. I appreciate it.'

'Would you like Mum to come?'

'Your mother? I don't know as she would want to.'

'She says she will if you would like her to. She won't push herself on you she says.' He did not reply, but sighed deeply, closed his eyes and appeared to drift off to sleep. Julia sat beside him looking at the tragic waste of the man she had always called Dad but had never really known. A man who had always been so alive and vital, who commanded instant respect and obedience from his staff, who excelled them all in strength and energy, who ran the Master's Arms with a Master's efficiency.

She knew what she must do. She would leave the telephone exchange without notice and quit her room. She need not leave her father even to collect things – her landlady could send them on, there was little enough to send. She pondered all that she would have to do – see the doctor, arrange for a day nurse, get advice on diet, exercise and how best to keep her father comfortable. She felt nervous of her own inexperience and longed for her mother to be there to advise her.

Her father slept, so she left his side and wandered round the flat, which was big and spacious. She perched on the corner seat between the two windows where she and her brothers had sat looking down on the changing scenes in the street below. She climbed the narrow stairs up to the attic full of junk where they had played hide and seek. The same junk, which had belonged to her grandparents, was there, a bit more dust and decay, but the same. She would have been outraged if anything had been changed! She went into the big kitchen, once so full of life and nice smells enticing to a child, but now cold and unused. She went into the bedroom she and her sister had shared and decided at once that she would occupy the same room. But one of the beds must go up to the attic – she could not sleep with Gillian's cold, empty bed in the room. She shuddered and returned to the kitchen to make a cup of tea.

Footsteps were heard on the stairs, and a man entered. He was youngish, cleanly dressed and carried a black bag. They met in the hallway and shook hands. He introduced himself as Dr Fuller.

'And I understand from Terry, the barman, that you are Miss Masterton, my patient's only living daughter?'

Julia nodded.

'I wish we had known about you a year ago. He said his family was dead.'

Julia felt herself blush with shame, and did not know what to say. Together they went into the sick room.

Expertly he examined the emaciated body. Julia winced to see the rib-cage exposed, with barely any flesh covering the bones. The doctor felt for enlarged lymph glands and neck rigidity. He palpated the chest at various points and listened through his stethoscope to the heart and the sounds of laboured breathing. He tested for muscular strength, which was almost nil. He looked into her father's eyes, and at his fingernails, which were a curious shape, Julia noticed. He examined the sputum in the pot. He said, 'You are doing nicely. Warmth, good food, and rest are what you need. I'm glad your daughter is here.'

'Yes. She has just come for the day. It's her day off work. It's nice to see her. A nice surprise.'

'I was hoping she would be staying,' said the doctor pointedly, knowing that Julia was just behind him.

'Oh no, no. She's got her own life to lead. She's doing well as a telegraphist. I don't want to be a drag on her. She's got her own friends, her own life.'

'I see,' said the doctor with a sigh. 'Well, I will return again in a few days.'

In the sitting room, Julia informed the doctor that she did intend staying, but had not told her father of her decision. She wanted to know more about his condition, and said that her four brothers and a sister had died of tuberculosis. The doctor told her that Mr Masterton had probably had a primary infection of the tubercle bacillus for many years, which had passed unnoticed. Any symptoms, such as fever or coughing, would have been put down to 'flu. However, about a year previously, a secondary infection had probably occurred, involving the mediastinal glands. 'I'm afraid that tuberculosis is now widespread throughout his lungs.'

Julia asked what treatment was available.

The doctor explained that treatment consisted of rest, warmth, good food, plentiful fluids, inhalations, postural drainage, fresh air and syrup of codeine linctus, and that later he would prescribe morphine.

Julia asked if her father would get better. The doctor looked unwilling to reply, but she insisted.

'I must know.'

'A year ago, my partner and I advised your father to go for six months' sanatorium treatment in the Swiss Alps. But he refused. He said he could not leave the pub for so long.'

'Typical,' said Julia angrily. 'He could never leave his pub, not even to save his own life. But do go on.'

'The clean air of the Alps might have saved his life, but it is too late now. Anyway, he seemed to improve for a while, or at least stabilise, and his decision seemed to be the right one. But two months ago he deteriorated rapidly. There is no drug available at this advanced stage that will effect a cure. In some cases, injection of sodium-gold thiosulphate is beneficial in diminishing the lung deposits, but we tried the gold injections weekly, with no effect. Your father, I am afraid, has now reached the stage of advanced phthisis, from which recovery cannot be expected.'

Julia sat quietly looking at the floor. She was not really surprised, just deeply sad.

'Can he go to a sanatorium now? The air of Poplar is notoriously bad, you know.'

The doctor smiled. 'Yes, I know, but there is no evidence that the air of Poplar causes tuberculosis. People living in ideal surroundings get the disease and do not recover. But your father cannot be moved now. It would kill him.'

Julia thought of her mother, toiling across Europe, a two-day journey by boat and train, with a sick child who had died shortly after arrival, and agreed with the doctor. 'So what can be done?' she whispered.

'You can make his life as comfortable as possible. He can eat what he likes, if he can eat at all. He can get up if he feels able to. Keep him warm. Inhalations are very soothing. You will need a nurse. I recommend the Nursing Sisters of St Raymund Nonnatus, an order of nuns who have worked in these parts for many years.'

Julia set about the massive task of tuberculous nursing with no knowledge or experience whatsoever. She did not tell her father of her plan to stay because she thought his pride might make him refuse her. Instead, she told him a story about having lost her job, and being unable to find another; that she had no money to pay the rent, and had been turned out of her lodgings.

Her father immediately said, 'That's hard, girl, you can come and stay here, of course, until you get on your feet again.'

After that he accepted her continued presence without question. He provided her with money to run their small ménage, to pay Mrs Weston for her cleaning, and to pay the doctor and the nurses, and for medicines. In fact, he was very generous, saying things like, 'Get yourself something pretty, a nice blouse or something. A young girl likes pretty things.'

He still kept a strict control of pub accounts. Ill as he was, and despite the fact he never went into the bar, he seemed to know exactly what was going on. Every morning Terry had to come upstairs and go through the previous day's sales. He had to give the number of customers in the bar, the number of sales and the quantity of stock consumed, and all was reckoned against the cash in the till, which was counted and entered in the ledger. Julia watched all this and marvelled that her father was so much in command. He seemed stronger while Terry was with him, and his mind was clear and focused. She also realised that it was only by maintaining such strong control that a publican could avoid being robbed by his staff. With hundreds of glasses of liquor being sold to customers every evening, it would be the easiest thing in the world to skew the money. Her father seemed to know from the daily sales what stock remained, and he placed all the orders himself and signed all the payment cheques. He was known by everyone as the Master, and his daughter came to admire his business acumen greatly. Her father would sink back on his pillows, exhausted and sweating, after Terry had gone; frequently he was coughing and trembling all over and needed his linctus and a cooling drink to get him over the ordeal. One day he said to Julia, 'Them doctors don't know anything about business. Wanted me to go away for six months, they did. That would have been a good day for the jackals if I'd gone, wouldn't it? There would have been nothing left by the time I got back.' He chuckled at his own astuteness, although Julia wondered what there was left of him through *not* going away to a sanatorium.

The doctor had advised she contact the Nursing Sisters, and as soon as Julia saw the heavy figure of Sister Evangelina lumbering upstairs she recognised her as the nun who had come to nurse her brothers when they were ill a decade previously. Sister was out of breath and grumpy by the time she got to the flat. She went straight to the sick room, sat down and demanded a cup of tea. Julia had expected a nun to be all holy water and prayers, but her opening remarks were about money.

'I will come each day, if you want me to, but it is going to cost you something, I warn you. We are an Order who nurse the poor. The Master of the Master's Arms is not poor. If you want me, you will have to pay handsomely, so that we can treat the poor for nothing. Take it or leave it and yes, two sugars please.'

Mr Masterton chuckled, which brought on a fit of coughing. Sister Evangelina sat drinking her tea, but watching him over the top of her teacup with an experienced eye. Eventually he was able to splutter, 'I agree, Sister, name your figure and I'll double it. There are thousands round here who can't afford to pay for the medical treatment they need.'

'Thousands?' she snorted. 'Tens of thousands would be nearer the mark. We see them all the time.'

She stared aggressively at Julia, who felt very small and didn't quite know what to make of the big nun.

'I suppose you don't know anything about good nursing, or any nursing at all, for that matter?'

Julia shook her head.

'No. I thought not. Ignorant girls. Dizzy young things. It seems to be my fate always to be landed with these flibbertigibbets. Well, I suppose you are better than nothing, so let's get on with it. Postural drainage is what the patient needs. Potions and pills and linctuses are all very fine, but they won't get the phlegm out of his lungs. Postural drainage,' she added emphatically and stood up. Julia was obliged to take a step backwards.

'In the bar I saw several trestle tables. That is what we need. Go to the bar and get the men to bring one up,' she commanded

Julia, who stood looking bewildered. 'Go on, go girl. Don't stand there gawping. And we will need a mattress.'

'A mattress?'

'That's what I said.'

'But we've got a mattress.'

'We will need another one. Now go on, go on. I haven't got all day, you know.'

Hastily Julia ran down to the bar. She was quite overwhelmed by the big nun, but she told two men to carry a trestle table upstairs, and then to fetch a mattress from the attic. The Sister looked at the equipment and grunted with satisfaction.

'Right, you fellows. Leave the table like that with the legs folded in, and lean one end against the bed, sloping gently – further up – yes that will do. Now pull that chest of drawers up to wedge it so that it can't slip. That will do nicely – now put the mattress over it. Good lads. Perfect.'

She glared hard at Terry.

'It's Terry Weston, isn't it?

He nodded.

'I thought as much. I knew you when you were about thirteen – you had eaten too much of something that didn't agree with you and couldn't get rid of it. Constipated for a fortnight, you were. I had to give you two enemas to shift it. Hope that taught you a lesson.'

Terry blushed scarlet, and the other man sniggered. Mr Masterton also laughed, which brought on the coughing again.

Sister shooed the men away, and when the coughing had subsided, she said gently, 'Now, Mr Masterton, we have to get some of that fluid off your chest. I want you to lie head down on the mattress. I am going to palpate your back, and show your daughter how to do it. I will help you to get into the right position.'

Julia marvelled at the gentleness of Sister Evangelina as she handled her patient. After behaving in such a brusque manner, it was unexpected. The nun was kind and respectful in every way as she helped Julia's father to get up and to lie face downwards on the sloping mattress. She explained that the position would drain fluid out of his lungs. 'Now I am going to palpate your back, cupping we call it, and massage from the lower lungs to the upper lobes, to try to shift some of the muck. We will need a bowl or a chamber pot for you to spit into, so fetch one, will you, nurse – I mean Miss Masterton?'

Julia did as she was bidden, then Sister began to work on her father's back. 'Watch me carefully,' she said, 'In a minute I am going to ask you to do it.' Her father coughed uncontrollably and brought up copious amounts of frothy fluid, streaked with thick ropes of greenish phlegm. 'You will feel better after this,' said Sister Evangelina to the sick man. 'Now come here, Miss Masterton. You have a go.'

Julia was terrified of touching her father's back, which looked so thin and fragile, but she could not disobey this commanding woman. 'That's right. Shape your hands like cups and slap from lower to upper lobes; keep going – round the sides also. Now some massage. You have the idea. You have a feel for it. Ten minutes is enough. Now cover your patient, he must be kept warm.' Then to Julia's utter astonishment the nun smiled and said, 'Good girl. Well done.'

To Mr Masterton she said, 'This must be done every day, twice a day. Your daughter can do it, and afterwards you must lie for about twenty minutes head down. It will make you feel a good deal better. I am going to leave you now, but I will call each day.'

Once they were in the sitting room, Sister turned to Julia and said abruptly, 'This will not cure your father. Nothing will cure him short of a miracle. But it will make him feel easier. Eventually he will drown in the fluid which accumulates in his lungs, but in the meantime it is our duty to make him as comfortable as possible. Apart from which I usually find that such drastic treatment encourages the patient into thinking that something positive is being done. This stimulates hope.'

She grunted and humphed, gathered up her things and plodded heavily downstairs. In the bar she called out, 'I'll be back tomorrow, Terry. In the meantime, keep 'em open, then you won't get bunged up again,' to the immense discomfort of the poor fellow and the hilarity of the lunchtime customers.

Julia nursed her father for three months, and during that time she grew to understand him more. His reticence and reserve appealed to her temperament; the way he shrugged off suffering won her admiration; his desire not to be a nuisance was touching; and his gratitude for the least thing she did for him was unexpected. His constant interest in and care for his pub was consistent with the man she had known throughout her childhood. She admired the huge effort he made each morning, going over the accounts with Terry, and she always stayed in the room in order to help her father, should he need help. Sister Evangelina came each day, and together they administered postural drainage and massage, and she saw the fortitude with which her father endured it. He always seemed a little better an hour later, so they continued.

He never openly showed affection, but one evening he squeezed her hand and muttered, 'You're a good girl, Julia, the only one left. Go to that cupboard and get the box out. I haven't seen it for years; we'll look at it together.'

Julia did as she was bid. Her father sat up in bed, his eyes bright, his breathing laboured.

'Open it, lass, will you? I can't any more.'

Opening the box, so long unopened, revealed more of her father than anything else could have done. Inside was a jumble of children's toys and books, colouring pencils, pictures drawn by a childish hand, a small teddy bear and a china doll. At the bottom was a wooden Noah's Ark.

'Get it out, Julie, we must look at it.'

Julia opened it up and took out the wooden animals. Her father chuckled.

'I remember you all playing with these. Do you?'

Of course she did, and the memory nearly choked her. He fingered the giraffe, and the lion, and the ghosts of her brothers seemed to enter the room.

'There's another box in there. Lift it out, will you?'

She did so, and it was full of toy soldiers. Her father handled them eagerly, his eyes bright.

'I bought these as a birthday present, once. The boys played with them for hours.'

The dying man closed his eyes.

'I can see them now, all over the floor with their soldier games.'

Julia looked at him, and a wave of tenderness swept over her. 'All gone, all dead,' he murmured, and his hand fell limply on the counterpane. But then he brightened. 'There's a little cotton bag in the bottom; pull it out.' Inside the bag were some hair ribbons and a child's bolero, the ones he had asked her to send to Gillian for her birthday when the family were in Skegness. He took the bolero, which was made of soft angora, and rubbed it up and down his cheek. 'Is there a card there? Read it to me, will you?' Julia read the card from Gillian, which said how lovely the bolero was, and how she wore it all the time and would not take it off. Her father chuckled. 'Wouldn't take it off, bless her,' but then his face crumpled, and tears started in his eyes. He turned his head away quickly, ashamed of his weakness. 'Go and get a cup of tea, there's a good girl.'

Julia left the bedroom in tears. So he had cared after all, and she had not known it. She lit the gas stove, put the kettle on and drew the kitchen curtains. The sounds from the pub were starting downstairs, but she hardly noticed them any more; they were just part of life. The singing and dancing would begin soon, but she no longer resented them. She sat down at the kitchen table and leaned her head on her arms and sobbed. Why was he dying now, just when she was getting to know him? He was the father she had never had but had always wanted, because all girls want a father to love.

The tears did her good. She stood up and washed her eyes in cold water, then made the tea and returned with it to the sick room.

Her father appeared to be asleep, with toys and books and childish things all around him, so she decided not to disturb him. She poured herself a cup of tea and sat down beside him. She took his hand, and he responded with a little squeeze; the other hand held the fluffy pink bolero. He stirred a little. 'Do you want that cup of tea, Dad?' she whispered. 'By and by,' he croaked, 'by and by,' and he drifted off to sleep again. She sat quietly beside him, as the sounds of 'Pack up yer troubles' floated upstairs. She shut the window, but he roused again. 'No, don't do that. It's nice to hear them enjoying themselves.' She opened it again and the shouts of '. . . . in yer ol' kit bag and smile, smile, smile' came flooding in. 'Smile,' he croaked. 'That's what we gotta do. It's a funny old world, eh, Julie?' And he drifted off into sleep once more.

Julia sat beside him for several hours; she couldn't bring herself to leave him. Darkness fell, and the tea grew cold. The noise from the pub ceased at closing time but continued in the street for a while. Raucous shouts and shrill cries grew fainter as the customers wandered or staggered away to their homes. A few tuneless attempts at a song, accompanied by a guffaw of laughter – and then all was quiet.

Julia fell asleep in her chair, and when she awoke the Master of the Master's Arms was dead, surrounded by children's toys.

THE MISTRESS

I saw pale kings and princes too
Pale warriors, death-pale were they all;
They cried – 'La Belle Dame sans Merci
Thee hath in thrall!'
'La Belle Dame Sans Merci', by John Keats

Julia was so accustomed to death in her family that she was neither afraid nor surprised when she found her father had died in his sleep. She waited till morning and then called the doctor. When Terry came up with the previous day's account of sales he questioned if they should close the pub for the day. She thought for a moment and then said no, her father would not have wished it – business as usual. But she told him to put a notice on the bar informing all customers and requesting quiet, out of respect for the Master.

Two days later a lawyer called. He informed Julia that she was the sole inheritor of the Master's Arms, of the buildings and all its assets, subject to a life annuity for Mrs Masterton. The will had been made six years earlier. Julia was shattered. The inheritance of the pub had not crossed her mind. If she had thought of it at all, it was only in a vague way, as though a business can carry on by itself. Her first words to the lawyer were 'What am I going to do?' He explained that she could sell the freehold to one of the big brewers, and that he would arrange the business side of things for her. 'You will be a wealthy woman,' he added.

Julia was a mere twenty-three years old, and the large inheritance overwhelmed her. When the lawyer had gone she wandered around the flat in a daze. She made her way down to the bar, and the staff and several lunchtime customers came over to her with words of sympathy. She went down to the cellar and looked at the huge barrels, the crates of stock and the bottles lining the walls. It was all hers. She felt numb with shock, and her mind was in turmoil. She returned to the flat and sat for a long time in the window seat overlooking the street. She watched the women gossiping or passing by, many pushing prams, going in and out of the little shops, some now and then making a furtive entry into a pawn-shop. Two barrow boys were arguing over a pitch. She heard children's voices from a nearby school. There was a street sweeper with his hand-cart. A woman flower-seller trundling along with her basket. A group of seamen in clogs and a Chinaman with a pigtail went past. A woman opposite was scrubbing and whitening her front doorstep. A shopkeeper in his long green apron was sweeping the pavement in front of his store. The lawyer had told Julia that she could sell and she would be a wealthy woman. But sitting in the window and watching the street scene had a calming effect on Julia, and she realised, for the first time, that she was amongst her own people, and that this was where she belonged. The memory of her father's hard work and pride in his achievement, and that of her grandparents, brought with it a proud and stubborn resolution: she would not sell, she would be the fifth-generation landlord of the Master's Arms.

The staff cheered when she told them of her decision, but were dubious, because she was a woman. They had not taken into account Julia's determination to succeed. Knowing that she was little more than a girl taking on a man's job, her instinct told her that she would have to be the undisputed boss from the very beginning.

She immersed herself in the business, taking over her father's office, and apart from cleaning it up a bit and introducing flowers and some pictures, she changed very little. She poured over the ledgers and on her own initiative drew a graph of sales and purchases throughout the year, which was pinned to the wall, giving an immediate visual record of profit and loss. She familiarised herself with suppliers and visited breweries and distilleries, causing quite a stir among the men, who had never seen a woman publican before, still less a young and pretty one. But Julia was always reserved and serious-looking, which did not invite cat-calls or lewd comments. In all this Terry was indispensable to her, and, knowing that she could not succeed without him, she raised his wages.

Each day she spent a great deal of time in the bar, watching how a pub was run, and admiring the skill and speed of the barmen. But when one of them slipped his arm around her waist and murmured that she needed a man's help now, and if they married they could make a real success of it, she slapped his face and sacked him. She also sacked one of the barmaids who took the liberty of calling her 'Julia', with the cold words 'My name is Miss Masterton.' There were no more 'Julias' after that, and the rest of the staff were quietly respectful. She had Terry's unqualified support, but she knew that she needed another man, preferably one with fighting skills, and she found one in Chubb, an ex-professional heavyweight with a broken nose and no front teeth. He was running to fat, and of limited intelligence, but the hammer fists and ingrown profile ensured that no one would knock his beer over to see how he took it. Chubb and Terry served her with dog-like devotion, and she rewarded them accordingly.

Within a few weeks she was known as the Mistress of the Master's Arms, a title in which she took great pride. Several of the big breweries offered to buy her out, but she refused them all, preferring to run a free house.

Every day she was in the bar, memorising and ordering stock, overseeing sales, bar and table service, and the hundred and one other things involved in running a pub. The local customers were intrigued by the new Mistress, who was always courteous and welcoming, but never over-friendly or familiar. She was even around during the sing-song and knees-up. She never joined in, but just stood quietly, watching and smiling. Chubb the Brawn was never far from her, and if anything got too rowdy a look from Julia and a movement from Chubb would put a stop to it instantly. In observing and analysing the people who came in, Julia realised that the pub and its atmosphere were an essential outlet for high spirits in her Cockney clients. One thing, however, had always made her unhappy, and that was seeing children hanging around the doors of the pub waiting for their parents. She was determined to do something about it. There was no point in refusing admission to the parent; they would merely move on to the next pub, and probably wallop the children as well. So she got the men to clear one of the stock rooms which was quite separate from the licensed premises, and turned it into a children's room. This was a completely new idea. A lot of people were scornful, but it worked, and sales increased.

It was 1937 when the Master died and Julia took over. Rumours of war were spreading all over Europe. No one believed, or wanted to believe, it could happen so soon after the last war, but Churchill thundered on about the dangers, and the Government dithered about rearmament. Two years passed, and in September 1939 war was declared. 'It will all be over by Christmas,' everyone said cheerfully. But it wasn't, and a year later on 30 September 1940, the bombing of London started with a ferocity hitherto undreamed of. For fifty-seven nights an average of 200 German bombers a night attacked London, aiming mainly at the Docklands. Acres of housing were destroyed, many were killed, and thousands of people made homeless. Noise, destruction, burning and death filled the streets, and each night nobody knew if they would live to see the morning.

The Master's Arms in Poplar was in the thick of it, and the chances of a direct hit, killing all inside, were pretty high. Julia felt she ought to close the pub and move to the safety of the countryside, but seeing the relief occasioned by the pub's warm and welcoming atmosphere made her hesitate. One day she was standing at the door, looking at the smoke and the devastation all around, and the rescue workers digging in the rubble for survivors, when a little old woman caught her eye. She was typical of the older generation of Cockneys – tiny, skinny, bright-eyed, toothless, with straggly grey hair beneath a greasy greyish cap and wearing a long, frowsty coat, of that indescribable colour created by age, damp and decay. She was standing in the street, smacking her lips and grunting to herself. An ambulance worker came up to her and said kindly, 'Are you all right, mother?' Quick as a flash she replied, 'All right? 'course I'm bleedin' all right! Vat bugger Hitler, 'e's bombed me 'ouse, 'ard luck, 'e's killed me ol' man, good riddance, 'e's got me boys – vey're all fightin' in ve war – 'e's got me girls, vey're somewhere, dunno where. But 'e aint got me. An' I got sixpence 'ere in me pocket, an' ve Master's Arms is open.' She grabbed his arm and grinned a toothless grin. 'So let's go in, mate, an' 'ave a drink an' a sing-song.'

That old woman banished Julia's indecision. She would not abandon her people. She would stick it out. If they wanted a drink and a sing-song, they should have it. She would not close the pub. Most of her staff were being called up into the services – all the young men went, including Terry – but she managed to keep going on a skeleton staff. Then a draft came from the Ministry requiring her services as an experienced telegraphist. She had to obey, so she worked all day in the telegraph office and all evening in the pub. Her office work was squeezed in after the pub closed. With a routine working day of about eighteen hours, she was always tired. But she survived, and the Master's Arms stayed open all through the war.

Julia had always been a remote, self-contained person, and the war years intensified this side of her personality. Life was hard, she could see the evidence all around her, and she could see little to smile about. She had loved her mother, whom she continued to meet occasionally, and her brothers and sisters, now dead; she had even grown to love her father at the very end of his life, when it was too late. But apart from that, love had not touched her and local people always said, 'She's a typical old maid.'

But one should never judge from appearances. Still waters run deep, and in wartime love affairs are intense, complicated, sometimes fleeting, but passionate.

Like a thunderbolt of God's grace, a man from RAF Intelligence Service walked into the telegraph exchange. He was twenty-five years older than she was, and married, but they loved with passionate intensity. They met seldom, and she never knew where he was stationed, because it was top security, but it made no difference. Their moments together were ecstatic and life-renewing. They gave themselves to each other, body and soul, because they both knew that they might never meet again. Death, if it came, would be swift and violent; it could come at any time, and neither would know the fate of the other.

It was 1945. Everyone knew that the war was coming to an end, and there was a lightness of heart in the air. In the Master's Arms each evening drinking and singing continued, and Julia watched her customers with quiet satisfaction. Against all odds the pub had never closed, and by a miracle it stood undamaged, alone amid streets of rubble.

And another miracle was about to happen; Julia realised that she was pregnant. At first she was fearful, but when she felt the quickening of new life within her, a thrill of unspeakable joy flooded her whole body. She was going to have *his* baby. Her love affair, lasting three years, had always been fraught with as much sorrow as joy; the stolen hours were always too brief, and the partings always agony. They both knew that, even if they survived the war, they would lose each other in the end, because he was a married man. The heartbreak was overpowering when the final parting came. But now his child was growing within her, and she could never be wholly separated from him. She thrilled with happiness. The child would always be with her, the consummation of her first and only love.

A baby girl was born and filled Julia's life with a happiness she had never dared hope for. All her maternal instincts of love and protection were focused on the baby and her life was emotionally complete. She continued to run the pub with her usual efficiency, and she engaged a nanny each evening when she needed to be downstairs in the bar. Terry had returned from war service and resumed his job, as manager, so she had more time to spend with her baby. People talked, of course, – people always do – and a baby born out of wedlock was a juicy subject for gossip. Some said, 'She's a dark 'orse,' while others said, 'She's no better 'an she should be,' but Julia was not perturbed. People had always talked about her, and she had always been indifferent to their comments. Nothing could spoil her happiness, and her staff noticed a softening in her eyes and a radiance in her features that they had never seen before.

It was 1957 when I first saw Miss Masterton, twenty years after she had taken over the Master's Arms from her father. It was my day off, which happened to be on a Saturday, and I had been showing my West End friends, Jimmy and Mike, and some of their set, around the Docks. We ended the day in the Master's Arms. There was a pleasant, relaxed atmosphere, and we settled down for a good session. The pub filled up as the evening wore on – local people on their night out, looking for fun. The war had changed much, but not the Cockney's appetite for bawdy enjoyment. A pianist started to bang out 'Doin' the Lambeth Walk, hoi!' and within seconds everyone joined in, *con belto* style. Glasses were raised with every 'oi!' which grew louder and louder with each refrain. Bodies swayed in rhythm, and beer was spilled. Our group sat in a corner and exchanged surprised glances. 'This is going to be fun,' we muttered. Then a group of girls got up, linked arms and started a side-kick routine to the 'Lambeth Walk', which went on and on, till they sank down exhausted amid cheers and whistles. 'Run rabbit run' followed, and several old music hall songs. Someone got up and acted as chorus master with an 'all together now . . .' and the pub was filled with raucous voices splitting their vocal cords. It was impossible to hear yourself speak, so we just sat back and enjoyed it.

One woman in particular caught my eye. She was standing behind the bar. She was about forty-five, was well-dressed and good-looking, but was not the typical barmaid. She was quietly pleasant to all her customers, but in a subtle way, seemingly detached from everything around her. Yet at the same time she was obviously watching everyone and everything that was going on. A group sitting by the door began to get a bit quarrelsome, one man shouting at and threatening another. The woman stepped out from behind the bar and walked towards the table. She did not say a word; she just looked at the two men and, somewhat shamefaced, they sat down. There was no more trouble. Her whole aspect exuded quiet self-confidence, but when you looked at her face there was something missing, something in the eyes that I could not define; a sort of blank, vacant expression, as though she was looking at people but not seeing them, or looking through and beyond them to something that was not there.

The boys were enjoying themselves and wanted to stay, but for me, the noise was getting a bit too ear-splitting for comfort, so I left early. As I walked back to the convent, the memory of the woman's face, and the look in her eyes, haunted me.

A few weeks later I saw her again, but it was a very different person from the woman I had seen in the pub. I was in All Saints Church with Sister Julienne. It was mid-afternoon, and the church was empty but for Sister and me. Then a woman staggered in. I did not recognise her at first, her hair was dishevelled, her eyes so red from weeping that she could hardly see, and her legs seemed barely able to support her. She looked wildly around her and clung to one of the pews for support. Sister Julienne went up to her to ask if she could help, but the woman did not answer. She took a couple of faltering steps forward and croaked, rather than spoke.

'Yes, this is the place. Six years ago it was. Here, in this church.'

She let out a low moan and staggered forward a few more steps.

'They stopped here, right here where I am standing. This is where they rested it, the little, little coffin. Six years ago to this day.'

She sank on to a seat and sobbed.

Sister asked if she could do anything to help.

'No. No one can help me. Nothing can bring her back. I just want to light a candle, and then I'll go.'

Sister helped her to the altar, and they lit a candle together and prayed. Then they sat quietly talking for a minute or two. Finally the woman stood up. She did not say anything, but she looked slightly more composed. She walked towards the spot where she had stopped before, where she said the coffin had rested. She stood silently for a few minutes and then with a firmer step walked out of the church.

I asked Sister if she knew the woman, and she told me it was Miss Masterton, owner of the Master's Arms. And then she told me the tragic story of the tuberculosis which had claimed nearly all her family, and lastly her little girl, aged six. The mother had nearly gone mad with grief, she had doted so on the child.

I told Sister Julienne that I had seen Miss Masterton in the pub, and something about her had caught my attention, perhaps the look in her eyes.

'Yes, there is something in the eyes of a woman who has lost a child that sets her apart from others. The grief and pain never go away. And for Miss Masterton it was all the more terrible because she was advised to be tested for the tubercle bacillus herself. Blood tests were taken showing that she was a carrier of the bacillus, and had been for a long time, but had never shown any signs or symptoms and had never succumbed to the disease herself. It is probable that she had infected her own daughter.'

THE ANGELS

While she could vividly remember things from long past, Sister Monica Joan's short-term memory seemed to be getting shorter and shorter. She appeared to have forgotten completely the unpalatable fact that she had been before the Court of the London Quarter Sessions on a charge of larceny only a few months previously. The prosecution had alleged that she had stolen jewels from Hatton Garden and initially all the evidence had pointed to her guilt. But a surprise witness proved her innocence. The trial had been a shock, to say the very least, for the convent, but for Sister Monica Joan it was as though it had never happened. She was her old self, delightful and entertaining, in her conversation, but in her behaviour she was becoming increasingly eccentric and unpredictable.

Sister had a niece, more accurately a great great niece, living in Sonning, Berkshire. They had not met or communicated for many years. One day Sister decided to visit her niece, and what is more she determined that a pair of fine Chippendale chairs which she had in her room should be presented to the woman as a gift. Accordingly, she left Nonnatus House early one morning while the Sisters were at prayer, and before Mrs B the cook or Fred the boiler man arrived. How she carried two chairs downstairs is impossible to conjecture, but she did.

Out in the street, she carried one chair to the corner and then came back for the other. She proceeded in this fashion to the East India Dock Road, where a policeman approached and asked her if he could help. Sister Monica Joan did not like policemen. She exclaimed, 'Tush, out of my way, fellow,' and rammed the chair leg into his stomach. The policeman decided to let her get on with it.

Sister reached the bus stop and sat down to regain her breath. A bus came, and the conductor, being a kindly soul, helped her on with her two chairs and put them in the luggage hold. When they reached Aldgate, he helped her off and pointed to where she could catch a bus to Euston, where she would have to change onto another for Paddington Station.

It was approaching rush hour when the bus trundled into Paddington. The bus stop was some distance from the railway station, so Sister left one of the chairs (Chippendale, of enormous value) at the bus stop whilst she carried the other to the station. Then she left that one in the station forecourt, and returned for the second. Once in the station things became easier for Sister Monica Joan, because she found a porter who loaded the chairs onto his trolley and took them to the train bound for Reading, were she would have to change onto a branch line for Sonning.

Meanwhile at Nonnatus House the alarm was raised. Sister Monica Joan was missing, and no one had a clue where she had got to. Mrs B was in tears. The police were informed but could offer no help. At lunchtime a phone call was received stating that a policeman had reported seeing a nun at six o'clock in the morning in the East India Dock Road, and that she had rammed a chair leg into his stomach.

'A chair leg!' cried Sister Julienne incredulously. 'What was she doing with a chair leg?'

'She was carrying a chair,' replied the duty policeman.

'But that's impossible. She is ninety, and it was in the East India Dock Road, you tell me.'

'I'm only telling you what the constable reported, ma'am. I'm not making anything up. Now, if you will excuse me, I have work to do. We'll keep an eye open for this missing nun, and if we have any more reports of her activities, you will be informed. Good day to you, ma'am.'

Sister went hastily to Sister Monica Joan's room and observed that not only one chair was missing, but two! Lunchtime conversation around the big dining table focused on nothing else, and prayers were said for Sister Monica Joan's safety.

The train reached Sonning station at about midday, and Sister Monica Joan telephoned her niece. There was no reply. So she decided to go with God and sat down on one of the chairs to have a little doze. A kindly porteress gave her a cup of tea. At about four o'clock she telephoned again, and this time she was lucky. Her niece was at home. Her astonishment at hearing from her great aunt after so many years, especially as she was waiting at the station with two chairs, can only be imagined. The niece came in her car to collect her aunt. Only one chair could be fitted into the boot, so the other had to be left on the pavement outside the station. It was still there when she returned a couple of hours later.

They telephoned the convent at about five o'clock. The niece said her aunt was tired but happy, and was welcome to stay for a few days if she wanted to. She added that she had received no warning of the intended visit, and that it was only by chance that she was at home at all, as her work often took her away for several days at a time. What would have happened to her aunt had she been away, she could not imagine. The telephone was passed to Sister Monica Joan, who in reply to Sister Julienne's anxious enquiries said, 'Of course I'm all right. Don't fuss so. Why should I not be all right? The angels look after me.'

The angels certainly had a heavy responsibility looking after Sister Monica Joan, and they could never relax their vigilance for a moment. Take the occasion when she nearly set fire to herself, for example. She had complained that the light in her room was insufficient, and that she could not see to read in bed; it was not good enough, something must be done. Obligingly, Fred, our odd-job man, ran a small cable up the wall and fixed a light just above her head. It was nothing fancy – just a bulb over which a small, fringed shade was placed. Sister Monica Joan was delighted. So simple; dear Fred – she could always rely on him, and now she could read in bed all night, if she wanted to.

She did want to, with alarming consequences. Since her bout of pneumonia, caused by wandering down the East India Dock Road in her nightie on a cold November morning, Sister Monica Joan had been favoured by being allowed to have her breakfast in bed. Mrs B usually took it up around 9 a.m., after we midwives and nurses had gone out on our morning visits. But the angels must have seen to it that Mrs B needed to be at the market by 9 a.m. that particular morning, and so she took Sister's breakfast up at 8 a.m. We were all in the kitchen having our breakfast, and the nuns were still in chapel. The house was quiet, except for the scratch-scratch of Fred raking out the boiler. A piercing scream, followed by louder repeated screams, shattered the calm. We girls and Fred rushed into the hallway, all shouting, 'What is it, where did it come from?' The chapel door opened, and the nuns ran out. (Nuns have been known to run, when the occasion demands!) The screams had stopped, but we could hear someone rushing about on the first floor. 'Stay where you are,' ordered Sister Julienne. 'Fred, come with me.' Disappointed at missing the drama, I waited with the others in the hallway. A smell of burning now filled the air. More running feet, more muffled voices, and smoke billowed along the corridor. Someone went to the bathroom, taps were turned on, windows were closed, banging and stamping was heard, and then Sister Julienne's calm voice: 'I think we have got it under control now. Thank God you came up when you did, Mrs B, otherwise I tremble to think of the outcome.'

Sister Monica Joan, protesting about being disturbed, was led out of her room and away from the smoke to the safety of the ground floor. Mrs B was in a very much worse state. She was pale and shaking, and needed several cups of strong tea fortified with whisky before she could tell us what had happened. Sister had had her new light on, with the pillows arranged so that she could sit up. The topmost pillow was touching the light bulb, and she must have fallen asleep. As Mrs B entered the room, a tiny flicker of flame no more than an inch high had leaped from the pillow. Mrs B screamed and dragged it from under the sleeping head. The open door and the movement had caused the pillow, which must have been smouldering for some time, to burst into flames. Her repeated screams brought help, and a rug thrown over the burning pillow and heavy stamping had controlled the fire. But the smoke was terrible, and they were lucky not to have been overcome by fumes. In the meantime Sister Monica Joan had sat on the bed saying, 'Gracious heaven! What *are* you doing?'

No one was hurt. The hem of Sister Julienne's habit was badly scorched, but she was not burned. They were all black with smoke and soot. But Sister Monica Joan was the least troubled of anyone. Either she genuinely forgot about it or decided that it would be expedient to do so (I could never be quite sure), but she did not refer to the incident again. When the light was removed from above her bed she said nothing, but she put on her hard-done-by look.

Then there was the occasion when Sister Monica Joan got stuck in the bath.

We girls first became aware that something was amiss when we heard movements and voices from the Sisters' floor during the period of the Greater Silence. This is the time after Compline, the last office of the day, and before Mass, the first of the new day, during which hours complete silence is normally observed in the monastic tradition. But on this occasion the Sisters were by no means observing the rule. First we heard one or two whispered words, then more, then a gaggle of anxious voices all talking at once, accompanied by banging on a door, and calls of 'Sister, can you hear us? Open the door.'

What was going on? We looked enquiringly at each other. Novice Ruth came running downstairs.

'Is Fred still here? Has he gone yet?' she called as she ran towards the kitchen. We didn't know, but then heard 'Fred, thank goodness you are still here. Come quickly to the second floor. We think you'll have to break down a door.'

Mysterious! Exciting! Thrilling! We girls looked at each other expecting more.

We heard more voices upstairs but didn't know what was going on. Fred came back down and passed us as we stood expectantly on the landing.

'What is it, Fred? What's up?'

'I'm goin' outside to see if ve winder's open.'

'The window? We thought it was a door.'

'It'll be easier.'

'Than what?'

'Than breaking ve door.'

And off he ran.

At this point Sister Julienne came downstairs and met Fred coming in.

'Yes, Sister. Winder's open. I reckons as 'ow I can do it.'

'Oh, Fred, you're wonderful. But do be careful.'

Fred assumed an heroic air.

'Don' choo worry 'bout me, Sister. I'm OK. We gotter ge' the 'ol lady safe, like. I'll get ve ladders.'

And off he ran.

Cynthia spoke. 'Sister, please tell us what is going on.'

'Well, the bathroom door is locked. It seems that Sister Monica Joan is in the bath and can't get out, but no one can get in to help her.'

Eager to get a slice of the action, I said, 'Fred's getting on a bit. I'm more agile than he is. Couldn't I go up the ladder?'

Sister looked at me knowingly.

'I have no doubt that you are more agile. But if you suggested to Fred that he was getting on and was no longer capable of going up a ladder he would be highly offended. We'll leave it to him.'

Twenty minutes later Fred came downstairs looking,

unusually for him, abashed. The fag that normally hung from his lower lip was not there. He looked different without it.

'What happened, Fred?' we chorused.

Knowing that we were agog with anticipation and that he was the only source of information, just to tease us he took out a battered tobacco tin from his pocket and started rolling another thin fag.

'Oh, Fred. Don't provoke. Tell us what happened.'

He lit his fag, scratched his head and looked at us with his south-west eye, before saying, 'Well, I reckon as 'ow I must be ve only bloke in England wot's seen a nun stark naked.'

'Oooh!'

He was warmed to his story by our reaction.

'Well, I gets up ve ladder to ve winder, like, an' pokes me 'ead in. "Be off with you, fellow," she calls out. 'I gotta ge' in, Sister,' I says. "Come back another day, if you must; it's not convenient at the moment." And she splashes water in me face. Well, I wasn't expectin' it, an' I nearly lost me balance.'

'Oooh, Fred. Poor Fred.'

He was really enjoying himself.

'But I grabs ve sides of ve winder an' hangs on, and says, "I'm sorry, Sister, but I gotta get in. You can't stay in 'ere all night. You'll catch yer death o' cold." Nah, tricky bit is ve bath's under the winder, so I 'as ter get in an' over the bath, wiv 'er in it an' not fall in meself.'

'How did you manage that, Fred?'

'Wiv difficulty 'an injinuity. Jest bein' smart, like.'

'Fred, you are so clever.'

'Nah, nah, jest smart like,' he said modestly. 'Worse fing was I drops me fag some'ow, an it floats around ve ole lady. Then I unlocks ve door, and Sisters come in, an' now I'm goin' a put me ladders away.'

'Would you like a cup of tea before you go, Fred?'

'Well now, vat's an invitation I can't resist, if you girls will 'ave one wiv me.'

Of course we would. We would like nothing better. So we all sat down in the big kitchen for a cup of tea and some of Mrs B's cake and a good old natter.

Upstairs we heard further sounds of movement and voices, then splashing of water and the gurgling of a waste pipe. Then no more. The Greater Silence had begun.

Sister Monica Joan was found in the bicycle shed one winter's night by Chummy who had been called out at about two o'clock. Again, the angels must have arranged it. If Sister had remained in the shed until morning she would probably have died of hypothermia; she was very thin, having no protective reserves of fat to cover her old bones. Chummy was getting her bicycle out when she heard a movement in the corner of the shed and thought it was a rat – we were all nervous of rats in dark places. She shone her torch over the area and was horrified, and indeed terrified, to see an arm move. Then an imperious voice, accustomed to being obeyed, ordered, 'Don't shine the light in my eyes like that! Fetch me a pillow if you want to be useful, but turn the light off.'

Sister Monica Joan was curled up in some old camping equipment, probably dating back to someone's Girl Guide endeavours. She was very cold and very sleepy, which is a dangerous combination. She resented being disturbed and tried to push Chummy away. 'Go away with your nasty lights and bothersome noise. Why can't I be left in peace?' Chummy carried her into the house and alerted the Sisters as she had to go out to a labouring mother. The Sisters covered the old lady with warm blankets and hot-water bottles and gave her hot drinks. Astonishingly she came to no harm, not even a cold in the nose.

I was in her room a few days later and referred to the night's adventure. She dismissed it as 'a lot of fuss about nothing'.

'Well,' I remarked, 'you were lucky that there was some old

camping equipment in the shed to cover you, or you might have died of cold.'

'Camping,' she said, 'such fun! We used to love it.' Her eyes were alight and her voice animated.

'Camping, Sister?' I exclaimed. 'You can't be serious. You've been camping?'

She was offended.

'Certainly, my dear. You don't imagine I have done nothing in my life, do you? We used to go camping often, my brothers and sisters, and some friends, with the maid and the manservant. It was wonderful.'

'A maid and manservant? Camping?'

'It was perfectly proper – a husband and wife in our service.'

'I wasn't thinking of the propriety of the arrangements But servants! Camping . . .' My voice failed me.

'We needed them, my dear. We needed the man to put up the tents and fetch the water and light the fires and things like that, and we needed the maid to do the cooking.'

'Well, if you put it like that, Sister, I suppose you did.'

I chuckled quietly, but I don't think she saw the joke.

One memorable Sunday afternoon Cynthia and I took Sister Monica Joan for a walk. The weather was beautiful, and we decided to take her up to Victoria Park, where there is a lovely lake, and where East Enders would gather with their children in sunny weather. But when the bus arrived it was full, so on the spur of the moment we changed our plan and took the next bus, which was going to Limehouse, and past the canal known as the Cuts. We thought we could have a walk along the towpath. The canal was dug in the nineteenth century to connect the River Lea to the Limehouse Reach of the Thames and was much used by commercial barges until the closure of the Docks in the 1970s. It was always a pleasant area for walking.

When we got there Sister said unexpectedly, 'I don't like the Cuts.'

'Why not, Sister?'

'A grim place. Bad associations.'

'What do you mean?'

'The place of suicides. In the old days, the bad old days, when there was no money, no work for the men, no food for the children, every week a cry would be heard: "Body in the Cuts, body in the Cuts," and always it was a woman. A poor, ragged, half-starved woman, driven to the limits of despair. Once a woman with a baby strapped to her body was dragged out, I was told.'

'Sister, how terrible. Shall we go away?'

'No. I want to go and see it for myself. I haven't been here for forty years, since Beryl died.'

Cynthia and I glanced at each other. We both wanted to hear the story, but didn't want to disturb her thoughts, in case they flitted off onto something quite unconnected, and the story was lost. But the dark water, barely moving, seemed to focus her attention, and she continued.

'They told me she jumped off Stinkhouse Bridge one night, and her body was dragged out the next day. I wasn't surprised. No one was. She had a brute of a husband, seven children, another expected, no money, and a hovel to live in – the usual story. It is only surprising more women didn't do it. Every child's fear, you know, was that one day things would get so bad that mother would jump into the Cuts.'

Sister Monica Joan raised her hand, took hold of the cross that hung around her neck and held it up over the canal. She called out, 'Be sanctified, you black and wicked waters. Rest in peace, Beryl, unloved wife, weeping mother. May the lamentations of your children sanctify these turgid deeps.'

Sister was in good form and continued, 'Do you know what that brute of a husband said when the vicar informed him that his wife was dead, and how she had died?'

'No. What?' we chorused.

'He said, my dears – the vicar himself told us – the husband said, "Spiteful cat. Spiteful to the last. She knowed as 'ow today's Newmarket day, and she knowed as 'ow I'm a delicate feelin' sort o' chap, so she goes an' kills 'erself jest to put me out of sorts for the races. I knows 'er nasty ways. Spite it was; pure spite." Then he walked out. The vicar was left alone in the derelict kitchen, with seven dirty, hungry children around him, for whom he would have to make some sort of provision, if the father wouldn't. Then the man returned. But he had no thoughts for his children. He walked jauntily up to the vicar, tapped him on the chest and said, "Now you listen 'ere, mate. I wont 'ave no funerals on Friday. Vat's Epsom day, see? No funerals. I wont 'ave 'er laughin' twice."

'That was the last the vicar saw of him. He didn't turn up for the funeral, which was on a Tuesday, and he simply abandoned his children. All of them ended up in the Workhouse.'

Sister Monica Joan said no more, and we continued walking. The sun was pleasant, and the ghosts of the past seemed long since asleep. Cynthia and I talked of our plans for the future. She was hoping to test her vocation in the religious life. I knew it was a huge step to take, requiring much thought and prayer, but I had always regarded Cynthia as a saint (or very nearly) and was not surprised. We came to a wooden seat and sat down, and she asked Sister's opinion.

'Do you think I am called to be a nun, Sister?'

'Only God knows. Many are called but few are chosen, my child.'

'What brought you to the religious life?'

'The conflict between good and evil. The eternal battle between God and the devil. I tried to resist the call, but it was too strong.'

The nun sat looking at the water. I ventured the question, 'Was there no other way?'

'For me, no. For others it is different. You do not have to be a nun to be at war with the devil. To be in the fight, on the side of the angels, is all that matters.'

'Do you believe in the devil?' I asked provocatively.

'Stupid, thoughtless child, of course I do. You only have to look at the record of the Nazis during the war to see the work of the devil.' The atrocities of the war were vivid in the minds of everyone.

She turned her head away from me scornfully. I had offended her, and she muttered, 'Thoughtless, empty questions,' but then said more gently to Cynthia, 'Test your vocation, my child. Become a Postulant, then a Novice. Time will reveal if you are truly called. It is a hard life, and doubts will always plague you. Just go with God.'

Mention of the Nazis brought to mind what Sister Julienne had told me some time earlier; that there was in Germany a community of Lutheran nuns, started in 1945 or 1946, just after the war, whose vocation was contemplative prayer and repentance for the sins of their fellow countrymen. The women lived a life of extreme privation, as near to concentration camp life as they could get: minimal food (the nuns were all close to starvation), scant clothing, no shoes, no heating in winter, and no beds, just a straw mattress and a thin blanket. And this life they lived in atonement for the sins of others. I had found this story deeply impressive, though I could not really understand the spiritual side of the vocation. I was grappling in my mind with the problems of sin, guilt, atonement, redemption, religious vocation and many unfathomable subjects, when abruptly Sister Monica Joan stood up.

'The water is not very deep,' she announced, 'I don't see how anyone could drown in it.'

'It is in the middle,' I pointed out. 'It takes cargo barges.'

'But you can see the bottom. Look, you can see the stones.'

'That's only at the edges. Anyway, the water level is low at the moment. I assure you it is deep in the middle.'

'I don't believe it. We shall see.'

Before we could stop her, and she was surprisingly nimble,

Sister Monica Joan had crossed the few steps to the canal and now stood ankle deep at the water's edge.

'There, I told you,' she cried triumphantly, 'the stories about people drowning in the Cuts are just fancy.' And she took another step towards the centre.

'Come back' screamed Cynthia and I in alarm. We leaped into the water beside her, but Sister was too quick for us.

'Don't be silly,' she called out, taking another step forward. But the Cuts was cut away, and instantly she fell forward into deep water.

Cynthia and I were not the only ones to hurl ourselves in after her. As many as a dozen East Enders dived, fully clothed, into the canal that Sunday afternoon. None of us need have bothered. It was immediately obvious that Sister Monica Joan could swim. Her habit did not absorb the water at once, and it floated around her like the wings of a huge black water-fowl. Her head was held high, and her white veil floated behind her like exotic plumage.

All might have been well, and Sister might have swum back to us, had it not been for the enthusiasm of three local lads who dived in from the other bank. They grabbed hold of her and began swimming back whence they had come.

'No, not that side!' I screamed. 'Come back – this side!' Everyone around, including those in the water, was screaming instructions. We all knew that if the boys landed Sister on the opposite bank there was no towpath exit to the bridge. But the lads did not or could not understand in all the confusion. They had pulled Sister to the middle of the canal and saw themselves as heroes. A powerful man, with muscles of oak and the speed of an Olympic swimmer, reached them first. He clouted one lad around the ear, pushed the other boy under, took hold of the protesting nun and swam back with her to our side.

Do not ask me how we got Sister Monica Joan to the convent. The whole process was too complicated and confusing. My memories are hazy: getting her clothes off with modesty and decorum; dozens of wet people offering advice; wondering what on earth to put on her; someone donating a raincoat, a cardigan, a baby's shawl; trying to find her shoes. The swimmer and another man got her to the Commercial Road by giving her a chair-lift. She sat regally on their crossed hands, holding their arms with perfect composure, as though a ducking in the Cuts were a regular experience. Someone must have stopped a lorry in the Commercial Road, because I remember the two men lifting Sister up into the lorry and settling her comfortably. She thanked them with queenly grace, and two tough, strong dockers blushed with pleasure. 'No trouble at all, ma'am,' they said. 'Any time. Good day, ma'am.'

Back at the Convent she was put to bed with hot-water bottles and hot drinks. She slept for twenty-four hours, and when she awoke, she appeared to have no memory at all of what had happened. She suffered no ill. It must have been the angels again.

TOO MANY CHILDREN

'I'm sorry, Mr Harding. Nothing can be done.'

'But you says we was top of the housing list.'

'You are. But there are building delays. Strikes. An electricians' strike.'

'We can move in wivout no electricity. We got no electrics where we are, so it don't matter.'

'I'm sorry, the Council cannot allow you to move into premises that are incomplete.'

'But I tells yer, it don't matter to us. We're desperate to move, anywhere'll do. Anywhere's better'n what we got.'

'It's out of the question, Mr Harding. The law is quite clear. Council premises must be adequate and suitable for the family applying for rehousing.'

The Council official shuffled his papers. His was an impossible job. Ten applicants for every house or flat being built. A housing list of thousands, every one of them clamouring for something better than the bomb-damaged buildings, the overcrowded and insanitary conditions in which they lived. But he had to follow the rules.

'Well, when vis electricians' strike's over, how long will it be? How long, eh?'

Bill Harding leaned forward menacingly. The official leaned back defensively.

'I don't know.'

Bill thumped the desk with his powerful fist.

''ow long? You must have some idea. How long's the strike gonna last? A week? Two weeks? Then we can move – yes?'

'I'm afraid not, Mr Harding. It's not just building delays. It's a question of size.'

'Size? What size?'

'Family size, Mr Harding. You have too many children. The Council at present is building two- and three-bedroom flats. We cannot allow a family of eight to move into a three-bedroom flat. We would have to provide a four-, or even five-bedroom flat or house for a family of this size. And at present the Council is simply not building five-bedroom flats.'

'But vat's daft. Three bedrooms is a luxury. More'n enough. We only gots one bedroom, and we all sleeps in it. We'd give anything for three bedrooms.'

'I'm sorry, Mr Harding. But we have our standards and our rules. We cannot rent a three-bedroom flat or house to a family of eight. It is simply not allowed.'

Bill had lost all his aggression, and despair overtook him. He sighed deeply and held his head in his hands. He had to get back to work. He had taken an hour off to see the Council, and it was like banging his head against a brick wall.

'Bloody red tape,' he groaned.

'I'm sorry, Mr Harding, really sorry. But the rules must be obeyed.'

Bill stood up and left without looking at the Council official, who, with a depressed and weary sigh, called, 'Next please,' knowing that the next interview would be as bad, or worse, than the last.

Bill slouched down the road towards the shipbuilder's yard, where he was a welder. He slunk against the wall and kicked a stone, hard. It shot across the pavement and hit a passing lorry. The stone ricocheted off and bounced back onto the pavement. A policeman saw what had happened and came over to Bill. No real damage had been done, but the copper tore a strip off Bill for dangerous and irresponsible behaviour. The incident did nothing to improve his humour – bloody red tape, bloody law. Well, his bloody job could wait; he needed a drink. He went into a pub and drank away his lunch hour until chucking-out time at two o'clock. He arrived back at the yard at 3 p.m., having been away since 11 a.m. The foreman came down on him like a ton of bricks. Bill swore obscenely at him and walked out. He walked around the streets until opening time at five o'clock and then got blind drunk.

Hilda made herself another cup of tea, lit a fag, and sat down at the table with her *Daily Mirror* propped up against the milk bottle. The two youngest children crawled around the floor, playing – thank God the older ones were at school and off her hands for a few hours. She couldn't face what she thought she knew. She sipped her tea and stared at the cracked wall and the huge damp stain on the grey-brown ceiling. It's gettin' bigger, she thought. When's the whole damn thing goin' to fall, that's what she wanted to know. No good talkin' to that landlord – you never saw him anyway, couldn't get past his agent, who only said if you don't like it get out, get your name on the Council housing list. Well they'd been on the damned list for five years, and look where it'd got them. Nowhere. Nuffink. Sweet Fanny Adams.

She poured herself another cup of tea, and laced it with sugar. Now this. She couldn't face it. Not another. But all the signs were there. She hadn't told Bill. Hadn't dared. Perhaps she should have told him before he went to the Council, but somehow she hadn't the courage. Wonder how he got on. He'd said he would be firm, wouldn't leave till he'd got the promise of a place, and a date. A date. That's what they wanted. A date to look forward to when they could leave this falling-down dump. She could wring that agent's neck. Last time she had pointed to the damp on the ceiling and asked for repairs, he had smiled and said it was a condemned property and that the Council wouldn't permit repairs because it was condemned. That's logic for you! She had heard the dripping last night as she lay awake wondering if she should tell Bill or not before he went to the Council, and the drips seemed to be getting closer.

They knew the roof had gone, but that was two storeys up, and the floors above them kept the rain out. But if the floors went, then there would be no roof over their heads. She must get Bill to go upstairs and lay a tarpaulin over the floor above. That would keep them dry for a bit, and then they might get a Council flat. Bill would be at the Council office now. He'd tell 'em.

The children were playing boats – floating matches on a bucket of water. One of them had an empty match box which the other wanted. He grabbed at it. The child screamed and lunged at his brother. 'Mind it,' shouted Hilda. But too late. They had tipped the bucket over, and water streamed across the floor. 'You little devils,' she shouted as she jumped up, and walloped them both. 'Look at the mess. Now I've got to clear it up.' She got a cloth and wiped up the water, wringing it out into the empty bucket. Well at least it's giving the floor a clean, she thought as she wiped and wrung. 'Now I've gotta go an' get more water. An' don't you touch anyfink while I'm gone,' she said menacingly. She picked up the bucket of dirty water. Might as well empty the pot while I'm downstairs. She pulled the chamber pot from under the bed and carried it down the creaking and rickety stairs. This stinkin' stairwell's worse than our rooms, she thought. At least we've made an effort to put a bit of paint on an' I try to keep them clean. No one's repaired or decorated this landing or these stairs for years. An' as for cleanin'. Well you might as well save your effort. She went out into the yard, to the lavatory with its asbestos roof and broken door and emptied the chamber pot. She pulled the chain – well at least it still flushes, but for how long? How long? How long would they have to wait in this hell-hole? She'd murder that landlord if she could get her hands on him.

Might as well do the washin', now I've got some clean water. She filled two saucepans and lit the gas stove on the landing, then went down again for another bucket of cold water. And now, just when the little one was out of nappies. Now this! She shut her mind to the possibility of more – yet more – nappies. She filled the tin bath – the one they all washed and bathed in – with hot water, added some soapflakes and started the daily chore with her dolly-board and a bar of Sunlight. The little ones clung to her skirts and wanted to help, but she pushed them away. A couple of hours later she had finished the washing, wringing, rinsing, mangling and hanging out. Well, at least it's a fine day. It'll soon be dry. That's one comfort. The little ones were clamouring for their dinner, and two of her children, those of primary school age, would be home for their midday meal. Thank God the others get theirs at school now. Saves a bit of trouble, anyhow. She had a small cupboard on the landing where she kept some food. Not too much, or it'd get pinched in this rotten hole. She pulled out a couple of tins of baked beans and some sliced bread. The grill sometimes worked – she tried it. Yes, it was working today. They could have beans on toast. Always enjoy it, they do.

The downstairs door opened, and two grubby children tumbled upstairs, pushing, shouting, laughing. 'Now shut yer noise, an' siddown, 'ere's yer beans on toast, and don't get it all over yerselves.'

She tried to eat a bit herself, but it made her feel sick. Oh no – another sign! Can't be much doubt. She'd have to see the doctor, she would.

After she'd packed the children off to school at two o' clock, she had to get some grub in for the evening. She went to the corner shop, the one she'd known since childhood, the one her mother got tick from when there was no money and no food in the place and a brood of half-starved kids. Well at least she wasn't always living on the breadline, not like her poor mum – at least she could feed her kids and not do without herself. Bill earned a good wage, and his job was secure, thanks to the Trade Union. She bought some more bread and half a pound of bacon. They could have fried bread and bacon this evening, then on reflection she added a large tin of beans. Well, at least they get some good food, bacon's more than she ever got when she was a kid, she mused. The two toddlers were restive and excited to be out, so she took them for a bit of a walk, not too far because she was tired, and she didn't want to go past the bomb site where the meths drinkers hung out. They scared her. She went down the street where she had played as a child, but it depressed her – all the windows boarded up, signs of demolition at the far end. Wearily she made her way back home.

Four o' clock and the brood would be home. She steeled herself for the rush and the noise. She prepared a large quantity of beans and bacon and fried bread. 'Now get that inside yer, an' go out an' play. An' take ve babies with you. I've had 'em all day, an' I'm just about up to here with 'em.' She raised her hand to her neck to indicate how high. The children gobbled down their food, and rushed out.

Hilda settled down to a quiet cup of tea and *Woman* magazine. It was the only time of day she got any peace – when the bigger children took the little ones off her hands. An hour later she thought, it's getting dark. The kids'd better be in. She went to the window and yelled down the street. No children in sight. They'll be on that bomb site, I'll be bound. I've told 'em not to. It's not safe. You wait till I get my hands on 'em, little devils. Muttering and grumbling, Hilda trudged off to the bomb site and gathered up her brood, cuffing each of the bigger ones round the ear as she did so. 'You jes' wait till I tells yer dad you've been down 'ere,' she shouted. The boys grinned and made rude faces and dodged out of her reach.

It was nine o'clock by the time they were all in bed, the four little ones in the bedroom, the two older ones in the cupboard – a decent-sized cupboard, she and Bill had agreed when they took the room shortly after the war, almost as big as another room. We can put all our junk in there, they had said, laughing.

Now it was full of kids! Still no Bill. What's happened to him? She sat down with another cup of tea and another fag.

At 10.45 she heard the front door bang and heard Bill singing down below. Her heart leaped – he's got good news – she jumped up to get another cup for him. He'd like a cup of tea before his meal, and then he could tell her the news. The door opened slowly, with Bill clinging to it. He swung into the room and leaned heavily against the wall, staring vacantly at her. Oh no, not drunk, she'd have to be careful, treat him gently, no questions, no chatter, she didn't want his fist in her face. Mrs Hatterton had got her nose broken only last week. But Bill's not like that, not really. She sat him down and took off his boots.

'Like some bacon and beans, eh, ducks?'

'Nope.'

'Cup o' tea?'

'Nope.'

''Ow about a nice bacon sandwich, ven?'

'Vat's more like it.' His eyes brightened a little.

She went to the gas stove on the landing, made two rounds and brought them to him. He hadn't eaten all day and devoured the first ravenously.

'Nice cup of tea to wash it down?'

He nodded. He was beginning to look more like himself.

He'll be all right after a good night's sleep. No trouble. You just need to know how to handle a drunk man, then you get no trouble. But her Bill wasn't like that anyway, wouldn't hurt a fly, but still you never knew, when the drink was on them. She went into the bedroom and pushed two children over to the far side of the bed so that there would be space for their father to lie down. She led Bill into the bedroom, quietly undressed him and held the chamber-pot for him to have a jimmy riddle. The pot was so full she had to go downstairs to empty it, and when she returned he was sprawled sideways across the bed, his feet and legs around two sleeping children.

There was no room for her, so she spent the night in a chair, wrapped in a coat.

She roused herself at six and went down to get some water. She made a pot of tea and buttered some bread, then she quietly shook Bill. 'Come on. You've got to get off to work,' she whispered so as not to wake the children. He struggled to his feet, sober, but somewhat the worse for wear. They sat at the table together. She lit a Woodbine, stuck it in his mouth and pushed his tea and bread towards him.

'You're a good girl, ducks,' he muttered, drawing on the fag.

'Well? What happened yesterday?'

'Happened? I got pissed, that's what.'

'No, afore vat. At ve Council.'

His mind slid backwards, and he groaned.

'Nuffink. Zilch. Gotta wait.'

'Wait! We've waited five years. I thought we was top of ve housin' list.'

'We are. But we still gotta wait.'

'Why?' she said savagely.

'Too many kids, vat's why.'

'How d'ya mean? They said all the kids 'ave to move to better, 'ealthier places.'

'I know. But we got too many. Council has to provide a four-bedroom 'ouse for two adults an' six kids. An' vey only builds two and fhree-bedroom places at the moment.'

'But we can manage with three bedrooms. We've only got one an' a cupboard here.'

'I tells ve bloke vat, but it makes no difference. It's rules – bloody rules.'

'I don't believe it. Vis place is fallin' down.'

'I told 'em so, an' vey say as what it's not Council property, so it's not ve Council's responsibility. We 'ave ter ask our landlord for repairs.'

'Fat lot of use that'll be. Look, let's get vis clear. Council has three-bedroom houses, but we can't 'ave one 'cause we got six children?'

'That's abou' it. We're stuck. Now I've gotta get off. Can't be late today.' The front door slammed, and footsteps hurried down the street.

THE ABORTIONIST

Hilda sat at the wooden table and lit another fag. She was stunned. Foremost in her mind was the suspicion that had been nagging at her for three weeks. What a blessing she hadn't told Bill! Only yesterday she thought she would have to, and then go to the doctor. Not now, no siree, no bleeding doctors. She'd see Mrs Prichard, who was well thought of in the area. She'd enquire in the corner shop. Someone would know how to find her. Hilda got the children up and packed them off to school, paying little heed to their demands and squabbles. Her mind was planning what she would have to do – the sooner the better, every day would count.

Discreet enquiries led her to Mrs Prichard. She had to be very careful. Back-street abortions were quite common in those days, but the practice was illegal, and both the client and the abortionist could be prosecuted if caught and would face a prison sentence if convicted. Every precaution was necessary.

Mrs Prichard and her daughter lived in a better class of house on the Commercial Road. To the police, local doctors, church and social workers, she was a herbalist, specialising in potions, known only to the mystics, for the cure of hay-fever, gout, arthritic knees and so on. Her front room was filled with bottles and phials. Her premises had been inspected several times by the public health authorities, who had found her remedies and treatments to be harmless, if ineffectual. Evidence of the more lucrative side of her business was nowhere to be seen. She had learned her trade from her mother, who had been an abortionist since the 1880s, and when the old lady died Mrs Prichard had inherited the equipment which had been stolen from a hospital about fifty years earlier.

Mrs Prichard was a well-upholstered lady. She wore smart suits and several gold chains over her ample bosom. Her face was heavily made up, and her eyebrows, plucked until nothing was left, were replaced by a thin pencil arc, reaching high into her forehead. Her hair was a colour that no woman of her age could hope to retain and was elaborately coiffed and curled. She greeted Hilda with a smile, and listened to her story sympathetically. When she spoke her voice was falsely genteel, an accent beloved by character actresses.

'Oh, my dear, what you got is stomach cramps. I sees a lot of it these days. The doctors don't know what to do with it. Don't know nothing, they don't. I can't think why they have all that training – they don't seem to learn nothing. Can't even treat a simple case of stomach cramps. Inflammation of the intestines, I calls it, dear. Going up or going down, it makes no difference, the intestines has a lot of work to do, and they get inflammation. Now what you need is some of my special stomach cramps mixture, dear. My own remedy, known only to myself. My dear deceased mother, who was a wise woman as ever there was one, passed the secret on to me on her death-bed. "Don't let anyone get it off of you," she says as she was dyin' like. "It's more precious than gold," she says. "Them doctors don't know nothing about it," she says, and then she expired, leaving me with the secret.'

Mrs Prichard wiped her eye and sniffed sadly as she went over to a counter. She took several bottles off the shelves, and with a measuring glass and a great deal of care, and with one eye shut, squinting against the light, she filled a bottle. Hilda was most impressed.

'That will be two guineas, dear, and worth ten of anyone's money, I can tell you. Now take a tablespoonful night and morning for five days. It will make the stomach cramps worse at first, but that is a sign that the potion is working, so don't stop taking it, will you, dear? It's got to get worse afore it gets better. If you don't get any bleeding, come back to me next week. My dear mother left me on her death-bed with other secret remedies for stomach cramps, known only to myself.'

Mrs Prichard pocketed the two guineas. Smiling and solicitous, she showed Hilda to the door.

'Now remember, dear, this is for stomach cramps. Mrs Prichard treats all sorts: headaches, migraines, ingrown toenails, flatulence, tennis elbow and stomach cramps. If anyone asks you, this potion is for them stomach cramps, which you 'ave been suffering of.'

Hilda took the potion as directed for five days. The taste was so revolting that it made her retch with each dose, and the pain in her stomach was intense. The third day she developed violent diarrhoea and vomiting, and spent most of the night in the outside lavatory. She sat curled up with pain on the rough wooden seat, trying not to cry out as the fluid poured from her. This'll get rid of it, she thought, and good riddance. In the morning she looked hopefully for signs of blood – but there were none. For three more days she put up with the pain and nausea and diarrhoea, trying to pretend to Bill and the children that nothing was wrong, but by the sixth day she was forced to admit that it had all been to no avail. She had lost no blood. She was still pregnant.

Hilda felt weak and shaky when she returned to Mrs Prichard, who in contrast looked splendid. Her hair had been newly dyed and was piled up on her head in layers of curled sausages. Her make-up was even thicker than before, and her lips and fingernails were a vivid red.

'Oh, my dear. These naughty cramps. Sometimes they really have to be swept away with a new broom. My dear mother always used to say that, if the cramps don't go with the old trusty broom, you've got to get out the new. Now it's up to you, dear. Do you want me to get out my new broom to sweep them clean away? I will have to come to your place, of course. Can't be done here. I ain't got the premises. And my daughter will have to come with me. I need her as my trusty assistant, you understand. And there must be no one around, no children nor husbands nor nothing like that, you understand? The decision is yours, dear.'

Hilda gulped, and felt sick.

'Will it hurt?' she murmured.

'Hardly a prick, my dear. I will give you a potion, my mother's secret mixture what she gave me when she was a-dying. It numbs the senses.'

'Is there no other way?'

'If the potion for cramps don't work, my dear, it means it's a real sticking, stubborn sort of cramp, and the only way is a new broom.'

'All right. When can you do it?'

'Wednesday morning. And it'll be twenty guineas. Ten guineas now, and ten when I've done. You won't regret a penny, my dear.'

Hilda went to the post office and drew out twenty guineas from the War Time Savings Account she had guarded so carefully to buy new furniture when she and Bill got their new place. She returned to Mrs Prichard, who took the money with 'You won't regret a penny, my dear. Till Wednesday.'

Hilda spent the next few days in an agony of doubt and indecision. Had she done wrong? Should she go through with it? She could cancel the whole thing and just have the baby. But the thought of a seventh baby in that horrible flat filled her with such dismay that she thought anything would be better. Should she tell Bill? She didn't know. Men are so squeamish, perhaps he'd rather not know. Then again he might start blabbing to his mates at work, and then, who knows where it might get to. Next thing they'd have the Law knocking on their door. She decided not to tell him.

On Wednesday, Mrs Hatterton opposite agreed to have the two little ones for the day, and the older children had all been sent to school with instructions to have school dinners and not to come back until four o'clock. Hilda waited with pounding heart. She had carried up several buckets of water, laid out clean towels and sheets and provided a few rolls of cotton wool. She didn't know what else to do. The waiting's the worst, she thought. There was a knock on the door at nine thirty, and she nearly jumped out of her skin, though she had been expecting it.

Mrs Prichard and her daughter entered. The two women were soberly, even drably, dressed in brown mackintoshes. They both had their hair wound up in curlers with a headscarf tied over the top, which was a common sight amongst East End women. They carried wicker shopping baskets from which protruded cabbages, leeks, turnip tops and brussel tops. They looked exactly like a couple of housewives coming back from market. It was a disguise to fool the police.

'Now, dear, the sooner we get on with this, the sooner it's over. Let me see your premises.'

Mrs Prichard mounted the rickety staircase going up from the foul-smelling hallway and wrinkled her sensitive nose in disgust.

'I'm not surprised, dear, that you wants to get rid of these stomach cramps.'

She looked round Hilda's rooms with a professional eye.

'Can't use the bedroom. We'll have to do it on the kitchen table. I will need some hot water. Where's the gas-stove? On the landing! That won't do. The hot water must be ready and in here. Now, can we lock the door? No? Why not? The door must be locked from the inside. Find the key. Ah, is that it? Good. Now clear the table. Draw those curtains; we don't want any prying eyes, do we, dear? Now dear, drink this. It's my mother's potion to numb the senses – and climb up on that table. Miriam, put that bucket there, and that bowl there, put those towels here, and get those sheets under her buttocks. I wants you to hold the knees against the chest, and to keep them there whatever happens.'

Miriam was a large, silent female, and she grunted her acquiescence.

Trembling, Hilda drank the potion as instructed and shakily climbed onto the table. She lay down in what is known medically as the 'lithotomy position', with her buttocks at the edge of the table, her legs drawn upwards and spread apart. Her head was spinning. A silky voice penetrated her hazy mind.

'Have you got the other ten guineas, dear? A professional person can't be expected to carry out professional duties without due payment.'

'On the shelf, in the brown pot,' Hilda answered thickly. Miriam went to the pot and took the money.

Mrs Prichard delved amongst the leeks and brussel tops and produced her instruments. They were exceedingly old and made of rough, unpolished steel, virtually impossible to sterilise – if, indeed, Mrs Prichard ever made any attempts at sterilisation. They consisted of a few ancient surgical instruments, such as forceps, dilators, curettes and a Higginson's syringe.

'Just a little prick, dear, you'll hardly feel a thing,' Mrs Prichard cooed, as she inserted her fingers into the vagina. Hilda felt no discomfort. This is going to be all right, she thought. The drug she had taken made her feel light-headed and sleepy.

Mrs Prichard glanced at her and muttered to her daughter, 'Keep her firmly in that position and have the towels ready.' She felt with her fingers until she thought she had located the cervix. She hissed, 'Keep her still now,' and with the forceps she grabbed the cervix and pulled it towards her. Hilda felt a pain like a knife stabbing her body, but she managed to suppress a scream. Holding the cervix quite firmly Mrs Prichard took one of the dilators and attempted to force it through the closed cervix, with no success. 'Too big,' muttered the abortionist and reached for a smaller dilator, which she pushed hard against the cervical orifice. Hilda felt pain like burning knives tearing her body apart. She opened her mouth to scream, but a towel was thrust in, pushing her tongue backwards and nearly choking her.

Miriam's weight held her legs fast against her body so that she could not move.

Mrs Prichard had a curette at her disposal. So she poked with it in a blind attempt to force entry through the cervix into the uterus. When she thought she had succeeded she started scraping around and continued scraping until blood began to flow. The pain was so intense that Hilda passed out, and when she regained consciousness she was vomiting, but the towel that had been thrust into her mouth was still there so she started choking. 'Pull that towel away; we don't want her to choke on us,' muttered Mrs Prichard.

The fresh blood flowed freely, but Hilda was unaware of it. She was conscious only of the vomit that was rising in her throat and of the towel being snatched away just in time, before she inhaled her own vomit, which would probably have killed her. She was aware of a silky voice saying, 'There now. A nice flow of blood. That's all you needed, dear. A nice new broom to sweep away them stomach cramps. You'll be all right now, dear. You might feel shaky for a day or two, but it'll soon pass, and you'll be fine. Now get up, dear. Yes, you can get up all right and go and lie on the bed for an hour or two. We'll do the clearing up. It's all part of the service. I pride myself on never leaving a mess behind.'

Hilda staggered to her feet and with the help of Miriam went to the bedroom. As she passed the end of the table she saw a bowl full of blood and blood dripping off the table onto the floor. Has that all come from me, she thought and clung to the towel the women had put between her legs. She vomited again. 'Have some more potion, dear,' said Mrs Prichard smoothly. 'It will ease the stomach and help you sleep. These cramps can be real nasty, can't they, dear?' Hilda drank the potion, and lay down on the bed. She drifted again into unconsciousness, a state that kept coming and going for the rest of the day.

The two women cleared up, after a fashion, Mrs Prichard muttering 'If she expects us to clean this hovel, she's got another think coming,' then left Hilda bleeding, shocked and semi-conscious.

Mrs Hatterton brought the toddlers back at three o'clock. She saw the state that Hilda was in and put two and two together. 'You poor soul,' she murmured. She took the children back to her place and returned with clean towels and sheets and carried fresh water up, because Hilda was raging with thirst. She took away the bloodied linen and packed the clean around the injured woman. Later she took the older children to her place too, and fed them, returning to Hilda several times to change the linen and to give her a drink. When she saw Bill returning at six o'clock, she stopped him in the street and told him his wife was ill. Nothing more. She told him that she would keep the children till her old man came back, but then they would have to return home. Bill just assumed that his wife had 'flu – 'She's bin a bit off colour lately.' He had no idea, and was aghast when he saw Hilda, deathly white, scarce able to move or speak. 'I'll get a doctor,' he said. 'No, no, don't, you mustn't,' was the woman's anguished reply. She had to tell him, but he did not comprehend. 'Women's troubles,' was his reaction. No man had anything to do with women's troubles. He made his tea and went out. Mrs Hatterton brought the six children back at seven thirty and put them to bed, two in the cupboard and the others on the sofa or in the cot which she pulled into the main room. She gave Hilda some more water and changed her linen again. 'You'll have to manage,' she said. She did not suggest getting a doctor. She knew, as Hilda did, that a doctor would probably mean police involvement and prosecution. These things had to be kept quiet. 'I'll be in tomorrow,' she said as she left.

Bill returned at ten thirty. He had been drinking, but was not drunk. Hilda looked no better. 'You sure you don't want no doctor?' he asked, concerned. She had to explain to him that a doctor was legally bound to inform the police of a criminal abortion. He didn't really understand, but the mention of police kept him silent. Seeing Hilda so pale and weak stirred his old tenderness for her. 'How about a nice cup o' tea, eh, duck?' he said kindly, 'do you good.' Hilda forced a smile, 'A cup o' tea would be nice. And Bill, thanks. Thanks for everything.' The children slept on.

It took about three weeks for Hilda to recover her strength. The bleeding stopped within a few days, but the shock, the pain and the general weakness kept her in bed for most of that time. Mrs Hatterton was good to her. She came in daily and saw the bigger children off to school. She cared for the toddlers, and did the washing, shopping, cooking and carrying of water up and down stairs. Mrs Prichard was not seen again. Her professional services did not include post-operative care.

BACK-STREET ABORTIONS

A woman's right to control her own body is so taken for granted now that younger people can scarcely believe that abortion used to be a criminal offence in the UK punishable by a prison sentence for the woman and the abortionist. The Criminal Abortion Act of 1803 was law for 165 years. It was only repealed in 1967.

There have always been women who wanted or needed an abortion. For rich women it was relatively easy – a clandestine visit to a secret address, often abroad, where a doctor working in an unregistered clinic would operate illegally, and usually successfully, leaving little damage to the woman. Sometimes it was possible to procure an abortion legally if two doctors, one a psychiatrist, would testify that the woman seeking the abortion was mentally and physically incapable of carrying the pregnancy to full term. It cost a lot of money, but the risk of prosecution was removed.

For poor women it was a different story. Most working-class people lived in a perpetual state of poverty, the whole family crowded into one, two or at most three rooms, with not enough food, lighting or heating. Contraception was inadequate, and women had too many children, far more than they could decently house or feed. Another baby was frequently a disaster. For single women pregnancy was a catastrophe, and many preferred suicide to the stigma of bearing an illegitimate child.

So millions of women sought an abortion. The first method attempted was usually a simple vaginal douche. But this was unlikely to work, because the fluid has to enter the uterus to be effective. If a caustic solution was used it caused chemical burns to the vagina and cervix.

Thousands of women tried medicinal ways of evacuating the uterus. Violent purgatives, such as a pint of Epsom Salts, were used. Gin and ginger, turpentine, raw spirit, aloes and sloes were also employed. None of them worked. Disreputable newspapers and journals advertised what they called 'cures for menstrual blockage' for a sum of money. These were poisonous and sometimes fatal. Quinine was common, and some 'cures' even contained arsenic or mercury.

'Wise women' have known for millennia that the black fungal growth on rye grain will induce an abortion. It was called 'ergot', and was also known to cause the deadly disease commonly called St Anthony's Fire. When I was a young pupil midwife doing my theoretical training at a teaching hospital, a colleague was having an affair with a doctor and she became pregnant. She stole a bottle of ergometrine from the ward medicine cupboard and took the tablets over a period of days until she aborted. She became terribly ill, but such was her desperation that she continued working throughout. If Matron had discovered that she was pregnant, my colleague would have been dismissed, and if it had come to light that she had been stealing ergometrine, her name would have been removed from the register (she was an SRN) and very likely reported to the police for prosecution under the Criminal Abortion Act.

Some women tried violent methods, such as falling downstairs, or half drowning, or taking a scalding hot bath, in the hope that they would provoke a spontaneous miscarriage. If the woman survived, she would usually still be pregnant, because one would virtually have to kill the mother before the foetus could be destroyed.

Driven to extremes by despair, women would go to unbelievable lengths in trying to make themselves miscarry. Knitting needles, crochet hooks, metal coathangers, paper knives, pickle spoons, curved upholstery needles, spokes of bicycle wheels have all been forced into the uterus by desperate women who preferred to do anything rather than continue the pregnancy.

How any woman could push an instrument through the closed os of her own cervix is more than I can imagine – but it has been done, times without number, sometimes successfully.

I have given talks to women's groups on the early days of midwifery. In the course of many of these talks, some lady in the audience has told us a story about a grandmother or great aunt who had induced an abortion on herself. I have heard many such stories, and in diverse circumstances, and they are all so dismally similar that the oral evidence cannot be in doubt.

One story, related by a lady at a Women's Institute meeting, will suffice: 'My aunt was a respectable single woman of thirty-five living with her mother, who was very proud of the family reputation. While on holiday my aunt became pregnant and tried to abort herself with a crochet hook. She bled profusely, and her mother found out what was going on. The old lady was so horrified at what the neighbours might say that at first she refused to call a doctor. It was not until it became obvious that her daughter would die that, in great secrecy, she summoned a doctor who performed an evacuation of the uterus and suturing on the kitchen table of their home, Afterwards he said, "this must not go beyond the walls of this house. No one but we three will know what has happened tonight." The story was not told in the family for forty years.'

The doctor had saved the woman's life but he had risked his career in doing so. Had the story become known and his name reported to the General Medical Council he would have been brought up before a disciplinary committee for professional misconduct. He might have got away with it by pleading that it was a life-saving emergency operation, but there would have been no certainty of exoneration and whatever the outcome such an experience would have been traumatic for a conscientious doctor.

The alternative to attempting to make oneself miscarry was a visit to an illegal abortionist. Back-street abortionists favoured one of two methods: the surgical procedure or the flushing-out method. Both are highly dangerous, and only a doctor trained in surgery is competent to conduct an abortion. However, that did not stop countless numbers of women practising for a fee. They had a vague idea of female anatomy and operated with improvised instruments such as those described, or with obsolete instruments often stolen from a hospital. There was no sterility, no anaesthetic, no proper lighting, and operations frequently took place on kitchen tables.

It is easy to push a metal object into the vagina, but the cervix lies at nearly a ninety-degree angle to the vaginal wall. Without surgical knowledge the instruments could easily miss the cervix and go straight through the vaginal wall. Working blind, abortionists had been known to push a sharp object into the bladder or rectum. If the instrument did enter the uterus, it was sometimes pushed right through and out the other side. Even if all these hazards were avoided, bleeding was frequently uncontrollable.

In my book *Call the Midwife*, I recall meeting Mary, a young Irish girl who was lured into prostitution. She told me the tragic story of her only friend in the brothel, who became pregnant. The madam called in an abortionist, who used the surgical method. The girl haemorrhaged and died in Mary's arms. Her body disappeared, and no one was prosecuted.

In 2004 a film about an abortionist – *Vera Drake* – was released. It is a brilliant film exploring the social dilemmas of the time. The film is probably regarded by millions as an accurate template of back-street abortions in the 1950s, but it does contain inaccuracies.

In the film, the flushing-out method was favoured. Vera Drake was seen supposedly pumping a solution of carbolic soap and water into a woman's uterus with a Higginson's syringe. But what she was doing was no more than a simple vaginal douche, which was unlikely to have any effect on the course of pregnancy because the fluid would only enter the vagina, not the uterus.

Flushing-out may seem less traumatic than the surgical method – in the film it is made to look very simple, even gentle – but it is still fraught with danger. Firstly, the caustic solution has to be exactly right; too weak and it will have no effect, too strong and it will burn the mucosa of the internal organs. Secondly the quantity of fluid and the rate of introduction into the uterus have to be accurate. One of the most severe pains a human being can endure is the sudden distension of a hollow organ. If too much fluid is pumped too fast into the uterus it could cause shock, a sudden drop in blood pressure, heart failure and even death.

At a talk I gave to the East London History Society in 2006, a woman in the audience told us that, in the 1930s, in the small Essex village where she was born, there was a bona fide midwife who was also an abortionist. She was a good practitioner, experienced and respected. A mother in the village came to her and said that her fourteen-year-old daughter was pregnant and begged her to carry out an abortion. The woman did not want to, but the mother pleaded so earnestly that eventually she agreed. The flushing-out method was used, and the girl died on the table. Mother and abortionist were sent to prison.

As nurses and midwives we often had to clear up the mess after a bungled abortion, especially when we worked on gynaecological wards. The outcome for these women was frequently chronic ill health. Conditions such as anaemia, scar tissue with adhesions, prolapse with chronic pain, incontinence, cystitis or nephritis could be expected, along with many others. Thrombosis of the leg was not uncommon. This could lead to a clot travelling in the bloodstream and lodging in the lungs. Anticoagulants were not available until the 1950s.

I have seen much mutilation and two deaths. The first was a girl of nineteen whose internal mucosa and cervix had been burned by a carbolic acid or some other caustic solution used during a flushing-out abortion. There was little we could do, and she lingered for a while, but she was in constant agony and died after a few days.

I recall another tragic woman, the mother of five children, who developed a massive sac of pus in the peritoneum after a surgical abortion. We tried to drain it without success, and for many weeks pus oozed from her abdomen. The five children coming into hospital just before their mother died can never be forgotten.

The Criminal Abortion Act 1803 was repealed in 1967. Knowing that I had been a midwife I was sometimes asked if I approved of it or not. My reply was that I did not regard it as a moral issue, but as a medical issue. A minority of women will always want an abortion. Therefore it must be done properly.*

* My thanks to the Marie Stopes Society for reading and approving this essay.

STRANGER THAN FICTION

Life, my dear Watson, is infinitely stranger than fiction; stranger than anything which the mind of man could invent. We could not conceive the things that are merely commonplace to existence. If we could hover over this great city, remove the roofs, and peep in at the things going on, it would make all fiction, with its conventionalities and foreseen conclusions flat, stale, and unprofitable.

The Adventures of Sherlock Holmes, by Sir Arthur Conan Doyle

A couple of months passed, and Hilda was just about able to cope with her household again, but the constant clamour of young children, incessant washing, endless meals to prepare and above all the squalid surroundings were dragging her down. She became more and more depressed, irritable with the children and quiet with Bill. He hadn't seen her like this before. They had always had fun together. Now she was a woman who hardly spoke. Sometimes he wondered what he had done wrong. He'd always been a good husband and a good father – or he'd tried to be – he'd always brought his money home, not like some of the blokes who drank all their money, and then beat their wives for not cooking a hot dinner for them.

Hilda roused herself and went to the Council. She was going to have it out with them. But she could have saved herself the effort. No four-bedroom houses or flats were available. They were scheduled for building next year, and the Hardings would be informed. Yes, they were top of the list, and they would be the first to be offered a place. In the meantime . . .

In the meantime, Hilda came close to throwing herself under a bus. But suicide is not so easy, and she balked at the actual fact of doing it. Life dragged on.

Another couple of weeks passed, and something strange was

happening in Hilda's body. At first she thought it was wind, and she took a dose of Epsom Salts. After a good clear-out, it seemed to settle down, and she thought no more of it. But a week later it came back, and then again with added emphasis. She put her hands on her tummy, and at that instant felt an unmistakable kick. With horror and disbelief the truth dawned upon her: the bleeding she had experienced must have come from a rupture to an artery, and the abortion achieved with so much pain and suffering, not to mention expense, had been a failure. She was still pregnant.

In a furious rage she took the bus to the Commercial Road and knocked on Mrs Prichard's door. The house was the same, the plush interior the same, Mrs Prichard – overdressed and over-painted – was the same, but gone the welcoming smile, the sympathetic voice, the womanly understanding.

'Well?' she demanded.

'You fraud. I'm still pregnant.'

'If you are going to descend to calling names of me, I've nothing to say to you.'

'Did you 'ear? I'm still pregnant.'

'You never was pregnant when I saw you. You had stomach cramps, if you cast your mind back, and I treated you for stomach cramps, with my dear deceased mother's secret remedies.'

'You liar. You did an abortion on me.'

'I did no such thing. And don't you call me a liar, you dirty little rat-bag.'

'You did, you stinking liar.'

'If you use that word again, you can leave my house. I'm a herbalist. I practise ancient remedies, passed on to me by wise women.'

'Then what did you do at my place, when you nearly killed me?'

'I came to your stinking hovel out of the kindness of my heart, because you kept a-pesterin' me with your stomach cramps. In the goodness of my nature, I do occasionally visit clients.'

'You nearly killed me.'

'Rubbish.'

'You did. The pain nearly killed me.'

'Well you look all right now.'

'No thanks to you, you bloody butcher.'

'Ooh, I can't stand this foul language any longer. I must ask you to be a-leave-taking of.'

'Not till I get my twenty guineas back.'

'Twenty guineas! What twenty guineas? I never heard such fairy-tales in all my life. I charged you two guineas for the secret herbal potion as was passed on to me by my dear deceased mother for the efficacious treatment of stomach cramps, remedies as what is known only to the select few.'

'Damn your dear deceased mother!'

'Oh, my poor mother. She would turn in her grave.'

Mrs Prichard took a lace handkerchief, and applied it to her mascara-ed eyes. Hilda was beside herself with rage.

'Are you goin' to give me back my twenty guineas what you took off me for a bungled abortion?'

'Excuse I, but I did not take twenty guineas off of you.'

Mrs Prichard walked swiftly to the door, her high-heeled shoes clicking as she walked.

'Miriam, dear. Come here, will you?'

Miriam entered, strong and silent, and stared hard at Hilda.

'This, er – lady, shall we say – this lady, Miriam, says that I took twenty guineas off of her. I did not. Did you receive any money, Miriam?

'No.'

'There you are, you see. Neither of us took any money off of you. You are fabricating, I'm afraid. I've met the likes of you before.'

'Then what did you do at my place, what nearly killed me?'

'Don't exaggerate. We gave you an enema for stomach cramps and left you well and comfortable.'

'An enema?'

'An herbal enema. That was all.'

'But it nearly killed me. I bled like a pig.'

'Piles, my dear. Piles. If you got piles what bleed in your – er – lower passage, you can hardly hold me responsible. Now, if you will excuse me, I have important work to do. I am expecting her ladyship, Lady Lucrecia, who won't hear of going to no one else for her migraines and dizzy spells.

'Damn you, d'you hear me, you painted ol' sow.'

'Oh, I have never been so insulted in all my life.'

Mrs Prichard patted her hair, her crimson fingernails fluttering. A gold bangle flashed on her wrist. It was an action calculated to make Hilda feel shabby.

Poor Hilda, clinically depressed, anaemic, weary, worn down by work and worry, still suffering from the pain inflicted by this woman, was sudderly made aware of her seven-year-old utility coat, her down-at-heel shoes, her straggly hair, her swollen hands and broken fingernails. The unspoken taunt drove her beyond the limits of self-control. She lunged out, trying to grab the blonde curls and pull them out by the roots, but Miriam stepped forward quickly and held her. Pinioned she screamed with frustration.

'You painted bitch, you, with yer false bloody eyelashes, and yer blonde wig and yer la-di-da accent. Yer nuffink but a sly, filthy, thieving ol' cow.'

'Oh, this is too much. If my dear deceased husband could hear you, he would defend me.'

'An' damn your dear deceased husband, an' all.'

'Now you're insultin' my hero hubby, Captain Prichard, what died an 'ero's death at the Battle of Agincourt in the last war. Miriam, show this person out.'

Miriam, strong, silent and menacing, took Hilda's arm, propelled her towards the street door and pushed her out onto the pavement. Blinded by tears, Hilda dragged herself back to her place – she always used 'place' in her mind; 'flat' was too posh a word for the dump. She bought four pounds of sausages and a couple of loaves at the corner shop. That would keep them quiet for the evening. 'Everything OK, Mrs Harding?' enquired the shopkeeper brightly. Nosy devil, always tittle-tattling, thought Hilda. 'Yes, everyfink's OK,' she said, sullenly. All that pain and suffering, all that time in bed feeling ill – and for nothing. She was back to where she started, and twenty guineas lighter.

In the evening, after the kids had gone to bed, she told Bill that the abortion had been a failure and she was still pregnant. He received the news in silence, drawing deep on his Woodbine. She'd seemed a bit off colour. So that was it.

'You're sure, are you?'

'Quite.' At least he didn't seem cross. Resentful, perhaps, but not cross.

'We've got too many kids as it is.'

'I know.'

'We can't do wiv any more.'

'I know.'

'Isn't there anyfink else you can do?' he asked hopefully, 'something what'll get rid of it?'

She sighed. If only he knew what she'd been through.

'I've tried. I've done everything I can, an' I'm still pregnant. There's nothing for it but to go through with it. I'm sorry, Bill.'

Then he did something surprising, something she had not expected. He took her hand. A simple gesture, but it made all the difference. He squeezed her hand and said, 'You don't need to be sorry, duck. It's my fault, as much as your'n. We've always had fun together, you an' me. That's the trouble – too much fun.' He grinned and winked at her. 'We'll see it through together. You'll see. As long as we sticks together, we'll see it through. There now, don't cry. Everythings gonna be OK. I'll go out and fetch a jug of ale. That'll see you right.'

When he had gone, Hilda dropped her head on the table and sobbed with relief. Just to know that she had the support of her Bill turned the tide of despair into a flood of hope. Nothing had changed, they still had too many children in a slum flat, and she was expecting another, but, as Bill had said, they would see it through together.

The story of Hilda and Bill was told to us by a friend and fellow midwife, Ena, who was attached to the Salvation Army Maternity Hospital in Clapton. The hospital had several district midwifery centres at the time, and Ena was based at the one in Hackney Road, Shoreditch, which bordered on our area. Consequently we often saw each other when we were out on our bikes. Their district was just as busy as ours, but when we had time we would meet and swap yarns. Most midwives in those days had some pretty ripe stories to tell, which provoked peals of laughter, or gasps of dismay from the rest of us, but Ena's story is the most astonishing and the most macabre that I have ever heard.

She first met the Hardings when there was a knock at the door late one afternoon. Ena opened it and a man stood before her. 'Can I help you?' she enquired. He did not say anything but just stood there, cap in hand, turning it round and round. 'Is anything the matter?' she asked. Still he said nothing. He pulled a packet of Woodbines from his pocket and with shaking fingers opened it and pulled one out. He stuck it in his mouth. 'Have you come to us for any reason?' Ena enquired, puzzled. He took a box of matches from his pocket and fumbled with it. His awkward fingers could not seem to pick one up. Ena noticed blood around the edges of his nails. 'Here, let me help you,' she said kindly, and took out a match, lit it and held the flame to his cigarette. He inhaled deeply.

'Now, can I help you?'

'Is you ve midwife?'

'Yes.'

'Well, it's come.'

'What's come?'

'Ve baby.'

'Whose baby?'

'My wife's.'

'Who is your wife?'

''ilda. Mrs 'arding.'

'Is Mrs Harding booked with us?'

'I dunno.'

'Let's get this straight. Your wife, Mrs Harding, has had a baby?'

'Yes.'

'When?'

'Abaht quar'er of an hour ago.'

'You mean it's just been born?'

'Yes.'

'Where?'

'At 'ome.'

'Who was with her?'

'I was.' He drew deeply on his fag and spat on the pavement. He seemed ill at ease and would not look at her. Ena was growing increasingly alarmed. A baby born before arrival (a BBA we used to call it) happened occasionally, but usually the midwife had been called in advance and literally could not get there in time.

'Did you call anyone?'

'Nope.'

'Why not?'

He drew on his fag again and chewed his bloodied fingernails. Ena was putting two and two together.

'Did you deliver the baby?' she enquired, incredulous.

'S'posin' I did?' he said defensively.

'Nothing. It's just unusual, that's all.'

He blew smoke into the air, still not looking at her.

'It just come. Quick like.'

'Well, I had better come if a baby has just been born. Your wife and baby will need attention. Do you think she was booked with us? If so, I'll get the antenatal notes.'

'Like I says, I dunno.'

Ena decided that looking for notes that might not exist would only be a waste of time. She went quickly to fetch her delivery bag. Many thoughts were racing through her mind: a baby just born would need attention, almost certainly the cord would not have been cut; the third stage of labour would have to be dealt with; perhaps the woman was bleeding. She returned. The man was still standing at the door. He had lit another fag.

'Where do you live?'

'Round ve corner.' He pointed to a near-derelict road where 90 per cent of the houses had been destroyed by the bombing, or had been boarded up as structurally unsafe.

'I thought no one lived in that road,' she said.

'We do, worse luck.'

'We'd better get to your wife and baby, then. Come on.'

Ena walked quickly down the road. He followed a step or two behind, dragging his feet.

'Which house?'

'Over the road. The one with the windows.'

She crossed the road and approached the front door. It was locked.

'Have you got a key?'

'Reckon so. Somewhere.' He fumbled in his pockets, seeming unable to find it.

'Oh, do hurry. You must have the key. You only left the house a few minutes ago.'

He grunted and continued fumbling. Eventually he produced it and opened the door.

Ena entered a foul-smelling hallway, and for the first time since the man had approached her, it occurred to her that this might be a trap. She felt a sharp stab of fear. Everything about the man was so strange. He had seemed ill at ease, or even shifty, since the beginning of the interview. She stifled a moment of panic when it occurred to her that perhaps the blood around his fingernails was not from the birth of a baby, but from something much more sinister. A derelict house in a bomb-destroyed street was not the sort of place in which a baby would be born. Yet the man had specifically asked for a midwife. If he had had any ulterior motive, he would have been more likely to ask for a nurse. His next words were reassuring. 'My wife's upstairs. You'll have to come up. Mind that broken step. Don't hurt yourself.' She controlled her fears and followed the man. He opened a door.

A woman was lying on the bed, staring vacantly at the ceiling. She did not speak, and neither did the man. 'Where is the baby?' asked the midwife. No one answered. 'Where is it?' she asked a second time. Panic was beginning to take hold of her once more. There was something menacing in the silence of the man and the woman. She looked from one to the other, but they both avoided meeting her eye. 'Where is the baby?' she demanded a third time, more emphatically. 'There,' said the woman, pointing to the floor.

Ena looked down and saw a chamber pot, overflowing with a gory, bloody mess, and two little white legs hanging over the side. She ran over to the pot. The mess she had seen was the placenta; the baby was head down in the chamber pot, covered by the placenta. Ena grabbed its legs and pulled the baby out. It was a little boy, quite limp and lifeless, suffocated by his own placenta.

Shock, horror and panic made her unable to speak. She was only young, scarcely more than twenty, and had seen nothing like this before. She wrapped the little body in a towel and tried mouth-to-mouth resuscitation; she tried milking the cord towards the body in a vain attempt to introduce new blood; she tried heart massage. All to no avail. The baby was quite dead.

'Why did you leave it like that?' she demanded hysterically.

'We didn't know what to do.'

'But you've had other babies? You must surely know that a baby cannot be left head down in a chamber pot.'

'No one told us what ter do. How was we to know?'

'Why didn't you call us earlier?'

'It was all so quick. There was no time.'

'Well why didn't you pick the baby up?'

Neither one answered. The woman continued to stare at the ceiling, while the man blew smoke at the window as he gazed out into the street.

'I must go and get the senior midwife. I don't know what to do.'

She left the room and ran downstairs, stumbling and nearly falling. Out in the street she had to lean against the wall for several minutes to control herself. It was only a few hundred yards round the corner, but her steps were unsteady.

The senior midwife called the police, then went to the house. Mr and Mrs Harding repeated their story to the police. The baby's body was taken for post-mortem examination.

The report stated that a normal baby at full term of gestation had been born. All internal organs – heart, brain, lungs, liver, kidneys, intestines, venous system – were well developed and normal, with full potential to support life. The lungs had expanded at birth, and the baby had taken several breaths, but the lungs were full of blood and amniotic fluid. The conclusion was that the baby had drowned in the fluids inhaled into the lungs.

A coroner's inquest was held a few weeks later, at which Ena was required to give evidence. She told them everything she knew. Mr and Mrs Harding were questioned. Hilda said that she was booked to go into the Salvation Army Maternity Hospital to have the baby. She said she had felt a few labour pains and had asked Mrs Hatterton opposite to get her husband and to look after her two youngest. Bill came back and was just getting ready to take her to hospital when she felt a bit wet, and wanted to go to the toilet. So she had sat down on the chamber pot, and it all just came away from her.

The senior midwife confirmed that this was perfectly plausible, and that occasionally a multigravid woman could feel little more than slight abdominal discomfort, and a bearing-down sensation, just as Mrs Harding had described, in which case, labour need take no more than about fifteen minutes from the start of contractions to delivery of the baby.

When the coroner asked the Hardings what they did next, both of them repeated their story that they didn't know what to do and no one was there to tell them. Mr Harding said that he'd thought the best thing would be to go round the corner to get one of the district midwives, which is what he did. By the time they got back, the baby was dead.

The coroner said that he found it very difficult to know what judgement to record. He found it hard to believe the story that the Hardings did not know what to do. On the other hand, he supposed that in the absence of a trained midwife or a doctor, two ignorant and unlettered people might really be at a loss to know how to act, especially if they were in a state of shock at the unexpected and rapid birth of a baby. Mr Harding had taken the course of action that seemed to them to be appropriate – he had gone to call a midwife. But it was too late.

In the event the coroner recorded an open verdict, which meant that the case was not closed, and that, if any further evidence came to light, it could be reopened and re-examined. But no further evidence was forthcoming.

THE CAPTAIN'S DAUGHTER

It was well that Chummy was on first call. Who else would have had the grit, the stamina and the sheer physical strength and courage to do what she did in the Docks that night?

Camilla Fortescue-Cholmeley-Browne came from a long line of 'Builders of the Empire'. District Commissioners and Colonels were her forebears. All the women seemed to be Lady This, That or the Other, and could not only run a garden party or a county ball for thousands but could also live in torrid isolation, maintaining the Hill Stations for their husbands the District Commissioners, who single-handedly governed areas the size of Wales. Whatever one may say about the British Empire, it certainly bred self reliance and courage in its administrators.

Chummy was typical of her family in this respect. In other ways, though, she was a misfit, because she was gauche, awkward and shy. Roedean and expensive finishing schools had been a failure. Chummy possessed no social graces whatsoever – a fact of which she was quite unaware – and she was always surprised and hurt when her mother let her know that she was an embarrassment to the family. The fact that she was over six feet in height and that she could not seem to control her long limbs did not help. She was always falling over or bumping into things, and after several disasters in public places her parents decided they could not take her anywhere. Many genteel and ladylike occupations were proposed, but after a fair trial, it had to be admitted that she was no good at any of them. 'Whatever are we to do with Camilla?' her mother would ask despairingly. 'She can't do anything, and no one is going to want to marry her.'

Demoralised and bewildered, Chummy accepted her role as the family failure. But the ways of man and the ways of God are not the same thing. Quite suddenly she found her vocation. Chummy was going to be a missionary. For this purpose she trained as a nurse and was an instant and brilliant success. Then she trained as a midwife, which is how we came to meet at Nonnatus House.

And, as I said, it was well that Chummy was on first call that night.

The telephone rang at 11.30 p.m., getting her out of bed.

'Port-of-London-West-India-Docks-nightwatchman speaking. We needs a nurse, or a doctor.'

'What's the matter? An accident at the docks?' asked Chummy.

'No. Woman ill, or somefink.'

'A woman? Are you sure?'

''Course I'm sure. Think I can't tell the difference?'

'No, no. I didn't mean that. No offence, old chap. But women are not allowed in the Docks.'

'Well, this one's 'ere all right. Captain's wife or somefink, the mate says. Least, that's what I think he's tryin' 'a say, because he can't speak no English. Just rolls his eyes and groans and rubs 'is tummy – vat's why I called ve midwives.'

'I'll come. Where do I go to?'

'Main gate. West India.'

'I'll be there in ten minutes.'

Chummy dressed in haste and went out into the night. It was windy. Not cold or raining, but a strong head wind made cycling slow, and it took Chummy nearly twenty minutes to reach West India Dock. The nightwatchman was sitting by the burning brazier next to the gate, which he unlocked.

'You bin a long time. Bloody wind, I s'ppose. Don't like ve wind.'

Chummy had never been inside the Dock gates before, and the place seemed eerie and alien in the darkness. The stretch of water in the basin looked vast, as she gazed down it, and the hulks of huge cargo boats loomed over the oily water. On the skyline numerous cranes criss-crossed each other. Some of the boats were dimly lit, but others were completely dark. The night watchman's coke fire glowed on the quay. The wind caused the water to splash and the rigging to tremble, making hollow moaning sounds.

'Swedish timber carrier on South Quay. Woman got a belly ache or somefink. Shouldn't be there, I told the mate, but I reckons as 'ow he never understood.'

Reluctantly he hauled himself up, left his comfortable little hut and tipped some more coke onto the fire.

'This way,' he sighed mournfully. 'Bloody women. Shouldn't be 'ere, I says. I've go' enough 'a do, wivout all vis.'

They made their way to the South Quay.

''ere we are. The *Katrina*. Yer rope ladder's there and yer guiders.'

He grabbed a rope, pulled it and shouted. A faint sound was heard about forty feet up. The watchman was thinking of his fire, and his cosy hut, and the sausages and fried bread he was going to cook. 'Bloody women,' he muttered, 'no offence to you, nurse.'

A head appeared over the side of the boat.

'Ya?'

'The nurse.'

'Bra. Valkommen. Tack.'

'Yer'll 'ave to climb ve rope-ladder. It's leeward o' the wind, an' won't rock too much. You can climb this, can't yer?'

Most women would have taken one look at the bulk of the ship towering above, at the slender rope ladder swinging dizzily in the wind, and said 'No'. But not Chummy.

'Right,' she said, 'Jolly-ho. But I think they will have to haul my bag up separately. I'm not sure I could carry it, and climb the ladder one handed.'

The watchman groaned, but tied the handle of the bag to a

rope and shouted to the men above to start hauling. Somehow they understood him, and Chummy watched it swinging upwards.

'Now for it,' she said, taking hold of the rope ladder.

'Ever done this afore?'

'We had a tree house when we were children, so I suppose you could say I've had some practice.'

'The 'ardest part is when you jumps off, because you're goin' to 'it the side of ve boat. But just hold steady and yer'll be all right. Ven you can start climbing.'

'Good egg. Thanks for the tip.'

The wind was blowing Chummy's gabardine raincoat in all directions. It was a heavy garment, and long, as required by nursing uniform standards.

'This bally thing's going to be a nuisance.'

She took it off. The nightwatchman looked at her. He was beginning to respect her, and his sausages and fried bread seemed less important.

'Yer skirts too long. You might catch yer foot in 'em.'

'Not to worry.' Chummy pulled her skirt up above her waist, and tucked it into her knickers. 'No need for false modesty,' she said cheerily.

She took hold of the ladder again and put a foot on the first rung.

'Go up a rung, so you pull ve ladder taut. Grab 'old of a rung above head height. Don't try holdin' the sides of ve ladder.'

'Thanks. Any other tips?'

'No. Just keep yer nerve, an' keep climbing. Don't look down or up. Keep a steady climb, and whatever yer do, don't stop. Jes keep it steady, an' you'll be all right.'

Chummy put one foot on a rung. 'Wizard show. Here we go,' she said, cheerily, feeling upwards for the next rung. She hauled herself up.

'Only another fifty to go,' she called out to the man watching as she reached upwards for another rung.

'I only 'ope to Christ them Swedes know 'ow to make a rope ladder,' he muttered to himself, 'a weak link could be ve death of 'er.'

'What did you say? I couldn't hear for the wind,' she called.

'Nuffink important. Jes' keep going, one hand, one foot. Keep it steady, and don't stop or look down.'

Chummy kept going. The wind was rocking the boat, and every now and then a sudden gust caught Chummy and blew her a few feet to one side. But she kept her nerve. She would have tougher things than this to face when she was a missionary. She remembered Miss Hawkins, a retired missionary and Matron of Queen Charlotte's, where she had done her early training. Matron Hawkins had taught all her students as though they were going to be up a creek without a paddle. Just keep going, old girl, thought Chummy.

She reached upwards and there was nothing. She groped around with her fingers, but no, nothing. Then she felt the wood of a broken rung swinging loose against her arm. Panic hit her, and she froze, leaning her head against the side of the ship. To be paralysed with fear can mean death, because the muscles are unable to respond. Chummy listened to her heart pounding and knew her breathing to be shallow and irregular. Her whole body was stiff. She sensed her danger. She was a sensible and highly trained nurse and knew that, if she could control her breathing she would begin to regain control of her muscles. She knew the breathing that she had taught others in ante-natal classes would help. Gradually she felt she could move. She brought her foot up to the next rung, which gave her a longer reach, and was able to grab the one above her head with her outstretched hand.

'That was a close shave,' she muttered to herself.

The nightwatchman had seen what had happened, and his heart was in his mouth.

'She's got guts, vat girl,' he thought. The men above were commenting in Swedish.

Chummy did not know it, but she had not far to go. She felt exhilarated now. Having successfully negotiated the danger of the missing rung, she felt she could tackle anything, and she even enjoyed the rest of the climb. Suddenly she heard voices close to her ear, and her hand touched the metal bars of the bulwarks. She climbed over the edge and stood flushed and breathless on the deck. For once in her life she was not confused or embarrassed to be surrounded by men, even though she was standing among them in her knickers.

'Whoops, cover your legs, old girl,' she said to herself as she let her skirt fall. They all laughed and clapped and cheered.

One of the men handed her the bag then another took her down to a cabin on the middle deck. He knocked and spoke in Swedish. The door opened, and a tall, bearded man appeared. He spoke rapidly to Chummy in Swedish, as though he expected her to understand him. A female voice from within the cabin called out in English, 'Don't try to explain, Dad, I can.'

Chummy entered the cabin, which was very small. A hurricane lamp swung from a hook and the atmosphere was suffocatingly hot. The woman, who was lying on a small bunk bed, was positively huge and not only filled the bunk but spilled out over the edge. She was sweating and dry around the mouth. Her eyes looked gratefully at Chummy. 'Thank God you've come,' she breathed, 'these men will be the death of me.'

The woman lay back and closed her eyes. Heavy blonde hair fell over the grey pillow. Beads of sweat covered her fat features, her chin was indistinguishable from her neck, which in its turn blended into a vast and pendulous bosom.

A small wooden crate in the cabin obviously served as both stool and table. Chummy sat down and took out her note-book.

'I'm glad you can speak English, because I need your case history.'

'My mother was English, my father Swedish. My name is Kirsten Bjorgsen. They call me Kirsty. I am thirty-five.'

'What is your address?'

'The *Katrina*.'

'No, I mean your permanent address.'

'The *Katrina is* my permanent address.'

'That is not possible. This is a trading vessel. It cannot be your permanent home. In any case, I'm told women are not allowed on the ships.'

Kirsty laughed.

'Well, you know, what the eye doesn't see . . .'

She laughed again.

'How long have you lived on the boat?'

'Since I was fourteen, when my mother died. We had a home in Stockholm, and I went to school there. But when she died my father brought me onto the *Katrina*. He is the captain.'

'I was informed that you were the captain's wife.'

'Wife? Who told you that? He's my dad.'

Chummy said no more on the subject, but enquired about the woman's condition.

'Well, I have a pain in my belly. It comes and goes.'

Chummy was beginning to put two and two together. 'When was your last period?'

'I don't know. I don't really take much notice of that.'

'Can't you remember at all?'

'Perhaps a few months. I'm not sure.'

'I need to examine your stomach.'

Chummy palpated the mountainous abdomen, which was all flesh and fat. It was quite impossible for her to tell whether the woman was pregnant or not. She took up her Pinards foetal stethoscope, but it sank about six inches into the abdomen, the flesh virtually covering it, and all that Chummy could hear was the gurgle and swish of intestinal movements.

The woman groaned – 'Ooh, you're hurting me. It's making the pain come back. Please stop.'

But the pain got worse. Chummy felt the lower abdomen and felt a hard round sphere beneath the flesh. When the pain had passed she said, 'Kirsty you are in labour. Didn't you know you were pregnant?'

Kirsty raised herself on her elbow. 'What?' she demanded, her eyes round and incredulous.

'You are not only pregnant. You are in labour. That's what your stomach pains are.'

'I can't be. You're wrong. I'm always so careful.'

'I'm not wrong.'

Kirsty lay back on the pillow. 'Oh no! What's Dad going to say?' she murmured.

'Which of the men on board is your husband?'

'None of them. And all of them. They are all my boys, and I love them all – well nearly all, anyway.'

Chummy was shocked. Kirsty read her thoughts and laughed a great belly laugh, which set all her flesh rippling.

'I'm what you call the "ship's woman". I keep the boys happy. My dad always says there's no fighting on a ship when the boys have a nice woman to go to. That's why he brought me here when mother died.'

Chummy was deeply shocked.

'You mean to say your father brought you here when you were only fourteen to be . . .' she hesitated, 'to be the ship's woman?'

Kirsty nodded.

'But that is shocking, disgraceful!' exclaimed Chummy.

'Don't be silly. Of course it's not. After my mother's death I couldn't stay in Stockholm by myself, and Dad was always at sea. So he took me with him. He explained what was expected of me. He couldn't keep me for himself, because that would cause trouble with the crew – so it had to be fair all round.'

Chummy felt she was choking.

'Your dad explained to you . . .?' Her voice trailed away.

'Of course. He was always fair, and he still is. But he's the captain, and he always goes first. The other boys have to wait their turn.'

'Your dad goes first?' said Chummy weakly.

'Well, he *is* the captain. It's only right.'

Chummy was thinking about the headmistress of Roedean, and what she would have said about the situation.

Kirsty continued, 'And I never have two at once. Dad wouldn't allow that. He has very high standards.'

'High standards!' Chummy gasped, and the standards enshrined on the coat of arms at Roedean School flashed through her mind – *Honneur aux Dignes*, 'Honour to the Deserving'. But Kirsty was happily babbling on.

'I love my father, I do. He's a lovely man. He has, how do you say it, the best bugger's grips you've ever seen.'

'Bugger's grips?!' Chummy felt weak from shock. This was a different world.

'You know, whiskers on his cheek bones. They're called bugger's grips. I like to brush them when he's relaxed, after he's done with me. Then he goes to sleep, often. It's like having a baby in my arms.'

Another contraction came, and Chummy sat with her hand on the lower abdomen until it passed. She could scarcely believe what she had heard and needed a few seconds to adjust. Kirsty chatted on.

'That's better. I feel all right now. I thought it was stomach cramps. I was eating green apples yesterday.'

'No, I assure you. You are in labour and you're going to have a baby.'

'But the boys always wear a rubber when they are doing it.'

'A rubber?' repeated Chummy enquiringly.

'You know – French letters, they call them in England, or *capotes anglaises*, as they say in France. Anyway, the men always wear one. Dad insists, and they wouldn't disobey the captain. And anyway, I make them put one on, or I put it on. Dad gets a great box of them. Five hundred at a time, when we come to a port. He's most particular.'

Chummy felt light-headed.

'Five hundred?' she murmured and stared aghast at Kirsty.

'And they are never reused – Dad insists on that – in case one splits, and I wouldn't know. So you see, I can't be pregnant. It must have been those green apples.'

Chummy couldn't reply to that, but was murmuring, 'Five hundred! How long does a box last you?'

'Oh, a few weeks. Dad would never let me run out. If it's a long voyage, he'll buy in two or three boxes. We always need them.'

'Always?'

'Well, the boys need me, and I'm always here for them. I'm the most important member of the crew, Dad tells me, because I keep the men happy, and happy men work hard. And that's what every captain needs – a hardworking crew.'

Chummy swallowed. She had entered a different world of morality and did not know how to respond. Kirsty must have read her thoughts because she patted her hand kindly.

'There now. Don't worry. You're only a young girl, and I can see you come from a different class. But it's all quite natural, and I've had a good life. I've travelled the world. Sometimes they can smuggle me ashore and I can have a look round the shops. I like that. I can buy a few pretty things, because Dad gives me money.

'Don't you do anything else – the cooking, or sewing, or something?'

'Oh no.' Kirsty squawked with laughter and slapped Chummy's shoulder. 'Don't you think I have enough to do with a crew of twenty? Sometimes it's one after another for hours on end. Do you think I could work after that? In any case, we have a ship's cook. He is the one who gave me those green apples yesterday. Oh . . .'

She doubled up with pain. Chummy felt the uterus; it was harder and more prominent. She had timed ten minutes since the last contraction. Labour was progressing.

Chummy had other things to worry about than Kirsty's

position on the boat. She was alone, in the middle of the night, on board a ship with no telephone and with a woman in labour. Furthermore the woman was a primigravida of thirty-five, who had had no antenatal care. She should go to hospital at once. But how? In the unlikely event of an ambulance arriving, the woman would be in no condition to climb down the rope ladder! If a doctor was called, would he climb *up* the rope ladder? Chummy remembered her climb, and the missing rung, and knew that she could not expect anyone else to do it. She was alone, and a cold hand gripped her heart. But in the same instant a voice whispered to her that she was going to be a missionary, and that this was just God's way of testing her. She prayed.

The contraction passed, and a new, strengthened Chummy spoke.

'You must stop all this nonsense about green apples. You are in labour, and your baby will be born within the next hour or two. I have to examine you vaginally, and I must have clean cotton sheets, cotton wool and something to act as absorbent pads, a cot to put the baby in, and hot water and soap. Now, where can I get all these things?'

Kirsty looked dumbfounded.

'You must call my father,' she said.

Chummy opened the door and called, 'Hi there!'

The big, bearded man entered, and Kirsty explained. He let out an oath and looked savagely at Chummy, as though it were her fault. But Chummy was taller than him and looked down on him with new-found confidence. The captain turned to go, but Chummy stopped him with a light touch on the arm. She said to Kirsty, 'Would you also tell your father that this cabin is quite unsuitable for the delivery of a baby, and that I will need somewhere better.'

Kirsty translated. The captain no longer looked savage. He looked at Chummy with respect. Then his whole expression changed, and his eyes filled with anguish. He kneeled down beside his daughter, took her huge body in his arms and rubbed his beard into the folds of her neck. He stood up with tears in his eyes and fled from the cabin.

Two more contractions came and went. They are getting stronger and more regular, thought Chummy. I hope the crew can get something sorted out quickly, because I need to move her, and she has to be able to walk.

The captain returned and said that the best cabin was ready. Kirsty sat up and heaved her great bulk off the bunk. With enormous difficulty she squeezed herself through the narrow doorway and along the gangways. Several men looked out of their cabins and patted her arms or shoulders. One man gave her a crucifix. They all looked anxious. The ship's woman was not only well used, she was well thought of.

The captain led them to a much larger cabin that was more appropriate in every way. Kirsty gave a cry when she saw it and embraced her father. He kissed her and turned to leave, but first he saluted Chummy in military fashion and bowed to her.

When the door closed, Kirsty said, 'This is the captain's cabin. He's so good to me, I tell you. What other captain would give up his cabin?'

'Well, under the circumstances, and considering he might be the father of the baby, I think it's the least he could do,' retorted Chummy dryly.

The captain's desk and all other naval paraphernalia had been pushed to one side. A large folding bed had been placed in the middle of the cabin, covered with clean blankets and linen. Kirsty looked at it and said, 'I didn't know they had these nice things on board.' A bowl was standing on a small table with jugs of hot water beside it, and soap and clean towels.

Another contraction came, and Kirsty grabbed the edge of the desk and leaned over it. She was panting and sweating. When it passed, she grinned and said, 'You must be right, nurse; this is more than green apples.' She went over to the bed to lie down.

'I still don't know how it happened. I'm so careful. Do you think one of the boys didn't put his rubber on, but told me he had?'

'I don't know. I haven't any experience in your line of business,' said Chummy truthfully, and they both laughed. A bond of female friendship and understanding was developing between them.

Kirsty said, 'You are nice. I'd like you to be my friend. I haven't had any girl friends since I left school, and I miss them. It's men, men, all the time. I never have the chance to talk to another woman. When I go ashore, which isn't very often, I look at the other women in the streets and think, "I'd like to talk to you and see how you live." But then it's back to the ship and off to sea again.'

'Do the lads ever talk to you?' asked Chummy, who was beginning to sense loneliness.

'Oh yes, some of them tell me all their troubles, they tell me about their wives and girl friends, and some tell me about their children. It's nice to hear about their children – it makes me feel part of the family.'

Secretly Chummy wondered if the compliment would be returned, but Kirsty was still speaking. 'But I must say most of them just want to be quick and have done with it. I don't mind, if that's what they want, but it's tiring, especially if I get ten or twelve who've only got half an hour before the next shift.' She puffed at the memory. 'You need some strength in my job, I can tell you. These men will be the death of me. Oooh, no, not again!' She threw her body back in pain and cursed in Swedish.

Chummy watched her carefully and made a note that contractions were now coming every seven minutes and lasting for approximately sixty seconds. She could feel the uterus firmly just above the pubic bone, but nothing higher, because abdominal fat occluded it. She longed to be able to hear the foetal heart and reassure herself that the baby was healthy, but it was impossible. She was going to make a vaginal examination. Perhaps that would reveal something. Suddenly she remembered the obligatory enema – that monstrous practice, sacred to midwifery – and abruptly forgot the idea. How absurd on a ship, and surrounded by men! She wrote in her notes: 'Enema not given'.

The pain passed, Kirsty relaxed with a sigh, and Chummy gave her a drink of water.

'I've got to examine you internally,' she said. 'That means I have to put my fingers into your vagina to assess where the baby is lying, and how close to birth it is. Will you allow me to do that?'

'Well, I'm used to that sort of thing, aren't I? But not for the same reasons!'

Chummy placed her delivery bag on the captain's desk and opened it. She scrubbed up and extracted a sterile gown, mask and surgical gloves and put them on. While she was doing so, it occurred to her that Kirsty had probably contracted syphilis during her career. Chummy had no practical experience of venereal disease, but from her classroom work she remembered that syphilis can usually be diagnosed by the hard, rubbery chancre on the vulva, whilst gonorrhoea is manifested by profuse greenish-yellow vaginal discharge. She recalled the midwifery tutor saying that a syphilitic woman very seldom carries to full term, because the foetus usually dies within the first sixteen weeks. She also remembered the next part of the lecture: that in the event of the baby going to full term, it was likely to be stillborn and was frequently macerated. Chummy felt queasy at such an idea. A macerated stillbirth could leave a midwife feeling sick and depressed for days, or even weeks – let alone the effect it had on a mother.

Chummy quickly put the thought from her. Another contraction was coming. She timed it to be seven minutes since the last one. Full dilation of the cervix was getting closer, and as she had been unable to assess the lie of the baby from external palpation, a vaginal assessment was imperative. When the contraction had passed, she said 'Now I want you to draw your knees up, put your heels together and then let your legs fall apart.'

Kirsty did this with great agility. Her lower limbs were surprisingly flexible. Her massive thighs not only flew apart, but her knees touched the bed on either side, revealing a vast, moist purple-red vulva. Chummy was a bit taken aback at the speed and efficiency with which the exercise was undertaken, and Kirsty must have seen her expression because she laughed. 'You seem to forget I do this all the time,' she said.

Chummy examined the external vulva carefully. She could neither see nor feel syphilitic chancre, nor was there any evidence of a foul-smelling and profuse vaginal discharge. Against all the odds, it seemed that Kirsty did not have venereal disease. It must have been her father's gifts of boxes of 500 rubbers at frequent intervals that had protected her. 'Bully for the captain!' thought Chummy.

Chummy did as every good midwife would do. She prepared to place two fingers gently in the vagina, but without the slightest effort her whole hand slid in. 'Great Scott! You could get a vegetable marrow in here,' she thought.

With easy access she could feel the cervix. It was three-quarters dilated, a head presenting, fairly well down, waters intact. She breathed a sigh of relief that the baby was lying in a good position for a normal delivery.

Then she felt something very strange. At first she thought it was part of the soft, undulating vaginal wall. She moved it with her fingers. It was not part of the vaginal wall. 'What on earth is it?' she wondered. It was attached above, and seemed to be hanging freely beside the baby's head. She palpated it with her fingers, and it moved a little. Chummy was feeling this strange thing and moving it about with her fingers, when she realized with horror that it was pulsating. She froze, and blind panic overtook her for the second time that night. She looked at her watch and saw that the thing was pulsating at 120 beats per minute. The pulsation was the baby's heartbeat. The cord had prolapsed.

Chummy said afterwards that in all her professional career she had never known a moment of such terror. She went shivery all over but could feel the sweat pouring out of her body. She withdrew her hand, and it was trembling. Then her whole body began to tremble. 'What can I do? What should I do? Oh please, God, help me!' She nearly sobbed aloud but controlled herself.

'Everything all right?' enquired Kirsty cheerfully.

'Oh, yes, quite all right.'

Chummy's voice sounded far away and faint. She was thinking back to her midwifery lectures: 'In the event of prolapse of the cord, an emergency Caesarean section is necessary.' She looked around the cabin, with the hurricane lamp swinging from the beam; at the portholes, black against the night sky; at the jugs of hot water and towels so thoughtfully provided; at her equipment laid out on the captain's desk, adequate for a normal birth, but no more. The ship moved in the wind, and she remembered her isolation and the impossibility of getting help. She trembled at her own inexperience and thought, 'This baby will die.'

Yet something else was stirring in her mind. The lecturer had not ended with 'a Caesarean section is necessary', but had continued. What else had the lecturer been saying? The pulsating cord, and the knowledge that a living baby depended on her for life, forced Chummy's mind back to the classroom. 'Raise the pelvis by instructing the mother to adopt the genu-pectoral position and sedate the mother. If the amniotic sac is unbroken it is sometimes possible to push the baby's head back a little and move the cord out of the way.'

Good midwifery is a combination of art, science, experience and instinct. It used to be said that it took seven years of practice to make a good midwife. Chummy had everything but experience. She possessed intuition and instinct in abundance. The amniotic sac was not yet broken. There might still be time to attempt the replacement of the cord. She must have a go. She could not sit and do nothing, knowing that the cord would be crushed as labour progressed, and that the baby would die.

'Raise the pelvis', the lecturer had said. Chummy looked at the massive thighs and buttocks of Kirsty, who probably weighed about thirty-five stone. A crane would be needed to raise her pelvis. The genu-pectoral position would be possible in a smaller woman, but Kirsty could no more roll over onto her front than a beached whale could. But only raising the pelvis would take pressure off the cord, and Chummy was resourceful. She remembered that a folding bed had been provided. If she folded up the legs at the head of the bed, but left the foot end standing, perhaps her patient could lie with her head and shoulders on the floor and her buttocks resting on the higher end of the bed. It was worth a try.

She explained what she wanted to Kirsty. She did not say anything about the cord or the gravity of the situation, because there was no point in alarming her unnecessarily. She merely explained about the bed, as though it was the usual way to deliver a baby.

With great difficulty Kirsty got to her feet, and Chummy crawled under the bed to collapse the legs so that the head dropped to the floor. That was easy; the difficult part would be getting Kirsty back onto it in the required position. The problem was solved by Kirsty. She calmly went to the raised end of the bed, sat on it, leaned backwards, then rolled her back down the bed. 'I do this all the time,' she said, splaying her legs apart.

Pressure would now be off the cord, Chummy thought with satisfaction – gravity would pull the baby back into the uterus, allowing a little extra space for the cord. But the advantage would not last for long, because the inexorable process of uterine contractions would push the baby forward. Time was short, and running out. Contractions were already coming every six minutes.

Chummy weighed in her mind whether or not to give pethidine to sedate her patient. It would relax her and might help when it came to replacing the cord. But on the other hand it would also sedate the foetus, and delivery was imminent. She decided against sedation. Kirsty seemed relaxed enough and would just have to bear the pain. The life and health of the baby were Chummy's main concern, and pethidine in its bloodstream would be an additional hazard.

A contraction was coming, and Kirsty groaned with pain. She threw her head around and tried to move her legs up to her body. 'Whatever happens, don't roll out of that position, Kirsty. It's perfect,' said Chummy.

'I must try to replace the cord before the next contraction,' she thought. The time between each would soon be only five minutes. The contraction passed, and Chummy said a quiet prayer for what she was about to do. She had never seen it done before and had received only one lecture on the subject, but it had to be enough, and with God's help it would be.

'I'm going to push you around a bit, Kirsty. Hook your knees over the edge of the bed, and hold on, so that you don't slip backwards with the pressure.'

Chummy slipped her gloved hand into the vagina. There was no perineal resistance, something she knew she could be thankful for. She felt the partly dilated cervix again, the forewaters protruding and the pulsation of the cord within. With her forefingers she felt around the baby's head – there must be no pressure on the fontanelle, she thought, because that could kill the baby at once. Her fingers were placed ready to push when the ship moved, causing them to slip. She had to find the correct position a second time. When she thought her fingers were rightly placed she pushed hard, but the head did not move. She felt the sweat running down her face and neck. 'It's got to,' she thought, 'it's got to go back.' So she pushed again. This time the head retreated slightly but not enough for the cord to be replaced behind it.

After the second unsuccessful attempt Chummy paused, trembling.

'Pressure, that is the only thing I've got to help me, massive pressure, and God be with me that I do no harm.'

Shaking all over, she leaned her head on the soft cushion of Kirsty's enormous thigh, trying to think clearly. The wind groaned outside, and the ship moved in sympathy. Her fingers slipped, and she withdrew her hand. If the amniotic sac broke, that would be the end: nothing could save the baby. Only the fact that the cord was still floating freely in the amniotic fluid made replacement a possibility.

Another contraction came. 'Five or six minutes can't have passed,' she thought. 'I can't have spent all that time achieving nothing.' She looked at her watch – it had been five minutes. Contractions were getting closer, and time was rapidly running out.

She saw the uterus heave with the muscular pressure of the contraction, and a plan formed in her mind. Looking at the uterus, her instinct told her that, if she applied reverse pressure externally, and internal pressure on the baby's head, she might be able to move it sufficiently to replace the cord. It was not a procedure that had been taught in the classroom, but something told her that it might work. With only five minutes, perhaps four, before the next contraction, she had to be successful, or the baby would surely die. The ship lurched as a great gust of wind hit the side, and Chummy prayed for calm during the next few minutes.

When the contraction passed Chummy said, 'Kirsty, I want you to listen carefully. Grip your knees over the edge of the bed again, and hold on. Just concentrate on holding your body still, because I am going to push hard, and you must *not* allow me to push you downwards.'

'I'll do my best, nurse. I have to be strong in my job. I don't suppose you can push any harder than a fifteen-stone first mate. I'll be all right.'

Chummy took her at her word. She inverted her left hand over the upturned uterus, just above the pubic bone. Being able to insert her whole hand into the vagina was a huge advantage. She cupped the palm of her right hand over the baby's head, stood up and took a deep breath.

'Hold on, Kirsty, don't let yourself slip. I'm going to push – now.'

Chummy was tall and strong. She exerted massive downward pressure internally and externally. The baby shifted two or three inches from her internal hand, but still she kept up the external pressure on the uterus. When she felt it was enough, she relaxed.

'That was hard! I don't know if I've had it harder than that. But I didn't move, did I?' said Kirsty.

Chummy did not reply. Her job was not done. She still had to replace the cord into the uterus. She felt for the cord, but it was not there. She stretched her finger inside the os and ran it around the rim, but could feel only the smooth, round surface of the baby's head. The cord had disappeared. Internal fluid suction, caused by shifting the baby, must have withdrawn the slippery cord without any further action being required from the midwife.

Chummy felt giddy with relief and leaned her head on Kirsty's capacious thigh. She giggled weakly.

'It's done, it's done, thanks be to God! And thanks to you, Kirsty. You didn't move. I couldn't have done it without you.'

'All in a day's work,' observed Kirsty casually.

The whole operation had taken only about thirty seconds. But Chummy sat trembling with relief for another two or three minutes, until her more practical side took over. Now that the baby was safe, how was it to be delivered? All sorts of questions tumbled into her mind. Kirsty looked quite comfortable, but could a baby be delivered in an upside-down position? She wondered what the midwifery tutors would say about that! On the other hand, moving this massive female might be a problem. Kirsty had rolled down the slope of the bed, but would she be able to roll up? The third stage of labour, the delivery of the placenta, was vitally important, and Chummy was not confident about the mother expelling a placenta upside-down. Kirsty would have to be moved. Then the cord came into her mind. Reverse pressure had made it withdraw into the uterus, but if Kirsty stood up, as she would have to, would the downward pressure displace the cord and make it slip forward again? Chummy could not be sure, but it might. The risk was too great. Kirsty would have to remain in her present position.

Chummy sat beside the labouring woman, listening to the wind and feeling the ship move beneath her. She was not really surprised by the extraordinary situation in which she found herself; after all she was going to be a missionary and she would have to be prepared for anything. She was a thoughtful, prayerful girl, and she thanked God she was being tested in this way.

She pondered the ugly situation in which Kirsty had been placed. First abused, probably raped, when she was fourteen by her father, and then confined to a ship for the pleasure of all the men, including her father. Yet, Chummy reflected, she seemed happy and content. Perhaps, as she had known no other life, it all seemed quite natural to her. The men were obviously fond of her – their concern as she struggled down the gangway was evident – and she was not ill-treated. Common prostitutes, pushed onto the streets by pimps and beaten up if they protested, had a much worse life, she thought.

Another contraction came, and the waters broke. Thank God I was able to replace the cord, she thought; it was only just in time. Labour was progressing fast, and Kirsty was wonderful. She had had no sedation but had barely murmured at the pain. Chummy could feel the head well down on the pelvic floor. 'It won't be long now,' she said aloud.

Kirsty groaned and pushed. When the contraction had passed she said, 'I've been thinking about this baby. I'm so glad now. I never thought I'd have one, because Dad always gave me the boxes of rubbers and said the boys must always wear them. So they did. But now I'm having a baby. And I'm glad.'

'I'm sure you are. A woman may not want a baby, but she's always happy when it comes,' said Chummy.

'I hope it's a little girl. I'd like a little girl. I have enough men. But I don't want her to have my life. It wouldn't be right for a young girl. I think Dad will understand if I talk to him. What's your name, nurse?'

'Camilla,' said Chummy.

'Oh, what a beautiful name. I want to give her your name, nurse, may I?'

'Of course. I should be honoured.'

'Baby Camilla. That's a lovely name.'

Another contraction came, only two minutes after the last, fiercer and longer. Kirsty had no vaginal or perineal resistance, so the head was able to descend quickly and easily. She gripped her hands until the knuckles showed white and pushed hard, forcing the weight of her buttocks against the end of the bed. In protest, the bed trembled and collapsed with a crash onto the floor.

The problem of an upside-down delivery had been solved! Mother and midwife were now on the floor, Kirsty floundering and pushing, Chummy desperately trying to control the situation.

Poor Kirsty was bewildered. 'What happened?' she kept asking. Chummy, who had narrowly missed having her hands crushed, tried to calm her.

'The bed broke, but the baby is all right, and if you are not hurt, no harm has been done. In fact it's a good thing, because delivery of your baby will be easier.'

Chummy's concern now was that the baby's head might be born too quickly. The slow and steady delivery of the head is what every midwife hopes for, but with no perineal resistance, this baby could well shoot out with the next contraction.

Another contraction came, and Kirsty raised her knees and braced herself to push, but Chummy stopped her. 'Don't push,

Kirsty, don't push. I know you want to and feel you must, but don't. Your baby's head will be born with this contraction, but I want it to come slowly. The slower the better. Concentrate on *not* pushing. Take little breaths, in-out, in-out, think about breathing, think about relaxing, but don't push.' All the time she was saying these words Chummy was holding the head, trying to prevent it from bursting out of the mother at speed. The contraction was waning, Chummy eased the slack perineum around the presenting crown, and the head was born.

Chummy breathed a sigh of relief. She had been concentrating so hard that she had not noticed the cramp in her legs as she squatted on the deck of the cabin; had not noticed the poor light cast by the hurricane lamp as it swung from a beam; had not noticed the movement of the ship, nor the occasional lurch as the wind hit it. All that she knew was that the miracle of a baby's birth would shortly take place, that the safe delivery was in her hands, and that the head had been born. Chummy kept her hand under the baby's face in order to lift it away from the hard floor and waited. Another contraction was coming. Chummy felt the face she was holding move.

'It's coming, Kirsty. You can push now. Hard.'

Kirsty drew her legs upwards and pushed. Chummy eased the shoulder out and downwards. The other shoulder and arm quickly followed, and the whole body slid out effortlessly.

'You have a little girl, Kirsty.'

Emotion flooded over Kirsty with such intensity that she could not speak. Tears took the place of words. 'Let me have her. Can I see her?' she spluttered, still floundering with her head on the deck, unable to lift her shoulders. Chummy said 'I am going to lay her on your tummy while I cut the cord, then you can hold her in your arms.'

The baby sank into the soft cushion of her mother's stomach. She was slightly blue around the mouth and extremities, but otherwise she seemed to have suffered no harm from the drama of labour. Chummy severed the cord and then held the baby upside down by the heels. Kirsty gasped and held up her hands protectively.

'Don't worry, I'm not going to drop her,' said the midwife, 'this is done in order to drain the mucus out of the throat, and to help breathing.'

Then she gave a short, sharp pat to the back of the baby, who at once gave a shrill yell. 'That's what I like to hear, let's have another one.' The baby obliged, crying lustily, and from outside the door a chorus of men's voices were heard cheering, shouting, whooping and whistling. They started to sing, in a united and raucous male voice. Kirsty called out to them in Swedish, but they were making so much noise they could not hear her. The captain's daughter was obviously very popular, and the men responded in their own way. 'I expect they will all get drunk now,' she said dryly.

Chummy wrapped the baby in a towel and placed her in the arms of her mother, who was weeping with joy. 'Are you all right on the floor like that?' Chummy enquired with concern.

'I've never been better in my life,' answered Kirsty. 'I would like to stay here for ever, cuddling my baby.' She gave a sigh of contentment.

Chummy now had to deal with the third stage of labour. In retrospect she would say that it was not the most comfortable third stage she had conducted, sprawled as she was across the floor, but at least it was uneventful.

Chummy washed Kirsty and cleared up the mess as best she could under the circumstances. The problem of how to get Kirsty up off the floor was her next concern. The mother obviously couldn't care less. She was cuddling, and cooing, and whispering sweet nothings to her baby. Calling the captain was Chummy's only option, but Kirsty was stark naked. Chummy's modesty shrank from the thought of exposing her patient, naked, to a crowd of men, until she remembered Kirsty's profession. She explained to Kirsty that help was needed and opened the door.

A dozen or more bearded faces appeared at the door, all

peering in. At once they started cheering and clapping again. Chummy beckoned to the captain, who strode in, shutting the door behind him. She indicated what was necessary, and he nodded. She took the baby from her mother and retired to a stool in the corner.

The captain was a big man, and strong, but for sheer body weight his daughter could easily have doubled him. He took both of her hands and pulled – the bulk shifted a few inches. He stood astride her body and pulled again; no result. He went to the door, shouted, 'Olaf, Bjorg!' and two massive men entered. He explained, and they nodded. He took her hands again, and one man stood behind each shoulder. As the captain pulled each man heaved until Kirsty was sitting upright. They gave a cheer. This is obscene, Chummy thought, I can't bear to look at that poor woman sitting there with her huge breasts swinging on the floor, and these men cheering. They were obviously debating how to get Kirsty onto a chair. The debate was long and contentious; each man had his own ideas. A chair was solemnly brought forward and placed behind the woman. The three men grabbed her torso and heaved once more. 'That's not the way to do it,' thought Chummy, who had been taught how to lift a heavy patient, 'you'll never get her up like that.' They didn't. After another debate, they tried again, the two men locking their arms under Kirsty's armpits, and the captain ready with the chair. 'That's more like it,' thought Chummy.

I have said that Chummy had cleared up the mess as best she could under the circumstances. But resources were minimal, and the deck of the cabin was still slippery in patches.

The two men lifting Kirsty nodded to each other, took a deep breath and heaved. Her bottom lifted about six inches from the deck. Olaf, on her left, moved his foot and trod on a slippery patch. He hurtled forward across Kirsty's body and Bjorg was thrown backwards. In his fall he flung his arm upwards and hit the hurricane lamp with such force that it shattered, plunging the cabin into darkness.

In the meantime Kirsty had acted. A desperate mother can do anything in defence of her child. As the lamp shattered she screamed, 'My baby,' pushed Olaf, who was lying sprawled over her, to one side, scrambled to her feet, and ran over to the corner where Chummy was sitting. She took the baby, enfolding her protectively to her bosom. When another hurricane lamp was brought in she could be seen by all the men sitting quietly on a chair, rocking her baby, with a sheet modestly draped around her.

When the cabin was cleared of men, Chummy set about making it into a suitable lying-in room for mother and baby. The bed was not broken, the legs had merely folded in on themselves so she fixed it up again for Kirsty. But there was no clean linen left after delivery, and her patient had no nightie. There was no cot for the baby, no means of bathing her, and no clothes for her. She explained her needs to Kirsty, who was not really listening, so she went to the door, opened it, and shouted, 'Olaf!' The biggest of the bruisers entered and stood to attention, looking ill at ease.

'Tell him I need more clean linen, two more pillows, some nightdresses and a dressing gown for you. Also I need some more hot water and more clean towels for me to bath the baby; a box or basket which I can make into a cot, and some soft linen or cloth that I can tear up and make into cot blankets.' She considered there was no point in asking for baby clothes.

Kirsty translated, and Olaf looked mesmerised. She repeated the instructions two or three times, and Chummy could see him desperately trying to activate his brain and memorise the list, which he was counting off on his fingers. He left the cabin, and Chummy set about clearing things up a little more and packing her delivery bag. She was beginning to feel tired. The drama of the night had kept the adrenalin pumping through her body, but now that all danger for mother and baby had passed, her limbs felt heavy and slow.

Olaf reappeared with an armful of stuff, and a second man brought in a jug of hot water. Chummy was able to bath the baby, with Kirsty eagerly watching and commenting at every stage. A basket, which smelled of fish, had been provided, and this Chummy transformed into a crib. She made up the bed with clean linen – but still there was no nightie. Chummy could not allow her patient to remain naked, so summoned Olaf again.

Kirsty explained what was wanted, and the man turned bright red. How very extraordinary, thought Chummy, that this man, who has regularly been having intercourse with this woman, should be embarrassed to have to fetch her a nightie!

He went away and came back with a bag full of women's clothing which he handed to Chummy without looking at her.

Breastfeeding was the next thing for Chummy to think about. One really wants to establish breastfeeding immediately after delivery and ensure that the colostrum is flowing and that the mother has, at least, a vague idea of what she should do. Kirsty's breasts were so huge that they rested on the bed on either side of her. The baby could easily be suffocated by these mammoth mammaries, Chummy thought, as she expressed some colostrum. She tried the baby at the breast, and the child, surprisingly, opened her mouth, latched on and sucked vigorously a few times. Kirsty was in an ecstasy of delight. Flushed, with sparkling eyes and radiant features, she looked quite different. She must have been a pretty young girl, thought Chummy, before she became the inert, sexually active queen bee in this hive of males.

By now, Chummy was so tired that she could scarcely stand. She sat down on a chair beside Kirsty, who was examining the baby's fingers and toes.

'Look. She has little fingernails. Aren't they sweet? Like little shells. And I think she's going to have dark hair – her eyelashes are dark, have you noticed?' Kirsty looked up. 'Are you all right, nurse? You don't look too good.'

Chummy muttered, 'I'll be all right. Do you think someone

might bring us a cup of tea? You could do with a cup also.'

Kirsty called out, and Olaf entered. She gave her instructions, and five minutes later he reappeared carrying a tray laden with good food and fresh coffee. He placed it on the captain's desk and then, rather sheepishly, took a quick look at the baby and sidled out.

'Did you see that?' said Kirsty incredulously. 'They're treating me like a lady.'

Chummy poured the coffee. The caffeine perked her up a bit, and she began to feel stronger. She knew that she would need to, because one more task faced her. She had to get down the rope ladder. She had another cup of coffee and a sweet pastry, which gave her some energy. She left, telling Kirsty that she would return later in the morning.

Up on deck the dawn was breaking. The wind had dropped, and thin shafts of red-gold sunlight filtered through the grey clouds. Seagulls were swooping and squawking. The docks looked beautiful in the half light, and the fresh, cold air stung her cheeks. One of the men was carrying her bag, and they all clustered around, cheering and clapping. Chummy walked to the side and looked over the edge. It looked a long, long way down, and the rope ladder looked flimsy. If I can do it once, I can do it again, she said to herself, putting her foot on the rail. Then she remembered her skirt, and the danger it presented. So without any inhibition – she who was chronically inhibited in the presence of men – she pulled it up, tucked it into her knickers and climbed over the side. Her main anxiety was the missing rung, but she knew roughly where it was, and was prepared for the gap. When it came it was not as hard to negotiate as she had expected, and with a sigh of relief she continued to the quayside. One of the men tied her bag to a rope and let it down for her. She untied it, released her skirt, waved to the men above, and set out for the dock gates, her body tired, but her whole being exhilarated with the joy of having successfully delivered a healthy baby to an eager and loving mother.

★

The nightwatchman was preparing to go home for the day. He collected his supper box, put away his frying pan, doused his fire and was sorting out the key to lock his hut, when two policemen approached the dock gates.

'Morning, nightwatch. Fair morning after the storm.'

The watchman turned. His fingers were stiff, and he was fumbling with the key, unable to find the keyhole.

'Dratted key,' he muttered. 'Fair morning? Fair enough. Don't like the wind.'

'Quiet night for you?'

'Quiet enough. Would 'ave been quiet, 'cept for bloody women gettin' in the way.'

'Women?'

'Yes, women. Shouldn't be 'ere, I say.'

The policemen looked at each other. They knew that the Port of London Authority was very strict on women entering the docks, especially since the previous year when a prostitute had slipped in the dark from a gangplank and drowned.

'Which vessel?' The policeman took out his notebook and pencil.

'The *Katrina.* Swedish timber merchant.'

'Did you see the women?'

'Saw one of 'em. A nurse. Her bicycle's over there. Don't know what to do wiv it. An' 'er coat an' all. Don't know what to do wiv it, neither.'

'A nurse?'

'Yes. Woman ill on the *Katrina*, so I calls ve Sisters, and a nurse comes.'

'You had better tell us what happened.'

'About eleven thirty. A deck hand, 'e comes to me, saying, "Woman, woman," rollin' his eyes an' rubbin' 'is stomach, an' groanin'. So I calls a doctor, but 'e's out, so I calls ve Sisters, an' a big lanky nurse comes, an' I takes her to the *Katrina*, South

Quay. Right plucky girl, she was. Climbs up ve rope ladder an' all.'

'What! A nurse climbed the ship's ladder in that wind?'

'I'm tellin' yer. Big plucky girl. Climbed up, she did. And a rung was missing near the top, an' all. I saw it wiv me own eyes, I did.'

'Are you sure?'

'Course I'm bleedin' sure. Think I'm bloody daft?' The nightwatchman was offended.

'No, of course not. What happened next?'

'Search me. She climbed on board, an' she's still there, for all I knows. Leastways she hasn't collected 'er bike, nor 'er coat, neiver.'

The two policemen conferred. This was a matter for the Port of London Police. The Metropolitan had no authority inside the ports. But was it true? Nightwatchmen, due perhaps to their solitary calling in the darkest hours, were known to fantasise.

The man was fumbling with his key again. He turned and glanced down the quay. 'There she is. That's 'er. Told yer, didn't I? Big lanky girl.'

The two policemen saw a female figure wandering towards them. Her footsteps were uncertain, and she staggered rather than walked. The ordeal of climbing down the rope ladder had taken the last reserve of Chummy's strength. One of the policemen stepped forward to meet her and took her arm. She leaned on him heavily, murmuring, 'Thank you.' He said, 'Haven't we met somewhere before?' She looked at him vaguely.

'I'm not sure. Have we?'

He smiled. 'It doesn't matter.'

She walked towards her bike. He said, 'I don't wish to be rude, nurse, but are you fit to ride a bike?'

She looked round and slowly gathered her thoughts.

'I'll be all right. I must admit I feel a bit queer, but I'll be all right.'

The bike was a big, heavy Raleigh, iron framed and ancient.

She took hold of the handlebars, but it felt so heavy she could barely move it. The policeman said 'Nurse, I really do not think you should ride that cycle, especially down the East India Dock Road just as the ports are opening and the lorries are coming in. In fact, in the name of the Law, I am telling you *not* to ride it. I am going to call a taxi.'

'What about my bike?' she protested. 'It can't stay here.'

'Don't worry about that. I will ride it back for you. You are going to Nonnatus House, I think. I know where it is.'

In the snug comfort of a London taxi Chummy fell sound asleep. She was confused and barely articulate on waking, so the driver had to help her out and then rang the bell for her. The Sisters were just leaving the chapel when it sounded. Novice Ruth opened the door to see a cab driver supporting Chummy and holding her bag. Her first reaction was to think that the nurse was drunk. 'Sit down here,' she said to Chummy. 'I'll fetch Sister Julienne.'

Sister Julienne came quickly, paid the cab driver and turned her attention to Chummy, who seemed unable to move.

'What is the matter, my dear?' She did not smell of drink. 'What has happened to you?' Perhaps she had been beaten up.

Chummy mumbled, 'I'm all right. Just feel a bit funny, that's all. Don't worry about me.'

'But what happened?'

'A baby.'

'But we deliver babies all the time. What else happened?'

'On a ship.'

'A ship! Where?'

'In the docks.'

'But we never go into the docks.'

'I did. I had to.'

'I don't understand.'

'The baby was born there.'

'You mean that a baby was born on a merchant vessel?'

'Yes.'

'How extraordinary,' exclaimed Sister Julienne. 'This requires further investigation. Do you know the name of the ship?'

'Yes. The *Katrina*.'

'I think you had better go to bed, nurse. You don't look yourself. Someone else can clean and sterilise your equipment. I must take your record of the delivery and look into this.'

Chummy was helped upstairs to her room, and Sister Julienne took the midwife's record to her office to study. She could scarcely believe what she read. She rang the doctor, and they agreed that they must examine the mother and baby on board the ship, and have them transferred to a maternity hospital for proper post-natal care.

They met at ten a.m. at the gates of the West India Docks. Sister looked very small and out of place. She explained to the porter that they must go aboard the *Katrina*, where a baby had been born during the night. He looked at her as though she were mad, but said that he would inform the Harbour Master.

A short time elapsed, and the Harbour Master arrived with the docking book in his hand. A berth had been reserved for the *Katrina* for three more days, but she had pulled anchor and sailed at eight a.m.

Sister was horrified. 'But they can't do that. There is a mother and baby on board, just delivered. They will need medical attention. It's the height of irresponsibility. That poor woman.'

The Harbour Master gave her a very dubious look, and simply said, 'Women are not permitted in the docks. Now, excuse me, but I must ask you to leave.'

Sister would probably have said more, but the doctor led her away.

'There is nothing you can do, Sister. They have gone, and if the captain has done a runner, frankly, I am not surprised. A ship's woman, as they are called, contravenes all international shipping laws. If a mother and baby were found on board the captain would be arrested. He would certainly be dismissed from service, he would be heavily fined and might have to face a prison sentence. It is no surprise that he left port three days ahead of schedule. By now the *Katrina* will be well out in the English Channel.'

ON THE SHELF

A knock at the door. Sister Monica Joan was in the hallway. I was just coming downstairs. She opened the door, then banged it shut and started to draw the bolts across. I went up to her.

'Sister, what's the matter?'

She did not answer coherently, but muttered and clucked to herself as she fumbled with the bolts; but they were large and heavy, and her bony fingers had not the strength with which to draw them.

'See here, child, pull this one, pull it hard. We must firm up the battlements, lower the portcullis.'

Another knock at the door.

'But Sister, dear, there's someone at the door. We can't keep them out. It might be important.'

She continued fussing.

'Oh, drat this thing! Why won't you help me?'

'I'm going to open the door, Sister. We can't keep people out. There might be someone in labour.'

I opened the door. A policeman stood there. But Sister was in readiness. She had her crucifix in her hand and held it forward with an outspread arm, thrusting it in his face.

'Stand back, stand back, I adjure you. In the name of Christ, retreat!'

Her voice was quavering with passion, and her poor old arm was trembling, so that the crucifix was rocking and shaking a few inches from his nose.

'You shall not enter. You see before you a Soldier of Christ, girt with the Armour of Salvation, 'gainst which the Jaws of Hell shall not prevail.'

The policeman's face was a study. I tried to intervene.

'But Sister, dear, it's not . . .'

'Get thee behind me, Satan. Like Horatio I stand alone on the bridge to face the Midian hordes. Lay down thy sword. Desist, thou Scourge of Israel.'

With that, she shut the door, then turned to me and gave me one of her naughty winks.

'That will see them off. They won't try again.'

Poor Sister. I understood her aversion to policemen and sympathised. But perhaps the policeman had called about something to do with our work. It would not have been the first time that a Bobby on the beat had been asked to 'go an' call ve midwife, deary. I reckons I'm in labour'.

'I'll go and see what he wants. But I won't let him in. I promise you, Sister.'

I opened the door a few inches and slipped out. Sister Monica Joan banged it shut behind me, nearly catching my ankle.

The policeman was standing in the street, looking as though he did not quite know what to do next. A bicycle was propped against the railings.

'You must excuse her. She does not like . . .'

Then I recognised him. It was the copper whom Chummy had knocked over when she was learning to ride her bicycle and who had also accompanied the police sergeant in his investigations about the stolen jewellery. I burst out laughing.

'Oh, it's you. We seem to meet a lot. What do you want this time?'

'I'm not here on police business. You can tell Sister and calm her fears. I've brought a bicycle back, that is all. I told the nurse I would.'

'Which nurse?'

'I don't know her name. The very tall one.'

'Chummy. What are you doing with her bike?'

'I sent her back by taxi, because I did not think she was in a fit condition to ride.'

'What?' I exclaimed, thinking he meant that she was drunk. 'When?'

'This morning at about six o'clock.'

'Good God! Where did you find her?'

'In the Docks.'

'In the Docks! Drunk and incapable in the Docks, at six o'clock in the morning! My God! This is a side of Chummy we knew nothing about. She's a dark horse. You wait till I tell the girls. Was it a wild party, or something?'

He was smiling. He was an interesting-looking man who was probably younger than he appeared. He had an ugly-attractive sort of face, and a scar ran up the side of his cheek almost to the cheekbone. This might have made him look grim, but as he smiled his dark eyes danced with humour.

'No. It was no party, and she was not drunk. I am not sure of the details, but apparently a baby was born on one of the ships, and your nurse Chummy went to deliver it.'

I knew nothing about the drama of the night and stared at him in amazement.

'I saw the nurse staggering along the quayside as my colleague and I were talking with the nightwatchman. It had been a stormy night, and he said that she had climbed up the rope ladder. So presumably she had to climb down again. When I saw her, she looked as if she were on the verge of collapse. She hardly knew where she was going. So I told her not to ride the bike and ordered a taxi. I am now returning the bike,' he added more formally, 'and would like you to sign for it.'

I signed, and he thanked me and turned to go. But then he hesitated and half turned back.

'I was wondering . . .' And then he stopped. Silence.

'Yes? Wondering what?'

'Oh, just thinking . . .' Another silence.

'Well, unless I know what you are thinking, I can't help you, can I?'

'No, of course not.' More silence. 'How is she?'

'Who? Chummy?'

'Yes.'

'Well, I don't know. I didn't know there was anything wrong with her.'

'I'm not sure. I hope not. She looked all in when I saw her, and . . .' His voice trailed off.

'Oh, that's nothing, I assure you. We are frequently "all in". Sometimes the work gets very heavy, and we are often out for long hours. It can be quite exhausting, sometimes. But we get over it. Chummy will, you'll see.'

'I hope so.' Another long silence, in which he looked as if he wanted to say more. I waited.

'Look, tell her I brought back the bike . . .' He stopped again; ' . . . I felt responsible for her in a way this morning, when I saw her staggering along the quayside. She hardly knew where she was going and would have killed herself on a bike in the East India Dock Road. I suppose I just wanted to reassure myself that she is all right now.'

'Well, I honestly don't know. And if you will excuse me, I have to go. I have the morning visits to make, and it's getting late. If you want to know how she is, you had better come back later.' He nodded. 'But come back when you are not on duty, and not in uniform. You might meet Sister Monica Joan again!'

A few days later we were relaxing in our sitting room. The pressure of work had subsided. Then there was a knock at the door. Trixie groaned.

'Here comes trouble. Someone in labour. Who's on call?'

She came back a few minutes later with a wicked grin on her face.

'There's a young man to see you, Chummy.'

'Oh whoopee! It must be my brother, Wizard Prang ! He's on leave from the RAF. Pilot, you know. Commissioned officer and all that. Don't know what he does, actually, now that the war is over, but he seems to enjoy it. Ask him to come up, old girl. Not too fast. We'd better tidy up, eh, girls?'

Cynthia, Chummy and I set about clearing away the dirty mugs, plates, papers, magazines, shoes and bits of uniform that were lying around the place. If Chummy's brother, Wizard Prang, was anything like his sister, and from the name it sounded as if he would be, this was going to be a rare treat.

A tall man entered the room. I recognised him at once as the policeman, in plain clothes. Chummy, who couldn't handle men, instantly went bright red and started spluttering. Trixie, who always liked to stir things up, said innocently, 'This is David, and he wants to see you, Chummy.'

'Oh, great Scott! Me? There must be some mistake. It can't be me.'

She swallowed hard, and her arm jerked sideways, knocking over a table lamp, which fell onto the record player, where our favourite 78 was spinning round. There was a ghastly screeching sound as the needle dragged across the record.

'Oh, clumsy clot! Oh silly me! Now what have I done?' Chummy's voice was distressed.

'You've ruined the Eartha Kitt, that's what you've done, you chump.' Trixie sounded cross. 'That was "Take It Easy", something *you* need to learn to do, you idiot.'

'Oh, sorry girls. Frightfully sorry and all that. I know I'm a liability. Here, I'll stop the dratted thing.'

Chummy moved, and there was another crash as she knocked over a table of coffee mugs.

'Lawks! What next?' was her anguished cry.

There was a guffaw of masculine laughter.

'David is the policeman you knocked over last year,' said Trixie wickedly. 'He wants to see you.'

'Oh, crikey! Not that again! I didn't mean . . .'

Chummy's voice trailed away into nothingness. Her embarrassment was all-consuming. David looked abashed, in the presence of four girls and a chaotic situation that somehow – he did not know how – he seemed to have provoked. Cynthia came to the rescue, her low voice easing the tension. She picked up the coffee mugs and scooped up the instant coffee from the carpet.

'Nonsense. Of course David hasn't come about last year's accident. Would you like a cup of coffee? There may be some bits of fluff in it, but you can pick them off when they float to the top.' With a few words she put everyone at their ease. 'We were talking about Chummy's extraordinary adventure in the Dock the other night.'

'That is why I came.' He turned to Chummy. 'It was a very brave thing you did. Are you all right now?'

'Lawks, yes. Nothing wrong with me. Bounce up like a cork, I do. But how did you know about it, actually?'

'I was there. I saw you coming along the quayside. Don't you remember?'

'No.' Chummy looked vague.

'Well, I do. I think I will always remember the way you looked when you got off that boat. You deserve a medal.'

'Me? Why?'

'For all that you did that night.'

'Oh, fiddlesticks. That was nothing. Anyone would have done the same.'

'I do not think so. I really don't.'

Chummy could not be induced to say anything more. She sat on the edge of her chair, stiff and awkward, looking as though she wished herself a thousand miles away.

The evening passed pleasantly. Policemen and nurses always have a lot in common. I had found from previous experience, living in nurses' homes, that if we wanted to throw an impromptu party, we only had to send an invitation round to the nearest police station, and we would be flooded with healthy young coppers, eager to try their chances. David certainly enjoyed himself, being the centre of the attention among four young girls, even though one of them was too shy to talk.

Inevitably, the conversation turned to Chummy's experience in the Docks, and in particular to the ship's woman, who held a morbid fascination for us. We were agog to hear more about the life of such a woman and tried to get Chummy to talk about her. But it was no use. Poor Chummy might have been able to be expansive with us girls, but in mixed company she was speechless with discomfort. In those days, it must be remembered, even amongst midwives who saw just about everything, sexual matters were either unmentionable, or referred to obliquely and with exaggerated delicacy. And the life of a ship's woman was in no way delicate!

We asked David if he had heard of such a character. He assured us that, although every crew might wish to have one, a ship's woman was pretty rare, because of the strict controls on trading vessels. 'But they do exist, as you have found out.' He looked sideways at Chummy with an amused grin. She persisted in looking at the carpet, biting her lips and chewing her fingernails.

The clock struck eleven. David stood up to leave. Cynthia said, 'This has been so nice. We do hope you will come again. Chummy, would you show David out, while we tidy up?'

Chummy reluctantly stood up and cast an appealing glance at Cynthia, who refused to notice her distress. In silence they left the room, and a few minutes later we heard the front door close.

Chummy reappeared, looking pink, giggly and bewildered.

'Well?' we all said in chorus.

'He has asked me to go out with him.'

'Of course. What did you expect?'

'Nothing.'

'Nothing?'

'No.'

'Well why do you think he came here, all dressed up in his best suit with a clean shirt and a new tie?'

'Was he? I didn't notice.'

'Of course he was. Anyone could see that.'

'But why? I don't understand.'

'Because he likes you. That's why.'

'He can't do. Not in that way, anyway. I'm not pretty. I'm not even attractive. I'm too big, and I'm clumsy and awkward. My feet are too big. I fall over things. I never know what to say to anyone. My mater can't take me anywhere. She says I'm on the shelf.'

'Well, your mater is an ass.'

David had been in the Arnhem debacle during the war. He had been in the Paratroop Regiment, which was a crack division. In the autumn of 1944, 30,000 troops were flown behind the enemy lines to capture the bridges spanning the canals and rivers on the Dutch/German border. At the same time, British tanks and infantry were mobilised to push through from the Allied front in Normandy to relieve the airborne troops. But things did not turn out as planned, and consequently the advance airborne divisions were cut off in enemy territory without supplies or reinforcements. David was one of the lucky ones who survived. Exhausted, filthy and half-starved, he and a handful of men had made their way through the woods to the British and American occupied territory. He had been in the war only for two years, from age eighteen to twenty, but the experience had left a lasting mark on his mind and character, as well as giving him the scar on his face.

After the war, he couldn't settle down in civilian life. He had scarcely had time before call-up to decide what he wanted to do, and after the danger and drama of the war everything seemed rather tame at home. He tried factory work, and a milk round, he worked in a garage and in a pub, but found satisfaction in none of these. His mother was worried, and his father impatient. 'Chopping and changing jobs all the time won't get you anywhere. You want to settle down. A nice steady job with a pension, that's what you want.' David privately thought that a steady job with a pension would be worse than death, so he changed his job again.

He had always been a quiet boy who read a lot. He was not particularly good at school, because none of the things the school taught seemed important to him. But he read voraciously, and his young mind and soul thrilled to tales of faraway places with strange-sounding names. He wanted to go to them all and learn about the people and their customs. The army had given him the chance to get away, but the horrors of war had shattered many of his romantic dreams.

But he did not like peacetime either, and the new job – assistant in a hardware shop – was worse than all the others. His father said, 'Stick to it, boy, you've got to learn to stick with things. When I was your age . . .'

But David was not a boy. He was twenty-five and more disturbed than he or anyone else had realised. One of the older men in the shop, a man who had been through the First World War, gave him the help he needed. They were sitting in the back of the shop eating their packed lunches, and David must have looked particularly down that day. They started talking and reminiscing. David spoke of the perilous crawl through the forest after Arnhem, and the man said, 'It's funny how times like that can be the best times of your life, in a twisted sort of way. It's the excitement, the adrenalin rush, the danger, the uncertainty. All these things make for intense living. You can't carry on here like this, weighing half a pound of six-inch nails and sharpening a chisel. You need more activity, or you'll go bonkers. Why not try the police? The Metropolitan are looking for recruits.'

David was twenty-seven when he entered Police Training College, and it was the best thing he could have done. He left home, leaving his mother fussing and worrying and his father criticising, and lived in the police hostel, where there were other young men who had been through the war. The training was harder than he could ever have imagined. There were hours of lectures on every aspect of crime, including assault, larceny, forgery, bribery, traffic offences, drink driving, rape, sodomy, buggery and much, much more. He had to be familiar with the Betting and Gambling Act, the Licensing Act and the Prostitution Act, to mention but a few. His head was spinning as he tried to take it all in. But an indifferent schoolboy who didn't find his lessons important turned into a police cadet who found everything meaningful, and he passed top of the examination. He then had two years on the beat as a probationer, during which time he was always with another constable, assigned to a section or a division. He found life on the streets even more fascinating than the college. It was a tough period, but he revelled in the challenge and determined to become a sergeant and inspector, with his ultimate sights set on chief inspector.

His parents were delighted. His father commented, with a chortle, that he not only had a steady job, but also a good pension. His mother started getting broody, and coyly mentioned that a 'nice girl' was what he needed.

But girls were as big a failure for him as all the dead-end jobs he had undertaken. He was quiet and rather shy and always conscious of the scar on his face. 'No girl will want me,' he thought. Also, a few unsatisfactory affairs had convinced him that girls were basically silly and self-obsessed. He wasn't interested in their preoccupations, and they weren't interested in the things that absorbed him. A few of the policewomen seemed interesting, but they were either married or going steady with someone else. He wanted a girl who could get her mind off her fingernails or her hair. One girl said to him archly, 'Do you like the way I have plucked my eyebrows?' He was aghast. Eyebrows? He had never noticed them. The girl was offended and provoked a quarrel. He wasn't really cross or disappointed. The incident confirmed in his mind that girls were a bit empty, and a man couldn't expect anything else.

That was until he saw Chummy staggering along the quayside. He had met her a few times before and he recalled with amusement the day she had propelled her bicycle into him and knocked him over, knocking herself out at the same time. She was a big, strong girl, but, as she weaved her way uncertainly towards the three men standing at the dock gates, he could see she hardly had the strength to carry her bag. His protective instincts were aroused. He had heard the extraordinary, garbled story from the nightwatchman about her going to see a woman on a boat and climbing the rope ladder, and he hadn't known what to make of it. At the time he knew nothing of a baby being born, nor of the perilous circumstances of the birth. He just thought, this is a girl who is different, whose main preoccupation is not her eyebrows or her fingernails, and after he had put her in a taxi, he determined to see her again.

His first visit left the convent in a flurry of excitement. Even the sisters were twittering with interest. It was the last thing anyone had expected. The evening of Chummy's first date was the occasion for unsolicited advice and useless assistance. First, what should she wear? She produced a few clothes from her wardrobe, none of them very attractive.

'You must have something new.'

'But what?'

We all borrowed and swapped each other's clothes, but nothing that we wore fitted Chummy, so in the end we sighed hopelessly and loaned her a pretty scarf. She was also in a dither over what she should talk about.

'I'm no good with boys. I have never been dated by a boy before. What am I going to say?'

'Look, don't be daft. He's not a boy, he's a grown man, and he wouldn't have asked you out if he hadn't any reason to think you are interesting.'

'Oh lawks! This is going to be a disaster, I know it. What if

I fall over, or say something bally silly? My mater says you can't take me anywhere.'

'Well, your mater's not taking you out, is she? Forget "mater". Think of David.'

The doorbell rang, and Chummy fell over the doormat, crashing into the door.

'Enjoy yourself,' we all whispered in chorus, but she didn't look as though she would.

We didn't see her when she came in, but after that first evening David's visits to the convent became more frequent, and Chummy went out more. She didn't say anything, to our keen disappointment, but became quieter and less of a good-old-chum, jolly-old-chum type of girl. We tried probing, of course, but the most we could get out of her was that 'Police work is very interesting. Much wider and more varied and interesting than you would think.'

'Anything else?' we asked, eagerly.

'What else?' she enquired innocently.

'Well . . . anything . . . sort of . . . interesting?'

'I've told him about my plans to be a missionary, if that's what you mean.'

We sighed deeply. It was hopeless. If all they ever talked about was the Metropolitan Police and missionaries, what future could there be? Poor old Chummy. Perhaps her mater was right, and she really was on the shelf.

It was another of those rush times. We were flying about. Eleven deliveries in two days and nights, post-natal visits, an ante-natal clinic, lectures to attend, and the telephone constantly ringing.

I was on first call, and thankful to be resting after a hectic night and day with no sleep. The phone rang. Wearily I picked it up.

'My wife's in labour. She told me to call the midwife.'

Hastily I collected my bag and looked at the duty rota to see who would now be on first call. Chummy's name was at the top of the list. I ran to her room and banged on the door.

'Chummy! I'm going out. You're on first call.'

There was no response. I banged again and burst into the room.

'You're on first . . .'

My voice trailed away, and I backed off, abashed, guilty of an unforgivable intrusion – it was one of those things you should never, ever do. Chummy was in bed with her policeman.

THE WEDDING

Chummy married her policeman and she also became a missionary. Mrs Fortescue-Cholmeley-Browne, her mater, tried to organise a society wedding, with a reception at the Savoy Hotel, but Chummy refused. 'You owe it to your family dear,' she said applying the pressure. Still she refused. She wanted a simple wedding in our local church, All Saints, to be conducted by our local rector, with a reception in the church hall. 'But we cannot announce in the *Times* that the reception will be in a church hall in the East India Dock Road!' Mater exclaimed in alarm. 'And what about photographs? I will have to inform *Tatlers* and *Society News*. The family expect it. We can't have the reporters and photographers coming to a church hall, of all things.'

But Chummy was adamant: no announcements, no photographers.

Next came the issue of a wedding dress. Mater wanted to take her to Norman Hartnell, the Queen's dressmaker, for a wedding gown. Chummy refused, even more emphatically. She wasn't going to be dressed up like a Christmas tree fairy. 'But you must, dear. We are all dressed by Hartnell.' No, she wouldn't budge. She would wear a tailored suit. 'But you must wear white, dear. Virginal white for a wedding.' 'I'm not entitled to,' replied Chummy wickedly. That put a stop to any further entreaties.

The wedding party left from Nonnatus House, and I am not at all sure that the Reverend Mother would have approved of the disruption it caused had she seen it. But she was far away in Chichester, so it did not matter. The Sisters were in a real flutter of excitement because nothing like this had ever happened in the convent, and we girls were in a state bordering on panic trying to get ready. Mrs B had been baking all week and was putting the finishing touches to delectable dishes on the last morning, but Fred the boiler man had to go into her kitchen to attend to the boiler, which nearly drove her wild, and we all thought she would walk out. Sister Julienne sorted them out and calmed the cook, which was just as well, because without her the reception would have been a flop.

Amid all the flurry of preparation the routine work had to be dealt with. We each had our usual list of ante- or post-natal visits, babies to bath, feeding to be supervised, and so on. In addition the general district nursing, especially the insulin injections, had to be attended to.

The day started badly for Trixie because she had washed and set her hair first thing and had then gone out on her bike to do her visits, so her hair was blown about, and when she got back it looked a mess. She kept wailing, 'What am I going to do with my hair? It's all over the place, and I can't do a thing with it!' Cynthia advised Vitapointe and gave her a tube, but Trixie in her hurry picked up a tube of foundation cream, which she smothered all over her hair. So then her hair was covered in grease, which looked a great deal worse. Cynthia advised washing it again.

'But it's too late. I can't go to a wedding with wet hair,' Trixie cried.

'Well, you certainly can't go to a wedding with pink face cream on your hair!'

Preparations started in earnest. A face pack was essential, then toning lotion; nails buffed and polished. Stockings were missing, or not matching, or laddered. A skirt had to be ironed.

'Be careful. It's too hot.'

'But I can't turn it down.'

'You'll have to leave it to get cooler.'

'I haven't time.'

'You'll have to. It will ruin the skirt if it's too hot.'

'Stupid thing. Why don't we get a better one?'

Hair clips had to be found, curlers taken out, lipsticks swapped, perfumes sniffed.

'I think I like the Musk.'

'The Freesia is more suitable for a wedding.'

'It's too light.'

'Well, the Musk is too heavy.'

'No it's not. Don't be such a misery.'

Eyes are the window to the soul, they tell us. But that was not good enough for us girls. Eyes needed serious embellishment. Eyebrows had to be plucked, eyelashes curled, eyeshadow blended, eyeliner drawn with trembling haste, mascara . . .

'Damn!'

'What's up?'

'This mascara's dried out.'

'Spit on it, then.'

'That's disgusting.'

'No it's not. Keeps it moist. Here have some of mine.'

'Not if you've been spitting on it, thank you very much.'

'Please youself.'

Trixie had decided that the only thing to do was to wash her hair again, and now she was frantically trying to dry it.

'This stupid dryer is useless. Haven't we got a better one?'

'I'll get mine.'

'Yours blows too hard. I tried it before.'

'Beggars can't be choosers.'

Accessories required careful thought. A brooch was pinned on, then taken off, a necklace tried, earrings swapped, bracelets considered. Scarves had to be compared.

'That one matches your dress, you know.'

'I think I prefer this one. It's a contrast.'

'No. Bit too dominant. Try that one over there.'

'How does that look?'

'Better, much better. I like it.'

'OK, then I'll wear it. No I won't. The silly thing will only get in the way. I won't wear a scarf at all.'

The only person who wasn't rushing wildly around preparing for the wedding was the bride herself. Chummy was perfectly calm and composed, and quietly smiling at the rest of us in our excitement.

'You sort yourselves out,' she said. 'I'm all ready. I will just go along the corridor and spend half an hour by myself in the chapel until it's time to go across the road to the church.'

One thing that had to be resolved was who should remain behind to be on call. Sister Julienne was adamant that we girls should all attend the wedding ceremony *and* the reception, so then came the discussion about which of the Sisters should remain at Nonnatus House.

'Weddings are for the young,' said Sister Evangelina. 'I'll stay behind.'

'No, no. That wouldn't be fair,' chorused her Sisters. 'We know you would like to go. We'll do a rota, and take it in turns.'

So that is what they did.

We left for the church, walked down the war-damaged road, past the bomb site that had been St Frideswide's church, round the corner, across the East India Dock Road to All Saints church on the south side of the road. No cars, no flowers, no bridesmaids – nothing like that. We could have been going out for an afternoon stroll. Chummy was wearing a simple grey suit, flat shoes, no make-up, no hat. She looked her usual self, but somehow more than herself, more than the Chummy we had grown to love.

The social division in the church was conspicuous. The Fortescue-Cholmeley-Brownes, oozing class, sat on one side of the aisle, and the Thompsons, shouting suburbia, sat on the other. We sat on Chummy's side with the nuns and several nurses from St Thomas's Hospital. On David's were half a dozen strapping young policemen. The policemen only came because David was popular, and for the chance of free beer. Also, they were intrigued. What on earth was a girl who wanted to be a missionary going to be like? And what, in the name of all that was holy, could they expect of a wedding party put on by a group of nuns.

They entered the church and were directed to David's side, where they sat self-consciously among the Thompson relatives. But when a crowd of young nurses entered in their wide skirts, their tight waists and high-heeled shoes, and sat down on Chummy's side, their spirits soared. They couldn't believe their luck and tried leaning sideways in the pews to make eye contact with nods and grins. But the girls ignored them, of course.

The nurses from St Thomas's had come because they found it hard to believe that Chummy was getting married at all. They had been convinced that she was firmly on the shelf, destined for a worthy spinsterhood. They were also, I'm sorry to say, condescending. 'Is it true that she's marrying a policeman, my dear? With all her connections, surely she could have done better than that? She must have been desperate, that's all I can say.' They sat demurely among the Fortescue-Cholmeley-Brownes, aware that a group of young men on the other side were trying to attract their attention, but deliberately turning their pretty heads to study the Stations of the Cross adjoining the opposite wall. The air was charged with testosterone, but the flirting had to be suppressed when Chummy entered on the arm of her father.

The wedding ceremony was beautiful, the love between these two like-minded young people filling the church with a golden light. Before God, and the present congregation, they pledged their life-long vows to each other and stepped out into the sunshine as man and wife.

At the reception the policemen made straight for the young nurses, who rapidly forgot their hoity-toity airs and graces. Everything looked set fair for a good old party. The Fortescue-Cholmeley-Brownes lined up for the ceremonial hand-shaking and introductions, but the Thompsons didn't know what to do and stood around looking sheepish, until Chummy rescued them with 'Oh come on, Mater, let's not bother with all that. Let's just mix. It will be much nicer.'

Mater's face, half-hidden by an exquisite hat, looked a trifle sour. She approached Mrs Thompson, David's mother.

'Are you related to the Baily-Thompsons of Wiltshire?'

'No.'

'Ah! Well-er-perhaps to the Thompson-Bretts of India?'

'I don't think so.'

'Well, you might be, you know. It was a large family.'

'I couldn't rightly say, madam. I don't know that any of my relations has been abroad. We come from Battersea, and we were all in trade.'

'Oh, really? How very interesting.'

'Yes. We have a nice little place, with a nice garden. Just right for a little child to run around in. You must come and have tea with me some day.'

'Enchanted.' With a pained smile, the lady inclined her head.

'And when we have grandchildren, we'll see a lot more of each other, I'm sure.'

'Oh, no doubt, no doubt. Delightful talking to you, Mrs Thompson.'

And the poor lady crossed the social divide to talk with her own set about the shortcomings of the other side.

Colonel Fortescue-Cholmeley-Browne, in grey tails and topper, opened conversation with Mr Thompson, in Moss Bros wedding hire and trilby.

'I say, old chap, let's have a snort together.'

'Don't mind if I do. You're paying for it.'

'Well, er, yes. Customary, you know. Noblesse oblige. Father of the bride, and all that.'

'And I'm father of the groom, so that makes us related, in a way.'

'Related!'

'Well, in a way.'

'I hadn't thought of it like that, I must say. Tell me a bit about yourself. I'm India, ex-army. Were you in the services?'

'Well yes, sir. I was staff orderly to the officers of the Third Riflemens' Division, East Sussex, in the First World War.'

'Staff orderly?'

'Yes, sir.'

'How interesting. How frightfully interesting.'

The colonel did not look at all interested. Soon he crossed the room to join his wife.

'Not a pukka sahib in the whole room. No one worth talking to.'

'She's really let us down. We never could take her anywhere, and I'm quite sure we never will. I suppose I must go round and "mix" with her friends as she puts it, but it will be the last time, I assure you. I think I will talk to that old lady sitting by herself over there.'

The old lady was Sister Monica Joan, who was fully absorbed with a dish of jelly and blancmange. Mrs Fortescue-Cholmeley-Browne approached her graciously.

'Can I introduce myself?'

Sister Monica Joan looked up sharply.

'Induce yourself? What! Induce yourself? My good woman, let it be known that I do not at all approve of inducing. A baby should come naturally, and the vast majority will, without the need for all these inductions. And what is a woman of your age doing being pregnant? It's indecent. And now you are asking me if you can induce yourself. Are you planning an abortion? Is that what? I tell you, it's illegal, and I'll have nothing to do with it. Be off with you.'

Poor Mater, shaken to the core, returned to her husband's side.

'I'm never going to get over this, never,' she murmured.

'Stiff upper lip, old girl,' retorted the colonel. 'This can't last for long, and then they're going to Sierra Leone, I understand.'

'Thank God for that. Best place for her,' said Mater emphatically.

Sister Julienne was quietly thrilled at the way Chummy had developed. Many girls had come to Nonnatus House aspiring to be medical missionaries, but somehow Chummy would always stand out in her mind. She gazed at the tall, happy girl standing at the other side of the room and fondly remembered her awkwardness when she first came to the convent, falling over things or walking into stationary objects. Above all she remembered Chummy learning to ride a bike with that nice boy Jack helping her. That was when the girl's true mettle first became apparent – she was indomitable. Sister Julienne chuckled to herself as she looked across the room at David, the policeman Chummy had somehow managed to run into and almost knock unconscious. So this was how the good Lord had planned it!

Sister Julienne was a deeply romantic soul, and she smiled to herself again as she remembered Jane and the Reverend Thornton Applebee-Thornton. Perhaps God had needed a bit of help there! She had never tried matchmaking before, but when the reverend gentleman had come from his mission in Sierra Leone to study the midwifery practice of the Sisters as a model for the medical services he wanted to introduce into his mission, she had shamelessly thrust Jane into his company. The success of her little plan had been spectacular. And now Chummy was going out to join them in Sierra Leone as the first trained midwife, while David had applied to the police force there.

Sister Julienne smiled around her at the happy faces, at Mrs B, in her element amid all the catering, Fred ambling around, moving chairs, clearing up, and obviously making wisecracks for the benefit of all. She looked across at the nurses from St Tommy's, who were roaring with laughter at the policemen, and thought how delightful it was to see young people enjoying themselves. And then her gaze fell on the frigid face of Mrs Fortescue-Cholmeley-Browne. This isn't right, she thought. I must go over and have a word with her.

After the usual pleasantries, Sister Julienne went straight to the point.

'Mothers and daughters seldom understand each other.'

'What makes you say a thing like that?' said Mrs Browne guardedly.

'Experience.'

'Experience? You have no children.'

'No, but I have a family. I am one of a family of nine, and I saw the tension between my mother and her five daughters. None of us lived up to her expectations. She did not attend any of their weddings. Not one! And when I took religious vows, she was outraged. I was embarrassing the family, she said. So you see, I know all about misunderstandings between mothers and daughters.'

Mrs Browne sat silent. She was not going to be drawn. After a moment's pause, Sister went on.

'Camilla is a fine young woman. You can be very proud of her. She has the makings of nobility in her. She has strength of character, steadfast pursuit of her goal and above all mental and physical courage. These are the qualities that built the British Empire.'

Sister Julienne had scored a goal. Mrs Fortescue-Cholmeley-Browne came from a colonial family. Her father had been official adviser to the Raj and administrator of Bengal. Her husband, the Governor of Rajastan. She knew all about the qualities that had built the British Empire. After a pause, she said, 'Well, I wish I could see it.'

'You will, I assure you. Mothers and daughters always draw closer to each other as the years pass. Camilla and David . . .'

Mrs Browne butted in: 'This David! This fellow she is marrying. A common policeman. I ask you! What sort of marriage is that?'

'He may be a common policeman, but I have every reason to believe he is a fine young man and will make a good husband. He has a heroic war record. He flew and landed behind the

German lines at Arnhem, you know, and not only survived, but helped others to survive.'

'I didn't know that.' The lady's face softened.

'No. Probably not. It is not the sort of thing he talks about.'

The time for speeches was drawing near. Sister Julienne felt she had no more than a few minutes alone with the mother of the bride, and must introduce some humour into the situation.

'Another thing. For years after he was demobbed from the army David's father (she pointed to Mr Thompson) strongly disapproved of his son. Nothing the boy could do was good enough for Mr T. So you see, the same misunderstandings and tensions can arise between fathers and sons. Often worse. The son does not live up to the father's expectations and earns his reproaches. And when he does succeed very often masculine rivalry can set in as the father desperately tries to beat his son at the very game he has initiated.'

For the first time that day Mrs Fortescue-Cholmeley-Browne burst out laughing. Chummy, who had been watching her mother apprehensively, looked across the room with amazement.

'Oh, how true. I know that syndrome all too well. My own husband shows a deadly rivalry with our son over sculling. The boy's far better than him, but he can't or won't see it. He is taking extra training courses and comes back exhausted, hardly able to move a muscle, and needs physiotherapy. He'll injure his back, or something, before he will admit defeat. I can't tell you what the atmosphere is like in our house sometimes with these two men competing against each other.'

The two ladies looked at each other, nearly creasing themselves with laughter but suppressing their giggles because the speeches were just about to start. Sister managed to whisper, 'I know *exactly* what you mean.'

The wedding speeches were predictable and charming. The colonel spoke with affection of his only daughter and said he was proud of her nursing career. We girls clapped and shouted,

'Hear, hear!' The best man said that David was a credit to the force, and Sierra Leone would be lucky to get him, and the policemen stamped and cheered.

The boys from the South Poplar Youth club band arrived and with them came a wedding guest who had been invited to the church, but had not come. We had all wondered why. This was Jack, a local lad of about thirteen who had been instrumental in teaching Chummy to ride a bicycle when she first came to Nonnatus House. He had turned up early and late, guiding her around the roads, helping her to steer and balance, shouting instructions as he ran along beside her until she had mastered the art. Then he had appointed himself to the position of bodyguard to keep away the local kids who teased her. As a 'thank you' the Colonel had given the boy a bicycle.

A close bond had developed between Chummy and Jack, and she had been surprised and a little sad that he had not come to her wedding. When he walked in, slightly behind the other boys, she shouted out, 'Jack! You've come – I'm so glad,' and rushed over to him. In her exuberance she would probably have taken him in her arms, but he quickly backed off with a 'Steady on, miss, steady on.' So she shook hands in the manner that boys of that age prefer. It would not do to shame him in front of the other lads.

Mrs B had held back a substantial part of the feast for the boys from the SPY club, knowing that it would be necessary, and while they were all tucking in, Chummy managed a few words with Jack.

'Well, I wouldn't miss your weddin', miss, but I didn't wanna come wiv all them toffs, like, so I comes wiv the lads, like, an' I gotta presen' for yer, miss. I made it in metalwork at school.'

He pulled a brown-paper package from his pocket and thrust it furtively into her hands, making sure that his back was turned to the others so that they couldn't see. 'It's fer you, miss.'

Then he turned quickly and blended in with the other lads.

Chummy returned to her husband and opened the parcel. It

was a tiny bicycle, carefully constructed out of wire and metal.

The SPY club band started up, somewhat out of tune but with plenty of rhythm, and the happy couple led the dancing. At seven o'clock they left to get the night train to Cornwall, where they were spending their honeymoon. A taxi came to take them to Paddington station, and a big crowd gathered outside the church hall to wish them well and see them off. Jack didn't stand waving with the rest of us. He ran round to the back of the hall, grabbed his bicycle and gave chase to the taxi, with Chummy and David looking out of the rear window in astonishment. He was a strong boy and a fast cyclist. He followed the taxi all the way and was on the platform to wave them off as the train steamed out of Paddington station.

TAXI!

Sister Monica Joan had recovered from pneumonia caused by wandering down the East India Dock Road on a raw November morning wearing only her nightie; had lived triumphantly through the shock, trauma and humiliation of having been accused of shop-lifting; had survived the ordeal of prosecution and a court case before judge and jury; and now, at the age of ninety-two, looked set for another decade.

It was a fine summer, and Sister Monica Joan had a number of relatives whom she decided she must visit. I have described earlier the niece living in Sonning-on-Thames, to whom she bequeathed two fine Chippendale chairs. Another niece and nephew with their three children lived nearer, in Richmond, which was still a tidy distance for a very old lady to travel alone by bus. But, undaunted, she set out.

I am not sure whether she told anyone where she was going (probably not), but once again there was general anxiety in the convent, because Sister Monica Joan was missing, it was eight o'clock and time for Compline. No doubt prayers were said for her safety, which must have caught the ear of the Almighty, or whoever oversees these small matters, because at that moment the telephone rang, and the niece in Richmond said that her aunt was with them, enjoying the company of the three children. Asked whether she could stay the night, the niece said it would be difficult, because they had only a small house, and there wasn't a spare bed, but her aunt was welcome to sleep on the sofa. At this point Sister Julienne made a tactical error, which she freely admitted later. A night on a sofa would have done Sister Monica Joan no harm whatsoever, but Sister Julienne hesitated and said she really ought to come back to the convent.

Thinking that it was too late in the evening to ask them to put her on a bus, Sister told them to put her in a taxi, which would be paid for on arrival.

It was a grave mistake, which in subsequent days and weeks led to a series of incidents that spun out of control. Sister Monica Joan had probably not been in a London taxi-cab since they were horse-drawn. As a professed nun she was vowed to a life of poverty, and if she travelled anywhere she took the bus or train, the cheapest available route. A modern taxi was a new and delightful experience.

At lunch the next day, Sister was full of her niece and nephew in Richmond, and their three delightful daughters. 'Such pretty gels, don't you know, so engaging.' She couldn't remember their names, but one of them, poor child, had spots. Such an affliction at that age. She would go that very afternoon to Chrisp Street market, to find something suitable for the one with spots.

She sailed around the market, oblivious to sideways glances and whispered warnings that went before her from the costers, who all kept a wary eye on her since they had been frustrated in their charge of petty theft.

She homed in on a new stall run by a woman with beads and flowers around her neck and in her hair, who sold herb and flower remedies and potions in pretty pots with exotic sounding names, guaranteed to cure anything. Ingrown toenails, gastric ulcers, piles, failing eyesight, toothache – all could be cured by her remedies. Sister Monica Joan was in a delirium of delight. This was what she had been looking for, all her life, she assured the woman behind the stall – an essence of marigold, a tincture of dog daisy, an infusion of dandelion, and all so simply explained in the little booklet. She poured over the booklet and compared it with her notes on astrology and life forces and earth centres and came to the happy conclusion that all had been revealed. Not only would the one with the spots, sweet child, be cured, but her future would be luminous.

*

The next day Sister Julienne had a rather nasty telephone call from the nephew, who said that his aunt had woken the whole house at three o'clock in the morning with a garbled story about flower essence, and if you have a bad toe rub it on your toe and it will get better, and if you have a tummy ache rub it on your tummy and the ache will go away, and if the one with the spots rubs it on her spots they will go away, and wasn't it wonderful? The nephew had replied that it was not at all wonderful. He and his wife had to go to work the next day, and the children had to go to school, and did she realise what time of the night it was? Sister Monica Joan had replied that yes, she thought she knew, but she was so sure the one with the spots ought to hear the good news straight away, so could she speak to her? The nephew had replied certainly not, it was ten past three, and the girl had to go to school. She was doing her O-levels and needed her sleep.

Sister Julienne was apologising and saying that she had no idea Sister Monica Joan was active in the middle of the night, when the nephew interrupted to say that that was not the end of the story by any means. About an hour later they were all woken again, and Sister Monica Joan explained that she didn't want the one with the spots to think she was being specially favoured, but spots were such an affliction at that age, didn't he know, nor did she want the two younger gels to feel left out, so she had a little present for them also, which she would give to them personally.

After that, the nephew said, he had disconnected the telephone, and Sister Julienne agreed that under the circumstances it was the best thing he could have done.

The following Saturday Sister Monica Joan decided to go to Richmond again. She discussed it fully with everyone around the big dining table. She must be sure to see those dear gels again, and how exciting to discover you have young and pretty great-nieces that you didn't know you had, and it reminded her of her own young days with her sisters in the big house and all the fun they used to have.

Sister Julienne was glad to know at least where she was going on this occasion, and telephoned the nephew to tell him to expect his aunt. She made quite sure that Sister Monica Joan had enough money for the bus fare.

But a humble London double-decker was not part of Sister Monica Joan's plans. Having once experienced the delights of a London taxi-cab, buses were out of the question. Oh, the pleasure and the grandeur of sitting alone in the spacious interior while a competent driver weaves his way through the streets. None of the awful business of having to get off one bus and wait anxiously for another. No standing around – just go straight from Poplar to Richmond (about fifteen miles through Central London). Sister Monica Joan was delighted with her new-found ease of transport. No fussing, looking for your bus pass. No fumbling for pennies and shillings to pay the bus conductor. And it didn't seem to cost anything. You just had to say, 'Payment will be met on arrival,' and off he went, dear man.

The nephew did not complain the first two times he was expected to finance the taxi-fare, but after the third occasion he put through a gentle phone call to Sister Julienne asking her, as tactfully as he could, if she could provide his aunt with sufficient money to pay for her own taxi. Sister, who with mounting alarm at the depletion of the convent's petty cash had paid for four return taxis, agreed that things were getting out of hand, and that she would have to do something, although she was not sure what. The nephew was particular to say that they were all delighted with his aunt's visits, and the girls adored her and would sit listening to her for hours. She was enchanting. It was just the taxi fares . . .

There was considerable discussion amongst the nuns as to how best to control the mounting problem. Sister Julienne had a very serious discussion with Sister Monica Joan about the vows of poverty, the need to economise for the sake of running the convent, the expense of taxi fares, and the need to take the bus wherever possible. Sister Monica Joan was very amenable and fully understood that she had been extravagant, so she agreed to take the bus in future. But perhaps she forgot. Or perhaps she could not resist the temptation when she saw a shiny black taxi-cab in the street. Or perhaps her intentions were good, but it was raining, and Sister Monica Joan could not abide the rain. Whatever the reason, the situation continued as before. Sister Julienne felt obliged to refund to the nephew all the taxi fares incurred to date, because a nun is the responsibility of the convent, and not of her family.

The Sisters had further discussions. At the start of her next journey Novice Ruth took Sister Monica Joan to the bus stop, put her on the correct bus, paid the bus conductor, and told him where she was to get off. But Sister Monica Joan was crafty, and she always got what she wanted. She thanked Novice Ruth kindly for her assistance, sweetly waved goodbye and quite simply got off at the next stop and took a taxi.

Things were going too far. Sister Julienne was obliged to inform the Reverend Mother Jesu Emanuel. Large sums of money were regularly leaking out of the convent funds, and she could not seem to control it. A Chapter meeting of all the Sisters at the Mother House in Chichester was convened, and the financial adviser was requested to be present. Thirty-two Sisters who worked in the Mother House attended, and many of them were very critical of Sister Monica Joan. Her behaviour was outrageous. She had first brought scandal to the Order through a court case for alleged theft, and now, instead of being humble and contrite as any other nun would be, she was spending money with reckless abandon. Why should they have to skimp and save and live a life of poverty while she was riding around London like a duchess?

The Reverend Mother pointed out to the younger Sisters that Sister Monica Joan had given over fifty years of dedicated service to the poorest of the poor, in conditions of unimaginable squalor, and it was the policy of the Order to allow privileges and comforts to elderly Sisters who had retired from nursing. Two or three of the elderly Sisters spoke up to say that they had also given lives of dedicated service to the poor and needy, and that they defined 'comforts and privileges' as jam on Sundays, or an occasional cup of tea in bed. They could not approve of taxis all over the place. It was a question of what was reasonable.

The Reverend Mother sighed; Sister Monica Joan had never been reasonable. She asked the financial adviser, an independent auditor and accountant, for his opinion.

The accountant said that he had carefully studied the finances of the Order, and had observed that Sister Monica Joan's dowry to the Order in 1906, when she made her life vows, was greater than that of all the other Sisters put together. In addition, a very large inheritance which she had received in 1922 on the death of her mother had immediately gone into the convent funds. Had it not been for these two large deposits of money, the accountant questioned whether the Sisters would have been able to continue their work at all.

That settled it. The Chapter ruled that finances should be made available to Sister Julienne to use at her discretion. There were still a few sour faces and mutters of 'not fair', which the Reverend Mother dispelled by saying that she was sure that all the Sisters would be relieved by the decision, as many would be anxious at the thought of an old lady roaming alone around London by bus – especially as her mind was wandering, as had been made clear by the recent scandal. 'Let's face it. She's senile and shouldn't be let out,' muttered one of the younger Sisters. To this the Reverend Mother replied sharply that the remark was uncharitable, and she would not countenance the thought of Sister Monica Joan being confined to the house like a prisoner.

Sister Julienne was relieved by the decision of the Chapter and was able to finance several more taxi fares to and from Richmond with no further anxiety. Nonetheless, she had another little talk with Sister Monica Joan about limiting the number of visits, the need for economy and the vows of poverty. Sister Monica Joan must have taken this to heart; perhaps her conscience had been pricked by the reminder of her life vows, or perhaps she just wanted a bit of diversion. After all, she had always been an adventurous soul, seeking out a challenge. The next thing we heard was that she had been seen by many witnesses standing at the traffic lights by the Blackwall Tunnel. When the lights turned red and the traffic stopped, she would totter into the road, round the front of the cars and lorries, tap on the window of a car, and ask the astonished driver to take her to Richmond.

Whatever might be said of nuns, thumbing lifts from strange men is not the way they are expected to behave. The reaction of the drivers can only be imagined. Sister Monica Joan would have been wearing the full monastic habit of her Order. If you were a businessman going to your next appointment, such an apparition weaving its way unsteadily into the road must have looked like a visitation from God – or perhaps the devil. When the apparition tapped on your window and started a long, convoluted yarn about pretty nieces in Richmond, and how she had got a new lotion from the woman in the market for the one with spots, but she suspected blackheads really, guaranteed to make them go away, and that was why she needed to get to Richmond, but buses were so difficult, you would probably have thought you were going a bit mad, particularly if the business lunch had been of the liquid variety.

Without exception the drivers refused, but Sister Monica Joan persisted in what to her mind was a perfectly reasonable request. The man had a car, and she did not, she would point out. It would surely be no inconvenience to him to make a small detour to Richmond? She knew the address – what was the difficulty? She was a lady inclined to become extremely cross and snappish if she did not get her own way, and many of the conversations ended in acrimony.

Several times, while she was still talking, the lights turned green, and the traffic started up again. Lorries in the free-moving lane passed alarmingly close as she stood in the road. The car driver, who would still be trying to reason with her, could not start, and there would be honking and hooting and shouts from frustrated motorists piled up behind. Eventually (and this happened several times) she would accept that the car driver was not going to Richmond and would not divert his journey to take her, and she would totter back to the pavement, only to try again when the lights turned red and another car stopped on the nearside lane.

After half a dozen such attempts she was caught in the act by two policemen, who observed her actions for a few minutes and then apprehended her for causing an obstruction to the traffic and for endangering her life and that of others. Sister Monica Joan was very sensitive about policemen and protested violently at finding herself between two of them, and being escorted back to the convent.

After this little escapade, Sister Julienne begged her to take taxis, and hang the expense.

A printed letter arrived for Sister Monica Joan from Wandsworth Borough Council, stating that a lady's hand bag containing a little money, a prayer book, a pair of spectacles and a set of false teeth had been found and awaited her collection at a lost property office in West London. Sister Julienne was taking no chances. A taxi was ordered to collect Sister Monica Joan, to take her to the address on the letter and to return her to the convent.

Four hours later the taxi returned. The driver said that when he reached West London, she said that she had forgotten or lost the piece of paper giving the address. She knew she should be going to a lost property office but she was not sure which one. So she had instructed him to drive to all the lost property offices in the area, which amounted to fifteen throughout Fulham, Putney, Chelsea, Wimbledon, Kingston, Twickenham and as far west as Hampton Court. No handbag was reclaimed. He must have missed the one where it was, he said. Anyway, the old lady seemed to have enjoyed herself. She'd had a nice day out. She had enjoyed going over Hammersmith Bridge so much that she had instructed him to go back, and then to go over it again, he said. He had looked after her and brought her home safely. The cost was so astronomical that Sister Julienne thought she would have to consult the Reverend Mother again. Where would it all end?

Novice Ruth was the first person up that morning. She was approaching her first year professional vows and wanted an hour of private devotion alone in the chapel before her Sisters joined her. The time was four a.m., and it being summer, the dawn was breaking and light was returning to the world. She walked quietly along the passage, turned the corner and found Sister Monica Joan lying on the floor. She was breathing, but her eyes were wide open and staring, her pulse was bounding and she was twitching intermittently. She had wet herself and could not be roused. Novice Ruth fetched a pillow and placed it under her head and wrapped a warm blanket around her. Then she telephoned the doctor and woke Sister Julienne. Together they carried the unconscious figure back to her room and laid her on the bed. Twenty minutes later the doctor arrived, examined the patient and confirmed what they had both suspected: Sister Monica Joan had had a stroke. She did not regain consciousness and died that evening, at the hour of Compline. The last words of the last office of the day are: 'Lord, grant us a quiet night and a perfect end.'

Peace at the hour of death is one of the greatest blessings that God can give. Death can be very terrible, but peace can transform it. Sister Monica Joan received no intrusive medical treatment, no drugs, no investigations into the cause of the stroke, no attempts to prolong her life or to delay her death. She received loving nursing care from her Sisters and was able to die in peace. This is the perfect end.

Her body lay at rest for two days in the convent chapel, and local people came to pay their respects. Then she was taken to the Mother House in Chichester for the funeral service.

The death of Sister Monica Joan affected me deeply. I had not expected her to die; I had somehow believed that she was indestructible. I could not reconcile myself to the loss. The magic and mystery of that extraordinary woman haunted me. Suddenly, all the beauty and fun and bewitchment that she encapsulated was gone, leaving me utterly bereft.

Aware of my state of mind, Sister Julienne said to me one day, with her usual twinkle, 'I was thinking about Sister Monica Joan this morning in chapel. Perhaps it was rather naughty of me, but the Old Testament reading about Elijah going up to Heaven in a fiery chariot prompted the thought. Don't you think perhaps that Sister Monica Joan went straight to Heaven by taxi?'

ADIEU

David and Chummy went to Sierra Leone. Chummy opened the first midwifery service at the mission station and ran the small hospital. David joined the police and became a senior officer in the force. They found the work harder and more demanding than they could ever have imagined, but they had the strength of youth and idealism to carry them through. Above all, they had the love to support and sustain each other in times of crisis. They stayed in Africa throughout their lives, and Chummy and I corresponded for a few years. They had a family, but she continued her work in a teaching capacity. She must have been desperately busy, and in the circumstances it is not easy to continue writing letters indefinitely to an old nursing colleague. We exchanged Christmas cards for a few years, but eventually they petered out. She was a unique character, and it was a happiness and a privilege to have known her.

Trixie was the only one of our small circle who did not continue nursing. She married a young man who had both feet firmly planted on the civil service ladder. He entered the diplomatic service, and Trixie went with him. I have often wondered how she managed, because diplomacy had never been her strong suit! I just could not imagine her in one of Her Majesty's Embassies. When I knew her, she was fun, quick-minded and clever, but sharp-tongued and brutally blunt. Perhaps she introduced a breath of fresh air into the unctuous atmosphere of the diplomatic service. She travelled with her husband to many of the big capitals of the world and became quite sophisticated, but cutting comments delivered with lightning rapidity remained her trademark.

I did not see much of Trixie during these years. It was not until the couple had retired to Essex, by which time we were both grandmothers, that we met again. I noticed a small granddaughter who looked exactly like Trixie when she was young. The little girl was about ten years old and had an answer to everything. She was an experienced manager already and bossed her three younger brothers around with consummate skill.

Trixie took me to the street market in Basildon, where we witnessed the daughters of Megan'mave at work selling their fruit and vegetables. Later, her comment was 'We never change, do we? And what is more, our children and grandchildren don't change.'

Trixie had certainly mellowed with the years.

Cynthia felt called to the religious life and was accepted as a Postulant and Novice in the order. She was a working Novice, as she was already a trained nurse and midwife. But the religious life is hard, and much is demanded spiritually and physically of any Novice. Cynthia's goodness and purity had always impressed me and had influenced me more than she ever knew, but perhaps her mind could not stand the strain. She had shown signs of clinical depression around the time of puberty, and this was a state of mind that beset her for many years. She left the order and became a hospital staff nurse, then returned to the convent to resume her life vows, but left again. Why does God so often cause good people to suffer so greatly? It is a question I have often asked myself. Sister Julienne turned the question the other way, and said, 'God loves greatly those whom he requires to suffer greatly.' This is a riddle wrapped in a mystery we cannot comprehend.

Cynthia limped through life for many years, in and out of psychiatric hospitals. Many drugs were prescribed, and also electric shock therapy. A true depressive lives a life of inner hell, which little or sometimes nothing can alleviate. My heart bled for gentle Cynthia, but there was nothing I could do to help.

At the age of thirty-nine she met a clergyman who was a

widower and had a son. They married, and his needs, mentally, were even greater than her own. Somehow the necessity to look after him and organise his life became the focus of her existence and cured her. We none of us can understand the complexities of the human mind. She became a very happy and successful vicar's wife and a health visitor. Her husband Roger was also a classical scholar. At the age of sixty-five he retired from the ministry, and for several years they lived like a couple of hippy teenagers. With no more than a rucksack each, and a budget of £3 a day, they roamed hundreds of miles across Greece, Israel, Jordan and Turkey, examining the architectural ruins of ancient civilisations. They slept in little cafés, on buses, under the stars on beaches, in fields, in olive groves and lemon orchards. They planned nothing, but simply went where the fancy took them.

After retirement, Cynthia's husband joined the Church of England World Mission Association. This meant that he could be asked to act as a locum for any church, at home or overseas, which was temporarily without a priest.

The couple were both about seventy years of age when the telephone rang one evening.

'This is the World Mission Association. Could you go to Lima? The vicar has just been shot.'

'Sounds nasty. Well yes, certainly. When do you want me?'

'The week after next.'

'I dare say we could go. I must ask my wife.'

Aside: 'Cynthia, could we go to Lima the week after next? The vicar has been shot.'

'Where's Lima?'

'Peru. South America.'

'Well, yes, I should think we could. A fortnight is enough time to pack things up here. For how long?'

To the telephone: 'Yes, we could go. For how long?'

'Three months. Six, perhaps. Not really sure.'

'That's all right. Send us details, flight tickets, etc., and we'll go.'

Cynthia – quiet, sensitive, depressive – led a life of high romance and breathtaking adventure in her old age that few of us would have dared contemplate, still less had the courage to carry out.

Some people have described my first book *Call the Midwife* as a spiritual journey, and they are correct – it is. I owe to the Sisters more than I could possibly repay. Probably they do not know how great is my debt. The words 'if God really does exist, then that must have implications for the whole of life' could not be dismissed. Sister Julienne and I spent many hours discussing these subjects, and the influence of her goodness has shaped my development. We corresponded, and I visited her all through my life, and I took my own children with me to the Mother House; we stayed in the caravan in the grounds of the convent.

I remained very close to her and always sought her prayers and wisdom at any difficult point in my life. She always guided me well. In 1991 Sister Julienne developed a brain tumour, and for the last three months of her life I visited her every Friday. It was an enriching experience, even though, or perhaps *because*, she was deteriorating week by week. Time was short, and getting shorter, in which to convey, if not in words, then in silent empathy, my love and gratitude. On the last Friday she was deeply unconscious, and it was obvious that her life was drawing to its end. She died two days later on Sunday morning – a beautiful day in June at the hour when her Sisters were saying Lauds, the first monastic office to greet the dawn.

It was a singular honour to be invited to attend her funeral at the Mother House. The service was the Requiem Mass for the dead as ordained by the Book of Common Prayer. The funeral of a nun is very quiet and reverent. Her Sisters do not mourn and grieve; they are more likely to express joy that a life given in the service of God is fulfilled. For them death is not an enemy. Death is seen as a friend.

At the end of the service, while plainsong was being chanted, one of the Sisters took up a pile of folded garments that had been lying on the altar throughout. The Reverend Mother came towards her with hands outstretched, palms facing upwards. The Sister placed the garments on the hands of the Reverend Mother, who turned and walked slowly towards the coffin. She placed the small burden on the centre of the coffin and turned and bowed to the altar. It was the folded habit, surmounted by the gold cross and rosary that Sister Julienne had worn all her professed life, and they went with her to her grave in the Sisters' cemetery in the convent garden.

Rest eternal, rest in peace, beloved Sister Julienne.

Sister Evangelina died some years ago. At her own request she was buried in Poplar, and not in the Sisters' cemetery at the convent. She had always been one of the people, and that is how she wished to be remembered.

Novice Ruth took her final vows and practised her calling for about twenty years. But in the mid-1970s she encountered a spiritual crisis, which in religious language is called 'the black night of the soul'. It is a most terrible experience, probably more shattering than the worst kind of divorce. It is well known and documented in monastic literature, and is a spiritual phenomenon to be dreaded, yet in some ways welcomed, as it is a testing of the soul and suffering can lead to an enriched spiritual experience. Sister Ruth was tormented for years with no respite and eventually renounced her life vows and left the order.

Sister Bernadette, an inspired midwife from whom I learned all the practical skills of the profession, also left the Order but for a very different reason. She worked faithfully all through the 1960s and '70s as a midwife. In the 1980s, when the HIV virus infected the Western world and when medical and nursing staff were vulnerable to being infected, she nursed AIDS patients at a time when the mortality rate was close on 100 per cent. Throughout the 1980s there had been debate in the Church of England about the ordination of women, and in 1993 the

General Synod voted that women could be admitted to the priesthood. Sister Bernadette could not take this. Deep religious conviction based on theology and history told her that it was wrong. She was in her seventies and crippled with arthritis, but she had the courage of her convictions to leave the Anglican Church. This meant that she would have to leave the Sisters with whom she had shared her life. She was accepted into a Roman Catholic order, where she lived the strict life of a solitary contemplative, devoting her time to prayer and meditation

Ambition is a double-edged sword. One side will cut through stagnation and lead to a new life; without ambition, mankind would still be living in caves. But the other side can be destructive, leading to feelings of loss and regret. I was ambitious, and my sights were set high. I was planning to be a hospital matron or at the very least a sister tutor, and I would have to climb the ladder of the nursing hierarchy. A district nurse and midwife was only a lower rung on that ladder. I did not really want to leave the Sisters, but I knew that, if I stayed with them, I would stagnate. I loved the Sisters and their devotional life, and I loved the fun and freedom of district work in the docklands, but to continue would have rendered me unsuitable for the discipline of hospital work, which was very strict indeed in those days. I left the Sisters in 1959 to become a staff midwife at the London Hospital, Mile End Road, where I enjoyed seeing more of Cockney characters. But it took a long time to settle down to the rigours and discipline of hospital routine. Eventually the move paid off, and after a couple of years I obtained my first junior sister's post at the famous women's hospital, the Elizabeth Garrett Anderson in the Euston Road (now sadly closed). Later I became night sister there, which in those days meant being in overall charge of the hospital throughout the night. Then I became ward sister of the Marie Curie Hospital in Hampstead.

I was climbing the ladder, as anticipated. But then I met a certain young man, and ideas of becoming a hospital matron seemed rather irrelevant. We have been happily married for about forty-five years at the time of writing. After our children were born I gave up full-time nursing, but continued part-time.

In 1973, after a twenty-year nursing and midwifery career, I left nursing altogether. All my life I had been a frustrated musician, and with intensive study, supported by my husband, I achieved a Licenciate of the London College of Music and later a Fellowship and started twenty-five years of music teaching.

IN MEMORIAM CYNTHIA

This book was dedicated to Cynthia as early as 2004, but she never read it. In June 2006 Cynthia died. She had had cancer six years previously, which had been successfully treated, and she and Roger had continued their adventures, but in 2004 he developed congestive heart failure, from which he died about eighteen months later. Clinical depression returned to cloud Cynthia's mind during his last illness, and then there was a recurrence of the cancer.

She died as she had lived, quietly, peacefully and with no fuss. Gently she let go of life, and had said to many people that death was what she wanted. She knew it was approaching, and was content. 'I hope I have been useful,' she whispered to me a few days before her death. Cynthia received her last communion and she, who was virtually sinless, made her confession and received Holy Unction.

Her stepson, her sister and I were with her during the last five days of her life, and on the final day, when to all appearances she was unconscious, I said to her slowly and clearly, 'I am so thankful I have been with you.' Her eyelids flickered, and she breathed rather than spoke the words, 'And so am I.' In my experience the dying always know who is with them and need the love they bring.

Cynthia was Godmother to my elder daughter, Suzannah,

who had sent a card to her during that week. It was a complete surprise to me, and I read it aloud to Cynthia. The words were so beautiful I cried as I read them, and Cynthia smiled her slow, sweet smile, and whispered, 'I remember too.'

It may seem pointlessly sentimental to those who do not know either character, but for me a testimonial to my dear friend is necessary, and so I quote my daughter's card in full:

Dear Cynthia,

I am thinking about you a lot at the present time, but most especially I am remembering past times and what you have meant to me over the years.

When I was a little girl, I remember dropping a bowl of jelly on the floor twice, and the second time the bowl broke! I was so upset I cried, but you didn't get cross.

I remember what fun it was when you took us up into the bell tower of Roger's church. You let us ring the bells – you said it wouldn't matter if all the people in the village thought it was the wrong time.

I remember sleeping in the caravan and being kept awake all night by the owls and the bells. More recently I remember visiting you when our girls were little. You took us for a lovely walk along the coast, and you made them a special pudding with smiley faces on.

Most recently you sent me some of your jewellery, and you patched up my old bear, which you made for me when I was christened.

All these things are memories I will treasure forever – they remind me of you, my Godmother. Over the years I have come to realise that you are essentially what a Godmother should be. Thank you for being you. Bless you, now and always.

Your loving God-daughter
Suzannah XXX

FAREWELL TO THE EAST END

The Sisters had opened Nonnatus House in the 1870s to meet the needs of women living in dire poverty. However, during the 1960s things began to change rapidly, and the old way of life vanished.

One by one the docks closed; air freight had replaced the old cargo boats, and the dockers became redundant. At the same time demolition of bomb-damaged and slum property started, and people were rehoused out of London in the new towns. For many this was life-shattering, particularly for the older generation who had lived their entire lives within a radius of two or three streets, close to their children and grandchildren. The rehousing programme tore apart the extended family, which had provided the unity and been the strength of East End life for generations. Families in the suburbs started a new, more affluent life, and began to feel ashamed of their old Cockney dialect with its distinctive accent, its idiosyncratic grammar, its delicious word order, its double and triple negatives, its back slang and rhyming slang. Sadly the old Cockney lingo virtually disappeared.

In the 1960s vast areas of London were torn down, and with them went the Canada Buildings. The heart went out of old Poplar.

I wandered around the Buildings after they had been evacuated. Where little girls had played hop-scotch and skipped, where boys had played football or marbles, where women in curlers and head scarves had gossiped and men exchanged racing tips, where teeming human life had been lived in all its rich fecundity was now a ghost town. Hollow sounds echoed up the walls of the high buildings, a dustbin lid rolled across the cobbles, a broken door swung against a wall. In the court, where costers had once trundled their barrows, stood rows of municipal rubbish bins. Where once there had been washing lines festooned with clean washing, broken lines now trailed in the dirt. Where the coalman with his horse and cart had sauntered in stood a notice – NO ENTRY. Stairways up which women had heaved everything, including a baby in its pram, were barricaded with the notice DANGER. Dark corners, where giggling and kissing had once been heard, were now filthy, piled high with detritus blowing in from the yard. Windows, where net curtains had fluttered, were boarded up. Doors that had always been open were now permanently closed. No movement, no life, no humanity. I left the Buildings and never went back.

IT IS FINISHED

The exodus of the traditional Cockney people affected the Sisters' practice, especially when the docklands became 'smart'. Newcomers did not know, nor particularly want to know, about the nuns. The National Health Service and the fashion of going into hospital to have a baby reduced their midwifery practice considerably. The advent of the Pill in 1963 brought it to an end altogether. Women, for the first time in history, had control over their own fertility, and the birth rate plummeted. Throughout the 1950s the Sisters had delivered around 100 babies per month. In the year 1964 that number had dropped to four or five.

The Sisters, who had done so much to help the very poor in the slums of Poplar, were no longer needed.

They had come to Poplar in 1879, when there was virtually no medical or nursing care, and their dedication and self-sacrifice had saved the lives of thousands of poor women. They were known and loved by everyone living in the area, but in the brave new world of modern technology, the nuns suddenly seemed absurdly old-fashioned. The history of these heroic women was forgotten.

This may seem a sad outcome. But the Sisters were first and foremost a religious order living under monastic vows in the service of God, and they did not look at it that way. A century earlier they had been called to nurse the sick and deliver the babies of those who could not afford medical attention. This vocation they had faithfully carried out for nearly 100 years. If the poor no longer needed them, they had fulfilled their mission and they were well pleased. 'It is finished,' were Christ's last words from the cross. A life's work fulfilled and finished is a triumph.

The nuns closed their nursing and midwifery practice and turned to other work – drug abuse, shelter for the homeless, working with the deaf, helping Asian women to integrate into British life, and in the 1980s they started working with AIDS patients. They continue to do these and other tasks into the new millennium.

In 1978 Nonnatus House was closed after ninety-nine years of service to the people of Poplar. The Sisters removed to the Mother House, to await God's calling for work – they knew not what or where. They left quietly and with no fuss. Perhaps only the local clergy and a handful of older people were aware that they had gone.

And here my tale ends, with the closure of Nonnatus House.

THE END

GLOSSARY

This glossary by Terri Coates MSc, RN, RM, ADM, Dip Ed.

Afterbirth. Also known as the placenta (see below). It is called the afterbirth because it is expelled from the womb after the baby has been born.
Amniotic fluid. The water that surrounds a baby in the womb.
Antenatal. The term used to describe the whole of pregnancy from conception to the onset of labour.
Anterior presentation. The back of the baby's head in labour will normally be in the front or anterior part of the mother's pelvis. The anterior presentation is the most favourable for the baby to adopt for a normal delivery.
Asphixia pallida. A newborn baby that has become very pale (grey/white) because there is no attempt to breathe and the heartbeat has become dangerously slow.
Atelectasis. An incomplete expansion of lobules (clusters of alveoli) or lung segments may result in partial or complete lung collapse. The collapsed tissue, unable to perform gas exchange, allows unoxygenated blood to pass through it unchanged, producing hypoxemia (deficient oxygenation of the blood). Atelectasis can be present at birth (incomplete expansion of the lungs), or during adulthood (from a collapsed lung). Prognosis depends on prompt removal of any airway obstruction, relief of hypoxia, and re-expansion of the collapsed lobule(s) or lung(s).

b.d. The medical shorthand used as an instruction on prescriptions to mean twice a day. From the Latin *bis die.*

Cervix. The cervix is the neck of the womb or uterus.

Caesarean section. An operation to deliver a baby through an incision in the mother's abdomen
Chloral hydrate. Chloral hydrate was a mild sedative and analgesic used in the early stages of labour. The drug was given as a drink with either water and glucose or fruit juice. Chloral hydrate is an irritant to the stomach and often caused vomiting, so is no longer used.
Contraction. A contraction is the intermittent tightening of the muscles of the uterus (womb) which are painful during labour.
Cord presentation. The cord is palpable at cervix through the intact membranes.
Crown. The top of the baby's head, usually the first part of the head to emerge. When the top of the head emerges it is said to crown.
Crowned. When the widest diameter of the baby's head is at the vaginal opening during delivery the head is said to have 'crowned'.
Curette. A surgical instrument that comes in different sizes and shapes that is used to scrape away unhealthy or unwanted tissue.

D and C. Dilatation and curettage (D and C) is an operation to remove any pieces of placenta or membrane from the uterus to prevent further bleeding or infection.
Dates. The date that the baby is due.

Eclampsia. Eclampsia is a rare and severe consequence of pre-eclampsia. It is characterised by convulsions and is an infrequent cause of death of a mother and unborn baby.
Ergometrine. Ergometrine is an oxytocic drug which makes the muscle of the uterus contract after delivery.
Eve's rocking. An outdated method of resuscitation. Chest compressions are more effective and are used with mouth-to-mouth resuscitation.

External Cephalic Version (ECV). Rotating the unborn baby or foetus into a position more favourable for a normal delivery.
Exsanguinate. Extensive blood loss. Possibly fatal.

First stage of labour. The first stage of labour is from the start of regular painful contractions until the cervix (neck of the womb) is fully open.
Forceps. Forceps are used to gently hold tissue during an operation or surgical procedures.
Full term. The length of a pregnancy is nine months (forty weeks). Full term is considered to be thirty-eight to forty-two weeks of pregnancy.
Fundus. The top of the uterus.

Gamgee. Absorbent tissue.
Gas and air machine. Gas and air was a popular form of pain relief for labour. The air has now been exchanged for oxygen, but the term 'gas and air' is still used. The 'gas' too has changed over the years: the 'gas' in current use is nitrous oxide.
Gestation. The gestation is the number of weeks of pregnancy.
Gluteous muscle. The gluteous or gleuteous maximus muscle is the large muscle in the bottom.

Higginson's syringe. A type of flexible syringe with a long nozzle usually used to administer enemas.

IM. Intra-muscular or into the muscle.
IV. Intra-venous or intra-venous infusion may be more commonly known as a drip (in this case blood).

Lobeline. A respiratory stimulant.
Left side. Positioning women on their left side for delivery was popular for a while. Women are now encouraged to choose the position for delivery that is most comfortable for them. The left side or left lateral position is rarely used.

Menorrhagia. Excessive menstrual blood flow.

Nurse. Title of nurse is now rarely used for or by midwives. Midwifery is an entirely separate profession. Many midwives were trained as nurses, but this dual qualification is now less common.

Obstetric forceps. Forceps used to grasp the foetal head to facilitate the delivery in a difficult labour.
Occipital protuberance. Or occiput is the back of the baby's head.
Os. The opening of the cervix which leads into the womb.
Otitis media. Inflammation or infection of the middle ear.
Oxytocic drugs. Drugs such as Oxytocin or Ergometrine that make the muscle of the uterus contract after delivery and are used to either assist the delivery of the placenta or control bleeding after delivery of the placenta.

Paediatrician. A doctor who specialises in the care of children.
Peritoneum. The lining of the abdominal cavity.
Pathology lab. Laboratory where samples of blood would be sent for confirmation of infection.
Pethidine. A drug used for pain relief in labour.
Perineum. The area of skin between the vagina and the anus.
Phthisis. Tuberculosis of the lungs. No longer in scientific use.
Pink eye. Conjunctivitis is also known as 'pink eye', an inflammation of the conjunctiva of the eye. The conjunctiva is the membrane that covers the eye.
Pinards. A simple trumpet-shaped stethoscope used by the midwife to listen to the baby's heartbeat before birth.
Pitocin. An early proprietary brand name for an oxytocic drug used for induction of labour or treatment of uterine inertia.
Pituitrin. A hormone produced by the pituitary gland, which helps enable lactation. The hormone also stimulates contraction of the uterus and was formerly used to help to induce labour.

Placenta. Also known as the afterbirth. The baby's life-support system supplying the baby with oxygen and nutrients and removing waste products while he/she is growing in the womb. The placenta also produces essential hormones during the pregnancy.

Postnatal. The time immediately following a birth when a midwife would continue to care for the mother and baby.

Post-partum delirium. A postnatal mental condition now known as puerperal psychosis. The less severe form is called postnatal depression.

Pouch of Douglas. A small pouch-shaped area situated behind the uterus and in front of the rectum.

Pre-eclampsia. A disease that is peculiar to pregnancy. The symptoms are: high blood pressure, protein in the urine and oedema (swelling).

Primigravida. A woman pregnant with her first baby.

Prolapsed cord. Occurs after the membranes have broken and the cord is found outside the uterus.

Restitution of the head. A normal corrective movement of the baby's head during delivery to bring it back into natural line with the shoulders.

Second stage. The second stage (of labour) is the time when the neck of the womb or uterus is fully open, and the mother starts to push until the delivery of the baby.

Special diet. It was thought that a restricted diet and restricted fluid intake would improve the symptoms of pre-eclampsia. It has now been proved that these restrictions had no effect upon the course of pre-eclampsia and are no longer practised. Pre-eclampsia is treated with rest and drug therapy.

SRN. State Registered Nurse.

Staphylococcus aureus. A bacterium that is commonly found on human skin and mucosa (lining of mouth, nose, etc.). It lives completely harmlessly on the skin and in the nose of about one-third of normal healthy people.

Staph infection. Staphylococcus aureus can infect wounds during or after childbirth or during surgical procedures. These infections may become serious.

Third stage. The third stage of labour is the time from the delivery of the baby to the end of the delivery of the placenta (afterbirth) and control of bleeding.

Transverse lie. Where the baby lies across the mother's womb (instead of parallel to the mother's spine) and so cannot descend through the pelvis for a normal birth.

Unstriped muscle. An outdated term for smooth muscle.

Volsellum forceps. Forceps designed to hold the cervix during gynaecological procedures.

BIBLIOGRAPHY

Sources for the 'Lost Babies' chapter

Booth, Charles, 'The Life and Labour of the People of London', vols. I–IX, *The Journals of the Royal Statistical Society*, 1887.

Booth, General William, *In Darkest England*, 1890.

Fishman, Professor W. J., *East End 1888*, Duckworth, 1988.

Fishman, Professor W. J., *The Streets of East London*, Duckworth, 1979.

Jordan, Jane, *Josephine Butler*, John Murray, 2000.

Keating, P., ed., *Into Unknown England 1866-1913*, Fontana, 1976.

Mearns, Andrew and Preston, William, *The Bitter Cry of Outcast London*, 1883.

William, A. E., *Barnardo of Stepney*, Allen and Unwin, 1943.

Sources for the 'Nancy' chapter

Jordan, Jane, *Josephine Butler*, John Murray, 2000.

Moberly Bell, E., *Josephine Butler*, Constable, 1962.

Petrie, Glen, *A Singular Iniquity (Campaigns of Josephine Butler)*, Macmillan, 1971.

Stafford, Ann, *The Age of Consent*, Hodder and Stoughton, 1964.

Williamson, Joseph, *The Forgotten Saint*, The Wellclose Trust, 1977.

Sources for the glossary

Ballière's Nurse's Dictionary, 7th edition, ed. B. Cape, Ballière Tindall, 1968.

Myles, M., *Text Book for Midwives*, ed. V. Ruth Bennett and L. K. Brown, Churchill Livingstone, 1999.

Stables, D., *Physiology in Childbearing with Anatomy and Related Biosciences*, Ballière Tindall, 1999.

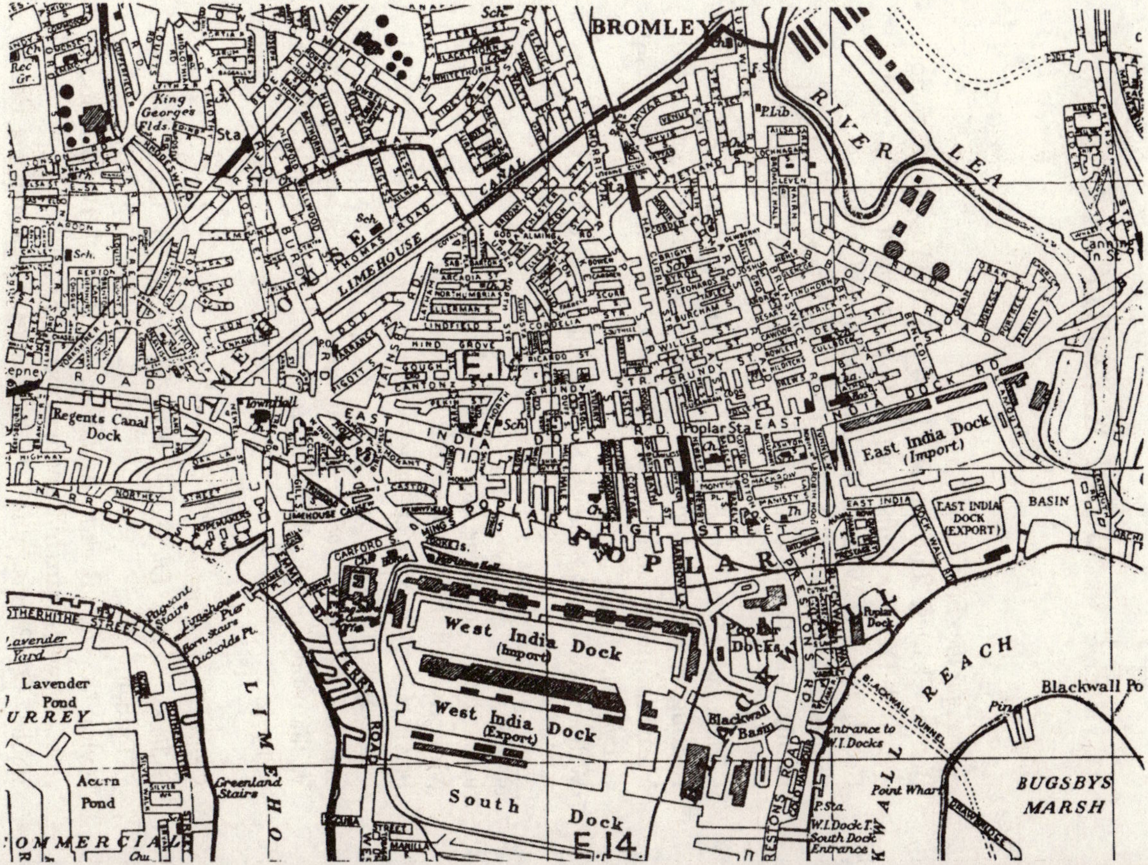

BROMLEY
RIVER LEA
LIMEHOUSE CANAL
LIMEHOUSE
POPLAR
East India Dock (Import)
EAST INDIA DOCK (EXPORT)
BASIN
West India Dock (Import)
West India Dock (Export)
South Dock
E.14
Regents Canal Dock
Poplar Docks
Blackwall Basin
BLACKWALL REACH
BLACKWALL TUNNEL
Blackwall Po
BUGSBYS MARSH
King George's Flds.
Lavender Pond
Acorn Pond
SURREY
COMMERCIAL
EAST INDIA DOCK RD.
POPLAR HIGH STREET
WEST FERRY ROAD
PRESTONS ROAD
NARROW STREET
Poplar Sta
Town Hall
Point Wharf
Entrance to W.I. Docks

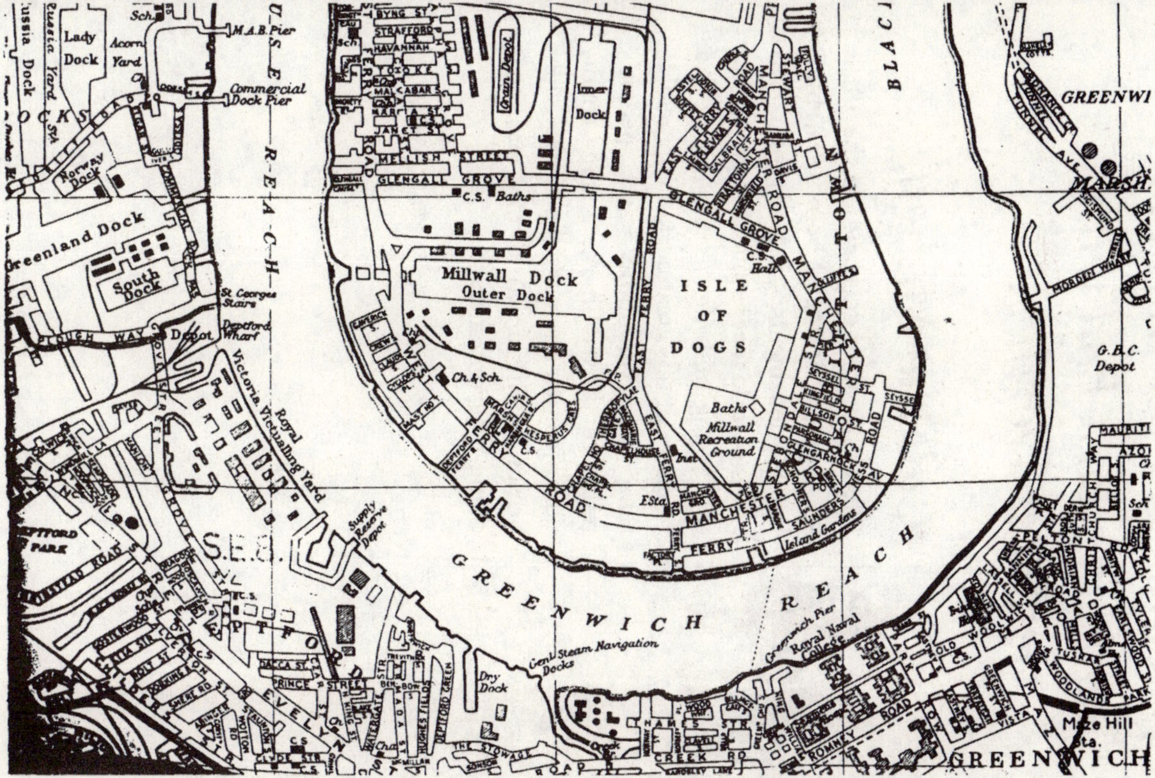

ISLE OF DOGS
Millwall Dock
Outer Dock
Inner Dock
Grain Depot
Millwall Recreation Ground
Baths
GREENWICH REACH
GREENWICH
Greenland Dock
South Dock
Norway Dock
Lady Dock
Acorn Yard
Russia Dock
Commercial Dock Pier
M.A.B. Pier
St Georges Stairs
Deptford Wharf
Royal Victoria Victualling Yard
Supply Reserve Depot
S.E.8.
DEPTFORD
Genl Steam Navigation Docks
Dry Dock
Greenwich Pier
Royal Naval College
Maze Hill Sta.
Island Gardens
MANCHESTER ROAD
GLENGALL GROVE
EAST FERRY ROAD
WEST FERRY ROAD
MELLISH STREET
ROMNEY ROAD
CREEK RD
EVELYN ST
PLOUGH WAY
G.B.C. Depot

Discover the lost world of London's East End with Jennifer Worth . . .

Call the Midwife

Life in London's docklands in the 1950s was tough. Brothels, bombsites, bug-infested tenements, gang warfare – this was the world that Jennifer Worth entered as a young midwife. Yet the beauty and romance of this great port, the incredible sense of community and people's resilience thrived in these slum conditions. Jennifer's remarkable story vividly brings to life a world that has now changed beyond measure.

ISBN: 978-0-7538-2383-5
£6.99

Available now in Phoenix Paperback

Shadows of the Workhouse

In the follow-up to bestselling *Call the Midwife*, Jennifer Worth returns to London's East End and the fascinating lives of the people she met there: orphaned siblings Peggy and Frank separated in childhood; young Jane broken by cruelty; and Sister Monica Joan who ends up in the High Court. A colourful and moving chronicle of a bygone era touched by the shadow of the workhouse.

ISBN: 978-0-7538-2585-3
£6.99

Available now in Phoenix Paperback